POETRY
for Students

Advisors

POETRY
for Students

Presenting Analysis, Context, and Criticism on Commonly Studied Poetry

VOLUME 26

Ira Mark Milne, Project Editor

Foreword by David Kelly

THOMSON
GALE

Detroit • New York • San Francisco • New Haven, Conn. • Waterville, Maine • London

THOMSON

GALE

Poetry for Students, Volume 26

Project Editor
Ira Mark Milne

Editorial
Jennifer Greve

Rights Acquisition and Management
Margaret Chamberlain-Gaston, Jacqueline Key,
Lisa Kincade, Robyn Young

Manufacturing
Drew Kalasky

Imaging and Multimedia
Lezlie Light

Product Design
Pamela A. E. Galbreath, Jennifer Wahi

Vendor Administration
Civie Green

Product Manager
Meggin Condino

ISBN-13: 978-0-7876-8716-8
ISBN-10: 0-7876-8716-2
eISBN-13: 978-1-4144-2934-2
eISBN-10: 1-4144-2934-7
ISSN 1094-7019

Printed in the United States of America
10 9 8 7 6 5 4 3 2 1

Table of Contents

Just a Few Lines on a Page

I have often thought that poets have the easiest job in the world. A poem, after all, is just a few lines on a page, usually not even extending margin to margin—how long would that take to write, about five minutes? Maybe ten at the most, if you wanted it to rhyme or have a repeating meter. Why, I could start in the morning and produce a book of poetry by dinnertime. But we all know that it isn't that easy. Anyone can come up with enough words, but the poet's job is about writing the *right* ones. The right words will change lives, making people see the world somewhat differently than they saw it just a few minutes earlier. The right words can make a reader who relies on the dictionary for meanings take a greater responsibility for his or her own personal understanding. A poem that is put on the page correctly can bear any amount of analysis, probing, defining, explaining, and interrogating, and something about it will still feel new the next time you read it.

It would be fine with me if I could talk about poetry without using the word "magical," because that word is overused these days to imply "a really good time," often with a certain sweetness about it, and a lot of poetry is neither of these. But if you stop and think about magic—whether it brings to mind sorcery, witchcraft, or bunnies pulled from top hats—it always seems to involve stretching reality to produce a result greater than the sum of its parts and pulling unexpected results out of thin air. This book provides ample cases where a few simple words conjure up whole worlds. We do not actually travel to different times and different cultures, but the poems get into our minds, they find what little we know about the places they are talking about, and then they make that little bit blossom into a bouquet of someone else's life. Poets make us think we are following simple, specific events, but then they leave ideas in our heads that cannot be found on the printed page. Abracadabra.

Sometimes when you finish a poem it doesn't feel as if it has left any supernatural effect on you, like it did not have any more to say beyond the actual words that it used. This happens to everybody, but most often to inexperienced readers: regardless of what is often said about young people's infinite capacity to be amazed, you have to understand what usually does happen, and what could have happened instead, if you are going to be moved by what someone has accomplished. In those cases in which you finish a poem with a "So what?" attitude, the information provided in *Poetry for Students* comes in handy. Readers can feel assured that the poems included here actually are potent magic, not just because a few (or a hundred or ten thousand) professors of literature say they are: they're significant because they can withstand close inspection and still amaze the very same people who have just finished taking them apart and seeing how they work. Turn them inside out, and they will still be able to come alive, again and again. *Poetry for Students* gives readers of any age good practice in feeling the ways poems relate to both the reality of the time and place the poet lived in and the reality of our emotions. Practice is just another word for being a student. The information given here helps you understand the way to read poetry; what to look for, what to expect.

With all of this in mind, I really don't think I would actually like to have a poet's job at all. There are too many skills involved, including precision, honesty, taste, courage, linguistics, passion, compassion, and the ability to keep all sorts of people entertained at once. And that is just what they do with one hand, while the other hand pulls some sort of trick that most of us will never fully understand. I can't even pack all that I need for a weekend into one suitcase, so what would be my chances of stuffing so much life into a few lines? With all that *Poetry for Students* tells us about each poem, I am impressed that any poet can finish three or four poems a year. Read the inside stories of these poems, and you won't be able to approach any poem in the same way you did before.

David J. Kelly
College of Lake County

Introduction

Purpose of the Book

The purpose of *Poetry for Students* (*PfS*) is to provide readers with a guide to understanding, enjoying, and studying poems by giving them easy access to information about the work. Part of Gale's "For Students" Literature line, *PfS* is specifically designed to meet the curricular needs of high school and undergraduate college students and their teachers, as well as the interests of general readers and researchers considering specific poems. While each volume contains entries on "classic" poems frequently studied in classrooms, there are also entries containing hard-to-find information on contemporary poems, including works by multicultural, international, and women poets.

The information covered in each entry includes an introduction to the poem and the poem's author; the actual poem text (if possible); a poem summary, to help readers unravel and understand the meaning of the poem; analysis of important themes in the poem; and an explanation of important literary techniques and movements as they are demonstrated in the poem.

In addition to this material, which helps the readers analyze the poem itself, students are also provided with important information on the literary and historical background informing each work. This includes a historical context essay, a box comparing the time or place the poem was written to modern Western culture, a critical overview essay, and excerpts from critical essays on the poem. A unique feature of *PfS* is a specially commissioned critical essay on each poem, targeted toward the student reader.

To further aid the student in studying and enjoying each poem, information on media adaptations is provided (if available), as well as reading suggestions for works of fiction and nonfiction on similar themes and topics. Classroom aids include ideas for research papers and lists of critical sources that provide additional material on the poem.

Selection Criteria

The titles for each volume of *PfS* were selected by surveying numerous sources on teaching literature and analyzing course curricula for various school districts. Some of the sources surveyed included: literature anthologies; *Reading Lists for College-Bound Students: The Books Most Recommended by America's Top Colleges*; textbooks on teaching the poem; a College Board survey of poems commonly studied in high schools; and a National Council of Teachers of English (NCTE) survey of poems commonly studied in high schools.

Input was also solicited from our advisory board, as well as educators from various areas. From these discussions, it was determined that each volume should have a mix of "classic" poems (those works commonly taught in literature classes) and contemporary poems for which information is often hard to find. Because of the interest in expanding the canon of literature, an emphasis was also placed on including works by international, multicultural, and women poets. Our advisory board members—educational professionals—helped pare down the list for each volume. If a work was not selected for the present volume, it was often noted as a possibility for a future volume. As always, the editor welcomes suggestions for titles to be included in future volumes.

How Each Entry Is Organized

Each entry, or chapter, in *PfS* focuses on one poem. Each entry heading lists the full name of the poem, the author's name, and the date of the poem's publication. The following elements are contained in each entry:

Introduction: a brief overview of the poem which provides information about its first appearance, its literary standing, any controversies surrounding the work, and major conflicts or themes within the work.

Author Biography: this section includes basic facts about the poet's life, and focuses on events and times in the author's life that inspired the poem in question.

Poem Text: when permission has been granted, the poem is reprinted, allowing for quick reference when reading the explication of the following section.

Poem Summary: a description of the major events in the poem. Summaries are broken down with subheads that indicate the lines being discussed.

Themes: a thorough overview of how the major topics, themes, and issues are addressed within the poem. Each theme discussed appears in a separate subhead and is easily accessed through the boldface entries in the Subject/Theme Index.

Style: this section addresses important style elements of the poem, such as form, meter, and rhyme scheme; important literary devices used, such as imagery, foreshadowing, and symbolism; and, if applicable, genres to which the work might have belonged, such as Gothicism or Romanticism. Literary terms are explained within the entry, but can also be found in the Glossary.

Historical Context: this section outlines the social, political, and cultural climate *in which*

the author lived and the poem was created. This section may include descriptions of related historical events, pertinent aspects of daily life in the culture, and the artistic and literary sensibilities of the time in which the work was written. If the poem is a historical work, information regarding the time in which the poem is set is also included. Each section is broken down with helpful subheads.

Critical Overview: this section provides background on the critical reputation of the poem, including bannings or any other public controversies surrounding the work. For older works, this section includes a history of how the poem was first received and how perceptions of it may have changed over the years; for more recent poems, direct quotes from early reviews may also be included.

Criticism: an essay commissioned by *PfS* which specifically deals with the poem and is written specifically for the student audience, as well as excerpts from previously published criticism on the work (if available).

Sources: an alphabetical list of critical material quoted in the entry, with full bibliographical information.

Further Reading: an alphabetical list of other critical sources which may prove useful for the student. Includes full bibliographical information and a brief annotation.

In addition, each entry contains the following highlighted sections, set apart from the main text as sidebars:

Media Adaptations: if available, a list of audio recordings as well as any film or television adaptations of the poem, including source information.

Topics for Further Study: a list of potential study questions or research topics dealing with the poem. This section includes questions related to other disciplines the student may be studying, such as American history, world history, science, math, government, business, geography, economics, psychology, etc.

Compare & Contrast: an "at-a-glance" comparison of the cultural and historical differences between the author's time and culture and late twentieth century or early twenty-first century Western culture. This box includes pertinent parallels between the major scientific, political, and cultural movements of the time or place the poem was written, the time or place the poem was set (if a historical work), and modern Western culture. Works written after 1990 may not have this box.

What Do I Read Next?: a list of works that might complement the featured poem or serve as a contrast to it. This includes works by the same author and others, works of fiction and nonfiction, and works from various genres, cultures, and eras.

Other Features

PfS includes "Just a Few Lines on a Page," a foreword by David J. Kelly, an adjunct professor of English, College of Lake County, Illinois. This essay provides a straightforward, unpretentious explanation of why poetry should be marveled at and how *Poetry for Students* can help teachers show students how to enrich their own reading experiences.

A Cumulative Author/Title Index lists the authors and titles covered in each volume of the *PfS* series.

A Cumulative Nationality/Ethnicity Index breaks down the authors and titles covered in each volume of the *PfS* series by nationality and ethnicity.

A Subject/Theme Index, specific to each volume, provides easy reference for users who may be studying a particular subject or theme rather than a single work. Significant subjects from events to broad themes are included, and the entries pointing to the specific theme discussions in each entry are indicated in **boldface**.

A Cumulative Index of First Lines (beginning in Vol. 10) provides easy reference for users who may be familiar with the first line of a poem but may not remember the actual title.

A Cumulative Index of Last Lines (beginning in Vol. 10) provides easy reference for users who may be familiar with the last line of a poem but may not remember the actual title.

Each entry may include illustrations, including photo of the author and other graphics related to the poem.

Citing Poetry for Students

When writing papers, students who quote directly from any volume of *Poetry for Students* may use the following general forms. These examples are based on MLA style; teachers may request that students adhere to a different style, so the following examples may be adapted as needed.

When citing text from *PfS* that is not attributed to a particular author (i.e., the Themes, Style, Historical Context sections, etc.), the following format should be used in the bibliography section:

"Angle of Geese." *Poetry for Students*. Eds. Marie Napierkowski and Mary Ruby. Vol. 2. Detroit: Gale, 1998. 8–9.

When quoting the specially commissioned essay from *PfS* (usually the first piece under the "Criticism" subhead), the following format should be used:

Velie, Alan. Critical Essay on "Angle of Geese." *Poetry for Students*. Eds. Marie Napierkowski and Mary Ruby. Vol. 2. Detroit: Gale, 1998. 7–10.

When quoting a journal or newspaper essay that is reprinted in a volume of *PfS*, the following form may be used:

Luscher, Robert M. "An Emersonian Context of Dickinson's 'The Soul Selects Her Own Society.'" *ESQ: A Journal of American Renaissance* Vol. 30, No. 2 (Second Quarter, 1984), 111–16; excerpted and reprinted in *Poetry for Students*, Vol. 1, eds. Marie Napierkowski and Mary Ruby (Detroit: Gale, 1998), pp. 266–69.

When quoting material reprinted from a book that appears in a volume of *PfS*, the following form may be used:

Mootry, Maria K. "'Tell It Slant': Disguise and Discovery as Revisionist Poetic Discourse in 'The Bean Eaters,'" in *A Life Distilled: Gwendolyn Brroks, Her Poetry and Fiction.* Edited by Maria K. Mootry and Gary Smith. University of Illinois Press, 1987. 177–80, 191; excerpted and reprinted in *Poetry for Students*, Vol. 2, eds. Marie Napierkowski and Mary Ruby (Detroit: Gale, 1998), pp. 22–24.

We Welcome Your Suggestions

The editorial staff of *Poetry for Students* welcomes your comments and ideas. Readers who wish to suggest poems to appear in future volumes, or who have other suggestions, are cordially invited to contact the editor. You may contact the editor via E-mail at: *ForStudentsEditors@gale.com.* Or write to the editor at:

Editor, *Poetry for Students*
Thomson Gale
27500 Drake Road
Farmington Hills, MI 48331-3535

Literary Chronology

1844: Gerard Manley Hopkins is born on July 28 in Stratford, Essex, England.

1877: Gerard Manley Hopkins's "Pied Beauty" is published.

1889: Gerard Manley Hopkins dies of typhoid fever in Dublin on June 8.

1892: César Vallejo is born on March 16 in Santiago de Chuco, Peru.

1919: César Vallejo's "The Black Heralds" is published.

1921: Hayden Carruth is born on August 3 in Waterbury, Connecticut.

1925: Gerald Stern is born on February 22 in Pittsburgh, Pennsylvania.

1927: Galway Kinnell is born on February 1 in Providence, Rhode Island.

1934: Sonia Sanchez is born on September 9 in Birmingham, Alabama.

1937: Alicia Ostriker is born on November 11 in New York City.

1938: César Vallejo dies.

1939: Frank Bidart is born on May 27 in rural southern California.

1948: Ciaran Carson is born on October 9 in Belfast, Northern Ireland.

1948: J. T. Barbarese is born on May 18 in Philadelphia.

1950: John Yau is born in Lynn, Massachusetts, shortly after his parents left Shanghai, China.

1952: Mary Ruefle is born in Pittsburg, Pennsylvania.

1956: Lucie Brock-Broido is born on May 22 in Pittsburgh, Pennsylvania.

1966: Galway Kinnell's "Another Night in the Ruins" is published.

1969: Julianna Baggott is born on September 10 in Wilmington, Delaware.

1983: Galway Kinnell is awarded the Pulitzer Prize in Poetry for his collection *Selected Poems.*

1987: Sonia Sanchez's "An Anthem" is published.

1996: Alicia Ostriker's "Mastectomy" is published.

1996: Hayden Carruth's "I, I, I" is published.

1997: Gerald Stern's "One of the Smallest" is published.

2000: Liz Waldner's "Witness" is published.

2000: Mary Ruefle's "Sentimental Education" is published.

2001: Julianna Baggott's "What the Poets Could Have Been" is published.

2002: John Yau's "Russian Letter" is published.

2003: Ciaran Carson's "The War Correspondent" is published.

2004: Lucie Brock-Broido's "After Raphael" is published.

2005: Frank Bidart's "Curse" is published.

2005: J. T. Barbarese's "Walk Your Body Down" is published.

Acknowledgments

The editors wish to thank the copyright holders of the excerpted criticism included in this volume and the permissions managers of many book and magazine publishing companies for assisting us in securing reproduction rights. We are also grateful to the staffs of the Detroit Public Library, the Library of Congress, the University of Detroit Mercy Library, Wayne State University Purdy/ Kresge Library Complex, and the University of Michigan Libraries for making their resources available to us. Following is a list of the copyright holders who have granted us permission to reproduce material in this volume of *PFS*. Every effort has been made to trace copyright, but if omissions have been made, please let us know.

COPYRIGHTED EXCERPTS IN *PFS*, VOLUME 26, WERE REPRODUCED FROM THE FOLLOWING PERIODICALS:

American Poetry Review, v. 27, July–August, 1998 for "Gerald Stern: An Interview," by Gary Pacernick. Copyright © 1998 by World Poetry, Inc. Reproduced by permission of the author.— *College Literature*, v. 31, winter, 2004. Copyright © 2004 by West Chester University. Reproduced by permission.—*Explicator*, v. 59, summer, 2001. Copyright © 2001 by Helen Dwight Reid Educational Foundation. Reproduced with permission of the Helen Dwight Reid Educational Foundation, published by Heldref Publications, 1319 18th Street, NW, Washington, DC 20036-1802.— *Hispania: A Teacher's Journal*, v. 35, May, 1952; v. 75, December, 1992. © 1952, 1999 The American Association of Teachers of Spanish and Portuguese, Inc. Both reproduced by permission.—*Irish Literary Supplement*, v. 25, fall, 2005. Reproduced by permission.—*Literary Review*, v. 40, winter, 1997 for "The Poetry of Gerald Stern," by Mark Hillringhouse. Reproduced by permission of the author.—*Nation*, v. 264, May 12, 1997. Copyright © 1997 by The Nation Magazine/The Nation Company, Inc. Reproduced by permission.—*Parnassus: Poetry in Review*, v. 22, spring–summer, 1997 for "The Importance of Small Floy Floy," by Eric Murphy Selinger. Copyright © 1997 Poetry in Review Foundation, NY. Reproduced by permission of the publisher and the author./ v. 29, 2006. Copyright © 2006 Poetry in Review Foundation, NY. Reproduced by permission of the publisher and the author.—*Poetry*, v. clxx, June, 1997 for review by John Taylor of *The Crack in Everything*. Copyright 1997 by the Modern Poetry Association. Reproduced by permission of the author.—*Poets & Writers*, v. 24, May–June, 1996; v. 29, May–June, 2001. Copyright © 1996, 2001 Poets & Writers, Inc. Both reprinted by permission of the publisher, Poets & Writers, Inc., 72 Spring St., New York, NY, 10012. www.pw.org.—*Prairie Schooner*, v. 76, fall, 2002. Copyright © 2002 by University of Nebraska Press. Reproduced from *Prairie Schooner* by permission of the University of Nebraska Press.—*Romance Quarterly*, v. 49, summer, 2002. Copyright © 2002 by Helen Dwight Reid Educational Foundation. Reproduced with permission of the Helen Dwight Reid Educational Foundation, published by Heldref Publications, 1319 18th Street, NW, Washington, DC 20036-1802.—***Women's Review of Books***, v. 14, March, 1997. Copyright © 1997 Women's Review of Books. Reproduced by permission.

COPYRIGHTED EXCERPTS IN *PFS*, VOLUME 26, WERE REPRODUCED FROM THE FOLLOWING BOOKS:

Baggott, Julianna. From ***This Country of Mothers***. Crab Orchard Review & Southern Illinois University Press, 2001. Copyright © 2001 by Julianna Baggott. All rights reserved. Reproduced by permission of Southern Illinois University Press.—Barbarese, J. T. From ***The Black Beach***. University of North Texas Press, 2005. © 2005 J.T. Barbarese. Reproduced by permission.—Bidart, Frank. From ***Star Dust***. Farrar, Straus and Giroux, 2005. Copyright © 2005 by Frank Bidart. Reprinted by permission of Farrar, Straus and Giroux, LLC.—Birns, Nicholas. From "John Yau," in ***Dictionary of Literary Biography, Vol. 312, Asian American Writers***. Edited by Deborah L. Madsen. Thomson Gale, 2005. Reproduced by permission of Thomson Gale.—Carruth, Hayden. From ***Scrambled Eggs & Whiskey: Poems, 1991–1995***. Copper Canyon Press, 1996. Copyright © 1996 by Hayden Carruth. Reproduced by permission.—Carson, Ciaran. From ***Breaking News***. Wake Forest University Press, 2003. Copyright © Ciaran Carson. Reproduced by permission.—Ferns, John. From "Gerard Manley Hopkins," in ***Dictionary of Literary Biography, Vol. 57, Victorian Prose Writers After 1867***. Edited by William B. Thesing. Gale Research, 1987. Reproduced by permission of Thomson Gale.—Frazier, Charles. From "Galway Kinnell," in ***Dictionary of Literary Biography, Vol. 5, American Poets Since World War II, First Series***. Edited by Donald J. Greiner. Gale Research, 1980. Reproduced by permission of Thomson Gale.—Hopkins, Gerard Manley. From ***Gerard Manley Hopkins: The Major Works***. Oxford University Press, 2002. Poetry © the Society of Jesus 1986, 2002. Republished with permission of Oxford University Press.—Kinnell, Galway. From ***Selected Poems***. Houghton Mifflin Company, 1982. Copyright © 1965, 1966, 1967, by Galway Kinnell. All rights reserved. All rights reserved.

Reprinted by permission of Houghton Mifflin Company.—Landrey, David W. From "Hayden Carruth," in ***Dictionary of Literary Biography, Vol. 165, American Poets Since World War II, Fourth Series***. Edited by Joseph Conte. Gale Research, 1996. Reproduced by permission of Thomson Gale.—Maier, Linda S. From "Cesar Vallejo," in ***Dictionary of Literary Biography, Vol. 290, Modern Spanish American Poets, Second Series***. Edited by Maria A. Salgado. Thomson Gale, 2004. Reproduced by permission of Thomson Gale.—Ostriker, Alicia Suskin. From ***The Crack in Everything***. University of Pittsburgh Press, 1996. Copyright © 1996, University of Pittsburgh Press. All rights reserved. Reproduced by permission.—Russell, William Howard. From ***The British Expedition to the Crimea***. George Routledge and Sons, 1877. Copyright © 1877.—Sanchez, Sonia. From ***Shake Loose My Skin***. Beacon Press, 1995. Copyright © 1995 by Beacon Press. All rights reserved. Reproduced by permission.—Stern, Gerald. From ***Last Blue***. W. W. Norton & Company, 2000. Copyright © 2000 by Gerald Stern. All rights reserved. Used by permission of W. W. Norton & Company, Inc.—Vallejo, Cesar. From ***The Black Heralds***. The Latin American Literary Review Press, 1990. Copyright © 1990 Latin American Literary Review. Reproduced by permission of the publisher.—Waldner, Liz. From ***A Point Is That Which Has No Part***. University of Iowa Press, 2000. Copyright © 2000 by the University of Iowa Press. All rights reserved. Reproduced by permission.—Yau, John. From ***Borrowed Love Poems***. Penguin Books, 2002. Copyright © John Yau, 2002. All rights reserved. Used by permission of Viking Penguin, a division of Penguin Group (USA) Ind.—Zimmerman, Lee. From ***Intricate and Simple Things: The Poetry of Galway Kinnell***. University of Illinois Press, 1987. Copyright © 1987 by the Board of Trustees of the University of Illinois. Reproduced by permission of the University of Illinois Press.

COPYRIGHTED EXCERPTS IN *PFS*, VOLUME 26, WERE REPRODUCED FROM THE FOLLOWING WEBSITES OR OTHER SOURCES:

From ***Contemporary Authors Online***, "Alicia (Suskin) Ostriker," www.gale.com, Gale, 2002. Reproduced by permission of Thomson Gale.—From ***Contemporary Authors Online***, "Ciaran Carson," www.gale.com, Gale, 2003. Reproduced by permission of Thomson Gale.—From ***Contemporary Authors Online***, "Frank Bidart," www.gale.com, Gale, 2005. Reproduced by permission of Thomson Gale.—From ***Contemporary Authors Online***, "Hayden Carruth," www.gale.com, Thomson Gale, 2004. Reproduced by permission of Thomson Gale.—From ***Contemporary Authors Online***, "Julianna Baggott," www.gale.com, Gale, 2003. Reproduced by permission of Thomson Gale.—From ***Contemporary Authors Online***, "Liz Waldner," www.gale.com, Gale, 2003. Reproduced by permission of Thomson Gale.—From ***Contemporary Authors Online***, "Mary Ruefle," www.gale.com, Gale, 2005. Reproduced by permission of Thomson Gale.—From ***Contemporary Authors Online***, "Sonia Sanchez," www.gale.com, Gale, 2003. Reproduced by permission of Thomson Gale.—Dellasega, Cheryl. "Mothers Who Write: Julianna Baggott," ***Writers Write: The Internet Writing Journal***, October–November, 2001. Reproduced by permission of the author.—Tranter, Nikki. For "Magical Things: An Interview with Julianna Baggott," ***PopMatters.com***, August 29, 2005. Reproduced by permission.

Contributors

Bryan Aubrey: Aubrey holds a Ph.D. in English and has published many articles on poetry. Entry on *The War Correspondent*. Critical essay on *The War Correspondent*.

Jennifer Bussey: Bussey holds a master's degree in Interdisciplinary Studies and a bachelor's degree in English literature. She is an independent writer specializing in literature. Entries on *After Raphael* and *An Anthem*. Critical essays on *After Raphael* and *An Anthem*.

Klay Dyer: Dyer holds a Ph.D. in English literature and has published extensively on fiction, poetry, film, and television. He is also a freelance university teacher, writer, and educational consultant. Entry on *Witness*. Critical essays on *Sentimental Education*, *Walk Your Body Down*, and *Witness*.

Joyce Hart: Hart has degrees in literature and creative writing. Entries on *Russian Letter* and *Walk Your Body Down*. Critical essays on *Russian Letter*, *Sentimental Education*, and *Walk Your Body Down*.

Pamela Steed Hill: Hill is the author of a poetry collection, has published widely in literary journals, and is an editor for a university publications department. Entry on *Curse*. Critical essay on *Curse*.

Sheri Metzger Karmiol: Karmiol holds a Ph.D. in English literature and is a university professor. Entry on *What the Poets Could Have Been*. Critical essays on *Russian Letter* and *What the Poets Could Have Been*.

David Kelly: Kelly is an instructor of creative writing and literature. Critical essays on *Russian Letter* and *Walk Your Body Down*.

Lois Kerschen: Kerschen is an educator and freelance writer. Entries on *The Black Heralds* and *One of the Smallest*. Critical essays on *The Black Heralds* and *One of the Smallest*.

Wendy Perkins: Perkins is a professor of twentieth-century American and English literature and film. Entries on *Mastectomy* and *Sentimental Education*. Critical essays on *Mastectomy* and *Sentimental Education*.

Claire Robinson: Robinson has an M.A. in English. She is a writer and editor and a former teacher of English literature and creative writing. Entries on *I, I, I* and *Pied Beauty*. Critical essays on *I, I, I* and *Pied Beauty*.

Carol Ullmann: Ullmann is a freelance writer and editor. Entry on *Another Night in the Ruins*. Critical essay on *Another Night in the Ruins*.

After Raphael

LUCIE BROCK-BROIDO

2004

Lucie Brock-Broido's "After Raphael" is the second poem in her third poetry collection, 2004's *Trouble in Mind*. It is a poem about grief and pressing forward in time. Having lost her parents, the speaker is faced with the process of grief, along with the realization that she herself is mortal. The same time that seems to stand still in deep sadness does not actually stand still and will take her along with it as it progresses. Then she too will grow old and will have to face the reality of her own death.

This poem is in many ways typical of Brock-Broido's style and voice. It is written in seemingly straightforward syntax but is complex in its thematic development and imagery. The poem reads naturally, but not casually. The subject of vulnerability and relationships is addressed introspectively, as is common in Brock-Broido's work.

AUTHOR BIOGRAPHY

Lucie Brock-Broido was born on May 22, 1956, in Pittsburgh, Pennsylvania. She completed her B.A. and M.A., both in 1979, at Johns Hopkins University, before earning an M.F.A. from Columbia University in 1982.

As a poet, Brock-Broido brings her complex, feminine voice to such topics as love, relationships, sorrow, culture, time, and art. Her style is spare, introspective, and symbolic, and she has

been compared to Emily Dickinson, Wallace Stevens, and Sylvia Plath. In addition to seeing her work published in literary journals and anthologies, Brock-Broido completed three published volumes of poetry: *A Hunger* (1988), *The Master Letters* (1995), and *Trouble in Mind* (2004), which includes "After Raphael." *A Hunger* was reprinted three times between 1988 and 1994. Considering the many volumes of poetry published every year to a dwindling readership, this book was an impressive debut.

Brock-Broido taught poetry and creative writing. She was an assistant professor of poetry at Harvard (1988–1993) and directed its creative writing program for a year (1992–1993). She was also an assistant professor of poetry for Bennington Writing Seminars (1993–1995). Starting in 1993, she taught poetry at Columbia University, first as an associate professor and later as a professor and director. In 1995, she also served as visiting professor of poetry at Princeton University.

Brock-Broido's poetry earned her critical acclaim and numerous awards and honors. Among these are a Grolier Poetry Prize in 1983, a National Endowment for the Arts Fellowship (1985, 1998), a Harvard-Danforth Award for teaching distinction (1989, 1990), *American Poetry Review*'s Jerome Shestack Poetry Prize, a Guggenheim Fellowship in 1996, and the American Academy of Arts and Letters' Witter Bynner Prize for Poetry in 1996.

POEM SUMMARY

In "After Raphael," the speaker describes her grief and the process she goes through as she deals with it. She begins by wondering if it is possible to talk about grief and loss without confronting the danger of love. She goes on to explain that she lost her father first, and then her mother. The speaker describes this time of grief as a "strange storm," after which her parents were "ruined down / From the boughs."

The speaker says, "I am sick of not loving and not / Sleeping well, of wanting spleen." Her description of her grief is that she has no one to love, that she is not sleeping well, and that she gravitates toward feeling melancholy. (The ancient Greeks believed in the four bodily humors, one of which was associated with the

spleen and responsible for melancholy.) Next, the speaker describes sheep carrying on with their lives, eating contentedly and growing fat. The next image is of a clock icing over, suggesting that in her home (as opposed to the outside world where the sheep graze), time is coming to a halt.

The speaker separates herself from everyone else in the next few lines, where she explains that she alone can "read incisions sanserif" and imagine when the "ghostpipes bloom at night." She goes on to comment that she can see the flowers "heathering the moors," a clear reference to time passing and life growing. Then comes the title reference: she refers to her world as "post-Raphaelite." She emphasizes that this life "*is true*." Another reference to time occurs when she remembers that she was little and is now middle, meaning she is no longer a child but is in the middle years of her life. To finish this thought, she faces the realization that she will one day grow old. Perhaps her parents died of old age because she expects to die not suddenly, like the break in a falcon's wing, but gradually. As she ages, she will not open and close in the rain like a flower.

THEMES

Grief

The speaker begins the poem apprehensive about discussing her grief openly when she states, "Perhaps it isn't possible to say these things / Out loud without the noir / Of ardor and its plain-spoken elegance." She feels that being open about her private pain might be emotionally dangerous, reveal her vulnerability, and force her to confront truths she may be unprepared to face. Still, the next three sentences state plainly what her pain is: "First, my father died. Then my mother / Did. My father died again." The speaker has lost her parents, and with no mention of siblings or other members of the family in the poem, the reader can assume that the speaker is an only child who now feels alone and perhaps abandoned.

She introduces an image of an apple tree after the "strange storm" of the first pangs of grief. The storm "ruined down" her parents from the boughs, leaving apples everywhere on the ground. This image communicates despair. The

TOPICS FOR FURTHER STUDY

- Using magazines, photocopies from books, printed images from the Internet, or pictures you create yourself, gather all of the images found in Brock-Broido's "After Raphael." You may want to add images you think are indirectly related to the poem (for example, one of Raphael's paintings). Create a collage with all of your images, making sure to incorporate a copy of the poem in your collage.

- "After Raphael" ends with the speaker's realization that she, too, is subject to the passage of time. She faces her own mortality when the poem ends. Based on what you know of the speaker, how do you think she will handle this realization? Write a poem in the style of Brock-Broido using the same speaker. Your poem should express how you think the speaker feels about her own limited time.

- Research in books or online the paintings and frescoes by Raphael. Choose between one and three that you think offer some insight into Brock-Broido's poem. Put together a slide show on your computer that shows the painting(s) you have chosen and explains how they shed light on the poem.

- "After Raphael" expresses pain without being overly emotional. Do you think there is more going on beneath the surface, or do you think this is representative of where she is in the grieving process? Choose three music selections that support your reading (or readings) of the poem and burn a CD. Create a CD cover with notes explaining your selections, and choose whatever cover art you think would be appropriate.

- Through books, articles, and therapy, psychologists help people understand and cope with grief. Research what they say about grief, and determine how the speaker is doing. If you can find enough information specific to the experience of losing one's parents as an adult, consider that in your analysis of the speaker. Write a report from the perspective of a researcher in which you evaluate the speaker's progress. You may want to give her a name to make the report easier.

---

apples represent the fruits of a living tree that, now torn from the tree, are dead. They are no longer part of the living tree but have been cast violently to the ground. The speaker's grief at this point is not a peaceful one, but a confusing and maddening one. Despite her calm tone, the speaker is undergoing intense turmoil.

The speaker's grief causes her to feel cut off from anyone she might love, and her broken heart is unlikely to love right now. Further, she cannot sleep, a common occurrence in times of depression or other strong emotions. Her sleeplessness is underscored when she later describes the ghostpipes (small white flowers) blooming at night with such abundance that they cover the moors. Her grief makes it impossible for her to sleep: she looks out her window at sheep in the day and flowers at night.

Mortality

Connected to the theme of grief is the theme of mortality. The speaker is grieving because she has been forced, apparently before she was ready, to confront the reality that the people she loves are mortal. Left behind when her parents die, she has no choice but to carry on with her life. She is a witness to the cycle of life, and her first reaction to it is a broken heart.

But as the poem continues, the speaker brings in images from nature—an apple tree, sheep, a falcon, and night-blooming flowers—all of which are also subject to a finite lifespan.

The image of the flowers is carried out in the final two lines, which describe a flower opening and closing in light rain. The speaker personalizes the cycle of life when she observes, "I was little; I am middle. Will I not / Grow old?" At this point in the poem, she has moved from her encounter with her parents' mortality to considering her own. She is akin to the apple tree, the sheep, the falcon, and the flower in that she too is part of the mortal world. The poem ends with this thought just dawning on her, as one realization in her grief.

Memory

When the speaker refers to the fact that her parents have died and a "strange storm" followed, she does so in the past tense. It is not until the ninth line that she moves into the present tense. This shift indicates that a period of time has passed between the first wave of grief and the present, although she is still moving through the grieving process. This shift is significant because it lets the reader know something about the speaker's perspective. This is not a poem about how it feels just after having lost a loved one; instead, it is a poem about the memory of that severe pain and the ongoing search for peace in the aftermath. Her memory of her parents is important and her grief is deep, and her memory of the initial pain of loss is so difficult that she begins the poem wondering if there is an appropriate way to discuss the subject at all.

Brock-Broido makes another important point about memory in the statements, "First my father died. Then my mother / Did. My father died again." There is no indication as to how much time elapsed between the speaker's father's death and her mother's death. What is important is that her mother kept her father's memory alive, directly and indirectly. As long as her mother was alive, the speaker could continue to relate to her father through her memories of their family life together. But the mother also kept the father's memory alive directly when she talked about him or referred to her own memories of their years together. Once the speaker's mother died, those last connections to her father died with her. And there is no one else, but the speaker herself, to keep those memories fresh and present. At this point in the speaker's grieving process, memory is a source of pain and sorrow instead of comfort and reassurance.

The paintings of Raphael may have been a point of departure for Brock-Broido in writing this poem
(© Peter Horree/Alamy)

STYLE

Free Verse

Free verse is written in a free style without the restraints of meter, rhythm, or rhyme. Lines may be of any length, contain complete or incomplete thoughts, and feature whatever structure the poet deems best for his or her purpose. In using free verse, many poets incorporate literary or structural devices as they see fit. Walt Whitman, for example, is known for his use of parallelism in his free verse.

In "After Raphael," Brock-Broido depicts grief and the realization that can occur during it through free verse. "After Raphael" demonstrates how she creates a style that is natural without seeming undisciplined. Brock-Broido's free verse in this poem is divided into irregular couplets, with the exceptions of lines 3 and 8, which stand alone for emphasis. Although Brock-Broido chooses to structure her poem this way, the structure is not arbitrary. Each couplet offers a self-contained thought, even when the sentence extends into the next couplet. For example, she writes, "All the Suffolk sheep stand still, eating / More, becoming fat and," then the next couplet picks up the thought with "Legible." At first glance, it may appear that she has divided the lines for the sake of the structure at the expense of meaning, but if that were the case, she would have pulled "legible" up to the end of the line above it. Instead, by separating that word, she suggests a pause in thought, which is followed by an unexpected word choice. The structure of the poem supports the natural flow of thought from the speaker.

Symbolism

Symbolism occurs in literature when a word stands for a recognizable object and for something else. For example, the Christian cross is a cross and also symbolizes the crucifixion of Jesus. Many poets who write spare verse rely on symbolism to imply additional meaning in the literal object, and Brock-Broido is no exception. As she describes her speaker's struggle with grief and mortality, she introduces symbols to allow the reader to understand the content at a deeper level. She describes the first wave of grief as a "strange storm," which effectively describes the unreal quality of going through grieving for parents. It is strange because it is not at all an everyday occurrence or one for which she could have prepared. It is also a storm because it is chaotic and intense and generates feelings of helplessness in the face of something bigger than she is. Brock-Broido's apple tree symbolizes not just a family tree, but a family from which its fruit has been torn away and ruined. The tree represents the family that they used to be, one that was living, vibrant, and inviting. The storm, however, knocks all the fruit to the ground, cut off from life and ruined. The fruit seems to symbolize family members, memories, or anything else good that comes from the family. Now that her parents have died, the tree is bare.

The sheep symbolize life going on just outside the speaker's window. She can see them, blissfully unaware of her pain. The clock symbolizes the speaker's pain. Brock-Broido describes the clock as freezing, as if the speaker's pain is causing time to come to a standstill. She does not want time to keep ticking because it takes her further from the ones she loves. Interestingly, it is just the crystal (or face) of the clock on which the ice crystals form. In reality, time is still passing even though the speaker does not see or acknowledge it. The clock's face is described as long, symbolizing the speaker's emotional state.

Sounds

Brock-Broido uses alliteration and assonance in "After Raphael." Alliteration is the repetition of identical consonant sounds at the beginning of words. Examples of alliteration are, "Perhaps it isn't possible," "strange storm," and "Suffolk sheep stand still." Assonance is the repetition of vowel sounds within words, and Brock-Broido uses it in "out loud without," "sleeping . . . spleen," "long-faced clock," and "grow old." Another literary device that relies on sound is the internal rhyme of "I was little; I am middle." In the midst of flowing free verse, the sudden interjection of a sing-song rhyme brings the reader's attention to it. This is the moment the speaker realizes the passage of time in her own life from the past to the present, and she begins to think about time passing from the present to the future.

Allusion

Allusion is any reference to something outside the literary work itself, to a person, event, or other literary work. The use of allusion assumes that the writer and the reader share the same frame of reference, and in that context, combining the allusion in the current work to the subject to which it refers allows for certain associations to be made. In "After Raphael," Brock-Broido refers to the Renaissance painter Raphael. Like other Renaissance painters, Raphael used perspective correctly in his paintings to create the illusion of space and depth even on flat surfaces. In some cases, the paintings were located in a certain place and the perspective in the painting corresponded to the architectural features of the room where the painting was displayed. In the immediate throes of grief, the speaker may feel that she has lost the perspective that made her feel like she knew where she was standing and where she was headed. Her perspective seems to be gone; her grief is large and engulfing. It is so large that it fills the space around her, including the objects she sees out her window (such as the sheep and the flowers at night) and the space in her own home (such as the clock face). Once she endures the pain and some time goes by, she will regain her perspective, and her sense of loss will get smaller as it recedes into the past.

HISTORICAL CONTEXT

Raphael, the Renaissance, and Pre-Raphaelitism

Brock-Broido's poem is named after the Renaissance artist, Raphael Sanzio. Raphael was born in 1483 in Urbino, Italy, to an artist named Giovanni Santi. Raphael first learned painting from his father, but after his death, Raphael went to study under Perugino, a celebrated artist. It was here that Raphael learned from the masters so well that his work was difficult to distinguish from theirs. In 1504, Raphael traveled to Florence to see the works-in-progress of Leonardo da Vinci and Michelangelo. He stayed there for four years, combining his mastery of Perugino's techniques with what he was learning from the works of Da Vinci and Michelangelo. While in Florence, Raphael was commissioned to paint holy family portraits for private patrons, many of which are considered masterpieces in modern times. Some of them feature only the Madonna and child, and it may be these paintings to which Brock-Broido's speaker in "After Raphael" refers. These beautiful renditions of families, including the mother and child, are the longed-for image of the speaker who is now orphaned. Because the speaker in the poem is grieving her parents, the reference to the "post-Raphaelite world" may refer to the loss of the union of parent and child as depicted in some of Raphael's paintings.

Raphael's work includes portraits, altarpieces, and frescoes. Raphael came to be regarded as one of the most important artists of the Renaissance. Scholars often point to his work, along with that of Da Vinci and Michelangelo, as representing the best of the High Renaissance (the time roughly between 1500 and 1525, considered by many scholars to be the pinnacle of Renaissance art). Perhaps the speaker in "After Raphael" means to evoke the burst of artistic expression of Raphael's time and his central position in it. Raphael may be a symbol for expression and growth, and after her parents' deaths, the speaker feels that such times are past.

Raphael's work can be seen in many places in Italy, including in the Vatican, which contains his famous fresco, "School of Athens." In works such as "School of Athens," his use of linear perspective creates the illusion of a huge space opening to the sky on a flat wall above a door. What is important about this perspective (to the Renaissance painters and to Brock-Broido's speaker) is that it allows the artist to portray accurately the way people and things are arranged spatially. Things that are far away are depicted as smaller, for example. Raphael died in 1520, and his body was buried in the Pantheon in Rome.

CRITICAL OVERVIEW

"After Raphael" is the second poem in the collection *Trouble in Mind*. Critics praised the collection for its elegance, imagination, and range of emotion. They found Brock-Broido's handling of loss in the poems to be honest, moving, and startling. In *American Book Review*, Catherine Daly had this to say about *Trouble in Mind*:

> What is poetry? In her third slim volume, Lucie Brock-Broido continues to answer that question with decorate verse and heightened language. Brock-Broido's poems are *ars poetica*—they are about poetry—but they are also about a life devoted to poetry, or a life converted into poetry, or poetry as a living, and therefore perishable, gesture.

Daly notes the influence of Wallace Stevens in this volume, adding that Brock-Broido "has used her own understanding of his poetic as the poetic in this volume of poems." Daly concludes, "*Trouble in Mind* is about the hall of mirrors that is writing poetry about the self as well as about poetry." Jahan Ramazani of *Virginia Quarterly Review* finds *Trouble in Mind* reveals the influence of Wallace Stevens, William Shakespeare, Emily Dickinson, and Gerard Manley Hopkins. Commenting on the melancholy mood of the volume, he writes, "For all the unrelieved despair of Brock-Broido's poems, the darkness visible of this volume is curiously resplendent."

A reviewer for *Publishers Weekly* hails the volume as "gorgeous and mournful, ornate and deeply felt." The reviewer concludes that Brock-Broido is a "poet who finds renewed languages for the recurrent dilemmas such [melancholic] hearts contain." In *Library Journal*, C. Diane Scharper remarks that Brock-Broido's poems are so personal and specific to her vision that they "are sometimes inaccessible." A *New Yorker* reviewer observes that Brock-Broido introduces dramatic, tragic characters alongside ordinary loved ones in the volume. The reviewer concludes that while lesser poets fail at elegiac verse, "in Brock-Broido's hands it yields great conceptual and syntactical variety."

WHAT DO I READ NEXT?

- Robin Behn's *The Practice of Poetry: Writing Exercises from Poets who Teach* (1992) provides strategies for aspiring poets to develop their technique with the guidance of numerous writing teachers. The book contains ninety exercises, along with essays to help would-be poets hone their craft.

- In 1988, Brock-Broido's debut collection, *A Hunger*, was acclaimed by critics and poetry lovers alike. Her subjects include analysis of time and American culture.

- *The Master Letters* (1995) is Brock-Broido's second collection of poetry. Based on three letters written by Emily Dickinson, this collection contains echoes of Dickinson while it puts forth Brock-Broido's unique poetic imagination and voice.

- *The Collected Poems of Wallace Stevens* (1990) provides readers with a basic understanding of Stevens' poetic vision and voice. Wallace Stevens inspired some of Brock-Broido's writing.

CRITICISM

Jennifer Bussey

Bussey holds a master's degree in Interdisciplinary Studies and a bachelor's degree in English literature. She is an independent writer specializing in literature. In the following essay, she explores the theme of time in Brock-Broido's "After Raphael."

Lucie Brock-Broido's "After Raphael" relates the grief experienced by a woman who recently lost her mother after having already lost her father. The speaker feels alone and orphaned, even though she is an adult. The speaker moves from describing her sense of pain and loss to the realization that one day, she will also grow old and have to face her own mortality. What ties these themes of grief and mortality together is

> THE CLOCK SIMULTANEOUSLY REPRESENTS TIME, WHICH THE SPEAKER PERCEIVES TO BE STANDING STILL, AND THE SPEAKER HERSELF, WHO IS ALSO 'LONG-FACED' (SAD) AND FROZEN BY HER OWN INABILITY TO MOVE FORWARD."

time, a subject that is a subtle undercurrent running through the poem. Brock-Broido addresses it through imagery and the speaker's feelings.

The first indication that time is going to be important in the poem occurs when the speaker decides to go ahead and talk about her grief and then sets it up with a chronology. In lines four and five, she states, "First, my father died. Then my mother / Did. My father died again." The words "first," "then," and "again" all denote sequence relationship to time. The speaker is in effect offering a timeline of the loss of her parents. The reference to her father dying again indicates that the father's memory had been kept alive through her mother. Memories are a critical element for spanning human experience through time, creating connection to the immediate and distant past. In this case, the mother's memories of the father and the speaker's memories of her father *with* her mother have allowed her to close up, to a degree, the time since she lost her father. She still has the mother's memories to comfort and encourage her. But when her mother dies, she feels that she has lost her father again on this other level. She loses all relationship with her parents, and she no longer has the benefit of interacting with the people whom she has known the longest. The way the speaker talks about her parents strongly suggests that she loved and respected them very much. In all likelihood, she continued to see her mother and probably came to her for advice and companionship. While she was alive, the mother surely offered her husband's perspective on things, too. So through her ongoing close relationship with her mother, the speaker was able to have the advantages of being parented when she needed it and having her oldest friendship when she needed that. Upon her mother's death, she lost the security, the friendship, the wisdom, and the sense of belonging. Now she has only her own memories, with no living connection beyond herself to connect her present self to her past self.

The next passage is stated in the past tense, so it is the speaker's telling of another memory. This time, the memory is of her experience when she was first hit with the loss of her parents. To her, it was a storm that decimated an apple tree, symbolizing her family. Trees are often used to represent families (as in family trees) because they have roots that go deep down and provide stability and history, while also displaying branches and leaves that indicate multidirectional life and generation. One root or one branch can be the source of numerous other outgrowths that represent entire families or, as in the case of this poem, a single individual who has a place in the tree but does not generate another branch. The speaker's break between lines 7 and 8 indicates a pause, either so she can decide what she wants to say or so she can collect herself emotionally. Either way, the memory of the tree is one that remains important to her. And both interpretations show that the speaker's utterance is spontaneous. Because it evokes such an emotional response from her, the reader can tell that this painful memory is preventing her from taking solace in pleasant memories.

After describing the tree, the speaker moves into the present and reveals her feelings directly. She is tired of feeling the way she does and of not being able to have what she wants. She longs for peace and rest, but instead she is lonely and melancholy. This is a very subtle use by Brock-Broido of time, but it indicates plainly the speaker's present. In the present, the speaker is emotionally stuck. Understandably, when the speaker looks out her window, she notices sheep standing still. This is very much a present-tense image, so present that time seems almost to have slowed down. The sheep are still. This leads into a direct reference to time when the speaker imagines that ice is forming inside her home, even on the face of a clock. The clock simultaneously represents time, which the speaker perceives to be standing still, and the speaker herself, who is also "long-faced" (sad) and frozen by her own inability to move forward. That the speaker says "the ice assembles / *Even* on the crystal of the long-faced clock" (italics added) indicates that the ice may be moving from the inside out. The emotional paralysis that she feels is beginning to affect her external reality. She now projects the

inability to move to her home, imagining that the very objects that personalize her living space have become victims of her grief. She is emotionally trapped by time; she grieves the past, is stuck in the present, and cannot figure out how to move into the future.

The speaker's sleeplessness is another example of how time is at a standstill in her world. She is unable to adhere to a normal routine of waking and sleeping hours, and the hours of the day begin to meld together into a constant span of time. Without the clear night and day demarcation, people often lose track of time and feel that time is moving slowly. The speaker's thoughts turn from night-blooming ghostpipe flowers to a realization that the world in which she lives "*is true.*" From here, she comes to a new realization, transitioned through the line, "I was little; I am middle." Now she understands that she is no longer a daughter, the youngest in the family. Her parents are gone, she is an adult, and she is now being taken by time toward her own mortality. She asks herself, "Will I not / Grow old?" Just as she is alone in her grief, she considers that she must face mortality alone. That does not mean that she is resigned to living out the rest of her years alone, and perhaps she will seek out new relationships or even pursue having a family of her own. These are issues outside the scope of the poem, but the speaker's gradual acceptance of reality and her place in time give relevance to such considerations.

Moving from the image of a broken falcon's wing that destines the bird to death, the speaker considers the opening and closing of flowers. This final image invites the speaker back into the normal flow of time because flowers open and close, usually according to the rising and setting of the sun. Unlike the speaker, they close at night to rest so they can open up for the sun in the morning. Even the flowers are part of the cycle of time every day, and the speaker is finally beginning to identify with that reality. The natural images throughout the poem serve to remind her that nature is in tune with time and change, and by realizing she is part of those cycles (even though it means the cycle of mortality), the speaker has hope of reconnecting with the world.

Source: Jennifer Bussey, Critical Essay on "After Raphael," in *Poetry for Students*, Thomson Gale, 2007.

SOURCES

Brock-Broido, Lucie, "After Raphael," in *Trouble in Mind*, Alfred A. Knopf, 2004, p. 4.

Daly, Catherine, "The Back Talk of the Dead," in *American Book Review*, September–October 2003, pp. 23–24.

Ramazani, Jahan, Review of *Trouble in Mind*, in *Virginia Quarterly Review*, Vol. 80, No. 3, Summer 2004, pp. 263–64.

Review of *Trouble in Mind*, in *New Yorker*, Vol. 80, No. 10, May 3, 2003, p. 107.

Review of *Trouble in Mind*, in *Publishers Weekly*, Vol. 250, No. 51, December 22, 2003, p. 54.

Scharper, C. Diane, Review of *Trouble in Mind*, in *Library Journal*, Vol. 129, No. 2, February 1, 2004, p. 92.

FURTHER READING

Black, Sophie Cabot, *The Descent: Poems*, Graywolf Press, 2004.

> Sophie Black is a modern poet whose work shares recurring themes and stylistic elements with Brock-Broido's work.

Chapman, Hugo, Tom Henry, Carol Plazzotta, et al., *Raphael: From Urbino to Rome*, National Gallery, 2004.

> Raphael's life and influences are discussed with the purpose of showing his development as an artist. The book includes more than ninety of his works, many in British collections.

Levy, Alexander, *The Orphaned Adult: Understanding and Coping with Grief and Change after the Death of Our Parents*, Perseus Publishing, 2000.

> Drawing on his personal experience and that of numerous other adults who have lost their parents, psychologist Alexander Levy offers explanation and reassurance so that other adults will know what to expect and how to care for themselves in coping with this particular type of grief. He also discusses how this experience often causes people to evaluate their own mortality.

Roberts, Neil, ed., *A Companion to Twentieth-Century Poetry*, Blackwell Publishing, 2003.

> Roberts compiled important and representative poetry from English-speaking writers all over the world. He presents here a wide range of styles, points of view, and cultural traditions in this volume of modern poetry.

Another Night in the Ruins

GALWAY KINNELL

1966

"Another Night in the Ruins," by Galway Kinnell, is a poem about spirituality and creativity told in seven sections. It was first published in the *Paris Review* in the spring of 1966. Kinnell later included it in his poetry collection, *Body Rags* (1968), which was a finalist for the prestigious National Book Award. The publication of this volume marked a high point in Kinnell's career as a poet; after this point Kinnell began to garner significant honors.

As a child, Kinnell loved the work of Edgar Allan Poe and Emily Dickinson, but as a mature poet, he considered himself a follower of Walt Whitman. Scholars of American literature assert that modern American poetry stems either from the tradition of Walt Whitman or from Emily Dickinson. Whitman is clearly evoked in Kinnell's passionate, sonorous style, and like Whitman's work, Kinnell's poems are concerned with spirituality, man's relationship with the natural world, and social issues.

"Another Night in the Ruins" draws heavily from the natural and spiritual world as the narrator examines his own process of creativity. The ruins referred to in the title are the metaphysical ruins of former works residing within the narrator of the poem. The narrator is seeking a way toward growth or rebirth as a writer. By the end of the poem, he comprehends that the fire of creativity is not a tool to be controlled, and he

Galway Kinnell (© *Oscar White/Corbis*)

knows instead his real work lies in trusting himself entirely to his creative passion.

AUTHOR BIOGRAPHY

Galway Kinnell was born February 1, 1927, in Providence, Rhode Island, to James Kinnell and Elizabeth Mills. He grew up in Pawtucket, Rhode Island, and as a child, loved the poetry of Edgar Allan Poe and Emily Dickinson. Kinnell was particularly drawn to the musicality and the loneliness that marked their works. In 1945, at age eighteen, Kinnell enlisted in the U.S. Navy. World War II ended that same year, and Kinnell returned home in 1946 to pursue studies at Princeton University. He graduated *summa cum laude* in 1948, alongside another future poet of fame, W. S. Merwin. Kinnell earned his Master of Arts degree from the University of Rochester in 1949.

Kinnell began his teaching career at the University of Chicago. After earning a Fulbright Fellowship, he lived and taught abroad, visiting universities in a variety of nations, including Iran, Australia, and France. Upon returning to the United States in the early 1960s, Kinnell became involved in the civil rights movement. He joined the Congress on Racial Equality (C.O.R.E.) in 1962. Kinnell's work with C.O.R.E. included assisting in voter registration and workplace integration in Louisiana, which led to his being arrested.

Kinnell was a poet-in-resident at various North American institutions, and he began winning awards soon after the publication of his first book, *What a Kingdom It Was* (1960). He won the National Institute of Arts and Letters Award as well as a Guggenheim Fellowship in 1962. Kinnell's second book of poetry, *Flower Herding on Mount Monadnock* (1964), continued to be one of his most popular, even after nearly five decades of his publishing poetry. *Body Rags*, the collection which includes "Another Night in the Ruins," was published in 1968. *Flower Herding on Mount Monadnock* and *Body Rags* were both finalists for the National Book Award. Kinnell received a Rockefeller Foundation grant in 1968 and a National Endowment for the Arts grant in 1969. Another popular book by Kinnell is *The Book of Nightmares* (1971), which consists of a sequence of ten interrelated poems drawing on the poet's experiences as a civil rights activist and Vietnam War protester. Kinnell won another Guggenheim Fellowship in 1974 and a prestigious MacArthur Fellowship in 1984. His collection, *Selected Poems*, won the Pulitzer Prize for Poetry and the National Book Award in 1983. Kinnell served as the state poet of Vermont from 1989 through 1993. In 2002, he was honored by the Poetry Society of America with the Frost Medal for Lifetime Achievement.

Kinnell married Ines Delgado de Torres in 1965, and they had two children together, who are sometimes featured in their father's poems. Kinnell and de Torres divorced twenty years later. He founded New York University's esteemed creative writing program and taught there until his retirement. He held the Erich Maria Remarque chair in creative writing and was also chancellor of the Academy of American Poets. After retirement, Kinnell left New York City to live full-time in Vermont.

MEDIA ADAPTATIONS

- An audio recording of "Another Night in the Ruins" is available at http://archive.salon.com/audio/the_paris_review/2001/04/30/lunch_three/ from the online magazine *Salon*. The reading, which lasts nearly eight minutes, was recorded in April 2001 as part of *Salon*'s celebration of National Poetry Month and also includes the poems "The Milk Bottle" and "The Frog Pond."

- *Galway Kinnell* is a compact disc that captures Kinnell's 1980 reading from his collection *Mortal Acts, Mortal Words*. The CD is 58 minutes long and includes an introduction by Allen Planz. It can be ordered at http://www.poets.org/ from the Academy of American Poets store.

- An audio recording of Kinnell's famous poem "After Making Love We Hear Footsteps" is available at http://www.poets.org/viewmedia.php/prmMID/15927 which is the website of the Academy of American Poets. The recording was made on March 18, 1980, at the Guggenheim Museum.

- Video of Kinnell reading "After Making Love We Hear Footsteps," is available at Bill Moyer's *Fooling with Words* series website, http://www.wnet.org/foolingwithwords/main_video.html which is a multi-poet project produced on PBS. This video was recorded at the 1998 Geraldine R. Dodge Poetry Festival and aired on PBS on September 26, 1999. A videocassette of the series is available at http://www.films.com.

- *Galway Kinnell* is a compact disc produced by the Poetry Archive. It is 54 minutes long and includes nineteen tracks of Kinnell reading his poetry. This recording, available for purchase from http://www.poetryarchive.org/poetryarchive/singlePoet.do?poetId=2637 was made on July 11, 2005, at the Audio Workshop in London, produced by Richard Carrington. The Poetry Archive made four of the poem tracks available for preview: "Blackberry Eating," "Oatmeal," "First Song," and "Lastness (section 2)."

- The hardcover edition of Kinnell's 2006 volume of poetry, *Strong Is Your Hold*, includes a compact disc audio recording of Kinnell reading all the poems published in this book, as well as related anecdotes. This collection and its accompanying CD, published by Houghton Mifflin, are available from book retailers.

POEM TEXT

1
In the evening
haze darkening on the hills,
purple
of the eternal, a last bird
crosses over, '*flop flop*,'   5
adoring
only the instant.

2
Nine years ago,
in a plane that rumbled all night
above the Atlantic,   10

I could see, lit up
by lightning bolts jumping out of it,
a thunderhead formed like the face
of my brother, looking nostalgically down
on blue,   15
lightning-flashed moments of the Atlantic.

3
He used to tell me,
"What good is the day?
On some hill of despair
the bonfire   20
you kindle can light the great sky—
though it's true, of course, to make it burn
you have to throw yourself in ..."

4

Wind tears itself hollow
in the eaves of my ruins, ghost-flute   25
of snowdrifts
that build out there in the dark:
upside-down
ravines into which night sweeps
our torn wings, our ink-spattered feathers.   30

5

I listen.
I hear nothing. Only
the cow, the cow
of nothingness, mooing
down the bones.   35

6

Is that a
rooster? He
thrashes in the snow
for a grain. Finds
it. Rips   40
it into
flames. Flaps. Crows.
Flames
bursting out of his brow.

7

How many nights must it take   45
one such as me to learn
that we aren't, after all, made
from that bird which flies out of its ashes,
that for a man
as he goes up in flames, his one work   50
is
to open himself, to *be*
the flames?

POEM SUMMARY

Section 1: Lines 1–7

"Another Night in the Ruins" begins with a description of setting in the first two lines. It is nighttime and the narrator is outside, or looking outside, at a hilly landscape. Lines 3 and 4, "purple / of the eternal" is a light reference both to aristocracy and spirituality. Purple is a color traditionally reserved for royalty. In this phrase, Kinnell is evoking awe, which is then stirred by a casual bird that flies by in lines 4 and 5. The bird is of the mortal, secular realm, emphasized by the silly "'*flop-flop*'" of its passing. The bird "crosses over" the hills in line 5, a turn of phrase that is also used colloquially to describe people who have died. This allusion to death is underlined by the frequent use of birds

in death symbolism. Birds have been described as harbingers of death or as those who carry away the souls of the dead. In the last two lines of this section, the narrator says he is "adoring / only the instant," a multilayered phrase referring both to the narrator's admiration of the bird, of the nighttime hills, and of the amorphous presence of a higher being.

Section 2: Lines 8–16

The second section recalls an experience from nine years earlier. Nine is a number of significance and power in Western folklore because it is comprised of three threes (three also being an important number). Here the narrator remembers a trans-Atlantic flight. The airplane passes through a storm and the poet sees, as described in lines 13 and 14, a thunderhead in the shape of his brother's face. The face is looking "nostalgically down" on the ocean as if it were a god looking down in its creation. This oblique spiritual reference reinforces those put forth in the first section. The layers of meaning here suggest the narrator's close (even familial) relationship to his own deity; the love and sorrow inherent in nostalgia; the storm as reference to the biblical story of Noah wherein the Earth was flooded for forty days and forty nights.

Section 3: Lines 17–23

Having remembered his brother, the narrator dwells on him further in the third section of the poem. The narrator remembers, in line 18, his brother scoffing, "What good is the day?" Lines 19 through 21 describe a bonfire that lights the nighttime sky. This image is reminiscent of the lightning over the Atlantic Ocean in the second section. The fire imagery of the second and third sections in connection with the narrator's brother invites an interpretation of the brother as a kind of fire god (for example, Zeus). The bonfire the brother speaks of is lit on "some hill of despair" although what causes the despair is not identified. Lines 22 and 23 introduce fear and excitement when the narrator's brother explains that one must jump into the fire to keep it burning. Literally this implies suicide by self-immolation. (Self-immolation is an extreme form of protest in which a person commits suicide in a public place by setting himself on fire and thus bringing attention to some injustice.) Figuratively, throwing oneself into the fire can be understood as giving into passion or even seeking release from despair through rash action.

TOPICS FOR FURTHER STUDY

- Creativity is a central focus for Kinnell in "Another Night in the Ruins." Write a poem in at least three sections that explores your ideas about creativity. As a class, have a poetry slam during which class members read their poems aloud.

- Kinnell is a renowned New England poet. In small groups, select poems by other New England poets and stage a dramatic presentation of these poems complete with costumes, props, and interpretive acting. Write a couple of paragraphs explaining why you selected these pieces and submit these to your teacher.

- What images stand out in your mind when you read "Another Night in the Ruins"? Write a short story or play whose action is based on what you see happening in Kinnell's poem.

- Two of the major subjects in Kinnell's poem are spirituality and creativity. Write an essay that examines the link between spirituality and creativity. Trade essays with another student. Do you agree or disagree with what your classmate wrote? Discuss your opinions and reasons in small groups.

- Select another poem by Galway Kinnell and read it. Create a visual interpretation of that poem using whatever medium you prefer: paint, collage, drawing, sculpture, or other media. Write a short paragraph explaining your piece and put your work on display along with the paragraph you wrote and a copy of the poem you are interpreting. How is this poem different from and how is it the same as "Another Night in the Ruins"?

- Choose one of the spiritual references in Kinnell's poem to research, making sure to select from a religious tradition other than one with which you are already familiar. Write a research paper explaining this reference in full, including its origin and contem-porary application. Examples from his poem include: flood stories; wicker man; holy bovine; drawing down the moon; fire in the head; and the phoenix.

- What environment speaks to you like the night-dark hills speak to Kinnell in this poem? It could be a place near where you live or someplace you've visited. It could be on a large scale or very specific and minute. It could be peaceful or it could be stimulating. Write a personal essay describing this place in detail and why it is important to you.

- Birds play an important part in the imagery of Kinnell's poem. Alone or in small groups, take a walk in the woods or a nearby park and count the number of birds you see as well as the different varieties of birds. Observe their behavior, coloring, and calls (binoculars help). Compare your observations to a field guide when you return from your walk. How many different birds could you identify? Write a brief essay describing what you saw.

- Choose six or more of your favorite poems and make digital audio recordings of them on the computer. If possible, enhance the tracks with some music or sound effects (but do not forget that the poems are the central focus). Make a CD compilation of your poems and trade them with your classmates or even share them with the whole school.

- In this poem, Kinnell uses a rooster to describe the moment of inspiration. If you were Kinnell, which kind of bird would you have chosen? Why? Is it local or exotic? Write a short essay describing this bird and why you like it better than Kinnell's rooster, paying special attention to your bird's place in other literary works.

Section 4: Lines 24–30

Line 24, the beginning of section 4, personifies the wind in the act of tearing "itself hollow." Carrying on into line 25, the narrator places this harsh wind in the abstract location of "my ruins." Ruined structures may be created by neglect over time and exposure to the natural elements, of which one is the wind. In this instance, the narrator refers to his own internal ruins, ravaged by a vicious wind. He then brings sound into this illustration with the words "ghost-flute," which evokes the eerie whistle of a hard-blowing wind, particularly when it catches on an edge or whips through a hollow structure. The narrator is building, line by line, a cold, wintry, wind-swept scene that is old, aged. Lines 28 and 29 describe the "upside-down ravines" of snowdrifts which capture this howling wind and amplify it. These hollowed-out drifts also capture the narrator's night-swept "ink-spattered feathers," drawing forth layered imagery of quills and of an old bird that is black or has black markings. Ink is a reference to writing and to the color black.

Section 5: Lines 31–35

In this short section, the narrator stops to listen—to the wind, for an answer, for a message? "I hear nothing," he reports in line 32. "Only / the cow . . . / of nothingness" has multi-layered meaning, referring simultaneously to the holiness of the cow (as exemplified in Hindi religion) and to its comical, mundane nature, a characterization more prevalent in the narrator's own Western culture. The silliness of the cow "mooing / down the bones" in the middle of this solemn, reflective poem, is emphasized in the last two lines. The narrator is outside, pondering seriously and listening closely to the natural world, only to be struck by the humor of the lowing of a mere cow. Perhaps here the natural world is telling the narrator, whether he hears it or not, that life cannot be taken so seriously all the time.

Section 6: Lines 36–44

The narrator next sees a rooster but carries this imagery of another bird back to the serious and spiritual. He sees the rooster search for grain in the snow—what must seem an impossible quest to those who are not birds. The rooster finds his grain in lines 39 and 40 and "rips / it into / flames," which returns the reader to the fire imagery of earlier. The last two lines describe fire coming from the rooster's head. This strange image is another spiritual reference masked by the mundane. The mundane is the red fleshy cockscomb on a rooster's head, which could figuratively be described as flames. Spiritually these lines are a reference to the fire in the head, a shamanistic description of one's experience with the divine.

Section 7: Lines 45–53

The last section is the culmination of the previous six, drawing them together into a greater meaning than each had individually. In line 45, the narrator wonders "how many nights must it take"—not days, months, or years. This poem takes place at night and never departs from that setting. In like 46, the narrator uses the phrase "one such as me," meaning a writer, as suggested earlier by the "ink-spattered feathers." Line 48 describes the phoenix, a mythical bird that is reborn following its own fiery death. The narrator is coming to terms with the fact that humankind—such as writers—are not like the phoenix because humans are not magically reborn in the fire that consumes them. This leaves unanswered the question then of *what* humans are. The narrator now understands that immersion in the fire—which is the fire of creation—is a different type of transmutation than the phoenix undergoes. Instead of rebirth, a person *becomes* the flames, that is, the creator. Just as the Bible describes God's creation of humankind as in His own image, so does Kinnell draw a similar circle in "Another Night in the Ruins": the poet, the fire, and the poet's works. His writing remakes him all the time, a never-ending cycle of change and expression.

THEMES

Birds and Transcendence

Transcendence, a state beyond material constraints, is a term often used to describe the spiritual. In Kinnell's poem, landscapes of nighttime hillsides, ruined buildings, snowdrifts, and bonfires are populated by a bird flying by, a man, a cow, and a rooster. The narrator's outward observations turn inward to the ruined eaves of his inner self, where a different storm rages, a relentless wintry death. The narrator draws the strength to reconnect himself to creativity from the words of his brother and the example of the rooster. In an interview for *Contemporary Literature* with Thomas Gardner, Kinnell describes his fascination with bird imagery as the inevitable tension of the bird's liminal state: "like everyone, I experience the contest between wanting to transcend and wanting to belong."

The scene is set in the first section when the narrator observes a lone, last bird "crosses over," wording which is suggestive of the threshold between the living and dead. The airplane of the second section is a man-made bird and, again, the narrator experiences a moment of wonder, faced with a thunderhead that bears a resemblance to his brother, looking down on the lightning-illuminated ocean. The third section goes right to the heart of the narrator's impending transformation. Here, his brother tells him of a bonfire that "can light the great sky" with the condition that the bonfire's fuel is man himself. Section 4 draws a parallel between the bird images and the narrator. This section is set in the narrator's internal landscape, which he describes as in ruins. In line 30, the narrator writes, "our torn wings, our ink-spattered feathers," an illusion to quills, to writing, as well as age and the avian. The fifth section lacks bird references, but this section is intended as a pause, a breath, in the cadence of the poem. The last two lines, "mooing / down the bones," suggest pagan transcendence, when a pagan high priestess draws down the moon, or goddess, into her own body for a short time. The rooster of section 6—that finds a grain in the snow and eats it up, symbolic of inspiration—marks the turning point of the poem, when the narrator finally understands what his brother told to him nine years before. "Flames / bursting out of his brow" is both a description of the rooster and also a description of a transcendent state of inspiration and creativity. The narrator communicates his understanding to the reader in section 7. He alludes to the phoenix, the mythical bird that ages, dies, burns, and is reborn from its own ashes. Now that he understands his own road to transcendence, he no longer unrealistically expects to burn and be reborn like a phoenix. His transcendent burning is not a tool for achieving creativity but rather the creative act itself.

Fire and Creativity

"Another Night in the Ruins" is rich in imagery drawn from the natural world, a common element in Kinnell's poetry. The four elements of

In the last section of this poem Kinnell suggests that when people "go up in flames" like the Phoenix depicted here, their job is to "be" the flames
(© Images.Com/Corbis)

earth, air, water, and fire are invoked in this poem, another nod toward pagan spirituality, which reveres the natural world. Earth is the "hill of despair" and the metaphysical ruins. Air is represented by the birds in the poem, the plane over the Atlantic, and the wind that "tears itself hollow / in the eaves of my ruins." Water is present in the Atlantic Ocean and the snowdrifts. Fire is present in the bonfires and suggested in the ashes of the phoenix, the flames of creativity so central to Kinnell's thesis. In the revelation of the final stanza, the narrator understands that he is not in control of what he creates but must instead submit to the chaos of conception: "to open himself, to *be* / the flames." The rooster ripping apart the grain it has found illustrates inspiration striking all of a sudden, both majestic and frightening. The narrator is haunted by his own, internal ruins of "torn wings," darkness, "snowdrifts," "ghost-flute," and wind. These ruins drive the narrator toward introspection and change. The narrator exists in darkness, the darkness of ruin and age. In seeking rebirth—creativity—the narrator is drawn toward fire and light. "On some hill of despair / the bonfire / you kindle can light the great sky." Even the lightning of the second section is a kind of fire although the narrator cannot be a part of it and looks on from afar, as a man to his god. Ultimately, the flames of creativity in Kinnell's poem are not flames of a passionate activity but rather the energy of being: "his one work / is / to open himself, to *be* / the flames."

STYLE

Imagery

Imagery is a literary device that uses information drawn from the five senses (sight, smell, touch, taste, and hearing) to create a picture in order to convey meaning. Kinnell anchors this poem with images. Rather than leave the night to a mere absence of light, he colors it and gives it life: "haze darkening on the hills," "lit up / by lightning bolts."

Flight is another reoccurring image. In the first section the narrator describes a bird flying at dusk, and then in the second section, he is in an airplane over the ocean. Wings and feathers are mentioned at the end of the fourth section and a rooster is the central image of the sixth section (although roosters are not necessarily known for flight). Flight and birds come together in the seventh, section where the narrator describes a bird flying out of its own ashes and then realizes that for man to go "up in flames," he must become one with the fire.

Kinnell uses some images in a more abstract way. "Purple / of the eternal" seems to refer to the dusky color of the sky at the beginning of night, when the last rays of the sun are dying on the horizon, leaving behind dark, richly colored hues. Similarly, "Adoring / only the instant" may describe the focus of the bird flying past, which appreciates the beauty of the brief moment of dusk before night arrives. This phrase may also refer to the narrator's own feelings as he looks out on this scene, caught up in the fleeting beauty. Another abstract image in Kinnell's poem is "ghost-flute / of snowdrifts." This image draws on the senses of hearing, touch, and sight. The "ghost-flute" is the eerie sound made by the

fierce wind. "Snowdrifts" refers to a winter of the spirit when things are at rest or have aged past a time of usefulness, of reproductive ability. "Mooing / down the bones" is a comical reference to the pagan ritual of drawing down the moon, wherein the high priestess enters a trance and is temporarily inhabited by the goddess. Kinnell is also referring to the musical instrument known as bones, usually made from a pair of cow or bull ribs. Imagery is extremely important in poetry, which may rely less on the narrative line and more on the feelings evoked by the author's choice of words to convey certain sensory impressions.

Meaning of Title

The title of this poem, "Another Night in the Ruins," is important to consider because it adds a whole other level of meaning. In using the word "another," Kinnell is drawing attention to the fact that the narrator's struggles are ongoing. The narrator has been here before and was likely unsuccessful in previous attempts to understand how to rise up out of his own ruins. The word "night" again emphasizes the time in which the poem is set. It is the light of understanding, of inspiration, of renewed vigor for creative work that shines through this nighttime meditation. These figurative forms of illumination are represented by the lightning and the bonfire, which are set against a backdrop of darkness. The "ruins" of the title anticipates the ruins mentioned in the fourth section. These are the narrator's psychological or emotional ruins, probably connected to creative writing as suggested in the "ink-spattered feathers" mentioned at the end of the same section. The hope suggested in this title, which seems full of despair, is that this time something will be different and the narrator will not go through this again. He sees this hope fulfilled in the last section when he finally understands the process by which his creative transmutation can be achieved with success.

HISTORICAL CONTEXT

Civil Rights Movement

Kinnell was involved with the civil rights movement in the United States in the 1960s, when "Another Night in the Ruins" was first written and published. The civil rights movement lasted

COMPARE
&
CONTRAST

- **1960s:** The U.S. military is involved in the Second Indochina War, known to Americans as the Vietnam War. Many Americans protest U.S. military involvement in the conflict and oppose mandatory military service (known as conscription or the draft). Young men are drafted right out of high school; some go to great lengths to avoid being sent to Vietnam, including fleeing to Canada, enrolling in college, or claiming conscientious objector status.

  Today: The U.S. military has been all-volunteer since 1973, although there is an attempt in 2003 to pass legislation reinstating the draft. The United States is involved in a long, drawn-out war in Iraq, which starts as a mission to recover weapons of mass destruction and overthrow Iraqi dictator Saddam Hussein but dissolves into a debilitating civil war. No weapons of mass destruction are found, but Hussein is executed in 2006. As in the Vietnam War, the conflict has no easy solution that is acceptable to the United States, but many Americans are clamoring for U.S. troops to withdraw and return home.

- **1960s:** The civil rights movement in the United States is at its peak and centered on equalizing the rights of people regardless of race. On August 28, 1963, more than 200,000 protestors gather in Washington, D.C., to take part in the March on Washington for Jobs and Freedom. Dr. Martin Luther King Jr. delivers his famous "I Have a Dream" speech from the steps of the Lincoln Memorial.

  Today: Popular perception is that the civil rights movement was successful, but many non-whites, religious minorities, and other marginalized citizens would argue that the struggle for equal rights in the United States is far from over. According to statistics available from the U.S. census, poverty rates in 2004 are 9 percent for whites, 10 percent for Asians, 22 percent for Hispanics, and 25 percent for African Americans. The fact is segregation continues despite laws prohibiting discrimination on the basis of race, religion, age, sex, or handicap.

- **1960s:** Popular poets include Allen Ginsberg ("Howl"), Denise Levertov (*Here and Now*), Frank O'Hara (*Lunch Poems*), LeRoi Jones (*Preface to a Twenty-Volume Suicide Note*; he later changed his name to Amiri Baraka), W. S. Merwin (*The Drunk in the Furnace*), Adrienne Rich ("Rape"), Robert Lowell (*For the Union Dead*), and Robert Creeley (*For Love*).

  Today: Popular poets living today include some of the same as those who were popular in the 1960s. Others are Maya Angelou (*Still I Rise*), Billy Collins (*The Trouble with Poetry*), Gwendolyn Brooks (*Blacks*), Rita Dove (*Mother Love*), Marilyn Hacker (*Desesperanto*), Jim Harrison (*Saving Daylight*), Mary Oliver (*Thirst*), and Saul Williams ("Not in My Name").

- **1960s:** Popular opinion holds that religion is in decline in the United States although statistics do not support this contention. Social and cultural issues such as civil rights, women's liberation, increased drug use, and the conflict in Vietnam cause Americans to ask the question, "Is God Dead?"—the title of a *Time* magazine article published in 1966.

  Today: According to a 2002 study conducted by the Pew Research Center, the United States is one of the most religious countries in the developed world with 59 percent of Americans reporting that religion is very important in their lives.

from approximately the mid-1950s until the end of the 1960s and was characterized by protest, civil disobedience, litigation, and other forms of social unrest that pushed for people to have equal standing under the law regardless of race, religion, gender, or sexual orientation. At this time, throughout the United States, blacks and whites were segregated in many schools, jobs, and businesses. Although black people were emancipated from slavery following the end of the U.S. Civil War in 1865, many were so impoverished and still ill-regarded by white people that they were systematically treated as second-class citizens. In May 1954, the U.S. Supreme Court ruled in *Brown v. Board of Education of Topeka* that racial segregation in public schools was unconstitutional. This crucial decision had a huge impact because many school districts across the country were not integrated. When Little Rock, Arkansas was pressed to integrate in 1957, the governor, Orval Faubus, called in the National Guard to prevent nine black students from entering a white school that they had sued for the right to attend. President Eisenhower intervened by dismissing the National Guard and bringing in U.S. Army soldiers to escort these nine black students to and from school and between classes.

Events escalated quickly after this Supreme Court ruling as high emotions erupted into action and reaction. A young black teenager, Emmett Till, was beaten and shot to death in Mississippi in August 1955 for allegedly whistling at a white woman. Rosa Parks refused to give up her seat on a Montgomery, Alabama, bus to a white passenger in December 1955, leading to a two-week bus boycott and the U.S. Supreme Court decision that segregated buses were unconstitutional. Following the successful Montgomery bus boycott, many civil rights protestors adhered to the strategy of non-violent protest. Sit-ins were frequent in the 1960s. Black people sat at lunch counters, in museums, in libraries, and other segregated public places, and when they were forcibly removed and arrested, they brought public attention to their cause. Many sit-in protestors asked judges for jail and no bail so as to put the financial burden of their arrest on the government by taking up jail space. Non-violent protestors also went on freedom rides across the southern states to take a stand for desegregation of bus terminals but were met with more dangerous reactions as the buses were sometimes attacked by people who believed in segregation.

In June 1963, President John F. Kennedy submitted his civil rights bill to Congress, which President Johnson saw passed in 1964. In 1965, the U.S. Congress passed the Voting Rights Act to eliminate poll taxes, literacy tests, and other methods of discrimination at the polls. One effect of these changes was that, in twenty years, the United States went from having barely one hundred elected black officials to over seven thousand. While the civil rights movement was caused positive change, few minorities living in the United States in the early 2000s would claim that the struggle for equal rights was over.

Vietnam War

Vietnamese nationalists (the Viet Minh) struggled for freedom from their imperialist occupier, France, in the First Indochina War (1946–1954). The Viet Minh were successful in their campaign against France, but their country quickly fractured into a northern communist state and southern anti-communist state once the French left. These two factions fought for control over all of Vietnam, leading directly from the First Indochina War into the Second Indochina War (1954–1979), known in the United States as the Vietnam War. What started out as a brutal civil war developed into an international outlet for cold war battles between the United States and the Union of Soviet Socialist Republics, also known as a proxy war. U.S. troops were present in Vietnam as early as 1950, but it was not until 1965 that large numbers of soldiers were deployed to aid the Viet Cong army of South Vietnam.

The warfare in Vietnam was unlike anything the U.S. military had previously encountered. Instead of clashes between large numbers of troops with an obvious winner and loser, the Viet Minh employed guerilla tactics. They attacked in small, mobile units, relying on surprise, knowledge of the landscape, and disguise. The U.S. military adapted, making wide use of chemical defoliants in an effort to expose the North Vietnamese forces, a choice that rendered much of the country's land dangerously toxic and infertile for years to come. The Vietnam War polarized Americans back in the United States. A significant number of people protested U.S. military involvement in Vietnam, which eventually led to Congress cutting off aid to the

South Vietnamese in December 1974. American troops were brought home, leaving South Vietnam vulnerable to the well-organized North Vietnamese army. The war ended on April 30, 1975, when Saigon, the southern capital, was taken by the Viet Minh.

The legacy of the Vietnam War is painful, in part because of the high numbers of casualties. The war was not restricted to Vietnamese territory and ranged far into the neighboring countries of Laos and Cambodia. Numbers of dead and wounded are still debated but can be estimated at 300,000 dead among the South Vietnamese and its allies out of a combined force of 1.2 million soldiers; and 600,000 dead among the North Vietnamese and its allies out of a combined force of 520,000. The harshest statistic is the one million civilians of Vietnam, Laos, and Cambodia who died. Then, too, the chemical defoliants, particularly the dioxin-containing Agent Orange, are alone responsible for the poisoning four million people, half a million birth defects, and significantly increased risk for various cancers. Veterans of the Vietnam War often also suffered from debilitating post-traumatic stress syndrome.

CRITICAL OVERVIEW

Kinnell has had an illustrious career as a poet from the very start, quickly coming to the attention of critics, such as Selden Rodman, as "the future of American poetry" with greats such as Robert Frost and E. E. Cummings aging. Kinnell's first volume, *What a Kingdom It Was*, was published in 1960. Rodman, reviewing for the *New York Times* was laudatory in describing Kinnell's epic "The Avenue Bearing the Initial of Christ into the New World": "I do not hesitate to call this the freshest, most exciting, and by far most readable poem of a bleak decade." Four years later, when Kinnell's second book of poetry, *Flower Herding on Mount Monadnock*, appeared, critical reception was still enthusiastic. In a review for the *New York Times*, De Witt Bell discusses how this new work displays "a new subtlety, depth and simplicity" and summarizes his review by describing this book as "memorable." Kinnell's style is often traced back to Walt Whitman, especially for its quality of inner reflection. Michael Goldman, writing for the *New York Times*, reviews Kinnell's third

collection, *Body Rags*, alongside a volume by the esteemed Robert Bly. Goldman gives a positive review, remarking on Kinnell's "growing reputation as a superior lyric poet."

Thomas Lask describes *The Book of Nightmares* as Kinnell's "most integrated book, a work of one mood." Lask's review describes an ever-maturing poetic voice, unafraid "to look at the underside of society." In another review of the same book, M. L. Rosenthal is cautiously positive, finding fault in a heaviness of the book that "needs stripping down." In conclusion, Rosenthal nonetheless enjoyed *The Book of Nightmares*: "the real power of his book comes from its pressure of feeling, its remarkable empathy and keenness of observation, and its qualities of phrasing—far more than from its structural thoroughness or philosophical implications."

Kinnell's retrospective, *The Avenue Bearing the Initial of Christ into the New World: Poems 1946–64*, was published in 1975 and reviewed by Christopher Ricks for the *New York Times*. Ricks writes: "The best of Kinnell, which is very good, comes when he resists the expected humorlessness of rural-piety poetry," a summary of the poet's early career. Kinnell's award-winning *Selected Poems* was published seven years later. Morris Dickstein, in his review, gives a glowing description of Kinnell's growth as a poet, concluding that Kinnell "has not been seduced by modernist obfuscation, technical cleverness or earnest, thin-lipped confessional self-display."

New York Times reviewer, Michiko Kakutani, writes eloquently of Kinnell's mid-1980s volume, *The Past*, noting that it is a further development and refinement of Kinnell's previous works: "An awareness of the evanescence of things suffuses the poems in this volume." Harold Beaver also gives *The Past* a good review and is clearly unsurprised at the poet's continued success: "Always there is this landscape with figures. Always the landscape embodies emotion without a hint of pastoral extravagance or natural fallacy." An anonymous reviewer for *Publishers Weekly* gave an inviting review of Kinnell's collection of poetry, *Imperfect Thirst*. The reviewer comments that some of the poet's "remarks to himself are needlessly self-referential" but that "his voice is unsurpassable" and covers a broad territory of expression and subject matter.

Ned Balbo, writing for *Antioch Review*, celebrates the breadth of Kinnell's poetry in his

WHAT DO I READ NEXT?

- *Leaves of Grass* (1855) is Walt Whitman's major work. Whitman continuously revised and republished this book until his death in 1895. Whitman, along with Emily Dickinson, is considered by scholars to be one of the parent-figures of the American poetic traditions. Kinnell regarded Whitman as one of his major influences.

- Kinnell's *The Book of Nightmares* (1971) is a sequence of ten related poems, which Kinnell was inspired to write after his experiences in support of the civil rights movement (including being arrested) and protesting the Vietnam War.

- *Judevine* (1991), by David Budbill, is a collection of poetry centered on the characters that inhabit the fictional rural town of Judevine, Vermont. Budbill is renowned for capturing local dialect, expressions, and personalities. *Judevine* was made into a play and an opera.

- *After Frost: An Anthology of Poetry from New England* (1996), edited by Henry Lyman, is a collection of poems from thirty New England poets, including Robert Frost, Galway Kinnell, Sylvia Plath, Donald Hall, and Louise Glück.

- *The Poems of Francois Villon* (1977) is translated by Kinnell from the original French. Villon is a fifteenth-century poet and thief, who composed his verse in prison and chose to write about the underworld he lived in rather than the more acceptable courtly ideals.

- *Robert Frost's New England* (2000), by Betsy and Tom Melvin, is a photographic guide to Frost's poetry. The book presents photographs chosen to convey some scenes Frost describes in his poems. Poems and photographs are presented side by side.

review of *A New Selected Poems*: "Kinnell continues to write superbly of heartbreak and affirmation, his vision clear and language supple." In

2006, Kinnell published his twelfth collection, *Strong Is Your Hold*, which includes a poem about the events of September 11, 2001, titled "When the Towers Fell." An anonymous review for *Publishers Weekly* writes, "Occasionally the poet veers too far toward silly, snapshot moments, but for the most part Kinnell injects the mundane . . . with meaning and passion." In all, critics generally praise Kinnell's work as it evolved through many books of poetry.

CRITICISM

Carol Ullmann

Ullmann is a freelance writer and editor. In the following essay, she discusses the relationship between creativity and spirituality in Kinnell's poem "Another Night in the Ruins."

"Another Night in the Ruins," by Galway Kinnell, examines a writer's struggle with creativity, and the perils and assurances inherent in the creative process. The narrator of the poem is a writer who, like Kinnell, draws inspiration from the natural world and seems driven to distraction by his own naturalist spirituality. In section 6, he watches a rooster find a grain— the inspired thought—and "rips / it into / flames. Flaps. Crows. / Flames / bursting out of his brow." Even before this direct illustration of inspiration is presented, the narrator is concerned with the nighttime hilly landscape and birds, both real and figurative. One bird he watches flying through the twilight. Another is part of himself, a tattered bird with "ink-spattered feathers." The final bird of the poem is the phoenix, mentioned indirectly in the last section. A phoenix is a mythical bird that dies a fiery death and then rises, reborn, from its own ashes.

Fire imagery is an important component of Kinnell's poem. This fire is not a fire of permanent destruction but one of creation and change. What the narrator struggles to understand over the course of the poem is that, like the real thing, his symbolic fire, and its resulting creations, are not controllable by man although fire is a tool of creation. In classical mythology, fire was a divine gift that man was given. The narrator comes to realize that he must give himself up wholly to the flames of his creativity for it to be fully unleashed and thrive. Through this magnificent process, he is lifted from depression and the

THE CENTRAL CONFLICT OF THIS POEM IS IN
THE NARRATOR AS HE COMES TO GRIPS WITH WHAT HE
MUST DO TO GROW AS A CREATIVE INDIVIDUAL."

ruins of old projects and previous failed attempts fall aside. Thus he can be born anew to new ventures, new productivity.

Kinnell also alludes to spiritual and religious symbolism throughout "Another Night in the Ruins." Flames bursting from the brow of the rooster is not only indicative of the catalytic moment of inspiration but also of the spiritual phenomenon known as fire in the head. Fire in the head refers to being touched by a divine spirit. It is not strictly possession because the deity does not take over. The person is instead sharing his mortal body, an experience that could be both intoxicating and terrifying. The central conflict of this poem is in the narrator as he comes to grips with what he must do to grow as a creative individual. Early in the poem, in section 3, as well as at the end, in section 7, the narrator is concerned with the idea that he has to give himself up to the flames. The flames he is talking about are those of his own passion and creativity. He is unsure about throwing himself in, as his brother told him to do. But then he reflects upon the wintry ruins of his former work and the mundane nothingness looming before him. The rooster arrives and shows him that fire is, indeed, the way. In giving himself to the fire of creativity, the narrator recognizes that "his one work / is / to open himself." Fire is transformative: That which it burns can never be restored. This irreversibility need not be looked upon as destructive, which is the narrator's fear. Fire is not a tool for him to master but a conduit through which he must move to become both tool and master.

Creativity begins with inspiration, a word whose roots are traced to breath. One of the definitions for inspiration has religious connotations of divine truths revealed to prophets. The etymology of the word, inspiration, is traced back to Hellenic times when the oracles of the gods—for example, Apollo's oracle at Delphi—would receive divine messages from vapors that mysteriously rose from the earth. Inspiration, in the more secular sense, occurs as a result of friction between ideas. This friction will eventually result in a spark (the inspired thought), which evolves into a new idea. Inspiration, for many creative people, is the easy part. Often they have more ideas than they have time to realize those ideas in an art form. Following inspiration, the work at shaping one's new idea begins, and this is when creativity comes into play. Metaphorically speaking, structures are built— buildings that will eventually wear, ruin, and tumble down, as seen in the narrator's internal ruins described in section 4.

Religion is a system of belief centered on the existence of a deity or of the human soul. Spirituality is a broader term, encompassing all that is intangible in human existence but requiring no specific belief system. Kinnell frequently expresses a spiritual inquisitiveness and sensitivity in his poetry, and "Another Night in the Ruins" is no exception. Here, the narrator's faith in his spirituality provides the means by which the narrator can map a way through his fear and become aligned with his creativity once more. After all, creativity is a part of spirituality. Origin stories are often a major aspect of religious belief. In these stories, the creation of the entire world and all of its creatures is explained, often in terms of divine expression. Set apart from animals, people are said to share in this mysterious power to create.

According to anthropological research, record of artistic expression first appears during the Upper Paleolithic period, approximately 40,000 years ago and when it does appear, it occurs in many places. As of the early 2000s, anthropologists continued to ponder *why* Upper Pleistocene hunters and gatherers created beautiful objects and images (for example, cave paintings, ivory carvings, and shaped stone beads). These things did not help them procure food as better tool technology would. One theory holds that prehistoric men and women may have developed spiritual beliefs at this time. They thus perhaps believed that these art works were spiritual aids for food procurement and for their protection.

Thus, creativity and spirituality are linked and together may have across the centuries been understood as capable of improving the human condition. For the narrator of this poem, creativity is a matter of concern to him as a writer; spirituality concerns him as a human. Throughout the poem, the narrator is probing his spiritual side for answers to his fears and uncertainties about the creative process. In sections 1 and 2, the narrator observes the natural world with awe. He watches a lone bird fly at dusk, "adoring / only the instant." The thunderhead in section 2 is a further sign of the narrator's spiritual link with the natural world. It is not until section 3, however, that the link between the narrator's creativity and his spirituality is revealed. Here the narrator remembers his brother's advice about coping with depression. His brother tells him that the inspiration, "the bonfire / you kindle," is the easy part: "To make it burn," when creativity comes into play, is the difficult part because "you have to throw yourself in." This surrender is an act of faith in one's ability to be creative.

The narrator's brother's advice was given nine years ago and, from the use of the word "another" in the title and from the ruins of section 4, it is clear the narrator either did not understand his brother or has failed to have faith in his own creativity. In section 5, the narrator continues to watch and listen to the night-darkened world, seeking inspiration. But he confesses, "I hear nothing." Coming upon a rooster in section 6, though, the narrator observes it picking through the snow for a grain. The snow is symbolic of death or sleep while the seed represents new life. Here the narrator finally understands inspiration as the rooster "finds / it. Rips / it into / flames." The fire the narrator has avoided all this time thus returns, and now, in section 7, he understands the role fire plays and his job in the creative process. He realizes he is not like the phoenix, born again from his own ashes after throwing himself into the bonfire of his inspired ideas, but rather, "his one work / is / to open himself, to *be* / the flames." To "open himself" means that he relinquishes control of his creativity to the idea itself; however, "to *be* the flames" also implies that in becoming one with the fire, the narrator will direct the transformation of his idea. It is a paradox worthy of classical literature: in order to control his creativity, he must give himself up to it completely.

Source: Carol Ullmann, Critical Essay on "Another Night in the Ruins," in *Poetry for Students*, Thomson Gale, 2007.

> THE END OF 'ANOTHER NIGHT IN THE RUINS,' FOR EXAMPLE, DISCLOSES EVEN AS IT INQUIRES: THE LESSON IS DEFINED AND AFFIRMED, EVEN IF IT REMAINS UNLEARNED."

Lee Zimmerman

In the following essay excerpt, Zimmerman explores the themes of isolation, struggle and unanswered questions—"revealing our inability to know truth but also our capacity to embody it"—in Kinnell's Body Rags. *Zimmerman also considers Kinnell's new approach to writing which he does not arrive at by "cultivating new concerns" but by transfiguring the old.*

Consider, for example, the opening poem of *Body Rags*, "Another Night in the Ruins." Its seven fragments suggest the extreme isolation in which the poem was actually begun; Kinnell had "bought an old ruined house in Vermont": "One night I stayed up all night mainly because I was too cold to sleep, and wrote a number of disconnected fragments, some descriptive of the place, some imagined, some memories" (*WDS* 34–35). These so-called "disconnected fragments," however, won't stay apart. Mind being shapely, they begin to arrange themselves around the images of birds, of "the instant," and especially of fire—images that combine in those "lightning-flashed moments of the Atlantic" glimpsed from a plane. From his lonely outpost, the poet, like the fragments, begins to make provisional connections. He hears "nothing," but this nothing is a *presence* that unites the internal world of "bones" with the external one of "the cow": "I listen. / I hear nothing. Only / the cow, the cow / of nothingness, mooing / down the bones." The poet's brother's absence (he's dead) might ultimately outweigh his presence (in memory), but by recalling and, in the conclusion, personally asserting Derry's teaching, Kinnell achieves a kind of empathy with him. The teaching itself expresses the self's communication with the world—"the bonfire / you kindle can light the great sky"—but also the price: "though it's true, of course, to make it burn / you have to throw yourself in . . ."

By withholding his own endorsement of this maxim until the end, Kinnell maintains tension between the obvious isolation in the poem and whatever empathy is finally established (in much the same way that the title holds together death ["Ruins"] and continuation ["Another Night"]). Despite its apparent fragmentation, the poem thus retains a sense of development; the double-edged empathy appears earned because it is clearly struggled for. Indeed, although the rhetorical elevation of the long last sentence and its repeated (and elaborated) formulation of the poem's "theme" convey a strong sense of resolution, the struggle is not yet over. As Yeats so often does, Kinnell hedges his strong rhetorical closure by ending with a *question:* "How many nights must it take / one such as me to learn . . . ?" Even as he affirms the truth of his brother's lesson, he demonstrates the difficulty of learning it. The poem thus remains "alive," straining forward, intimating fulfillment but remaining unfulfilled:

How many nights must it take
one such as me to learn
that we aren't, after all, made
from that bird which flies out of its ashes,
that for a man
as he goes up in flames, his one work
is
to open himself, to *be*
the flames?

There is an undertone of frustration and complaint in these lines, as if they read, "How many *more* nights must it take?" The apparent difficulty in taking Derry's words to heart illustrates how much further *Body Rags* goes beyond Kinnell's previous work in putting the self in question. Throwing yourself on the bonfire—*being* the flames—surpasses just standing on the pulse and loving the burning earth ("Alewives Pool," *WKW*) or merely spying on a forest flower whose "invisible life . . . / Goes up in flames that are invisible" ("Flower Herding on Mount Monadnock," *FH*). If you stand on the burning earth, you must personally catch fire. In his efforts to do without the "scaffolding or occasion" to which the earlier poems still partly clung, to structure his verse wholly on the meanderings of his awareness, Kinnell here evidences his growing capacity to commit himself more directly, to "dig" deeper—to "*be* / the flames."

Still, as I have suggested, a great reluctance always accompanies these efforts. And the prosody mirrors this ambivalence. Examining an earlier version of the lines quoted above (one that, except for the lowercase line openings, looks more like a passage from *Flower Herding* than *Body Rags*)—

that for a man
as he goes up in flames, his one work
is to open himself, to *be* the flames?

—Howard remarks: "It is interesting to see that in his final version of these lines, Kinnell literally opens himself, breaking apart the language until it illustrates the aperient nature of all such poetry" (316). But even as the lines open out, their extreme irregularity—the syntax-splitting line breaks, the unpredictable mix of long and short lines—creates a tension indicative of the concomitant difficulty. To open, for Kinnell, is indeed to break apart. Thus, where Whitman easily plunges right into the world, Kinnell approaches it more gingerly, with more fits and starts, like the rooster in section 6, searching for food:

Is that a
rooster? He
thrashes in the snow
for a grain. Finds
it. Rips
it into
flames. Flaps. Crows.
Flames
bursting out of his brow.

If "the lines are the river bed," they don't often allow smooth flowing. Rather, strewn with hidden obstructions, they reroute, temporarily dam, and only finally permit climactic release, the kind of outrush that we see in the famous last line of "The Bear."

The final image of "Another Night in the Ruins" is of jumping into flames. But, as in *Crow*, life goes on. Even though "we aren't, after all, made / from that bird which flies out of its ashes," in the beginning of the volume's very next poem, "Lost Loves," the poet has survived a conflagration: "On ashes of old volcanoes / I lie dreaming." The volcano's death, and the prospect of his own, provokes nostalgic dreams of other "deaths"—his lost loves. But soon, as Andrew Taylor suggests, "the poem changes from nostalgia to an affirmation of the vitality of change." A tadpole "dies" as a tadpole, but—retaining its identity—is born anew as a frog:

And yet I can rejoice
that everything changes, that
we go from life
into life,

and enter ourselves
quaking
like the tadpole, his time come, tumbling
   toward the slime.

"Quaking" intimates the potential violence of such self-transfiguration (perhaps the old volcano is only dormant) and recalls Yeats's sexual "shudder" that accompanies bloody historical succession. But at the same time the juxtaposition of that one-word line with the long concluding one accomplishes a release of tension that reinforces the rejoicing. The concluding line also testifies that, tumble and thrash about as it will, *Body Rags* at its best retains the craftsmanship (if not the manners) that Davie so admired in the very early work. Assonance is carefully controlled ("come, tumbling") and shades into internal rhyme (like/time/slime), while the alliterated, hard-edged *t*'s (tadpole/time/tumbling toward) finally relax into the amorphous, sensual mix of sibilance and liquidity ("slime"), like the tadpole wriggling free of its old form.

"'Lost Loves' is structured on, and expresses, a transformational process," Taylor proposes, "which is basic to almost all the best of Kinnell's poetry. . . . First, through suffering of some kind the poet undergoes a death of the self, of a conscious self. He goes 'from life.' However, this does not involve death as we usually think of it. Rather, it is a withdrawal to a pre-human or preconscious state, an 'animal' state, consistently represented by animal imagery, in this case, the tadpole. This animal image is the second component. The third is a rebirth, a moving back 'into life,' and is accompanied by a variety of emotions, the most characteristic being rejoicing, wonder, or awe" (229). Although few poems employ this pattern as straightforwardly as "Lost Loves" or "The Bear," many make a more oblique use of it. In "How Many Nights," for example, the paradigm is slightly submerged. The emphasis falls on the third stage, the "moving back 'into life,'" as the poet, after many nights, emerges into morning; he hears the breath of sleeping animals

   and above me
   a wild crow crying '*yaw yaw yaw* '
   from a branch nothing cried from ever in my
      life.

Kinnell reports that some of his friends were unsure "whether I'd thought of the crow as benign or as an unwelcome presence" (*WDS* 4). But if the crow is not exactly "benign," the outrushing last line (itself venturing forward, enacting the speaker's release) unambiguously evinces the thrill of discovery itself—little matter of what. Kinnell advises that "we take seriously Thoreau's dictum, 'Be it life or death, we crave only reality'" (PPD 67). One good dictum deserves another: the crow makes it new for the poet. But, for Kinnell a discovery of the world is a discovery of the self; the poem's initial setting, "the frozen world," is finally renamed: "my life." Thus, he explicates the end of "How Many Nights" by writing a "bit of verse" called "The Mind":

   Suppose it's true
   that from the beginning, a bird has been
      perched
   in the silence of each branch.
   It is this to have lived—
   that when night comes, every one of them
   will have sung, or be singing.
   (WDS 4)

An explication of the explication: "I was thinking of those diagrams . . . that show the brain in the shape of the tree. At moments of full consciousness all the birds would be singing. Whether or not the crow's cry is beautiful mattered less to me than that this hitherto mute region comes into consciousness" (*WDS* 4).

Taylor's paradigm also structures "Night in the Forest," one of the "moment" poems in *Body Rags* that extends from those in *Flower Herding*. The opening—"A woman / sleeps next to me on the earth"—presents a version of the first stage ("the death of a self, of a conscious self"), while the "cocoon sleeping bag" in which the woman sleeps is a vestige of the second stage ("a withdrawal to a pre-human or pre-conscious state, an 'animal' state"). "A strand / of hair flows" from her bag, "touching / the ground hesitantly, as if thinking / to take root": a withdrawal involves the danger of *not* returning, of merging into the earth, rather than remaining conscious but isolated. Kinnell, however, isn't bound by these two choices. In the third stage, the "moving back 'into life,'" the focus shifts to the poet himself, who now bears within himself an echo of the world: "I can hear / a mountain brook / and somewhere blood winding / down its ancient labyrinths. . . ."

The poem concludes:

> And
> a few feet away
> charred stick-ends surround
> a bit of ashes, where burnt-out, vanished
>   flames
> absently
> waver, absently leap.

Drawing on the poetics of "The Poem," these lines themselves waver like flames, rise and fall capriciously, leap high and suddenly flicker out, and in this they illustrate one way that Kinnell breaks open his poetry in *Body Rags*. We have seen the effect already at the end of "Another Night in the Ruins," where in this sense the work of the verse itself also is to "*be* / the flames" The whole of "In the Anse Galet Valley" forms another striking example. "Clouds / rise ... and sink," "A straw torch / flickers," and "fer-de-lances / writhe," but these fluctuations describe the movement of the verse as well as the events of the poem. It ends:

> The fer-de-lances
> writhe in black winding-skins,
> the grail-bearers go down, dissolving.
> What question could I have asked, the wafer-
>   moon
> gnawed already at its death-edge?

"What question could I have asked?": doubt squared. Certainty twice removed, a question about a question, an interrogative cast in a conditional—trafficking in liminality, how little one knows! Going "from life / into life"—surviving—so much is jettisoned. Yeats wrote about modern poets, "we sing amid our uncertainty": we may embody truth but we cannot know it, and where truth cannot be known questions and uncertainties will proliferate. And proliferate they do, from the first pages of *Body Rags* to the last—especially at the conclusion of poems, where doubts traditionally are resolved, not left hanging.

The opening and closing poems, ending with questions, frame the volume in mystery. First: "How many nights must it take ...?" Finally: "what, anyway, / was that sticky infusion, that rank flavor of blood, that poetry, by which I lived?" In between, "What question could I have asked ...?" and "How many nights / have I lain in terror ...?" (this single-sentence poem doesn't end with a question mark but the subject-verb inversion nevertheless indicates an interrogative). Sometimes a question occurs *near* a poem's end, but the remaining lines don't answer it directly,

relating instead a sensory experience, shifting away from "knowledge" and toward "embodiment," away from what we cannot know and toward what we can. In "Getting the Mail," for example, a question arises:

> And touching
> the name stretched over the letter
> like a blindfold, I wonder,
> what did *getting warm* used to mean? ...

Kinnell does open the letter, but the promise of a verbal answer goes unfulfilled. Instead a different sort of fulfillment follows—aural, not rational; we are thus, typically, both answered and not answered, given satisfaction and left unsatisfied:

> And tear
> open the words,
> to the far-off, serene
> groans of a cow
> a farmer is milking in the August dusk
> and the Kyrie of a chainsaw drifting down
>   off Wheelock
> Mountain.

At the end of "Night in the Forest" the flames are simultaneously present and absent, a paradox that crystallizes in the odd coupling of the final two words—"absently leap." And in asking an unanswered question, "Last Songs" seeks a poetics—couched in a conditional—based on a mysterious "it" that can be gestured toward but not precisely defined:

> Silence. Ashes
> in the grate. Whatever it is
> that keeps us from heaven,
> sloth, wrath, greed, fear, could we only
> reinvent it on earth
> as song.

This kind of double ending—withholding but asserting, revealing our inability to know truth but also our capacity to embody it—provides many of Kinnell's poems in *Body Rags* with what Barbara Herrnstein Smith has termed "anti-closure": their conclusions avoid "the expressive qualities of strong closure"—obviously anathema to a singer amid uncertainty—"while securing, in various ways, the reader's sense of a poem's integrity." The withholding precludes strong closure, while the assertion secures the sense of an ending; even as a question conveys ignorance, it can also express discovery—discovery of what precisely to ask. The end of "Another Night in the Ruins," for example, discloses even as it inquires: the lesson is defined and affirmed, even if it remains unlearned. In "The Bear" the poet is left "wondering," but at the same time we feel something climactic has been revealed (the concluding question is thus sometimes quoted out of context—as an epigraph to a student literary magazine or a newspaper interview—as if it conveyed some great Truth about Poetry). One reason is that this conclusion sifts through the hallucinatory confusions of the poem to arrive at the center of things: "What was that thing? What was this all about anyway? What am *I* about?" Moreover, that central thing *is* named, even as it is wondered about: it is a "sticky infusion," a "rank flavor of blood" and finally (out with it now) "poetry" itself. The poem's true subject, hidden throughout, making its claims only implicitly, is finally, dramatically unveiled. *Voilà!* ...

Source: Lee Zimmerman, "Romanticism in the Rag-and-Bone Shop: *Body Rags*," in *Intricate and Simple Things: The Poetry of Galway Kinnell*, University of Illinois Press, 1987, pp. 95–103.

Charles Frazier

In the following essay, Frazier gives a critical analysis of Kinnell's work.

Galway Kinnell was born in Providence, Rhode Island. He received an A.B. from Princeton University in 1948 and an M.A. from the University of Rochester in 1949. Kinnell served in the U.S. Navy in 1945-1946. He married Ines Delgado de Torres and has two children, Maud Natasha and Fergus. He was supervisor of the liberal arts program at the University of Chicago's downtown campus from 1951 through 1954, after which he taught at the University of Grenoble and later at the University of Iran as a Fulbright Professor. He has been poet-in-residence at Juniata College in Huntingdon, Pennsylvania; Colorado State University; Reed College in Portland, Oregon; the University of California at Irvine; and the University of Iowa. Kinnell also served as a field worker for the Congress of Racial Equality. He has been the recipient of numerous awards and grants, among them a National Institute of Arts and Letters Award (1962), two Guggenheim Fellowships (1962, 1974), a Rockefeller Foundation grant (1968), a Longview Foundation Award (1962), a National Endowment for the Arts Grant (1969-1970), and *Poetry* magazine's Bess Hokin and Eunice Tietjens Memorial prizes (1965, 1966), and a Pulitzer Prize in 1983 for *Selected Poems*.

> THE FIRST POEM, 'ANOTHER NIGHT IN THE RUINS,' ESTABLISHES THE CENTRAL CONCERNS OF THE VOLUME. KINNELL THINKS OF THE DEATH OF HIS BROTHER AND THE NOTHINGNESS THAT DEATH REPRESENTS, AND HE ONCE MORE ATTEMPTS TO FIND CONSOLATION FOR LOSS AND SUFFERING."

Kinnell's poetry has been devoted to a remarkably consistent, though by no means limited, range of concerns. The subjects and themes to which he has returned again and again are the relation of the self to violence, transience, and death; the power of wilderness and wildness; and the primitive underpinnings of existence that are disguised by the superstructure of civilization. Kinnell's approach to these topics is by way of an intense concentration on physical objects, on the constant impingement of the other-than-human on our lives. As he indicates in one of his many interviews, for him the nonhuman is a realm charged with meanings we hardly understand:

> If the things and creatures that live on earth don't possess mystery, then there isn't any. To touch this mystery requires, I think, love of the things and creatures that surround us: the capacity to go out to them so that they enter us, so that they are transformed within us, and so that our own inner life finds expression through them.

The roots of this feeling lie in primitive rituals of propitiation through which man identifies himself with the physical world of animals, plants, and inanimate objects to beg a kind of forgiveness for some transgression, usually the taking of an animal's life in hunting. It is a ritual filled with the dual awareness of the regrettability and the necessity of death. Most of Kinnell's best poetry is in this propitiatory mode, evoking natural objects, creatures, and landscapes to come to terms with and attempt to transcend temporality. The transcendence that results is, however, not always comforting; indeed, one of the criticisms leveled at Kinnell most frequently is that his poetry is bleak and harsh, death-obsessed, devoid of affirmation. Yet this harshness is not just fashionable cynicism, for as Joseph Langbaum says, "Kinnell, at a time when so many poets are content to be skillful and trivial, speaks with a big voice about the whole of life."

In terms of form, Kinnell has moved, like many poets of his generation, from traditional rhyme and meter in his earliest work to free verse. Seeing rhyme as a limitation on the possible directions a poem may take and the possible meanings it may develop, Kinnell has reacted against Robert Frost's often quoted statement that writing free verse is like playing tennis without a net: "It is an apt analogy, except that the poem is less like a game than like a journey, where there are so many real obstacles in the nature of the case that it would be a kind of evasion to invent additional, arbitrary, verbal ones." In developing his sense of the potentiality of free verse to correspond not to some external pattern but to what he calls "the rhythm of what's being said," Kinnell points most often to Walt Whitman, rather than to Ezra Pound or William Carlos Williams, as the single greatest formal influence on his poetry. Whitmanesque roughness and colloquiality make themselves felt not only in the longer, looser poems like "The Avenue Bearing the Initial of Christ into the New World" and "The Last River," but also in the shorter, more personal lyrics.

Kinnell first began seriously writing poetry during his undergraduate years at Princeton, where he and W.S. Merwin were friends. Selected poems from this early period were published under the title *First Poems 1946-1954* in a limited edition in 1970, and poems from this period are included in the 1974 collection *The Avenue Bearing the Initial of Christ into the New World: Poems 1946-1964*. Although Donald Davie expresses admiration for a few of these poems, especially "The Feast," which he calls "exquisitely civilized and mannerly," many readers would agree, at least in part, with J.F. Cotter's opinion that "Kinnell has done himself a disservice in digging up his juvenilia." Certainly these poems display a derivativeness and an absence of distinctive voice that is perhaps understandable in very early work, but they also hint at the direction Kinnell's later poetry takes. Many of the poems have for their subjects the outdoors, and they frequently take place at night, a combination that appears over and over in Kinnell's poetry. But the poems are marred by a strained delicacy only partially attributable to the formal artificiality and self-consciousness. They seem pale in comparison with the later, more vigorous and harsher work.

What a Kingdom It Was (1960) was Kinnell's first published book of poems, and Ralph Mills has written that it "can be viewed in retrospect now as one of those volumes signaling decisive changes in the mood and character of American poetry as it departed from the witty, pseudo-mythic verse, apparently written to critical prescription, of the 1950's to arrive at the more authentic, liberated work of the 1960's." In this volume Kinnell begins developing his own material and angle of vision. Many of these poems deal with a sense of transgression or loss, which leads to a need for propitiation or reconciliation. In "First Song" three boys transform cornstalks into violins and awaken in themselves a sense of aesthetic awareness coupled with a loss of innocence: "A boy's hunched body loved out of a stalk / The first song of his happiness, and the song woke / His heart to the darkness and into the sadness of joy." The transcendence accomplished through the intercession of crude physical objects is typical of Kinnell's work as a whole, just as is the double awareness in the final line of the darkness and sadness that lie at the core of life. Another poem of childhood, "To Christ Our Lord," examines a boy's feelings toward killing a bird for Christmas dinner. His guilt becomes transformed by the ritual nature of both the dinner and the act of killing:

> Now the grace praised his wicked act. At its
> end
> The bird on the plate
> Stared at his stricken appetite.
> There had been nothing to do but surrender,
> To kill and to eat; he ate as he had killed,
> with wonder.

Here the boy's sense of wonder at the processes of life and death, his new awareness of the mystery at the basis of existence, is the necessary propitiatory gesture.

Similarly, "The Descent," "Freedom, New Hampshire," and "Seven Streams of Nevis" concern death and an adult's sense of loss and guilt requiring some recompensatory action. In these poems the darkness of Kinnell's attitude toward life, for which he has been criticized, becomes obvious, for memory and wonder provide the only recompense for loss, and as the conclusion of "Freedom, New Hampshire" indicates, these are distinctly inadequate:

But an incarnation is in particular flesh
And the dust that is swirled into a shape
And crumbles and is swirled again had but
     one shape
That was this man. When he is dead the grass
Heals what he suffered, but he remains dead,
And the few who loved him know this until
     they die.

The final poem of the volume, the long, Whitmanesque "The Avenue Bearing the Initial of Christ into the New World," continues the theme of loss, carrying it out of the personal and into the communal. The poem's unusual title refers to Avenue C in New York City, and the poem takes as its subject the ethnic, primarily Jewish, inhabitants of the street. Through the progression and compilation of naturalistic detail, it soon becomes apparent that behind the images of waste and loss, the garbage, junk, and dead fish, lies the ultimate loss of the holocaust. The physical and human landscape of waste that is Avenue C provides an objective counterpart to the earlier, more personal expressions of loss, and it leads to a recognition of the universality of suffering: "everything / That may abide the fire was made to go through the fire."

Flower Herding on Mount Monadnock (1964), Kinnell's second book of poetry, breaks little new ground beyond *What a Kingdom It Was*, although it extends his use of rough, conversational free verse and establishes more firmly the natural, physical world as his primary setting. In poems like "Tillamook Journal (2nd version)," "On Hardscrabble Mountain," and "Middle of the Way," he devotes even more attention than before to precise evocation of the things of the physical world. In these poems the speaker is alone, traveling through the wilderness, and very much aware of his separation from the natural world and of the dangerous emptiness that surrounds him. To combat this separation and emptiness, he continually calls the names of the things around him in order to place himself into a relationship with them and thus to establish a context. The result is a poetry of nouns to fill the void. The physical world and the emptiness behind it are in constant tension, as in "On Frozen Fields" when, after a noun-filled description of a walk at night, Kinnell gives this propitiatory prayer in reminder of the emptiness:

You in whose ultimate madness we live,
You flinging yourself out into the emptiness,
You—like us—great an instant,
O only universe we know, forgive us.

Such dual awareness is also evident in "Middle of the Way" when the speaker says, "I love the earth, and always / In its darkness I am a stranger," but its fullest expression is in "Flower Herding on Mount Monadnock." In this segmental poem, a favorite structure for Kinnell, the self is a much more apparent and undeniable presence in contrast with the physical world. In the climb up the mountain the speaker's body provides nouns for the poem just as do the animals, plants, and other objects he encounters. But the forces of emptiness and death enter when he sees a flower and realizes that physical objects are no stay against transience:

The invisible life of the thing
Goes up in flames that are invisible
Like cellophane burning in the sunlight.
It burns up. Its drift is to be nothing.

In *Body Rags* (1968), a book selected for special mention by the poetry judges for the National Book Awards, Kinnell's work becomes more consistently forceful, and the dominant imagery of fire and darkness becomes more apparent. The first poem, "Another Night in the Ruins," establishes the central concerns of the volume. Kinnell thinks of the death of his brother and the nothingness that death represents, and he once more attempts to find consolation for loss and suffering. What he arrives at is close, although clearer in attitude, to the ending of "Flower Herding on Mount Monadnock." He opposes the darkness with fire:

How many nights must it take
one such as me to learn
that we aren't, after all, made
from that bird which flies out of its ashes,
that for a man
as he goes up in flames, his one work
is
to open himself, to *be*
the flames?

Since consumption in the flames is unavoidable, the only recourse is intensity, and throughout *Body Rags* Kinnell uses the imagery of darkness and fire to push his poetry toward such heightened experience.

Sometimes the drive for intensity seems strained, as in "The Last River," but more often it succeeds, as in "The Burn," "Last Songs," and "Night in the Forest." But certainly the two best and most intense poems in *Body Rags* are "The Porcupine" and the often anthologized "The Bear." In these poems Kinnell seeks entrance into a primitive state of identification with the nonhuman. In "The Porcupine" the speaker identifies with the porcupine's suffering and emptiness. The poem describes in ghastly detail how a porcupine is shot from a tree, hooks itself on a branch, lands on the ground, and runs until it falls dead, its entrails played out behind it; and near the poem's conclusion the speaker, calling himself the "Saint / Sebastian of the / sacred heart," makes the association with the creature complete by saying:

> I have fled, have
> jogged
> over fields of goldenrod,
> terrified, seeking home,
> and among flowers
> I have come to myself empty, the rope
> strung out behind me
> in the fall sun
> suddenly glorified with all my blood.

In "The Bear," an even more violent poem, the identification with the nonhuman and with suffering and horrible death leads to visionary experience and to the essence of poetry itself. The poem concerns an Eskimo who wounds a bear internally with a coiled, sharpened wolf rib and then follows its bloody spoor across the tundra for days until the bear dies. The hunter then opens the bear, climbs inside, and in a dream becomes the wounded bear. When he awakes, the experience of identification through suffering and death is total and transforming, for, as the hunter says:

> the rest of my days I spend
> wandering: wondering
> what, anyway,
> was that sticky infusion, that rank flavor of
>   blood, that
> poetry, by which I lived?

In the harsh world of these poems, violence, death, and nothingness become the essence of life and of art, and the only reconciliation is intensity of experience.

Kinnell's most recent poetry, the long poem *The Book of Nightmares* (1971), was received with considerable praise, and, although the central concern is still with emptiness and the imagery of darkness and fire still dominates, the poem modifies the bleak vision of *Body Rags*. Joseph Langbaum calls this long poem, made up of ten related segments beginning with the birth of Kinnell's daughter and ending with the birth of his son, "an unforeseeable leap forward for Kinnell." Langbaum goes on to identify the subject of the poem as "the attempt of the lonely soul, existing in a world where community has broken down, to reforge connections." It is significant in Kinnell's development as a poet that the connections he seeks to establish in *The Book of Nightmares* are much more with the cycles of human existence.

In the second section of the poem, "The Hen Flower," Kinnell stresses man's inability to open himself to death, to "throw ourselves / on the mercy of the darkness," as does the hen. In the other segments, he goes on, largely through the births of his children and through identifying himself with a dying derelict, to seek consolation for death in the human world. This search is not completely successful, for the awareness of mortality and the threat of nothingness is only heightened by the fragility and helplessness of the young children, as in these lines addressed to his daughter, Maud, in "Little Sleep's-Head Sprouting Hair in the Moonlight":

> And yet perhaps this is the reason you cry,
> this the nightmare you wake screaming from:
> being forever
> in the pre-trembling of a house that falls.

The recognition at the end of the poem that "Living brings you to death, there is no other road" is, however intensely felt, nothing new for Kinnell, but the advice he gives his son embodies a double-edged, lighthearted fatality that is not present in the earlier work:

> Sancho Fergus! Don't cry!
> Or else, cry.
> On the body,
> on the blued flesh, when it is
> laid out, see if you can find
> the one flea which is laughing.

The affirmative tone of this conclusion is certainly relative, but the shift in attitude is significant. Consolation for suffering and death is no longer flame, as in "Flower Herding on Mount Monadnock" and "Another Night in the Ruins"; it is now laughter.

Kinnell has said that in the future "Whatever I do will be different from *The Book of Nightmares*,", and that "It would be foolish to go on in the same way." Kinnell's future poetry should prove interesting, but it would be unreasonable to expect major departures or the opening of drastically new ground in the poetry following *The Book of Nightmares*. His poetry has not, over the years, developed through distinct major phases, nor has it undergone radical changes. It has instead grown and evolved slowly and continuously, approaching again and again a handful of fertile major themes in a distinct and personal voice.

Source: Charles Frazier, "Galway Kinnell," in *Dictionary of Literary Biography*, Vol. 5, *American Poets Since World War II, First Series*, edited by Donald J. Greiner, Gale Research, 1980, pp. 397–402.

SOURCES

Balbo, Ned, Review of *A New Selected Poems*, in *Antioch Review*, Vol. 59, No. 1, Winter 2001, p. 121.

Beaver, Harold, "Refuge in the Library, on the Farm and in Memories," in *New York Times*, March 2, 1986, p. BR14.

Bell, De Witt, "Wonders of the Inner Eye," in *New York Times*, July 5, 1964, p. BR4.

Dickstein, Morris, "Intact and Triumphant," in *New York Times*, September 19, 1982, p. 33.

Goldman, Michael, "Joyful in the Dark," in *New York Times*, February 18, 1968, p. 12.

Kakutani, Michiko, "Mortality and Love," in *New York Times*, November 2, 1985, p. 15.

Kinnell, Galway, "Another Night in the Ruins," in *Selected Poems*, Houghton Mifflin, 1982, pp. 67–68.

Kinnell, Galway, and Thomas Gardner, "An Interview with Galway Kinnell," in *Contemporary Literature*, Vol. 20, No. 4, Autumn 1979, p. 427.

Lask, Thomas, "The Makers and Their Works," in *New York Times*, September 1, 1971, p. 35.

Pew Global Attitudes Project, *Among Wealthy Nations . . .: U. S. Stands Alone in Its Embrace of Religion*, Pew Research Center for the People & the Press, December 19, 2002.

Review of *Imperfect Thirst*, in *Publishers Weekly*, Vol. 241, No. 39, September 26, 1994, p. 57.

Review of *Strong Is Your Hold*, in *Publishers Weekly*, Vol. 253, No. 41, October 16, 2006, p. 34.

Ricks, Christopher, "In the Direct Line of Whitman, The Indirect Line of Eliot," in *New York Times*, January 12, 1975, p. 241.

Rodman, Selden, "A Quartet of Young Singers," in *New York Times*, September 18, 1960, p. BR50.

Rosenthal, M. L., "Under the Freeway, In the Hotel of Lost Light," in *New York Times*, November 21, 1971, p. BR77.

FURTHER READING

Kinnell, Galway, *Body Rags*, Houghton Mifflin, 1968.
In his third collection, Kinnell is concerned with mortality and the material world. This volume collects some of his most frequently anthologized poems, including "Another Night in the Ruins," "The Bear," and "The Porcupine."

———, *Walking Down the Stairs: Selections from Interviews*, University of Michigan Press, 1978.
Through selections from his own interviews, Kinnell shares his thoughts on his work and poetry in general.

Nelson, Howard, ed., *On the Poetry of Galway Kinnell: The Wages of the Dying*, University of Michigan Press, 1988.
In this volume, Nelson has collected reviews and articles—both flattering and scathing—about Kinnell, his books, and his individual poems. Critics include Joseph Bruchac, Tess Gallagher, Donald Hall, and Harold Bloom.

Zimmerman, Lee, *Intricate and Simple Things: The Poetry of Galway Kinnell*, University of Illinois Press, 1987.
Zimmerman examines six volumes of Kinnell's work, observing a paradox of conflicted desires which informs Kinnell's verse. Zimmerman's dynamic writing makes this critical study a comfortable book to read.

An Anthem

SONIA SANCHEZ

1987

Sonia Sanchez's poem "An Anthem" first appeared in 1987's *Under a Soprano Sky* and later was included in *Shake Loose My Skin* (1999), a collection of previously published and new poems. "An Anthem" is written in free verse broken into stanzas of varying lengths. In it, Sanchez celebrates her African-American heritage with vibrant descriptions of dance and music. Alongside this celebration is a call for courage to stand up for peace and compassion. It is a poem of resilience that acknowledges some of the ills of the world without giving up hope or identity.

Sanchez uses many styles of writing in her poetry, ranging from haikus and sonnets to free verse. "An Anthem" is representative of her work in that the style suits the content, and the content is perfectly in line with her canon of work. Throughout her career, Sanchez has written about the importance of peace, even when pursuing it is uncomfortable or dangerous. Her writings about African-American themes often have a collective application, as "An Anthem" does. Although the speaker in the poem asks for personal courage, the word "we" dominates the poem.

AUTHOR BIOGRAPHY

Originally named Wilsonia Benita Driver on September 9, 1934, poet Sonia Sanchez was reared in the American South. She was born in

Sonia Sanchez (*Photograph by Marion Ettlinger. Reproduced by permission*)

Birmingham, Alabama, and her mother died in childbirth when Sanchez was only a year old. Sanchez was reared by her grandmother until she also died when Sanchez was only six years old. At this time, she and her siblings returned to Harlem to live with their father, who was a schoolteacher. It was also at this time that Sanchez began to write. The loss of her grandmother and the development of a stutter prompted her to find expression through writing. In Harlem Sanchez learned the dialect of the street that would later characterize so much of her writing. In New York, she learned that racism was not confined to the South, although its northern manifestation was different.

Sanchez acquired much of her education in New York, first earning her bachelor's degree at Hunter College before attending New York University for post-graduate study. She went to Ohio to attend Wilberforce University, where she completed her doctorate. As a professor and lecturer, Sanchez has worked all over the United States, including San Francisco, Pittsburgh, New York City, Amherst, and Philadelphia. In addition to being a respected teacher and scholar, Sanchez won awards for her other activities, her poetry, children's books, her other publications, and her work as a social activist. Over the course of her career, Sanchez was honored by her peers, readers, and literary organizations. Her honors include a PEN Award (1969) and Arts Fellowship (1993–1994), a grant from the National Institute of Arts and Letters (1970), a Lucretia Mott Award (1984), an American Book Award from the Before Columbus Foundation for *homegirls & handgrenades* (1985), a Pennsylvania Governor's Award in the humanities (1989), an Oni Award from the International Black Women's Congress (1992), a Roots Award from the Pan-African Studies Community Program (1993), and a Legacy Award from Jomandi Productions (1995).

Sanchez was committed to encouraging other literary voices; earlier in her career, she refused royalties on her books because she wanted to invest in her publishers and encourage them to publish works by other young writers. Her own work was influenced by the writings of Langston Hughes, Malcolm X, Countee Cullen, and Gwendolyn Brooks.

Her first published book was a collection of poetry, *Homecoming* (1969). Sanchez's next volume, *We a BaddDDD People* (1970), is a collection of poems with a specifically African-American point of view. In it, the poet emphasizes the strength and character of a people with a unique identity. The 1973 collection, *Love Poems*, was published after Sanchez aligned herself with the Nation of Islam; as a result, the perspective reflects a stronger emphasis on building unity among African Americans. *I've Been a Woman* (1978) demonstrates Sanchez's growth as a poet and as a woman. Here, she writes to share wisdom and encouragement. In 1987, *Under a Soprano Sky* was published. The poems contained in this volume are grounded in the real world; Sanchez addresses issues and topics of the day, and she conveys general truths through telling individual stories. *Wounded in the House of a Friend* (1995) is difficult for many readers. Sanchez explores the pain and harshness of difficult experiences. From drug addicts to rapists to betrayal, nothing is off-limits as Sanchez seeks to lay bare the worst of the human condition. In 1999, *Shake Loose My*

Skin was published. "An Anthem" appears in this collection. This poem is an expression of Sanchez's love for her heritage and the need for courage when people take to the streets in protest. It is in content and style representative of much of her work.

As a social activist, Sanchez has been committed to racial and gender equality. She has taught many courses at the college level on black studies, has participated in demonstrations, and has expressed through her writing her vision for peace and freedom. During the late 1960s and early 1970s, her desire for racial equality led her to join Malcolm X's Black Muslim organization, but she eventually left. Although she supported the religion and the discipline, she was frustrated by its treatment of women. She continued to speak out against inequality and negative stereotypes, although she admits that being so outspoken came at a personal and professional price. Often labeled as a radical, she endured the backlash of government agencies, peers, and even a landlord. Still, her commitment to her beliefs came first.

As of 2007, Sanchez was teaching at Temple University in Philadelphia.

POEM TEXT

(for the ANC and Brandywine Peace Community)

Our vision is our voice
we cut through the country
where madmen goose step in tune to Guernica.

we are people made o fire
we walk with ceremonial breaths   5
we have condemned talking mouths.

we run without legs
we see without eyes
loud laughter breaks over our heads.

give me courage so I can spread   10
it over my face and mouth.

we are secret rivers
with shaking hips and crests
come awake in our thunder
so that our eyes can see behind trees.   15

for the world is split wide open
and you hide your hands behind your backs
for the world is broken into little pieces
and you beg with tin cups for life.

are we not more than hunger and music?   20
are we not more than harlequins and horns?

are we not more than color and drums?
are we not more than anger and dance?

give me courage so I can spread it
over my face and mouth.   25

we are the shakers
walking from top to bottom in a day
we are like Shango.
involving ourselves in acts
that bring life to the middle   30
of our stomachs

we are coming towards you madmen
shredding your death talk
standing in front with mornings around our
    waist
we have inherited our prayers from   35
the rain
our eyes from the children of Soweto.

red rain pours over the land
and our fire mixes with the water.

give me courage so I can spread   40
it over my face and mouth.

POEM SUMMARY

"An Anthem" begins with a statement of unity: "Our vision is our voice." The speaker then explains that "we" go all over the country seeking out those who are in favor of war. In the next stanza, the speaker identifies who she and her group are, but she does it in figurative terms. She says that they are people of fire and ceremony who speak with condemned mouths. In other words, they are people of strength, determination, and heritage who continue to speak out even though they are rebuked for it.

The third stanza continues to describe the speaker and her people as having wisdom and purpose. They can do things in their hearts that they do not have to do physically. She says, "we run without legs," meaning that they can move forward or away without physically going anywhere at all. She also says that they "see without eyes," indicating that they know things apart from what they actually see. Their understanding is greater than their direct experience. Her statement that "loud laughter breaks over our heads" indicates joy and camaraderie in the culture of their community.

The next two lines appear three times in the poem. They are: "give me courage so I can

TOPICS FOR FURTHER STUDY

- Choose two African American female poets and select two poems by each poet that you think are typical of each poet's work (either in terms of content or form). Choose one other poem by Sanchez besides "An Anthem" so that you have two of her poems. Compare and contrast the six poems and create a presentation that gives a little bit of background information on each poet, along with your observations on the poems. Your presentation can be in whatever format you choose.

- Observe African dance and celebration. Drawing from your observations on the costumes, music, energy, and meaning, write a poem capturing your impressions.

- Research Sanchez's life to find out more about her social activism. Do you think there is a connection between her motivation to write and her motivation to bring about change? Can you think of other people who fit the same profile? Write an introduction to a biography of Sanchez in which you explore the relationship between writing and working for social change.

- Sanchez was born in the South and lived there for part of her childhood before moving to New York. Read about these two areas during the years Sanchez was there as a child and teenager. What historical, economic, and cultural characteristics and events were most prominent? How might these realities have influenced her? Draw up a two-sided chart presenting the major factors in each area. Illustrate your chart with drawings, photos, maps, and any other visual elements. Write a conclusion explaining how you think these factors influenced Sanchez in adulthood. You may want to look for additional poems to support your assertions.

- "The Anthem" mentions Soweto. Read more about what happened in Soweto, what "Soweto" means, and what the long-term ramifications were for the riots there. What is apartheid and what is its status today? Write about your findings in a magazine article, locate photos to go with it, and format it to look like a magazine spread.

---

spread / it over my face and mouth." The speaker acknowledges that she needs courage to face problems or conditions in the world that demand attention. Her previous reference to war suggests that she asks for courage to advocate peace. It is interesting that here she moves from "we" to "me," so that the reader knows that the speaker is part of a community and she embraces its heritage and culture, but she asks for personal courage. She confronts difficulties that she will have to fight alone, and she wants to be prepared. She describes courage as something that can be given to someone, and it is something that is worn right on a person's face and is expressed in a person's words.

The speaker returns to describing her people, and now she likens them to a secret river, a life source that is unrecognized. The women working and marching, moving like a river, can see what is hiding behind trees. In this stanza, Sanchez introduces the motif of singing and dancing. The dancing is depicted as "shaking hips," and their voices are depicted as "thunder."

The sixth stanza describes divisiveness and conflict in a world "split wide open." Sanchez writes that "the world is broken into little pieces / and you beg with tin cups for life." The speaker then asks if she and her people are not more than hunger, music, harlequins (clowns in traditional European theater), horns, color, drums, anger, or dance. This is her way of demanding that her community be respected as a whole rather than dismissed or relegated to a single aspect of their history or culture. Again she repeats the lines about courage.

The next two stanzas are the poem's longest, at six lines each. In the first, the speaker relates the fact that her people are always moving, usually from the top to the bottom. She refers to the thunder god, Shango, a deity in Yoruban culture. (The Yoruba are a West African ethnic group.) In the second of these two stanzas, the speaker addresses the enemy for the first time, the "madmen" with their "death talk." She warns them that she and her people are not afraid and that they are going on the offensive to stop their madness and their destruction. The protesters are strengthened by nature (the sun and the rain) and by injustice in the world ("children of Soweto"). (Soweto, an acronym for southwest townships and a city formed in 1991 near Johannesburg, South Africa, was the scene of a 1976 uprising by black students against apartheid in which hundreds were murdered.)

The speaker closes the poem with an image of red rain (which could be interpreted as blood), and the fire of her people mixing with water. She says their fire "mixes with the water," which means in this context not that the water douses the fire but rather that the fire ignites and spreads with the blood. To finish the poem, the speaker repeats for the last time, a plea for "courage so I can spread it / over my face and mouth."

Nelson Mandela at a rally of ANC supporters, one of the groups that is lauded in this poem (AP Images)

THEMES

Courage to Protest

In the repetition of the words, "give me courage so I can spread / it over my face and mouth," Sanchez asserts the speaker's plea, almost as a prayer, for courage to face seemingly overwhelming obstacles. She wants to wash in this courage and drink it. The speaker needs to acquire courage, and she is eager to wear it on her face and to speak it with her mouth. An important point about courage is that it is not the absence of fear, but the willingness to do something despite the fear. That is the speaker's position: She is not brimming with her own courage; she is afraid. She asks for courage in order to carry on with what she is committed to do: wage and protest against injustice and suffering

In the third line, the speaker identifies what intimidates: "madmen goosestep[ping] in tune to

Guernica." The reference here is to the 1937 destruction of the Basque city of Guernica by a combined air attack of Nazi German and Fascist Italian air forces. The leveling of this city was considered by Nazi commanders as an experiment to see what destroying a city requires militarily and a chance for pilots to get experience in dropping bombs. The attack laid waste the city, and an estimated two thousand people, mostly women and children, were killed. The speaker is enraged by this event and all other events in which people, who only really want to live their lives, are murdered by madmen. The speaker's protest in this poem joins that made by the painter Pablo Picasso who made a large painting, entitled *Guernica*, as an antiwar protest. In the face of the horrors of war and the carnage wrought by violent attacks on protesters, as occurred in Soweto, the speaker asks for courage to yell in the streets and vigorously confront politicians in an all out effort to assert human rights.

Ethnic Pride

The ethnic pride in "An Anthem" is difficult to miss. The speaker identifies struggles that bring her people together against common enemies of human rights, and she offers the spirit of her people as the force to stop oppression. From the first line ("Our vision is our voice"), the speaker establishes a community created by a similar philosophy. These protesters have a single vision and a single voice.

Beginning in the second stanza, the speaker introduces imagery that calls to mind African dances and ceremonies. She says they "walk with ceremonial breaths," which suggests ceremonies charged with purpose and passion. The refrain, "give me courage so I can spread / it over my face and mouth," seems to link ceremonial face painting with wearing courage in the modern world.

Other references to African dances reinforce the theme of ethnic pride. Words and phrases like "shaking hips," "color and drums," "anger and dance," Shango, and Soweto, all work to reveal the speaker's pride in her African ethnicity and the strength she finds in that identity.

STYLE

Repetition

Sanchez uses two literary devices of repetition in "An Anthem" to underscore images and ideas that are central to the poem's meaning. The first device is anaphora, a type of parallelism. Anaphora is repetition of the same word or words at the start of two or more sentences. Walt Whitman famously uses it in *Leaves of Grass*. In "An Anthem," Sanchez uses it to create thematic and structural unity. The sentences in the second and third stanzas begin with "we" just as lines 21–23 repeat "are we not." These chant-like repetitions create a strong sense of unity or solidarity. It is the speaker's way of saying that "we" are not going away and "we" need to be heard. The central idea of the poem is one of protest, of in-the-street chanting, and this form of repetition underscores that idea.

The other repetitive device Sanchez uses is refrain. A refrain is a phrase or sentence that is repeated within a poem or song, generally at the end of a stanza or in some other predictable way. The refrain in this poem is the plea or prayer:

"give me courage so I can spread / it over my face and mouth." This is the only thing the speaker asks for outright, but she repeats it to create a sense of urgency, of immediate confrontation and need for empowerment. Three times she repeats these lines, the third occurring in the final lines, which is an emphatic and powerful site in a poem. The last lines, especially ones that have been repeated, create the reader's final impression of the poem.

Allusion

An allusion is a reference within a literary work to a historical event or person or to another work of art. For example, classical allusions may refer to mythology; biblical allusions refer to stories or people in the Bible; and literary allusions refer to stories or characters from other literary works. In three places, Sanchez uses allusion to pull meaning into her poem. In the third line, she refers to the "goosestep," a word used to describe the Nazi soldiers in parade march, which is characterized by a strong forward kick. She also mentions Guernica, which is the name of the Basque city which was destroyed in 1937 by Nazi and Fascist bomber pilots and is also the name of Picasso's anti-war protest painting. The historical place and the painting give specific examples of the type of enemy the group in the poem protests against. They "cut through the country" where Fascists march to the "tune" of urban decimation.

In the tenth stanza, the speaker infuses her group of protesters with the power of Shango, the thunder god or sky father worshipped in Africa and South America, where he is called Changó. Shango was the main god of the Oyo people, West Africans who were enslaved and taken to Brazil and the Caribbean islands. In all, Shango came to symbolize African resistance to slavery. By alluding to this god, the speaker makes references in an economical way to all multiple historical instances of racial injustice. Finally, the mention of Soweto is a reference to both the economic inequities and the race riots that began in this township area near Johannesburg in 1976. She says nothing of the riots or the murder of school children, only that the protesters see through the eyes of Soweto children, meaning that they too witness racial prejudice, oppression, and brutality. This allusion pinpoints the type of oppression that the speaker and her group rise up to challenge.

COMPARE
&
CONTRAST

- **1987:** By writing about what conditions they believe need changing, African American women continue the tradition of such protest writers as Harriet Beecher Stowe, Zora Neale Hurston, and Gwendolyn Brooks. Prominent African American women whose writing calls for change, justice, and freedom include Toni Morrison, Maya Angelou, Nikki Giovanni, and Alice Walker (whose *The Color Purple* won a Pulitzer Prize in 1983), and Gloria Naylor (whose *The Women of Brewster Place* won the National Book Award in 1983).

  Today: African American women's voices are still heard through the works of writers with vision for the betterment of society and for black women, in particular. Toni Morrison (who won the Nobel Prize for Literature in 1993) and Maya Angelou are still important voices, along with newer voices, such as Edwidge Danticat and Pearl Cleage.

- **1987:** Apartheid (the official segregation of races) is still in effect in South Africa. It is a system that perpetuates the political and economic powerlessness of non-Europeans. Under apartheid, people are legally categorized by race and then assigned to live in certain areas based on those categories. In addition to political power through voting, rights denied to non-Europeans include access to education and adequate medical care. In response, twenty-five nations, including the United States, have trade sanctions against South Africa.

  Today: As of 1994, the apartheid system is no longer legal in South Africa. Thanks to the political, social, and economic pressures of numerous organizations, and the dedication of South Africa's president, Nelson Mandela, who headed the country from 1994 to 1999, apartheid was dismantled. Today, all citizens enjoy equal rights and participate in the political process.

- **1987:** Dictatorships exist in several countries. In Chile, under Augusto Pinochet Ugarte thousands of Chileans are imprisoned, tortured, and killed, while others disappear. In Iraq, Saddam Hussein imprisons, tortures, and kills groups and individuals who oppose his regime. Hussein commits genocide against Sunni Muslims and Kurds, and unknown thousands die. In the Philippines, Ferdinand Marcos is recently driven into exile (1986) by the people after decades of martial law, human rights violations, corruption, and nepotism.

  Today: In North Korea, dictator Kim Jong Il keeps the country completely closed from the rest of the world. He uses resources to build the military rather than feed starving North Koreans in the midst of drought and famine. Terrorist organizations are more organized that ever before. However, Saddam Hussein is found guilty of genocide and hanged, leaving Iraq in a turmoil as it attempts to form a new system of government.

HISTORICAL CONTEXT

War and Political Violence in the Mid- to Late 1980s

The mid- to late-1980s witnessed war and political violence in many countries. During the first half of the 1980s, the Ayatollah Khomeini instituted terrorism against his people in Iran to subject them to his rule. Among his methods was execution of his own people, including underage children and youths, political personnel, and adherents to minority religions. In 1985, Juan Peron, the leader of a junta in Argentina, and four of his commanders were convicted of human rights violations against the Argentinean people during Peron's military rule. During the hearings, the atrocities committed during the repressive rule came to light. U.S. president Ronald Reagan and Soviet leader Mikhail Gorbachev began arms negotiations to keep nuclear weapon build-up under control because a nuclear war would be devastating and self-defeating. Beginning in 1986 and lasting almost two years, trials against 476 members of the Sicilian mafia took place. The trials brought to light the violence and intimidation used by the mafia in its pursuit of power and wealth. Ultimately, sentences were passed down for 338 of the defendants, with prison terms sentenced and a total of more than ten million dollars in fines.

Shango

Shango is a prominent figure in Nigerian Yoruba mythology. He has other names in other cultures, but the character of the deity is consistent. Based on the fourth king of Oyo, Shango was deified after his death. There are various legends regarding his birth. In one legend, Shango is the son of Aganju, the god of fire; this is pertinent to "An Anthem" because of Sanchez's references to her people being of fire.

He is the ancestor of the Yoruba, the god of thunder and weather, and he is symbolized by a double-sided axe that represents justice and discipline. Shango has come to symbolize African resistance to European domination. He is also closely associated with music and dance. According to tradition, worship of Shango enables followers to be possessed by his very spirit, which gives them strength, discipline, and calm in the face of great difficulty.

Soweto

Racial tensions in South Africa came to a head on June 16, 1976, when protests against the government and the police resulted in a full-scale riot in Soweto, a township outside Johannesburg. The protest involved ten thousand students who challenged the new school policy of teaching in Afrikaans, the language of the Dutch minority who ruled South Africa. In truth, the protests that June were aimed at hundreds of laws meant to tighten further the oppression of black South Africans. Conditions were harsh, and black Africans, although they outnumbered the whites, endured poverty, unemployment, inadequate health care, and no voice in the government. In contrast, white South Africans had far greater power, opportunity, wealth, and resources, despite the fact that they were the minority. This unequal treatment was coupled with a system of racial segregation known as apartheid.

Leaders, including Desmond Tutu, had warned officials that the people of Soweto would not stand for being treated badly much longer and that its youth were likely to take action. The protests in June began nonviolently, with students carrying signs, but the conflict intensified, and police used tear gas, which led to students throwing rocks, which escalated to gunfire. Students were joined by others who helped overturn police vehicles, set fires, and attack white people. The protests spread to other parts of South Africa, and violence erupted in other townships. The riots tragically resulted in the deaths of seven hundred black Africans and the injuries to five thousand more in Soweto alone; estimates for the whole country are several thousand. The Soweto riots led to outright rebellion that remained intense for months. Besides the dramatic increase in violence, the Soweto riots led to the formation of guerrilla groups, liberation organizations, and black pride. Apartheid came under attack as it never had before.

CRITICAL OVERVIEW

Under a Soprano Sky is a collection of poetry that explores themes of racial identity and empowerment. These themes are also handled in "An Anthem." Sanchez also muses on the troubles of modern life, including the loss of her brother from AIDS and the young generations' ignorance of their heritage as a source of pride and identity. In response to *Under a Soprano Sky*, Kamili Anderson of *Belles Lettres* comments that Sanchez "may be the most undeservedly underspoken of contemporary women poets in America." Anderson calls the collection "hot enough to melt rock" yet "introspective and intricate." Contrasting Sanchez's work to that of her peers, Anderson notes, "Few poets write with more succinctness or intensity." Echoing Anderson's sentiments is Joanne Veal Gabbin, contributor of a chapter about Sanchez in *Southern Women Writers: The New Generation*. Gabbin finds that in *Under a Soprano Sky*,

> the mature voice of the poet is giving expression to the sources of her spiritual strength, establishing and reestablishing connections

that recognize the family-hood of man/wom-ankind, and singing ... of society's strange fruit sacrificed on the altars of political megalomania, economic greed, and social misunderstanding.

Author and interviewer, Joyce A. Joyce has spent considerable time with Sanchez. In *Ijala: Sonia Sanchez and the African Poetic Tradition*, Joyce assesses the poet's various collections. She remarks that *Under a Soprano Sky* shows growth, as it brings "to maturity the poet's skillful use of lyricism and images that first became apparent in the new poems collected in *I've Been a Woman* (1978)." Joyce explains that *Under a Soprano Sky* is less confrontational and aggressive than Sanchez's earlier work. This book, Joyce states, "is a *revolutionary* collection in which the poems reflect the poet's inward movement and a desire ... to strengthen and change herself in order to continue her struggle to change the world."

Regarding 1999's *Shake Loose My Skin* appeared (in which "An Anthem" appeared for a second time), Sanchez's readers and critics were enthusiastic. Because this book contains selections from six prior collections along with a handful of new poems, it offers a record of Sanchez's growth as a writer and philosopher. In *Booklist*, Donna Seaman characterizes Sanchez as an "outspoken and unflinching poet, innovative in her improvisation on meter and form." Seaman adds that Sanchez has the ability to give "shape and sound to every shade of mood." Jabari Asim of *American Visions* calls Sanchez "one of the most admired poets of her generation" and applauds "the depth and passion Sanchez brings to her life and her work." *Library Journal*'s Ron Antonucci boldly states that the "indomitable Sanchez is on fire" in *Shake Loose My Skin*. Ann K. van Buren points out Sanchez's success in showing that topics such as drug abuse, racism, and poverty are appropriate for poetry. They write that *Shake Loose My Skin* "leaves one in awe of the stretches of language Sanchez has helped to legitimize throughout her career."

Critics frequently evaluate Sanchez's poetry from the perspective of effective social activism. "An Anthem" fits neatly in this area. In *Heart & Soul*, Dahna Chandler notes that after decades of commitment, Sanchez is still writing her "unwavering call to arms." A reviewer for *Publishers Weekly* finds "Sanchez is at her best when enacting power struggles rather than

WHAT DO I READ NEXT?

- Robin Behn's *The Practice of Poetry: Writing Exercises from Poets who Teach* (1992) is a practical way for aspiring poets to gain insight and guidance from numerous writing teachers. The book contains ninety exercises, along with essays to help readers hone their poetry-writing skills.

- In the mid-1950s, Sanchez studied with Louise Bogan at New York University. *The Blue Estuaries: Poems: 1923–1968* (1995) presents Bogan's work.

- Joyce A. Joyce's *Ijala: Sonia Sanchez and the African Poetic Tradition* (1997) covers over thirty years of Sanchez's work. The critical analysis is written in a style accessible to a wide audience.

- Sonia Sanchez's *I've Been a Woman: New and Selected Poems* (1985) provides a unified vision of Sanchez's female-centered poetic voice and expresses her hopes for other women.

- Claudia Tate's *Black Women Writers at Work* (1983) presents the results of Tate's interviews with fourteen female writers that focused on their writing process and how their ethnicity has played a part in their creativity. Writers include Toni Morrison, Gwendolyn Brooks, Maya Angelou, and Sonia Sanchez.

merely rallying political support in easy battle-cries." Yusef Salaam of *New York Amsterdam News* reported about Sanchez's being honored at the Langston Hughes Festival in New York. He quotes Joyce as stating that "Sanchez's primary focus in her work is 'group survival,' the growth and development of African peoples and humanity." Joyce also stated that Sanchez's poems "are not emotional quick-fixes, but contain a power to propel the reader or listener 'to action.'" This description perfectly describes "An Anthem" and many other poems of hers about social injustice.

CRITICISM

Jennifer Bussey

Bussey holds a master's degree in Interdisciplinary Studies and a bachelor's degree in English literature. She is an independent writer specializing in literature. In the following essay, she provides an overview of African dance as an important context for Sonia Sanchez's "An Anthem."

In most cultures, dance has an important place. In fact, the diversity of dance styles is so great that cultures can be recognized by their traditional dances, even by someone with only a passing knowledge of dance history. What is it about dance that speaks so clearly to and about a culture? In Sonia Sanchez's "An Anthem," the poet weaves dance and music imagery into a poem that makes strong statements against war and injustice and about the need for courage. Central to the message of the poem are the descriptions of African dance and dancers because from them comes a sense of identity, community, and roots. A study of specific African dances would require volumes, as each tribe and culture has developed its own dances over centuries. Here, African dance is discussed in general terms in order to shed light on why and how Sanchez uses it to bring energy and depth to her poem.

In African culture, dance has played important social, religious, symbolic, military, and occupational roles. In most cases, a dance holds a primary purpose but is carried out in such a way that secondary functions are also served. For example, a hunter's dance may be intended to show the tribe how an animal was killed and to acknowledge the animal's spirit, but it also showcases the athleticism and skill of the hunters who perform the dance. Similarly, a dance performed in a particular Yoruba town is meant to honor Mother Earth, but it also disparages immorality and draws sharp contrasts with its depiction of the genders.

Even the most casual observers may notice that dances often draw distinctions among tribal members based on age, status, occupation, or gender. Dances often give different segments of the tribe an opportunity to express themselves in ways that are suited to their age or gender. Dances for older members are generally slower and more elegant; dances for young women are often flowing and feminine; and dances for mid-life men are often energetic and forceful. Some

> IN THE EARLY 2000S, MODERN DANCERS CONTINUE TO LEARN AND EMBRACE TRADITIONAL AFRICAN DANCE, MUSIC, AND COSTUMES. AFRICAN AMERICANS COMMITTED TO PRESERVING THEIR HERITAGE INCLUDE THE CULTURAL TRADITIONS OF MUSIC AND DANCE."

tribes even use dance to signal transitions from one age group to another, which is especially important when youths are admitted to adulthood. In these cases, dances often indicate readiness and desirability for marriage or serve as an initiation into a new social group. Dances for young men serve a secondary purpose of providing exercise and conditioning to keep them in shape for fighting and hunting. Dances also function to separate by status, as leadership within the tribe can be identified within certain dances. Dance can affirm leadership, show loyalty to leaders, and honor past leaders of the tribe.

Dance and religion are closely intertwined in African cultures as a way to create union between the body and the spirit. Dances are used as an extension of religious powers when they are performed to cast out evil spirits, call on fertility gods, and demand discipline in purification rituals. Dancers who perform in rituals are trained for many years, often beginning very young. In some cases, as in the worship of Shango (who is mentioned by Sanchez in "An Anthem"), dances represent the worshippers being overtaken by the spirit of the deity. Other qualities of dances to Shango are expressed in Sanchez's poem. Yoruba priests express Shango's thunderous rage by rhythmic and rapid pounding on drums, rolling their shoulders, and stomping their feet. Related to religious ceremonies are other ceremonies such as weddings and funerals. These are accompanied by dances traditional within each society. Wedding dances are celebratory and symbolic, while funeral dances are performed to complete burial, provide comfort, and honor the dead and the dead person's legacy.

Military dances can be performed to relate ancestral history, recall great heroes of the tribe, and honor the military, in general. They also energize the warriors as they prepare for battle, generate a strong sense of camaraderie among them, and give the tribe an opportunity to express admiration and gratitude to them. The demanding dances require physical fitness, thus showing the warriors' strength while providing exercise. Similarly, other male groups dance together to commemorate success in harvest, hunting, or building. These dances present stylized movements specific to the group's role, such as casting nets or growing crops.

Numerous dances are known as masquerades because they involve masks of some kind worn by some or all of the participants. This is relevant to "An Anthem" because the refrain, "give me courage so I can spread / it over my face and mouth." These words describe courage as something that covers the speaker's face like a mask. In masquerades, a dancer is often chosen (and his identity kept secret) to represent the deity by wearing a mask or cloth over his head and face. Other dances involve performers wearing masks to represent animals, spirits, or qualities. Masks, like dance movements, can be highly symbolic. A mask of an animal might just represent the animal in the context of a hunt or a story, or it may symbolize a quality such as power, strength, or status. Some of the dances feature masks so heavy that the dancer can barely move at all while wearing them. This is intended to strip the dancer of freedom and encourage purification and discipline.

The central role of dance in African cultures is evident in its continuation among slave groups in the Americas. In fact, slave groups often created new dances in traditional styles to represent their experience as slaves. Because slaves were assimilated into their new cultures, their dances became blends of the traditional African styles and the new styles they learned in the Americas. The extent of this blend depended on how large the slave group was (larger groups had more success in preserving the original dances than smaller ones) and how often new slaves from Africa were added. Interesting to the context of this essay, West African societies such as the Yoruba (indirectly referred to in Sanchez's poem through the allusion to Shango) were the sources of the dominant dance styles.

Music accompanies dance, and African music has a distinct quality. Drums and other instruments that are pounded or scraped are common across African cultures. Often dancers' costumes include rattles on the costumes themselves or on straps worn around the ankles. All of these instruments reinforce the importance of rhythm in African dance. In some areas, instruments such as flutes and horns are used.

In the early 2000s, modern dancers continue to learn and embrace traditional African dance, music, and costumes. African Americans committed to preserving their heritage include the cultural traditions of music and dance. These dances include those of Africa as well as those of slave ancestors. Notable choreographers in this area include Katherine Dunham, Alvin Ailey, and Talley Beatty. The preservation of dance is not limited to performance, however, as proven by Sanchez. With her energetic descriptions of "ceremonial breaths" and "shaking hips," Sanchez brings life to "An Anthem." She describes a community that runs, sees, and laughs loudly. But she cautions that they are more than cultural elements like music, horns, color, drums, and dance. Still, through cultural unity, she believes that with courage, she and the other protesters can stare down "madmen" war makers and bring justice to a world that desperately needs it.

Source: Jennifer Bussey, Critical Essay on "An Anthem," in *Poetry for Students*, Thomson Gale, 2007.

Thomson Gale

In the following essay, the critic gives a critical analysis of Sanchez's work.

In addition to being an important activist, poet, playwright, professor, and a leader of the black studies movement, Sonia Sanchez has also written books for children. She introduced young people to the poetry of black English in her 1971 work *It's a New Day: Poems for Young Brothas and Sistuhs*, created a moral fable for younger children in 1973's *The Adventures of Fat Head, Small Head, and Square Head*, and produced a collection of short tales for children in 1979's *A Sound Investment and Other Stories*. As William Pitt Root noted in *Poetry* magazine: "One concern [Sanchez] always comes back to is the real education of Black children."

Sanchez was born Wilsonia Benita Driver on September 9, 1934, in Birmingham, Alabama. Her mother died when she was very young, and

FEATURING VERSE FROM HER OLDER PUBLICATIONS, AS WELL AS FOUR NEW ENTRIES, *SHAKE LOOSE MY SKIN* OFFERS A SAMPLING OF SANCHEZ'S WORK SPANNING OVER THIRTY YEARS. IN HER POEMS, SHE TACKLES TOPICS RANGING FROM BIGOTRY TO POVERTY TO DRUG ABUSE."

she was raised by her grandmother until she too died when the author was six years old. Her father was a schoolteacher, and as a result she and her siblings spoke standard English instead of a southern or black dialect. It was not until she and her brother rejoined her father in Harlem, New York, when she was nine years old, that Sanchez learned the speech of the streets that would become so important to her poetry. Sanchez also stuttered as a child; this led her to writing, which she has done since she was very young.

Sanchez also learned about racism at a very young age. She recalled in an interview with Claudia Tate for Tate's *Black Women Writers at Work:* "I also remember an aunt who spat in a bus driver's face—that was the subject of one of my first poems—because he wanted her to get off as the bus was filling up with white people. . . . Well, my aunt would not get off the bus, so she spat, and was arrested. That was the first visual instance I can remember of encountering racism." She did not leave racism behind when her family moved north, however. She told Tate that "coming north to Harlem for 'freedom' when I was nine presented me with a whole new racial landscape." Sanchez continued, "Here was the realization of the cornerstore, where I watched white men pinch black women on their behinds. And I made a vow that nobody would ever do that to me unless I wanted him to. I continued to live in the neighborhood, went to that store as a nine-year-old child, and continued to go there as a student at Hunter College. When I was sixteen to eighteen they attempted to pinch my behind. I turned around and said, 'Oh no you don't.' They knew I was serious." She has been fighting racism and sexism ever since.

After graduating from Hunter College in 1955, Sanchez did postgraduate study at New York University. During the early 1960s she was an integrationist, supporting the ideas of the Congress of Racial Equality. But after listening to the ideas of Black Muslim leader Malcolm X, who believed blacks would never be truly accepted by whites in the United States, she focused more on her black heritage as something separate from white Americans. She began teaching in the San Francisco area in 1965, first on the staff of the Downtown Community School and later at San Francisco State College (now University). There she was a pioneer in developing black studies courses, including a class in black English.

In 1969, Sanchez published her first book of poetry for adults, *Homecoming*. She followed that up with 1970's *We a BaddDDD People*, which especially focused on black dialect as a poetic medium. At about the same time her first plays, *Sister Son/ji* and *The Bronx Is Next*, were being produced or published. In 1971, she published her first work for children, *It's A New Day: Poems for Young Brothas and Sistuhs*. Shortly afterwards, she joined the Nation of Islam, also referred to as the Black Muslims. Sanchez enjoyed the spirituality and discipline of the religion, but she always had problems with its repression of women. She explained to Tate: "It was not easy being in the Nation. I was/am a writer. I was also speaking on campuses. In the Nation at that time women were supposed to be in the background. My contribution to the Nation has been that I refused to let them tell me where my place was. I would be reading my poetry some place, and men would get up to leave, and I'd say, 'Look, my words are equally important.' So I got into trouble." Sanchez stated: "One dude said to me once that the solution for Sonia Sanchez was for her to have some babies. . . . I already had two children. . . . I fought against the stereotype of me as a black woman in the movement relegated to three steps behind. It especially was important for the women in the Nation to see that. I told them that in order to pull this 'mother' out from what it's under we gonna need men, women, children, but most important, we need minds." She added: "I had to fight. I had to fight a lot of people in and outside of the Nation due to so-called sexism. I spoke up. I think it was important that there were women there to do that. I left the Nation during the 1975-76 academic year."

While she was a Black Muslim, however, Sanchez produced her second children's book, *The Adventures of Fathead, Smallhead, and Squarehead*. A moral fable about a pilgrimage to Mecca, the tale began as a story for her own children. In an interview with *African American Review* contributor Susan Kelly, Sanchez remembered, "my children had asked me to make up a story one night in New York City before we moved to Amherst. They would always say, 'Read, read, read!' So I would read to them. And one night, they said, 'Don't read; make up a story.'" The resulting tale became *The Adventures of Fathead, Smallhead, and Squarehead*.

Other Sanchez books of interest to a teen-aged audience include *Shake Loose My Skin: New and Selected Poems*. Featuring verse from her older publications, as well as four new entries, *Shake Loose My Skin* offers a sampling of Sanchez's work spanning over thirty years. In her poems, she tackles topics ranging from bigotry to poverty to drug abuse. "This collection should draw wide attention to the consistency of Sanchez's achievement," believed a *Publishers Weekly* contributor. *Library Journal* critic Ann K. van Buren found that this book "leaves one in awe of the stretches of language Sanchez has helped to legitimize."

Because of the political nature of most of her writings and her involvement in black power causes, Sanchez feels that her academic career has suffered from persecution by government authorities. She told Tate: "While I helped to organize the black studies program at San Francisco State, the FBI came to my landlord and said put her out. She's one of those radicals." Sanchez continued: "Then I taught at Manhattan Community College in New York City, and I stayed there until my record was picked up. You know how you have your record on file, and you can go down and look at it. Well, I went down to look at it, because we had had a strike there, and I had been arrested with my students. I went to the dean to ask for my record, and he told me that I could not have my record because it was sent downtown." Sanchez said: "That's when I began to realize just how much the government was involved with teachers in the university. I then tried to get another job in New York City—no job. I had been white-balled. The word was out, I was too political. . . . That's how I ended up at Amherst College, because I couldn't get a job in

my home state. That's what they do to you. If they can't control what you write, they make alternatives for you and send you to places where you have no constituency."

After leaving Amherst, Sanchez eventually became a professor at Temple University in Philadelphia, Pennsylvania, where she has since taught for many years. She has also edited several books, and contributed poetry and articles on black culture to anthologies and periodicals. Summing up the importance of Sanchez's work, Kalamu ya Salaam concluded in *Dictionary of Literary Biography:* "Sanchez is one of the few creative artists who have significantly influenced the course of black American literature and culture."

In her interview with Kelly, Sanchez concluded, "It is that love of language that has propelled me, that love of language that came from listening to my grandmother speak black English. . . . It is that love of language that says, simply, to the ancestors who have done this before you, 'I am keeping the love of life alive, the love of language alive. I am keeping words that are spinning on my tongue and getting them transferred on paper. I'm keeping this great tradition of American poetry alive.'"

Source: Thomson Gale, "Sonia Sanchez," in *Contemporary Authors Online*, Gale, 2003.

SOURCES

Anderson, Kamili, "Giving Our Souls Ears," in *Belles Lettres*, Vol. 4, No. 2, Winter 1989, p. 14.

Antonucci, Ron, Review of *Shake Loose My Skin*, in *Library Journal*, Vol. 129, No. 6, April 1, 2004, p. 64.

Asim, Jabari, "A Revival with Sonia Sanchez," in *American Visions*, Vol. 13, No. 1, February–March 1998, p. 27.

Chandler, Dahna, "Poetry in Our Voices," in *Heart & Soul*, Vol. 7, No. 2, April–May 2000, p. 32.

Gabbin, Joanne Veal, "The Southern Imagination of Sonia Sanchez," in *Southern Women Writers: The New Generation*, University of Alabama Press, 1990, p. 183.

Joyce, Joyce A., "The Continuing Journey of Sonia Sanchez: From *homegirls & handgrenades* to *Wounded in the House of a Friend*," in *Ijala: Sonia Sanchez and the African Poetic Tradition*, Third World Press, 1996, p. 133.

Review of *Shake Loose My Skin*, in *Publishers Weekly*, Vol. 245, No. 51, December 21, 1998, p. 63.

Salaam, Yusef, "Sonia Returns Victorious and Honored," in *New York Amsterdam News*, Vol. 90, No. 48, November 25, 1999, p. 21.

Sanchez, Sonia, "An Anthem," in *Shake Loose My Skin*, Beacon Press, 1999, pp. 75–76.

Seaman, Donna, Review of *Shake Loose My Skin*," in *Booklist*, Vol. 95, No. 12, February 15, 1999, p. 1028.

Van Buren, Ann K., Review of *Shake Loose My Skin*, in *Library Journal*, Vol. 124, No. 2, February 1, 1999, p. 93.

FURTHER READING

Joyce, Joyce A., *Conversations with Sonia Sanchez (Literary Conversations)*, University Press of Mississippi, 2007.
> Joyce has spent considerable time with Sanchez over the years, having the opportunity to interview her about her craft and her purpose in writing. In this collection of interviews, readers learn about how Sanchez's writing craft and subject matter have changed over three decades, during which time Sanchez was an activist, mother, and teacher.

Ling, Peter J., and Sharo Monteith, eds., *Gender in the Civil Rights Movement*, Routledge, 1999.
> Ling and Monteith have compiled an anthology of writings exploring the role of gender issues during the American civil rights movement. The essays address important events, legislation, key figures, and philosophies.

Sanchez, Sonia, *The Adventures of Fathead, Smallhead, and Squarehead*, Third Press Review of Books, 1973.
> Among Sanchez's best known children's books, this is the story of three friends who gain insight about what is really smart and what is really dumb.

Stone, Ruth M., *Africa (Garland Encyclopedia of World Music)*, Routledge, 1997.
> This volume includes a wealth of information about Africa and how music and dance are an integral part of African culture. Stone covers general topics about music, dance, ritual, and expression, but also discusses subjects specific to certain regions. The book includes a CD.

Young, Kevin, *Jelly Roll: A Blues*, Knopf, 2003.
> Young is an African American poet whose writing is influenced by music of all kinds. In this collection, readers see how everything from jazz to classical music informs his poetic vision and expression.

The Black Heralds

CÉSAR VALLEJO

1919

In the early 2000s, César Vallejo was considered Peru's greatest poet, and the first line of "The Black Heralds" was said to be known by every Peruvian. Written after his move to Lima from a country village in 1916, the poem was included in a collection to be published in 1918, but Vallejo waited to issue the book until Abraham Valdelomar, an avant-garde writer, could add an introduction. However, Valdelomar died suddenly, so Vallejo released the book in 1919. There has been a confusion about the date of publication ever since. The collection was praised by Vallejo's own artistic community; however, there were few sales and few reviews. The public was accustomed to *modernismo* and symbolism in verse, not Vallejo's emotional and social outcry.

As time would show, *The Black Heralds* was actually the most traditional of Vallejo's works, a blend of modernistic influences and the unique style of structure and language that he developed even more in later works. Nonetheless, the basic themes addressed in *The Black Heralds* remained important elements in all of his poetry: suffering, compassion, and the various components of existential anguish. All of these elements find expression in the title poem. "The Black Heralds" opens the collection and sets a tone for the rest of the book of bitter sentiments and blasphemous rebellion, as well as a compassionate understanding of suffering. Although his first book of poetry, *The Black Heralds* was the last of Vallejo's works to

be translated into English. Two later publications of the title poem can be found: in the 1990 English edition of *Los Heraldos Negros*, the translation by Kathleen Ross and Richard Schaaf; and in the 2006 collection *The Complete Poetry of Cesar Vallejo*, the translation by Clayton Eshleman.

AUTHOR BIOGRAPHY

César Abraham Vallejo was born on March 16, 1892, in Santiago de Chuco, Peru, the youngest of eleven children in a family of mixed Spanish and indigenous heritage. After graduating from high school in 1908, Vallejo attempted to attend college but had to withdraw because of a lack of funds. So he went to work as a clerk in his father's notary public office, then in the office of a mining company. He worked as a tutor to the children of a wealthy mine owner and as a cashier in the accounting office of a sugar plantation. Added to his rural upbringing, these experiences furthered his concern about the social injustices in Peru. In 1913, he formally enrolled at the University of Trujillo, where he graduated with a bachelor's degree in 1915 and later earned both a master's degree in Spanish literature and a law degree.

During his college years, Vallejo joined a progressive circle of writers and intellectuals. Within this group, he discovered Latin American modernism and French symbolism, as well as political radicalism. After a few tumultuous romantic involvements, Vallejo moved to Lima in 1917. He took a job as a teacher and later principal of a prestigious private school but was fired after he refused to marry the woman with whom he was having an affair. This event, coupled with the death of his mother, prompted him to visit his home. Once there, Vallejo found himself unintentionally involved in a violent uprising. Although innocent, Vallejo was charged as an instigator and spent three months in jail. He was released on parole, but the experience embittered him for the rest of his life.

Vallejo won the Peruvian National Short Story Contest in 1921. However, his first two books of poetry, *The Black Heralds* (1919) (which contains the title poem) and *Trilce* (1922), were ill-received, so Vallejo moved to Paris in 1923. He worked for a press agency and continued with his own writing, but for the rest of his life he barely made enough money to support himself.

In the late 1920s, he participated in communist activities and visited the Soviet Union three times. After an arrest in Paris, Vallejo moved to Madrid and was allowed back in Paris only when he promised to refrain from all political activities. He did so until the outbreak in 1936 of the Spanish Civil War whose republican cause reinvigorated his political involvement. Consequently, he visited Spain twice and saw for himself the horrors of war, which inspired the acclaimed poetic collection, *Spain, Take This Cup from Me* (1937).

Besides poetry, Vallejo wrote a novel, *Tungsten* (1931), as well as numerous articles and essays, and five plays that were never published or produced in his lifetime. He married Georgette Philipart in 1934, and after he died of a lingering fever in Paris on April 15, 1938, she published his final collection of poetry, *Human Poems*, in 1939.

POEM TEXT

> There are blows in life, so hard ... I just don't
>   know!
> Blows as from God's hatred; as if, before them,
> the backwash of everything suffered
> welled-up in the soul ... I just don't know!
>
> They are few, but they are ... They open
>   dark furrows   5
> in the fiercest face and in the strongest back.
> Perhaps they are the steeds of barbarian Attilas,
> or the black heralds Death sends us.
>
> They are the deep falls of the Christs of the
>   soul,
> of some worshipping faith Destiny blasphemes.   10
> Those bloody blows are the crackling
> of some bread burning up on us at the oven door.
>
> And man ... Poor ... poor man! Turns his
>   eyes, as
> when a slap on the shoulder summons us;
> turns his eyes wild, and everything lived   15
> wells-up like a pool of guilt in his gaze.
>
> There are blows in life, so hard ... I just don't
>   know!

POEM SUMMARY

Stanza 1

The first line of "The Black Heralds" is one of the most memorable in Spanish poetry: "There are blows in life so powerful . . . I just don't know!" The intensity of the poem is immediately established with the subject of the painful blows and the questioning they engender, although a question is not asked but is left to the reader's imagination by the ellipsis before the answer, "I just don't know!" The line is the cry of the oppressed as they struggle to understand why life is so hard.

In the second through fourth lines, Vallejo says that these blows are as terrible as if they were from "God's hatred." These blows are so strong that they are capable of causing all the memories of one's suffering to well up, capable of causing the pain to rise up from the depths of the soul to the surface. However, the author repeats the use of the ellipsis to create a pause that makes the "I just don't know" phrase that follows into an outcry of exasperation and frustration, as if to question his own analogy or to emphasize the impossibility of knowing why terrible things happen.

Stanza 2

Here the narrator says that even when there are only a few hard blows in one's life, any of them can cause deep wounds, "dark furrows," in even the "fiercest face and in the strongest back." The word "dark" may simply be a reference to the usually darker, redder skin color of scars, but it may also mean "dark" as in the black depths of the soul that the furrows represent or as in the dark recesses of the mind that are repressed after trauma.

In the third line, Vallejo compares the blows to "the steeds of barbarian Attilas." This phrase is a reference to the notorious historical figure, Attila the Hun, ruler of a tribe of warrior nomads who terrorized the Roman Empire for a number of years in the middle of the fifth century. Attila was known as the Scourge of God, so an allusion to this barbaric invader is fitting in a poem that in the previous stanza talked about "God's hatred."

Another comparison of the blows is made in the fourth line to "the black heralds Death sends us." The word "angel" is from the Greek word "angelos" meaning messenger, and another word for messenger is herald (in some translations of this poem the word messenger is used instead of herald), although herald carries the connotation of one who makes an announcement. Vallejo is probably making a reference to the concept of an Angel of Death that is sent by God to guide the dead on their journey to heaven or hell. Whether the murderous barbarian or

TOPICS FOR FURTHER STUDY

- Look for two other existential poets and compare their works to that of Vallejo. What are the common themes among these poets? List and describe these themes and note the different ways that each poet finds to express the same theme.

- Which elements of modernism can be found in "The Black Heralds"? Identify the characteristics of modernism and then discuss whether it is possible to assess meter and rhythm when working with a translation.

- Write a biographical analysis of Vallejo's reason for leaving Peru. Did he find what he was seeking in Paris? How did living in Paris affect his life and works? Justify your answers with specifics.

- What was it about communism that attracted Vallejo? What was in his background, education, or lifestyle that led him to communism? Why did he travel to Russia and involve himself in the Spanish Civil War? Write an essay explaining the relationship of Vallejo to communism.

- Besides poetry, Vallejo wrote journalistic articles, short stories, essays, and novels. Put together a list of his other works and discuss their impact and value in the body of his life's work.

those who pronounce death, the idea is that the blows of life bring terror and devastation.

Stanza 3

Continuing to make comparisons, in this stanza Vallejo does not say that the blows cause falls to the ground, but that they are falls, "deep falls of the Christs of the soul." It is an odd phrase that combines the cause and effect. The image that is evoked is that of Christ as he fell three times carrying his cross on the road to Calvary. Therefore, the falls are those of "some worshipping faith" that teaches hope and salvation, a faith that "Destiny blasphemes" because it is a useless faith to those who live and die in such misery.

In one last comparison, Vallejo writes the "bloodstained" blows are like the "crackling / of some bread burning up on us at the oven door." Perhaps the blows are described as bloodstained to make a connection to the red color of the fire that is burning the bread. Bread is often called the "staff of life" because it has been for millennia a staple in the diet of humans, so the burning bread represents the life that is being consumed by the blows of tragedy. The bread does not even get out of the oven, does not make it past the door to perform its life-affirming purpose before it is destroyed by forces that do not allow individual fulfillment.

Stanza 4

In the last of the four-line stanzas, Vallejo turns to describing the recipient of the blows: "And man . . . Poor . . . poor man!" Here, the speaker pauses in his complaint about the blows to express sympathy for the plight of the poor human and to emphasize the depth of the tragedy of the laborer through the pauses inserted by the ellipses. Vallejo then paints an image of the worker who, when summoned to further labor, looks over his shoulder with eyes as wild as those of a caged animal, eyes crazed by the madness of it all. In those eyes is a reflection of the experiences of life, the "backwash of everything suffered" mentioned in the third line of the first stanza. It is as if it these experiences of hardship were deserved for some unknowable sin.

Stanza 5

The last stanza repeats the first line of the first stanza. The effect is to emphasize the depth of the desolation and despair felt by the speaker about human limitations, the harshness of life, and life's mysteries.

THEMES

Suffering

The indigenous Peruvians, descendents of the great Incans, were subjected to centuries of abuse and exploitation by Spanish colonial rule. Half Indian and a speaker of Quechua, Vallejo shared this heritage and observed its effects in his provincial village and on the plantation where he worked for a time. The suffering he witnessed is reflected in "The Black Heralds," in which the speaker's life is characterized as filled with agony that cannot find expression in words but leaves the speaker frustrated and despairing. Typical of all oppressed peoples, the subject of the poem cries out for relief from the brutality of existence yet quells desperation with a fatalistic sadness about the condition which seems his destiny. Nonetheless, there is a hint of the pride of a mighty people who hunger for their rightful place, so long lost. The suffering described is both physical and emotional: blows that leave wounds in the flesh, damage faith, and drive a person to crazed desperation and confusion.

Life, Death, and God

Vallejo was greatly disturbed by questions concerning the reason for life. The specter of the grave tormented him because of his view that life is a steady march toward death. In "The Black Heralds," the title is a reference to the "black heralds sent to us by Death," and the "deep falls of the Christs of the soul" alludes to the final walk that Christ made going to his crucifixion. Perhaps Vallejo does not believe that Christ ever reached Calvary or enacted a resurrection to save humankind because in this poem the blows that cause the soul to fall are ongoing. The argument here is that a merciful God who gave the world a savior would not behave as does the hateful God that Vallejo depicts. These sentiments provide the reason that the message in "The Black Heralds" is described as questioning and challenging God, if not being outright blasphemous. Definitely, the message is one of acute, painful frustration at being unable to determine why life is so hard.

Existential Anguish

"The Black Heralds" is an excellent example of existential anguish. The poem contains classic descriptions of the existentialist experience: trying to create meaning from a world that has no meaning but is empty and confusing; trying to understand the purpose of an existence that makes no sense; trying to establish the freedom and responsibility of the individual in relation to established ethics and morality; trying to endure the hardships of life when there seems to be no valid reason or reward to do so. Angst is often associated with existentialism because there is so much anxiety, guilt, and isolation that comes with individual responsibility and that stems

In this poem, Vallejo likens the blows of God to "the colts of barbaric Attilas," the fifth century Hun who led his horde on rampages through Asia and Europe (Getty Images)

from unanswered questions about causation and human suffering. A possible conclusion is that there is no meaning to life because there is only a path to nothingness, but Vallejo tells readers that he just does not know what to conclude.

STYLE

Repetition

Repetition is a signature device that Vallejo used throughout his career as a poet. The opening line of "The Black Heralds" is repeated as the last line for emphasis and to create an enclosed structure or circle. This enclosure may represent the prison of life that constrains humanity with time limits and physical limitations or the freedoms taken away by government and social status. The phrase, "I just don't know," not only ends the first and last lines of the poem but also the first and last lines of the first stanza in order to underline the frustration of the inexplicable.

In the seventeen lines of "The Black Heralds," Vallejo uses the word "blows" four times: in the first and second lines to establish blows as the subject, in the eleventh line, to remind the reader of the topic, and then in the last line to emphasize the importance of the blows. In addition, Vallejo uses the ellipsis before each of the "I just don't

know" phrases as if the speaker runs out of words and sighs or cries out, "I just don't know." The ellipsis is also used in line 5 to create a change of thought, and in line thirteen ("And man . . . Poor . . . poor!") to stretch out and emphasize the pathetic nature of humans. Vallejo also uses the similar phrases "welled up" and "wells up" in lines four and twelve as another way to provide a connection between the first and the last sections of the poem. Thus repetition serves to tie the poem together and as a type of rhythmic device like a metronome keeping the beat.

Ellipses

Ellipsis points are not only used to indicate omissions from a quotation but also are used by writers to give the reader the impression that the narrator is experiencing faltering speech. The ellipsis, which consists of three spaced periods, indicates a long pause, or a thought that has trailed off and will not be completed, or will be left for the reader to complete. Sometimes a writer will use an ellipsis rather than a dash or a colon just to catch the reader's attention.

In the case of Vallejo and "The Black Heralds," the ellipsis is used six times in seventeen lines with great dramatic effect. In the famous opening line, Vallejo starts with an attention-grabbing statement about the hardships of life, but instead of reaching some profound conclusion about the bad times people all encounter, he cuts off the speaker with an ellipsis, who then says "I just don't know!" The reader immediately knows that this is a poem of frustration. The poet wants to talk about the tragedy of life, but the speaker lets the reader know right away that he does not have any answers to the mysteries of life. Twice more in the poem, Vallejo uses the ellipsis and the speaker's exasperated "I just don't know" to express the sense of being at a loss for an explanation.

In the first line of the second stanza, Vallejo trails off with an ellipsis after the speaker says, "They are few; but they are" before saying what the blows are. It is as if the speaker changes his mind about discussing what the blows are because he then starts a new sentence talking about what the blows do. The ellipsis after "but they are" also gives the impression that "are" means "exist" as in "They are few, but they still exist."

In the first line of the fourth stanza, Vallejo inserts ellipses for emphasis and to slow down the reading. "And man . . . Poor . . . poor!" highlights the pathetic nature of "poor" and once again gives the impression of an incomplete thought as if it is too painful to go into detail about the wretchedness of the human condition.

Beyond Modernismo

Much is made of the influence on Vallejo of the modernismo (modernista) movement. There were a number of famous Latin American writers who were writing in this style in the late nineteenth century and early twentieth century, but the first of note was the Cuban poet Jose Marti, and eventually Chilean Ruben Dario became the master of the movement. Vallejo was well aware of these other poets and their works because they created a frenzy of interest in literature that carried over into politics and economics and caught the attention of the world, even affecting literary ideas in Spain. The characteristics of modernismo included beautiful landscapes, a crafted verse that sometimes became an artifice of mannerisms, colorful imagery, and elegant, musical language. Modernistas Leopoldo Lugones and Julio Herrary y Reissig added surprising images that were admired and imitated by Vallejo. Although these elements can be seen in *The Black Heralds*, Vallejo was already departing from the movement in his first work by moving into darker, more realistic subjects and themes of social protest as well as dropping

the typical rhetoric and ornamentation of the style. It is difficult to judge a translation for the patterns and rhythms of modernismo that may have been present in the original Spanish version, so English readers must rely on the expertise of scholars to verify that the influence is there, especially when the subject, tone, and concentrated phrases of *The Black Heralds* are so different from what a reader would expect from modernismo.

Surrealism

Native Americans use symbols and images to express themselves and their mystic fatalism, so it was natural for Vallejo, with his indigenous heritage, to embrace surrealism, a style that uses dreamlike images and suggests the unconscious or subconscious in a psychological way. Surrealism liberates the poet from literary conventions such that language can be ambiguous and ironic as it breaks the rules of logic and reason in its multiple images and irregular rhythms. In "The Black Heralds," the irregular rhythms come from the pauses inserted by the use of ellipses to change the course of the thought. The language of Vallejo's images in this poem is not as ambiguous as one would expect from a surrealist. Rather, they are created with common language and objects, but there is the surrealistic multiplicity of images, and they lead to careful thought and interpretation about the psychological as well as physical torture endured by the abused person Vallejo depicts.

There is no difficult language in "the backwash of everything suffered," "open dark furrows in the fiercest face and in the strongest back," "bloodstained blows," "crackling bread burning up at the oven door," or "like a pool of guilt, in his look." Backwash, furrows, bloodstained, pool and guilt are all terms that are understandable, but combined as they are in the phrases that create the image, they are beautifully crafted to readily conjure a vivid picture in the mind of the reader. The images created from literary and religious allusions—"steeds of barbaric Attilas," "black heralds Death sends us," "deep falls of the Christs of the soul,"—are more difficult at first but are not beyond the average reader's ability to grasp. Images are intended to appeal to the senses, and the images in "The Black Heralds" manage to cover four of the five: sight, hearing, touch, and smell. Coming one upon another in rapid succession in a relatively short poem, they bombard the reader in a powerfully effective way.

COMPARE
&
CONTRAST

- **1918:** In Russia, the Bolsheviks execute the Romanov royal family, setting up a series of events that eventually lead to Russia becoming a communist country. At the same time, Vallejo lives in Lima and is acquainted with political activists to whom he is attracted because of his experience with rural poverty and plantation labor and his disillusionment with religion. Thus begins his eventual involvement in the communist movement.

  Today: The power of communism is diminished greatly around the world since the breakup of the Soviet Union, although China and North Korea have communist systems, and Hugo Chavez of Venezuela gains world attention as a great admirer of the last icon of Central American communism, Cuba's Fidel Castro.

- **1918:** World War I, described as the war to end all wars, comes to a conclusion, leaving the European continent, and the colonies of European countries, in an unsettled and bitter situation. After moving to Europe, Vallejo becomes involved in these issues, earning political exile from France from 1930 to 1932 and campaigning against fascism in the Spanish Civil War from 1936 until his death in 1938. One of Vallejo's last great collections of poetry, *Spain, Take This Cup from Me*, comes from this endeavor.

  Today: World War I does not end all wars. Rather, the terms of the Treaty of Versailles that arrange the cessation of warfare in 1918 come to be seen as a leading cause of World War II, which is more global. The treaty terms include the creation of new countries and border divisions that contributes to present-day conflicts in Israel, Palestine, Iraq, Iran, and other parts of theMiddle East.

- **1918:** Post-war sentiments change modernism from a call for change while respecting the past to a call for a complete remake of the worldview around new technologies and philosophies. This rebellion against emotionalism typically rejects any call to copy the past or return to the classics.

  Today: Modernism becomes mainstream by the 1930s and remains so until the late twentieth century when media-influenced postmodernism begins mixing elements of pop culture with electronics; postmodernism is characterized by open-endedness and collage and a self-referential irony that questions the foundations of cultural and artistic forms.

- **1918:** Vallejo prepares his first book of poetry for publication, beginning his career as a writer in several genres that is to gain him little fame and virtually no income during his lifetime.

  Today: Vallejo is considered the greatest of all Peruvian poets; new editions of his writings and works of criticism about him continue to be published.

HISTORICAL CONTEXT

History of Peru

Peru had been inhabited for thousands of years when, in the twelfth century, the Quechua-speaking Incas established an empire that lasted until the Spanish conquest in 1533. Peru remained a colony until 1821, then went through a number of upheavals before a period of stability started in 1844. A republican constitution was in effect from 1860 until 1920, but Peru did not have its first civilian president until 1872. Foreign debts for a costly program of public works, followed by a war with Chile, caused the Peruvian government to allow foreign capitalists in 1889 to form the Peruvian Corporation, headquartered in

London, to mine up to three million tons of the country's valuable guano deposits, control the railroads for sixty-six years, and receive annual payments of eighty thousand British pounds. The arrangement averted economic disaster for Peru, but the Peruvian people hated the loss of national control and prestige.

There followed a power struggle between the Creole upper class and liberals who urged social and economic reform. The Democratic Party was formed and won the presidency in 1895 with promises of direct suffrage, increased local self-determination, and public schools. This effort, which resulted in positive economic development, was followed by the rule of Augusto Leguia y Salcedo from the Civilian Party from 1908 to 1912 and 1919 to 1930. Although a dictator, Leguia expanded sugar and cotton production and settled a boundary dispute with Chile. In 1920, he supported a new constitution that provided for the protection of Indian lands from sale or seizure. However, the provision was not enforced, leading indigenous Peruvians to organize and attracting members to the Communist Party.

During this time César Vallejo received his college education and wrote his first book of poetry, *The Black Heralds*. Both of Vallejo's grandmothers were natives, and he grew up with knowledge of the Indian language Quechua, which he used occasionally in his poems. While working on a plantation to earn money for college, Vallejo saw the harsh living conditions of the exploited workers. Given his background and the mood of the times, it is no surprise then that the opening poem of his first collection should deal with the oppression of the masses.

Post–World War I Artistic Movements

From the late 1800s to 1918, the modernist movement existed as a corollary to the Industrial Revolution and mechanization. Modernists advocated adaptation of society in all its aspects to rapid technological changes; traditional forms of art, literature, and social organization simply would not suffice. Therefore, a period of worldwide revolution in all the arts ensued with the belief that anything new and unrelated to the past is better than what is old and traditional.

The writings of Charles Darwin and Karl Marx helped to establish modernism since they challenged established worldviews, both religious and social, and questioned various romantic

notions, for example about the innate superiority and decency of humans. At the same time, the impressionist painters took art outdoors and argued that people do not see objects so much as they see light itself as it shines on objects and transforms them. Symbolist writers expressed a theory that since language is itself symbolic in nature, writers should seek words for their sound and texture. Adding to these breaks with traditional thought was Sigmund Freud, the so-called father of psychology, who said that people perceived the world through a filter of their own basic drives and instincts, thus making reality subjective. Philosopher Friedrich Nietzsche advocated that vision is more important than facts or things. Consequently, impressionism, symbolism, along with the work of Freud and Nietzsche, influenced the progression toward abstraction in art and literature. Freedom of expression, experimentation, radicalism, and primitivism, the belief that nature provides truer and more healthful models than culture, were stressed.

Following such catastrophic upheavals in the social order as the Russian Revolution and World War I, modernism changed from a movement that recognized its link with the past even while questioning tradition to a movement that encouraged overturning the status quo. It was obvious that humanity was not morally progressive and reality was questionable, so surrealism, the movement that uses illogical, dreamlike images and events to suggest the unconscious, was born in an age that also fostered cubism and jazz.

In South America, modernism or modernismo replaced nationalism as the predominant trend in literature and followed the symbolist and Parnassian schools in espousing that art should be for art's sake. The modernistas wrote about exotic matters and experimented with language. Leading this movement were Jose Asuncion Silva of Colombia and Julian del Casal and Jose Marti of Cuba. The movement reached its height with Nicaraguan Ruben Dario (1867–1916) whose fundamental collection, *Azul* (Blue), was published in 1888. These writers influenced the up-and-coming poet, César Vallejo, who quickly moved beyond them to embrace surrealism and create his own unique style. His experimentation with language is an indication that he, too, rejected the traditional and the familiar. In the process, he joined many other Latin American writers who chose social protest for their themes. From the late nineteenth century on, Peruvian writers stressed analyzing society and exposing the conditions of the poor, especially Peruvian natives.

CRITICAL OVERVIEW

Many early works of writers are amateurish and only hint of the talent that later blossoms as the skills mature. In the case of Vallejo, however, the first line of the first poem, "The Black Heralds," has become a super star in the world of poetry, and the collection of the same name in which this poem appears, Vallejo's first published collection, continued into the early 2000s to rate serious academic study among literary scholars.

Efrain Kristal, writing for the *American Poetry Review*, suggests that the palpable intensity of the first line is what makes it one of the most well-known lines in Latin American poetry. Kristal says that the strong pathos is "not in the words that can be recited but in the silence of the ellipsis. One feels the breath knocked out of the poetic voice" as he expresses the "impotence of a suffering humanity."

In her article on Vallejo for *Hispania*, Phyllis White Rodríguez points out that the "strong notes" that open the poem set the tone of the piece, and the poem itself contains the themes that pervade the rest of the collection. She adds that *The Black Heralds* "is a tremendous shout of sadness and grief, of contradiction and protest."

Similarly, Ivan Arguelles, writing a review for the *Library Journal* about *The Black Heralds* states: "From the very first line . . ., the discerning reader is convinced that what follows will be a profound literary experience, a life perceived from a harrowingly surrealistic perspective." Arguelles also comments on Vallejo's rare ability to express the human condition and notes that this first book of poetry "already reveals the complex intellectual, emotional, and spiritual qualities that characterize his later work."

Speaking of the collection as a whole, Kristal adds that *The Black Heralds* "marks the turn, in Hispanic poetry, from the symbolist aesthetic . . . to an unprecedented level of emotional rawness which eventually stretched the Spanish language beyond it grammatical possibilities." David Biespiel, writing for the Poetry Foundation about Vallejo's language in his first

WHAT DO I READ NEXT?

- A complex and groundbreaking work, Vallejo's second book of poetry, *Trilce*, contains seventy-seven poems filled with creative syntax and punctuation and abstruse images. Published in 1922, the work contorts the Spanish language with Incan phrases and medical terminology to express very personal emotions.

- *Complete Later Poems: 1923–1938*, translated by Valentino Gianuzzi and Michael Smith and published in 2005, contains all of Vallejo's poetic works from the time he moved to Paris until his death, including *Poemas Humanos*, or *Human Poems*, Vallejo's last and possibly finest book of poetry.

- Vallejo wrote *Tungsten: A Novel* (translated by Robert Mezey and published by Syracuse University Press in 1988) to expose the situation of the exploited native Peruvians in the tungsten mining industry. Popular in the U.S.S.R. and Spain when first published, it is the narrative that goes along with the picture he depicted in "The Black Heralds" and one of the earliest social-realist novels from Spanish America.

- Ruben Dario's *Selected Writings* (2005) is an English translation of some of the best poetry of the modernismo leader from Nicaragua who was a notable influence on Vallejo.

- "The Black Heralds" was written in the style of Paul Verlaine's "Art Poetique," which appeared in a 1913 anthology that Vallejo read and appears again in *Selected Poems*, a 2000 publication of selected poems by Verlaine.

- Pablo Neruda of Chile is considered by many to be South America's greatest poet. *Neruda and Vallejo: Selected Poems* (1993) presents some of Neruda's poetry with a selection of Vallejo's poetry and is an excellent study of these two masters of the craft.

work, states: "Sometimes blasphemous, other times merely irreverent, *The Black Heralds* surrealistic imagery, tone, diction, and themes confront pastoral traditions, colonialism, and religious conformity."

The publishers of the Kathleen Ross and Richard Schaaf 1990 translation of *The Black Heralds* write on the inside flap of the cover of the book a summation of the critical judgment of Vallejo's first collection, saying that it "shows a mystical and social vision that penetrates the deepest recesses of the human spirit and consciousness. . . . [and] ushers in the dawn of a new poetry in Perú." Concerning the famous initial lines of the title poem, the publishers add that they "probably mark the beginning of Peruvian, in the sense of indigenous, poetry." However, just as the narrator in "The Black Heralds" represents all humanity, Vallejo's opening line and first collection of poetry contain universal themes that appeal to all readers.

CRITICISM

Lois Kerschen

Kerschen is an educator and freelance writer. In this essay, she compares the differences found in various translations of the Vallejo poem "The Black Heralds" and comments on the possible changes in tone and meaning that these differences can make.

It is said that every Peruvian knows the opening line of "Los Heraldos Negros," the title poem to César Vallejo's first book, published in 1919 in Lima: "Hay golpes en la vida tan fuertes . . . Y no sé!" Translated into English, this line from "The Black Heralds" is: "There are blows in life so hard . . . I just don't know!" Or is it? The book was, of course, written and published in Spanish, so English readers have to rely upon the quality of the translation to be able to discern the tone and meaning of Vallejo's poetry. Depending on the interpretation of the translator, any given word could appear in two, three, or more variations, and some of the variations could convey quite different connotations.

Poetry is very subjective, intentionally so. The poet may have one thing in mind when writing the poem, but the reader gets something else out of it—and that is okay. Everyone does some interpreting while reading prose or poetry, according to each person's own schema, that is,

> THE POINT IS THAT TRANSLATORS COME INTO THE JOB WITH DIFFERENT AGENDAS AS WELL AS KNOWLEDGE, AND CRITICS ARE LIKELY TO FIND FAULT WITH THEIR EFFORTS ONE WAY OR ANOTHER."

the individual's own world view based on that person's individual knowledge and experience. Within reason, and following certain basic rules of language, the poem nonetheless means whatever it means to each person, including the translator. The definition of a word, its literal meaning, is the first consideration, but then the connotations come into play and can change the entire meaning of a line. "No act shows the provisional nature of reading and writing as does translation, a series of decisions and revisions themselves subject to infinite questioning and revising," states Alfred J. MacAdam in a 1980 review of Clayton Eshleman's translation of *Cesar Vallejo: The Complete Posthumous Poetry*.

Critics often comment on the difficulties of the translator's job. Julio Ortega, writing for *Latin American Writers*, states: "Vallejo is perhaps the most complicated poet of the Spanish language. . . . the hermetic [airtight] work of Vallejo is nearly impossible to translate." However, Efrain Kristal, writing a critique of Eshleman's 2006 book, *The Complete Poetry of Cesar Vallejo*, for *American Poetry Review* says that Eshleman has shown that "impossible to translate" is not the same as "impossible to paraphrase," and he "renders Vallejo's paradoxes with ease, and his linguistic unconventionalities with instinctual acumen."

In the introduction to her translation of *The Black Heralds*, Rebecca Seiferle asserts: "Reading and translating Vallejo has been a long process of trying to meet him on his own terms, to discover what those terms were within the contexts of his particular time and, finally, taking his word for it." How well Seiferle succeeds is questioned by Christopher Maurer in an article for *New Republic* about her translation of Vallejo's *Trilce*, and one can assume that these remarks could apply to *The Black Heralds* as well. Maurer complains that Seiferle has only a "tenuous hold on the Spanish language." In addition, Seiferle appears to be trying to excise from Vallejo the colonization that she sees in other translations. Despite the many critics who find evidence of Vallejo's indigenous background in his poetry, which is fairly evident from his use of some native language terms, Seiferle finds these allusions to be parodies of Indian culture rather than romantic nostalgia about rural and native life. In the same article, Maurer reviews Eshleman's translation of *Trilce* and finds it to be a high risk for accuracy, calling Eshleman a "verbal stunt man." The point is that translators come into the job with different agendas as well as knowledge, and critics are likely to find fault with their efforts one way or another.

The translation provided by Kathleen Ross and Richard Schaaf in their 1990 publication of *The Black Heralds* was reviewed by Asunción Horno-Delgado for *American Book Review*. Her comments touch on several of the issues involved in translation that could apply to any work:

> The Spanish-speaking reader will feel compelled to quibble with some of the translations . . . for the English translations sometimes render a Romantic overtone totally absent in Vallejo's poetry. Several other subtleties of the original Spanish are lost, as inevitably happens in translations of poetry. The translation loses some gender-based shades of meaning that are virtually impossible to translate from Spanish into English, and also those wonderful diminutive forms of Spanish that do not exist in English. Still, the magic of this poetry does survive in English, despite such absences. In general, this translation is well done and an invitation to enjoy the pleasure of the text.

For example, regarding the first line of "The Black Heralds," is it that the "blows in life" are hard, powerful, strong, violent, or heavy? In the 1990 translation of the book by Kathleen Ross and Richard Schaaf, the choice is "hard." In the 2006 edition of Clayton Eshleman's *The Complete Poetry of Cesar Vallejo*, it is "powerful." In Eshleman's 1979 book, Cesar Vallejo: The Complete Posthumous Poetry, the choice is "strong." In a 1995 article by Vallejo scholar Edward Hirsch, it is "violent." In *Cesar Vallejo: Selected Poems* translated by H. R. Hays in 1989, it is "heavy."

From this list, it is obvious that Eshleman changed his mind between 1979 and 2006 from "strong" to "powerful." Since Eshleman has spent four decades studying Vallejo and won the National Book Award for his 1979 translation of *The Complete Posthumous Poetry* (in partnership with Jose Rubio Barcia), it would seem that he has the expertise in Spanish and on Vallejo to make an accurate choice. So, is the 2006 version more correct simply because more years of study have passed since the first translation and Eshleman has a better understanding of Vallejo's intent? Does the mood of the translator have an effect on the interpretation just as the mood of the reader does?

Complicating matters for the translator of poetry is the difficulty of choosing a word that not only conveys the original meaning but also the rhythm and meter of the poem. Perhaps the three-syllable word "powerful" was considered too long for the line by one of the translators who chose the one-syllable "hard" or "strong" or the two-syllable "heavy." Line two presents another issues of interpretation: Hays uses "Blows like God's hatred," while Eshleman uses "Blows as from the hatred of God." The latter is less of a comparison of the blows to God's hatred and more of a connection between the blows and God's hatred—the blows are not "like" God's hatred, they actually come from God's hatred. Eshleman's translation seems more powerful and sinister.

There are some translations that even an English-only reader or an amateur reader of poetry may question. For example, an essay for *The Dictionary of Literary Biography*, by Linda S. Maier, cites a translation of "Yo no sé!" as "I can't answer!" instead of "I don't know!" or "I just don't know!" Even a first-semester Spanish student knows that "No sé" is the expression for "I don't know" because that is the reply used often by students in answer to the teacher's questions. Although the phrase certainly could be interpreted to mean "I can't answer," the more common usage is simply "I don't know." Since "I can't answer" is more formal, few people cry out in frustrated anguish: "I can't answer!" Rather, they will shout "I don't know!" to express their loss of words for an explanation of their desperate situation, or as Ross and Schaaf translated the phrase "I just don't know" using "just" for further emphasis. Nonetheless, Edward Hirsch, a frequent writer on Vallejo, uses a translation in a 1995 article that has "I can't answer!" This translation uses "violent" for "hard" in the first line, but calls the poem "The Black Riders," which is totally different from all the other references. Here again, it is hard to understand how anyone could get "riders" out of "heraldos," unless one focuses on Attila's steeds. Some translations use "messengers" for "heralds." At least that is closer, but "messenger" carries less the connotation of bringing an announcement than "heralds" conveys. Is Death more likely to send a message or a pronouncement?

The Maier article also translates the third and fourth lines of "The Black Heralds" as "the deep waters of everything lived through were backed up in the soul." The better translations use "undertow" for "deep waters," which has more of a sense of danger and being pulled down. Preferred translations also use "suffering" for "lived through," which again carries more a sense of pain; things "lived through" could be joyous occasions, too. Eshleman in 1979 uses the stronger "undertow" but follows that with "flowed into our souls," which seems too gentle a phrase for an undertow. A worse choice, though, is using "backed up" instead of "welled up," which sounds more like a backed up sewer system than the rising of repressed emotions. Are the emotions backing up in the soul to places where they could hide more deeply, or are they welling up to the point of being released in an explosion of reaction? Depending on the translation, it is hard to tell if the flood of emotions is flowing forward or backward. Ross and Schaaf use the similar term "backwash," and Hays uses "dammed up." These two choices carry the same idea of being held or pushed back as the translation in Maier's article, but "dammed up" carries the meaning of being forcibly held back by structures that humans tend to build around their emotions and is, therefore, more powerful than merely being "backed up," as in a traffic jam or backwashed like water at a marina.

The questions that a critic could ask about a translator are numerous: Did the translator lean too heavily on dictionaries and literary sources? Was the translator sensitive to the everyday subtleties of the language? Did the translator take into account idiomatic usage? How well does the translator know the poet, his life, his idiosyncrasies, the emotions he would have put into his poetry? With Vallejo, was his Spanish really mixed with the Quechua language, or did his experimentation with the Spanish confuse translators about the source of his words and phrases? In addition, did he use words that were mispronounced by the rural, uneducated people of his village and thus may appear to be something different from what they are? Did Vallejo have in his language words from his indigenous, backwater upbringing that appear archaic to translators but were in popular usage where he lived? Since Vallejo experimented with language, is a word choice a neologism—a made-up word—for which there is no match in English?

With all these variables, it is no wonder that the seventh line of "The Black Heralds" might have the barbarians of Attila the Hun's army riding ponies, colts, or steeds, although it is frankly hard to imagine warriors riding ponies or colts. Steeds are noble, spirited horses bred for war and thus would seem to be the best word choice. Even plain "horses" would be better than ponies or colts whose size and youth make them unsuited for battle. However, MacAdam quotes Jorge Luis Borges, the great Argentinean writer as saying, in a commentary on the various translations of Homer, that "No translation is, in the last analysis, better than any other. Even the worst translation may succeed in communicating to the reader some aspect of the original absent in the 'better' translation." Beauty is in the eye of the beholder because beauty is subjective, poetry is subjective, and translation, besides the language skills required, is ultimately subjective, too.

Source: Lois Kerschen, Critical Essay on "The Black Heralds," in *Poetry for Students*, Thomson Gale, 2007

Linda S. Maier

In the following essay, Maier gives a critical analysis of Vallejo's work.

Although he published relatively little during his lifetime and received scant critical acclaim, César Vallejo has come to be recognized as one of the most important and complex poets of the Spanish language, one of the foremost poets of Spanish America, and the greatest Peruvian poet of all time. His literary production includes essays, novels, short stories, plays, and a screenplay; but his reputation rests primarily on his poetry, much of which appeared posthumously. Vallejo's chief contribution to poetry is his innovative use of language to communicate intense, authentic emotion and to convey both personal and existential anguish. His verse is marked by a strong sense of compassion and filled with Christian imagery that in his later works is fused with Marxist ideology. Vallejo's poetry has influenced generations of Peruvian and other Spanish American poets to undertake further experiments with poetic language and technique.

The youngest of seven boys and four girls, César Abraham Vallejo was born on 16 March 1892 in Santiago de Chuco, a small town in an agricultural region of the Andes Mountains in northern Peru, to Francisco de Paula Vallejo Benites, a notary public and district official, and María de los Santos Mendoza Gurrionero. Both of Vallejo's grandfathers were Spanish Jesuit priests, and his grandmothers were Chimú Indians. Vallejo received a traditional Catholic upbringing and was encouraged by his parents to consider the priesthood. After attending primary school in his hometown, he began secondary school in 1905 at the Colegio Nacional de San Nicolás (St. Nicholas National High School)—known as the "Athens of the Andes"—in Huamachuco, where he first began writing poetry.

Vallejo graduated from high school in 1908 and took a job as a clerk in his father's notary public office. Later he worked in the office of a mining company in Quiruvilca, between Santiago de Chuco and Huamachuco; as a tutor on a country estate; and as an assistant cashier in the accounting office of a sugar plantation near Trujillo, the capital of the department of La Libertad on the northern Peruvian coast. He was forced to abandon college plans twice during this period because he could not afford the cost of university study.

In 1913 Vallejo enrolled at the Universidad Nacional de La Libertad (La Libertad National University) in Trujillo. He completed a humanities degree in 1915 with a thesis titled *El Romanticismo en la poesía castellana* (Romanticism in Castilian Poetry). The thesis, which was published in 1954, is divided into a description of the origins of Spanish Romanticism and a review of typical Romantic traits of Spanish poets, including Manuel José Quintana, José de Espronceda, and José Zorrilla. Vallejo studied law at the university from 1915 to 1917 but did not complete work for a degree. To support himself as a student he taught botany and anatomy at the Centro Escolar de Varones No. 241 (Middle Boys' School No. 241), where he contributed scientific explanations in verse to the

IN *LOS HERALDOS NEGROS* VALLEJO OFTEN CLOAKS SOCIAL AND EXISTENTIAL THEMES IN RELIGIOUS IMAGERY; HE CONTINUED TO DO SO THROUGHOUT HIS CAREER."

school magazine, *Cultura Infantil* (Children's Culture), and later at the Colegio Nacional de San Juan (St. John National School), where one of his pupils was the future novelist Ciro Alegría.

In Trujillo, Vallejo had failed romances with two women, María Rosa Sandoval and Zoila Rosa Cuadra, who merged into the figure of "Mirtho" in his early verse. He belonged to a progressive circle of writers and intellectuals known as the *bohemios* (bohemians) or "Trujillo group," which also included artist and journalist José Eulogio Garrido; politician Víctor Raúl Haya de la Torre; philosopher and journalist Antenor Orrego; poets Óscar Imaña, Francisco Sandoval, and Alcides Spelucín; and painter Macedonio de la Torre. His reading expanded from medieval and Golden Age Spanish literature to embrace the works of Americans Ralph Waldo Emerson and Walt Whitman, Spaniard Miguel de Unamuno, Uruguayan José Enrique Rodó, French symbolists, and Modernista poets such as Rubén Darío of Nicaragua, Julio Herrera y Reissig of Uruguay, Juan Ramón Jiménez of Spain, Amado Nervo of Mexico, and José Santos Chocano of Peru. Vallejo began to publish his poetry in *La Industria* (Industry) and *La Reforma* (Reform), local newspapers edited by Garrido and Orrego, and to recite it publicly. *La Industria* said of one of his readings in a 13 October 1916 review: "Es aún novicio casi, pero en él se apunta una preciosa promesa" (Though still a novice, he promises bright hopes for the future).

In 1917 Vallejo moved to Lima, where he conducted newspaper interviews with the prominent Peruvian literary figures Abraham Valdelomar (whose pseudonym was "El Conde de Lemos" [Count Lemos]), José María Eguren, and Manuel González Prada and came into contact with the city's two leading groups of writers and intellectuals: one led by Valdelomar, the editor of the experimental magazine *Colónida*, and the other by essayist and political activist José Carlos Mariátegui. In 1918 he began teaching at the Colegio Barrós (Barrós High School), one of the city's finest private schools. That year his mother, who is lovingly portrayed in his early verse, died, but Vallejo was unable to return home for her funeral. Also in 1918 Valdelomar wrote of Vallejo in the Lima journal *Sud-América*: "Hay en tu espíritu la chispa divina de los elegidos. Eres un gran artista, un hombre sincero y bueno, un niño lleno de dolor, de tristeza, de inquietud, de sombra y de esperanza.... tu espíritu, donde anida la chispa de Dios, será inmortal, fecundará otras almas y vivirá radiante en la Gloria por los siglos de los siglos. Amén" (The divine light of the chosen is in your spirit. You are a great artist, a good and sincere man, a child filled with pain, sadness, and anxiety, with both pessimism and hope.... your spirit, where God's inspiration dwells, will be immortal and enrich others and blaze in Glory forever and ever. Amen).

When the founder of the Colegio Barrós died in September 1918, Vallejo became principal and led the reorganization of the school as the Instituto Nacional (National Institute); but an unhappy romantic involvement with a woman named Otilia, the sister-in-law of one of his colleagues, cost him his job. Subsequently, he held a short-lived post as an elementary teacher at the Colegio Nacional de Guadalupe (Guadalupe National School).

Vallejo's first collection of poetry, *Los heraldos negros* (translated as *The Black Heralds*, 1990), was printed in mid 1918 but not distributed until the following year. The title conveys the melancholy tone of the volume and announces a bleak worldview in which life heralds inevitable death. The sixty-nine poems are divided into an introductory text and six unequal sections, of which only two form thematic units: "Nostalgias imperiales" (Imperial Nostalgia), on the Peruvian countryside, and "Canciones de hogar" (Songs of Home), on the connection between happiness and family. The other poems are grouped arbitrarily and treat personal, social, and existential themes, and many incorporate Christian symbolism and allusions. *Los heraldos negros* is a transitional work that marks both a continuation of Spanish American Modernismo and the emergence of Vallejo's original poetic voice. Like the Modernista masters Darío,

Herrera y Reissig, and Leopoldo Lugones of Argentina, Vallejo employs traditional forms, including sonnets as well as heptasyllabic (seven-syllable) and hendecasyllabic (eleven-syllable) verses, which lend musicality to his work. Moreover, he assimilates common Modernista motifs, such as idyllic landscape description and blending of mysticism and eroticism. On the other hand, Vallejo's poems exhibit greater social awareness and a more extensive use of ordinary language than most Modernista verse.

The title poem sets the pessimistic tone of the book:

> Hay golpes en la vida, tan fuertes . . . Yo no sé!
> Golpes como del odio de Dios; como si ante ellos,
> la resaca de todo lo sufrido
> se empozara en el alma . . . Yo no sé!
>
> (There are blows in life so violent . . . I can't answer!
> Blows as if from the hatred of God; as if before them,
> the deep waters of everything lived through were backed up in the soul . . . I can't answer!).

The pastoral compositions are also imbued with sadness; and while Vallejo equates happiness with home and family, the loss of his brother, commemorated in the elegy "A mi hermano Miguel" (To My Brother Miguel), represents the dissolution of the family unit. Similarly, Vallejo's love poems, such as "Setiembre" (September) and "Heces" (Down to the Dregs), depict painful personal experiences.

In *Los heraldos negros* Vallejo often cloaks social and existential themes in religious imagery; he continued to do so throughout his career. For example, in "El pan nuestro" (Our Daily Bread) he expresses concern for the underprivileged but is incapable of taking action to help them; in his imagination he distributes bread to them like the priest giving out the Host during the Eucharist. Bread is both the physical and the spiritual staff of life:

> Se quisiera tocar todas las puertas,
> y preguntar por no sé quién; y luego
> ver a los pobres, y, llorando quedos,
> dar pedacitos de pan fresco a todos.
> Y saquear a los ricos sus viñedos
> con las dos manos santas
> que a un golpe de luz
> volaron desclavadas de la Cruz!

(I wish I could beat on all the doors,
and ask for somebody; and then
look at the poor, and, while they wept softly,
give bits of fresh bread to them.
And plunder the rich of their vineyards
with those two blessed hands
which blasted the nails with one blow of light,
and flew away from the Cross!).

Vallejo compares human existence to a game of chance in which humanity, alone and defenseless, must struggle for survival in a hostile universe. In "Los dados eternos" (The Eternal Dice) God is a gamester incapable of managing the world:

Dios mío, y esta noche sorda, oscura,
ya no podrás jugar, porque la Tierra
es un dado roído y ya redondo
a fuerza de rodar a la aventura,
que no puede parar si no en un hueco,
en el hueco de inmensa sepultura

(My God, in this muffled, dark night,
you can't play anymore, because the Earth
is already a die nicked and rounded
from rolling by chance;
and it can stop only in a hollow place,
in the hollow of the enormous grave).

Vallejo's first poetry collection characterizes life as meaningless anguish and God as impotent, indifferent, and, possibly, even nonexistent.

Having lost two teaching jobs and published an unnoticed volume of poetry during his two and a half years in Lima, Vallejo decided in mid 1920 to return to his hometown. Stopping along the way in Huamachuco, he publicly recited several poems that were not well received and defiantly predicted "Llegaré a ser más grande que Rubén Darío y tendré el orgullo de ver a la América prosternada a mis pies" (One day my poetry will make me greater than even Rubén Darío, and I will have the pleasure of seeing America prostrated before my feet). He arrived in Santiago de Chuco during festivities in honor of the town's patron saint. Vallejo and nearly twenty other individuals were accused of instigating a riot on the final day of the celebration that resulted in one death, the looting and burning of the town's largest business, and an assault on the municipal telephone and telegraph offices. Vallejo went into hiding but was arrested three months later, in early November, and spent 112 days in prison in Trujillo. Although he was allowed to have books and visitors and to

write, his prison experience embittered him and led to his later stories and poems exposing the world's arbitrary cruelty. During his incarceration his poem "Fabla de gesta (Elogio del Marqués)" (Heroic Fable [in Praise of the Marquis]) was awarded second prize in a municipal competition commemorating the centennial of Peru's declaration of independence.

Released in late February 1921, Vallejo returned to Lima and resumed teaching at the Colegio Nacional de Guadalupe. In late 1921 his story "Más allá de la vida y la muerte" (Beyond Life and Death) won first prize in a literary contest; it was published in the Lima magazine *Variedades* (Variety), along with a photograph of the author and three illustrations, the following year.

Also in 1922 Vallejo published *Trilce* (translated, 1973), his second book of poetry and the last to appear during his lifetime. Comprising poems written between 1918 and 1922 and including a preface by Orrego, *Trilce* signals a radical break with tradition and has come to be viewed as one of the major texts of avant-garde poetry in Spanish. Vallejo's knowledge of the international avant-garde movements that were occurring at the time the volume was published was derived principally from his reading of literary journals from Spain such as *Cervantes*, *La Esfera* (The Sphere), *España* (Spain), and *Ultra;* his relative lack of familiarity with the European avant-garde makes his achievement all the more notable.

Vallejo had originally intended to publish the volume as "Cráneos de bronce" (Bronze Skulls) under the pseudonym César Perú; the title he used, *Trilce*, is a neologism that is generally interpreted as a combination of *tres* (three) or *triple* (triple) and *dulce* (sweet). The volume consists of seventy-seven poems designated by Roman numerals rather than by titles. As in *Los heraldos negros*, Vallejo explores personal and universal existential issues; but this time he does so in a raw, idiosyncratic style. Past happiness is juxtaposed with present anguish as the family unit disintegrates with the deaths of its members. The poet's mother embodies this lost paradise in poem XXIII: "Tahona estuosa de aquellos mis bizcochos / pura yema infantil innumerable, madre" (Radiant bakery of those my sweet rolls / pure infantile innumerable yolk, mother). In poem LXI a visit to his family home produces nostalgia when the poet encounters only an empty house:

> Esta noche desciendo del caballo,
> ante la puerta de la casa, donde
> me despedí con el cantar del gallo.
> Está cerrada y nadie responde

> (Tonight I get down from my horse,
> before the door of the house, where
> I said farewell with the cock's crowing.
> It is shut and no one responds).

In poem XVIII Vallejo's prison experience becomes a metaphor of the human struggle against all limitations:

> Oh las cuatro paredes de la celda.
> Ah las cuatro paredes albicantes
> que sin remedio dan al mismo número

> (Oh the four walls of the cell.
> Ah the four bleaching walls
> that inevitably face the same number).

Vallejo blends conventional techniques such as antithesis, oxymoron, paradox, and free verse with neologisms; awkward alliterations; harsh sounds; linguistic and syntactic distortions; reiterations; enumerations; innovative capitalization, punctuation, and spacing; reverse writing; archaisms; idiomatic and regional expressions; and slang. In poem XXXII he invents words and uses numbers and discordant sounds to describe a sweltering afternoon in which heat and noise block human activity:

> 999 calorías.
> Rumbb. . . . . . Trrraprrr rrach. . . . . chaz
> Serpentínica u del bizcochero
> enjirafada al tímpano.
> Quién como los hielos. Pero nó.
> Quién como lo que va ni más ni menos.
> Quién como el justo medio

> (999 calories.
> Roombbb. . . . . . Hulllablll llust. . . . . ster
> Serpenteenice of the sweet roll vendor
> girafted to the eardrum.
> Lucky are the ices. But no.
> Lucky that which moves neither more nor less.
> Lucky the golden mean).

Because of its difficult and hermetic nature, *Trilce* was generally ignored by critics and was despised by those who did notice it. In his October 1922 review in the Lima weekly *Mundial* (Universal) Luis Alberto Sánchez called

the book "incomprensible y estrambótico" (incomprehensible and outlandish) and wondered, "¿Por qué habrá escrito *Trilce* Vallejo?" (Why did Vallejo ever write *Trilce?*).

In 1923 Vallejo published a collection of short stories and a novella. *Escalas melografiadas* (Melographic Scales) is divided into two parts, "Cuneiformes" (Cuneiforms) and "Coro de los vientos" (Choir of Winds). The stories in the first section, several of which Vallejo composed in prison, may be considered prose versions of poems in *Trilce*. The macabre stories in the second section reflect the influence of Edgar Allan Poe. The short novel *Fabla salvaje* (Savage Fable) also shows Poe's influence: set in the Andes, it explores the psyche of an Indian peasant who imagines his wife's infidelity.

After losing his teaching job because of a reduction in staff, Vallejo moved to Paris in June 1923. Not fluent in French and having, at first, neither regular employment nor permanent living quarters, Vallejo began to suffer the ill health that endured for the rest of his life. His father's death in 1924 added to his woes.

From 1925 to 1927 Vallejo was employed as a secretary at the newly created Ibero-American Press Agency and served as a correspondent for various Spanish and Spanish American periodicals, including *Amauta* (Inca Elder), *Bolívar*, *El Comercio* (Commerce), *Cromos*, *Estampa* (Print), *Mundial*, *La Razón* (Reason), *Revista de Avance* (Advance Review), *Variedades*, and *La Voz* (The Voice). His journalistic pieces generally report on European political, social, and cultural life. One of his essays, "Contra el secreto profesional" (Against Professional Secrets), published in *Variedades* in 1927, deals with the deficiencies of contemporary Spanish American writing; it was republished in book form in 1973. He also earned money from literary translations and Spanish-language tutoring and received a scholarship to continue his legal studies.

In Paris, Vallejo met Costa Rican sculptor Max Jiménez, Spanish painter Juan Gris, Chilean poet Vicente Huidobro, and Spanish poet and literary critic Juan Larrea, who became one of the foremost experts on his work. Vallejo and Larrea started a literary magazine, *Favorables-Paris-Poema;* only two issues appeared, in July and October 1926. Contributors included Gris, Huidobro, Chilean poet Pablo Neruda, French Creationist poet Pierre Reverdy, and the founder of the Dada movement, Tristan Tzara. Also in

1926 Vallejo was listed in the *Índice de la nueva poesía americana* (Index of New Spanish American Poetry), edited by Huidobro, Peruvian poet Alberto Hidalgo, and Argentine writer Jorge Luis Borges.

In 1926 Vallejo began writing a novel about the Incas, "Hacia el reino de los Sciris" (Toward the Kingdom of the Sciris), but never completed it. In the following year he published in the Lima journal *Amauta* a prose piece, "Sabiduría" (Wisdom), that he later included in his protest novel, *El tungsteno: La novela proletaria* (Tungsten: The Proletarian Novel, 1931; translated as *Tungsten*, 1988). Vallejo also tried his hand at drama, though he destroyed the manuscript for his first play, originally titled *Mampar* and retitled *Cancerbero* (Goalkeeper). He composed two other plays: *Moscú contra Moscú* (Moscow vs. Moscow), retitled *Entre las dos orillas corre el río* (Between the Two Shores Runs the River), about a Russian princess whose daughter is a communist activist, and *Lockout*, on a labor-movement theme. Neither was published or produced during Vallejo's lifetime, but both are included in a two-volume edition of his dramatic works that appeared in 1979—more than forty years after his death.

From 1926 to 1928 Vallejo lived with Henriette Maisse. He had begun attending communist workshops and lectures, and in 1928 he traveled to Moscow with the intention of relocating there; but he changed his mind and returned to Paris. In 1929 he moved in with a neighbor, Georgette Phillipart, with whom he returned to the Soviet Union that year. During this second trip Vallejo interviewed the poet Vladimir Maiakovsky, who committed suicide the following year. Vallejo's leftist activities resulted in his expulsion from France in December 1930, and he and Phillipart moved to Madrid.

Shortly after his arrival in the Spanish capital, Vallejo joined the Communist Party and witnessed the proclamation of the Spanish Republic. He continued to earn a living from translation and contributions to Spanish and Spanish American magazines, though his sentimental short story about an Indian boy, "Paco Yunque," was rejected as too sad for young readers and remained unpublished until after his death. A series of articles chronicling his travels in the Soviet Union, "Un reportaje en Rusia" (A Report on Russia), appeared in the Madrid magazine *Bolívar* in 1930 and served as the basis of his *Rusia en 1931: Reflexiones al pie del Kremlin* (Russia in 1931: Reflections at the Foot of the Kremlin), published the following year. In the book Vallejo describes the new social order emerging in the Soviet Union and sets out his own manifesto for the future. Recommended by the Asociación del Mejor Libro del Mes (Book of the Month Club), whose selection committee included such prominent Spanish writers and literary critics as Azorín (pseudonym of José Martínez Ruiz), Ricardo Baeza, Enrique Díez-Canedo, and Ramón Pérez de Ayala, *Rusia en 1931* went through three printings in four months and became the second-best-selling book in Spain after *Sin novedad en el frente* (1929), the Spanish translation of Erich Maria Remarque's *Im Westen nichts neues* (1928; translated as *All Quiet on the Western Front*, 1929). Vallejo began writing *Rusia ante el segundo plan quinquenal* (Russia in the Face of the Second Five-Year Plan) after a third trip to the Soviet Union in October 1931 to participate in the International Congress of Writers, but the work remained unpublished until 1965.

In 1931 the Spanish writers José Bergamín and Gerardo Diego brought out a second edition of *Trilce* that led the Paris reviewer Pierre Lagarde to claim that Vallejo had invented Surrealism before the Surrealists. His greatest literary success during his lifetime, however, came that same year with the publication of his best-selling proletarian protest novel *El tungsteno*. Written in a realistic style and set in the fictional Andean village of Quivilca, the novel is based on Vallejo's firsthand observations of the deplorable conditions in the mines of Quiruvilca. The two main characters are the heroic Indian miner Servando Huanca and the intellectual mine accountant Leonidas Benites. The plot, designed to incite outrage, includes the gang rape of an Indian woman who subsequently dies, the perversions of two wealthy brothers, the conscription of workers for the mines, and a labor revolt that ends in bloodshed.

In early 1932 Vallejo received permission to return to Paris on the condition that he refrain from political activity. With no fixed residence or steady employment, Vallejo was reduced to poverty; nevertheless, he and Phillipart were married in 1934. Between 1932 and 1936 he unsuccessfully submitted for publication three works in three genres: a collection of essays,

El arte y la revolución (Art and Revolution), which was finally published in 1973; a satirical play about Peruvian political life, *Colacho hermanos o Presidentes de América* (The Colacho Brothers; or, Presidents of America), which was included in the 1979 edition of his plays; and a volume of poetry, "Nómina de huesos" (Payroll of Bones), which was incorporated into his posthumous *Poemas humanos: 1923-1938* (1939; translated as *Poemas humanos: Human Poems*, 1968). Some of his other poetry was included in the *Antología de la poesía española e hispanoamericana, 1882-1932* (Anthology of Spanish and Spanish American Poetry, 1882-1932), edited by Federico de Onís in 1934.

The outbreak of the Spanish Civil War in July 1936 prompted Vallejo to resume his political activity. He solicited money in the street to support the Republican forces, was one of the founders of the Spanish American Committee for the Defense of the Spanish Republic, and worked on the committee's bulletin *Nuestra España* (Our Spain). He went to Spain twice during the war; on the second trip he attended sessions of the International Congress of Anti-Fascist Writers in Barcelona, Valencia, and Madrid and visited the battlefront.

In hopes of making money, Vallejo drafted a screenplay titled *Charlot contra Chaplin* (Charles against Chaplin); it was never produced. He also completed a tragedy set in Incan Peru, *La piedra cansada* (The Tired Stone); despite strong support from the Spanish poet and playwright Federico García Lorca, however, it was not produced during his lifetime and was first published in the 1979 edition of his theatrical works. Between September and December 1937 Vallejo composed the poems that were published in 1940 as *España, aparta de mí este cáliz: 15 poemas* (Spain, Take This Cup from Me: 15 Poems; translated as *Spain, Let This Cup Pass from Me*, 1972). He also devoted a significant amount of time to correcting, revising, and editing his unpublished poetry.

Vallejo became bedridden on 13 March 1938. The Peruvian embassy paid to have him placed in a clinic, where, after suffering from delirium and losing consciousness, he died on the morning of 15 April 1938. The International Association of Writers in Defense of Culture organized and financed Vallejo's funeral and burial in the Montrouge cemetery in south Paris; among the eulogists was French avant-garde writer Louis Aragon. In the 1960s Vallejo's widow purchased a new tombstone and had his remains transferred to Montparnasse cemetery.

Georgette de Vallejo and her friend, historian Raúl Porras Barrenechea, brought out Vallejo's unpublished poetry the year after his death under the title *Poemas humanos*. The volume includes 108 poems, some dated and others undated; they are in no chronological or thematic order with the exception of the last fifteen, the poems that were republished separately in 1940 as *España, aparta de mí este cáliz*. Critical opinion on the organization and interpretation of Vallejo's posthumous poetry varies. Some critics believe that his entire European production should be considered as a unit. Others divide it into the poems written between 1923 and 1937 and the fifteen poems of *España, aparta de mí este cáliz*. Still others suggest a three-part division, comprising the undated poems, which are assumed to have been written between 1923 and 1936, the dated poems from 1936 to 1938, and the poems of *España, aparta de mí este cáliz*.

The texts of *Poemas humanos* further expand Vallejo's fusion of personal and existential themes and also reflect his heightened political commitment: as in much of his previous poetry, human beings are depicted as weak, defenseless orphans, alone in a hostile universe; and political issues are addressed in poems about hunger, homelessness, and unemployment. He contrasts the absurd, chaotic present, filled with problems and class conflicts, with an ideal future based on human solidarity.

In "Palmas y guitarra" (Palms and Guitars) love offers a temporary refuge in the midst of war:

> Ahora, entre nosotros, aquí,
> ven conmigo, trae por la mano a tu cuerpo
> y cenemos juntos y pasemos un instante la vida
> a dos vidas y dando una parte a nuestra muerte.
> Ahora, ven contigo, hazme el favor
> de quejarte en mi nombre y a la luz de la noche teneblosa
> en que traes a tu alma de la mano
> y huímos en puntillas de nosotros
> (Now, between ourselves, right here,
> come with me, bring your body by the hand
> and let's dine together and spend our life for a moment
> in two lives, giving a part to our death.

Now, come with yourself, do me the favor
of complaining in my name and by the light
  of the teneblous night
in which you bring your soul by the hand
and we flee on tiptoes from ourselves).

All the same, death is inevitable; and Vallejo predicts his own death in "Piedra negra sobre una piedra blanca" (Black Stone on a White Stone):

Me moriré en París con aguacero,
un día del cual tengo ya el recuerdo.
Me moriré en París—y no me corro—
talvez un jueves, como es hoy, de otoño

(I will die in Paris with a sudden shower,
a day I can already remember.
I will die in Paris—and I don't budge—
maybe a Thursday, like today is, in autumn).

In "Intensidad y altura" (Intensity and Height) Vallejo describes the challenges of aesthetic creation:

Quiero escribir, pero me sale espuma,
quiero decir muchísimo y me atollo;
no hay cifra hablada que no sea suma,
no hay pirámide escrita, sin cogollo.
Quiero escribir, pero me siento puma;
quiero laurearme, pero me encebollo.
No hay toz hablada, que no llegue a bruma,
no hay dios ni hijo de dios, sin desarrollo

(I want to write, but out comes foam,
I want to say so much and I freeze;
there is no spoken cipher which is not a sum,
there is no written pyramid, without a core.
I want to write, but I feel like a puma;
I want to laurel myself, but I stew in onions.
There is no spoken cough, which doesn't end
  in mist,
there is no god nor son of god, without
  unfolding).

But in the face of poverty and adversity, Vallejo says in "Un hombre pasa con un pan al hombro" (A Man Walks by with a Stick of Bread), art is inconsequential:

Un hombre pasa con un pan al hombro.
¿Voy a escribir, después, sobre mi doble?

Otro se sienta, ráscase, extrae un piojo de su
  axial, mátalo.
¿Con qué valor hablar de psicoanálisis?

Otro ha entrado a mi pecho con un palo en
  la mano.

¿Hablar luego de Sócrates al médico?

Un cojo pasa dando el brazo a un niño.
¿Voy, después, a leer a André Breton?

Otro tiembla de frío, tose, escupe sangre.
¿Cabrá aludir jamás al Yo profundo?

(A man walks by with a stick of bread on his
  shoulder.
Am I going to write, after that, about my
  double?

Another sits, scratches, extracts a louse from
  his armpit, kills it.
How dare one speak about psychoanalysis?

Another has entered my chest with a stick in
  hand.
To talk then about Socrates with the doctor?

A lame man passes by holding a child's hand.
After that am I going to read André Breton?

Another trembles from cold, coughs, spits
  blood.
Will it ever be possible to allude to the profound I?).

On another level, *Poemas humanos* alludes to the ordeals of existence in general and proposes a collective solution to personal and human problems. In "Hoy me gusta la vida mucho menos" (Today I Like Life Much Less) and "Los nueve monstruos" (The Nine Monsters) Vallejo describes modern humanity's existential anguish, as he writes in the latter:

I, desgraciadamente,
el dolor crece en el mundo a cada rato,
crece a treinta minutos por segundo, paso a
  paso,
y la naturaleza del dolor, es el dolor dos veces
y la condición del martirio, carnívoro, voraz,
es el dolor, dos veces
y la función de la yerba purísima, el dolor
dos veces
y el bien de sér, dolernos doblemente.

¡Jamás, hombres humanos,
hubo tánto dolor en el pecho, en la solapa,
  en la cartera,
en el vaso, en la carnicería, en la aritmética!

(AND, unfortunately,
pain grows in the world every moment,

grows thirty minutes a second, step by step,
and the nature of the pain, is the pain twice
and the condition of the martyrdom, carniv-
     orous, voracious,
is the pain, twice
and the function of the purest grass, the pain
     twice
and the good of Being, to hurt us doubly.

Never, human men,
was there so *much* pain in the chest, in the
     lapel, in the wallet,
in the glass, in the butcher shop, in arithmetic!).

Vallejo reveals his increasing exaltation of the proletariat in "Los mineros salieron de la mina" (The Miners Came out of the Mine): "¡Salud, oh creadores de la profundidad!... (Es formidable)" (Hail, oh creators of the profundity! . . . [Tremendous]).

España, aparta de mí este cáliz is generally regarded as the best and most important literary text to emerge from the Spanish Civil War. The fifteen poems had first been printed in the Republican-controlled part of Spain in September 1938, but all copies were destroyed before distribution. After Vallejo's death the texts were included at the end of *Poemas humanos;* the following year, in Mexico, exiled Spanish poet Emilio Prados edited *España, aparta de mí este cáliz*, prior to its publication in 1940. Vallejo's friend Larrea wrote the preface, "Profecía de América" (American Prophecy), and Pablo Picasso contributed an ink portrait of Vallejo. The title echoes Christ's prayer in the Garden of Gethsemane to be released from his imminent sacrifice and conveys the hope that the Spanish Republic may be spared the ravages of war. Incorporating biblical discourse and imagery, the volume glorifies the Spanish Republic and presents a Christian vision of Marxism. The Spanish Civil War symbolizes human suffering and the struggle to create an ideal world, or New Jerusalem. Though the Spanish Republic is compared to a mother offering love and protection, the Republican militiaman endures Christ-like agony and personifies and redeems humanity. In "Himno a los voluntarios de la República" (Hymn to the Volunteers for the Republic) Vallejo describes Republican volunteers as humanity's heroic saviors:

Voluntarios,
por la vida, por los buenos ¡matad
a la muerte, matad a los malos!
Hacedlo por la libertad de todos,

del explotado y del explotador,
por la paz indolora—la sospecho
cuando duermo al pie de mi frente
y más cuando circulo dando voces
y hacedlo, voy diciendo,
por el analfabeto a quien escribo,
por el genio descalzo y su cordero,
por los camaradas caídos,
sus cenizas abrazadas al cadaver de un
     camino!

(Volunteers,
for life, for the good ones, kill
death, kill the bad ones!
Do it for the freedom of everyone,
of the exploited and of the exploiter,
for a peace without pain—I glimpse it
when I sleep at the foot of my forehead
and even more when I travel around
     shouting—
and do it, I keep saying,
for the illiterate to whom I write,
for the barefoot genius and his lamb,
for the fallen comrades,
their ashes hugging the corpse of a road!).

In "Masa" (Mass) international solidarity on behalf of the Spanish Republic brings about resurrection:

Al fin de la batalla,
y muerto el combatiente, vino hacia él un
     hombre
y le dijo: "¡No mueras; te amo tanto!"
Pero el cadáver ¡ay! siguió muriendo.
. . . .
Entonces todos los hombres de la tierra
le rodearon; les vió el cadáver triste,
     emocionado;
incorporóse lentamente,
abrazó al primer hombre; echóse a andar . . .

(At the end of the battle,
the combatant dead, a man came toward him
and said: "Don't die; I love you so much!"
But oh God the corpse kept on dying.
. . . .
Then all the inhabitants of the earth
surrounded him; the corpse looked at them
     sadly, moved:
he sat up slowly,
embraced the first man; began to walk . . .).

Despite his declaration of faith in the Republic, Vallejo hints in the title poem at the possibility of its fall:

si la madre
España cae—digo, es un decir—
salid, niños del mundo; id a buscarla!

(if mother
Spain falls—I mean, it's just a thought—
Out, children of the world, go and look for
    her!).

In contrast to the avant-garde poems of
Trilce, Vallejo's posthumous poetry uses more-
traditional forms and techniques. Employing
free verse as well as standard verse forms, such
as heptasyllabic and hendecasyllabic lines, these
poems are longer and make use of reiteration
and enumeration. Vallejo reclaims the religious
tone of his first poetry collection and instills it
with political connotations.

Though he published little and was critically
underestimated during his lifetime, César Vallejo
is regarded today as one of the great poets of the
twentieth century and one of Spanish America's
most original poetic voices. His poetry, much of
which appeared after his death, conveys his deep-
seated compassion and treats general themes
relating to human existence in a fresh way. His
remarkable combination of individuality and universality has resulted in his posthumous elevation
to canonical status.

Source: Linda S. Maier, "César Vallejo," in *Dictionary of
Literary Biography,* Vol. 290, *Modern Spanish American
Poets, Second Series,* edited by María A. Salgado,
Thomson Gale, 2004, pp. 331–45.

Adam Sharman

*In the following essay excerpt, Sharman asserts
that traditional indigenous Andean Culture influenced Vallejo's first book* Los Heraldos Negros,
*particularly in the concept of time, even though
Vallejo was positioned in the modern world.*

Vallejo's first collection of poetry, *Los heraldos negros,* makes space consciously, indeed
self-consciously, for traditional indigenous
Andean culture, though only by confining it
largely to a discrete section revealingly named
"Nostalgias imperiales." Broadly speaking,
indigenous Andean temporality is here figured
as something predominantly past, something
remote, or as that which stands outside time,
something eternal. Thematically, the *modernista*
exoticization of the pre-Colombian is unmistak-
able in this section; technically, so too, the
preference for synaesthesia. Despite the incorpo-
ration of an Andean thematics and lexicon, there

is a preciousness that jars. I shall comment on
just a selection of Vallejo's poems that have the
narrow remit mentioned above.

In the second of the four sonnets that comprise the poem "Nostalgias imperiales," the
"anciana pensativa" ponders the past in a manner redolent of the way in which the aged mariner of Darío's "Sinfonía en gris mayor"
contemplates distant lands. Whereas he meditates through a haze of tobacco smoke, she,
cipher for pre-Colombian Andean cultures,
muses while spinning, that is to say, while practicing one of the culture's great crafts. Vallejo
depicts the *anciana pensativa* as active in elaborating a thread of continuity with the cultures,
but also as in a state of petrification—"cual
relieve / de un bloque pre-incaico"—as though
she were a fossilized relic-detail of another, celebrated Andean technological past. In the third
sonnet, the oxen are compared to kings weeping
over defunct domains. The atmosphere is melancholic, senescent, decadent; in the oxen's
"widowed pupils" the dreams have no memory
of the time they are supposed to revivify, not
because they are supposed to revivify, not
because they are gloriously timeless, but because
the past is so remote . . .

The three sonnets that comprise "Terceto
autóctono" strike a different note, that of festival
time. They process the festival's sights through
the sound of the traditional song form, the *yaraví,*
and process both the sights and sounds through
the conventional visual and rhythmic form of the
modernista sonnet. The *féte galante* of Darío's
"Era un aire suave" becomes an autochthonous
festival. The second line of the Darío poem,
"el hada Harmonía ritmaba sus vuelos," is syl-
labically reworked in the third line of Vallejo's
opening sonnet such that the source of music is
not Greek harmony, but the humble, telluric
plough: "Es fiesta! El ritmo del arado vuela."
The synaesthesia continues in a conceit that
binds together color and music, sight and sound
in the idea of an ancestral connection (blood) to
the Incan worship of the sun (sacrifice) . . . The
conceit is taken up in the last line of a final stanza
that gives full recognition to the processing of
Christian materials by pre-Colombian beliefs . . .

The stanza acknowledges the temporality
that dominates the hybridization (it is a *modern*
sun-god) *and* takes its distance from the traditional (the modern sun-god is *for the other,* . . .)
The second sonnet abounds in *couleur locale*

raised to epic proportions (the shepherdess's traditional clothing wraps her in a "humildad de lana heroica y triste"); while the last one depicts a river as drunk as the festival-goers as it simultaneously celebrates and mourns a time before time... The three poems attempt a species of indigenization of symbolist topoi, or "aquenando hondos suspiros" as Vallejo puts it in the first sonnet in a stanza that sounds like a distorted echo of the opening verse of "Era un aire suave," replacing the violins with Indian *quenas*. Ultimately, however, the poems clothe the indigenous in a symbolist aesthetic, such that the quotidian *quechua* words require italicization while the high-literary tropes of personification and hyperbaton remain the norm...

The poem "Aldeana" continues the use of synaesthesia, mimicking the mournful monotony of the *yaraví*. In it the time of the Indian is again figured alternately as the non-time of eternity or the time of death and the past, of "idilios muertos." But in "Los arrieros," from the section "Truenos," is where we find the most explicit and most revealing statement of cultural difference expressed as temporal disjuncture. There the poetic persona watches an Indian *arriero* heading slowly for the sierra with his donkey. As the indigenous subject distances himself in space, the "I" distances him in time... The two characters may live in the same place, the poem seems to suggest, but they do not live in the same time. I take seriously the expression "desde un siglo de duda" that Vallejo uses to position himself discursively as one removed from the representative of traditional Andean culture. Vallejo is conscious of his own modernity, of the legacy of doubt bequeathed by the death of God. Caution should attend efforts to make him into a prophet of multitemporal heterogeneity. For temporality is just what is denied to the *arriero*. The poem ends by making the place of the Indian into the locus of an altogether different time, the non-time of eternity... The neologism highlights the temporal difference (the Iron Age versus the Modern Age) at the same time as it suggests, speaking strictly against the idea of eternity, the deterioration (the rusting, the oxidization) of the latter.

The obvious conclusion at this point, namely, that Vallejo is a modern, cut off from tradition and uncontaminated by it, is the one to be avoided. It is untenable to draw a clear distinction in the case of Vallejo's production between a subject matter that would be ancient (that is, pre-Colombian culture) and an aesthetic form that would be modern (symbolism). Not only is the "ancient" culture resignified in the modern era, as we saw in "Terceto autótono"; symbolism itself, as Raymond Williams observes, is at once symptomatic of its own historical time *and* expressive of an ancient, traditional temporality. Synaesthesia may well have invoked the contemporary moment through its appeal to immediate sensory experience; it also sought to tap in to a timeless spiritual realm: "Characteristically, in the Symbolists, as clearly in Baudelaire and again in Apollinaire, [the] form of poetic revelation involved a fusion of present synaesthetic experience with the recovery of a nameable, tangible past which was yet 'beyond' or 'outside' time." In other words, symbolism can only be erected as a representative of the modern to the extent that it bears witness to the differential character of modernity itself (which would precisely never quite be itself). Williams's observation guards against the totalizing proclivities of the concept of temporalities, which we here use because of its explanatory value, but against which we must remain vigilant.

There is much more to be said about *Los heraldos negros* in what concerns its thematic and technical innovations and general poetic worth. I have dwelt on "Nostalgias imperiales" and certain contiguous poems for the specific, limited purpose of demonstrating that it is not enough to provide a taxonomy of the lexical and larger discursive elements of Vallejo's poetry that appear to articulate a specifically Andean indigenous vision of things. The most hackneyed tourist guidebook can effortlessly accommodate such a lexicon, the presence of which may betoken not a speaker's familiarity with the material but the distance from that reality with which he or she tries to populate the pages. It is noticeable in Vallejo's later poetry just how often the cultural and topographical references to Andean things are accompanied by the presence of exclamation marks (see "Gleba," "Los mineros salieron de la mina," and "Telúrica y magnética"), as though the author could not mention these things without an ironic voice. Not a dismissive irony, to be sure, but one that operates between a Marxist hyperbole celebrating the workers as Promethean force (such as that applied to non-Andean subjects in "Parado en una piedra") and a discourse that cannot quite have faith in them as realities rather than hyperboles...

Source: Adam Sharman, "Semicolonial Times: Vallejo and the Discourse of Modernity," in *Romance Quarterly*, Vol. 49, No. 3, Summer 2002, pp. 198–201.

Leslie Bary

In the following essay excerpt, Bary explains that Vallejo's poetry is so difficult because of his experimentation with language and his unique use of established literary movements. His verse may appear simple but often has a message contrary to appearances.

The almost notoriously difficult poetry of César Vallejo (Peru, 1892–Paris, 1938) is often defined as political for what are in fact largely biographical reasons—the poet's humble background and well-known militancy on the Left—which his writing refracts in themes such as the defense of the poor and solidarity with the Republican cause in Spain. A thematic understanding of the "political" in this poetry ascribes static, (classically) representational qualities to the work that tend to iron out Vallejo's originality along with his difficulty—thus ignoring the depth of his own thought on the relationship between politics and aesthetics.

Literary histories commonly pair Vallejo with his contemporary Pablo Neruda because both are highly acclaimed, Left-oriented writers who first arose in the heyday of the avant-garde period. Yet the simple style and clear message of socially conscious poetry such as Neruda's in *Canto general*, intended to make the poem available to an ill-educated public and unrecuperable to a bourgeois literary tradition, typify an esthetic very different from Vallejo's, whose most politically committed poetry is, in a seeming paradox, also nearly unreadable by traditional standards. Vallejo, in his critical writings, which question both the human value of the avant-garde style in poetry and the poetic force of Maiakovski's political verse, constantly ponders the question of how to restore the social content of words without creating a propagandistic literature. This question parallels a central problem in the contemporary critical debate: how can literature generate meaning without falling into the trap of representation or logocentric discourse? An examination of the political bases and implications of Vallejo's stylistic difficulty is crucial, then, to any reading of his work not based on paraphrase or on the study of isolated images. In what follows, I want to suggest that Vallejo is difficult because meaning (and hence the

THE DISCOVERY OF LANGUAGE AS MEDIATION IS CENTRAL TO BOTH MODERN POETRY AND CONTEMPORARY LITERARY THEORY."

"political") in his work is neither constituted, as it is for the more traditional "social" poets, as a task primarily of representation; nor is it conceived as a question of the "interruption" of representation, that indeterminacy of meaning which according to much post-structuralist theory is in itself politically subversive. Rather, Vallejo's difficulty is that of a poetry which disturbs accepted configurations of thought, but also pushes us to participate in the creation of a new cognitive mode. Ever aware of the opacity of words, Vallejo stretches their ideological boundaries. Rather than claim to redeem language or lead us to a clear space beyond its turbulent surface, Vallejo strives within it to set in motion what he calls in one of his notebooks "el rigor dialéctico del mundo objetivo y subjetivo" (Vallejo 1977: 90).

I

The discovery of language as mediation is central to both modern poetry and contemporary literary theory. After the Romantics' voyage towards the limits of language, summed up by Rubén Darío at the end of the nineteenth century ... after the avant-garde's emphasis on linguistic productivity at the level of the signifier over the referential function of art; and especially after the description of the world as text in so much recent literary and cultural theory, it has become commonplace to conclude that the apprehension of heterogeneous impulses and self-ironic stances in our literary and cultural texts are the last possible horizon of their reading, as well as the only possible "non-repressive" critical attitude. The self-positioning of this critical development specifically at the *end* of interpretation claims not to presuppose a former harmony among language, perception and "truth," but it does seem to depend on a general *belief* in such a harmony—a belief which deconstruction, as it is most commonly practiced, undertakes to dispel.

Recent work by critics such as Djelal Kadir, Mary Layoun, and Kum Kum Sangari has shown that the current crisis of representation in Western literature and theory, along with its attendant demise of the subject and also the "recognition" of the links between literature and politics, are constitutive rather than culminating characteristics of "Third World" (or, perhaps more specifically, post-colonial) literatures. As the Inca Garcilaso, himself the product of a hybrid culture, suggested early in the seventeenth century, the duplicity of language is primordially evident in the colonial situation—a situation in which different languages correspond to radically different cultures, and the dominant language is an imported one. Post-colonial discourse inherits the consciousness of this duplicity: the status of language (as well as that of "meaning" and "truth") is always already in question.

Vallejo's poetry dramatizes this situation. His disarticulation of "language" and "world" in all of his poetic production, and his declarations in his first collection of poems, *Los heraldos negros* (1919), that he doesn't know the source of the "golpes en la vida" and that he was born "un día / que Dios estuvo enfermo," even as they echo generalized modern sentiments like the death of God and the loss of connections with an origin, place these notions at the base of his poetics rather than as final realizations. *Los heraldos negros* does not merely register the decline of *modernista* "correspondances" and a supposed naturalness of linguistic representation. In fact, in this collection Vallejo does something quite different: situating himself, as Julio Ortega says, on the margins of these traditions (108), he shows the unities they presuppose to have been originally insubstantial. As it systematically empties images of plenitude or solace (such as "home," "origin," and "God"), Vallejo's writing also devalues the terms in which they have been constructed. What elsewhere are organizing images and allusions appear here (in Ortega's words) as discursive residue (109).

The *Los heraldos negros* sonnet "Unidad" (1988) can, for example, be read as rather simple allegory of Christian hope for resurrection after death, if we focus on the final tercet as a resolution or redemption of the crisis evoked in the first three sections of the poem. Here the metaphorical . . . of the first tercet, which folds into itself the images of time and death presented in the quatrains, is superseded . . . Above the web of human structures and human doubt, the light-infused hand holds up a bit of lead. This is the same lead that in the quatrains was a bloody bullet, now made divine "en forma azul de corazón." Thus the problematic images of the first half of the poem are apparently transmuted; the "hand that limits" seems to be supplanted by the Hand that comforts, that resolves, that leads us beyond limits.

Yet the leap of faith this ending asks us to make also works to intensify the gap between its discourse and that of the first three stanzas, and the resolution asserted rings false at least as much as it rings true. Because the apparent resolution comes so close to the traditional "mysteries" of resurrection/redemption, it is hard to be sure that the blue heart and "great Hand" of the final tercet are not further forms of the "hostile idea" and reddened bullet that two stanzas earlier gave form to the "great Mystery". . . . In fact, the instability of the terms that structure the poem—among them the leaden (bullet-like) quality of the blue heart, the transformation in the second quatrain of the moon, traditionally an emblem of poetic inspiration and authority, into a gun-barrel, . . . and the questionable power of the admonition "cede y pasa" in the first tercet to banish the frightening images of the quatrains—seems to suggest that there is actually no secret behind the symbols and structures we use to interpret our experience, which could be revealed so as to unify and explain them.

The reading of "Unidad" I propose, then, is that in counterpoint to its title, the poem is more about disjunctions than about unity; or, to put it another way, that it is not about the sort of Symbolist or theological unity that its final images seem, at one level, to imply. The putative resolution of the poem's paradoxes in the final tercet is actually only a kind of overlay. So the discourse of unity is not treated by the poem as a natural, organic thing but as an artificial construct, an imposed form.

Another *Los heraldos negros* poem, "Absoluta", very directly presents the idea of "unity" as an alien and alienating *discourse*. The "unidad excelsa" called for in the fourth stanza stands in sharp contrast to the failure of its attempted embodiment in the first three, and is invalidated, even as a principle, in the fifth and final one, where the "linderos," the spatial and temporal boundaries that "God" and "Love" ought to be able to conquer, are themselves the "irreducibly disdainful" victors, and the "doncella plenitud del 1" is metaphorically host to serpents, wrinkled so that part of its surface is hidden, and crossed by a shadow...

As is even more clearly the case in the poem entitled "Comunión", the tenuously balanced thematics of love and religion used to evoke physical and spiritual plenitude here are actually seen from the perspective of the great distance between the speaker and the language he uses. In both poems, what attempt to be unifying (and comforting) metaphors are made to expose their own inadequacy. (In "Comunión" this gesture becomes painfully comical, when the speaker tries, and fails, to assuage his sexual guilt by comparing the body of his beloved to the river Jordan, and her open arms to a redemptory cross.) At the close of "Comunión," furthermore, Vallejo's speaker tells us he was born on Palm Sunday and not in Bethlehem: his origin does not coincide with that of the episteme that has given him his metaphors. He enters, so to speak, in the middle of an already-written story, and at the beginning of its crisis.

I am arguing that the gap in these poems between the speaker and his language is not the same as the gap between present fragmentation and ideal unity we can see in poets like Baudelaire and in part of the Spanish American *modernista* tradition. Although Vallejo here uses the readily available vocabulary of fragmentation and unity, or even spleen and ideal, he seems to do so precisely because this is the only available vocabulary in the place and time he is writing. He is, in other words, attempting to insert himself into a patently problematic discourse because he has as yet found no other. His simultaneous appropriation by and problematization of pre-existing literary and cultural discourses grows, in his later work, into a will to speak from their ruins.

Source: Leslie Bary, "Politics, Aesthetics, and the Question of Meaning in Vallejo," in *Hispania: A Teacher's Journal*, Vol. 75, No. 5, December 1992, pp. 1147–49.

Phyllis White Rodriguez

In the following essay excerpt, Rodriguez examines Vallejo's collection Los Heraldos Negros, *including the title poem, in terms of the types of messages the poet expressed. Vallejo, she says, combined the cry of the peasant, the shout of the modern reformer, and the voice of Everyman in this first work.*

Who is César Vallejo? One could answer: He is the authentic interpretation of the "pueblo peruano" in its agonizing thirst for fulfillment; or: His poetry is the shout of contemporary tragedy; or: He is the expression of the anguish in the destiny of man. However we choose to describe him, he remains the same. César Vallejo is a poet, a Peruvian poet, who, through the beauty he created, has left us an artistry both simple and magnificent, and who has pointed the way to the rebirth of Peruvian expression.

He was born in 1892 or 1893 in Santiago de Chuco, a provincial Andean town in northern Peru. This is a land of mountain solitude, of cosmic sadness, of bleak crags and peaks and sultry valleys. Santiago stands at 10,500 feet. It is a town of steeply inclined, deserted streets, of patios, of cackling hens and musical brays, where the sparrows roost in the discolored tile roofs, and the aroma of the fields greets the women washing clothes in the river, the workers arriving with their yoked oxen and burros, the scratching, ragged Indians mingling with the yelping dogs. Of such things is the poetry of César Vallejo during his first epoch.

Leaving this isolated mountain corner, where his days had been full of the sweetness of family life, Vallejo began his studies in Trujillo, later making an abrupt change to the capital. In the same year, 1918, he published *Los heraldos negros*, his first book of poetry. It was greeted with coldness and indifference. Lima, still resounding with the brilliant modernism of Chocano and addicted to Valdelomar and the symbolist Eguren, could not receive this poetry so full of social emotion and human content, with a tenderness neither forced nor intellectual. *Los Heraldos Negros* is a tremendous shout of sadness and grief, of contradiction and protest. The years have increased its importance until, in Peru at least, there is a consuming interest in anything written by Vallejo...

If we should classify this book, we would say it is postmodernistic, with attendant symbolism, faint echoes of Darío and Herrera y Reissig emanating from the verses. But it is an independent modernist, as seen by the absence of rhetoric and ornamentation, and a more human and pathetic approach.

We are in the presence of an independent poet, whose subjective grief is identified with that of the Indian race. In this rests its Peruvian essence, for the true mestizo is a product of two bloods, and to deny one is to take away from the whole. We have the Indian's nostalgic attitude, his subjective tenderness of evocation. How well the symbolist cycle lends itself to interpreting the spirit of the Indian, who tends to express himself in symbols and images. This melancholic nostalgia is a sentimental thing, the nostalgia of the exile, of absence. We can see the tragedy of the Indian faced with four centuries of oppression. We sense his resignation, his mystic fatalism. Vallejo's indigenism flows as naturally as the Quechuan words he sometimes uses . . .

This is the nostalgia of the countryside he knew and loved. This is the silent somber Indian in the brooding sadness of the little towns of Peru. Only once, in "Terceto autóctono," is the Indian momentarily happy in his own way . . .

The odor of sadness, the feeling of age and decay and solitude that belong to the Peruvian landscape are notes Vallejo strikes again and again. Here is the breath of Peru. Here is the bitter-sweet poignancy of vain regret. Of what? Only Vallejo knows, and the vast somberness of Peru. . . .

Certainly Vallejo is greatly troubled with the reason for life, and the cold breath of the tomb is ever reaching out toward him. He is by turns questioning and pessimistic, seeing life as a continual march toward the grave . . . The reader may find that his greatness shines out more clearly when he is expressing universal grief than when he confines himself to gnashing of teeth and wringing of hands over his own grave. In the typical Vallejoesque manner is the vivid "La cena miserable." We are all shown seated at a table, waiting, waiting, with the bitterness of a child who wakes up at midnight crying from hunger . . .

Then the pendulum swings the other way and he is given over to the suffering of others in his poem "El pan nuestro" that ends . . .

Vallejo often talks to God, shifting from almost blasphemous imprecations to speaking gently, as to any suffering person. . . .

But always Vallejo was on his feet, speaking as one person to another.

The last portion of his book is called "Canciones de hogar." These are portraits of his family, lovingly drawn. They are beautiful in their simplicity and sincerity, in their obvious loving devotion to parents, to brothers and sisters. Through all his life, the wrinkles smooth out when Vallejo thinks of his family, his childhood.

He is at his happiest then, expressing himself with tremulous emotion. He is at home. . . .

Source: Phyllis White Rodriguez, "Cesar Vallejo," in *Hispania: A Teacher's Journal*, Vol. 35, No. 2, May 1952, pp. 195–97.

SOURCES

Arguelles, Ivan, Review of *The Black Heralds*, in *Library Journal*, Vol. 115, Issue 6, April 1, 1990, p. 118.

Biespiel, David, "Reading Guide: César Vallejo: The Ambassador of South American Surrealism," http://www.poetryfoundation.org/features/feature.guidebook.html?id=177374 (accessed September 20, 2006).

Eshleman, Clayton, trans., *The Complete Poetry of Cesar Vallejo*, University of California Press, 2006, as cited in Efrain Kristal, "César Vallejo," in *American Poetry Review*, Vol. 34, No. 3, May–June 2005, p. 25.

Eshleman, Clayton, and Jose Rubia Barcia, trans., *Cesar Vallejo: The Complete Posthumous Poetry*, University of California Press, 1978, as cited in Alfred J. MacAdam, "¡Viva Vallejo! Arriba España!" in *Virginia Quarterly Review*, Winter 1980, p. 187.

Hays, H. R., trans., *Cesar Vallejo: Selected Poems*, Sachem Press, 1981, as cited in Julio Ortega, *Latin American Writers*, Vol. 2, Charles Scribner's Sons, 1989, p. 730.

Hirsch, Edward, "Poetry: Cesar Vallejo," in *Wilson Quarterly*, Vol. 19, No. 4, Autumn 1995, p. 98.

Horno-Delgado, Asunción, "The Plural 'I,'" in *American Book Review*, Vol. 13, No. 2, June–July 1991, p. 22.

Kristal, Efrain, "Cesar Vallejo," in *American Poetry Review*, Vol. 34, No. 3, May–June 2005, p. 25.

MacAdam, Alfred J., "¡Viva Vallejo! Arriba España!" in *Virginia Quarterly Review*, Winter 1980, p. 185.

Maier, Linda S., "César Vallejo," in *Dictionary of Literary Biography*, Vol. 290: *Modern Spanish American Poets, Second Series*, edited by Maria A. Salgado, Thomson Gale, 2004, p. 336.

Maurer, Christopher, "Through a Verse Darkly," in *New Republic*, Vol. 209, No. 2, July 12, 1993, p. 34.

Ortega, Julio, "Cesar Vallejo," in *Latin American Writers*, Vol. 2, Charles Scribner's Sons, 1989, pp. 727–28.

Rodriguez, Phyllis White, "Cesar Vallejo," in *Hispania*, Vol. 35, No. 2, May 1952, p. 195.

Ross, Kathleen, and Richard Schaaf, trans. *The Black Heralds*, by César Vallejo, Latin American Literary Review Press, 1990, jacket flap.

Seiferle, Rebecca, "Cesar Vallejo : The Thread of Indigenous Blood," in *The Black Heralds*, by César Vallejo, Copper Canyon Press, 2003, p. 1.

St. Martin, Hardie, "Ring-Master in the Vallejo Circus," in *American Book Review*, Vol. 15, No. 3, August–September 1993, p. 6.

Vallejo, César, "The Black Heralds," in *The Black Heralds*, translated by Kathleen Ross and Richard Schaaf, Latin American Literary Review Press, 1990, p. 17.

FURTHER READING

Hart, Stephen M., and Jorge Cornejo Polar, *César Vallejo: A Critical Bibliography of Research*, Tamesis Books, 2002.

> A comprehensive guide to scholarship about Vallejo, this book, produced by a well-known Vallejo scholar, lists sources of information and provides helpful evaluations of the materials that are available.

Ortega, Julio, "Cesar Vallejo," in *Latin American Writers*, Vol. 2, 1989, pp. 727–38.

> An analysis of Vallejo's work arranged chronologically with brief biographical information, this article presents excerpts in both Spanish and English and examines their poetic characteristics in a highly readable fashion.

Starn, Orin, Ivan Degregori, and Robin Kirk, eds. *The Peru Reader: History, Culture, Politics*, Duke University Press, 1995.

> This book provides a broad spectrum of in-depth information about multiple aspects of Peru, including introductions to and excerpts from several of its authors.

Tapscott, Stephen, ed., *Twentieth-Century Latin American Poetry: A Bilingual Anthology*, University of Texas Press, 1996.

> This collection of lyrical works from seventy-five poets, including Vallejo, provides helpful introductions to and evaluations of the writers as well as a selection of some of their most notable poetry.

Curse

FRANK BIDART

2002

Frank Bidart's "Curse" is addressed to the masterminds of September 11, 2001—those who planned and carried out the attacks on the World Trade Center in New York City and the Pentagon in Washington, D.C., and those who crashed an airliner into a field near Shanksville, Pennsylvania. As the title suggests, the poem is a harsh and bitter indictment of these terrorist acts, and Bidart leaves no room to doubt the loathing he feels toward the perpetrators. That said, "Curse" does not rave in predictable angry language or trite sentiment. Instead, Bidart approaches this sensitive topic in a methodical and provocative manner that causes readers to think, regardless of any already-formed opinions they may have.

"Curse" is a relatively short poem, but its carefully chosen words, precise style, and intense message provide a dramatic comment on one of the most world-changing events in modern history. Ironically, Bidart relies on an early-sixteenth-century form of cursing a vile act or individual to express his dismay over an event that occurred in the early twenty-first century. The blending of old-style damnation with contemporary resolve makes this poem a memorable statement on a single day in U.S. history that dominated headlines for several years.

"Curse" was published in 2005 in *Star Dust*. It appeared previously in the spring 2002 issue of *Threepenny Review* and was subsequently posted

Frank Bidart (© *Jerry Bauer. Reproduced by permission*)

on that journal's website. However, readers should be aware that poems on the Internet may not appear as they do in printed publications. In this case, the line breaks in "Curse" on the *Threepenny* site are not the same as they appear in *Star Dust*.

AUTHOR BIOGRAPHY

Frank Bidart was born in rural southern California on May 27, 1939, and grew up on a potato farm owned by his father as part of a thriving family business. As of 2007, Bidart Brothers was still one of the largest diversified farming operations in Kern County, California. But Bidart knew at an early age that he did not want to follow in his father's footsteps to become a farmer. Instead, Bidart was interested in the theater and movies, and he dreamed of becoming an actor or a film director.

Although the family ran a prosperous business, Bidart's father and mother were not as successful in their personal lives. When Bidart was five years old, his parents divorced, and he

was raised primarily by his mother. After a somewhat tumultuous childhood and adolescence, Bidart started classes at the University of California at Riverside, where he mixed literature and philosophy studies along with his interest in theater and film. Ultimately, he turned his attention to poetry, although he never completely relinquished his flare for the dramatic or his love of theatrical performance. He simply found a way to work those passions into his poems.

As an undergraduate, Bidart enjoyed the work of such notable twentieth-century poets as Robert Lowell, T. S. Eliot, and Ezra Pound. He especially enjoyed Pound's *Cantos*, a lengthy series of works that showed Bidart, among other things, that poetry could encompass virtually any subject in the world—a premise he would adopt for his own work and that figures heavily into his unusual topics and characters.

After Bidart completed his undergraduate degree at University of California, he began graduate studies at Harvard University. Although he never earned a degree from Harvard, he did meet accomplished poets and teachers there whose work would ultimately influence his own. Robert Lowell was a teacher, mentor, and friend whom Bidart greatly admired and respected. In general, his experiences at Harvard led to his own serious attempt at becoming a poet—an endeavor that paid off with the 1973 publication of his first collection of poems, *Golden State*.

Several collections followed over the next thirty-some years, with *Star Dust*, appearing in 2005 and including the poem "Curse." Although much of Bidart's poetry is noted for its atypical, often controversial, subjects—his personas include a pedophile, a murderer, and an anorexic woman, among others—it is also highly regarded for its strength of language, graphic imagery, and intensity.

Bidart's work has been honored with various awards and nominations, including the Bobbitt Prize for Poetry (1998) and nominations for the Pulitzer Prize, National Book Award, and National Book Critics Circle Award—all for *Desire* (1997). His chapbook, *Music Like Dirt* (2003), was a finalist for the Pulitzer Prize and was republished two years later as the first section of *Star Dust*.

MEDIA ADAPTATIONS

- *Frank Bidart, the Maker* is a twenty-eight-minute documentary on the poet, produced by "Art Close UP," a monthly TV series from WGBH in Boston. Filmmaker Jay Anania visits Bidart at his home in Cambridge and accompanies him to his classroom at Wellesley College. The 2004 documentary includes an interview, readings, and discussions of Bidart's poems. People may contact WGBH for information on the availability of a copy.

- In 1992, the Academy of American Poets produced a CD of Bidart and C. K. Williams reading selections of their poems. Bidart reads six short poems and his lengthy dramatic monologue, "Ellen West." This is a two-disc set that runs eighty-eight minutes and is available online at poets.org from the academy's Poetry Audio Archive.

- As of 2007, a recording of Bidart reading a selection of poems was available at http://wiredforbooks.org/frankbidart/ on the Wired for Books website. The reading runs just over fifty-three minutes.

POEM TEXT

May breath for a dead moment cease as jerking
* your*
head upward you hear as if in slow motion floor
collapse evenly upon floor as one hundred and ten
floors descend upon you.
May what you have made descend upon you.   5
May the listening ears of your victims   their
  eyes   their
breath
enter you, and eat like acid
the bubble of rectitude that allowed you
  breath.
May their breath now, in eternity, be your
* breath.*   10

Now, as you wished, you cannot for us
not be. May this be your single profit.

Of your rectitude at last disenthralled, you
seek the dead. Each time you enter them

they spit you out. The dead find you are not
  food.   15
Out of the great secret of morals, *the imagina-*
tion to enter
the skin of another, what I have made is a curse.

POEM SUMMARY

Line 1

The explication of "Curse" depends as much on understanding its style as its language. Bidart is noted for his quirky punctuation and presentation of words, such as using all capital letters or italics. In this poem, he uses italics and gaps in lines to emphasize his point, but what he does *not* use is just as important. The first line, for instance, may be confusing initially because it lacks the commas it needs to make the meaning easier to grasp. If it were punctuated as "*May breath, for a dead moment, cease, as, jerking your,*" its message would be clearer.

Starting the sentence with the word "May" is in keeping with the title of the poem, as the speaker expresses a wish or desire for what is to follow. What follows is the beginning of the "curse" that the speaker wants to befall the targets of his hex. Specifically, the first line expresses the speaker's desire for the "you" in the poem (here, plural) to be so shocked at what is happening that they lose their breath for a moment and jerk in response to the scene. The fact that the moment is "dead" foretells the sorrow and death that underlie the main focus of the poem.

Lines 2–4

These lines identify the subject of the poem, as indicated by the reference to "*one hundred and ten / floors*" collapsing. Each tower of the World Trade Center had 110 floors that burned and collapsed on September 11. Here, the speaker's desire is that those responsible for the attack should have to experience *in slow motion* the same horror of being trapped in a crumbling skyscraper. The hope that it occurs slowly implies the speaker's yearning for the attackers to suffer as long as possible. He wants them to *hear* the floors falling *evenly*, one on top of the other, above their heads until finally all the floors "*descend upon you.*"

Line 5

This line employs the old "eye for an eye" concept of retribution. Just as the terrorists of September 11 "made" the World Trade Center fall, killing nearly three thousand people, the speaker wishes for the same to happen to them. Another common saying that this line brings to mind is, "You reap what you sow." At the heart of the speaker's curse is the desire for the terrorists themselves to experience terror.

Lines 6–7

In these lines, Bidart uses word spacing to slow down the action of the poem. By offsetting "your victims," "their eyes," "their / breath," he effectively halts each image long enough for the reader to grasp it completely. The idea is that the attackers should have to consider very deliberately the human beings they have killed. Ears, eyes, and breath are all real and physical, and they suggest the strong, haunting connection that the speaker wants the terrorists to feel with their victims.

Lines 8–9

The anger displayed in these lines is biting, but controlled. Referring to the previous two lines, the speaker wants the terrorists to be so plagued by their actions that their victims' breath may actually "enter" their bodies and become vile and destructive, "like acid." The part of the terrorists that the speaker wants the acid to "eat" is important to note: it is "the bubble of rectitude that allowed you breath." "Rectitude" means righteousness or morally correct character or behavior. It is a form of goodness that generally implies sternness and strict adherence to a set of rules. The word appears twice in "Curse" and carries much weight in the evaluation of the terrorists' mindset. While it seems contradictory to apply any word that has to do with morality or righteousness to people who commit heinous crimes, the speaker uses "rectitude" to describe the killers' beliefs that they are justified in attacking a country, regardless of the loss of innocent life. He suggests that it is their sense of self-righteousness that gives them life and purpose in the first place.

Line 10

The message in line 10 sums up the ultimate purpose of the curse. It may be paraphrased this way: May you identify so closely with your dead victims that it is as though you now must breathe for them. Once again, Bidart uses italics to stress the significance of this single line.

Lines 11–12

Line 11 introduces an "us" into the poem, referring to people in general in a post-9/11 world—perhaps Americans in particular, but, more broadly, anyone emotionally affected by the events of that day. The arrangement of the words in these two lines appears awkward, but they also read like the archaic language used to cast curses centuries ago. "You cannot for us / not be" means that, just as the terrorists "wished," their existence and their acts will never be forgotten by those left behind. The speaker hopes that this fact is the killers' "single profit"—the one and only infamy they enjoy.

Lines 13–14

In line 13, the word "rectitude" appears again, but now the terrorists are "disenthralled," or set free, of it. Describing them as "at last disenthralled" alludes to the hijackers' own deaths on September 11, as they supposedly achieved everything they desired in their own "moral" sense. Themselves deceased, they now "seek the dead," trying to "enter them" just as the terrorists entered their living victims on the final day of their lives.

Line 15

This line indicates the defiance and disgust that the victims feel toward their killers. In death, they have the power to "spit . . . out" whatever unwelcome thing tries to enter their mouths. In the end, they have the strength to prevent the terrorists—and, more specifically, the terrorists' philosophy—from becoming a source of energy or nourishment. They are "not food" for the dead.

Lines 16–17

The final two lines of "Curse" allude to a line from the prose work *In Defense of Poetry*, by nineteenth-century poet Percy Bysshe Shelley. In the "Notes" section at the end of *Star Dust*, Bidart writes: "Shelley in his *Defense of Poetry* says that 'the great secret of morals is love'—and by love he means not affection or erotic feeling, but sympathetic identification, identification with others." In his poem, Bidart puts a twist on Shelley's benevolent intention, turning *"the imagination to enter / the skin of another"* into a curse, instead of an attempt to sympathize with someone. The goal is to have the terrorists receive just and equal punishment for the act

TOPICS FOR FURTHER STUDY

- Where were you on September 11, 2001? Write an essay expressing your thoughts, actions, and emotions on that day. Include an assessment of how your feelings may or may not have changed since then and why.

- Research the roots of the word terrorism and present your findings to your class. Concentrate on the historical events surrounding the coining of the word and be prepared to answer questions on how it has evolved into the way Americans in particular define it in the early 2000s.

- Terrorists, both before and after September 11, 2001, cited the existence of the State of Israel—and U.S. support for it—as a reason for the violent response to a nation they consider an intrusion on Palestinian territory. Research the history of the region and write an essay that takes into account the opposing viewpoints, being careful to be fair to both.

- Since its beginning in 2003, the war in Iraq has elicited mixed and increasingly negative reactions from people around the world, especially Americans. Take on the role of a politician and prepare a speech either in favor of or against the war and try to persuade your audience to vote for you and the ideals you support.

they have committed. In essence, the speaker condemns them to suffer the same as they have caused others to suffer.

THEMES

Equal Retribution

The most obvious theme in "Curse" is the justification of "an eye for an eye" punishment for those responsible for the September 11, 2001,

terrorist attacks on the United States. The curse that the speaker places upon the terrorists calls for equal retribution for their acts: "May what you have made descend upon you" and "*May their breath now, in eternity, be your breath.*" In these lines, the speaker's wish is more figurative than literal, as he speaks in general terms of what has been "made" on this day and the eternal repercussions for the deeds committed. His curse is more precise, however, in lines 3 and 4, in which he calls for the same number of floors to collapse on the attackers as they caused to fall on the people in the World Trade Center.

The idea of equal retribution is, of course, symbolic in this poem because the hijackers are already dead—dying alongside their victims when the planes crashed. But this obvious fact is overshadowed by the very compelling desire for revenge, even if it is only emblematic. The speaker acknowledges the deaths of the terrorists toward the end of the poem, but he seeks their punishment, regardless. He is glad that they are "spit . . . out" each time they try to "enter" the dead, and he appears to enjoy telling them that they "are not food" for the ones they killed. While symbolic retribution does not cause any actual harm to the intended persons, it may have a cathartic effect on the one who wants revenge. That seems, at least, to be the case for the speaker here.

If the "you" in the poem applies only to the infamous nineteen hijackers of 9/11, then the speaker's curse can be only a symbol of his anger and wish for revenge, since the attackers cannot be brought to justice. If, however, the "you" covers anyone who had a hand in planning the attacks, then the possibility for justice—or retribution—continued after September 11, 2001. Most likely, those addressed in the poem account for more than the nineteen men on the airliners. The theme of equal retribution easily applies to both the deceased hijackers and their still living fellow terrorists.

The Act of Making

Much of Bidart's late twentieth-century and early 2000s work, including the poems in *Star Dust*, explores the theme of making things. While this sounds broad and undefined, Bidart is actually taking a close look at the myriad of things that human beings create—from the obvious invention of concrete objects to the

A marine preparing a target sheet for firearms practice showing the face of al-Qaeda leader Osama Bin Laden in Fallujah, Iraq (Cpl. William Skelton/Getty Images)

pair the attackers' acts with just and equal payback, step by step until the curse is complete. The poem reads as though it describes something being made from the ground up—layer added upon layer until the construction is finished. Ironically, what the speaker builds will ultimately lead to destruction, just as what the terrorists made led to destruction. If the act of making is central to human desire, as many of the poems in *Star Dust* suggest, Bidart shows here that its *negative* side is just as powerful, just as desirable as its positive.

STYLE

Free Verse

Free verse is poetry that does not rhyme or have a regular meter—poetry that is literally *free* of traditional conventions and restrictions. Its popularity is often traced back to nineteenth-century French poets such as Arthur Rimbaud and Jules Laforgue but is easily recognizable in the works of twentieth-century American poets such as William Carlos Williams, Carl Sandburg, and Marianne Moore. By the end of the twentieth century, free verse was the most common form of poetry being written. But the most important thing to keep in mind about free verse is that the style does *not* mean that a poem is completely without distinctive cadence, form, or structural complexity. "Curse" is an apt example of just how structured a free verse poem can be.

more intangible making of art, war, friendship, enemies, love, and so forth. Sometimes *making* is a positive endeavor, but it may be negative and detrimental. In "Curse," what is *made* is most certainly negative.

The word "made" is used twice in the poem, in lines 5 and 17. In both instances, it is aligned with an adverse notion—what the terrorists have made should come back to haunt them and what the speaker has made is a curse. From the outset, the poem builds toward the final statement, "what I have made is a curse." The hex is constructed from a series of statements beginning with the word "May," followed by the description of what the speaker wishes to befall his targets. Each one involves a form of punishment that the "you" in the poem should suffer for the suffering they created. In essence, the speaker's act of making is a mirror image of what the architects of 9/11 made.

In the first statement, the speaker wishes for the terrorists to experience the same fate as their victims, looking up only to realize many floors collapsing upon them. His subsequent statements

Bidart is noted for his unusual punctuation, capitalization, and word spacing—all to draw special attention to a line or a single word or to emphasize a certain point. For example, in some works he capitalizes words or entire lines in an attempt to shout at the reader, "Hey, this is important!" While he does not use unexpected capitalization in "Curse," he does rely on italics and spacing to make the poem more effective.

The four italicized lines that begin the poem indicate right away that they are significant in setting up the message of the entire work. Not all the lines that begin with the word "May" are italicized, but line 10 is—an implication that it is as important as the first four lines and also serves to complement them with a similar subtlety in making a "deadly" wish. The portions of lines 16 and 17 that appear in italics are emphasized because "*the imagination to enter / the skin of another*" expresses the mechanism through which the curse works. These words encompass the core of the poem's theme.

Besides italics, Bidart also uses extra line and word spacing to emphasize his point by slowing down the reader long enough to contemplate what he is saying. The first four lines are double spaced, even though they essentially comprise a sentence or at least a single thought. But the impact of their message is made even stronger by having them read separately and slowly, rather than running them together in a typical single-spaced verse. He uses the same tactic in lines 6 and 7, but here he also adds extra spaces between words to slow down the reading even more. The blank space between "victims" and "their" and "eyes" and "their," as well as the line break between "their" and "breath," all serve to decelerate the reading of the poem, forcing the reader to take in the full impact and weight of each word.

Finally, Bidart separates lines 10 and 11 with an odd dot that divides them by four line spaces. The first word in line 11, "Now," implies movement in the poem, from the first part entailing the elements of the curse to the second part, or present, in which the elements of the curse are in place. While the dot may be unusual, it provides an abrupt and necessary break between the poem's set-up and its conclusion. The curse is concocted above the dot, and it is "made" after the dot.

HISTORICAL CONTEXT

Terrorism and the United States

Some people, especially Americans, became familiar with the term "terrorism" on September 11, 2001, and believe this is the date the United States first encountered it. In fact, the United States had been battling terrorists for decades, responding in a variety of ways to such incidents as the kidnappings of U.S. diplomats in Latin America in the late 1960s and 1970s; the murder of two U.S. diplomats in Sudan in 1973; the takeover of the U.S. Embassy in Iran in 1979; the suicide bombings of the U.S. Embassy and U.S. Marine barracks in Lebanon in 1983; the bombing of the World Trade Center in 1993; and the suicide bombing of the *USS Cole* in 2000. While the U.S. government met some of these acts with CIA operations and secret meetings with leaders of the nations involved, others were met with military strikes and a no-concessions policy

against the perpetrators. Since the September 11 attacks, the response has been primarily swift and decisive military action.

The first U.S. military campaign following the terrorist attacks on U.S. soil began in October 2001 in Afghanistan, where Osama bin Laden and his Al-Qaeda network of terrorists had thrived for years. The ruling Taliban government was toppled, but large pockets of remaining Taliban fighters and their Al-Qaeda colleagues took refuge in the nation's vast mountainous regions and began to rebuild their forces, emerging little by little in subsequent years in a bid to retake Afghanistan from the control of the new U.S.-backed government and international troops. By 2005, Islamic extremists in Afghanistan had strengthened enough to conduct several deadly terrorist attacks and assassination attempts on government officials, as well as gain control of small towns in remote areas.

The initial destruction of the Taliban and hundreds of Al-Qaeda operatives did not diminish terrorist activities elsewhere in the world, as evidenced by the first Bali, Indonesia, bombing in 2002; the Riyadh, Saudi Arabia, bombing in 2003; the Madrid, Spain, bombing in 2004; and the two bombings in London and the second attack in Bali in 2005. While these were some of the most deadly, high-profile terrorist activities during those years, many other smaller-scale suicide bombings, kidnappings, shootings, and beheadings occurred in dozens of countries around the world.

In 2003, U.S. and coalition forces invaded Iraq and quickly defeated the Iraqi military, bringing down Saddam Hussein's regime in a few weeks. Although President George W. Bush declared major combat operations over in Iraq on May 1, 2003, the anti-American insurgency that developed among various Iraqi factions did not prove so easily put down. War in Iraq continued in the following several years, although by 2007, it seemed to be more a military campaign against radical insurgents than against an official military opponent.

The sentiment expressed by Bidart in "Curse" toward the terrorists of 9/11—or terrorists in general—is shared by many people around the world, not just Americans. In the months following the attacks in New York, Washington, D.C., and Pennsylvania, the sense of outrage, patriotism, and desire for justice, if not revenge, permeated the thoughts, speech,

WHAT DO I READ NEXT?

- Bidart's highly acclaimed *Desire* (1997) was nominated for several prestigious awards. The underlying theme of this volume is that human beings cannot choose what brings them joy—joy chooses the individual.

- *An Eye for an Eye Makes the Whole World Blind*, edited by Allen Cohen and Clive Matson and published in 2002, is a collection of works by over one hundred poets from all across the United States, writing in response to the September 11 terrorist attacks. Many of the poets project themselves into the minds and bodies of the victims, as well as the firefighters, police officers, and hijackers. Poets include Lawrence Ferlinghetti, Robert Creeley, Lyn Lifshin, and Diane di Prima.

- After September 11, 2001, journalist and teacher Samar Dahmash-jarrah wanted to do something to dispel the stereotypes that many Americans believed were true about Muslims and Arabs. The result was *Arab Voices Speak to American Hearts*, written with coauthor/editor Kirt M. Dressler and published in 2005. The book is compiled from interviews with Arabs and Muslims living outside the United States who agreed to answer over a hundred questions that Dahmash-jarrah gathered from interested Americans. The authors believe that most of the responses are surprising to Americans and Westerners in general.

- Critic Thomas M. Allen's lengthy article "Frank Bidart's Emersonian Redemption" (in *Raritan*, Vol. 25, No. 4, Spring 2006, pp. 95–114) presents an interesting comparison of the poems in Bidart's *Music Like Dirt* and the nineteenth-century poetry of Ralph Waldo Emerson. The author's basic argument is that the nation Bidart tried to disown as a young poet became a backdrop for many of his later works, as he evolved through a love/hate relationship with U.S. history, values, and landscape. Allen likens Bidart's use of common language to that of Emerson's, who also included American themes and subjects in much of his work.

and actions of many people, and especially many U.S. citizens. Over the following five years as U.S. and other casualties in Afghanistan and Iraq increased, much of the initial fervor was replaced by disillusionment and skepticism that the war on terror in either country could ever be won. Instead, many people came to believe that terrorism would continue, echoing Bidart's assertion that, "Now, as you wished, you cannot for us / not be."

CRITICAL OVERVIEW

Bidart's poetry has been well received by critics, scholars, and readers in general, since the publication of his first collection in the early 1970s.

His reputation is based primarily on his work in dramatic monologue—a type of poem popular during the Victorian period in which a one speaker delivers an oftentimes lengthy speech explaining his or her feelings, actions, or motives. Bidart's choice of rather unusual characters (murderers, rapists, an anorexic woman, among others) may be seen as an attention-getter, but his ability to develop the monologue in realistic, compelling, yet poetic style earned him high praise.

In the late 1990s and early 2000s, Bidart turned more toward writing shorter poems, while still retaining the passionate voice and provocative language of his lengthy monologues. Many poems in *Star Dust* reflect the new style, and this collection received very positive reviews. A comment in the "Editor's Corner" for *Ploughshares* notes that "Bidart illustrates with unforgettable passion that the dream beyond desire is rooted in the drive to create." Writing for the *Library Journal*, critic Barbara Hoffert says that *Star Dust* "offers bold yet perfectly calibrated poetry that celebrates the act of making. . . . Bidart is back doing something he's done with verve since 1965: making poetry." In his review of the collection for *Harvard Review*, critic Jonathan Weinert claims that *Star Dust* "carries the imprimaturs of greatness." He goes on to say that the poetry "interrogates the act of making, which Bidart considers an imperative of being rather than a choice." While many acts of making are positive, Weinert asserts that "The architects of 9/11, addressed directly in "Curse," represent its hellish negative." Weinert concludes his review by stating that Bidart is "not only one of our most challenging poets, but also one of our most responsible."

CRITICISM

Pamela Steed Hill

Hill is the author of a poetry collection, has published widely in literary journals, and is an editor for a university publications department. In the following essay, she examines "Curse" as an anathema, explaining the origins of the word and considering how the religious overtones of the poem suggest the theological roots of its subject.

The word, curse, typically connotes a wish for harm or punishment placed on an individual or group of people. It is often associated with the supernatural, usually evil, such as curses conjured in rituals of witchcraft or black magic. But curses also are found in records of traditional religious doctrines such as the Christian Bible, the Muslim Qur'an, and the Jewish Torah. In these works, they often imply a desire for the target of the curse to be deprived of the blessings of a supreme being and to suffer the consequences of being abandoned by goodness. Many times, the curse is inspired by a need for justice—that one bears punishment for the harm he or she has caused others. Bidart's poem "Curse" is based on this latter principle.

Regardless of one's association with the terrorist events of September 11, 2001, or opinion on the actions of U.S. and international armed

> IN THE ORIGINAL GREEK, ANATHEMA MEANS SOMETHING LIFTED UP AS AN OFFERING TO THE GODS, OR, LATER, TO GOD. AS SUCH, IT TOOK ON THE ROLE OF A SACRIFICE, OR SOMETHING TO BE CAST OUT OR SLAUGHTERED."

forces since that day, no one can deny that the magnitude of the attacks was unprecedented in U.S. history and that many people—Westerners, in particular—have paid more attention to the Middle East and the world of Islam than they ever may have otherwise. Initial reactions ranged from fear of and anger toward all Muslims to a call for greater compassion and understanding among people of all faiths and cultures. As of 2007, neither extreme dominated the process of moving beyond 9/11.

Among the countless number of poems written in commemoration of that day, "Curse" is interesting in that Bidart attempts to respond to it on a level equal to the purported reasoning of those who planned and committed the attacks: in their minds, crashing the planes was justified by Allah (God). In spite of the fact that Muslims insist that violence is not condoned or encouraged by Islamic laws, terrorists typically use their own interpretation of the Qur'an to defend their acts. Bringing religion into it seems to excuse the violence. In "Curse," Bidart employs both subtle and overt religious overtones to meet the terrorists of 9/11 on their own terms.

In the "Notes" section at the end of *Star Dust*, Bidart writes this about "Curse": "The poem springs from the ancient moral idea . . . that what is suffered for an act should correspond to the nature of the act. . . . Identification is here called down as punishment, the great secret of morals reduced to a curse." Even the language he uses to explain the work carries religious overtones, and the word that comes to mind in regard to "ancient moral idea," "what is suffered for an act," and "reduced to a curse" is *anathema*—a word originating in Greek theology.

Anathema is both an interesting and confusing word, all for the same reason. In the original Greek, anathema means something lifted up as an offering to the gods, or, later, to God. As such, it took on the role of a sacrifice, or something to be cast out or slaughtered. Eventually, any positive connotations of the word were lost, and anathema came to mean something evil or damned. In the Christian Bible, the word *herem* (or *haram*) is the equivalent of anathema and is used to describe one who is condemned to be cut off or exterminated. In some interpretations of Christian doctrine, it refers to a formal excommunication from the church, someone officially banished from the holy community—in other words, one who is cursed.

The final phrase of Bidart's poem announces his intention in creating it: "what I have made is a curse." More specifically, what he has made is an anathema. The language and temper of "Curse" are somber, even funereal in places: "*May breath for a dead moment cease*"; "May what you have made descend upon you"; "*May their breath now, in eternity, be your breath.*" These lines are spoken with solemn clarity and determination, seemingly uttered by an authority with the power to make the stated wishes come true. Each time the word "may" repeats adds another layer to the curse that is being created, and it also adds to the ceremonial tone of the entire poem. The single lines and couplets and the repeated use of "may" make the poem read like a melancholy chant heard in religious rituals.

Before and after 9/11, Islamic extremists invoked the teachings of the Qur'an to justify their acts of violence, and many were heard using the name of Allah in taped messages before carrying out suicide attacks on primarily Western targets. While people of all faiths, including moderate Muslims, tried to downplay the notion that the war on terrorism was a religious war, terrorists played *up* that idea in order to incite anger in the Islamic world, where some believers might come to think that the entire religion is under attack. In "Curse," it is not Islam that is damned—only those who would try to defend murder as a self-righteous, holy cause in the name of Islam.

The aspect of Bidart's poem that makes it especially interesting is the parallel method he uses to bring a metaphorical justice to the 9/11 hijackers—one in name only, of course, since they perished along with their victims. From the first line to the last, the poet builds his anathema one step at a time, starting with a chilling allusion to the collapse of the World Trade Center and a wish that the terrorists endure the same horror. While the first four lines are presented in italics for apparent emphasis, they do not shout at the reader or at the hijackers. Instead, these opening lines quietly and methodically say, "I curse you to suffer the same fate of being crushed by one hundred and ten floors falling upon you as you caused to happen to people in the World Trade Center on a Tuesday morning in September." As simple—and as terrifying—as that.

Bidart's use of the word "rectitude" also suggests the moral or religious roots of the poem's subject. The most fundamental element of terrorists' rationalization of their violent acts is the assertion that they are morally correct in committing them. "Rectitude" implies "righteousness," and the latter is generally associated with things that are good, virtuous, honorable, even saintly. Bidart states that it is a "bubble of rectitude" that allows terrorists to exist in the first place. Later, when they are "disenthralled" of that notion, their one pathetic option is to "seek the dead" who want nothing to do with them.

The notion of seeking the dead implies an otherworldly endeavor, also pointing to the spiritual basis of the poem; but even when Bidart steps outside the normal realm of religious subject matter, the tone still sounds like a hallowed, ceremonial rite. He solemnly tells the terrorists that the victims they try to "enter" do not want them and, in fact, "spit [them] out" like some vile, inedible thing in their mouths. The statement "The dead find you are not food" is a grim and final assessment of the 9/11 attackers' dismal fate. It denies them the glory of the supposed martyrdom they believed their suicide missions would bring. In short, the contention that their own deaths are revered by Allah and, therefore, sanctified by Islam is simply another attempt to rationalize their acts.

Bidart's allusion to Shelley's phrase "the great secret of morals," from *Defense of Poetry*, is a fitting conclusion to "Curse"—mainly, because it turns Shelley's purpose on its head, just as terrorists turn religion on its head to meet their own sense of reasoning. The nineteenth-century poet says the secret of morals is "love." The twenty-first-century poet says it is "*the imagination to enter / the skin of another.*" By identifying so closely with the subjects of his poem, Bidart uses the secret to create a curse—anything but the "love" that Shelley intended.

Although the word anathema is never used in this poem, its implication runs throughout. The language, the style, and the themes all point to a controlled, methodical placement of a curse on a specific target—a punishment as old as the biblical "eye for an eye." While there is a general sense of revulsion, even hatred, expressed in "Curse," Bidart never succumbs to raw anger or emotional tirade. Instead, his desire for retribution is outlined carefully in a step-by-step ceremonial damnation of the 9/11 terrorists. His decision to address such a event obviously speaks to his ability as a poet, but it also makes a much stronger case for his cause. Ranting and raving may be expected. But quietly building an anathema against his subjects proves to be both haunting and spiritual, in kind.

Source: Pamela Steed Hill, Critical Essay on "Curse," in *Poetry for Students*, Thomson Gale, 2007.

Garth Greenwell

In the following essay review, Greenwell argues that Bidart's poetry has evolved from lengthy dramatic monologues in which theatrical performance by the characters outweighs any attempt to be lyrical. Greenwell also describes his definition of "lyric" as "short, intimate, and musical" and claims that the poems in Star Dust *provide the best evidence that Bidart has become a lyric poet.*

I intend my title as something of a provocation: Frank Bidart has largely been seen, and until recently for good reason, as anything but a lyric poet. The early poems for which he is best known—"Herbert White," "Ellen West," "The War of Vaslav Nijinsky"—are long dramatic monologues, powerfully theatrical in their gestures and in the extremity of their subjects' psychic states. In their forms and the textures of their language they are not just unlyrical; they stand nearly as a rebuke of lyricism. In an attempt to capture the nuances of a speaking or declaiming voice, they nearly always refuse themselves the recognizable music that is the traditional grace and accompaniment of lyric poems.

Bidart's new work shares with the old a striking thematic boldness. But, in a turn that has gone largely unnoticed, his recent collections have made increasing use of precisely those lyric resources rejected in the early poems. Beginning with the new work included in his collected

> BIDART'S NEW USE OF THE LYRIC HAS GRANTED HIM ACCESS TO EMOTIVE REALMS ALMOST ENTIRELY UNEXPLORED IN THE EARLY POEMS: REALMS OF TENDERNESS, OF UNVICIOUS LOVE, OF ELEGY UNTOUCHED BY BITTERNESS OR RAGE."

volume, *In the Western Night* (1990), Bidart has turned away from the improvisatory sprawl of the early work—what he has called its "homemade quality"—to take up instead the discipline of regular stanzas and, if not a quantifiable or precise meter, then something at least closer to a regular pulse. The poems have grown more lavish in their rhetoric, framing sentences and lines in elaborate and often graceful figures, taking on at times an almost Renaissance gleam. But these figures—most often of repetition: chiasmus, epanalepsis, polyptoton—seem in Bidart's poems less virtuosic decoration than emblems for the excruciating machinations of an inevitable and, more often than not, tragic fate: If the poems at times attain a kind of formal perfection, it is accompanied less by the click of Yeats's closing box than by the clang of a prison door. Yet most important change in Bidart's practice is at once more fundamental and harder to demonstrate: the poems' increasing delight in the sensual pleasures of word and image, their increased commitment to the pursuit of beauty.

This shift is even more evident in Bidart's new collection, *Star Dust* (2005). But I don't intend to argue that his career is usefully described by any sort of "breakthrough narrative," and I don't dispute the clarity of signature that any of his poems from any period displays. It is true that lyric forms appear in his early work (a sonnet in his first book, a villanelle in his second), and that passages even in the early long poems exhibit richness of sound. It is also true that some of the new poems avoid such richness, and that several others ultimately turn away from or subvert the beauty they approach. And yet, with these caveats in mind, there remains a marked difference between the poems of his first book, *Golden State* (1973), and those of *Star Dust*.

Gradually, in a way unforeseeable from his early books but without relinquishing their startling, often violent originality, Frank Bidart has made himself a lyric poet.

By "lyric," I mean both a certain kind of poem—short, intimate, and musical—and also a certain use of language, one that emphasizes the sensual features of rhyme, alliteration, assonance, rhythm, and stress, and especially those features arranged with some sense of pattern. To gauge the ascendancy of lyricism in Bidart's recent work, some comparisons are in order. Consider this excerpt from "Ellen West," the crowning achievement of Bidart's second collection, *The Book of the Body* (1977). In a characteristic passage, Ellen meditates on the sources of her anorexia, rejecting her first description of her illness as "a childish / dread of eating":

> —Then I think, No. The ideal of being thin
>
> conceals the ideal
> *not* to have a body—;
>   which is NOT trivial …
>
> This wish seems now as much a "given" of
>   my existence
>
> as the intolerable
> fact that I am dark-complexioned; big-boned;
> and once weighed
> one hundred and sixty-five pounds …
>
> But then I think, *No.* That's too simple,—
>
> without a body, who can
> *know* himself at all?
>
>   Only by
> acting; choosing; rejecting; have I
> made myself—
>
>   discovered who and what *Ellen* can be …
>
> —But then again I think, *NO.* This *I* is
>   anterior
>
> to name; gender; action;
> fashion;
>
> MATTER ITSELF,—
>
> … trying to stop my hunger with FOOD
> is like trying to appease thirst
>
>   with ink.

The strength of this passage lies in its depiction of what Coleridge called "the drama of thought," the mind falling back repeatedly in the fight to deny itself comfort and illusion. In the first of its three parts, each of which is a stage of argument, Ellen allows herself the grandeur of a pedigreed ascetic ambition ("the ideal / *not* to have a body"), a grandeur tenable only in the context of the sort of robust and sustaining metaphysics that Bidart's poems have always found *un*tenable. In the second, Ellen strips away the illusion of that grandeur to entertain, for a moment, a sense of success in willed self-shaping ("discovered who and what *Ellen* can be"), her starvation an exercise of terrible freedom. Only with her third attempt does she discover what is in fact helplessness before a dilemma that allows for no sense of metaphysical vocation, only metaphysical despair: " … trying to stop my hunger with FOOD / is like trying to appease thirst / with ink." Ellen's great disciplined attempts to master her hunger have been as misguided as the struggles of others to cure her: They have all mistaken the ground and object of her need.

It is typical of Bidart's monologues that Ellen's last simile suddenly indicts writing as a comparable act of futility. His narrators, each of them stationed at extremities of illness or insanity, are all in some way artists, by turns aspiring (Ellen, who writes poems), accomplished (Nijinsky and, in the new collection, Cellini), or plagued by aesthetic longings for order and sense-making that have been horribly misdirected (the necrophiliac murderer Herbert White, who longs "to *feel* things make sense"). Bidart insists that we see these figures as something more than pathological "cases." He is interested in extreme psychic states as illustrative of our commonly more muted lives, and he wants us to acknowledge the implication of our natures in the grand dramas of his poems. In doing so, he aligns himself with a tradition that includes not only psychologists like Freud and William James (who defends the generalizing use of the extreme case in *Varieties of Religious Experience*) but also that now-beleaguered strand of humanist literary thinking that encourages us to make of Oedipus or Faust or Lear mirrors for ourselves. Bidart's long poems are arduous and discomforting lessons in what he calls, following Shelley, "the great secret of morals, *the imagination to enter / the skin of another.*" We cannot dismiss Ellen West as a "case"; we must confront her in the full nobility of her intelligence and acknowledge the shared urgency of her quest.

But what of the passage's formal properties? Ellen's "drama of thought" is set in variable lines, stretching toward the right margin in moments of confident assertion, breaking for doubt and the more difficult work of argument. With each turn ("Then I think, No"; "But then I think, *No*"; "But then again I think, *NO*") the voice intensifies, marked by slight alterations of phrase ("then," "but then," "but then again"), and by Bidart's characteristically heavy punctuation. The passage is as nearly free from regular meter as English can manage; there's no ghost of pentameter, no Eliotic cadence to structure the verse. And yet the language is organized by a distinctive prosody, determined not so much by stress or accent as by punctuation—semi-colons where the syntax calls only for commas, dashes joined (sometimes jarringly) with other marks—as well as italics and capitalization.

In short, this is highly crafted language, the function of which is to indicate the urgencies and hesitations of a voice. This it does very well. But its expressive resources pale beside those of the lyric, which enables, in the highest achievements of the mode, the smallest formal choice to carry a significant charge. There are two defects by which Bidart's early work is occasionally marred, and his avoidance of lyric resources is a source, I think, of both. The first is a sometimes choking over-reliance on heavy punctuation and typography. The problem is that the potential for variation is quickly exhausted: To indicate volume or pitch or stress, for instance, one can italicize, capitalize, italicize *and* capitalize, italicize *and* capitalize *and* add an exclamation point, and then one is very nearly out of options. Such a system is far less rich in expressive possibilities than is traditional prosody. The poem in which Bidart seems to exhaust those possibilities, and in which his punctuation and typography are most distracting and at times infuriating, is "The First Hour of the Night." Consider these lines, which take as their subject the fall of the dream of reason:

Its *PREMISE*,—

the Neo-Platonic Christian-Humanist
CONFIDENCE that the world's obdurate
contradictions, terrifying
unintelligibility,

can be *tamed* by CLASSIFICATION,—

... Time
now has effaced.

Punctuation detracts from these powerful lines: I can't imagine a voice in which "tamed" carries less force than "confidence" or "classification," or

understand why "contradictions" and "unintelligibility" are relegated to typographical obscurity.

If the lines quoted above suffer from melodramatic typography and punctuation, the second flaw of Bidart's early work is occasional melodrama of statement or situation. I feel this, for example, in the opening of "Confessional" (from *The Sacrifice* [1983]), when the speaker finds his cat hanging, strangled by his mother; or in the otherwise beautiful Maria Callas section of "Ellen West," when Ellen remembers Callas's rapid and drastic weight loss: "—The gossip in Milan was that Callas / had swallowed a tapeworm. But of course she hadn't. // The *tapeworm* / was her *soul* ..." One can't help feeling, even with the best will in the world, that the absurdity of the metaphor is lost on the poem. Similarly, Bidart's earliest poems occasionally lapse into the bathos that so frequently mars the confessional project, as in the seventh section of "Golden State": "How can I say this? / I think my psychiatrist / *likes* me ... / ... / he greets my voice // with an interest, and regard, and affection, / which seem to signal I'm worth love." And yet, without obscuring or excusing these faults, one should note that they stem from Bidart's most admirable qualities: his defenselessness; his refusal to reject, in an ironic age, the language of true feeling; and his relentless pursuit of thematic ambitions more commonly, in current American practice, relinquished to prose.

This is a long way to have come for a comparison. But consider, as an example of Bidart's new style, a lyric from *Desire* (1997), "Overheard Through the Walls of the Invisible City." It is quoted here in full:

... telling those who swarm around him his
    desire
is that an appendage from each of them
fill, invade each of his orifices,—
repeating, chanting,
Oh yeah Oh yeah Oh yeah Oh yeah Oh yeah

until as if in darkness he craved the sun, at
    last he reached
consummation.

—Until telling those who swarm around him
begins again

(we are the wheel to which we are bound).

Bidart has found, in his most successful lyrics, a way to inhabit short forms without compromising the scope of his thematic ambition:

This little poem could serve nicely as a *précis* of *Desire*. In its odd arrangement of clauses, it is reminiscent of a fourteenth-century *Ars Subtilior* score (a style briefly exhumed in the last century by the gloriously eccentric George Crumb), the musical staves curving to meet in the shape of a circle or a heart. The syntax reads almost—leaving aside for a moment the final parenthesis and end stop—like a single sentence cut in two and rearranged, with the initial clause ("Until telling those...") placed perversely after the period. But things are not quite so neat. The parts of the poem don't mesh; no arrangement will yield a complete sentence, as the poem (again excepting the final, autonomous line) has no primary verb. Instead, it presents a series of dependent structures, participial and prepositional phrases, and clauses of indirect statement.

This suggests a grammar of stasis, a suggestion underscored by the repetition, in the penultimate line, of the poems opening words: "telling those who swarm around him." But the repetition has come, as so often in Bidart, with a difference. In the first line, "telling" functions as a verb: Its elided subject is the man directing the scene; he is the master of his actions and of the actions of those to whom he speaks. A dramatic reversal is enacted by the penultimate line: Note that here the entire verbal phrase of the first line ("telling those who swarm around him") functions not verbally but nominally, and has itself become the impersonal subject of "begins." The man as agent is no longer even implied; he is trapped within a process that has usurped all agency in the poem, grammatical and otherwise.

This is not just clever wordplay. Dramatically, the poem is a circle, as a first glance at the syntax suggests: The same actions cycle *ad infinitum*, giving the lie to the illusion of "consummation" which provides the brief, unstable respite of the seventh line's full stop. But psychologically the poem enacts, in its syntax, a progression similar to that of the passage quoted from "Ellen West": The fantasy of the will gives way to passivity before the "radical givens," as Bidart has called them, of our nature. The final summation—"(we are the wheel to which we are bound)"—does not so much extend this argument as provide it with an emblem, the inescapable Catherine wheel that is at once our torment and our nature, and that the poem, in the weird misalignment of its syntax, becomes. One may quarrel (though I do not) with the Augustinian view of human nature to

which the poem, like Bidart's work generally, subscribes, but one cannot deny the high fineness of its craft. It exalts us in the peculiar way art exalts us: by placing us in contact, in Pound's beautiful and modest formulation, "with something arranged more finely than the commonplace."

My argument has been that Bidart's poems have grown formally richer, subtler and more varied, in his three most recent books. But he is still first and foremost a poet of ideas. Each of his collections has circled more or less tightly around a particular theme, what Bidart has described as a "territory." The subjects he has chosen run little risk of exhaustion: the relationship of soul and body, the problem of guilt, the force of desire, and now, in *Star Dust*, "the human need to make."

The book is structured like the two that precede it (taking as an autonomous volume the new poems of *In the Western Night*), with several short lyrics prefacing a single long poem. This is a congenial structure for Bidart, one well-suited to his circling examinations: The short pieces stake out a book's territory and the long poem explores it. Bidart has acknowledged that his territories overlap, that, as he puts it, "the great issues are not separate from each other. There should be a side-chapel in each structure for each crucial issue." Certainly *Desire* did not (how could it?) lay its theme to rest, and several of the most affecting poems in the new volume are love poems. But even among "the great issues," "the human need to make" is an especially capacious theme for this poet. Certainly it has occupied him since his earliest books, and as a result these poems often allude to or recall his old work.

"Advice to the Players," a prose piece from the first section of the new book (this section, *Music Like Dirt*, appeared separately as a chapbook in 2002), makes clear the breadth of Bidart's construal of "making." It includes, of course, art; but for Bidart, *being is making: not only large things, a family, a book, a business: but the shape we give this afternoon, a conversation between two friends, a meal.* The challenge, not only for the artist but for anyone determined to live meaningfully, is to make "something commensurate to [one's] will to make"; failure to do so renders the need to make "a curse, a misfortune." One sees, in the light cast by this new volume, even more clearly the extent to which many of Bidart's dramatic poems—especially "Ellen West," "The Arc," and "Herbert White"—are meditations on the failure to make, and on the ease with which the ambition, the desire to mean, if frustrated, can lead to suffering and horror.

Not only the monologues have been haunted by the idea of this failure. In "Confessional," Bidart wrote of his mother:

> She had no profession,—
>
> she had painted a few paintings, and written a handful of poems, but without the illusion
>
> either were any good, or STOOD FOR HER . . .
>
> She had MADE nothing.
>
> *I* was what she had made.

In *Music Like Dirt*, Bidart returns to the family dramas that so tormented his first three books, and it is among the more moving aspects of the new work that the anger and futility of those early poems have given way to a less excoriating compassion. In a beautiful poem, "Stanzas Ending With the Same Two Words," Bidart addresses his father with a new tenderness:

> At first I felt shame because I had entered through the door marked *Your Death.*
>
> Not a valuable word written unsteeped in your death.

The poem ends with an echo of *Hamlet* (echoed already, of course, in the title "Advice to the Players") that makes of the son's art an elaborate vengeance:

> *Kill whatever killed your father*, your life turning to me again said before your death.
>
> Hard to grow old still hungry.
> You were still hungry at your death.

The short poems that follow *Music Like Dirt*, presumably written since the publication of the chapbook, are the finest and most beautiful lyrics Bidart has written; the best of them are among the finest lyrics of his generation. ("Hadrian's Deathbed," a translation of "*Animula vagula blandula* " that diminishes the original, obscuring its richness of sound and lightness of touch, is the section's sole failure.) While the poems of *Music Like Dirt* generally address acts of explicit making, these lyrics are more oblique, often taking as their subject *un* making. The section opens, for instance, with "Curse," a cry of grief at the attacks on the World Trade Center. In "Knot," a woman's

hand has been unmade by injury or age or stroke; in "Romain Clerou," Bidart returns to the scene of his mother's death; "Song" addresses the unmaking of the self that is, the poem suggests, the necessary preamble to any significant act of creation: "Whatever for good or ill / grows within you needs / you for a time to cease to exist." But the most extraordinary poems here are love poems, albeit of an unsettling kind: "The Soldier Who Guards the Frontier," "Phenomenology of the Prick" (a poem marred only by its monstrous title), and "Star Dust."

The act of making considered in the first of these poems is not only imaginary but, if I'm reading it correctly, impossible. Here are the opening three stanzas:

> On the surface of the earth
> despite all effort I continued
> the life I had led in its depths.
>
> So when you said cuckoo
> hello and my heart
> leapt up imagine my surprise.
>
> From its depths some mouth
> drawn by your refusals of love
> fastened on them and fattened.

Each stanza asks to be read in the light of what follows it. Thus the nature of the relationship between the speaker and the "you" of the poem becomes clear only in the third tercet; with the disclosure of "your refusals of love," the unarmored delight of the second stanza takes on enormous poignancy ("my heart / leapt up" is a nod, of course, to Wordsworth). This poignancy, in turn, reveals the cost hinted at by the first stanza's "effort." Having been rejected by a man he loved, the speaker attempts a life free from him, "on the surface," while the life of fixation and true significance continues unacknowledged in the "depths." "Drawn" by and fed on that refusal is an impossible creation, the "creature / born from our union in 1983," as the poem's fourth stanza has it: the soldier of the poem's title.

Both the date and the weird, violent image of feeding ("fastened on them and fattened") recall the title poem of Bidart's collected volume, "In the Western Night," which is uncharacteristically labeled with the year and place of its composition: "*Berkeley, California; 1983.*" It too is a sort of love poem, its tone alternately angry and tender, and the relationship it memorializes would seem to be the one the new poem remembers. In the third section of "In the Western Night," the speaker, having declared of the beloved who has refused him that "THIS MAN IS STONE...NOT BREAD," turns his anger abruptly and movingly upon himself: "The man who tries to feed his hunger / by gnawing stone // is a FOOL; his hunger is // fed in ways that he knows cannot satisfy it."

And yet something *has* been nourished, if not satisfied, in the new poem's recapitulation of this image. The second half of the lyric turns away from the "you" of the first four stanzas to the soldier of the title:

> He guards the frontier.
> As he guards the frontier he listens
> all day to the records of Edith Piaf.
>
> Heroic risk, Piaf sings. Love
> is heroic risk, for what you are impelled
> to risk but do not
>
> kills you; as does, of course this voice
> knows, risk. He is addicted
> to the records of Edith Piaf.

It may be difficult to feel, from these excerpts, the great deal of work that form is doing in the poem: In the context of seven end-stopped tercets, the single enjambment between the second and third stanzas here carries enormous force. Bidart has replaced the heavy punctuation and typography of his early poems with the kind of emphasis that only pattern—by providing opportunities to depart from pattern—allows. The departure here is perfectly timed: The poise of the tercets is broken at the poem's realization of a double bind, the fatal nature of both "risk" and the avoidance of risk.

The frontier this soldier guards is that of experience, the line between a life lived at risk in the world—the world of love and betrayal and of the reckless gamble of art—and a life avoided. But the self-congratulation that this seems inevitably to preface is thwarted, because the poem finds neither alternative bearable. The final stanza makes clear this ambivalence: "He lives on the aroma, the intoxications / of what he has been spared. / He is grateful, he says, not to exist." In the movement from "aroma" to "intoxications" there is a great longing for the world, and yet the poem gives us no reason to dismiss the soldier's claimed gratitude. Insight, for Bidart, nearly always involves the revelation or recognition of a double bind ("Man needs a metaphysics. / He cannot have *one*"; "this '*tradition*' that I cannot / THINK MY LIFE //

without, nor POSSESS IT within"). He is a poet for whom the endeavor to live a meaningful and conscionable life often seems nearly hopeless.

"Start Dust," another deeply affecting poem of failed love, presents a scene of momentary clarity between two men that is very like grace, a scene from which the beloved turns irrevocably away. But it is a poem that communicates immediately and powerfully, and that outruns both criticism and praise. I want only to note how unique it is in Bidart's work, and how nearly unprecedented it is for him in its pursuit of lushness. Consider a single sentence:

> That night
>
> dense with date palms, crazy with the breath-
> less aromas of fresh-cut earth,
>
> black sky thronging with light so thick the
> fixed
>
> unbruised stars bewildered
> sight, I wanted you dazzled, wanted you
> drunk.

Propelled by a powerful and consistent pulse and reveling in every extravagance of sound, this presents a texture of language entirely removed from the austerity of "Ellen West." (The one poem that anticipates it in Bidart's oeuvre is "Dark Night," a glorious translation from St. John of the Cross first published in the collected volume.) It reminds me, I am surprised to say, of nothing so much as that most rhapsodic of our poets, Hart Crane. Consider these lines from the third section of "Voyages": "Past whirling pillars and lithe pediments, / Light wrestling there incessantly with light, / Star kissing star through wave on wave unto / Your body rocking!" Bidart pulls back, at the last moment, from the kind of ecstatic froth that Crane works himself into, and one is grateful for the restraint: Rhapsody has yet, in this poet, to trump intelligence.

I have suggested that Bidart's turn to the lyric is a response to a technical crisis: Having exhausted the resources of the prosody he developed for his early work, Bidart has turned to new prosodies, which happen to be old prosodies. Like a great many of his contemporaries across the arts, he has shifted from an experiment divorced from tradition to one drawn from tradition. But a poem like "Star Dust" shows that technical replenishment has not been his only reward. Bidart's new use of the lyric has granted him access to emotive realms almost entirely unexplored in the early poems: realms of tenderness, of unvicious love, of elegy untouched by bitterness or rage. The resources of the lyric tradition have not just provided Bidart with new rhythms and tonalities; they have given him access to new territories of feeling.

"The Third Hour of the Night" furthers the sequence of long poems begun in *In the Western Night* and continued with the magnificent culminating poem of *Desire*. As in its predecessor, both of the poem's narratives have source texts. But where the central story of "The Second Hour" was spun from a few hundred lines of Ovid, the source for the primary narrative of the new poem is the sprawling, disjointed, maddening, often quite marvelous *Autobiography* of the sixteenth-century Florentine goldsmith and sculptor, sodomite and murderer, Benvenuto Cellini. Cellini's voice is mercurial—now burnished, now vulgar; now defiant, now pandering; now angry, pleading, despairing, boasting— and Bidart wisely chooses not to attempt to match or mimic it; his Cellini speaks with greater measure and care than the original, though still with pronounced shifts of tone and cadence. All of this makes Cellini sound like the typical Bidart narrator, who tends to have a less than placid inner life. But Cellini is a new sort of character for this poet: Unlike Nijinsky, Ellen West, or Herbert White, he is in no exceptional, fundamental way flawed. He is not insane or ill or even unusually, for the times, homicidal. In the rogues' gallery of Renaissance artists his is not an extreme case; colorful as his life is, the scandals and trials of, say, Marlowe or Gesualdo or Caravaggio would provide for narratives of far more dramatic transgression. And there is an even greater difference that sets this narrator apart from the others: He is granted a moment of real—not deranged or illusory—triumph.

As in several of Bidart's long poems, the structure of "Third Hour" is operatic: Narration proceeds more or less as recitative, interrupted by brief passages of greater lyrical charge. His re-telling of Cellini's story is selective, and many of the more colorful bits have been left out: There's no mention here of the sack of Rome, or of Cellini's heroic part, at least as he tells it, in defending the Pope. Instead, Bidart focuses on the making of Cellini's masterpiece, his bronze statue of Perseus, and on the forces that jeopardize it. These include fickle patrons; matter itself, which resists the forms that imagination

and will would impose on it; and finally that aspect of the self which the first section of the poem calls "the beast within," which "will use the conventions of the visible world // to turn your tongue to stone."

The poem is too long to discuss here in full, but two passages exemplify these themes and display the lyric resources on which Bidart has come increasingly to depend. Bidart has always built his long poems out of shorter parts, whether the numbered sections of sequences like "Golden State" and "Elegy" or the less formal divisions of "Ellen West" and "The War of Vaslav Nijinski." But in his most recent long poems—"Second Hour" and "Third Hour"— some or these shorter sections have a formal integrity that makes them nearly autonomous. Consider this section, spoken by a voice that is not Cellini's:

> *In the mirror of art, you who are familiar with*
> *   the rituals of*
> *decorum and bloodshed before which you are*
>
> *silence and submission*
>
> *while within stone*
> *the mind writhes*
>
> *contemplate, as if a refrain were wisdom, the*
> *   glistening*
>
> *intrication*
> *of bronze and will and circumstance in the*
> *   mirror of art.*

This is reminiscent, in its reach and vatic authority, of certain sections of "Second Hour," and it serves a similar purpose: to implicate us in the drama of the poem's persona. But "implicate" is too tame a word: The repetition of "in the mirror of art" is emblematic not just of "mirroring," but of capture. And yet I'm tempted to read the central image—of the mind writhing "within stone" despite outward submission to worldly power—as suggesting not futility but aesthetic promise. One thinks of the unfinished statues of Michelangelo, and of the familiar observation that their subjects seem to be emerging from the marble, needing the chisel not to shape but to reveal them, to set them free. Though "free," Bidart's last line would seem to argue, is a mistaken notion. "The mirror of art" is never free of the forces that resist it; it is made, rather of their "intrication."

That intrication is achieved only through acts of the highest defiance. Exhausted by the labor of his Perseus, Cellini sleeps while the bronze for the statue is heated, and while he sleeps, he dreams:

> The old inertia of earth that hates the new (as from a rim I watched)
>
> rose from the ground, legion—
>
> truceless ministers of the great unerasable ZERO, eager to annihilate lineament and light,
>
> waited, pent, against the horizon:—
>
> some great force (*massive, stubborn, multiform as*
> *earth, fury whose single name is LEGION,*—)
>
> wanted my Perseus not to exist:—
>
> and I must defeat them.

This is writing of high drama and thrilling beauty, recalling Webster and Marlowe in the dark extravagance of its sounds. Bidart is often discussed as a "difficult" poet, which would seem to be the fate of any writer who takes seriously the life of the mind. So it is worth remarking how engagingly readable his poems are, how often they delight through the sheer suspense of their narratives. This is not something, in the early twenty-first century, one can often say of our poets. I can't think of another passage of recent verse that rivals in its visceral excitement Cellini's eventual triumph; it may be that one has to look to a very different poet, John Berryman, for its nearest equal.

"After sex & metaphysics,—" Bidart writes at the poem's end, "... what? //What you have made." It hardly matters that Cellini's triumph is, by the world's logic, short-lived, that he is imprisoned for sodomy and able to achieve little else of any ambition, save his *Autobiography*. His triumph in making his Perseus stands as the most intense moment of affirmation in all of Bidart's work, the accomplishment of an act of making "commensurate to [his] will to make." It is not compromised even by the much shorter third section of the poem, a terrifying narrative of unmaking that sets Bidart's *oeuvre*, as it stands, in a circle, returning (though with crucial differences) to the world of his first poem, "Herbert White"—a world where "anybody can kill anybody / with a stick."

While I have been lavish in my praise for the new poems, it is important to acknowledge Bidart's limitations. It may be fair to say, as critics have, that his fascination with extremity has blinded him to the common passions of ordinary men and women. Certainly his unremitting seriousness has kept him from the full gamut of human feeling, and one may need reference to Milton for a poet so nearly humorless. Yet Bidart has always shown the virtue of dissatisfaction with his own work, and his new poems make toward these faults gestures of repair. In a poems like "The Soldier Who Guards the Frontier," there is a new lightness of touch ("cuckoo / hello and my heart leapt / up"), and in his recent poems on his parents, and in the elegies for Joe Brainard in *Desire*, there is a welcome descent from the heights of tragedy to a more recognizably human world. But it's difficult, in the end, not to cherish even Bidart's faults. The humorlessness, the occasional melodrama, the hint of strain in the voice: All are symptoms of his singular virtue of ferociousness. It is this ferociousness—in his increasingly constant pursuit of beauty, his refusal of the comfort of our common allusions, and his devotion, however despairing, to the ideal of an intelligible life—that grants Bidart, among our current poets, an eminence almost without rival.

Source: Garth Greenwell, "Frank Bidart, Lyric Poet," in *Parnassus: Poetry in Review*, Vol. 29, Nos. 1 & 2, 2006, pp. 330–47.

Thomson Gale

In the following essay, the critic gives a critical analysis of Bidart's work.

Frank Bidart first gained the attention of critics with *Golden State* and *The Book of the Body*, introspective verse collections that were published during the 1970s. On the basis of Bidart's early work, David Lehman, in a *Newsweek* assessment, called him "a poet of uncommon intelligence and uncompromising originality." In the early 1980s Bidart wrote *The Sacrifice*, which furthered his reputation as a prominent voice in American poetry. Much of Bidart's work, critics suggest, focuses on the origins and consequences of guilt. Among his most notable pieces are dramatic monologues presented through such characters as Herbert White, a child-murderer, and Ellen West, an anorexic woman. "Part of his effectiveness comes simply from his ability as a storyteller," commented Michael Dirda in *Washington Post Book World*. "You long to discover what happens to his poor, doomed people."

"

Bidart grew up in California, where he developed a love for the cinema. He entertained thoughts of becoming an actor when he was young and later, at the time he enrolled in college, considered becoming a film director. His plans began to change, however, when he was introduced to literature at the University of California—Riverside. While an undergraduate, he was introduced to such critical works as *The Liberal Imagination* by Lionel Trilling and *The Idea of a Theater* by Francis Fergusson—both of which exerted a strong influence on his early attitudes toward literary expression. He also became familiar with the work of notable twentieth-century poets T. S. Eliot and Ezra Pound. In a 1983 interview with Mark Halliday, which is included in Bidart's *In the Western Night: Collected Poems, 1965-90*, the poet spoke of how reading Pound's cantos, long works which were first released in 1917, introduced him to the potential of poetry to encompass a wide range of subjects: "They were tremendously liberating in the way that they say that anything can be gotten into a poem, that it doesn't have to change its essential identity to enter the poem—if you can create a structure that is large enough or strong enough, *anything* can retain its own identity and find its place there."

After graduating from the University of California—Riverside, Bidart continued his education at Harvard University. He was not, however, certain of where his course of study would lead him. Bidart related in his interview with Halliday: "I took classes with half my will—often finishing the work for them months after they were over; and was scared, miserable, hopeful. I wrote a great deal. I wrote lugubrious plays that I couldn't see had characters with no

character. More and more, I wrote poems." Bidart's first attempts at poetry were, by his own admission, failures. "They were terrible; no good at all," he continued in his interview. "I was doing what many people start out by doing, trying to be 'universal' by making the entire poem out of assertions and generalization about the world—with a very thin sense of a complicated, surprising, opaque world outside myself that resisted the patterns I was asserting. These generalizations, shorn of much experience, were pretty simple-minded and banal."

After honing his craft, Bidart submitted his work to Richard Howard, who was then editor of a poetry series at Braziller. Howard decided to publish Bidart's poetry in a volume titled *Golden State*, which was released in 1973. In the title poem to Bidart's debut collection, a son and father vainly attempt to understand and accept one another. The poem, presented as an address to the father, is divided into ten separate sections. Critics remarked on the autobiographical nature of the piece and on the sparse quality of the language that Bidart employs throughout the work. Other poems in the collection also touch upon the relationship between parent and child. In his interview Bidart discussed how he came upon the theme of family that enters into some of the poems in *Golden State:* "When I first faced the central importance of 'subject matter,' I knew what I would have to begin by writing about. In the baldest terms, I was someone who had grown up obsessed with his parents. The drama of their lives dominated what, at the deepest level, *I* thought about."

Also included in *Golden State* is "Herbert White," a poem which is presented through the voice of a psychopathic child-murderer and necrophiliac. In his interview with Halliday Bidart stated that his intent in writing the piece was to present "someone who was 'all that I was not,' whose way of 'solving problems' was the *opposite* of that of the son in the middle of the book. The son's way ... involves trying to 'analyze' and 'order' the past, in order to reach 'insight'; Herbert White's is to give himself a violent pattern growing out of the dramas of his past, a pattern that consoles him as long as he can feel that someone *else* has acted within it." According to several reviewers, the dramatic monologue, which opens the collection, is the most notable work in the book. Sharon Mayer Libera, in her *Parnassus* assessment, stated that

"Bidart's achievement, even a *tour de force*, is to have made [Herbert White] human. The narrator's gruesome adventures become the least important aspect of the monologue—what is significant is his reaching out, in a language both awkward and alive, for the reasons he seeks power over his experience in peculiar and violent ways."

In Bidart's second collection, *The Book of the Body*, he includes several poems which feature characters who are struggling to overcome both physical and emotional adversity. The book opens with "The Arc," in which the author presents the musings of an amputee, who at the beginning of the poem provides instructions on how to care for his stump. Bidart also gives voice to Ellen West, a woman with anorexia, a condition which causes her to starve herself continuously because she is dissatisfied with the appearance of her body. Based on a case study by noted psychiatrist Ludwig Binswanger, "Ellen West" was regarded by Edmund White in *Washington Post Book World* as "a work that displays Bidart's talents at their most exacting, their most insistent."

In the opinion of several reviewers, Bidart's work gains strength by disregarding the conventions of poetry. In an appraisal of *The Book of the Body*, Helen Vendler of the *Yale Review* stated that "Bidart's method is not narrative; unlike the seamless dramatic monologues we are used to, his are spliced together, as harrowing bits of speech, an anecdote, a reminiscence, a doctor's journal notes, a letter, an analogy, follow each other in a cinematic progression." Reviewers have also often drawn attention to liberties that Bidart takes when spacing his words and lines in his poetry and when punctuating and capitalizing the English. In his interview with Halliday Bidart explained that "the only way I can sufficiently . . . express the relative weight and importance of the parts of a sentence—so that the reader knows where he or she is and the 'weight' the speaker is placing on the various elements that are being laid out—is [through] punctuation. . . . Punctuation allows me to 'lay out' the *bones* of a sentence visually, spatially, so that the reader can see the pauses, emphases, urgencies and languors in the voice."

The Sacrifice, released in 1983, received widespread praise from reviewers for its insightful poems, many with a guilt theme. Central to the volume is a thirty-page work titled "The War of Vaslav Nijinsky." The title character in the poem is a dancer who pays witness to World War I and eventually loses his sanity. Feeling responsible for the injustices inflicted upon humanity during the conflict, Nijinsky offers penance by performing a dance in which he enacts his own suicide. As with most of his poetry, "The War of Vaslav Nijinsky" went through a series of revisions with Bidart experimenting with language and punctuation throughout its development. "The Nijinsky poem was a nightmare," he remarked in his interview. "There is a passage early in it that I got stuck on, and didn't solve for two years. Undoubtedly there were a number of reasons for this; the poem scared me. Both the fact that I thought it was the best thing I had done, and Nijinsky's ferocity, the extent to which his mind is *radical*, scared me. But the problem was also that the movement of his voice is so mercurial, and paradoxical: many simple declarative sentences, then a long, self-loathing, twisted-against-itself sentence. The *volume* of the voice (from very quiet to extremely loud) was new; I found that many words and phrases had to be not only entirely capitalized, but in italics." In reviewing the poem, *Newsweek*'s Lehman offered praise for Bidart's technique of alternating portions of the dancer's monologue with prose sections on Nijinsky's life. According to Lehman, "the result combines a documentary effect with an intensity rare in contemporary poetry." Also included in Bidart's third collection is "Confessional," in which he presents the musings of a person who places himself in the role of a patient undergoing psychotherapy. The piece was regarded by Don Bogen of *Nation* as "one of the most intelligent and moving poems on family relations" to be published at the time.

Although he has written in a variety of forms, Bidart is best known for his dramatic monologues of troubled characters like Herbert White, Ellen West, and Vaslav Nijinsky. In his interview Bidart discussed how he is able to write dramatic monologues through voices different from his own: "Once I finally get the typed page to the point where it does seem 'right'—where it does seem to reproduce the voice I hear—something very odd happens: the '*being*' of the poem suddenly becomes the poem on paper, and no longer the 'voice' in my head. The poem on paper suddenly seems a truer embodiment of the poem's voice than what I still hear in my head. I've learned to trust this when it happens—at that point, the entire process is finished." Later in the interview he commented on his approach toward expression through language as a whole, remarking that "again and again, insight is dramatized by showing the conflict between what is ordinarily seen, ordinarily understood, and what now is experienced as real. Cracking the shell of the world; or finding that the shell is cracking under you."

Bidart's *Desire* was nominated for the triple crown of awards—the Pulitzer Prize, the National Book Award, and the National Book Critics Circle Award—and received the 1998 Rebekka Bobbitt Prize from the Library of Congress for the best book of poetry published during the previous two years. In reviewing the volume for the *Boston Phoenix* online, Elizabeth Schmidt wrote that "the use of autobiography in [Bidart's] work is a coded, highly intricate enterprise, and his poetry is some of the most difficult and painstakingly original written in America in the last thirty years, weaving quotes and philosophical fragments, vivid detail and stupefying abstraction, into a linguistic matrix that rarely follows the standard rules of punctuation and syntax." "Previously, most of Bidart's longer efforts were dramatic monologues," wrote Stephen Burt in the *New Leader*. "Here they are third-person narratives, unconfined by a persona's voice. Little else has changed, though, in his basic formula, least of all the initial shock of immersion that his poems occasion. To enter a Bidart poem is to enter a world of literal and figurative violence." Burt called "Adolescence," a found poem about sexual assault that Bidart created from anonymously published prose, "an extreme example."

The first part of *Desire* consists of thirteen short poems, including a memorial to artist Joe Brainard, who died of AIDS. Daphne Kutzer wrote in *Lambda Book Report* that this section "includes the few overtly homosexual poems in the volume, although the underlying premise of the entire volume—that we cannot choose what will bring us to ecstasy, it chooses us—certainly resonates for gay readers." William Logan said in *New Criterion* that these poems "prepare the psychology of 'The Second Hour of the Night,' a masterwork whose first part is as good as anything Bidart has done, juxtaposing the memoirs of Berlioz, whose wife died slowly and horribly, with the death of the poet's mother. The not-so-subtle merger of Bidart's mother and Berlioz's wife, in

the erotics implicitly embraced, is the most important psychological gesture in these poems."

The second part is a recounting of Ovid's tale of Myrrha's incestuous love for her father, Cinyrus. In an *Antioch Review* article Molly Bendall compared Bidart's translation with that of Horace Gregory, saying that "characteristically, Bidart has chosen to make the psychological tension more available and succinct rather than allowing it to remain latent." *Nation* reviewer Langdon Hammer wrote that the poem "is, in a sense, the worst case that could be made against desire: Sex makes people miserable; it leads them to destroy others and themselves. Yet Bidart converts his poem into an affirmation of embodied love. The 'precious bitter resin' into which Myrrha's tears are changed tastes bitter and sweet, like *Desire* as a whole. That it is a gay man who has created this book, many years into the age of AIDS, makes the balm a little more bitter, a little more sweet." Hammer noted that the "preexisting forms" in *Desire* include writing by Dante, Marcus Aurelius, and Catullus. "Bidart's mind," continued Hammer, "like Ezra Pound's, is full of writing. The experience he records is first of all the experience of a compassionate, intensive reader. What he cares about most is not the content of prior texts but what it feels like to enter them, and then to carry them inside you."

Poetry contributor David Yezzi wrote that Bidart's message is that "it's our inner struggles that inexorably define us." Kutzer said, "In a short review like this, I cannot possibly do justice to the beauty, horror, complexity, and passion of this poem, and indeed of all of Bidart's poetry." Adam Kirsch wrote in the *New Republic* that "while Bidart's poetry is, on the surface, about unpleasant things and people—monomaniacs, anorexics, transgressors—his treatment of them is not at all repellent; it is positively glamorous. His ostentatious violation of decorum and conventional morality is not shocking to the reader, but actually flattering to him, because it suggests that he, too, contains dark and tumultuous depths. The awe that the reader feels at Myrrha, or Nijinksy, or West, he is allowed to feel also at himself."

Bidart told *Lambda Book Report* interviewer Timothy Liu, "I think 'The Second Hour of the Night' is a poem I've been trying to write all my life. . . . I wanted to write a poem that questioned love, and in some sense, to punish love as far as one could—and see what remained. Not out of the illusion that one could destroy the desire for love, but to devour as many sentimentalities and delusional aspects as possible, certainly to question the traditional assumptions about love."

Andrew Rathmann wrote in *Chicago Review* that *Desire* shows Bidart "to be perhaps less agonized and more resigned to the existential, erotic, and familial contradictions that had occasioned so many of his earlier works. These contradictions are no less intolerable than before (and his exposition of them is no less shockingly, daringly articulate), but Bidart in this book seems at least somewhat attracted to the idea of praising what cannot be altered. This takes the form of accepting desire as one's fate." *Booklist* reviewer Ray Olson called *Desire* "literature of the highest order, written to be carefully and slowly read and rewarding such reading with wonder-struck appreciation of human love."

Source: Thomson Gale, "Frank Bidart," in *Contemporary Authors Online*, Thomson Gale, 2005.

SOURCES

Bidart, Frank, "Curse," in *Star Dust*, Farrar, Straus and Giroux, 2005, pp. 25–26.

———, Notes, in *Star Dust*, Farrar, Straus and Giroux, 2005, p. 83.

"Editor's Corner," in *Ploughshares*, Vol. 31, No. 2–3, Fall 2005, p. 232.

Hoffert, Barbara, "Best Poetry of 2005," in *Library Journal*, Vol. 131, No. 7, April 15, 2006, p. 80.

Weinert, Jonathan, Review of *Star Dust*, in *Harvard Review*, Vol. 30, June 2006, pp. 167–69.

FURTHER READING

Armstrong, Karen, *Islam: A Short History*, Modern Library, 2000.

This popular introduction traces the history of Islam from its origins through to modern times, explaining the various sects, the central points of the Qur'an, and the effects of Western civilization over the centuries. Published in 2000, the book does not reflect an attitude about or response to the events of 9/11.

Chomsky, Noam, *Failed States: The Abuse of Power and the Assault on Democracy*, Henry Holt, 2007.

In this carefully documented study, Chomsky explains how the Bush administration's actions after 9/11 transformed the United States into an imperialist power, one eschewing both international and domestic law and endangering itself and the world in military escalation.

Hennessy, Christopher, *Outside the Lines: Talking with Contemporary Gay Poets*, University of Michigan Press, 2005.

Despite its title, this book does not concentrate on the sexual preferences of the poets, and Bidart's homosexuality is mentioned only in an offhand manner in his discussion of the controversial subjects he often chooses for his poems. He also talks about what he feels is most fundamental in his writing and his blending of mind and body in many of his works.

Kowit, Steve, *In the Palm of Your Hand: The Poet's Portable Workshop*, Tilbury House, 1995.

Kowit provides background and how-to information, strategies, and exceptionally fine models by known and unknown poets, all in a readable text intended to support interested readers in improving their skills in writing poetry.

I, I, I

HAYDEN CARRUTH
1996

In 1996, American poet Hayden Carruth published his poem "I, I, I" in his collection, *Scrambled Eggs & Whiskey: Poems 1991–1995*. At that time, Carruth was already an established and popular poet who had published many collections of poetry since 1959. While he is viewed as a proponent of twentieth-century modernism, he defies categorization and, indeed, has consciously resisted it. In his poetry, Carruth moves easily between free verse and verse written in rhyme and meter.

Scrambled Eggs & Whiskey: Poems 1991–1996 was generally well received by critics and won a National Book Award in poetry for the poet in the year 1996. "I, I, I" is written in non-rhyming free verse. Thematically, the poem is a poetic version of the *bildungsroman* (a novel dealing with the development or coming-of-age of a young protagonist). It raises and, to some extent answers, questions about self-identity through a memorable boyhood experience of the speaker. The poet's treatment of the experience is highly personal but shows the influence of existentialism and Eastern mysticism. The poem appears to be autobiographical, in that it is written in the first person and the speaker's physical appearance matches that of Carruth himself.

AUTHOR BIOGRAPHY

Hayden Carruth was born on August 3, 1921, in Waterbury, Connecticut, to Gorton Veeder

Hayden Carruth (Portrait by John Reeves. Reproduced by permission of John Reeves)

Carruth, a newspaper editor, and Margery Barrow Carruth. He received a B.A. in journalism from the University of North Carolina at Chapel Hill in 1943 and an M.A. in English from the University of Chicago in 1947. During World War II, Carruth served for two years in the United States Army Air Corps. From 1949 to 1950, he was the editor of *Poetry* magazine. He was associate editor at the University of Chicago Press from 1950 to 1951, and project administrator for Intercultural Publications, the publishing project of the Ford Foundation, from 1952 to 1953.

In 1953, Carruth suffered an emotional breakdown and was admitted to a psychiatric hospital in White Plains, New York. His doctors encouraged him to write as a means of therapy, and he kept journals and wrote poetry.

He left the hospital in 1955, and for the next five years, Carruth lived a life apart from the mainstream of society in his parents' house in Pleasantville, New York. He subsequently lived for two years in Norfolk, Connecticut. From 1962 on for a period of eighteen years, he and his third wife, Rose Marie Dorn, lived in

seclusion in the woods of northern Vermont, mixing with the local farmhands and writing about the rural poor. This was not an ideologically motivated move; Carruth's chronic psychiatric disorders had made life in a city and work in an office or classroom intolerable.

In 1970, Carruth was appointed advisory editor for *Hudson Review*, a position he held for twenty-five years. From 1977 to 1981, he was the poetry editor of *Harper's* magazine. In 1979, Carruth accepted a professorship at Syracuse University, where he worked until his retirement in 1991.

Carruth's failed suicide attempt in 1988 paradoxically heralded a positive phase in his life. He notes in his essay "Suicide" (cited by Eric Murphy Selinger in his article on Carruth, "The Importance of a Small Floy Floy") that since childhood, he had been struck by a sense of "the purposelessness of it all, of existence as such." Even the most beautiful or compelling things, he writes, "were pointless." In contrast, after his suicide attempt, he reflected, "I discovered in suicide a way to unify my sense of self, the sense which had formerly been so refracted and broken up."

Politically, Carruth described himself as an anarchist. He publicly opposed the Vietnam War, and, in 1998, refused an invitation from President Bill and Hillary Clinton to attend a celebration at the White House, on the grounds that the government only cared about the interests of those for whom poets and the poor were irrelevant. In 2003, galvanized by President George W. Bush's announcement of the U.S. invasion of Iraq, he posted a poem of protest on the website of Poets Against War (http://www. poetsagainstwar.com/chapbook.asp#Carruth).

Carruth published many books, chiefly of poetry but also a novel, four books of criticism, and two anthologies. His subject matter varies widely but includes man's place in the universe and in nature, rural people and their lives and work, human relationships, and jazz music, which many critics believe influenced his poetry. One of his most admired poetry collections is *Brothers, I Loved You All* (1978). The book in which "I, I, I" appears, *Scrambled Eggs & Whiskey: Poems 1991–1995* (1996), won the National Book Award for Poetry for Carruth in 1996. Later works are *Selected Essays & Reviews* (1995); *Reluctantly: Autobiographical Essays* (1998); *Doctor Jazz: Poems 1996–2000*

(2001); and *Collected Shorter Poems 1946–1991* (2001). A poetry anthology edited by Carruth, *The Voice That Is Great within Us* (1970), was in the early 2000s still considered one of the finest collections of contemporary American poetry.

The many prizes, grants, and honors awarded to Carruth include the University of Chicago's Harriet Monroe Award (1960), Guggenheim Fellowships (1965, 1979), National Endowment for the Arts Fellowships (1968, 1974), the Lenore Marshall Poetry Prize for *Brothers, I Loved You All*, the Shelley Prize of the Poetry Society of America (1979), and the Ruth Lilly Poetry Prize (1990). In 1988, he was named a senior fellow of the National Endowment for the Arts.

Carruth's first three marriages ended in divorce. He has a daughter by his first wife, Sara Anderson, and a son by his third, Rose Marie Dorn. In 1989, Carruth married the poet Joe-Anne McLaughlin. As of 2006, they lived in Munnsville, New York.

POEM TEXT

First, the self. Then, the observing self.
The self that acts and the self that watches. This
The starting point, the place where the mind
  begins,
Whether the mind of an individual or
The mind of a species. When I was a boy   5
I struggled to understand. For if I know
The self that watches, another watching self
Must see the watcher, then another seeing that,
Another and mother, and where does it end?
And my mother sent me to the barber shop,   10
My first time, to get my hair "cut for a part"
(Instead of the dutch boy she'd always given me),
As I was instructed to tell the barber. She
Dispatched me on my own because the shop,
Which had a pool table in the back, in that   15
Small town was the men's club, and no woman
Would venture there. Was it my first excursion
On my own into the world? Perhaps. I sat
In the big chair. The wall behind me held
A huge mirror, and so did the one in front,   20
So that I saw my own small strange blond head
With its oriental eyes and turned up nose repeated
In ever diminishing images, one behind
Another behind another, and I tried
To peer farther and farther into the succession   25
To see the farthest one, diminutive in
The shadows. I could not. I sat rigid
And said no word. The fat barber snipped
My hair and blew his brusque breath on my nape
And finally whisked away his sheet, and I   30
Climbed down. I ran from that cave of mirrors

A mile and a half to home, to my own room
Up under the eaves, which was another cave.
It had no mirrors. I no longer needed mirrors.

POEM SUMMARY

Lines 1–5

In "I, I, I," the speaker tells of an incident that happened in his boyhood. If it is assumed that Carruth is describing his own experience, this would have taken place in the 1920s. The speaker begins by describing his understanding of the nature of his self from the point of view of mature adulthood. The self is divided into two aspects: the self and the observing self; "The self that acts and the self that watches." He now knows that this realization, this self-awareness, marks the point where the mind of an individual or of a species begins.

Lines 5–9

The speaker shifts back in time to his boyhood. He struggles to understand the nature of his self. He can grasp the idea of the first self that watches, but the fact that he ("I") can know this watching self means that there must be another "I" who is the knower, a self beyond the first watching self. If he can know this other watching self, then there must be yet another self, watching that watching self, and so on to infinity. As the speaker asks, remembering the bewilderment of his boyhood, "where does it end?"

Lines 10–13

The speaker remembers an important incident in his childhood that related to his questions regarding the self. His mother sends him to the barbershop to get his hair cut. She tells him to inform the barber that he needs it to be "cut for a part," with the hair parted on one side. It is the first time that he has been to the barber's for a haircut, as prior to this, his mother has always cut his hair in a "dutch boy" style—the kind of haircut that results from placing a bowl on a child's head and cutting around it.

Lines 13–18

The boy's mother sends him to the barbershop on his own because the shop has a pool table in the back. In the small town where they lived, this was the men's club, and women never ventured

TOPICS FOR FURTHER STUDY

- Write an essay in which you compare and contrast "I, I, I" with William Wordsworth's poem "Lines Written a Few Miles Above Tintern Abbey." What differences and similarities do you see between the spiritual experiences described in each poem? How does each speaker respond to his experience, and what are the implications or consequences of the experience for him?

- Write a poem about an experience (spiritual or otherwise) that changed your life. You may use free verse or rhyme and meter as you wish. Write a short paragraph on what was gained or lost from writing in verse as opposed to writing your account in prose.

- Research the topic of coming of age and initiation ceremonies in at least two different cultures and create a class presentation on your findings.

- Write an essay in which you relate the experience of the boy speaker in Carruth's "I, I, I" to your own and/or your friends' childhood or teenage experiences. In your view, how usual is his experience and his response to it?

- Research the topic of spiritual experiences from history and the present day. Write a report about the different types of experience and give your view of what is happening in each case.

there. He wonders whether it was his first excursion into the world on his own and concludes that it may have been.

Lines 18–28

The boy sits in the barber's big chair. In front of him on the wall is a huge mirror, and behind him on another wall is another mirror. He looks at his image in the mirror in front of him. His image is reflected by the mirror behind him, so that he sees a reflection of his "small strange blond head" repeated in ever diminishing images, one behind another. He strains to see the farthest one, but cannot. He sits rigidly in silence.

Lines 28–34

The barber finishes cutting the boy's hair. He blows the pieces of hair from the boy's neck and removes the sheet that he has put around his shoulders. The boy climbs down from the chair. He runs from "that cave of mirrors," the barbershop, to his home a mile and a half away. He goes to his room under the eaves of his house, and it seems to him to be another cave. There is one difference, however: this cave has no mirrors. The boy realizes that he no longer needs mirrors. He has reached an understanding that makes them redundant.

THEMES

The Nature of the Self

"I, I, I" explores the nature of the self, a topic that the speaker has come to understand better as an adult than he did as a child. The poem presents the concept that there are two selves: one that acts and another that watches or witnesses the action. Carruth is describing the moment of individuation, when the self becomes conscious of the self and the concept of *I* is born: "The starting point, the place where the mind begins." Although it is a moment in time, it is also a state of being, in that it is possible to maintain a simultaneous awareness of the self that acts and the self that watches in everyday activity. Indeed, the boy in the poem has this experience and struggles to understand it; his adult self maintains this experience and has understood it, thanks to the episode in the barbershop.

The concept behind Carruth's poem is that of the dual nature of the self. This concept suggests that one part of the self, the small individual self, is engaged in action in the material world. The other part, the large self, which is eternal in its nature, does not act, but silently witnesses the small self's actions. It remains uninvolved and serene. This concept is common in Eastern mystical traditions. It is found in ancient Indian texts, Buddhist thought, and the writings of some Christian theologians, including St. Augustine and Meister Eckhart.

The poet, as a young boy, is struck by the idea that people have multiple "selves" as he sees his image reflected into infinity through mirrors set opposite each other, as these are (© Age Fotostock/Superstock)

As a boy, the speaker finds the implications of this idea difficult to grasp. He finally reaches understanding through the incident in the barbershop, which graphically illustrates and makes concrete what previously was only an abstract idea. He looks in the mirror and sees an infinite number of images of himself receding into the "shadows," an image that connotes death. Afterwards, he no longer needs the mirrors that showed him his small self, because he knows the nature and destination of this small self: death.

Coming of Age

There are elements of the boy's experience at the barbershop that are reminiscent of a coming of age or moment of maturation such as might be described in a *bildungsroman*. In particular, some elements of the experience connote an initiation ceremony into manhood such as are performed in certain cultures, including some Native American and African societies. Common aspects of these traditional ceremonies are that the boy leaves his mother to symbolize his new independence and spends some time alone. The speaker in "I, I, I" also leaves his mother behind, since the place where he is going (the barbershop) is a male domain for two reasons: first, a barber is a hairdresser for men, and second, the shop has a pool table at the back, and playing pool is a traditionally male pastime. The ceremonial nature of the occasion is foreshadowed by the momentous phrase, reminiscent of an adventure story, "no woman / Would venture there."

The sense of initiation is reinforced by the fact that this is his first trip to the barber, and it is possibly his first lone excursion into the world. In addition, the barbershop is described as a "cave," and his own room, on his return from the barber, has become "another cave." Caves, or huts from which all light is blocked out, are traditional sacred locations for initiation ceremonies. The idea is that in the darkness and silence of the cave, distractions that pull the senses outward are minimized, so that the attention can be turned within. The cave in such ceremonies has a dual symbolic aspect: it is both a tomb in which the old self is laid to rest and a second womb from which the initiate is born into a new phase of life. Even the cutting of hair is an important ritual in many cultures. It symbolizes a purification of the old life and a new beginning, as, for example, in some Christian orders of monks and nuns, where the hair is cut when a novice takes vows to enter the order.

All initiation ceremonies aim to ensure that the initiate returns to his home changed in some way: he is wiser, more independent, more of an adult. The boy in Carruth's poem is no exception. He returns home no longer needing mirrors in which to see the reflection of his small self, since he has gained some knowledge of who he is.

STYLE

Imagery

"I, I, I" is filled with imagery of contrasting size. The boy speaker and his mother live in a "Small" town; when he gets to the barbershop, the boy sits in a "big" chair; the walls in front of him and behind him hold "huge" mirrors; his head is "small"; the image of his head in the mirror is repeated "In ever diminishing images"; the barber is "fat" and, therefore, bigger than he is; after his haircut, he "Climbed down" from the chair. The overall effect is to emphasize the boy's smallness in a big world. Infinity is bigness drawn out to the ultimate extent, and the image of the small boy peering into the unfathomable distance is a graphic representation of the theme of the poem: the small self being faced with the concept of infinity. The contrast gives an impression of the insignificance and unreality of the small self, and this is reinforced by the strangeness of the boy's face to himself and the repetition of the images of his head. The small self becomes depersonalized, an object which is almost disowned. This is in line with Eastern traditions such as Hindu and Buddhist thought, which view the small self as fundamentally unreal and teach that it is part of the *maya*, or illusion, of the material world. In these traditions, this concept is not thought of as an abstract or theoretical idea, but as the subjective experience of many people, regardless of culture, religion, or belief.

The barber contrasts with the boy in other ways than size. To the barber, with his quick, snipping movements and "brusque breath," the boy's visit means only another haircut. The barber is in a different world from the boy: he inhabits the everyday world in which time and space are the governing realities and in which speed and efficiency matter. The boy, on the other hand, experiences a moment outside time and space and beyond his familiar small world. Sitting rigid and wordless, he witnesses the dissolution of the ego, the small self that inhabits the world of time and space. He finds himself face to face with death.

The Run-on Line

In poetry, a run-on line is one in which the end of the line does not correspond with a completed unit of meaning. "I, I, I" contains many run-on lines, with commas or periods often occurring within the lines to mark a pause, known as a caesura. The caesura can be used to emphasize what follows or to add the power of silence to what has gone before it. There is a particularly remarkable series of caesuras in a significant part of the poem. The line "To see the farthest one, diminutive in" contains a comma to mark a pause, as the boy strains his eyes to see the most distant image of his head in the mirror. The next line intensifies the boy's effort and failure to bring infinity within the grasp of his senses: "The shadows. I could not. I sat rigid / And said no word." The comma of the previous line has become three periods in just one and a half lines. The pauses are longer and weightier as the power of thought, words, and ideas fails in the presence of infinity. The boy's awed silence is not merely described, but enacted by means of the insistent caesuras.

Repetition

Carruth repeats certain words in the poem to reinforce the meaning. Lines 2 through 8 has many recurrences of variants on the word *watch*, which serve to emphasize the progression to infinity of the concept of the watcher, the knowing and conscious self that is conscious of the small, acting self. Lines 7 through 9 repeat the word *another*, which has a similar effect, drawing attention to the endless repetition of the knowing self to infinity; the word recurs in line 24, as the boy sees the repeated series of images of himself. Lines 25 and 26 echo "farther . . . farther . . . / farthest" as he strains to see the most distant image. The repeated words also express the ever-onward march of the boy's busy and bewildered mind as he seeks to force

COMPARE
&
CONTRAST

- **1920s:** Society in small towns in the United States is to some extent gender-segregated, in that there are places where women do not generally venture. These include public bars, pool rooms, and barbershops.

  Today: Gender segregation has largely disappeared. Both women and men frequent bars and pool rooms, and men's barbershops have in many cases been replaced by dual-gender hair salons.

- **1920s:** Ideas prevalent in existentialist and Eastern philosophies are known in some circles of the intelligentsia and academe, but they are not known or discussed in society

in general, particularly, perhaps, in small towns in the United States.

Today: Elements of existentialist and Eastern thought are widely disseminated throughout society, for example, through films, popular books, television, and magazines. Eastern religions are taught in religious education classes in schools and colleges. The mystical aspects of religions and New Age ideas are popular with increasingly widespread discussion of spiritual experiences. Consequently, some of the fear and isolation that has often surrounded such experiences in the West has dissolved.

---

it to contain the uncontainable. Significantly, these repetitions end with a series of caesuras (the comma in line 26 and the three periods in lines 27 and 28) as the seemingly unstoppable activity of his mind freezes into silence.

Free Verse

Though Carruth frequently writes poetry in rhyme and meter, he has written "I, I, I" in free verse, meaning that there are no rhymes and the meter is irregular. This contributes to the informality of the poem, which approximates everyday speech. The ordinariness of the presentation and setting contrasts with the somewhat momentous experience of the boy. Carruth thereby draws attention to the profound possibilities within the mundane events of people's lives and emphasizes the central role of the subjective experience in interpreting the world.

HISTORICAL CONTEXT

Existentialism and Eastern Thought

Carruth long had an interest in the philosophy of existentialism, and its influence on his work is discernible from the time of his 1964 publication

of a book-length imaginary dialogue with the French author and philosopher Albert Camus (1913–1960) entitled *After "The Stranger": Imaginary Dialogues with Camus.*

Existentialism is a philosophy that attempts to understand the fundamentals of the human condition and its relation to the world. It eschews externally located absolute values such as reason and religious doctrine and rejects the notion that life has an inherent meaning, instead emphasizing that each individual must evolve his or her own subjective values. As a result, subjective experience is seen as being of paramount importance. According to music critic Annie Holub in her review of "Nowhere Man: Considered to Tears (I Like Red Recordings)" for the *Rhythm & Views* section of the *Tucson Weekly*, Hayden Carruth defined existentialism as "the reestablishment of the individual in the face of Nothingness and absurdity." This is also an apt summary of the theme of "I, I, I." The "Nothingness and absurdity" lie in the boy's bewildered imagining of an endless series of watching selves, ending with the exasperated question, "and where does it end?" The "reestablishment of the individual" lies in the boy's attempt to make some sense of his experience in the barbershop.

The boy's sense of alienation is emphasized by his response to the sight of his own reflection, which seems both unfamiliar and foreign: "my own small strange blond head / With its oriental eyes." The "oriental eyes" both reflect a fact of Carruth's physical appearance and recall his interest in Eastern thought. For example, the Chinese poet Tu Fu (712–770) forms the subject of Carruth's poems "A Summer with Tu Fu" and "Peace on the Water," and "Rubaiyat" refers to the Persian poem, the *Rubaiyat of Omar Khayyam*, attributed to the Persian mathematician Omar Khayyam (1048–1123). All these poems appear in *Scrambled Eggs & Whiskey: Poems 1991–1995*.

Insofar as it is possible to generalize about the many traditional philosophies of the East, it is safe to say that they excel in such self-reflection as is enacted in "I, I, I." They lay greater emphasis than is found in the Western philosophical traditions on the subjective experience of the self, and they offer frameworks that define the relationship of the individual self to the material universe and to the infinite, or divine.

Carruth's speaker's "oriental eyes" alert the reader to a philosophical framework that is not native to the small American town where he and his mother live but that has its home in the Eastern countries. This philosophical framework may seem incongruous in the mundane small-town setting of the barbershop, but that is part of the point of the poem. The alienated boy who finds his own image "strange" finds answers to his questions of identity in the kind of self-examination that is central to philosophies of distant Eastern countries. He does not have to move outside his own small world to find those answers, but this is because the philosophies of the East are based on subjective spiritual experience, which is universally available to everyone, even a boy sitting in a barbershop in a small town in the United States.

The boy receives an answer to his question, "where does it end?" in the barbershop. He finds that it (the watching self) does not end but stretches to infinity. Infinity cannot be grasped or seen by the senses, but lies "in / The shadows," an image that suggests death. Whether this lends meaning to the boy's life is not made explicit, but it is clear that he gains an understanding that

makes him independent of the mirrors, and the small self that they symbolize.

CRITICAL OVERVIEW

When *Scrambled Eggs & Whiskey: Poems 1991–1995* appeared in 1996, the critical reception of the collection was generally positive. Though no critic picked out "I, I, I" for particular comment, the poem was posted on various websites and is anthologized in *The Autumn House Anthology of Contemporary Poetry*, edited by Sue Ellen Thompson (2005).

Eric Murphy Selinger concludes his essay on Carruth, "The Importance of a Small Floy Floy," with a consideration of *Scrambled Eggs & Whiskey: Poems 1991–1995*, calling it a "first-rate new collection." Selinger credits the collection with two qualities widely praised in Carruth's poetry, spontaneity and emotional honesty, in his commendation of the poet's "apparently off-the-cuff, heart-on-sleeve verses." This comment could easily apply to "I, I, I."

Ray Olson, reviewing the collection for *Booklist*, notes the influences on Carruth of the poets Ezra Pound and William Carlos Williams, concluding, "Contemporary American poetry doesn't get any richer than this." In her review of the collection for the *Christian Science Monitor*, Elizabeth Lund writes, "Hayden Carruth has never been afraid to wrestle with life's hardest questions." Lund notes that the poems in the collection are "straightforward and simple," and, agreeing with Selinger, she remarks on their honesty. However, she adds, "the magic is missing," and writes, "One would hope for more of the stunning music and imagery that occasionally allows the work to change the reader as well as challenge."

The anonymous reviewer for *Publishers Weekly* calls the collection "bittersweet, sometimes celebratory, occasionally rueful," adding that it is "generally moving" but "uneven." The reviewer writes that Carruth's poetry is "at its best when it mixes colloquial diction with an elegiac lyricism," a comment which could apply to "I, I, I." The reviewer adds that when the colloquial takes over, Carruth's verse becomes "almost flat." The reviewer concurs with other critics that the collection illustrates "the openness and honesty with which Carruth addresses

WHAT DO I READ NEXT?

- Carruth's *Brothers, I Loved You All: Poems, 1969–1977* (1978) is widely considered to be his best collection of poems. It covers a variety of themes, including the insanity of society, the people and natural environment of Vermont, and the jazz music that he loves.

- Carruth's *Reluctantly: Autobiographical Essays* (1998) is a collection of essays in which the poet discusses with characteristic honesty his suicide attempt, hospitalizations, nervous breakdowns, divorces, and other disappointments, alongside his successes, joys, and creative life.

- Ralph Metzner's *The Unfolding Self: Varieties of Transformative Experience* (1998) is a popular yet scholarly book that uses stories and metaphors to look at the different stages of spiritual growth, bringing sense and order to what for many is a challenging or even frightening experience.

- The poet William Carlos Williams exercised a considerable influence on Carruth's work, and readers who enjoy Carruth's poetry may appreciate that of Williams. Williams's poetry is characterized by its honesty, its clarity of thought and expression, and its concreteness of imagery. Many of his best poems are collected in *William Carlos Williams: Selected Poems* (2004).

---

the world" and notes "the mixed compassion and outrage with which he responds to it."

The power of "I, I, I" is identified by Matthew Miller's general comment in *Midwest Quarterly* on Carruth's body of work that it is especially distinguished by its "truth value." The brand of truth for which Carruth strives and often achieves, Miller writes, is not the truth of the ego in narcissistic reverie, nor is it "the presumption of objective truth handed down from the twin mountains of religious and intellectual

tradition." It is "the truth of impassioned subjectivity . . . as Carruth puts it . . . 'the whole individual subjectivity, the spirit-body-soul.'"

CRITICISM

Claire Robinson

Robinson has an M.A. in English. She is a writer and editor and a former teacher of English literature and creative writing. In the following essay, she examines how "I, I, I" illustrates an idea of the self that runs through the ancient Indian and other spiritual traditions.

When the author Roger Housden included a poem by Hayden Carruth in his book *Ten Poems to Last a Lifetime*, he wrote by way of introduction, "Carruth, a social realist and a political radical, is wary of mysticism, yet his work carries some of the most penetrating insight—spiritual insight—to be found anywhere." Indeed, Carruth's poem "I, I, I" addresses the fundamental paradox of the Upanishads, one of the ancient Indian texts known as the Veda: "By what . . . should one know the knower?" Lest this should seem an impossibly obscure question, Carruth asks the same question in his characteristically clear language at the beginning of "I, I, I." There is "The self that acts and the self that watches." But if the speaker of the poem knows the self that watches, then there must, logically, be another watching self beyond the first watching self, and this other watching self must be the knower. Every watching self, in order to be known, demands another knower beyond itself. The speaker cannot comprehend how this never-ending process can conclude: "and where does it end?"

Carruth is describing a common spiritual experience of people of every culture and of all shades of religious belief and non-belief: that there is an aspect of the self that is involved in activity in the world, and an aspect of the self that does not act, but stands apart and silently witnesses the busy-ness of the acting self. The first self is frequently called the small self or ego, the self that identifies with the material world, with change, with time and space constraints, and with the fears and anxieties that come from a feeling of individuality and separateness from the rest of creation. The second self (sometimes capitalized as Self) is sometimes described as the large self and is the self that feels

> **A PERSON IN THIS STATE HAS CEASED TO IDENTIFY THE SELF WITH THE MATERIAL WORLD OF THE SENSES, BUT HAS YET TO ATTAIN THE BLISSFUL EXPANSION OF THE SELF INTO UNION WITH GOD; HE IS ALONE, BETWEEN TWO WORLDS, WITH NOTHING."**

serenely uninvolved with the bustle of activity. It stands beyond time and space and beyond the separations and divisions of the material world.

The Upanishads describe the two aspects of the self as follows:

Two birds, companions (who are) always united, cling to the self-same tree. Of these two, the one eats the sweet fruit and the other looks on without eating. On the self-same tree, a person immersed (in the sorrows of the world) is deluded and grieves on account of his helplessness. When he sees the other, the Lord who is worshipped and his greatness, he becomes freed from sorrow.

In the Christian tradition, St. Augustine (cited in *The Principal Upanisads*) wrote of the "two virtues . . . set before the soul of man, the one active, the other contemplative." The first is engaged in "toil" that cleanses the heart to prepare it for the vision of God, and the other enables the person "to repose and see God"; the first is bound by time and space, the second eternal.

If the self can be brought to identify with its expanded aspect, then, depending on the person's belief system, the experience may be felt as being at one with the creator, God, infinity, eternity, or the transcendent. Those people who consciously experience this state describe it as a unified state of being, a feeling of being at one with God or with the universe as a whole, and as profound bliss or peace.

Mystical traditions, including those of Hindu, Buddhist, and Christian origins, teach that the process of witnessing activity from the point of view of the transcendent can be consciously cultivated through meditation. It also appears to happen involuntarily to many people who have had near-death experiences. Equally, it can occur through extreme circumstances such

as a serious illness or a life-threatening experience. People who become very absorbed in an activity, such as sportspeople or musicians, often describe so-called peak experiences in which they seem to stand apart from the self that performs the activity. Finally, it can happen in periods of transition, for example, in puberty, or in the moments of transition between different states of awareness, such as passing from sleep into the waking state. Carruth's boy speaker appears to be in just such a period of transition, when he takes his first trip into the world unaccompanied by his mother.

Mystics often describe the ultimate conclusion of the experience, the expansion of the self into the infinite, as one of pure bliss. However, many people initially find the process of getting to that point disturbing or frightening. This is because it can seem to involve the diminishment of the small self to a point smaller than the smallest before it expands to become bigger than the biggest, into infinity. Carruth's poem features a graphic enactment of the diminishment of the small self, in the form of the receding images of the self in the mirrors to an infinite degree of smallness. There is no blissful sense of expansion into infinity. Insofar as a conclusion to the experience can be located, it is "in / The shadows," an image that connotes darkness and death. To the boy, the experience does not seem pleasant; in fact, it is so disturbing that he sits "rigid" and speechless while it takes place and runs home as fast as he can immediately afterwards. The boy has the first half of the experience, the diminishment of the ego, but seems unwilling or unable to pass through the Biblical "eye of a needle" (Matthew 19:24) into infinity. His experience is incomplete.

The boy's experience is reminiscent of the song by the American songwriter and guitarist Jimi Hendrix, "Room Full of Mirrors":

I used to live in a room full of mirrors
All I could see was me
Then I take my spirit and I smash my mirrors
And now the whole world is here for me to see.

Many writers have used the symbol of passage through and beyond a mirror to mark the transition into another, wider world of expanded potential from which the protagonist returns transformed. These writers range from the French poet, playwright, and filmmaker Jean Cocteau in his film *The Blood of a Poet* to the

English author Lewis Carroll in his book *Alice Through the Looking Glass.*

The boy's experience in the barbershop may be understood as an example of the *dark night of the soul*, a phrase coined by the sixteenth-century Spanish poet and mystic St. John of the Cross to describe a period of desolation in spiritual development. A person in this state has ceased to identify the self with the material world of the senses, but has yet to attain the blissful expansion of the self into union with God; he is alone, between two worlds, with nothing. The silence into which the speaker of "I, I, I" falls is a recognition that the self has passed into a state beyond words; his rigidity suggests the rigid fear of death. The *dark night of the soul* generally precedes a surge in spiritual development and the discovery of a greater meaning to life. Carruth does not explicitly say whether this occurs to the boy speaker. However, the episode clearly marks a milestone in his development, as afterwards, he no longer needs the mirrors that showed him the nature of the self. He knows that the small self is an illusion that he can leave behind, but he does not yet know the reality that lies beyond.

Source: Claire Robinson, Critical Essay on "I, I, I," in *Poetry for Students*, Thomson Gale, 2007.

Thomson Gale

In the following essay, the critic gives a critical analysis of Carruth's work.

"Now and then a poet comes along whose work ranges across wide and diverse territories of form, attitude, and emotion—yet with the necessary intelligence that belies a deep, lifelong engagement with tradition—so that variance never seems mere experimentation or digression, but improvisation," wrote *Midwest Quarterly* contributor Matthew Miller. "Hayden Carruth is such an artist."

The [National Book Award] won by Carruth in 1996 for his collection *Scrambled Eggs and Whiskey* provided a grace note for a long academic and literary career that has seen the author become known as an proponent of twentieth-century modernism. Though recognized primarily as a critic and editor, Carruth is also, according to the *Virginia Quarterly Review*, "a poet who has never received the wide acclaim his work deserves and who is certainly one of the most important poets working in this country today.... [He is] technically skilled, lively, never less than

> CHARACTERIZED BY A CALM, TIGHTLY CONTROLLED, AND RELATIVELY 'PLAIN' LANGUAGE THAT BELIES THE INTENSITY OF FEELING BEHIND THE WORDS, CARRUTH'S POETRY ELICITS PRAISE FROM THOSE WHO ADMIRE ITS WIDE VARIETY OF VERSE FORMS AND CRITICISM FROM THOSE WHO FIND ITS PRECISION AND RESTRAINT TOO IMPERSONAL AND ACADEMIC."

completely honest, and as profound and deeply moving as one could ask." Characterized by a calm, tightly controlled, and relatively "plain" language that belies the intensity of feeling behind the words, Carruth's poetry elicits praise from those who admire its wide variety of verse forms and criticism from those who find its precision and restraint too impersonal and academic.

Commenting in his book *Babel to Byzantium*, James Dickey speculated that these opposing views of Carruth's work may result from the occasionally uneven quality of his poetry. In a discussion of *The Crow and the Heart*, for example, Dickey noted "a carefulness which bursts, once or twice or three times, into a kind of frenzied eloquence, a near-hysteria, and in these frightening places sloughing off a set of mannerisms which in the rest of the book seems determined to reduce Carruth to the level of a thousand other poets. . . . [He] is one of the poets (perhaps all poets are some of these poets) who write their best, pushing past limit after limit, only in the grip of recalling some overpowering experience. When he does not have such a subject at hand, Carruth amuses himself by being playfully skillful with internal rhyme, inventing bizarre Sitwellian images, being witty and professionally sharp."

American Poetry Review critic Geoffrey Gardner, who characterized Carruth as "a poet who has always chosen to make his stand just aside from any of the presently conflicting mainstreams," said that such linguistic playfulness is typical of the poet's early work. He attributes it to Carruth's struggle "to restore equilibrium to the soul [and] clarity to vision, through a passionate command of language," a struggle that gives much of his poetry "a Lear-like words-against-the-storm quality." Continued Gardner: "I won't be the first to say Carruth's early work is cumbered by archaisms, forced inversions, sometimes futile extravagances of vocabulary and a tendency of images and metaphors to reify into a top heavy symbolism. . . . But the courage of [his] poems can't be faulted. From the earliest and against great odds, Carruth made many attempts at many kinds of poems, many forms, contending qualities of diction and texture. . . . If the struggle of contending voices and attitudes often ends in poems that don't quite succeed, it remains that the struggle itself is moving for its truthfulness and intensity. . . . Carruth uniformly refuses to glorify his crazies. They are pain and pain alone. What glory there is—and there are sparks of it everywhere through these early poems—he keeps for the regenerative stirrings against the storm of pain and isolation."

In his essay, Miller looked at one major influence on Carruth's poetry. "Carruth's relationship to jazz music has been lifelong," he noted, "and it has expressed itself on many different levels in his work." Carruth produced an essay, "Influences: The Formal Idea of Jazz," in which he described his personal feelings about the musical genre. He did read the prominent poets Ben Johnson, William Yeats, and Ezra Pound, but added that "the real question is not by whom I was influenced, but how." To Miller, Carruth's early grounding in traditional poetic forms prepared him to "improvise" later on, much like the way jazz musicians often study classical music early in their training: "The discipline must precede the rejection of discipline."

In Carruth's poetry, that means using an external, fixed poetic structure upon which to launch improvisation. But even when he works in a spontaneous, "jazz" mode, his "poetic improvisation does not mean the abandonment of form or rhyme," declared Miller, "nor does it limit itself to any particular attitude or emotion. . . . What improvisation ultimately amounts to is structure becoming a function of feeling, whatever that feeling may be." Miller pointed to *Brothers, I Loved You All* as a prime example of Carruth in his spontaneous prime.

Like many poets, Carruth also turns to personal experience for inspiration; however, with the possible exception of *The Bloomingdale*

Papers (a long poetic sequence Carruth wrote in the 1950s while confined to a mental hospital for treatment of alcoholism and a nervous breakdown), he does not indulge in the self-obsessed meditations common among some of his peers. Instead, Carruth turns outward, exploring such "universal opposites" as madness (or so-called madness) and sanity or chaos and order. He then tries to balance the negative images—war, loneliness, the destruction of the environment, sadness—with mostly nature-related positive images and activities that communicate a sense of stability—the cycle of the seasons, performing manual labor, contemplating the night sky, observing the serenity of plant and animal life. But, as Gardner pointed out, "Carruth is not in the least tempted to sentimentality about country life. . . . [He recognizes] that it can be a life of value and nobility in the midst of difficult facts and chaos." Nor is he "abstractly philosophical or cold," according to the critic. "On the contrary," Gardner stated, "[his poems] are all poems about very daily affairs: things seen and heard, the loneliness of missing friends absent or dead, the alternations of love for and estrangement from those present, the experiences of a man frequently alone with the non-human which all too often bears the damaging marks of careless human intrusion." Furthermore, he said, "Carruth comes to the politics of all this with a vengeance. . . . [His poems] all bear strong public witness against the wastes and shames of our culture that are destroying human value with a will in a world where values are already hard enough to maintain, in a universe where they are always difficult to discover. Carruth does not express much anger in [his] poems. Yet one feels that an enormous energy of rage has forced them to be."

Concluded Alastair Reed in the *Saturday Review*: "[Carruth's] poems have a sureness to them, a flair and variety. . . . Yet, in their dedication to finding an equilibrium in an alien and often cruel landscape, Vermont, where the poet has dug himself in, they reflect the moods and struggles of a man never at rest. . . . His work teems with the struggle to live and to make sense, and his poems carve out a kind of grace for us."

In the 1990s, the appearance of anthologies and collections of Carruth's verse and prose allowed critics to assess his career as a whole. In reviewing *Collected Shorter Poems*, which appeared in 1992, *Poetry* contributor David

Barber called attention to the rich diversity of the poet's oeuvre: "Hayden Carruth is vast; he contains multitudes. Of the august order of American poets born in the Twenties, he is undoubtedly the most difficult to reconcile to the convenient branches of classification and affiliation, odd man out in any tidy scheme of influence and descent." Somewhat deceptively titled, *Collected Shorter Poems*, which won the 1992 National Book Critics' Circle Award, is not a comprehensive volume but is comprised of selections from thirteen of Carruth's previously published volumes, together with many poems appearing for the first time. Writing in the *Nation*, Ted Solotaroff found the volume to be a welcome opportunity for giving a "full hearing" to "a poet as exacting and undervalued as Carruth generally has been." Solotaroff highlighted two characteristics typifying Carruth's poetic achievement. First, he describes him as a "poet's poet, a virtuoso of form from the sonnet to free verse, from medieval metrics to jazz ones." Secondly, Solotaroff drew attention to the moral seriousness of Carruth's work as a critic of contemporary poetry, claiming that the poet "has also been, to my mind, the most catholic, reliable and socially relevant critic of poetry we have had in an age of burgeoning tendencies, collapsing standards and a general withdrawal of poets from the public to the private sector of consciousness."

The 1993 volume *Collected Longer Poems* received similar praise from many critics, who felt that this collection contained much of the poet's best work. Anthony Robbins, commenting in *American Book Review*, characterized Carruth's poetry as being "grounded in the traditions of Romance, in *entre-les-guerres* modernism revised in light of mid-century existentialism, and in his own personal forms of nonviolent anarchism." Both Robbins and *Bloomsbury Review* contributor Shaun T. Griffin called attention to the importance of the volume's opening selection, "The Asylum," which details the poet's experiences of being hospitalized for a breakdown. Griffin judges these "among the most honest and harrowing in the volume," maintaining that "they ring with the compelling voice of despair; the wind floats through them, and the reader finds himself staring at the November landscape, leafless, dark, and dormant."

Carruth's prose discussions of poets and poetry were anthologized in the 1995 volume *Selected Essays and Reviews*. Spanning thirty years of his critical writing, this collection was enthusiastically received by critics, who singled out for particular praise the essays on Alexander Pope, Edwin Muir, and Paul Goodman. In the following year, Carruth published *Scrambled Eggs and Whiskey: Poems 1991-1995*, a volume that centers on meditations of such themes as politics, history, aging, nostalgia, guilt, and love, a book that would garner [for Carruth] the National Book Award in 1996. Another collection, *Doctor Jazz: Poems, 1996-2000*, was written as Carruth approached his ninth decade and includes a fifteen-page elegy to the author's daughter, Martha, who died in her forties of cancer. That poem in particular "refuses to release us until its final syllable," said *Library Journal* reviewer Fred Muratori.

In 1998 Carruth turned to a different form of self-narrative with *Reluctantly: Autobiographical Essays*. These essays—the words of a self-described "old man in his cave of darkness, regretting his arthritis and impotence and failing imagination"—speak frankly of his often troubled life, including treatment for depression, debilitating phobias, and a nearly successful suicide attempt. Peter Szatmary, writing in *Biblio*, found the "fractured" nature of Carruth's life reflected in his prose: "At its best, [*Reluctantly*] isolates idiosyncratic clarity. At its worst it betrays arbitrary self-indulgence." In a similar vein, "fragmentary" was the word used by Ray Olson of *Booklist* to describe the memoir, though Olsen also characterized the book as a "powerful autobiography." A *Publishers Weekly* critic had a similar impression, saying the *Reluctantly* shows that "although life is messy and unpredictable, it is possible to survive, to write well and to salvage from the wreckage a redemptive dignity."

Carruth once told *CA:* "I have a close but at the same time uncomfortable relationship with the natural world. I've always been most at home in the country probably because I was raised in the country as a boy, and I know something about farming and woodcutting and all the other things that country people know about. That kind of work has been important to me in my personal life and in my writing too. I believe in the values of manual labor and labor that is connected with the earth in some way. But I'm not simply a nature poet. In fact, I consider myself and I consider the whole human race fundamentally alien. By evolving into a state of self-consciousness, we have separated ourselves from the other animals and the plants and from the very earth itself, from the whole universe. So there's a kind of fear and terror involved in living close to nature. My poems, I think, exist in a state of tension between the love of natural beauty and the fear of natural meaninglessness or absurdity.

"I think there are many reasons for poets and artists in general to be depressed these days. . . . They have to do with a lot . . . [of] things that are going on in our civilization. They have to do with the whole evolution of the sociology of literature during the last fifty years. Things have changed; they've turned completely around. I don't know if I can say it briefly but I'll try. When I was young and starting to write poetry seriously and to investigate the resources of modern poetry, as we called it then, we still felt beleaguered; modern poetry was still considered outrageous by most of the people in the publishing business and in the reading audience at large. We still spoke in terms of the true artists and the philistines. We felt that if we could get enough people to read T. S. Eliot and Wallace Stevens and e. e. cummings and William Carlos Williams and other great poets of that period, then something good would happen in American civilization. We felt a genuine vocation, a calling, to try and make this happen. And we succeeded. Today thousands of people are going to colleges and attending workshops and taking courses in twentieth-century literature. Eliot and Stevens are very well known, very well read; and American civilization has sunk steadily, progressively, further and further down until most of the sensible people are in a state of despair. It's pretty obvious that good writing doesn't really have very much impact on social events or national events of any kind. We hope that it has individual impact, that readers here and there are made better in some way by reading our work. But it's a hope; we have no proof."

Source: Thomson Gale, "Hayden Carruth," in *Contemporary Authors Online*, Thomson Gale, 2004.

Eric Murphy Selinger

In the following excerpt, Selinger refers to Carruth's divided nature as a poet: there is the self that is tough and philosophical and views poetry as pointless, and the self (to borrow the words from a Carruth poem, the "Small Floy Floy") that is subtler, more tender, more charming, and appreciative of the power of love and music to make something beautiful out of nothing.

Carruth dedicates his first-rate new collection, *Scrambled Eggs & Whiskey,* to his wife, the woman who "lives with me / and is my love." The echo of Christopher Marlowe's "The Passionate Shepherd to his Love" is unusually overt. But this is a book that keeps calling to mind the shepherd's promise to give his darling "beds of roses / And a thousand fragrant posies," even if his modern incarnation is a little the worse for wear. "Let's make a bouquet of lilac / For our old bedside table," one poem proposes; "Then the fragrance in the night / Will make me form-i-dable." The jokey forced rhyme suits Carruth's engaging self-portrait. But it also hints at Flatfoot Floogie facts other pieces make clear. This is a lover, after all, who must visit "the banker, the broker, those strange / people, to talk about unit trusts, / annuities, CDs, IRAs, trying / to leave you whatever I can after / I die" ("Testament"). As Sir Walter Raleigh wrote in his answer to Marlowe, "The Nymph's Reply to the Shepherd," the pleasures of both love and verse will "soon break, soon wither, soon [be] forgotten." This husband and wife, both poets, know that source too.

Near the end of *Scrambled Eggs & Whiskey,* Carruth's wife challenges him to write "a poem that will prepare me for your death." He doesn't exactly jump at the invitation. ("A jay slanted down to the feeder and looked at me behind my glass and squawked. / Prepare, prepare." The echo of Frost's "Provide, Provide!" sets him off as much as the nagging reminder. "F—— you, I said, come back tomorrow.") He knows, after all, how easily any such poem can slip into mere platitude or sob. In a way, though, the book as a whole is his answer. Some poems call quits to old quarrels, whether with his parents ("Flying into St. Louis") or with Frost ("February Morning"). Others take up the poet's longstanding political concerns. "This is the summer of war in Bosnia," one poem begins; "A few summers ago the war was somewhere else." From a man who's written about (and against) wars in Abyssinia, Algeria, Korea, and Viet Nam, such weariness is understandable. And it's no wonder he slips into the self-irony of *A Summer with Tu Fu,* where the two poets are simply "two old guys" who are "confronting their final / futility after years of futile awkwardness / in the world of doing." (The hooting long "oo" s are a nice touch, and almost carry the dead weight of that second "futile.") But Carruth's radicalism has survived those blues; and one believes his confession that the thought of "everyone comfortable and warm / *The great pain assuaged* " is, for him at least, "a moment / of the most shining and singular sensual gratification" ("Ecstasy").

As I read *Scrambled Eggs*, I kept thinking of my initially enthusiastic, then wary, more critical response to *Brothers, I Loved You All*. Was I moved by the ache and consolation of "The Camps" or by the refugee scenes it described? By the verse he writes for his adult daughter "in the crisis of forever inadequately medicated / pain," or by the simple fact that she has cancer? The Small Floy Floy of sentimentality is at once "the worst and best" of our failures, Carruth insists, refusing to throw his poems off course to avoid it. And, I'll confess, I found myself won over, not least by the graceful composition of the volume, which starts with the poet alone, about to take some sleeping pills and wine and slip off to bed, only to bring him back as a lover and a fighter and a father and a writer, as casual as you please. ("What is this poem," he wonders for a moment in "Isabel's Garden, May 14," "—is it / necessity or an exercise? I am too old / to think about this any more," he decides.) A closer look at his most apparently off-the-cuff, heart-on-sleeve verses also reminded me, however, of how long he's been at this "grubbing art." Even when he slips off key he plays with the grace of Pee Wee Russell, the clarinetist who, as Carruth writes elsewhere, once "picked up / his horn and blew / a mistake so lovely" that tears came to a smartass critic's eye. Consider the last poem, the collection's title piece and a new addition to the poet's fine body of verses on jazz:

> Scrambled eggs and whiskey
> in the false-dawn light. Chicago,
> a sweet town, bleak, God knows,
> but sweet. Sometimes. And
> weren't we fine tonight?
> When Hank set up that limping
> treble roll behind me
> my horn just growled and I
> thought my heart would burst.
> And Brad M. pressing with the
> soft stick, and Joe-Anne
> singing low. Here we are now

> in the White Tower, leaning
> on one another, too tired
> to go home. But don't say a word,
> don't tell a soul, they wouldn't
> understand, they couldn't, never
> in a million years, how fine,
> how magnificent we were
> in that old club tonight.

There's an easy, after-hours lilt to those first lines, as "bleak, God knows" winks a rhyme at "Chicago" and the twin long "ee" s of "sweet" and "bleak" ask the wallflower final syllable of "whiskey" for a dance. And you can trace the echoes all the way through, as the breathy "e" of "Eggs" comes back in "set" or the "i" of "whis-" in the "limping / treble roll." When Carruth turns that "roll" to "growled," in line eight, hitting the new sound hard, the poem grins. There's even a nod to "Paragraphs" in the phallic humor: the way he uses his wife the singer's name to pivot from Brad's "soft stick" to a scene in the "White Tower," ending with a memory of "that old club" where they swung the blues. Even clichés like "don't tell a soul" or "never / in a million years" find a home in this heady, friendly, artful interplay.

Is the performance really "magnificent?" That's the whiskey talking, or the scrambled eggs. But in this poem and much of this new collection—hell, throughout his long career, particularly when he writes of jazz and love—Carruth has earned the right to call himself "So / good, so good." And sometimes, with the Floogie pressing, and the Floy Floy swinging low, he's done better than that. He's been *fine*.

Source: Eric Murphy Selinger, "The Importance of a Small Floy Floy," in *Parnassus: Poetry in Review*, Vol. 22, Nos. 1–2, Spring–Summer 1997, pp. 277–79.

Roy Scheele

In the following essay interview, Carruth evaluates modernism and postmodernism, discusses who influences him, talks about Ezra Pound, his lifelong interest in jazz, his fondness of Vermonters, and gives a brief autobiography.

It is billed as "an evening with Hayden Carruth," and the audience gathering in the wood-paneled lounge on the University of Nebraska at Lincoln campus buzzes with excitement as it awaits the arrival of the well-known poet and editor of *The Voice That Is Great Within Us* (Bantam, 1970). Literary figures associated with the university—Willa Cather, Loren

> **OUR OWN HISTORY, HE SAYS, IS BUILT ON THE BONES OF OUR NATIVE PEOPLES. 'IF YOU CAN'T BE BOTHERED TO WRITE ABOUT THINGS LIKE THAT,' HE ALMOST SHOUTS, 'YOU CAN'T BE BOTHERED TO WRITE ABOUT ANYTHING!'"**

Eiseley, and Mari Sandoz prominent among them—look on, seemingly bemused, from their photographs along one wall. Then, at one end of that row of photographs, a door opens, and Carruth comes in. Suddenly the room is still.

As he is introduced the poet looks bemused himself. Introduction over, he leans forward slightly, holding himself in readiness for the first question. It comes from a student, his long hair in a ponytail, who asks for an evaluation of modernism/postmodernism. Carruth gives a very succinct summary of modernist literature, says that as a movement it is dead, though its landmark achievements—the works of Joyce, Eliot, et al.—live on. He suggests that young poets today should be thinking of what poetry will be like in the 21st century. "I have no idea," he says, "but I know it will be very different from what we have had, and from what we have right now."

Someone asks about early influences. Shakespeare and Mother Goose, he replies, and the audience titters, but he is serious; the Mother Goose rhymes, he notes, inculcate in young readers and listeners a sense of the syncopated line, and he recommends to the audience Theodore Roethke's essay on the Mother Goose poems ("Some Remarks on Rhythm," *On the Poet and His Craft: Selected Prose of Theodore Roethke,* University of Washington Press, 1965). Responding to a question about the major themes in his poetry, he says, "My poetry is about the spiritual dimension of human experience." When asked about Eastern influences on the poems in *Tell Me Again How the White Heron Rises and Flies Across the Nacreous River at Twilight Toward the Distant Islands* (New Directions, 1989), he speaks of his admiration for the classical Chinese poets and refers to them as part of "The Grand

Community," a phrase of poet Paul Goodman's that he uses to indicate the great writers of the past. It is important to him, he says, to feel connected to such literary ancestors as Li Po, Euripides, Herodotus, and Emily Dickinson.

Toward the end of the hour-long session, someone in the audience wants to know Carruth's views on Ezra Pound's anti-Semitism: should Pound's virulent prejudice weigh against his work? Carruth replies that every reader has to decide that for himself. So far as he is concerned, Pound's prejudice and political judgment are things to be wished away, but they do not negate Pound's worth as an innovator and stylist. He follows this up by saying that he feels young writers should be aware of prejudice and injustice both in general and in the world immediately around them. He tells of the systematic slaughter of Indians in Nova Scotia, where the British offered a bounty of £20 for each Indian scalp—man, woman, or child's—and how this resulted in the extermination of the native population. Our own history, he says, is built on the bones of our native peoples. "If you can't be bothered to write about things like that," he almost shouts, "you can't be bothered to write about anything!" Abruptly he thanks the audience and rises, leaving us as he found us—in silence. After a moment we recover ourselves and begin to clap, but he is already at the door; and our applause follows him down the hallway like a patter of rain.

Walking across campus to my car, under a cold, star-bright February sky, I think of Carruth's honesty and intensity. Earlier he had said that every good writer he has known has also been a good person, and it is clearly important to him to be as good a person as he can be; his writing is an extension of that conviction. What I have gleaned from the evening is a first-hand impression of the man himself and a better sense of how to read his poems. When I get home I pick up my copy of *Collected Shorter Poems* (Copper Canyon Press, 1992) and begin to reread.

I see him again the next day. He has come to Doane College in Crete, Nebraska, for lunch and a late afternoon reading. He wears a gray herring-bone tweed jacket, a checked shirt with open black collar, and tan slacks. Though initially nervous, in a few moments he is chatting amiably with the small group of students and faculty that has gathered in a private dining room. He sips at a cup of coffee as he reminisces and responds to questions.

We talk about his fondness for cryptograms, stemming from his service as a cryptographer in Europe in World War II, then talk of his long stint—from the 1950s through the 1970s—as a freelance reviewer and editor. He calls this his "hack work," though anyone familiar with Carruth's reviews knows what an astute and even-handed critic he has been. Looking back on this period, when he and his family lived primarily on the small income from his reviewing and editing, he marvels at having survived such hand-to-mouth conditions, but it was exhilarating too, he says, and good for his poetry. At the time he was living in the country in northern Vermont, and his days were occupied with work around the farm; in the evening he would read for his reviewing assignments and then go out to the shed near the house and write the reviews. Only when he had all other obligations taken care of would he allow himself to begin work on a poem, often at three or four in the morning. He remembers frequent all-night sessions that concluded with a walk down to the mailbox to post a manuscript just as the sun was coming up. He had to read so much on assignment in those days, he says, that he hardly reads anything for pleasure anymore.

Carruth has an impish sense of humor and something of the iconoclast about him, and now, as we discuss his teaching at Syracuse University in the 1980s, he berates, in the presence of academics, the whole idea of requiring research papers. We should not be surprised to get back tentative or plagiarized papers, he says, for we are fostering an entirely unnatural situation in which the student is being asked to submit the product of his or her own forming sensibility to the judgment of an expert in the subject. It is an exercise in futility, he feels, and he says that he has never read a student research paper that wasn't stilted as a result. Instead, he suggests, teachers should be assigning nothing but personal essays. I notice the students' eyes light up at this.

When he has eaten and had a smoke I sit down with him in a large quiet room nearby, and we make small talk as I fiddle with a lapel mike, which I decide, for comfort's sake, to place on the table in front of him instead of clipping to his jacket. I begin by asking him about his days as an undergraduate at the University of North Carolina (UNC).

Lawrence Ferlinghetti was at UNC with Carruth, "But," he says, "I don't recall that we ever met"; so was Theodore Weiss. The people he knew well were, like Carruth himself, interested in journalism: among his friends were Louis Harris, the pollster, and Richard Adler, author of *Pajama Game* and other Broadway musicals. Carruth worked on the college daily and thought at one time that he would become a newspaperman, but he discovered that he was too shy to do a proper interview or go out and gather the news. He feels that he was a good editor and columnist, however, and he thrived on the pressure of a deadline. "I liked the idea of writing something in the afternoon and then seeing people read it the next morning at breakfast. That was exciting to me."

After the war, when Carruth was a graduate student at the University of Chicago, Robert Hutchins (whom he calls "the greatest university administrator ever—at least since Erasmus") was chancellor, the faculty included scholars of worldwide reputation such as Jacques Maritain, and Saul Bellow and Paul Goodman were fellow students. Those years were pivotal to Carruth's development as a poet. He says that he had never even heard of T. S. Eliot before arriving in Chicago, but "As soon as I got into the bookshops along 57th Street I was reading Eliot and Williams and Stevens and all the rest of them just as avidly as I could, and that's when I became truly serious about my own poetry."

In 1949 Carruth became editor of *Poetry,* a position that he occupied for two years and found enormously enjoyable. "I think the biggest literary boost in a way that I ever got was sitting in the editor's chair, which was in a very small room with a very old battered desk, and the walls all around behind me and up above my head just filled with back issues. The magazine had been going since 1912. And I could pluck one of those issues down and blow the dust off it and there would be a poem by, say, Wallace Stevens. What more could you want?"

While discussing Carruth's work, I discover his great affection for the up-country Vermonters he has written about in his monologues and narrative poems. We talk about the humor in his poems, often based on the laconic and sometimes exaggerative qualities characteristic of New England speech. As one widely read in

19th-century American dialect literature, he relishes his characters' semi-literate speech and their propensity to tell stories on themselves as a means of handling disappointment and hardship. He admires their capacity for hard work, the physical labor that is at the heart of life in the country, the rural impetus toward interpersonal relationship and community. Many of the poems from the years Carruth spent in Vermont deal with labor, either as focus or backdrop. In the meditative "Essay on Love," for example, the speaker expresses his feelings for "my best friend, Rose Marie" by cutting and stacking firewood for her and, near the end of the poem, thinks of labor as "the only meaning."

Carruth writes in meter, free verse, and syllabics with equal facility, a fact which can be partly accounted for by his lifelong interest in jazz. He constantly entertains the possibilities of improvisation in his poems, and I ask him whether the syllabic quatrains of "Essay on Love" derive from this impulse. Yes, he says, they probably do. We get to talking about the many good modern poets whose works are on the verge of being forgotten, and Carruth observes that this has doubtless always been true; he mentions Winfield Townley Scott and Conrad Aiken as poets who are seldom read anymore. He has a particular admiration for Aiken and rates his work as highly as Pound's. And Aiken's anthology *Twentieth-Century American Poetry* (Modern Library, revised edition, 1963), Carruth tells me, served as his model in compiling his own highly successful anthology, *The Voice That Is Great Within Us*.

Late that afternoon, Carruth and I are sitting in the front row at the bottom of the small tiered auditorium at Doane, an audience of perhaps 100 at our backs, waiting out the last few minutes before I introduce him. By now his slight nervousness has left him. I recall that the first time he was scheduled to give a reading, he became so nervous he ran out on his audience before he had said a word. As we talk about various things I am wondering how his reading in person will compare with his masterful performance on the cassette collection. *Eternity Blues* (Watershed Foundation, 1986).

It was this recording that drew me to a closer reading of Carruth's work. It gave me my first inkling of how his poems sound to *him*, and I heard there, in a way I had not, except intermittently, in my earlier desultory reading, his quiet

power and range of subject matter. As the poems are read, one's impression of mastery grows: from "The Ravine," the meditation on a landscape with which the tape begins, to the jaunty "November Jeans Song," and what may be the best of Carruth's monologues, "Regarding Chainsaws," on through the pure Yankee humor of "Crow's Mark," and the austere lyricism of "The Oldest Killed Lake in North America," to "The Impossible Indispensability of the Ars Poetica," the amazing love lyric with which the recording ends. And when the listener turns reader, the poems are as shimmering and finally realized on the page as they are on the tape.

When I have introduced him he steps to the lectern and graciously thanks me. He has noticed me playing with the sound system and gauged its tendency to produce feedback; now, leaning a little to his right, away from the microphone, to compensate, he begins with "Regarding Chainsaws." I can hardly believe my ears: his live performance is nearly as good as the recording. Everyone laughs at the predicament of Old Stan, who has driven his Powerwagon through the back of the barn and into the manure pit, then howls when his wife asks. "Stan, what's got into you?" and Stan replies, "Missus.../ain't nothing got into me. Can't you see?/It's me that's got into this here pile of shit." From this point on the audience is his.

He reads several more poems from the tape ("Crow's Mark," "The Cows at Night") interspersed among twenty-some lesser known poems. One of these "I Tell You for Several Years of My Madness I Heard the Voice of Lilith Singing in the Trees of Chicago," alludes, if only through its title, to Carruth's nervous breakdown and hospitalization in the mid-1950s. Another, "Emergency Haying," is a monologue in unrhymed tercets whose range of reference and tone is all the more impressive for the poem's being so firmly rooted in an act of labor. He reads a number of haiku and several sonnets, including the witty "Well, she told me I had an aura," and concludes with "None," the next-to-last poem in *Collected Shorter Poems*, a meditation on Greek and Navajo conceptions of death and the afterlife. When he is finished reading there is a moment of great stillness, and then thunderous applause.

I shake his hand, thank him, and stand by as several people come down front to talk to him and ask him to inscribe copies of his books. After a while, engaged in conversation with a colleague, I notice that Carruth is no longer there. He is seated in the last row of the sloping hall, near the exit, examining a tin whistle that a woman has drawn from her tote bag. In a moment he is playing an Irish air on the instrument; the last of the hangers-on all turn to watch and listen. When he is done he hands the whistle back to the woman, and I hear him thank her. He has made, for the few of us still there, this parting gesture, a kind of exclamation point to the afternoon he has spent with us, a time during which he has offered, again and again, without stint, the gift of himself.

Source: Roy Scheele, "Hayden Carruth: The Gift of Self," in *Poets & Writers*, Vol. 24, No. 3, May–June 1996, pp. 45–49.

David W. Landrey

In the following essay, Landrey gives a critical analysis of Carruth's work.

Hayden Carruth first published a poem in 1946, and his poetry, essays, and anthologies now approach forty volumes with no sign of abatement. He has, moreover, by his own estimate written several thousand pieces for newspapers, magazines, and anthologies. He is often called a poet's poet, and his aid to and promotion of others has been remarkable. His eclectic anthology, *The Voice That Is Great Within Us* (1970), a survey of American poetry from Robert Frost to its date of publication, has been widely used and continues to be highly regarded. Carruth's influence and importance have grown markedly in the last decade, especially with the publications of his historical/mythical epic, *The Sleeping Beauty* (1982); *Collected Shorter Poems* (1992), which won the National Book Critics Circle Award in 1993; and *Collected Longer Poems* (1994). Furthermore, his essays and reviews, now collected in four volumes, including *Suicides and Fazzers* (1992), constitute a major overview of the craft of American poetry since World War II.

Carruth has been an editor of *Poetry* (1949-1950), associate editor at the University of Chicago Press (1950-1952), the project administrator for Intercultural Publications of the Ford Foundation (1952-1954), the poetry editor of *Harper's* magazine (1977-1981), and advisory editor for *The Hudson Review* (1970-present). His many prizes, grants, and honors include the University of Chicago's Harriet Monroe award

"AGAINST THE UBIQUITOUS DECAY OF LIFE CARRUTH IN HIS MOST RECENT VERSE AND ESSAYS TAKES HIS STAND MAINLY IN TWO ALTERNATIVES: LOVE AND CYNICISM."

(1960), Guggenheim Fellowships in 1965 and 1979, National Endowment for the Arts fellowships in 1968 and 1974, the Shelley Prize of the Poetry Society of America (1979), Senior Fellow of the National Endowment for the Arts (1988), and the Ruth Lilly Poetry Prize (1990). Carruth is a member of American P.E.N., the Poetry Society of America, and the Academy of American Poets.

Born in Waterbury, Connecticut, Carruth's primary formative experience was of small-town and country life. He reports in an interview with David Weiss in *In the Act: Essays on the Poetry of Hayden Carruth* (1990) that his father, Gorton Veeder Garruth, a newspaperman, editor, and writer of verse, once told him, "Don't ever take any job that isn't a service to the community." Carruth has heeded this advice. His mother, for whom he wrote a long elegy in 1985, was Margery Barrow Carruth. His education includes a B.A. in journalism from the University of North Carolina (1942) and an M.A. in English from the University of Chicago (1948). Before his emergence on the literary scene, he served two years in Europe during World War II as a member of the Army Air Corps.

Carruth has been married four times, the first three ending in divorce. He married Sara Anderson on 14 March 1943. He has a daughter by that marriage, Martha Hamilton. He married Eleanore Ray on 29 November 1952. His third marriage, to Rose Marie Dorn on 28 October 1961, produced his son, David Barrow, whom he calls "the Bo." The family lived for eighteen years in Johnson, Vermont, a period Carruth in *Suicides and Fazzers* recalls "afforded me the opportunity to put everything together, the land and seasons, the people, my family, my work, my evolving sense of survival (for when I'd been in the hospital the doctors had told me I'd never again have anything like a normal life), in one tightly integrated imaginative structure. The results were my poems, for what they're worth, and in my life a very gradual but perceptible triumph over the internal snarls and screwups that had crippled me from childhood on." Carruth married poet Joe-Anne McLaughlin on 29 December 1989. The couple resides in Munnsville, New York.

Although Carruth has said that he abhors repetition and has always employed a diversity of forms, some of his own invention, he has almost methodically examined and reexamined a cluster of themes and concerns. In "Influences: The Formal Idea of Jazz," an essay collected in *Sitting In: Selected Writings on Jazz, Blues, and Related Topics* (1993), Carruth writes that having poetry rather than music as his articulation of his lifelong absorption in jazz may account, "in part for the sorrow that appears to emanate from the center of my poems. . . . Poetry for me was, and is, second-best to jazz." Carruth's sorrow also has other powerful roots. He writes of the decline of the nation, especially of family farming, of the distraught lives of ordinary people, and of the destructive history of power politics; in the process, he often proclaims himself a "philosophical anarchist." To convey the starkness of these issues he recurs to such aspects of hard natural beauty as the stone, winter, birds, and trees as well as to the idea of "nothing," his own continuing struggle with psychological problems, and the voices of the men and women of his milieu. An abiding interest in philosophy, especially existentialism, underpins Carruth's thought. He has special interests in Søren Kierkegaard, Arthur Schopenhauer, Jean-Paul Sartre, Martin Heidegger, Immanuel Kant, and Albert Camus. Although he says in *Suicides and Jazzers*, writing with passion of his own attempted suicide in 1988, that "every artist of the second half of the twentieth century knows that his or her working life is in at least one sense a resounding defeat," he maintains an elemental love of life.

In November 1953, after six years in Chicago, followed by his first divorce and second marriage, Carruth entered Bloomingdale psychiatric hospital in White Plains, New York, where he remained for fifteen months. He has often said that the time there did not help and may have made matters worse, but it clearly became a central issue in his early poetry and has never quite disappeared from his work.

Part of his treatment consisted of his writing about the experience between November 1953 and January 1954, an effort that resulted in *The Bloomingdale Papers*, a volume not published until 1975 when his friend, the artist Albert Christ-Janer, persuaded Carruth to let the University of Georgia Press publish it. Despite the depth of his personal despair, Carruth was sensitive to the problems of his fellow inmates and to the madness of the larger world. "I think of it as a paradigm of the general quality of life in this country during the 1950s," he says in his preface, "Explanation and Apology, Twenty Years After." Taking "exile as the experience *par excellence* of the mid-twentieth century," Carruth writes:

> The bitcheries of Madison Avenue
> Where I lost my mind, where pigs that
>   learned to read
> Talk money wise around the urn of love; . . .
> The catalogue of our misfortunes, oh
> How long it is, so have the false men
>   prospered!

While he had not been able to function in the face of the "false men," he ends the book with a plea for his daughter:

> That some small wisdom always may endure
> Amidst your weariness; that lovers may
> Be kind to you; that beauty may arouse
> You; that the crazy house
> May never, never be your home: I pray.

After emerging from the hospital Carruth settled in New England, where for the next twenty-four years he spliced together a bare living. From 1955 to 1960 he lived a secluded life in his parents' house in Pleasantville, New York. From 1960 to 1962 he lived in Norfolk, Connecticut, in a place provided by poet and publisher James Laughlin, who also provided Carruth with many writing and editorial tasks. (Carruth's friendship with Laughlin has been an enduring one. In 1994 Carruth wrote a warmly appreciative introduction to Laughlin's *Collected Poems*.) Besides working the land, the insomniac Carruth did reviews, ghostwriting, and editing at all hours. He fitted writing his own poems into spare moments.

The products of these years were his first three published volumes and the creation of his special form, the paragraph. In 1990 he explained that his invention of this fifteen-line form was influenced by a sonnet of Paul Goodman . . . in which he displaced the final couplet and put it in the middle after the octet. . . . So when I invented the paragraph I put a rhymed couplet in the middle, a tetrameter couplet, and in a way the whole history of what I did with the paragraph was to get around that terrible barrier, that terrible problem I'd given myself, because having a rhymed couplet in the middle tends to break up the poem terribly and I had to find ways to flow through that.

Carruth's first collection, *The Crow and the Heart, 1946-1959* (1959), includes poems written before, during, and after his Bloomingdale stay. The most important poem is the thirteen-part "Asylum," written in 1957 and later revised as the first section of *For You* (1970), his first effort using the paragraph form. Gaining perspective on his experience at Bloomingdale and musing on its relationship to the century's problems, Carruth plays on the meanings of *asylum*. He notes that "The nation was asylum when we came" and asks "is not the whole earth / Asylum? Is mankind / In refuge?" In the penultimate section, he asserts that "ultimately asylum is the soul"; but he ends the poem on a cryptic note: "Here am I—drowned, living, loving, and insane."

Journey to a Known Place (1961), written in 1959, takes a large step away from what Carruth calls in the introduction to *The Bloomingdale Papers* his "spirit caged and struggling." The four-part poem depicts a Dantean movement of the spirit through the primal elements, cast as a journey across a frozen land, a descent to the depths of the sea, an awakening on shore, and a soaring guided by an eagle and its song. The poem concludes, "Aspiring now in sun's cascading element,"

we make
Each in his only ascertainable center,
The world of realization, the suffered reality,
Through which comes understanding.

The understanding attained, however, is not presented as a permanent haven.

The Norfolk Poems, 1 June to 1 September 1961 (1962) completes Carruth's Connecticut period. In this third collection he begins to examine his neighbors, to grapple with their fading world, and to make contact with the land. Disparaging the proclivity to make "the stone a thing that is less than stone, / A dolmen, a god," Carruth writes,

the stone is a greatness, itself in its grain,
Meaning more than a meaning, and more
    than a mind
May diminish.

Thus Carruth moves to new stages of his thought, holding tightly to the forms of the natural world yet seeking a personal transcendence.

The first books published by Carruth during his long Vermont sojourn were *North Winter* (1964) and *After the Stranger: Imaginary Dialogues With Camus* (1965), both of which he worked on at the same time in 1963. The experimental nature of each book no doubt fed the other. In *After the Stranger* a painter named Aspen (Carruth is fascinated by the shimmering qualities of the aspen tree) recognizes his entrapment in his loft and in his work. Rather like the painter in Franz Kafka's *The Trial* (1925) or like Joseph Grand in Camus's *The Plague* (1947) Aspen is obsessed by a single motif, in his case a stone, which he constantly reconceives on canvas. To begin his liberation, he moves to Paris and engages for the balance of the book in conversation with Camus, mostly about the motives of the character Meursault in *The Stranger* (1942) and what, if anything, he attains. The result is Aspen's gradual emergence into painting things other than the stone and his finding love in the person of Dora. Instrumental in his change is Dora's former lover, D'Arrast, who bears the name of the protagonist of Camus's short story, "The Growing Stone," which was published in America in 1958.

In her contribution to *In the Act*, Maxine Kumin describes "North Winter" as "a tone poem in 57 strophes, subtly modulated here and there with little skips and riffs of typographical invention. Not 'concrete' poetry, but lightly shaped, like a homemade loaf." The blending of form, subject, and precise language is stunning. Carruth, who points out that he used no personal pronouns in the poem, leads his reader through winter's stages to a rebirth. In strophe 12 he urges the reader not to think of snow as chaste but to think

of stags raging down
the rutting wind and of northern
passion crackling like naked trumpets
in the snow under the blazing aurora.

In strophe 57, the poet emerges in spring, "brushing the / mist from his shoulders" to discover

water water
the pools and freshets
wakening
earth glistening
releasing the ways of the
words of
earth long frozen.

A section titled "AFTERWORD: / WHAT THEPOETHADWRITTEN," inspired by the 1909 arctic expedition of Commdr. Robert E. Peary and Matthew Henson, concludes the poem:

north is the aurora north
is deliverance emancipation . . .
. . . north is
nothing. . . .

For Carruth existential acceptance is essential, but like Aspen in *After the Stranger* he has grown to new realms.

During the next decade Carruth settled in to his milieu, restructuring his Vermont home, enjoying family life, listening to the voices of those around him, and infusing his spirit with jazz. Building toward the major work *Brothers, I Loved You All: Poems, 1969-1977* (1978), he yet had to take some important soul-searching steps. "The Smallish Son" from *Nothing for Tigers: Poems 1959-1964* (1965) underscores the pain that continued to flow from Carruth's early years:

Listen,
I who have dwelt at the root of a scream forever,
I who have read my heart like a man with no
hands
reading a book whose pages turn in the wind,
I say listen, listen, hear me
in our dreamless dark, my dear. I can teach
you complaining.

But Carruth also heeds his own command to listen, as his close friend and fellow poet David Budbill points out in *In the Act* "This ability to *listen* to the world both outside and inside the self and then attempt to articulate what you hear is rife throughout Hayden's work." In *Nothing For Tigers* Carruth goes on to speculate on "Freedom and Discipline," addressing "Saint Harmony" and discovering that

Freedom and discipline concur
only in ecstasy, all else
is shoveling out the muck.
Give me my old hot horn.

In "Fragments of Autobiography" from *Suicides and Fazzers* Carruth recalls, "Once in 1965 I was able to give myself a whole month. I don't remember how this came about, but I wrote 'Contra Mortem,' a poem in thirty parts, doing one part a day for thirty days. . . . This poem remains my personal favorite among all the poems I've written." Published by Carruth's own Crow's Mark Press *Contra Mortem* (1967) is a reflection on "Being" and "Nothing" that concludes:

Such figures if they succeed are beautiful
because for a moment we brighten in a blaze
of rhymes
and yet they always fail and must fail
and give way to other poems
in the endless approximations of what we feel
Hopeless it is hopeless Only the wheel
endures It spins and spins winding
the was the is the will be out of nothing
and thus we are Thus on the wheel we touch
each to each a part
of the great determining reality How much
we give to one another Perhaps our art
succeeds after all our small song done in the
faith
of lovers who endlessly change heart for heart
as the gift of being Come let us sing against
death.

In this poem Carruth arrives at his clearest statement of the absurdist paradox and sets forth the terms of the rest of his work.

After revising five of his previously published long poems in *For You*—a book that traces the poet's journey from the asylum outward into the world—Carruth took his last major step toward *Brothers, I Loved You All* in the collection *From Snow and Rock, from Chaos* (1973). In poems such as "Emergency Haying" he identifies with his close friends, in this case Marshall Washer, and expresses the agony of work on the diminished farms of Vermont. His role as poet-participant is clear in "The Ravine":

These are what I see here every day,
not things but relationships of things,
quick changes and slow. These are my sorrow[.]

In the entry on Carruth in *DLB 5* William Koon called *Brothers, I Loved You All* by far his best work. He adds, "Carruth seems to have endured his personal agony, his Bloomingdale, and emerged a more complete poet." Carruth opens the volume with "The Loon on Forrester's Pond," hearing the bird's cry:

it came from inside the long wilderness
of my life.

He realizes that the bird's laugh is

a vestige, the laugh that transcends
first all mirth
and then all sorrow
and finally all knowledge, dying
into the gentlest quavering timeless
woe. It seemed
the real and only sanity to me.

In this and other poems of the collection Carruth shows a deep understanding of both his spirit and surroundings. In the long poem "Vermont" he captures the geography, language, and feeling of the state in a cascade of wit.

Galway Kinnell's praise of *Brothers, I Loved You All* in his "Foreword" to *The Selected Poetry of Hayden Carruth* (1985) could apply to much of Carruth's later work:

One of the most striking things about his work is his ability to enter the lives of other people . . . and tell their tales. . . . I think this is so because he knows them through their speech. There is a reciprocity in all this, however. In telling their tales, he finds a means to express his own inner life. He gives them a voice, they give him a language.

The voices are those of his "brothers," in one sense all of humankind but particularly the jazz musicians who have given music to his language.

In the twenty-eight-part "Paragraphs" from *Brothers* he loosens (as he calls it) his invented form. The poem concludes with a vision of the recording session of "Bottom Blues" by Albert Ammons, Lips Page, Vic Dickenson, Don Byas, Israel Crosby, and Big Sid Catlett that occurred while the poet was fighting in World War II:

A day very solid February 12th, 1944
cheerless in New York City (while I kneedeep
elsewhere in historical war
was wrecking Beauty's sleep
and her long dream) [.]

He conveys "a moment ecstatic / in the history / of creative mind *and* heart" and prays,

Ah,
holy spirit, ninefold
I druther've bin a-settin there, supernumerary
cockroach i' th' corner, a-listenin, a-listenin,,,,,,
than be the Prazedint ov the Wurrurld.

In *If You Call This Cry a Song* (1983) Carruth continues his exploration of others' voices, deepens his analysis of political and social corruption, and enlarges his use of jazz rhythms. "Marvin McCabe" is the dramatic monologue of a man rendered inarticulate by an auto accident

who is now thought to be "good for nothing" by his father. McCabe says of Carruth,

He's listened to me so much
he knows not only what I'm saying but what
I mean to say, you understand?—that thought
in my head. He can write it out for me.

The poem is a bitter portrait of the failure of community. At its conclusion Carruth and McCabe seem to be speaking as one:

It isn't because we're a joke, no,
it's because we think we aren't a joke—that's
     what the whole universe is laughing at.
     It makes
no difference if my thoughts are spoken or
     not,
or if I live or die—nothing will change.
How could it? This body is wrong, a misery,
a misrepresentation, but hell, would talking
     make
any difference? The reason nobody knows me
is because I don't exist. And neither do you.

Seemingly in the same spirit of negation is "On Being Asked to Write a Poem Against the War in Vietnam." He says he has done so and has written against many other wars as well,

and not one
breath was restored
to one
shattered throat[.]

But, as Wendell Berry observes in *In the Act,*

Mr. Carruth's protest poem is a poem against reduction. On its face, it protests—yet again— the reduction of the world, but its source is a profound instinct of resistance against the reduction of the poet and man who is the poet. By its wonderfully sufficient artistry, the poem preserves the poet's wholeness of heart in the face of his despair. And it shows us how to do so as well. That we would help if we could means that we will help when we can.

While the collection also features rollicking, jazzy poems such as "A Little Old Funky Homeric Blues for Herm" and "Who Cares, Long As It's B-Flat," perhaps its masterpiece is "Loneliness: An Outburst of Hexasyllables," another powerful poem of anguish. The poem was written, Carruth recalls in *Effluences from the Sacred Caves: More Selected Essays and Reviews* (1983), "in extreme emotion—agitation, depression, bitterness"—that is evident in its concluding lines:

I know that
I am a fool and all

men are fools. I know it
and I know I know it.
What good is it to know?

And yet Carruth's artistic integrity convinces the reader that the poet's spirit will prevail. His loneliness is like the snow-sculpted tree, "made by / the whole of motioning, / all in a concert."

Throughout the 1970s Carruth worked on the verses of his long poem *The Sleeping Beauty*, in which he reveals a sweeping vision of human history. He begins the 125-paragraph sequence in his favorite setting:

Out of nothing.
This morning the world was gone;
Only grayness outside, so dense, so close
Against the window that it seemed no season,
No place, and no thought almost,
Except what preys at the edge of thought,
    unknown;
But it was snow.

From "A presence gathering," at once beauty—"which is also love"—and his own consciousness, the poem begins.

Carruth identifies three principal "persons" in the poem, beginning with the princess from the fairy tale:

Oh, begin
In all and nothing then, the vision from a name,
This Rose Marie Dorn,
Woman alive exactly when the Red Army came
To that crook of the Oder where she was born,
Woman who fled and fled in her human duty
And bore her name, meaning Rose in the
    Thorn,
Her name, the mythologos, the Sleeping Beauty.

In a note included in *Collected Longer Poems* Carruth explains the allusion to his wife—"Because their family name was Dorn, her parents named her intentionally after the story of *Dornröschen* , and from this the poem sprang"—though he asserts that "nothing beyond this in the poem should be construed as a personal reference." The second person is the prince who would in his arrogance awaken Beauty but who "knows the horror of being / Only a dream."

Third is the poem, who must make
Presence from words, vision from seeing,
This no one that uniquely in sorrow rejoices
And can have no pronoun.

Throughout the poem, one may also hear "the echo of coincidental voices" as Carruth traces "this beauty in its centuries of wrong," *beauty* meaning not only the princess but the quality, especially as it is manifested in the spirit of art. As Sleeping Beauty dreams, the prince appears in many guises, as historical figures and events and as abstract entities—all beginning with the letter *H*. From Homer to Hayden, Carruth reveals Beauty's exploitation "In this history of the Slaughter / Of the Innocents." In section 108, where "Its peculiar name is Hydrogen Bomb," Carruth asks,

Yet was not each
Dream always precisely made for this power
At the heart of darkness, this violence, this
    beast
Of non-existence hulking beyond your horror?

Among the counterpoints of the poem are a woman's face in stone looking upward through the water of a brook and the voice of Amos, a Vermont farmer long dead. Carruth uses such images to gain perspective on the centuries of horror.

Sleeping Beauty is certainly a masterpiece. In his essay from *In the Act* Sam Hamill describes the poem as "perhaps Hayden Carruth's grandest achievement. It is astonishingly inclusive, making use of his enormous narrative skills as in *Brothers, I Loved You All*, formal without being awkward or selfconscious, lyrical in its execution and epic in its proportion, sweeping in its broad affections and horrors. Squarely in the American romantic-mythopoeic tradition, *The Sleeping Beauty* is a sustained visionary icon of our culture. It returns to us a spirit now too often missing in our poetry, one which dares the sustained experience, a spirit which encourages as many literary lions as housecats."

In 1979, as he relates in "Fragments of Autobiography," Carruth was worn out from the Vermont years of hard labor and needed money to send his son to the university. "The system had snagged me after all," he admitted. Although he somewhat reluctantly accepted a professorship at Syracuse University, where he would work until his retirement in 1991, he was entering into a new era of productivity.

The first published result of the Syracuse period was *Asphalt Georgics* (1985), a collection in which Carruth incorporates a whole new cast of voices—with names such as Septic Tank, Capper Kaplinski, and Art and Poll—in an examination of urban life. Carruth exposes the vacuity of life caused by strip malls and housing subdivisions, but as in his earlier work his characters emerge with a stubborn dignity. The quirky quatrains of his "Georgics" seem suited to capture a diminished modern life. The poem "Cave Painting," for example, reviews the progressive extinction of species, down to "our own / fixed and impoverished being":

> We were with them. They went away.
> And now every bell in
> every tower in every village
> could toll the tocsin
> of our sorrow forever and
> still not tell how across
> all time our origin always
> is this knowledge of loss.

The theme of loss dominates *The Oldest Killed Lake in North America: Poems, 1979-1981* (1985), titled after Syracuse's Onondaga, dead from pollution. Also lost are clean air and most human values. In "The Sleeping Beauty (Some Years Later)," Carruth writes that "The face in the water is gone" and records that the brook in which the face appeared is filled with the "damp dregs / of all the world."

Against the ubiquitous decay of life Carruth in his most recent verse and essays takes his stand mainly in two alternatives: love and cynicism. *Sonnets* (1989) presents a long sequence about rediscovered eroticism and political anger. Even though he knows "our country has no use for how / value survives" and lives "in a system more absolute / than any kingdom, for now the State is god," he is sustained by physical love and the love expressed in the act of writing. "The kiss is one and egoless," he proclaims; and although "my poems too are incorporated" in the system, he writes:

> Always I wanted to give and in wanting was
> the poet. A man now, aging, I know the best
> of love is not to bestow, but to recognize.

In *Tell Me Again How the White Heron Rises and Flies Across the Nacreous River at Twilight Toward the Distant Islands* (1989), Carruth argues that "The poem is a gift, a bestowal" and "is for us what instinct is for animals, a continuing and chiefly unthought corroboration of essence." In this volume of mostly longline poems, he adopts his posture as cynic. In "The Incorrigible Dirigible," the opening meditation on the alcoholism he has shared with Raymond Carver and John Cheever (a condition conquered by all three), he depicts Cheever and himself in a long discussion: "We

were men buoyant in cynicism." In "Suicide" from *Suicides and Fazzers* he reveals a new joy in life after his 1988 suicide attempt: "My dictionary says: 'The Cynics [in ancient philosophy] taught that virtue is the only good, and that its essence lies in self-control and independence'.... For me virtue is indeed the only good." The act of creation is his virtue, for "the artist must not only work but *live* in a state of devotion to things greater than himself."

In his influential essay, "The Act of Love: Poetry and Personality," collected in *Working Papers: Selected Essays and Reviews* (1982), Carruth defines *personality* as "the whole individual subjectivity, the spirit-body-soul." When that personality has been realized in a poem, he asserts, "It is no longer an object; it transcends objects." That realization he calls love. In "Sometimes When Lovers Lie Quietly Together, Unexpectedly One of Them Will Feel the Other's Pulse" from *Tell Me Again How the White Heron Rises and Flies Across the Nacreous River at Twilight Toward the Distant Islands* he presents a moment in mid August when he feels no less than the pulse of the world itself, his ultimate lover: "And for a while I was taken away from my discontents / By this rhythm of the truth of the world, so fundamental, so simple, so clear."

Carruth currently is working with David Budbill to revive the reputation of the turn-of-the-century writer of sketches and stories Rowland Robinson. His *Collected Shorter Poems* includes a concluding section titled "New Poems, 1986-1991" in which he has written passionate elegies for friends George Dennison and Raymond Carver, and he has recently published *Scrambled Eggs & Whiskey, Poems 1991-1995* (1996) and *Selected Essays and Reviews* (1996).

Source: David W. Landrey, "Hayden Carruth," in *Dictionary of Literary Biography*, Vol. 165, *American Poets Since World War II, Fourth Series*, edited by Joseph Conte, Gale Research, 1996, pp. 92–101.

SOURCES

Carruth, Hayden, "I, I, I," in *Scrambled Eggs & Whiskey: Poems 1991–1995*, Copper Canyon Press, 1996, p. 44.

Hartman, Steven, "Who Is Hayden Carruth?" in *Writers Online*, Vol. 3, No. 2, Spring 1999, http://www.albany.edu/writers-inst/olv3n2.html (accessed December 7, 2006).

Hendrix, Jimi, "Room Full of Mirrors," http://www.sin-gulartists.com/artist_j/jimi_hendrix_lyrics/room_full_of_mirrors_lyrics.html (accessed December 7, 2006).

Holub, Annie, Review of "Nowhere Man: Considered to Tears (I Like Red Recordings)," in *Rhythm & Views*, *Tucson Weekly*, June 26, 2003, http://www.tucsonwee-kly.com/gbase/music/Content?oid = 47238 (accessed December 7, 2006).

Housden, Roger, *Ten Poems to Last a Lifetime*, Random House, 2004, http://www.randomhouse.com/catalog/display.pperl?isbn = 9781400051137&view = excerpt (accessed December 8, 2006).

Lund, Elizabeth, Review of *Scrambled Eggs & Whiskey: Poems 1991–1995*, in "Themes of Family, Struggle in National Book Awards," in *Christian Science Monitor*, November 12, 1996, p. 14.

Miller, Matthew, "A Love Supreme: Jazz and the Poetry of Hayden Carruth," in *Midwest Quarterly*, Vol. 39, No. 3, Spring 1998, p. 307.

Olson, Ray, Review of *Scrambled Eggs & Whiskey: Poems 1991–1995*, in *Booklist*, Vol. 92, No. 16, April 15, 1996, p. 1409.

The Principal Upanisads, edited and translated by S. Radhakrishnan, George Allen & Unwin, 1953, reprint, 1974, pp. 201, 575, 686.

Review of *Scrambled Eggs & Whiskey: Poems 1991–1995*, in *Publishers Weekly*, Vol. 243, No. 9, February 26, 1996, p. 101.

Selinger, Eric Murphy, "The Importance of a Small Floy Floy," in *Parnassus: Poetry in Review*, Vol. 22, No. 1–2, 1997, pp. 257, 274, 275, 277, 278.

FURTHER READING

Fu, Tu, *Selected Poems of Tu Fu*, translated by David Hinton, New Directions, 1989.
Tu Fu (712–770) is widely considered to be China's greatest poet, and he is one of Carruth's favorites. His highly personal poems tell of his own and his family's experiences in a period of history fraught with such disasters as famines, floods, and civil war, as well as the simple pleasures of life. David Hinton's translation has garnered much critical acclaim.

Kaufmann, Walter, *Existentialism from Dostoevsky to Sartre*, The World Publishing, 1956, reprint, Plume, 1975.
Kaufmann provides a readable anthology of existentialist writings for the lay reader. In his illuminating commentaries on the various writers, which includes Jean-Paul Sartre, Albert Camus, and Søren Kierkegaard, he emphasizes that existentialist thinkers revolted against traditional philosophies and resisted categorization.

Pound, Ezra, *ABC of Reading*, New Directions, 1960.
In this enjoyable, clear, and accessible work, the modernist poet Ezra Pound, whom Carruth cites as an important influence, gives advice on how to develop the sensitivity to appreciate and get the most out of reading literature. The book contains a selection of passages from great literature.

Upanisads, translated by Patrick Olivelle, Oxford University Press, 1998.
The Upanishads form the core spiritual thought of the Vedas, the scriptures of ancient India. They have had a profound influence on philosophers, artists, and writers, including Ralph Waldo Emerson, Samuel Taylor Coleridge, Arthur Schopenhauer, and Ludwig Wittgenstein. They also influenced Buddhism and existentialism. They explore the nature of consciousness, spiritual experience, and man's relationship to the universe and to God. Parts of the text are difficult, but other parts are immediately accessible.

Weiss, David, ed., *In the Act: Essays on the Poetry of Hayden Carruth*, Hobart & William Smith Press, 1990.
This collection of critical work on Carruth's poetry includes essays by Philip Booth, Wendell Berry, Maxine Kumin, David Weiss, Anthony Robbins, Sam Hamill, William Matthews, Geoffrey Gardner, and Carolyn Kizer. It examines Carruth's contribution to twentieth-century American poetry and provides a useful introduction for students.

Mastectomy

ALICIA OSTRIKER

1996

In the mid 1990s, Alicia Ostriker was diagnosed with breast cancer. She expressed her feelings about this traumatic experience, which resulted in a mastectomy and a long, painful recovery, in her collection of poems, *The Crack in Everything*. When it was published in 1996, the book confirmed her reputation as one of America's finest poets. The fourth section of the collection, titled "The Mastectomy Poems," deals directly with her response to each stage of her cancer: the diagnosis, the surgery and treatment, and the aftermath. In one of the most powerful poems of this sequence, "Mastectomy," the speaker describes her interaction with the doctor who performed the surgery and imagines how he removed her breast. The poem becomes a poignant exploration of one woman's struggle to understand and cope with the physical and emotional consequences of this disease.

AUTHOR BIOGRAPHY

Alicia Ostriker was born on November 11, 1937, in New York City, to David, a civil service employee, and Beatrice Suskin, both of whom had earned bachelor degrees in English. Ostriker grew up in a housing project in New York City where her mother read Shakespeare and Browning, among others, which inspired a love of literature in her and prompted her to write her own poetry. Ostriker earned a B.A. from

Alicia Ostriker (*Photograph by J. P. Ostriker. Reproduced by permission of Alicia Ostriker*)

been translated into French, Italian, German, Japanese, Hebrew, and Arabic.

Ostriker has received numerous honors and awards. Some of these are a National Endowment for the Arts Fellowship (1976–1977), the Pushcart Prize (1979, 2000); a Rockefeller Foundation Fellowship (1982); a Guggenheim Foundation Fellowship (1984–1985); and the William Carlos Williams Prize in 1986 for *The Imaginary Lover*. She was named a National Book Award finalist, received the Paterson Poetry Award, and the San Francisco State Poetry Center Award, all in 1996, for *The Crack in Everything*, which contains the poem "Mastectomy."

In 1958, she married Jeremiah P. Ostriker, a professor of astrophysics, with whom she had two children. As of 2007, she was teaching English and creative writing at Rutgers University.

Brandeis University in 1959 and an M.A. (1961) and a Ph.D. (1964) from the University of Wisconsin. A year later, she began teaching at Rutgers University.

Ostriker's first book of poems, *Songs*, was published in 1969. By the time her collections *The Mother/Child Papers* (1980) and *A Woman under the Surface* (1982) appeared, her reputation as an important American poet had been established. In 1986, her controversial treatise on literary feminism, *Stealing the Language*, was published. After that, she continued to write poetry, dealing with personal as well as spiritual topics and essays on gender and literature.

Ostriker's work has been published in various periodicals, including the *American Poetry Review*, *New Yorker*, *Atlantic Monthly*, *Paris Review*, *Nation*, *Poetry*, and the *New York Times Book Review*. Her poems and essays have also been published in anthologies, including *Our Mothers, Our Selves: Writers and Poets Celebrating Motherhood* (1996); *Worlds in Our Words: Contemporary American Women Writers* (1997); *Best American Poetry* and *Yearbook of American Poetry* (both in 1996). Her poems have

POEM TEXT

for Alison Estabrook

I shook your hand before I went.
Your nod was brief, your manner confident,
A ship's captain, and there I lay, a chart
Of the bay, no reefs, no shoals.
While I admired your boyish freckles,   5
Your soft green cotton gown with the oval
    neck,
The drug sent me away, like the unemployed.
I swam and supped with the fish, while you
Cut carefully in, I mean
I assume you were careful.   10
They say it took an hour or so.

I liked your freckled face, your honesty
That first visit, when I said
What's my odds on this biopsy
And you didn't mince words,   15
One out of four it's cancer.
The degree on your wall shrugged slightly.
Your cold window onto Amsterdam
Had seen everything, bums and operas.
A breast surgeon minces something other   20
Than language.
That's why I picked you to cut me.

Was I succulent? Was I juicy?
Flesh is grass, yet I dreamed you displayed me
In pleated paper like a candied fruit,   25
I thought you sliced me like green honeydew
Or like a pomegranate full of seeds
Tart as Persephone's, those electric dots
That kept that girl in hell,
Those jelly pips that made her queen of death.   30
Doctor, you knifed, chopped, and divided it

Like a watermelon's ruby flesh
Flushed a little, serious
About your line of work
Scooped up the risk in the ducts   35
Scooped up the ducts
Dug out the blubber,
Spooned it off and away, nipple and all.
Eliminated the odds, nipped out
Those almost insignificant cells that might   40
Or might not have lain dormant forever.

POEM SUMMARY

Stanza 1

"Mastectomy" begins with the speaker addressing the doctor directly, explaining her feelings about the operation. Then it jumps back and forth in time from before to during the operation. She begins with a description of their interaction before the surgery when she shook his hand, appreciating his confident manner. She compares him to a ship captain and his view of her as a map of the bay with no reefs (underwater ridges of coral or rock) or shoals. A shoal, here used as a noun, has several definitions: a group of fish swimming together, a group of people or things, or an underwater sandbank that is visible at low tide in shallow water. Here, it most likely suggests a sandbank since that, coupled with the reef, connotes a barrier.

While the speaker appears to have confidence in the doctor, she suggests that he is young or looks it with his "boyish freckles." She then begins her description of the surgery as she notes that she lost consciousness under the anesthesia. When she describes how the drug sent her "away, like the unemployed," she notes her powerlessness. She feels like she is underwater while unconscious, like she "swam and supped with the fish." The speaker assumes that while she was under, the doctor performed the operation carefully; she learns later the operation took about an hour.

Stanza 2

The speaker shifts back in time at the beginning of this stanza to her first office visit with the doctor when she learned that she had cancer. She again refers to the doctor's "freckled face," which she liked at that first meeting, along with his honesty when she asked him about the odds

TOPICS FOR FURTHER STUDY

- Read some of the other "Mastectomy Poems" in *The Crack in Everything* that focus on different stages in Ostriker's experience with the surgery, such as "The Bridge" (which chronicles her pre-op experience) and "Normal" (which depicts her struggle to adapt to the loss of a breast). Compare these other poems to "Mastectomy" in an essay, focusing on what Ostriker says about the different stages that women go through when they must deal with breast cancer and a mastectomy.

- Write a poem or short story about the speaker's life and attitude toward the surgery and her body ten years after the operation.

- Interview women who have undergone a mastectomy and present a PowerPoint presentation on your findings about their experiences and views of the treatment they received.

- Research the causes and treatment of breast cancer and give a presentation to your class on your findings.

that the biopsy would prove that she had cancer. He immediately told her, without mincing words, that she had a one-out-of-four chance of having the disease. She imagines that his diploma hanging on his wall "shrugged" at his estimate of her chances, probably because she did have cancer even though her odds were good. At the end of the stanza, she notes his experience: he has seen "everything" from his "cold window onto Amsterdam," all of the "bums and operas," and that filled her with enough confidence in him to choose him to perform her surgery.

Stanza 3

In this stanza the speaker uses a series of images to describe her body as the doctor performs the operation. She asks the doctor whether her flesh was "succulent" and "juicy" like the fruit she later names. The image of flesh as grass is rather obscure here. Grass is a living thing like flesh

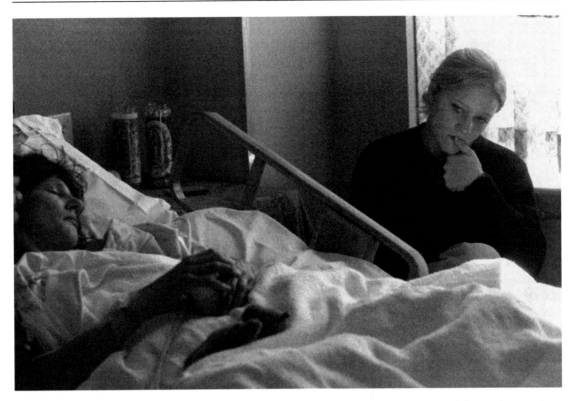

Undergoing a mastectomy is physically and emotionally challenging for a woman and those who are close to her (© Phototake Inc./Alamy)

unless it becomes detached, and it also serves as a groundcover. One could compare that to how flesh covers the body's organs. Anesthetized, the speaker dreams about her flesh not as grass but as ripe fruit while the doctor makes his incisions. First, she imagines her flesh as candied fruit that the doctor "displays," then as green honeydew and then "like a pomegranate full of seeds."

This last metaphor she extends to the mythological figure of Persephone, the goddess of the underworld and daughter to the Greek god Zeus and the mortal woman, Demeter. Dazzled by her beauty, Hades abducted Persephone and pulled her down into the underworld. When Zeus intervened, Hades agreed to release her after giving her a pomegranate. When Persephone ate some of its seeds, a spell was cast over her, which forced her to return to Hades four months out of each year. Ostriker refers to Persephone's pomegranate seeds as "electric dots / That kept that girl in hell" and "made her queen of death." Here, the speaker correlates the image of the seeds to the cancer cells in her body.

She then shifts her focus to the doctor cutting out the cells in her flesh, which she likens to a watermelon. She describes him as serious about his work as he operates, trying to "[eliminate] the odds" that cancer exists in the breast and surrounding tissue cells and may kill her if these parts are left in her body. The poem ends on an uncertain note. She is not sure that the excised cells would have developed into cancer if left in her body.

THEMES

Identity

As the speaker in the poem tries to comprehend her experience with breast surgery, she must deal with the physical and emotional changes that occur as a patient confronts and undergoes mastectomy. Before and during the early part of the surgery, she sees herself in traditional feminine images. She imagines her breast as "succulent" and "juicy" like ripe fruit, suggesting that before the operation she felt womanly and fertile. As the surgeon removes her breast, the fruit metaphors shift to verbs associated with incision, chopping, and serving, as though the fruit associated with sexual attraction is now just a lump of matter to be handled with a knife and cleaned. This transition suggests that the speaker's self-image is undergoing a transformation, too. The poem concludes in an open-ended way, without the speaker having found a new identity. The poem ends with a question about whether, had she not had the surgery, cancer would have developed in the excised parts. Here Ostriker suggests that establishing a new sense of self after such a traumatic procedure is difficult and takes time beyond the surgery.

Innocence and Death

Ostriker's allusion to the myth of the Greek goddess Persephone ties into her themes in the poem of innocence and death. Persephone was abducted by Hades and brought to the underworld. The pomegranate seeds that she was forced to eat become a symbol of the speaker's cancer cells. Like Persephone, she was an innocent who should have beaten the one-in-four odds that she had cancer. In that sense she was "abducted" by fate. Her discovery of the cancer threatens to make her the "queen of death" as well. The two are also linked by the image of barrenness. During the months that Persephone was forced to remain in the underworld, winter occurs. The speaker alludes to her own barrenness when the symbol of her fertility, her breast, is removed, and she no longer uses fruit metaphors to describe her flesh. Ostriker's use of the myth of Persephone connects the speaker's plight with a universal pattern of birth and death and the seasons of the year. Moreover, the ratio stated, one in four, suggests that winter or death is correlated with cancer, while the three remaining are correlated to the other three seasons of the year, spring, summer, and fall, times of sowing, growing, and reaping.

STYLE

Free Verse

Free Verse, also referred to as open form, does not contain set patterns of meter, rhyme, and stanza. Rhythm emerges from the repetition of words or phrases or in line breaks. Ostriker's use

of free verse in the poem gives readers a sense that the speaker's observations are spontaneous, that she is thinking out loud about her experiences. This sense is heightened by her use of simple declarative sentences, such as the opening lines: "I shook your hand before I went. / Your nod was brief, your manner confident."

Rhythm is achieved in a variety of ways but does not follow any set pattern. The first two lines form a couplet ending with the words "went" and "confident" as do those in the first two lines of the third stanza, "juicy" and "me" but that end-line rhyming pattern appears no where else in the poem. Also, Ostriker undercuts the standard form of the couplet in the second line of the third stanza when she does not end a thought with the rhymed word. After the word "me," the thought continues on the next line: "In pleated paper like a candied fruit." Ostriker also uses repetition to establish rhythm. In the second stanza, for example, she repeats the image of the freckled face of the doctor, and in the second stanza, she twice uses the verb, to mince. She uses a partial repetition when in the third stanza she notes that the doctor "spooned" her flesh away "nipple and all," and in the next line, she insists that he "nipped out / Those almost insignificant cells." The final instance occurs in the third stanza when the speaker is describing how the doctor "scooped" the cancer from her "ducts." Ostriker's refusal to follow traditional poetic patterns seems in keeping with the personal nature of her speaker's experience with this operation.

HISTORICAL CONTEXT

Breast Cancer

The most common, worldwide form of cancer in women is breast cancer, which in the early 2000s constitutes about 7.3 percent of all cancers. One estimate is that between one in every nine to thirteen women who live in Western countries to the age of ninety is diagnosed with this form of cancer, which is the second most fatal for women after lung cancer. The chances of getting breast cancer increase with age, but younger women who develop it often do so in more aggressive forms. Less than 1 percent of the total number of cases occurs in men.

Damage to DNA is thought to be the leading cause of the cancer, indicating a strong inherited risk, but a direct cause for most incidences is unknown. Some studies have shown environmental influences, such as diet and alcohol consumption, to be factors. Other risk factors include a high density of breast tissue, the onset of menstruation at twelve years or younger, menopause that occurs at fifty-five or older, first pregnancy at thirty or older or no pregnancies, and long-term use of oral contraceptives and hormone replacement therapy.

Breast cancer in the early stages is difficult to detect since it has no symptoms. It is usually discovered through a mammography or the detection of a lump in the breast, under the arm, or above the collarbone. Other symptoms include nipple inversion or discharge and skin changes in the breast. Regular self-examinations of the breast and mammography are highly recommended for the detection of breast cancers, especially for women over fifty.

Mastectomy

The most common treatment of breast cancer when it is localized is the removal of the tumor, called a lumpectomy, which is usually followed by hormonal, chemo-, or radiation therapy. When the cancer is found in surrounding tissue, the surgeon may perform a mastectomy, the surgical removal of the breast. Traditionally, the entire breast was removed when cancer was discovered, but in the late 1990s and early 2000s, more options were considered after diagnosis. Sometimes women who have a high incidence of breast cancer in the family decide to undergo a mastectomy as a preventative measure.

Different types of mastectomy include simple (all breast tissue is removed but surrounding lymph nodes and pectoral tissue beneath the breast are left in tact), modified radical (breast tissue and some lymph nodes are removed), and radical (breast tissue, nodes, and pectoral tissue are removed). Some operations preserve the skin of the breast so that reconstructive surgery can be performed.

Radical mastectomies were the most popular form of breast surgery before the 1980s when the modified radical took its place. By the end of the twentieth and beginning of the twenty-first centuries, more concern was shown for breast conservation. As a result, lumpectomies, node dissections, and radiation became more frequently the chosen treatments.

CRITICAL OVERVIEW

Reviews for *The Crack in Everything* were overwhelmingly positive, and several critics singled out the "Mastectomy Poems" for special notice. Doris Earnshaw in her review of the collection for *World Literature Today* finds the tone of the poems "sober and honest" with a "warmth at heart" and insists that "Ostriker puts no barriers of arcane language between herself and her reader." Earnshaw also praises her "acute observation" in the poems. Marilyn Hacker, in her article "Tectonic Shifts," calls Ostriker "an important American poet" and suggests that the collection affirms "the poet's unique and contradictory role, at once storyteller and witness, s/he who makes of language not a prison but a prism, refracting and re-combining the spectrum of human possibilities."

In her review for *American Book Review*, Sharon Dolin describes the collection as "a mature work filled with wisdom about personal grief and the world," written by a poet with "enormous range." Dolin praises the poems' "study in compassion for the self and others" and their focus on "what we can and cannot master, and to what we can at least bear witness." Patricia Monaghan, in *Booklist*, finds that the "distinguished" Ostriker "writes with calm authority and almost rocklike solidity," proving herself to be "a poet singing at the top of her form." She also points out how immediate and private the poems can feel as one reads them: "although hers is a public voice of great clarity, her poems also possess a quality of being overheard, and reading them can seem like finding an especially lyrical journal or chancing upon a great opera singer practicing in the shower." Putting the same sentiment a different way, a reviewer in *Publishers Weekly* insists that Ostriker's "accomplished poems ... are grounded in the details of a woman's daily life and speak with the appeal of an intelligent, sympathetic friend." This reviewer concludes, "Ostriker confronts middle age and mortality with deft touch and wry humor."

Alison Townsend in *Women's Review of Books* claims that Ostriker "writes about something terrible, transforming it with the intelligence and beauty of her art" and "from a level of awareness that is both heartbreaking and healing, precisely because it encompasses so much loss." She finds that "one of Ostriker's greatest strengths as poet has always been the

WHAT DO I READ NEXT?

- Ostriker wrote twelve poems in *The Crack in Everything* (1996) that center on her experience with undergoing a mastectomy. The speaker in these poems focuses on her responses to the diagnosis, the surgery, and the aftermath as she tries to adjust to her new body. One especially poignant poem is "Normal," which focuses on others' as well as her own response to the operation.

- Ostriker's controversial treatise on literary feminism, *Stealing the Language*, was published in 1986. This work proposes that only women can have an authentic voice when constructing female literary characters.

- *The Cancer Journals* (1980), by Audre Lorde, is a courageous chronicle of Lorde's struggle with breast cancer and radical mastectomy and the support she received from her community of women. Lorde was one of the first to speak out about the harsh reality of the surgery and its aftermath.

- *How Cancer Works* (2003), by Lauren Sompayrac, defines the ten most common cancers and explains causes and treatments.

---

lack of separation between self and world in her work," which is "immediate, passionate and direct" with "an intimacy that startles the reader." Though her poetry is "often tender," Townsend claims that Ostriker "is overall witty and urbane, a poet of intellect whose voice is filtered through an acute social consciousness." Her poems "all speak with authenticity and authority . . . helping us to approach our own terrible stories in the process."

Townsend reserves special praise for "The Mastectomy Poems," which, she insists, are "strong, touch-minded, lyrical poems" that describe "the experience of mastectomy . . . with clarity and grace." Her poetry "offers us a different perspective on loss, damage or fear and its

transformation through the ritual of poem-making." A reviewer in *Virginia Quarterly Review* claims that "The Mastectomy Poems" are "simply stunning," while Steven R. Ellis in the *Library Journal* finds that they "convey the experience of mastectomy in a frank and liberating clarity but always with the riddle of an illness underneath."

The *Publishers Weekly* reviewer argues that Ostriker's observations in these poems "cut as clean and sharp as the surgeon's scalpel" as her readers "become immersed in her sensibility that 'tragedy / Is a sort of surrender.'" Monaghan finds the "Mastectomy Poems" are "moving" in their focus on "the push-pull of public and private voices." "In this sequence," she writes, "Ostriker's impressive craft rises to meet a demanding subject so fully that these poems stand among the classics of the poem-sequence genre."

CRITICISM

Wendy Perkins

Perkins is a professor of twentieth-century American and English literature and film. In this essay, she explores Ostriker's focus on the transforming power of poetry.

The title of Alicia Ostriker's collection of poems *The Crack in Everything* alludes to an interpretation found in the writings of the Kabbala, a mystical Jewish doctrine that includes stories of the creation of the world. One such story focuses on the cracking of the vessel, representing the world, into which the first light was poured. Humans were directed by God to repair the brokenness of the world. The title also refers to a line from a song by Leonard Cohen, which Ostriker uses for the collection's epigraph: "There is a crack, a crack in everything / That's how the light gets in." Both of these allusions relate to the theme of the poems in the collection, including "Mastectomy," in which Ostriker explores how poetic language can express the experience of a woman whose world has "cracked" after she is diagnosed with breast cancer.

The twelve mastectomy poems that appear at the end of the collection chronicle the stages a woman who has breast cancer experiences. In "Mastectomy," she confers with her doctor whom she has chosen to perform the operation and then describes what she imagines happened during the surgery. The cancer has created a significant crack in her world which she needs to repair. Yet ironically, as Cohen's song suggests, that very crack allows light in. Here the light becomes the poetic process of putting experience into words that express the emotional pain the speaker endures as she struggles to understand what is happening to her.

In "Class," another poem in the collection, Ostriker insists, "The teacher's job is to give [her students] permission / To gather pain into language." She tells them to *Write for the sake of the silenced. / Write what makes you afraid to write.* Ostriker gives a perfect example of this instruction in "Mastectomy" as she gathers the pain into a poetic language of cancer, breaking the silence caused by the fear of imagining what it is like to lose a breast.

Ostriker juxtaposes direct, declarative statements with detailed metaphors as she finds the language to express the reality of the speaker's experience. The speaker's keen, straightforward observations create a personal, almost conversational tone, as if she is thinking out loud. She does this when she describes the doctor, to whom she addresses her observations about him and about her surgery. Here Ostriker's free verse adds to the effect of individualizing the speaker's experience as her lines sound more like prose than poetry: "I assume you were careful. / They say it took an hour or so."

The speaker's direct tone as she details the doctor's characteristics reveals the confidence she has in him. He appears capable yet youthful with "boyish freckles." He is honest when the speaker asks about her odds, not "mincing words," which is why she chose him to "cut" her. He flushes during the operation, "serious / About [his] line of work." She adds a note of

irony, however, when she imagines his medical diploma "shrugg[ing] slightly" when he tells her that her odds of her getting cancer are only one out of four, a direct response to a complex question. She soon learns that even a capable, experienced doctor, who has "seen everything" from his "cold window onto Amsterdam," can get the odds wrong.

Ostriker moves from direct to metaphoric language whenever she describes the speaker's cancer or the surgery she endures. Through the use of a series of metaphors, the speaker tries to find the right images to understand and express her experience. Her initial use of figurative language occurs in the first stanza when she describes herself lying on the operating table. Here the doctor becomes "a ship's captain" while she is a chart of the bay unfurled before him. Her confidence in him is reflected by her determination that there are no "reefs, no shoals" on the chart—no impediments to his successful navigation.

She extends the maritime metaphor a few lines later when she describes the effect that the anesthesia has on her. She feels as if she is underwater, swimming and eating with the fish, a rather peaceful and benign image. That tone, however, is modulated by her likening herself to the unemployed after "the drug sent [her] away." Here she suggests the powerlessness she feels regarding her body and what is happening to it. She can neither prevent the cancer from spreading, nor can she ensure that the doctor will perform the operation successfully, which she notes when she admits that she can only "assume" that he was careful.

In the third stanza, Ostriker begins a series of fruit metaphors that are used to characterize the way the speaker feels about her breast as it is being removed. This series is linked to the previous stanza when she uses the word "minces" to describe what the surgeon does in the operating room. In the operating room, he becomes a dark chef, as he "display[s]" the speaker's flesh "in pleated paper like a candied fruit." She knows that flesh is nondescript as "grass," little more than a covering for the important bodily organs, yet dreams about her own as ripe fruit. She wonders whether her flesh was "succulent" and "juicy" as "green honeydew," "a pomegranate full of seeds, or a watermelon" when he made his incision.

She extends the image of the pomegranate full of seeds to the Greek goddess Persephone, who, after eating some of the seeds from that fruit given to her by Hades, was forced to return to the underworld for a few months every year. "Those electric dots ... kept that girl in hell" where, for those few months, she became "queen of death." The speaker imagines the seeds of Persephone's pomegranate as the cancer cells in her own breast, "jelly pips" that could also keep her in hell and make her the queen of death if they spread throughout her body.

The ripe fruit images suggest the speaker's feelings of fecundity and femininity, values associated with breasts. After the doctor is done knifing, chopping, and dividing her flesh, the fruit images, along with her sense of herself as a woman, disappear. At the end of the operation, he "scooped" up the ducts and the blubber, "spooned it off and away, nipple and all" in order to "[eliminate] the odds" that she will die.

The poem ends on an ambiguous note. The speaker does not know whether the cells that the doctor has removed along with her breast were "insignificant" or not. She acknowledges that they "might / Or might not have lain dormant forever," and thus she comes to an acceptance of her mortality and the part that luck plays in it, for this is an answer that she will never find. She is left with the experience of losing her breast, which she has tried, as part of the grieving process, to put into words in order to understand. In this sense, then, through the transforming power of poetry, while she may not be able to repair the crack in her world, she has been able to let some light through it.

Source: Wendy Perkins, Critical Essay on "Mastectomy," in *Poetry for Students*, Thomson Gale, 2007.

Thomson Gale

In the following essay, the critic gives a critical analysis of Ostriker's work.

Alicia Ostriker has published nine books of poetry and several works of feminist literary criticism that examine the relationship between gender and literature. In a comment that applies to both Ostriker's poetry and criticism, Amy Williams in *Dictionary of Literary Biography* noted how Ostriker "consistently challenges limitations. For discovery to take place there must be movement, and Ostriker refuses to stand still; each volume tries to uncover anew what must be learned in order to gain wisdom, experience, and

> TO QUOTE PATRICIA MONAGHAN IN *BOOKLIST*, THE POEMS ARE 'GROUNDED IN THE DETAILS OF A WOMAN'S DAILY LIFE AND SPEAK WITH THE APPEAL OF AN INTELLIGENT, SYMPATHETIC FRIEND,' MAKING THE WORK FEEL AS IF IT POSSESSES 'A QUALITY OF BEING OVERHEARD.'"

identity. She is a poet who breaks down walls." In the *Women's Review of Books*, Adrian Oktenberg wrote: "One of the great pleasures in reading Ostriker is hearing her think out loud; putting her humanity fully on the page is one of her strengths as a writer." Calling Ostriker "America's most fiercely honest poet," *Progressive* contributor Joel Brouwer observed that she "puts the reader to work, and she blenches at nothing that experience offers up." According to Williams, Ostriker's voice is "personal, honest, and strong; her poetry incorporates family experiences, social and political views, and a driving spirit that speaks for growth and, at times, with rage."

In Ostriker's criticism, she argues that literature written by women can be tracked as a tradition. In *Stealing the Language: The Emergence of Women Poets in America*, she asserts that women writers have produced poetry that is "explicitly female in the sense that the writers have chosen to explore experiences central to their sex." Furthermore, in their search to find an aesthetic that accommodates this expression, Ostriker claims that women poets are "challenging and transforming the history of poetry. They constitute a literary movement comparable to romanticism or modernism in our literary past."

These claims have evoked a wide range of response from reviewers. Frieda Gardner, writing in the *Women's Review of Books*, agreed that women have brought new subject matter to American poetry; the "thematic landscape" of literature now includes poems on "women's quests for self-definition, on the uses and treachery of anger, ... female eroticism and, most impressively, on women poets' sweeping revision of Western mythology," according to Gardner. However, "lots of male poets grew fat on the 'butter and sugar' Ostriker calls peculiarly feminine," Mary Karr pointed out in a *Poetry* review. Reviewers also questioned the notion that poetry by women is unified by the concentrated "drive for power" that Ostriker sees in it. Nonetheless, stated Karr, "those predisposed to feminist criticism will eagerly take up these pages. At the other extreme, certain critics and philosophers will shudder at the very thought of women generating language, a practice they interpret as exclusively masculine."

The Nakedness of the Fathers: Biblical Visions and Revisions (1994) offers "an imaginative and spiritual dialogue with characters and narratives of the Old Testament," wrote Lynn Garrett in *Publishers Weekly*. By exploring both men's and women's stories from the Bible—from Adam and Eve to Job and Job's wife—and speaking through their voices, Ostriker attempts to offer a more humanized and modernized reading of the Bible, and in doing so, she attempts to reconcile the revisionism of feminism with the traditions of Judaism. She presents Esther through the lens of a post-Holocaust family party, and shows Job's wife as a bystander who must accept the "casual brutality of this world," according to Enid Dame in *Belles Lettres*. Ostriker's book is as grand and comprehensive as her subject, offering, noted Dame, "a retelling-with-commentary of Jewish scripture intertwined with a brilliant web of poems, stories, personal memoirs, scholarly observations, and speculative meditations." Ultimately, it is "in the reclamation of the *Shekhina*, or female aspect of God," stated Dame, that Ostriker finds a reconciliation between Judaism and feminism.

Dancing at the Devil's Party: Essays on Poetry, Politics, and the Erotic drew a great deal of praise for its observations on a multitude of poets, from John Milton and William Blake to Maxine Kumin and Lucille Clifton. *Pif Magazine* reviewer Rachel Barenblat maintained that, "for Ostriker, poems are both crucial and relevant. She respects poems, the way one respects magic or religion or anything that smacks of the ineffable." Noting that Ostriker approaches her subject matter with "passion and precision," Barenblat concluded: "Ostriker's criticism is grounded in her impressive knowledge of American literary traditions and their adherents. ... This is a strong, compelling and beautiful collection of essays. I recommend it highly." In her review of the same title,

Oktenberg stated: "As we follow [Ostriker] into her reading, we are more and more illuminated, not only intellectually but with a palpable, physical sense of expansion, and even spirituality. This is the best writing—it gets you at all levels." The critic concluded: "I would . . . recommend this book, and unhesitatingly, as one of the finest I have ever read."

In addition to her reputation as a feminist literary critic, Ostriker is also an accomplished poet. In 1986, the Poetry Society of America awarded her the William Carlos Williams Prize for *The Imaginary Lover*, and two of her works have been finalists for the National Book Award. Ostriker "is at her best when most urbane and ironic" in these poems that look back at marriage from the perspective of midlife, said *Times Literary Supplement* contributor Clair Wills. "The actions are melodramatic, but the recording consciousness is steady," Patricia Hampl related in the *New York Times Book Review*. Since the poems often reflect on disappointment or loss, they have an elegiac tone. More noticeable, however, "is Mrs. Ostriker's tendency to locate a sustaining force for the rest of life—a force that is both passionate and honorable," Hampl observed. "This is evident in lines from 'Everywoman Her Own Theology,' in which Ostriker declares: 'Ethically, I am looking for / An absolute endorsement of loving-kindness.'" At times, says Hampl, the poems lack music, but they charm the reader with their "candor and thoughtfulness."

Green Age (1989) is a book of poems that blends "personal time, history and politics, and inner spirituality," wrote Williams. As Robyn Selman noted in *Village Voice*, Ostriker's title denotes "the stage in a woman's life—after her children have left home, after the death of her parents—when her sense of herself is clear and muscular: a time of loss, but also of heightened awareness and passion." Ostriker offers love poems, poems which are forceful and persuasive, and poems which, according to a *Publishers Weekly* reviewer, "sympathize and nurture, affirming life," as when the poet states: "Friend, I could say / I've been alive a half a dozen moments / but that's not true / I've been alive my entire time / on this earth / I've been alive."

The pieces in *The Crack in Everything* are "accomplished poems," declared a *Publishers Weekly* reviewer. To quote Patricia Monaghan in *Booklist*, the poems are "grounded in the details of a woman's daily life and speak with the appeal of an intelligent, sympathetic friend," making the work feel as if it possesses "a quality of being overheard." The topics of some of Ostriker's poems range from the rape of a mentally retarded girl by her high school classmates to the bombing of MOVE in Philadelphia, so that her poems feel, according to a *Publishers Weekly* reviewer, as though "a broad-based politics enters this work routinely, like the morning news." The long sequence, "The Mastectomy Poems," which concludes the collection, movingly address the poet's successful treatment for cancer, "in a frank and liberating clarity," stated Steven Ellis in *Library Journal*, as Ostriker refers to how "cells break down, their membranes crushed / Where the condemned / Beg for forgetfulness."

The Little Space: Poems Selected and New 1968-1998 expresses itself as an autobiography in poetry form, as the volume begins with the birth of Ostriker's child and moves through the changes that age wreaks in relationships between mates, between parents and children, and within the poet's sense of herself. Nominated for a National Book Award, *The Little Space* was described by Judy Clarence in the *Library Journal* as a "lively and moving collection," containing poems that "move into deeper levels of mystery and spirituality." A *Publishers Weekly* contributor maintained that the poems are "simultaneously funny and tragic, intense and conversational, politically charged and personally graphic," and that the book reveals a writer "with a rare intelligence."

Ostriker told *CA:* "All poets have their chosen ancestors and affinities. As an American poet I see myself in the line of Whitman, Williams, and Ginsberg, those great enablers of the inclusive democratic impulse, the corollary of which is formal openness. As a student I wrote in traditional closed forms, as did they—before they discovered the joy and meaning of open forms. To write in open forms is to improvise. Improvisatory verse is like doing a jazz solo: we know what we've just done, and the next line has to be connected to it, has to grow out of it somehow, but there is an essential *unpredictability*. This is an American invention because we act, in America, as if the future is partly shaped by the past, but is not determined by it. We are (a little bit) free. As a poet of the spirit, I have always been inspired by the great heterodox visionaries—Whitman since childhood, Blake since my student days, and H. D. since the 1980's when I

discovered that she was not a minor imagist but the exquisite peer and rival of T. S. Eliot and Ezra Pound. Wrestling with the Bible, I am Blake's daughter; trying to imagine the divine Feminine, I am H. D.'s child. I am also in love with the poetry of Lucille Clifton, whom I believe to be the most important spiritual poet writing today. And then there are John Donne, George Herbert, and Gerard Manley Hopkins. As for the women poets who have influenced my poetry and my life, they are probably countless—but among them are Emily Dickinson, Louise Bogan, Edna St. Vincent Millay, Muriel Rukeyser, Adrienne Rich, May Swenson, Sylvia Plath, Anne Sexton, Maxine Kumin, Marge Piercy, June Jordan, Sharon Doubiago, Sharon Olds, Ntozake Shange, Toi Derricotte, and (as said before), H. D., and Lucille Clifton.

"People who do not know my work ask me what I write about. I answer: love, sex, death, violence, family, politics, religion, friendship, painters and painting, the body in sickness and health. Joy and pain.

"I try not to write the same poem over and over. I try to stretch my own envelope, to write what I am afraid to write. Composing an essay, a review or a piece of literary criticism, I know more or less what I am doing and what I want to say. When I write a poem, I am crawling into the dark. Or else I am an aperture. Something needs to be put into language, and it chooses me. I invite such things. 'Not I, not I, but the wind that blows through me,' as D. H. Lawrence says.

"I write as an American, a woman, a Jew, a mother, a wife, a lover of beauty and art, a teacher, an idealist, a skeptic. Critics seem often to remark that I am 'intelligent'—but I see myself also as passionate. Actually, I am a combination of mind, body, and feelings, like everyone else, and I try to get them all into play.

"When I give poetry readings, my hope is to make people in my audience laugh and cry. They often do. The gamble is that my words will reach others, touch their inner lives. When I write literary criticism, I try to see and say clearly what is actually there in the work of other poets. Teaching is extremely important to me, my students are important, I try my best to awaken them to the delight of using their minds. Although clarity is unfashionable, I encourage it. When I teach midrash writing workshops—midrash is an ancient genre which involves elaborating on Biblical stories and characters—I want people to discover how powerfully the Bible speaks to the issues of our own time: gender roles, family dynamics, social class, freedom and slavery, war and peace, fear of the stranger, and the need to overcome that fear. These are my issues, too."

Source: Thomson Gale, "Alicia (Suskin) Ostriker," in *Contemporary Authors Online*, Thomson Gale, 2002.

Marilyn Hacker

In the following review, Hacker focuses on the sometimes conflicting identities in the poems in the collection. She argues that the poems reaffirm "the poet's unique and contradictory role, at once storyteller and witness... [of the] spectrum of human possibilities."

Alicia Ostriker's work joins the humanitarian's unalienated will to ameliorate suffering and share what's of value (which energizes progressive political engagement) to the humanist's hunger to re-engage with and continually redefine intellectual (specifically literary, also spiritual) traditions: the pedagogical passion. She is a Blake scholar and a Bible scholar, a feminist critic whose work continues to germinate a wider-branching, inclusive literary purview, a Jew whose writings are informed by, while they interrogate, that heritage and history. She is a mother and a teacher. She is also an important American poet, whose writing is enriched, and enriches its readers, by all those sometimes conflicting identities.

The Crack in Everything is her eighth collection of poems (and her thirteenth book). Ostriker is not a "difficult" poet, demanding of the reader a primary concern with the construction (or deconstruction) of literary edifices: She is a Socratic poet, who engages the reader in complex examinations by means of simple questions, deceptively simple declarative sentences.

> I picked the books to come along with me
> On this retreat at the last moment
>
> In Chicago, Petersburg, Tokyo, the dancers
> Hit the floor running
>
> We say things in this class. Like why it hurts.
>
> I called him fool, she said
> It just slipped out

A series of homages to other ordinary/extraordinary women frames the book's first half. Two dramatic monologues, spoken by a middle-class and a working-class woman, confronting the end (or not) of marriage, are followed, mirrored, by

> *... MASTECTOMY SEEMS TO ENTER ALMOST OFFHANDEDLY INTO THE DISCOURSE, UNTIL THE READER REALIZES HOW IT INFORMS THE EARLIER STANZAS ABOUT THE DANCE OF RANDOMNESS, THE FALLING INTO THE BODY OF ILLNESS AS WE'VE FALLEN INTO OUR BODIES AT BIRTH."*

two magnificent portraits of known artists—the painter Alice Neel and the poet May Swenson—in which Ostriker meticulously details the way various ordinarinesses can coalesce into genius.

After a vivid introductory stanza in which all the senses are called to witness, in counterpoint with a litany of American brand names, Neel, quintessential urban American painter, speaks (through the poet) for herself:

> You got to understand, this existence is it,
> I blame nobody, I just paint, paint is thicker than water,
> Blood, or dollars. My friends and neighbors are made
> Of paint, would you believe it, paintslabs and brushstrokes
> Right down to the kishkes, as my grandfather would say.
> Like bandaged Andy, not smart enough to duck.
>
> Palette knife jabs, carnation, ochre, viridian.

—and continues, relentlessly, to recount her descent into and emergence from mental illness.

Swenson's portrait is structured on word-and-eye-perfect observation: of a tortoise, which generates the image of the child-poet examining the animal, and the mature poet's own not untortoiselike, equally cannily observed physical presence. "Amphibian, crustacean?" Ostriker asks, to begin, and concludes, "It's friendly. Really a mammal." A modest inference to which Swenson would readily have assented, as she'd have been pleased to be glimpsed in her own naturalist's glass.

These strains meet in the book's long centerpiece, "The Book of Life," addressed to sculptor Sheila Solomon, whose work readers won't know as they do Neel's and Swenson's. The theme of the poet's and sculptor's correspondences and their differences, as artists, as friends, as Jews, as parents, interweaves with descriptions of the sculptor's work and workplace, and with the story of a third friend, who died of cancer in early middle age:

> You started the eight-foot goddess
> The year Cynthia spent dying,
> The same year you were sculpting
> Her small bald head
> Fretting you couldn't get
> The form.

In five sections, seven dense pages, "The Book of Life" is more like the notebook (writers' "books of life") from which a complex poem might be drawn. "Figurative sculpture is dead," the sculptor is told, but persists in her own (figurative, majestic) vision. This poem, with its doubled or tripled levels of narration and description, left me wishing for what I equate with the figurative in poetry: the fixed structure of accentual-syllabic form to order its plunges and ascents through the sculptor's studio and garden, the friends' shared history. (Ostriker is, in general, a poet whose formal strategies inspire confidence, and seem the outer manifestation of the poem's intentions, whether in the Sapphic echoes of the triplet stanzas of the epithalamium "Extraterrestrial," the clear-cut free-verse couplets of the May Swenson tribute or the Augustan rhymed pentameter, witty and elegiac, of "After the Reunion.")

Ostriker is a teacher by vocation, one feels, not just economic necessity: a poet/scholar who teaches not only "creative writing" but the creative *reading* that sustains the republic of letters. Many poets and novelists teach. Ostriker (along with Toi Derricotte and Marie Ponsot) is one of the few who has written about, recognized and re-created the pedagogic relationship as one of the quintessentially human connections, as fit a subject for poetry as erotic love or the changes spring rings on a meadow. Her students, as individuals or cohered into a class, are present in a group of these poems, where the dynamic that fuels a class's work together is examined—not a lecturer imprinting young minds blank as new tapes but a multivocal conversation, a collective expedition:

> All semester they brought it back
> A piece at a time, like the limbs of Osiris.

Generous as she is, Ostriker can permit herself the rueful professorial aside that the one student who "gets" Emily Dickinson, after the teacher's inspired cadenza on her poems, is "the boy/ Who'd had four years of Latin/In high school and loved Virgil." And, activist as she has always been, Ostriker cannot view the university in a vacuum, peopled only by students and teachers. "Lockout," the poem that opens the university sequence, is spoken largely by a middle-aged Latino security guard, aware of how the imported hegemony of English has inflected his life and the lives of the continent's native peoples.

The contemplative poem "After Illness" makes graceful reference to gratuitous, inevitable bodily destiny, different but equally mortal for each individual:

> What is a dance without some mad randomness
> Making it up? Look, getting sick
> Was like being born,
>
> They singled you out from among the others
> With whom you were innocently twirling,
> Doing a samba across the cumulonimbus,
>
> They said *you*, they said *now*.

Three pages, two sections later, still in a cropped triplet stanza, the poet/speaker refers to "my mastectomy"—but in a subordinate clause of a sentence whose (conditional) object, and objective, is "mourning" and "feeling," counterbalanced by imagined indulgence of an improvident infatuation; the conclusion is that any consciously determined subject matter of meditation "By definition isn't it!" In this elegant philosophical play, ... mastectomy seems to enter almost offhandedly into the discourse, until the reader realizes how it informs the earlier stanzas about the dance of randomness, the falling into the body of illness as we've fallen into our bodies at birth. The balance between the raw, unresolved mourning for Cynthia in "The Book of Life" and this almost ludic intrusion of the harsh word "mastectomy" with its vulnerable "my" prepares the reader for the book's concluding and conclusive achievement, "The Mastectomy Poems," a twelve-poem sequence.

In the book's preceding sections, Ostriker has displayed a virtuoso register of styles, voices, forms: the dramatic monologue/ word-portrait; the aphoristic or fable-like narrative in meter and rhyme; the pedagogical "I" addressing a plural "thou"; the quotidian anecdotal that shifts subtly into the meditative or the surreal. She deploys all of these in "The Mastectomy Poems" to create a mosaic of a woman's changing inner and outer life as she undergoes this ordeal (become so horrifyingly common as to resemble a rite of passage). All the while, given the book's structure, in the augmented formal echoes of its preceding themes, she reiterates as subtext that the breast cancer survivor is, chastened and changed, the same woman, the same artist and citizen, that she was before—she who praises other women (here, a breast surgeon) in the exercise of their vocations:

> I shook your hand before I went.
> Your nod was brief, your manner confident,
> A ship's captain, and there I lay, a chart
> Of the bay, no reefs, no shoals

a sensual/social woman:

> I told a man *I've resolved*
> *To be as sexy with one breast*
> *As other people are with two*
> And he looked away

a lyric economist of meter and rhyme:

> And now the anesthesiologist
> Tells something reassuring to my ear—
> And a red moon is stripping to her waist—
> *How good it is, not to be anywhere*

a teacher and member of the academic community:

> First classes, the sun is out, the darlings
> Troop in, my colleagues
> Tell me I look normal. I am normal.

Always, though, underneath the surface, under the "Black and red China silk jacket," is the shocked, transformed body, the "skinny stripe," "short piece of cosmic string" of the mastectomy scar, at once sign of escape and *memento mori*.

Omnipresent, too, the scar's double, is the lost breast, also with a double significance, first as instrument of pleasure, self-contained sustenance, bodily benignity, badge of responsible womanhood: "my right guess, my true information," transformed into a kind of time bomb, storehouse of explosives, inert but dangerous matter:

> Jug of star fluid, breakable cup—
> Someone shoveled your good and bad
>   crumbs
> Together into a plastic container . . .
> For breast tissue is like silicon.

And the breast, or the ghost breast, marks mortality now even more than the scar:

Carry me mama. Sweetheart,
I hear you, I will come.

"The River" concludes: the generative constant rescue mission of maternity thus transformed into the poet's prescience of death.

Abruptly, the sequence's next, last poem begins and ends with the speaker back in the quotidian world of work and talk: "The book-bag on my back, I'm out the door"—a teacher again, with the vivacity and accoutrements of a young student in her self-description. "Winter turns to spring/The way it does," and she unthinkingly answers the anxious "*How are you feeling*" with anecdotes about family and work. The "woman under the surface" is back on the surface, in her disguise as an ordinary worker-bee, an ordinariness like that which camouflages the genius of Swenson and Neel in their poem-portraits. But this section is titled "Epilogue"—which gives us the double message that, despite the brisk exit-line, the poem's real conclusion is the haunted one of "The River."

One section of "The Mastectomy Poems" has an epigraph—referring to "an ordinary woman"—from a poem by Lucille Clifton. Clifton too was treated for breast cancer, a few years after Ostriker. Some, only some, of the contemporary American writers who are living with, or who have succumbed to, breast cancer are, in no particular order: Pat Parker, Audre Lorde, Susan Sontag, Maxine Kumin, Eve Kosofsky Sedgwick, Penelope Austin, Edith Konecky, Hilda Raz, Patricia Goedicke, June Jordan, myself; black, white, Jewish; fat, thin and middling; lesbian, straight (and middling); childless and multiparous "And"—to borrow the title of a poem by Melvin Dixon about friends lost to AIDS—"These Are Just a Few."

The Crack in Everything: Is it a shift in the earth's tectonic plates, the purposeful Zen flaw in a ceramic vase that individualizes its perfection, the long pink keloid ridge on a newly flat chest? All of the above. This is not a polemic, a book with an aim, a recovery manual. It reaffirms the poet's unique and contradictory role, at once storyteller and witness, s/he who makes of language not a prison but a prism, refracting and recombining the spectrum of human possibilities.

Source: Marilyn Hacker, "Tectonic Shifts: A Review of *The Crack in Everything*," in *Nation*, Vol. 264, No. 18, May 12, 1997, pp. 54–57.

John Taylor

In the following review, Taylor finds a wide range of subjects and themes in the collection. In "The Mastectomy Poems," he finds that the "disparate cracks" that the speaker observes in others, appear in the speaker's own world.

Alicia Suskin Ostriker's new collection may at first surprise the reader with its multifarious subject matter (the "everything" referred to in the title), but this impression of heterogeneity takes on a compelling significance and justification by "The Mastectomy Poems," the fourth and last section. Here the disparate "cracks" that have been observed in others and in various societal phenomena fissure all the way back to the empathic observer, that is, brutally converge on the poet herself. "You never think it will happen to you," she avows in the first of twelve candid poems, "Then as you sit paging a magazine ... / Waiting to be routinely waved good-bye / ... the mammogram technician / Says *Sorry, we need to do this again.* " Ostriker describes her operation (a powerful poem is addressed to her doctor), meditates on "What Was Lost," before investigating her feelings as she recovers. During her convalescence, for instance, she breaks off an icicle, declaring it to be "A brandished javelin / Made of sheer / Stolen light / To which the palm sticks / As the shock of cold / Instantly shoots through the arm / To the heart—/ I need a language like that."

Ostriker indeed seeks a language capable of taking on "the extremes" (as she puts in "Marie at Tea"), which is to say that she strives to perceive the malefic, debilitating, or cancerous fractures beneath the smooth, deceiving surfaces of reality. This pursuit is admittedly arduous. "What the eye instantly consents to," she specifies in "Still Life: A Glassful of Zinnias on my Daughter's Kitchen Table," "Language stumbles after / Like some rejected / Clumsy perpetual lover ... / Encouraging himself: maybe this time / She'll go with me." Yet struggling with language is not the only difficulty. It is remarkable how often Ostriker mediates reality through the creativity of others. Poems here concern, allude to, or invoke Wittgenstein, Rothko, van Gogh, May Swenson, Elizabeth Bishop, Wallace Stevens, Shostakovich, Plato, Chekhov, Rumi, T. S. Eliot, Emily Dickinson, *et al.* Is their presence perhaps sometimes more self-hindering than enlightening? Even the last Mastectomy Poem concludes with Ostriker running off with

a "bookbag on [her] back." Several *engagé* poems—memorably, those set in Somalia or at a rape trial where the victim is a retarded girl—likewise seem reactions, however justifiably indignant, not to what Ostriker has eye-witnessed (or experienced in her own body) but rather to what she has learned through the news media.

This is not to suggest that Ostriker's bookbag is overly burdensome; only that the problem of "paying attention"—not just to extraordinary events, but also to zinnias on a kitchen table—functions here as a sort of Achilles' heel for the poet. Her occasional under-estimations of the ordinary, as opposed to her eagerness to point up the dramatic, work like insidious cracks weakening or diverting the emotional intensity of some of these poems. Perhaps the poet relies, in places, not confidently enough on her own perceptive gifts, although her talent is evident in the arresting detail of "Locker Room \Conversation" or in the delightful opening poem, which depicts dogs plunging "straight into / The foaming breakers // Like diving birds, letting the green turbulence / Toss them, until they snap and sink // Teeth into floating wood / Then bound back to their owners." This canine image of "passionate speed / For nothing, / For absolutely nothing but joy" is the touchstone—not yet marred by illness or moral iniquity—against which the reader will measure the destructive cracks in everything else. Interestingly, some longer poems begin as detailed, firmly-structured narratives, then conclude in fragments or with an oblique, even dissociated, twist—a sign, too, that a former wholeness has crumbled. This quality is particularly striking in a diary-like poem, "Taylor Lake," where Ostriker first relates a family hike in the mountains, then abruptly records the tale of a man who has sat down with children in a sandbox.

Too many poems, however, include facile pronouncements. In "The Vocabulary of Joy," for example, Ostriker exclaims her "happiness" while she watches a laughing, racially-mixed family—a sentiment that she cannot convey more graphically, however, for she adds only: "Though surely you know what I mean / In the late twentieth century // When I say this." It is a pity that Ostriker has not dissected her "happiness"; such remarks in any case dull the vibrancy of the present, which she had nevertheless evoked with gusto: "Father to shoulders hoists / Their slender redhead daughter, who // Laughs and shouts, pulling his hair, / *You're fun, Daddy.*" "Lockout" similarly perks our interest in a campus security guard who helps the poet unlock her office door; yet we never get to know this man, for the poem turns to the way he was treated at school: "They hit my hands with rulers and made me eat soap / For speaking my own language, Spanish." We sympathize, but the poem goes no further than this revelation of organized brutality; the security guard is ultimately used as a mere political symbol.

This tendency to take stands crops up even in the complex, ambitious long-poem, "The Book of Life," which is a challenging exploration of Judaism. A few cumbersome lines ("She used to describe the folk music scene in America /— *Before money made a hole in it* / *And the joy spilled out*") distract from the poignancy of a folksinger's death. "Her daughters assembled," writes Ostriker, "As she slept and woke, slept and moaned. / They made the decision to switch / To the intravenous." This simple, moving scene illustrates our (once again) late-twentieth-century manner of seeing off our parents and loved-ones. In contrast to allusions to ever-shifting socio-economic realities, do not these grave gestures and the random, telling remembrances that follow ("A pair of buttersoft, cherry-red / Italian gloves ... / her tragicomic love affairs, / Her taste in flowers, Catalan cooking, / Shelves of tattered blues and flamenco records"), suffice in giving us the essential—a lasting, universal emotion?

Source: John Taylor, Review of *The Crack in Everything*, in *Poetry*, Vol. CLXX, No. 3, June 1997, pp. 174–77.

Alison Townsend

In the following review, Townsend finds the poems in the collection both "heartbreaking and healing." She claims that Ostriker forges a strong connection between self and world, and is "immediate, passionate and direct."

Rilke once said, "Perhaps everything terrible is in its deepest being something that wants help from us." Each of these three poets writes about something terrible, transforming it with the intelligence and beauty of her art. Against the backdrop of the Vietnam War and her brother's suicide, Roseann Lloyd confronts incest, abuse and alcoholism. Lucille Clifton writes movingly of cancer and mastectomy. Alicia Ostriker examines illness and healing from

> **OSTRIKER WRITES FROM A LEVEL OF AWARENESS THAT IS BOTH HEARTBREAKING AND HEALING, PRECISELY BECAUSE IT ENCOMPASSES SO MUCH LOSS."**

breast cancer, as well as the power of poetry in an imperfect and increasingly dangerous world.

Near the end of the title poem in *War Baby Express*, Roseann Lloyd asks "What is left, then, at the end of grief?" The response is "a voice that bears witness/ to human pain." Lloyd's luminous second collection bears witness to the development of that steady and authentic voice against nearly overwhelming odds.

The speaker in these poems goes on a journey propelled by loss: beginning with the drug overdose of her artist brother at 21, and continuing through the losses inflicted by sexual abuse and battering, the poems in the opening section comprise the landscape the poet traverses to move from "a place of pain" to the peace attained at the end of the book.

The metaphor of the journey first appears in the incantatory "Angles of Vision." In this hypnotic gathering of evidence, the speaker literally walks herself back through her terrible memories, knowing that when I'm walking it's the movement that counts thinking whatever flits across my mind the way a cat tracks each purple shadow catching the grass &

> when I'm walking I let
> myself think about the
> doctors who thought my
> symptoms indicated a
> tumor buried deep inside
> my head

Here are the after-effects of incest. The walking in the poem provides a perfect meditative structure for remembrance that is both rhythmic and obsessive, that permits the speaker to link seemingly disparate experiences into a coherent whole. As she walks, she allows herself to think about the unthinkable: incest, its lingering physical and psychological symptoms, her father's violence toward her brothers, her brother's suicide, her husband's "violent silence" in the face of it all. The poem walks/works its way through the past, up to a present where the speaker is "not afraid any more':

> walking up the canyon . . .
> up through
> the knapweed up to
> the purple lupine the fringed
> gentian the scarlet gilia
> & on up to the shooting stars
> walking into my life walking
> up the canyon I never
> reach the end of

Reading this poem, I had the feeling that the rhythm of the body, the actual walking woman, had made it possible.

One of the pleasures of reading Lloyd's work derives from her completely unobtrusive technical skill. In "Angles of Vision" she uses repetition, mid-line caesuras and lack of punctuation to capture the halting, eliding movement of memory and mind on the page. In other more directly narrative poems, such as the stunning "Cloud of Witnesses, All Saint's Day" and "County Mental Health Clinic, 1976," she employs a longer, almost Whitmanesque, iambic line and mostly endstopped couplets that underscore the pain and solemnity of wife abuse.

> When I told the story of how he beat me up, why, and how,
> his face cracked like neglected plaster
> in an empty house.
> I could never believe it was happening.
> It was always a shock to be slammed
> sideways against a door.
> He was careful not to break my glasses.
> Bruises—raw umber—don't show on
> the back of the head.

These lines have a cumulative power that builds into one of the most affecting poems of witness I have read in recent years.

The feature of Lloyd's work I find most appealing is what I can only describe as her undefendedness. There is no pretense or posturing in these poems. This is a poet who has fought to understand things exactly as they are, and is not afraid to name them. Despite the painful stories at the core of this book, it is full of redemption and grace. In one of my favorites, "Tenderness," the poet sits in the hospital with a sick friend:

> I want to tell you
> how your hand held on to mine like a
> life-line
> & you said, will you stay until If fall
> asleep
> & I sat there for a long time
> & felt close to you peaceful in the white,
> still room holding you to earth.

Long one of my favorite poets for the courage of her art, in this collection Lloyd is both stylistically original and emotionally whole, transforming the landscape of loss into one of possession.

The journey Lucille Clifton undertakes in *The Terrible Stories* begins in the interior and moves outward into the world. This movement is established in "Telling Our Stories," which serves as introduction and overture to the collection. The speaker recalls being summoned by a mysterious "fox that came every evening to my door/ asking for nothing." Trapped by fear, the speaker hopes to "dismiss her." But she cannot escape the message the fox brings:

> child, I tell it was not
> the animal blood I was hiding from,
> it was the poet in her, the poet
> and the terrible stories she could tell.

She enters into an almost shamanic relationship with this fox, who represents her instinctual/animal/creative self. Though her malaise is never named, it is clearly one of the soul, something that the fox knows about. In "One Year Later" she wonders

> what if, . . .
> entering my room,
> brushing against the shadows,
> lapping them into rust,
> her soft paw extended,
> she had called me out?
> what if, . . .
> I had reared up baying,
> and followed her off
> into vixen country?
> what then of the moon,
> the room, the bed, the poetry
> of regret?

The poet has not followed the fox, and yet by meditating on its image, something in her is transformed. In "a dream of foxes," the fox vanishes, becoming "a lovely line/ of honest women stepping/ without fear or guilt or shame/ safe through the generous fields."

The "terrible stories" Clifton tells in this collection are all powerful. But I found the most affecting sequence in the book to be "From the Cadaver," the poems about cancer and mastectomy. "What is the splendor of one breast/ on one woman?" she asks. In "lumpectomy eve" she describes the sense of loss "all night it is the one breast/comforting the other." And in "1994" she describes the fear of waking "into the winter/ of a cold and mortal body/ thin icicles hanging off/the one mad nipple weeping."

There is no self-pity here, however. What is here is a willingness to embrace our collective experience—"you must know all about this," she says, "from your own shivering life." Finally, there is hope. In the wonderfully spirited "hag riding," we wake with the speaker "to the heat of morning/ galloping down the highway of my life" when

> something hopeful rises in me
> and I lob my fierce thigh high
> over the rump of the day and honey
> i ride i ride

Clifton's stripped-down lines, characteristically direct and unadorned language, lack of punctuation and gem-like metaphors all work to create a poetry so concentrated it bypasses the cerebral, traveling straight to the heart. Gritty and determined, these are poems that look mortality in the eye.

In "The Class," in Alicia Suskin Ostriker's eighth collection, *The Crack in Everything*, the speaker/teacher says her job is to give her students "permission/ to gather pain into language," to make an art that is not "divisible from dirt,/ from rotten life," because, she believes, "Against evidence . . . / Poetry heals or redeems suffering," even if it is "not the poet who is healed,/ But someone else, years later." Ostriker examines subjects as diverse as "weightless/ unstoppable neutrinos/ leaving their silvery trace/ in vacuum chambers," a Times Square bag lady in her "cape of rusty razor blades," three million dead "stacked . . . like sticks" in winter, or the "nectar/ in the bottom of a cup/ This blissfulness in which I strip and dive." This world is seen against the undercurrent of mortality that pulses beneath even the most optimistic poems.

Ostriker writes from a level of awareness that is both heartbreaking and healing, precisely because it encompasses so much loss. She searches for what, in the title of one poem, she calls "The Vocabulary of Joy," noting how very difficult indeed it is to "define . . . happiness,/

Though surely you know what I mean/ In the late twentieth century// when I say this."

The book moves from examinations of contemporary events to meditations on art and artists, to musings about the meaning of existence, to the closing, more immediately personal poems on age, illness and healing. Part of search is the search for self in mid-life. Don't I know you from somewhere?" the speaker asks in "Neoplatonic Riff." "Didn't I use to be you?" "Looking like a grownup, but still/ Crayoning in the outlines, a good child,/ A good committee member," she finds herself in her fifties, still trying to figure out who she is.

One of Ostriker's greatest strengths as poet has always been the lack of separation between self and world in her work. Immediate, passionate and direct, even the more public poems in this collection possess an intimacy that startles the reader. Capable of personifying subjects as diverse as a California surfer, a migrant, even a "globule" of transparent life, Ostriker also testifies to the horrors of our time. In poems like "The Russian Army Goes Into Baku" and "The Eighth and the Thirteenth" she looks at cruelty and violence with a fierce and unblinking eye.

> In the splendid extended sequence "The Book of Life," she reflects on the strength of spirituality and the friendships of female creators. "To whom shall we say/Inscribe me in the book of life," she asks—

> To whom if not each other
> To whom if not our damaged children
> To whom if not our piteous ancestors
> To whom if not the lovely ugly forms
> We have created,
> The forms we wish to coax
> From the clay of nonexistence—
> However persistent the voice
> That rasps hopeless, that claims
> Your fault, your fault—
> As if outside the synagogue we stood
> On holier ground in a perennial garden
> Jews like ourselves have just begun to
> plant.

Here, in one seamless stanza, the speaker embraces self, family, friends, creative work and spirituality, making what must die away into life.

Like Clifton, Ostriker describes the experience of mastectomy, writing a path though the "riddle" of illness with clarity and grace. "You think it will never happen to you," she begins, whirling us into diagnosis, surgery and recovery with the peculiar intimacy of the second person.

There is shock here. The post-op scar is a "skinny stripe/ That won't come off with soap/ A scarlet letter lacking a meaning . . . / It's nothing." There is grief: "Was I succulent? Was I juicy./ you sliced me like a green honeydew." There is rage. The poet is careful never to say "the thing that is forbidden to say," never invites her colleagues "to view it pickled in a Mason jar." There is healing: "Like one of those trees with a major limb lopped/ I'm a shade more sublime today than yesterday." And finally, in the delightfully understated "Epilogue: Nevertheless," there is recovery. "It actually takes me a while," she says, "To realize what they have in mind" when friends ask how she is feeling. Bookbag on her back, she is out the door, to whatever comes next. These strong, tough-minded, lyrical poems take us there too.

Though they begin from similar emotional points of reference, each of these three poets offers us a different perspective on loss, damage or fear and its transformation through the ritual of poem-making. Lloyd, whose work I find most direct, accessible and affecting, speaks in a voice that is both intimate and individual. Reading her is like sitting with a friend at a kitchen table, exchanging confidences over tea. Clifton, by contrast, is a myth-maker: her condensed, gem-like poems cast their spell from some source near the center of existence. Ostriker, though often tender, is overall witty and urbane, a poet of intellect whose voice is filtered through an acute social consciousness. But all speak with authenticity and authority, claiming the events of their lives and helping us to approach our own terrible stories in the process.

Source: Alison Townsend, "No Pain, No Gain," in *Women's Review of Books*, Vol. 14, No. 6, March 1997, pp. 12–13.

SOURCES

Dolin, Sharon, "How the Light Gets In," in *American Book Review*, Vol. 18, No. 6, September–October 1997, pp. 23, 24.

Earnshaw, Doris, Review of *The Crack in Everything*, in *World Literature Today*, Vol. 71, No. 1, Winter 1997, p. 156.

Ellis, Steven R., Review of *The Crack in Everything*, in *Library Journal*, Vol. 121, No. 6, April 1, 1996, p. 87.

Hacker, Marilyn, "Tectonic Shifts," in *Nation*, Vol. 264, No. 18, May 12, 1997, pp. 54, 57.

Monaghan, Patricia, Review of *The Crack in Everything*, in *Booklist*, Vol. 92, No. 17, May 1, 1996, p. 1485.

Ostriker, Alicia Suskin, "Mastectomy," in *The Crack in Everything*, University of Pittsburg Press, 1996, pp. 88–89.

Review of *The Crack in Everything*, in *Publishers Weekly*, Vol. 243, No. 18, April 29, 1996, p. 63.

Review of *The Crack in Everything*, in *Virginia Quarterly Review*, Vol. 73, No. 1, Winter 1997, p. 29.

Townsend, Alison, "No Pain, No Gain," in *Women's Review of Books*, Vol. 14, No. 6, March 1997, pp. 12, 13.

FURTHER READING

Benedet, Rosalind, and Bob Hogenmiller, *After Mastectomy: Healing Physically and Emotionally*, Addicus Books, 2003.

> Benedet, an experienced oncology nurse who has helped hundreds of women recover from mastectomies, offers important guides to emotional and physical recovery, including reconstruction options. Hogenmiller provides detailed photographs of the surgery and of the healing process.

Lucas, Geralyn, *Why I Wore Lipstick to My Mastectomy*, St. Martin's Press, 2004.

> The twenty-seven-year-old author, producer of the television show *20/20*, chronicles her bout with breast cancer, including her emotional response and coping strategies pre- and post-surgery.

Perkins, David, *A History of Modern Poetry*, Vol. 2: *Modernism and After*, Belknap Press, 2004.

> Perkins examines the works of individual poets published up to the twenty-first century as well as important movements such as modernism, beat poetry, and confessional poetry. He notes the distinctiveness and the interconnectedness among the poets in these movements and addresses the critical response to them over the years.

Spiegelman, William, *How Poets See the World: The Art of Description in Contemporary Poetry*, Oxford University Press, 2005.

> Spiegelman investigates how poetry makes connections between the word and the image and offers insight into the processes of reading and interpretation. He also explores how word and image are influenced by biographical and cultural factors.

One of the Smallest

GERALD STERN

1997

Gerald Stern's poem "One of the Smallest" was first published in the journal *Poetry* in January 1997. A four-page poem, it is the first section of six sections in Stern's twelfth book of poetry, *Last Blue*, published in 2000. Stern did not start publishing poetry until 1971, when he was forty-six years old, but by 1973, he had received a National Endowment for the Arts grant to be a master poet for Pennsylvania, and he received numerous awards afterward, including the National Book Award in 1998 for his collection of poetry entitled *This Time: New and Selected Poems*. *Last Blue* was also well received as a continuation of Stern's emotional, exuberant expression of himself in surreal images. Using the first person, the narrator becomes a sort of Everyman based on Stern's own background and memories. "One of the Smallest" is typical of Stern's work in that it includes abundant imagery taken from elements of the natural world such as animals, plants, and a river. A poem about death and rebirth, "One of the Smallest" follows a ray of sunshine through multiple locations and transformations as a life force that is compared to and connected with a person's life span.

AUTHOR BIOGRAPHY

Born on February 22, 1925, Gerald Stern grew up in a rough neighborhood in Pittsburgh, Pennsylvania. His parents, both Eastern European

Gerald Stern (© *Nancy Kaszerman/ZUMA/Corbis*)

MEDIA ADAPTATIONS

- Gerald Stern gave a reading of "Roses" from his book *American Sonnets* for the Griffin Trust for Excellence in Poetry. As of 2007, video of this reading was available on the Griffin Poetry Prize website.

- On November 23, 1998, Elizabeth Farnsworth interviewed Gerald Stern for the *PBS Online NewsHour*. As of 2007, both a print and an audio version were available at PBS website.

immigrants, were Orthodox Jews who sent him to a religious school, but he stopped practicing his faith shortly after his bar mitzvah. In childhood, Stern suffered from anti-Semitism; moreover, at age eight, he experienced the traumatic death of his nine-year-old sister Sylvia to spinal meningitis. In 1947, he graduated from the University of Pittsburgh, served in the U.S. Army Air Corps, and then earned his master's degree from Columbia University in 1949. Although he began writing poetry in college, Stern taught college English for most of his professional career.

After graduation, Stern went to Paris for a year of travel and study at the Sorbonne, and it was there that he became seriously interested in poetry. Upon his return to New York, he entered a doctoral program at Columbia but left a year later to become the headmaster at a private school. He married Patricia Miller in 1952, and in 1953, they went back to Europe for three years. He eventually taught high school in Glasgow, Scotland. Upon his return to the United States, Stern began his college teaching career, holding positions at Temple University, Indiana University of Pennsylvania, and Somerset County College. From 1982 to his retirement in 1995, he held a tenured position at the Writers' Workshop of the University of Iowa. Throughout these years, he was also a visiting professor at several other universities. He and his wife had two children, but the couple divorced in the late 1980s.

Stern did not publish his first book of poetry, *Rejoicings*, until 1971, when he was forty-six years old. Among more than a dozen subsequent collections of poetry are *Lucky Life* (1977, Lamont Poetry Selection Award); *This Time: New and Selected Poems* (1998, National Book Award); *Last Blue* (2000), which contains "One of the Smallest"; *American Sonnets* (2003, Griffin Poetry Prize); and *Everything Is Burning* (2006). He is also the author of a book of personal essays, *What I Can't Bear Losing: Notes from a Life* (2003).

Stern has received many other honors, including a Guggenheim Fellowship, five National Endowment of the Arts Fellowships, the Governor's Award for Excellence in the Arts for the State of Pennsylvania, the PEN Award, a chancellorship in the Academy of American Poets, and the Ruth Lilly Prize and the Wallace Stevens Award for a lifetime of achievement in poetry. A lyric poet who emphasizes lessons from memories and nature, Stern has made a significant contribution to American literature.

POEM TEXT

> Made of the first gray light
> that came into my room,
> of the hole itself
> in the cracked window blind,
> thus made of sunshine, thus made of   5
> gas and water, one of the
> smallest, smallest, made of
> that which seizes the eye,
> that which an eagle needs

and even a mole, a mole, a
rabbit, a quail, a lilac,
it was uncreated. I
fought for it, I tore down
walls, I cut my trees,
I lay on my back, I had a
rock to support my head, I
swam in two directions,
I lay down smiling, the sun
made my eyes water, what
the wind and the dirt took away
and what was abraded and what was
exhausted, exhausted, was only
a just reflection. The sun
slowly died and I much
quicker, much quicker, I raced
until I was wrinkled but I was
lost as the star was and I
was losing light, I was dying
before I was born, thus I was
blue at the start, though I was
red much later, much later,
for I was a copy, but I was
something exploding and I was
born for just that but fought
against it, against it. The light
of morning was gray with a green
and that of evening was almost a
rose in one sky though it was
white in another—at least
in one place the light comes back—
and I disappeared like a fragment
of gas you'd call it, or fire,
fragment by fragment I think,
cooled down and changed into metal,
captured and packaged as it will be
in one or two more centuries
and turned then into a bell—
not a bridge, not a hammer—
really the tongue of a bell,
if bells will still be in use then,
and I will sing as a bell does,
you'd call it tolling—such
was my burst of light seen from
a certain viewpoint though seen from
another, another, no sudden
flash but a long slow burning
as in the olive tree burning,
as in the carob, as slow as the
olive, still giving up chocolate
after two thousand years, that's
what we lacked, our light
was like the comet's, like a
flash of fosfur, a burst
from a Spanish matchbox, the wood
broken in two, the flame
lasting six seconds—I counted—
that is, when the fosfur worked,
two or three lives lived out
in a metal ash tray, one of them
nothing but carbon, one of them
wood part way, poor thing that

10

15

20

25

30

35

40

45

50

55

60

65

70

died betimes, one snuffed out
just at the neck where the pinkish
head was twisted the wrong way
and one of them curling up
even after burning, thus the
light I loved stacked in a box
depending on two rough sides
and on the wind and on the
gentleness of my hand,
the index finger pressed
against the wood, the flash
of fire always a shock,
always new and enlightening,
the same explosion forever—
I call it forever—forever—
sitting with my mouth open
in some unbearable blue,
bridal wreath in my right hand,
since this is the season, my left hand
scratching and scratching, the sun
in front now. How did dogwood
get into this yard? How did
the iris manage to get here?
And grow that way? I live
without a beard, I'm streaked
with a kind of purple, my hands
are folded and overlapping, I
love the rain, I am
a type of Persian, where I am
and in this season I blossom
for fifteen hours a day, I
walk through streams of some sort—
I like that thinking—corpuscles
bombard my eyes—I call it
light—it was what gave me
life in the first place—no no
shame in wandering, no shame
in adoring—what it what it
was was so primitive
we had to disturb it—call it
disturbing, call it interfering—
at five in the morning in front of
the dumpster, at six looking down
on the river, a little tired from
the two hundred steps, my iris
in bloom down there, my maples
blowing a little, I was
a mole and a rabbit, I was
a stone at first, I turned
garish for a while and burned.

75

80

85

90

95

100

105

110

115

120

POEM SUMMARY

Lines 1–8

"One of the Smallest" is a long poem without
stanzas. Rather than simply say that there is one
long thread that runs through the whole poem
tying it together, it would be more accurate to

say that there is one long thread running through the poem as if placed there by a sewing machine gone berserk, zigzagging unevenly as Stern's thoughts ricochet down the poem. However, there are divisions that can be made according to subject and punctuation.

The poem starts with "one of the smallest" things in existence, a ray of light. The "first gray light" of morning finds its way through a tiny hole "in the cracked window blind" in the narrator's room. Sunshine, "made of gas and water"—a reference to the gaseous composition of the sun and the way sunlight reflects off particles of water—although the "smallest, smallest" microscopically small, can still catch the eye in an otherwise darkened room.

Lines 9–23

The sunlight is needed by living creatures, and Stern lists among them an eagle, a mole, a rabbit, a quail, and a lilac. He emphasizes the mole by repeating, "even a mole, a mole" because even though the mole lives mostly underground, it, too, needs sunlight. As a human, the narrator needs sunlight so much that he says, "I tore down walls, I cut my trees," to allow more sunlight to reach him. He enjoys the sunlight by sunbathing while lying on his back with "a rock to support" his head, swimming, and then drying in the sunlight, even if the bright sun can make his eyes water. Stern notes the passage of time in a reference to "the wind and the dirt" wearing away the surface of the earth as he segues into the segment of the poem that deals with death.

Lines 23–35

As the day and the years progress, the sun "slowly died." When the sun sets, it appears to die out, but it is actually dying over millions of years, while the narrator is dying "much quicker, much quicker." The narrator describes life as a race "until I was wrinkled" by old age, but he and the star are both "losing light." The narrator says, "I was dying before I was born," because from the moment life begins it is on a journey to death. At birth, the narrator describes himself as "blue" perhaps in reference to those babies who are born a little blue because before birth they did not get sufficient oxygen. A healthy baby will turn red when crying, and the narrator says, "I was red much later." The redness is Stern's color for life, "a copy" of the sun exploding down the path of life, but the narrator is inescapably born for death, even if he "fought against it."

Lines 35–43

In the first line, Stern refers to "the first gray light," and he returns to that image in line 36 as a comparison to the evening sky that is "rose" in one sky and "white" in another. The narrator actually says "a rose," perhaps to create an image of an evening sky when the varied colors are layered like the petals of a rose. The white sky may be equivalent to the bright light to which one is supposed to go at death, the "one place the light comes back" in the darkness that is death. At this point, the narrator says, "I disappeared like a fragment of gas . . . or fire." Choosing to use the words gas and fire again, Stern is making connections to the gases and fire of the sun in the disintegration of the narrator's life.

Lines 44–52

Eventually, Stern wants to resurrect the narrator, but first the fiery, gaseous fragments are cooled and transformed into metal and then, after "one or two more centuries," made into a bell. Some people who believe in reincarnation or multiple lives believe there may be large time gaps between lives and perhaps that is why Stern provides a length of time before the metal finally gets made into something. The narrator insists that he is made into a bell and "not a bridge, not a hammer"; more precisely, he envisions becoming "the tongue of a bell" because he wants to "sing as the bell does."

Lines 52–62

The burst of light that exploded the narrator's being into gaseous fragments is one viewpoint, but, the reader is told, there could be another way of looking at his death. Perhaps instead his was a "long slow burning" fire as one might have with a slow-burning wood such as that of the olive or carob trees, two trees still in existence after thousand of years. The narrator says that is what is wrong with human life: it is more like the comet's flash of fire than like the plants that have lasted on earth longer than humans.

Lines 62–85

Even more short-lived is the flame on a match. Stern describes in detail the composition and function of a match and a matchbox. Anyone who has ever used a match is reminded by Stern's description of exactly the process of striking a match, letting it burn, and how it looks afterwards. Readers can almost smell the "fosfur" (usually spelled phosphor), hear the striking of the match, count with the narrator through the six seconds that the flame lasts, and see the curled remains of matches in the ash tray. The matchbox is also vividly described with its stack of matches, the two rough striking areas on the sides of the box, and how one holds a match to light it. No matter how common the action, the narrator says that the "flash of fire" is "always a shock," because one never knows when the match will catch fire and when it will not. Besides, the making of fire simply by scratching a treated piece of wood against a rough surface still seems like magic, so the experience is always new and enlightening because each match starts a new fire.

Lines 86–93

Speaking of forever, time has apparently passed, and the narrator finds himself once again in his yard, once again starting out blue with his mouth agape, perhaps from the surprise of the transition. The narrator is immediately able to discern the season because he has a bridal wreath in his right hand, so it must be June, the month of weddings. Why is his left hand scratching? Is he clawing his way back into life? Stern is a poet of place, so the narrator is located in a yard that has a dogwood tree and an iris.

Lines 93–102

Is the narrator looking at the iris, or has the narrator become the iris in a new life? He says he is without a beard, and irises have what is called a beard in the center of the flower, but he also says that he is streaked with purple, a common color for irises, and that his "hands are folded and overlapping" just as the iris's large petals appear to be like folded hands. As a plant, he loves the rain and "blossoms for fifteen hours a day" in the summertime sunlight.

Lines 102–121

In this last section of the poem, the narrator shifts back to being a human who walks "through streams of some sort." As the sunlight bombards his eyes, he likes to think that the sun is what gave him "life in the first place." The next several lines ponder how natural it might be, as primitive peoples did, to worship the sun for its life-giving properties. Instead, modern people sometimes see the sunlight as "disturbing, call it interfering" when in its pervasiveness it lights up the area around the dumpster "at five in the morning" or shines on the river at six. The narrator describes being "a little tired from the two

TOPICS FOR FURTHER STUDY

- Stern is Jewish and has written poems about the Holocaust as well as many other subjects. He is often called a Jewish poet. In a small group, discuss whether heritage or subject matter makes someone a *Jewish* poet. For reference, look up his poem "Soap" or his poem "Adler."

- Gerald Stern did not publish his first book of poetry until 1971 when he was forty-six years old. After that he published more than a dozen books and earned numerous prestigious awards. Research the time in Stern's life before 1971 and write a brief biography of the man before his career as a poet.

- Why is Stern called the modern Whitman? Make a list of the characteristics of the poetry of each man and compare them. Is it valid to say that Stern writes in the style of Whitman? Defend your answer in a written answer or a presentation to your class, with specifics from your list.

- In 1982, Stern began teaching at the Writers' Workshop at the University of Iowa and remained there until his retirement at the age of seventy in 1995. The Iowa Writers' Workshop is one of the most famous schools for aspiring writers of all genres in the United States. Make an online search for other colleges that offer degrees in professional or creative writing. If you wanted to be a writer, where would you go and why? Explain your answer to your class.

- Stern won the National Book Award in 1998. What is this award and why is it so prestigious? How many genres does it cover? Make a comparison of the National Book Award to the Pulitzer Prize. Compare lists of recent winners. Report your findings in a brief, bulleted format.

hundred steps." Are these steps a reference to the one or two centuries in line 46 that it took for the metal to be made into a bell? Or does Stern have a backyard that has two hundred steps down to the river? Regardless, his iris is blooming and his maple tree is blowing in the wind. All is well. He has been a mole, a rabbit, a stone, maybe a bell and an iris, or at least shared life and the need for fire and sunshine with them. Life is "garish," a bright flash of many colors, and then a burning of human energy.

THEMES

Light versus Darkness

A career-long theme for Stern was that of light versus darkness, that this natural contrast or conflict is inherently important to humans in both a biological and an emotional way. "One of the Smallest" incorporates light and darkness with life, death, and rebirth. The narrator of the poem says that light "was what gave me life in the first place," and Stern makes this connection between light and life throughout the poem. In lines 9–11, he asserts that the plants and animals need sunlight. In the same way, the narrator needs sunlight so much that he tears down walls and cuts down trees to get more of it. Stern describes a scene in which the narrator is soaking up the sun outdoors by sunbathing and swimming. The implication is that his energy and his joy come from the sunlight. However, the sun is dying and so is the narrator. By "losing light," he disappears into fragments, but he reappears into his sunlit yard after an explosion of light brings him back to life. A popular image of death is going into the light, but for the narrator of the poem death is darkness, an absence from the world until his essence is remade and brought back to life by the fire of light. Although the word "light" is used many times in "One of the Smallest," the words "dark" and "darkness" are not because death is equated to darkness or the loss of light. So, although there are allusions to death in this poem, the emphasis is on the power of light to generate life and rebirth, a power so strong that even "one of the smallest" particles of light can awaken a person to a world of joy.

Memory and Nostalgia

Memory for Stern is as much a device as a theme; he uses memories to generate poetry. The idea, however, is to encourage readers to take a trip down memory lane with the narrator of the poem for the purpose of sharing memories and comparing them to the readers' own. Perhaps whatever the "I" of the poem learns from his memories serves as a lesson for readers, too. Stern is not being didactic or nostalgic in a heavy-handed way; rather, the memories are an opportunity for thoughtful examination that might lead to a resurrection of goals and the search for paradise that Stern feels is a central quest for all humans. Nostalgia prompts one to look back and gain perspective about events in one's past. At the same time, it prompts one to bring the pieces of one's life together in order to blend past, present, and future into a cohesive whole, of applying logic to the emotions lingering from the past. In "One of the Smallest," the speaker in the poem remembers a past life spent in sunshine and nature. Death takes that life away for a while, but light, the energy of fire and the sun, gives it back. The interim period is a remembrance of the fragments of his essence being made into the tongue of a bell, remembering how slowly the olive and carob trees burn and how long they have been a part of the earth's resources, remembering in detail the construction and use of a matchbox and matches. Stern's narrator imagines being transformed into a bell's tongue. The close-up look at the matches provides a way to come back to the fire and light that will rekindle his life and place him once again in his yard, where he does not remember the dogwood and the iris, but time has gone by and there is a new world to experience in the warmth of the life-giving sunlight that he appreciates so much.

Rebirth

A frequent subject in storytelling, mythology, and religion, rebirth can be portrayed as spiritual, as a metaphoric rectification of one's life, or as a some kind of reincarnation. The symbols of rebirth include baptism, the rites of spring, the rise of the mythic phoenix from the ashes, and so on. Whether used in the *Odyssey*, *Rime of the Ancient Mariner*, or *Groundhog Day*, the theme is a familiar one that usually involves uprooting the subject who then journeys to the new life. Rebirth is used frequently by Stern as a device for becoming free of inner conflict and the past's burdens, a type of cleansing. In "One of the Smallest," rebirth takes place after a transformation through time and matter. It is described as the reincarnation of the narrator into an iris, but also possibly into a mole, rabbit, stone, and then perhaps back into a human who can once again

The spiritual journey of death in this poem is symbolized by contrasting images of light and dark drawn from nature (© Images.Com/Corbis)

relish the joy of light and nature. Perhaps the narrator has been all of the these things at different times as the molecules of nature evolve and transform, just as the molecules of the sun bring life to everything.

STYLE

Lyric Poetry

Lyric poetry, the dominant form of the twentieth century, does not tell a story; it has a single narrator, not the poet, who speaks in first person. This "I" is a distinguishing feature of lyric poetry and is used to express a state of mind, present an argument or a justification, make an observation, or contemplate a problem. Readers of lyric poetry need to identify the type of person speaking and the listener to whom the narrator is speaking. Stern's poems are based on his memories, but he does not reveal the source of those

memories, nor does he regard the speaker as his personal mouthpiece. Rather, the speaker is a contemporary representative person, more singular than the Everyman of Whitman and other poets. In "One of the Smallest," the "I" gives individuality to an experience that yet could be the life and fate of anyone.

Free Verse

The most commonly used style of poetry in modern times is free verse. While it does not have strict metrical patterns, fixed line lengths, or ending rhymes, it qualifies as poetry because of its rhythms and sound patterns. Students of free verse should look for divisions within a poem (not just stanza divisions but divisions from one line to the next), line length, repeated syntactical units, imagery patterns, sound devices, and word choices. Assonance, alliteration, and internal rhyme are used to create the desired sound qualities, while repetition of words and phrases with the same syntactical structure is used to create a rhythm. Another way to create rhythm is by constructing phrases of about equal length. In "One of the Smallest," Stern uses word and phrase repetition liberally. Line length can also help to convey emphasis or create tension. For example, a series of long lines followed by one short line might signal a commentary on the preceding lines or the solution to a problem. "One of the Smallest" has lines of almost equal length throughout, which may signal that Stern wants the reader to keep going, to keep reading with the speed that the passage of time takes with one's life. Stern is known for his use of imagery from nature, and "One of the Smallest" is replete with free verse patterns of flora and fauna, sunshine, and water.

Colors

An important part of the imagery that Stern uses is color. *Last Blue* is the title of the collection in which "One of the Smallest" is the first entry, and blue is a dominant color throughout the poems in the book. In "One of the Smallest," the word "blue" appears only twice, once describing the narrator's color at birth, "blue at the start," and "sitting with my mouth open in some unbearable blue," but six other colors help to paint the landscape: gray (twice), as in the "first gray light that came into my room" and "The light of morning was gray"; red, the color he becomes after the blue of birth; green, "the light of morning was gray with a green"; white, the evening light was like a rose, "though it was white"; pinkish, "the pinkish head" of the match; and purple, "I'm streaked with a kind of purple," like the iris. Imagery is intended to appeal to the senses, and use of colors helps to convey a vivid picture to the reader.

Sensuality of Nature and Physical Things

Stern is noted for his extensive use of images from nature. The things he names, such as plants and animals, give concreteness to his abstract expression and give readers something familiar to cling to as they try to follow the narrator's associative thoughts. In "One of the Smallest," the reader finds an eagle, a mole, a rabbit, a quail, a lilac, an iris, and dogwood, maple, olive and carob trees. There is a river, a stream, a yard, sunrises, and sunsets; in all, Stern sees nature as an integral part of the human experience. Also, his belief in the human need to find the lost paradise causes him to fill his landscapes with the abundant garden people may associate with paradise. Stern glorifies nature and its importance to the human environment. The renewal of life, part of nature's cycle, finds its way into Stern's poetry, as it does in the story of life, death, and rebirth that is "One of the Smallest."

HISTORICAL CONTEXT

Poetry in the 1990s

Post–World War II poetry in the United States could be categorized into definite schools, and discussions centered on traditional forms versus free verse, or academic study versus experimentation. In the 1980s, there were still definite boundaries between competing styles, but change occurred in the 1990s when reality in poetry became totally relative to the imagination of the poet. This change is referred to as the postmodern movement, and it held to no rules as it mixed varying viewpoints with psychology and experimentation with language. American poetry showed the influence of overseas and in film techniques (such as the split screen and shifting angles) and fostered diversity among women and various ethnic groups, thus joining in the burgeoning global literature movement. The result was a public interest in poetry that in the early 2000s continued to be at an all-time high. Colleges increased the number of creative writing programs, poetry slams and readings were well attended, and the Internet opened a vast exchange among poets, aspiring poets, and readers. The introduction of the World Wide Web in 1992 led to paperless, experimental poetry that is technology-driven and includes graphics, animation, and hypertext links.

Poetry in the 1990s dashed off in all directions as if the doors were opened to a big new world, and poets raced to see where they could take the genre. Consequently, in the early 2000s, it became almost impossible to typify the poetry of this decade. Anthologists had to narrow their titles to categories in this time period; for example, women's writing in the 1990s; ethnic writers; jazz poetry; cowboy poetry; hip-hop; poetry of nature, of wit, of family, etc. It could be said, though, that there were two major starting points for this new adventure from which the genre grew: first, poetry of the self, as influenced by Robert Lowell and the confessional poets of the 1950s and 1960s whose impact continued to be felt for decades, and, second, poetry of the world as typified by Elizabeth Bishop. The latter type was like a narrative, setting scenes centered on detail. The two roots of postmodernism were polar opposites and in between fell all the new poetry with various themes. Both Lowell and Bishop influenced Stern, who won the National Book Award in 1998. However, Stern definitely falls into the category of poetry of the self, which explores the psyche and expresses very personal emotions.

In addition, a study of the Pulitzer Prize winners of the decade shows a tendency toward the negative. Doom and gloom were common themes of the 1990s, perhaps because of the increased concern for the earth's environment that can be found in the poetry of the time. Whatever the cause, the negativity did not prevent the world of poetry from becoming larger and more diverse. It is hard to make a short list of notables in the field, but a few American names of import in the 1990s are Jorie Graham, Louise Gluck, Philip Levine, Charles Wright, Robert Pinsky, and Yusef Komunyakaa.

Reincarnation

An essential belief of some religions is reincarnation, the idea that the essence of a person can come back from death to live again, perhaps many times. Some religions assert that reincarnation can be cross-species, that a person may come back as an animal, for example. The idea is that the soul gains new experiences and learns in each life until spiritual perfection is achieved, at which time the sequence of birth, death, and birth ends. If the person errs with one life, then the next life could be as a lower species or in a lower station. Reincarnation is a central teaching of Hinduism, Jainism, and Sikhism, as well as to many Native American and Inuit traditions. It was also believed by some ancient Greeks, Romans, and Egyptians. Some modern New Age philosophies subscribe to the idea of reincarnation. Scientologists believe in immortality and that one is not born into another life but into another body. Buddhists believe in a continual momentum of ever-changing life, but they do not believe the individual entity or soul returns. Rebirth as used in literature usually means a spiritual renewal that is symbolized by death and rebirth, although mythology and folklore are full of stories about people who come back from the grave, often as ghosts or spirits. The theme of rebirth is generally used by writers to explain going through some kind of catharsis or dramatic life-changing turning point. Stern's "One of the Smallest" leaves the interpretation of rebirth or reincarnation up to the reader.

CRITICAL OVERVIEW

Many critics warmly received Stern's *Last Blue*. For example, Carlos Reyes, writing on the collection for the book review section of *Willamette Week Online*, points out that, "like wine, [Stern's] work only gets better with age. This is a rare book where each new reading brings us further insight into our existence." A reviewer for a volume on *American Writers*, Jonathan N. Barron agrees, commenting that "One of the Smallest," is a "visionary, even apocalyptic, tale of death, rebirth, and regeneration." As to singing, noted *Booklist* critic Donna Seaman says that Stern "levitate[s] out of the ordinary to take in the big picture and to feel the lift, the free-floating, singing bliss of life."

The focus on common events drew the notice of John Taylor, in his review of *Last Blue* for *Antioch Review*. Taylor writes that Stern's twelfth book of poetry is "composed in a vigorous first person and focused on the vagaries" of daily life. Taylor notes the extraordinary way that Stern presents ordinary things: "Stern's serpentine,

WHAT DO I READ NEXT?

- Stern won the National Book Award in 1999 for *This Time: New and Selected Poems*. This collection contains selections of Stern's best poetry from his seven previous volumes as well as new poems, and the collection shows remarkable consistency in theme and style through the years.

- *Everything Is Burning* is Stern's 2006 collection of poetry, published when the poet was eighty-one years old. As he did before, Stern based the poems on his own life and his Jewish-American heritage, but there seems to be a wider range of emotions and subjects in this volume.

- In 2003, Stern published a memoir, *What I Can't Bear Losing: Notes from a Life*, a reminiscence that includes explanations about the development of his writing style.

- Since Stern is often compared to Walt Whitman, a good companion to the study of Stern's poetry is Whitman's 1855 masterpiece, *Leaves of Grass*, which is available in various editions.

- Stern admits to preferring elements of Emily Dickinson to Walt Whitman. Multiple editions of her poetry are available, including a 2006 edition, entitled *Complete Poems of Emily Dickinson*.

- Stern recommends to readers the work of poet Rainier Maria Rilke (1875–1926), whose popularity increased after Galway Kinnell and Hannah Liebmann published *The Essential Rilke* in 2000.

- As a young man, Stern sought out W. H. Auden, whose *Collected Poems* are available in a 2007 edition from Modern Library.

kaleidoscopic verses combine, as in a Cubist collage, unexpected juxtapositions or contradictory viewpoints." Taylor further comments: "Capricious, amusing and sometimes suddenly poignant in their imagery, these poems exhibit mobility and uprootedness as paradoxically constant themes." He concludes that the collection has a "plucky, if melancholy, spirit." A reviewer for *Publishers Weekly* agrees: "The language is far from ordinary.... The poems still rely on Stern's inimitable blend of coiled anger, love of life and raffish, on-the-outside-looking-in wit."

Concerning *Last Blue*, a *Ploughshares* reviewer finds: "This is a sparer Stern than we're used to . . . he's writing now with a tighter focus, as though he had to make every word count. The best news is he does." But the reviewer for *Publishers Weekly* assures readers that Stern has remained true to his established style and that "While there are few surprises here, the quality of the poems is consistently quite high, and the voice behind them remains winning and companionable." In all, Stern won praise from many reviewers.

CRITICISM

Lois Kerschen

Kerschen is an educator and freelance writer. In this essay, she uses Stern's own words from his interviews to show how Stern's poetic practices were applied in "One of the Smallest."

It is common practice in the study of literature to examine the life of the author in hopes of finding clues to the inspiration behind the work. Often researchers can learn about the literary philosophies and creative practices of poets prior to the twentieth century only through any writings they or their learned admirers left behind on the subject. Since newspapers, radio, television, scholarly journals, and the Internet have proliferated, information about every variety of artist usually takes just a quick investigation. A further advantage of studying a modern writer is the likely availability of interviews with the author. Although some are reclusive and rarely give interviews, Gerald Stern has granted a number of them, as well as writing literary articles of his own. Besides, Stern has been a teacher most of his life and as such is inclined by the nature of the profession to share his knowledge with others. Therefore, reading his interviews can provide insight into his work. Specifically, it is interesting to see if what he preaches is what he practiced in "One of the Smallest."

Jeffrey Dodd, Elise Gregory, and Adam O'Connor Rodriguez conducted a 2005 interview

> TRYING TO KEEP UP WITH WHERE STERN IS GOING REQUIRES A MENTAL GYMNASTICS THAT FEELS LIKE BEING SHOT INTO A PINBALL MACHINE, AND YET THERE ARE NO VAGUE ALLUSIONS SENDING THE READER TO THE DICTIONARY."

with Stern for *Willow Springs*, a literary magazine produced at Eastern Washington University. In this interview, Stern talks about the process by which he arrives at a poem: "I begin with language. I don't begin with ideas, I don't begin with images. I begin with words." In regards to "One of the Smallest," the reader may then wonder if the poem began with the word "sunlight" and then Stern thought about when sunlight has made an impression on him, such as the first light of morning. "Language is everything," Stern continues to explain in the *Willow Springs* interview. He says, "I let the words transform me, carry me, literally, to places and experience. Occasionally, I'll actually think of an experience, relive an experience. You'll read a poem that might describe an experience, but it starts with language." So, in "One of the Smallest," Stern went from the thought of that first morning light and let the thought carry him to what the ray of light touches, who sees it, how it feels when multiple rays warm him outdoors, and then arrives at a comparison of light to life which, when it fades, becomes death.

Similarly, in a 2002 interview with Gary Pacernick for the *American Poetry Review*, Stern says that he allows himself to "just move along as the spirit, if you will, takes me. God knows what that spirit is. Call it the muses, call it unconsciousness, guilt, shame, love, hope, memory." Stern describes this process to Pacernick as an associative way of writing in which "one thing leads to another." The reader can then see how, once the ray of light leads Stern to a comparison with life and death in "One of the Smallest," he moves on to the death of the narrator, an interim time as a bell tongue, and then rebirth.

In Greek mythology, the muses were the nine goddess sisters who served as patrons and sources of inspiration for the arts and sciences.

For Stern, perhaps the muse of poetry is still around to guide him and in "One of the Smallest," this associative method of Stern's is obvious. Thoughts run down the page with only a few commas and a rare period to give pause. The poem's opening sentence, if it can be called a sentence, runs for twelve lines. The next two sentences run eleven and twelve lines, but the fourth sentence runs from line 35 to line 92! Trying to keep up with where Stern is going requires a mental gymnastics that feels like being shot into a pinball machine, and yet there are no vague allusions sending the reader to the dictionary. All the terms are everyday language, and for an abstract work, there are sufficient logical connections to enable the reader to hang on for the whole ride. Everyone has seen sunlight peeking through a window shade. Everyone has seen pictures of, if not actual, eagles, moles, rabbits, quails, lilacs, dogwood, and irises. Readers have seen bells, bridges, hammers, and matchboxes, and understand the point about olive and carob trees. The abstract nature of the poem comes in its ideas, but Stern describes everyday, concrete objects with words that are piled and scattered about, words that, as he says, carry him to places and experiences, words that fly wherever the spirit guides them, to express those thoughts and his feelings. Stern told Sue William Silverman in an interview for *Fourth Genre*: "What I believe...is that there is a subordinate or superior body or mind that is writing, organizing for you, and you must submit to that body or mind. It's inchoate or invisible, without making it too mystical or being too Freudian about this." Put in its simplest terms, Stern summed up the process for Silverman by saying: "I just write and hope it's good."

Stern wrote in a 1999 essay for *American Poetry Review*: "Poetry helps people live their lives through its music," through poetry's "exquisite interpenetration of these two things, moral force and tenderness, or brute power and tenderness." Stern's words may run pell-mell down the page in "One of the Smallest," but there are the commas, periods, and dashes to create pauses as well as repetition of words and phrases, and parallel structures to create the meter, the beat of the music. In five places, he repeats words side by side. Then in lines 46 through 51 he scatters the word "bell." In lines 21 through 22, there is a short structural repetition, "what was abraded and what was exhausted," followed by an extended structural repetition in line

26 through 33 with "I was" repeated eight times to set up a progression of changes. Using this repetition definitely sets up a rhythm and serves as a sort of refrain in the music of the poem. Other repeated words and phrases follow in the rest of the poem but become slightly less frequent as Stern gets into detail with his comparisons and then brings his poem to its conclusion.

Stern also referred to the music of poetry in his Silverman interview, telling her that "In poetry, the music comes first, and I would never write a bad line, or what I consider a bad line, in order to get some content into the poem." Content in the poem is the story that Stern tells. He admitted to Elizabeth Farnsworth in an interview for the *Jim Lehrer News Hour* that he is like "the ancient mariner who grabs people and says: 'Listen, I have to tell you something. I have to explain myself.' I suppose as I'm explaining myself to others, I'm quintessentially explaining myself to myself." Nonetheless, his poems are not confessional, nor do they express what he thinks about issues. Rather, they are his way of enabling the reader to participate in the spiritual journey that the muses allow him to pursue. There are no issues in "One of the Smallest," just the journey as he imagines it, and he invites his readers to tag along so they can experience the same feelings. As Stern emphasized to Farnsworth, his poems "don't relay the adventure of my life. I become, in effect, at the best, representational, so that my life is the reader's life, that the reader can zero in on those aspects of my life as I reveal them, that he can say, yes, that's what happens to me." The simple, concrete language that Stern uses helps readers relate to Stern's life and recognize similarities to their own lives.

For Stern to call upon aspects of his own life in his poetry, he has to draw on past experiences, but not in a sentimental or nostalgic way. Although Jane Somerville reports in the *American Poetry Review* that Stern proposes, "'Maybe the subject of the poem is always nostalgia,'" he clarifies this statement by saying that "'conventional nostalgia fits'" are only "echoes of the real thing...authentic nostalgia is 'the essential memory.'" This type of memory, Stern says, has "great psychic roots with true and terrifying aspects of rupture and separation." The pain of separation, Stern further asserts, stems from the loss of paradise. Living in the modern world automatically means not living in paradise, and humans instinctively are trying to re-create paradise and envision a future world. Somerville records Stern as saying, "I see it as an intense desire to be reunited with something in the universe from which we feel cut off. I see it as a search for the permanent." All of these elements are present in "One of the Smallest." Nostalgia as memory is seen in the first part of the poem in the picture of the narrator cutting down trees, basking in the sun, and swimming, then later being in the yard and seeing flowers, trees, and a river. Whether Stern ever actually cut down trees is not the point. These are all real things that he has seen or witnessed. They are brought to mind by his original subject of sunshine and are connected as he automatically goes on his search for paradise, for his Garden of Eden. The permanency he seeks lies in the fact that the garden is there in his first life, and even after his rebirth, the garden is there again. He is reassured that paradise will always be there.

"One of the Smallest" wonderfully exemplifies the use of memories to describe the small joys of life that a person embraces until they disappear "like a fragment of gas" or fire. Stern picks up on the idea of fire in line 42 and carries it through three manifestations until line 85: fire changing the fragments into metal that can be used in the making of a bell, the slow burning wood of the olive and carob trees, and the fire that is produced by a match. These three examples are all taken from memories about seeing how metal and a bell are made, memories about how slowly olive and carob trees burn, and detailed recall of the parts of a match and how a match works. The joyful memories are what make the eventual separation at death so painful. As Stern says, this is a loss that humans can hardly bear to face, so Stern turns the story of "One of the Smallest" into one that describes death as a transformation into a new life, giving hope that there may yet be a future and a paradise in a garden with dogwoods and irises.

Source: Lois Kerschen, Critical Essay on "One of the Smallest," in *Poetry for Students*, Thomson Gale, 2007.

Gary Pacernick

In the following interview excerpt, Pacernick asks Stern to share his thoughts about Walt Whitman (to whom he is often compared), Emily Dickinson, W. H. Auden, and Ezra Pound in connection with their influences on his poetry. Stern is also asked how maturity has affected his poetry.

[*Gary Pacernick:*] *The person who introduced you at your reading at Barnes & Noble yesterday said you're often compared to Whitman, that you're a reincarnation of Whitman, which is not terribly accurate. But he's influenced most of the American poets who followed him. And in your poem,"Lucky Life," again from that earlier volume, I see a lot of Whitman there. And of course in a lot of the other poems: the use of catalogs and parallel structure. Of course one could argue that you got that from the Hebrew prophets. And your affirmation of self, your kind of manic joy and energy remind me of Whitman. And then even the very title,"Lucky Life." Any thoughts about Whitman?*

[Gerald Stern:] I love Whitman, and in the long poem "Hot Dog," which is in *Odd Mercy,* one of the two principle figures, characters, personalities, voices, in that poem is Whitman. The other is Augustine. I present them as kind of polar opposites, for good or ill, correctly or incorrectly. And Whitman even as a literal figure in the poem. There's a section of that poem where he is dying; he's dead. When I wrote that, and in the poem itself, I'm lying on my back in his little bed in the last house he lived in in Camden, New Jersey. I actually was there and I was doing that.

I love Whitman. I don't love all of Whitman. There's a lot of Whitman that is repetitive, flat, excessive. But when he's on, there's no one like him. In "Song of Myself," he's elusive, he's a genius, he's brilliant, and he's smart. And I love that Whitman. I don't know how it happened that there are so many connections between him and me. There are with Whitman and many contemporary poets. One could say the same thing of Galway Kinnell, one could say the same thing of Allen Ginsberg, to a degree Philip Levine, to a degree Robert Bly. Maybe me more than the others or maybe a little less than some of the others. Certainly less than Ginsberg; I think even less than Kinnell.

I find myself getting a little angry and resisting it. But resisting it has nothing to do with Whitman as a poet. It's got to do with what seems to me too easy an identification. Resisting the connection. Maybe I want to be more "original" and not be derivative; maybe that's an element. As far as the two grand masters, Dickinson and Whitman, I find that Dickinson is the one that continues to interest me more. She is the one I read more. The last time I went to

Europe, I took two books with me. Dickinson's Letters and Dickinson's Poems. I didn't take "Song of Myself."

What that means I don't know. Psychologists, Jungians, tell us about the opposites. I don't know what I can say about Whitman that is not obvious: his expansiveness, his openness, his liberal view of the world, his sense of an open future, his belief in redemption through unforeseen ways, his use of ideology and various ideologies metaphorically rather than literally. So that at the end, for example, of "Song of Myself" where he's almost a Christ figure, and I think possibly that was deliberately in his mind when he wrote that poem, he says, "Look for me somewhere else." He says, "It's time to explain myself. Let us stand up." I love that Whitman. That humorous, serious Whitman.

It's interesting about Whitman. He speaks very little about the Jews. I'm sure he loved the Jews. I'm sure he had a good nineteenth-century liberal vision of Judaism, if he thought about it. I don't think he thought about it a lot. Certainly he's an important element in Yiddish and Hebrew thinking. There are many, many early translations of Whitman into Yiddish and into Hebrew. But Whitman does not have a Jewish taste. There is humor in Whitman but it's a different kind of humor. I think that quality in me that is nervous, ironic, mean, even nasty, elusive in my way, derives from another place than Whitman. I think there are other connections. One doesn't always know the connections. Certainly Yeats is a connection, certainly Marlowe, Shakespeare, Christopher Smart, Eliot and Pound, Stevens in different ways, Williams, Coleridge. Coleridge very, very much so. But I don't reject it, I'm just trying to elaborate on this. I'm not speaking against Whitman. God love Whitman.

What about Dickinson, though? I mean, I was surprised when you said—

I know. I saw the look of surprise on your face. I don't know what I can say about it. I love her metaphors. I guess the thing about her I love the most is her mystery, her elusiveness, and her metaphysics. I love how she presents every poem as a kind of problem to be solved. I do the same thing, in a way. Whitman doesn't do that. I love, of course, her music. I love her bizarre imagination. I love her grotesqueries. I don't like the mechanical rhymes and the woodenness.

You have a poem about Auden.

Yes.

In Paradise Poems, "In Memory of W. H. Auden."

Which is of course a paraphrase of his "In Memory of W. B. Yeats."

Ah, that great elegy.

"Earth receive an honored guest;/ William Yeats is laid to rest."

Did you meet him? In the poem you make it seem like you met him.

I met him, yes. Several times.

What kind of personal impact did he have on you and of course what kind of impact did he have on you as a poet through his poetry?

Well, it's interesting that, when I first started to think about poetry, memorize poetry, read poetry, and even write poetry in my early, early twenties, one of the poets I read intensely was Auden. I loved Auden, and I thought that Auden was my maître, my master. The interesting thing was that in many ways we were absolute opposites. He was ironic, intellectual, academic (maybe not academic), formal, coming from quite a different tradition with a different view of things, a different use of language. Yet I loved him, I loved his songs and sonnets, I loved his elegies, I loved his biographical poems (about Forster, about Freud, about Yeats and so on).

I read him eagerly and avidly. I knew poem after poem of his by heart, and I still do. And yet he was not a true influence. Really someone like Marlowe was more of an influence. Someone like Isaac Rosenberg. Certainly someone like Yeats or Pound. I visited Auden in the early fifties. I had just written a long poem with the absurd title of "Ishmael's Dream." It was an outsider's outsider poem, I spent a year at it. I was living in Paris, writing at a little desk every day, ten, fifteen lines. I had no idea what it was about. One didn't have Xerox machines in those days. My poor fiancé at the time, later my wife, typed up ten, twelve copies of this long poem.

I sent one copy to Auden. He asked me to come see him. He was living in the West Village then, Christopher Street, I believe. It was going to be a laying on of hands. I thought, this was it. And I remember spending a long, long afternoon, a half day with him. There were some other people in the apartment, and I was this innocent, almost ignorant, Pittsburgher, kind of an intellectual tough. I remember I and my friends spent an hour discussing what clothes I would wear. Should I wear a suit and be a neo-academic? Should I wear a sweater and pants and not shave and be a Pittsburgh ruffian. Well, they were talking about theater and cheese and God knows what. I knew Velveeta cheese. I mean, what did I know about cheese, coming from Pittsburgh. And it was a long day, and finally I said to him, "Mr. Auden, what about my poem?" He looked at me, and he said, "Oh, I really liked the last ten lines." A kind of a lyric at the end of the poem. And I was furious at him for years for that.

Of course it was inevitable. I was writing ecstatic poetry without focus. Now I'm writing ecstatic poetry with focus. At least I hope so. It took me a long time to focus. It was inevitable that he would say what he did say. Later I took a course with him at the New School, on the sonnet. He was brilliant, he could talk for hours. And I've always loved the man! I think there was a grand decline in his later years, and he became more and more English and more and more Anglican, though I think poems like "In Praise of Limestone," and some of the other later poems, are great poems, and I think he is being redeemed as an important poet. That's my relationship with Auden.

Your poem called "Near Perigord" in Paradise Poems *has the same title as one of Pound's poems.*

Right.

Pound was an influence, as you said, on yourself and so many other people. He's emerged as the most important poetry person of the twentieth century. Can you forgive him for his hatred of Jews and his pro-Fascist and pro-Nazi stance during the Second World War? And along with that, how can such a person influence Jewish poets?

You know, Pound often would defend himself and his relation to Jews and the libel, as he saw it, by saying that so many of his friends were Jewish, and they were. "Some of my best friends." As far as Pound's influence on me, I was obsessed with Pound and fascinated with him and his work, including "Personae" and *The ABC of Reading* as well as *The Cantos.* I admired so many things about him, even his rigidity and his formality and his assumption of being a guru. The teacher, the only teacher. We were looking for such a man. I think he has written some extraordinary poems. But I think *The Cantos* is a flawed poem. I think it's flawed because he was flawed. I think it's unfinished, undeveloped. It is not a great poem. I think there are parts of it that are extraordinary. The parts that are extraordinary are really lyric

outbursts. The poem doesn't have a superstructure. Maybe a long poem can't have such a superstructure in our time, connected with a core belief. Clearly I love those parts of that poem, for example the part which he wrote in 1945 when he was in prison.

The Pisan Cantos.

The Pisan Cantos. One loves those poems. But I find them flawed, too. I mean, there's a lot of self-pity and a lot of self-congratulation and self-forgiveness in those poems which now I find objectionable and even abhorrent. His influence on me has been in an overwhelming sensitivity to language and to the urgency and importance of the poem, and that's his influence on all the poets. Merwin and Kinnell and so on. Levine. Rich. He's taught me to be precise, to try to be precise about language, to make the words be authentic, to reject Victorianism, as he understood it as a young man. It's language where he's the major influence. And the importance of literature, where literature had become like almost a, well, I hate to say it, a kind of religion to us.

As far as his philosophy, as far as his Jew baiting: disgusting, vile, abhorrent, unforgivable. As far as Ginsberg's forgiving him in the famous incident that's recorded in the *Parish Review* interview, Pound embracing Ginsberg, Ginsberg embracing Pound, Pound saying it was a suburban prejudice, whatever the hell that means, Ginsberg kissing him and forgiving him, I find that to be sheer bulls——. I can't forgive Ginsberg for that stupidity. Ginsberg has no right to forgive Pound. For whom? For the Jews slaughtered? Of course Pound didn't slaughter Jews. Pound possibly didn't even know about the camps. Possibly. We're talking about words here, we're not talking about actions. That's another complicated subject. I don't forgive that in Pound. Pound never asked for forgiveness. That is unforgivable. The sad thing about it is his defenders, his critics, never truly accounted for that aspect of Pound, Pound as fascist, as Jew baiter, as racist.

That aspect of Pound I can't forgive. But most of all, seen from a literary point of view, it was the central flaw in his writing, and in his soul, that prevented *The Cantos* from being a great poem. My dear friend, Jack Gilbert, whom I grew up with in Pittsburgh and who adores Pound, tries to separate the fascistic poems from the others. I think that's a mistake.

I think that you can't ignore Pound's fascism. It's a critical part of his thinking, or it became so at a certain point in his life. Was he crazy? Was Hitler crazy? Of course he was crazy. So *nu*, what does that mean? Does that answer the question?

You're forty-one. Does that kind of maturity give you a new, fresh perspective or vision? Let's put it this way: has your vision changed, do you think, since you've become mature?

Of course it has, but not just the vision. You know, one changes physically, psychologically, spiritually, as one gets older. One can't resist it, one can't help it. There's new joy and there's new sadness. There are sadnesses you absolutely forget about, they seem so unimportant, and new sadnesses that enter. Obvious ones. Closeness to death, for example. There's also new joys, surprisingly enough. I'm more joyful now than I've ever been in my life. I have periods of absolute elation. To some degree it's connected with the satisfaction that I did what I wanted to do in this life, quite frankly. To the degree that I didn't do exactly what I wanted to do, there's sadness, or if I didn't achieve what I wanted to achieve in my way, you know? The language changes in the poems, the subject matter changes. On one level, I'm writing longer poems in order to work out the matter. On another level I've also started to write shorter lyrics again.

A friend of mine said recently to me, "You know, the poems of yours I really like," and I took this as a kind of criticism, "are your shorter lyrics that your were writing in *Rejoicings* and *Lucky Life*. Later the longer poems are interesting, but they don't have the intensity of the shorter lyrics." I don't agree, but I listened to what she said. I'm trying almost deliberately to know what's happening by itself; also, to return to the shorter lyric. I think I'll be doing that. The language changes, the focusing changes, the point of view changes. It's hard to talk about it without being just banal; talking about the wise old man, or the gray beard, or wisdom or knowledge. I prefer to talk about knowledge rather than wisdom. It's knowledge. I seek, and knowledge does not mean information, and it does not mean scholarship. Knowledge is, for me, a deeply emotional, intensive, energetic, mystical quality. ...

Source: Gary Pacernick, "Gerald Stern: An Interview," in *American Poetry Review*, Vol. 27, No. 4, July–August 1998, pp. 43–44.

> STERN IS A POET OF DEEP INTIMACY AND OF PERSONAL KNOWLEDGE WHO IS NOT AFRAID OF LETTING HIS NARRATOR FACE THE TRUTH OF HIS PAST NOR OF HIS FEELINGS."

Mark Hillringhouse

In the following review, Hillringhouse describes the consistency of the style and techniques of Stern in regard to his use of metaphor, his play upon the senses, and his intimate expression of truth, poignancy, and compassion. Hillringhouse says that Stern vacillates between self-burial and rebirth, and follows two currents: his Jewish past and his present as a poet.

Gerald Stern is a poet I can keep coming back to with new interest and amazement. He is not experimental. He doesn't try to change his style with each new book. There is no attempt at postmodern abstraction. He writes emotionally charged poems that speak with directness and sincerity and that pay close attention to physical detail and the many nuances of human joy and sorrow. He is a poet who is sensitive to the slightest changes in light, color, texture or sound. Particular attention is paid to the hands and the fingers and the mouth, the sense organs of touch. Stern is above all else a sensuous poet, rubbing, stroking, caressing. This is how he moves.

He is a metonymic poet, letting a part of one thing stand for another, displacing the meaning from one image onto the next, creating new meaning out of old contexts. There are certain poetic ingredients that go into every poem: There is place description; an evocation of memory; a ritual of self-burial; there is nature: moles, opossums, spiders are used as totems for his alter ego. Trees, flowers, and birds are named as a part of this ceremony. There is resolution in the form of beatitude.

In his background there is a shtetl past inherited from his parents and imported to the new world from Eastern Europe. There is nostalgia for the old cramped quarters of that world. There is a beloved sister who died tragically at a young age, a circle of boyhood friends, sensitive, intellectual youths who would pursue poetry. There is an Upper West Side past as a graduate student at Columbia University. There's a daughter, a son, an ex-wife and other women who trail him in memory as he moves from his fifth-floor walk-up in New York City to his houses in Pennsylvania and Iowa.

Stern writes elegies for love. There are sad and tender poems addressed to his deceased mother, poems to friends, poems about his bitter-sweet and angry youth, oedipal struggle, poems about getting older, of finding, finally, a state of grace. Half the new book *Odd Mercy* is a thousand-line poem entitled "Hot Dog" which is broken into seventeen segments. It is a New York poem of the Lower East Side, the Polish and Jewish quarters, the grubby immigrant life, the vagrants, the meanness and sweetness of it all. In another way, the poem is a form of "Prelude" about the growth of the poet's mind as he discovers his identity.

Half of the time Stern's poetry is buried in an idealized youth of the narrator who shovels and digs through his memory to uncover the talismans and fetishes of his growing up. These talismanic psychic connections have the narrator walking in a semi-conscious state and living in two worlds, but the new world that replaces the old world is shabby, rude, obscene, superficial, insulting. It's the ugly "McPresent." It's New York destroyed or old traditions eroding, lost, gone forever: old department stores, cafeterias, former apartments, disappearing, forgotten except by the narrator. The tone is always elegiac or vatic. These are poems of exile, poems of exodus, of being the only Jew in a land of goyim. That connection is extended to other artists, poets, painters, musicians, who like Jews are celebrated for their own battles with the Philistines.

Stern vacillates between two opposite poles, from self-burial, or some low form of animal death, to rebirth on a higher plane. This tendency to bury himself under the earth or to immerse himself under water is a symbolic attempt to free himself from the burden of his own childhood, the life he rejected, the Orthodox world of his parents. In *Odd Mercy*, in the long poem "Hot Dog," this struggle becomes obvious in several places and much of the writing wrestles with this dilemma:

> ... When I was thirteen I left
> shul Yom Kippur afternoon and sneaked
> back to my house; I ate a Bartlett pear

and I was free a little, but my stomach
was almost burning from my fear. I threw
the core into the toilet, my mother and
     father
never found out. That night at supper we ate,
I remember, some fruit and cheese but they
were irritable from fasting and from standing
half the day. That pear, I know, always helped
     me.
It made me stubborn. It gave me certain
     detachment.
It kept me hidden. I can be in the middle of
anything because of that pear ...

(Further on in the same poem he writes)

> ... I was able
> When I was twenty to stay underwater for
>   three
> whole minutes—under a dock; it would have
>   been longer
> except they pulled me up. I found a way
> to exhale a little, and float—in the dark—
>   the light
> was above me, and behind me; they were
>   angry
> and frightened that I stayed so long, and I
> was sad to come up ...

There are two main currents in Stern's work. One flows out of the cities of an industrial, prewar, ghettoized past where the narrator was formed, and another flows into the here and now where the narrator has to struggle to locate himself in a meaningful way. Or, as the poet/narrator writes in a poem called "Diary":

> I am at last that thing, a stranger in my own
>   life,
> completely comfortable getting in or getting
>   out of my own
> Honda,
> living from five cardboard boxes, two small
>   grips,
> and two briefcases.

This strange sense of alienation comes from two sources, from trying to be a poet and from being Jewish. In the third section of "Hot Dog" the narrator argues the differences:

> ... What I loved
> was arguing with a Lutheran over the law
> and watching him suffer; over three coffee
>   cups
> a couple I knew reached out, they may have
>   been Quakers

or radical Catholics, they were loving, they
    stood for
reason, above all else; we talked for an hour
about the forbidden—milk and meat—
    Maimonides
was at their side, he was their coach; they
    argued
hygiene and nourishment and toxic qualities
while I was for obedience to the book,
for its own sake, and slavery to the words . . .

The book referred to is the Torah, but it is also
the commitment to poetry, to being compelled to
write poetry and to struggle with the language as
another form of devotion. There is strangeness
and alienation in moving out of one world and
into another. And this, ironically, is where Stern
is able to get much of his subject matter, by
traveling through the culture he lives in as both
a native and a tourist.

His narrator examines these lives and tries
to make connections to the parallel world of
nature where there are always two forces, the
force of light and darkness, heat and cold, life
and death. The parts of the body, like separate
entities, contain their own individual memories.
Each poem describes a season in miniature, the
weather of a particular city street, or backyard
garden, or a few feet of muddy riverbank. In this
physical world the narrator always performs
two actions or motions, one to the left and one
to the right. There is constant duality. This is
Stern's metaphysical dance, his way of living in
two worlds. "Birthday," the opening poem, is a
good example:

It is that they spend so much time in the sky
that bluebirds have streaks of red across
    their chests;
and it is that—except for the robbing of their
    houses—
they come north for my birthday bringing
    the light
of southern Texas with them. Every year
I am able to do the mathematics
and stand like another bird—outside my
    door—
with one foot in and one foot out, half-
    looking
for the first light and whisper one phrase or
    other—

The narrator acts as a kind of human fulcrum
and attempts to achieve a balance between dual
forces, the relentless forces of nature which are
absolute and the forces inside the mind of the

narrator where a joyful sadness is brewing. This
double reference is a ubiquitous feature of
Stern's work and can be found in almost every
poem. Within his duality there is one symbolic
direction for punishment, loathing or scorn, and
another direction for forgiveness, grace and
redemption. One direction is for self-sacrifice,
falling one way for love, one way for poetry,
and for transcendence. The other direction is
for touching the mind and the past. There's
hope for a second chance behind this meditation
coupled with the movement of nature. This
becomes clearer towards the end of the poem:

when the thaw comes and the birds begin to
    swell
with confusion and a few wild seeds take
    hold
and the light explodes a little I lie down
a second time, either to feel the sun
or hear the house shake from the roar of
    engines
at the end of my street, the train from North
    Dakota
carrying sweeteners to Illinois, moving
forward a single foot, then backwards
    another,
one of those dreary mysteries, hours of
    shrieking
and banging, endless coupling, the perfect
    noise
to go with my birthday . . .

Onto this stage of the narrator's drama enters
the world of human activity, noise and machi-
nery. It is an infernal intrusion, the noise of the
present age, and it fills the narrator sometimes
with horror and sometimes with sorrow.

Noise is another frequent element with
many dimensions. There are many voices of
many decibels, tenors singing and birds war-
bling. There are also many unpleasant sounds:
animal roaring, screeching, shrieking, sobbing
and moaning, and there are groans, gasps for
air, snorting and raging. There is also silence. It
is in that silence that the poet waits and listens.
Stern is like Keats in his garden listening to
nightingales. And though this country lacks
that enchanting species, a native crow will do
for the final section of Diary:

An American crow, a huge croaker, a
    corvus,
who caws four times, then caws five times at
    six
in the morning will be my thrush,

and I will turn from painted door to hanging
    spider to crooked
curtain rod
to hear his song. . . .

before coming down together
for an early breakfast
and an hour or two of silent reading . . .

Stern's first book, *Rejoicings*, was about loss, separation, getting rid of shame and guilt. There's a quiet anger in those poems. There's the bitter-sweet taste of youth ending, there's the serenity of special places, of finding the grid locations of the soul. The poems "The Unity," "The Poem of Life" and "On The Far Edge of Kilmer" from that collection exemplify the pattern that his best work would take in *Lucky Life* and in later books such as *The Red Coal* and *Paradise Poems* where Stern hits his stride.

Two signature poems emerged out of *Lucky Life*: "The Power of Maples" and "At Bickford's." They are like Psalms. The speaker addresses himself in prayer. There is the same type of parallel structure found in Psalms whereby one phrase is followed by another, repeating the same idea yet transcending it with metaphorical leaps. In "At Bickford's" the "I will" anaphora could be taken right out of Exodus, God talking to Moses, going back and forth from "you" to "I." In *Lucky Life* the center of his later work emerged and developed into the poetic longing to simplify and unclutter existence thereby reducing it to its timeless essentials. *Odd Mercy* returns to this theme.

It's a theme embodied in the desire to live the life of the mind. One of the poet's poetic quests is for true knowledge—the simplicity of knowing. He seems to want to return to the foundations of philosophy, to the pre-Socratics, when it was possible to reduce matter and existence to a single permanent substance. All this so he can ponder the fate of the things he loves and cherish them one more time before they vanish. In the last stanza of the poem "Bitter Thoughts" he tries to capture this desire:

maybe I'll find a harp, or the end of a lute
with a wire attached, maybe the wind will
    sing
for me—there on the granite curb—and
    maybe
knowledge will come and I will understand it
once and for all, the light that first existed,
    the
struggle between imperishables, what I
    thought of

for most of my life, near a water-stained
    lampshade
that saved the world and an overcoat that
    renewed it.

In reading Stern's poetry I can connect the lines of the final stanzas of his first book to the end of *Odd Mercy*, over twenty years apart, and not feel any discontinuity in the writing. He has never steered away from his passion. Reading him I become more acutely aware of what things matter most in my own life. Stern is a poet of deep intimacy and of personal knowledge who is not afraid of letting his narrator face the truth of his past nor of his feelings. There is a tender moment of confession between mother and son near the end of "Hot Dog" that gives the reader the impression of eavesdropping:

. . . My mother only once
told the truth about her father, the saint
who sent his boys to work when they were
    twelve
so he could sit there reading. "He never
    kissed me
once," she said, "he never touched me." She
    was
eighty-five when she said that, she would
    have
eight more years; we talked at the end, we
    learned
to love each other.

If Gerald Stern were a painter he would be a Chagall, floating colorful dreams and memory in a mysterious upside down world. Or, if he were a composer, he would be a Dvorak, rhapsodic, full of melodic contours and the haunting rhythms of gypsy folk music. There is much I have learned from him about where to locate a poem. He is able to find poetry in places others have overlooked or neglected, and he is able to write poems about what has been left behind or about objects that have been discarded. Few have his poignancy or his compassion.

Source: Mark Hillringhouse, "The Poetry of Gerald Stern," in *Literary Review*, Vol. 40, No. 2, Winter 1997, pp. 346–51.

SOURCES

Barron, Jonathan N., "Gerald Stern," in *American Writers*, Supplement IX, edited by Jay Parini, Charles Scribner's Sons, 2002, p. 17.

Dodd, Jeffrey, Elise Gregory, and Adam O'Connor Rodriguez, "A Conversation with Gerald Stern," in *Willow Springs*, No. 56, February 11, 2005, p. 15.

Farnsworth, Elizabeth, "This Time," in *Online NewsHour*, November 23, 1998, p. 3, http://www.pbs.org/newshour/bb/entertainment/july-dec98/stern_11-23.html, (accessed September 18, 2006).

"*Last Blue* by Gerald Stern," in *Ploughshares*, Fall 2000, p. 230.

Pacernick, Gary, "Gerald Stern: An Interview," in *American Poetry Review*, Vol. 27, No. 4, July–August 1998, p. 41.

Review of *Last Blue*, in *Publishers Weekly*, Vol. 247, No. 8, February 21, 2000, p. 83.

Reyes, Carlos, Review of *Last Blue*, in *Willamette Week Online*, http://www.wweek.com/editorial/2729/1691/ (accessed October 21, 2006).

Seaman, Donna, Review of *Last Blue*, in *Booklist*, Vol. 96, No. 14, March 15, 2000, p. 1319.

Silverman, Sue William, "A Conversation with Gerald Stern," in *Fourth Genre*, Vol. 6, No. 1, Spring 2004, p. 113.

Somerville, Jane, "Gerald Stern and the Return Journey," in *American Poetry Review*, Vol. 18, No. 5, September–October 1989, p. 39.

Stern, Gerald, "How Poetry Helps People to Live Their Lives," in *American Poetry Review*, Vol. 28, No. 5, September–October 1999, pp. 22, 23.

———, *Last Blue*, W. W. Norton, 2000, jacket flap.

———, "One of the Smallest," in *Last Blue*, W. W. Norton, 2000, pp. 13–16.

Taylor, John, Review of *Last Blue*, in *Antioch Review*, Vol. 59, No. 3, Summer 2001, p. 639.

FURTHER READING

Genovese, Peter, "A Singer of Everyday Life: At 74, Gerald Stern Is Finally Getting Recognition," in *The Star-Ledger*, April 13, 1999, p. 57.

This article for a Newark, New Jersey newspaper, close to where Stern lives, is a short but information-packed overview of Stern's life and works and the literary criticism of his poetry.

Hamilton, David, "An Interview with Gerald Stern," in *Iowa Review*, Vol. 31, No. 2, 2001, pp. 148–56.

This interview, conducted in 1999, covers mostly biographical material, including a more personal look at Stern's parents and his time in Paris than found in generic biographies.

Somerville, Jane, "Gerald Stern Among the Poets: The Speaker as Meaning," in *American Poetry Review*, Vol. 17, No. 6, November–December 1988, pp. 11–19.

Somerville is an authority on Stern, and this article is her analysis of Stern's use of the narrator in his poetry.

———, *Making the Light Come: The Poetry of Gerald Stern*, Wayne State University Press, 1990.

After writing a number of articles about Stern, Somerville wrote this in-depth examination of the work Stern produced from 1977 to 1990.

Stitt, Peter, *Uncertainty and Plentitude: Five Contemporary Poets*, University of Iowa Press, 1997.

This book is a study of five American poets of note who were contemporaries in the 1990s. The chapter on Stern is called "Weeping and Wailing and Singing for Joy." Stitt is an eminent critic and the publisher of the highly regarded literary journal *Gettysburg Review*.

Pied Beauty

GERARD MANLEY HOPKINS

1877

The British poet Gerard Manley Hopkins is often described as an early modern poet ahead of his Victorian time. This is perhaps why, while he wrote "Pied Beauty" in 1877, in common with most of his other poetry, it was first published twenty-nine years after his death. It appeared in the first collected edition of his poems, *Poems of Gerard Manley Hopkins*, edited by Robert Bridges (1918). The poem subsequently appeared in the second complete edition of Hopkins's poetry, published in 1930. As of 2006, "Pied Beauty" was available in *Gerard Manley Hopkins: The Major Works*, edited by Catherine Phillips (1986).

"Pied Beauty" is one of the first poems that Hopkins wrote in the so-called sprung rhythm that he evolved, based on the rhythms of Anglo-Saxon and ancient Welsh poetry. His aim was to approximate the rhythms and style of normal speech, albeit speech infused with a religious ecstasy and enthusiasm that are characteristics of his poetry. The poem also embodies Hopkins's innovative use of condensed syntax and alliteration. It is written in the form of a curtal or shortened sonnet, another of Hopkins's stylistic inventions. Thematically, the poem is a simple hymn of praise to God for the "dappled things" of creation. God is seen as being beyond change but as generating all the variety and opposites that manifest in the ever-changing world. Hopkins is best known as a nature poet and a religious poet,

Gerard Manley Hopkins (Harry Ransom Humanities Research Center, University of Texas At Austin, Photography Collection. Reproduced by permission)

and "Pied Beauty" perfectly exemplifies both these aspects of his work.

AUTHOR BIOGRAPHY

Gerard Manley Hopkins was born on July 28, 1844, in Stratford, Essex, England, to Manley Hopkins, a marine insurance adjuster, and Catherine (Smith) Hopkins. He was the first of their nine children. His parents were devout High Church Anglicans. The family had a lively interest in religion and the creative arts. Manley published a volume of his poetry the year before Hopkins's birth and frequently reviewed poetry; Catherine was a keen reader, and the young Hopkins and his siblings involved themselves in literature, music, and painting.

Stratford was becoming industrialized during Hopkins's boyhood, and in 1852, the family moved to the then more rural area of Hampstead,

north of the city of London, in the belief that it would provide a healthier environment.

Hopkins attended Highgate Grammar School from 1854 until 1863. He won the poetry prize and a scholarship to Balliol College, Oxford, where he studied from 1863 to 1867. At Oxford, he was strongly influenced by the aesthetic theories of the essayist and literary critic Walter Pater, who was one of his tutors, and of the art critic and social commentator John Ruskin. Literary influences included the Anglican poets George Herbert and Christina Rossetti. It was during his Oxford years that Hopkins began to question the religion in which he had been brought up. He came under the influence of John Henry Newman (later Cardinal Newman), one of the founders of the Oxford movement (also called Tractarianism), which aimed to bring the Anglican Church back to its Catholic roots. In 1845, Newman had converted from the Anglican faith to Roman Catholicism. In 1866, Hopkins, to the consternation of his parents, also converted to Catholicism and was received into the Catholic Church by Cardinal Newman himself. The following year, Hopkins graduated with a first-class degree in classics.

In 1868, Hopkins joined the Society of Jesus, often called the Jesuits, with the aim of becoming a Jesuit priest. He gave up writing poetry and burned his poems, believing that they had no place in the life of someone who was committed to God. Only when he read the writings of the theologian Duns Scotus (1265–1308) in 1872 did he decide that poetry might be compatible with his religious vocation. He was also encouraged to return to writing poetry by his mentors in the Society of Jesus. In 1874, while Hopkins was studying theology in North Wales, he learned Welsh. He began to adapt the rhythms of Welsh poetry to his own poetry, evolving a metrical system that he called sprung rhythm. He put his metrical theories into practice in a radically innovative poem, "The Wreck of the Deutschland," about the 1876 sinking of a ship that carried five Franciscan nuns, exiles from Germany. Over the next year, Hopkins continued to use sprung rhythm in some of his most famous sonnets, including "God's Grandeur" and "Pied Beauty" (both written in 1877).

After he was ordained as a priest in 1877 and until 1881, Hopkins did parish work in Sheffield, Oxford, and London, and then in the slums of the three industrialized cities, Manchester, Liverpool, and Glasgow. He followed this work with three years of teaching Latin and Greek at Stonyhurst College, Lancashire. In 1884, he was appointed professor of Greek and Latin at University College, Dublin. This period of his life was marked by depression, precipitated partly by his overly conscientious marking of hundreds of student examination papers. He suffered a period of religious doubt, which led to his writing a series of sonnets characterized by spiritual despair, including "Carrion Comfort" and "No Worst, There is None" (both c. 1885). Hopkins died of typhoid fever in Dublin on June 8, 1889. He appears to have overcome his low spirits before he died, and according to W. H. Gardner in *Gerard Manley Hopkins (1844–1889): A Study of Poetic Idiosyncrasy in Relation to Poetic Tradition*, his last words were reported to be, "I am so happy."

Apart from a few uncharacteristic poems that appeared in periodicals, Hopkins did not publish his poetry during his lifetime. His friend, the poet Robert Bridges (1844–1930), whom Hopkins met at Oxford, arranged the publication of the first volume of his poetry in 1918.

POEM TEXT

Glory be to God for dappled things—
  For skies of couple-colour as a brinded cow;
    For rose-moles all in stipple upon trout that swim;
Fresh-firecoal chestnut-falls; finches' wings;
  Landscape plotted and pieced—fold, fallow, and plough;   5
    And áll trades, their gear and tackle and trim,

All things counter, original, spare, strange;
  Whatever is fickle, frecklèd (who knows how?)
    With swíft, slów; sweet, sóur; adázzle, dím;
He fathers-forth whose beauty is pást change: 10
    Práise him.

POEM SUMMARY

Stanza 1, lines 1–2; stanza 2, line 11

"Pied Beauty" opens and closes with variants of the two mottoes of St. Ignatius of Loyola, the founder of the Society of Jesus (Jesuits), of which Hopkins was a member. As cited by Peter Milward in *A Commentary on the Sonnets of G.*

M. Hopkins, the two mottoes are: "Ad majorem Dei gloriam (To the greater glory of God) and Laus Deo semper (Praise be to God always)." Milward points out that it is customary for pupils in Jesuit schools to write an abbreviated form of the former motto, A. M. D. G., at the beginning of each written exercise, and the latter motto, L. D. S., at the end. Thus Hopkins appears to be treating his poem as an exercise in the Jesuit tradition.

Line 1 begins a hymn of praise to God for creating "dappled things" that embody the "Pied Beauty" of the title. These are things of mottled or variegated hue that display variety and pairs of opposites (such as light and dark). The whole of stanza 1, the sestet of the curtal sonnet, consists of a number of such things. Line 2 gives two examples of dappled things. In a simile, the poet likens "skies of couple-colour" to a "brinded" or striped cow, since both are of two contrasting colors.

Stanza 1, lines 3–4

The poet turns his attention to the river, where trout swim, their skins showing rose-colored markings "all in stipple," meaning spots such as an artist might create by using small touches of the brush, a technique known as stippling. Then the poet draws attention to the windfalls from chestnut trees. When chestnuts hit the ground, their dull brown shells break open to reveal reddish-brown nuts within, which the poet likens in a metaphor to coals that break open in a fire and glow red. He notes the wings of finches, which are of varied colors.

Stanza 1, lines 5–6

The poet broadens his vision to take in the landscape. This is not an untouched, virgin landscape, but a landscape worked and shaped by man: it is "plotted and pieced," meaning divided into sections or plots. A "fold" is an enclosure for sheep; "fallow" refers to a field left for a period of rest between crops; and "plough" refers to a field tilled in preparation for crop planting. All these references include, by implication, man's intervention in the natural landscape. In line 6, the poet draws more direct attention to man, this time in the form of his trades and the clothes and tools associated with them. The trades are spoken of in terms of their neatness and orderliness: "gear and tackle and trim," with "trim" perhaps suggesting the sailboats of fishermen.

TOPICS FOR FURTHER STUDY

- Write an essay in which you compare and contrast "Pied Beauty" with John Keats's poem "Ode to a Nightingale" or Dylan Thomas's poem "The Force That Through the Green Fuse Drives the Flower." What does each poem reveal about the relationship between man, God, and nature?

- Write a poem on any topic using sprung rhythm and alliteration. You may use any number of syllables per line, but you must keep to a set number of strong stresses per line (as in Hopkins's "Pied Beauty," you may vary the number by one only). You may use rhyme or not, as you wish. Write a short separate paragraph on how the techniques of sprung rhythm and alliteration helped or hindered the meaning of the poem. Finally, perform your poem and read your paragraph to a group.

- Hopkins's poems often move between a personal, sensual experience to a philosophical reflection. Write an essay discussing this movement with relation to at least three of his poems.

- Identify some images that recur in Hopkins's poems, and write an essay on how they relate to the themes of the poems.

- Read about Hopkins's religious life and views, and create a class presentation in which you relate your findings to his poetry.

Stanza 2, lines 7–8

In the quatrain of the curtal sonnet, the poet leaves behind the concrete examples of dappled things of stanza 1. He turns his attention inward, to his reflections on the abstract qualities he admires in "dappled things." He appreciates their oddness, uniqueness, and rarity, all of which contribute to their preciousness. His use of the words "fickle" and "freckled" to describe these things is noteworthy, as these are both

qualities that were neither admired nor appreciated in the Victorian age. "Fickle" was most often applied to inconstant lovers (more frequently women) and unstable and capricious people. Many ladies with freckled complexions employed poisons and potions to try to remove the marks and attain the uniformly pale color that was fashionable. The poet's description of these things as "counter," as well as meaning contrary to expectation and therefore unusual, suggests an opposition to the mainstream of opinion. The interjection of "who knows how?" adds an element of wonder and mystery.

Stanza 2, lines 9–11

The poet describes the way in which the dappled things are "fickle, frecklèd": they embody pairs of opposite or contrasting abstract qualities. Those mentioned are swiftness and slowness, sweet and sour, and brightness and dimness. In conclusion, the poet returns to the theme he introduced in the first line: the creator of all this variety, change, and contrast is God, "whose beauty is past change." He ends with a simple half-line consisting only of the exhortation, "Praise him."

THEMES

Nature's Variety and God's Unity

"Pied Beauty" is a hymn of praise to the variety of God's creation, which is contrasted with the unity and non-changing nature of God. This variety is embodied in the "dappled things" of nature, as detailed in the sestet of the curtal sonnet. The significance of these things lies in the union of contrasting or opposite qualities in one being or aspect of creation. Thus bi-colored skies and streaked cows display contrasting hues; the "rose-moles" on the trout stand out against the background color of the skin; finches' wings have bars of contrasting colors; broken-open chestnuts show a bright color inside against their dull-colored outside; and the worked landscape consists of divisions that separate one part from another.

The "Fresh-firecoal chestnut-falls" seems to open up a moral and personal aspect to the theme of variety. The idea of the broken-open chestnuts revealing a shining hidden glory within symbolically suggests that a humble, unremarkable, or flawed exterior can conceal a beautiful, divinely

This poem praises God for creating the dappled things in nature, pointing to the perfect balance that is created when imperfection is introduced (© RF Company/Alamy)

inspired soul. This suggestion is picked up by the ambiguous adjectives "fickle, frecklèd," which are commonly used to describe things of which the Victorian mainstream did not approve, such as inconstant lovers and less-than-flawless complexions. From the point of view of the visual arts (Hopkins was a keen painter), these elements represent asymmetry, or broken symmetry. Whereas an even-colored object or being displays symmetry, a dappled object or being displays asymmetry. In the visual arts, the power of a painting, drawing, or sculpture comes from the interplay between symmetry and broken symmetry. In terms of poetry, this might be expressed in terms of regular rhythm (symmetry) and broken rhythm (asymmetry). In giving thanks to God for "All things counter, original, spare, strange," Hopkins includes in his hymn of praise people and other beings who are different, unusual, and (figuratively speaking) swimming against the mainstream. It can be no accident that such words were repeatedly applied to Hopkins's poetry, which was stylistically and thematically so far ahead of its time that readers found it odd, difficult, and even incomprehensible. Hopkins was

aware of this, writing in a letter of February 15, 1879, to Robert Bridges (reproduced in *Gerard Manley Hopkins: The Major Works*), "No doubt my poetry errs on the side of oddness." In "Pied Beauty," oddness and contrariness are brought into the fold of God's diverse creation.

Man and his environment are also unified. The landscape is not one of untouched nature, but one that is formed and shaped by man, to such an extent that it is defined by the activities of man within it: the sheepfold, the land that man has ploughed, and the land that he has left to rest between crops. At a time when the Industrial Revolution was prompting many writers and thinkers to lament the growing gap between man and the countryside, and the consequent destruction of the countryside by the manufacturing activities of man, this poem is a celebration of the oneness between rural man and his land. Hopkins portrays man as just another organic part of God's creation, enfolded into the landscape, not a force that is destroying that creation. The "trades" that he mentions are not the searing, smearing, and blearing trades of that other poem of 1877, "God's Grandeur," but trades that bring man into a cooperative and order-creating relationship with creation, embodied in the neatness of the image, "their gear and tackled and trim."

Piedness or variety is unified and embodied by each being named in the poem. Thus, though the cow is bi-colored, it is a single being and thereby represents a unity of contrasting elements. There is unity in diversity too in the poet's juxtaposition of contrasting beings or elements. Thus the solid, familiar form of the cow is set against the unbounded, infinite skies or heavens, just as the various, finite, and ever-changing forms of creation are set against the oneness, infinity, and constancy of God. In the second stanza, the theme is broadened to include abstract qualities that are opposite or contrasting in the same way in which, in the concrete examples of the first stanza, the colors on the cow and the trout are opposite or contrasting. To unify such abstract opposites as swift and slow, bright and dark, is a greater imaginative stretch than envisaging contrasting colors on an object, but such is the momentum of the poem that nothing could seem more natural. The poem concludes with the ultimate expression of piedness: God and his creation, the one and the many. The one and the many, however, are ultimately one, the God that is praised in the extremely simple, disyllabic final line before the poem drops into the silence of contemplation.

STYLE

Sprung Rhythm

Hopkins based his sprung rhythm on the metrical systems of Anglo-Saxon and traditional Welsh poetry, and he used this rhythm for much of his poetry. Sprung rhythm is based on the number of stressed syllables in a line and permits any number of unstressed syllables. Each foot consists of a first strongly stressed syllable, which either stands alone or is followed by unstressed syllables. Generally there are between one and four syllables per foot. An example from "Pied Beauty" is line 1, which can be scanned thus: "Glory | be to | God for | dappled | things," with four strong stresses falling on "Glo-" in the first foot, "God" in the third foot, "da-" in the fourth foot, and "things" in the fifth foot. The strong stresses in all feet except

the second fall on the first syllable of the foot; even in the second foot, the stress is stronger on the first syllable than the second. Most lines of this poem have four or five strong stresses.

An additional feature of sprung rhythm is the free use of juxtaposed stresses without intermediate unstressed syllables. Examples from "Pied Beauty" include "all trades," "swift, slow," and "Praise him." In the last two of these examples, Hopkins has signaled to the reader that both syllables should have strong stresses by marking them with his customary acute accent. In the first example, he has marked "all" with a strong stress, and if the reader takes account of the sense, he or she must also stress the next word, "trades."

Compound Words

In his poetry, Hopkins uses an extraordinarily high number of compound words in order to convey meaning in a graphic and condensed form. Sometimes, it is difficult to work out whether these are adjectives, nouns, or verbs, which creates ambiguity and complexity. Examples from "Pied Beauty" are "couple-colour," "rose-moles," "Fresh-firecoal," and "chestnut-falls." Hopkins's use of compound words is a deliberate borrowing from the Anglo-Saxon and Welsh poetic traditions.

Alliteration

Alliteration is the repetition of initial consonant sounds in neighboring words. An example from "Pied Beauty" is "fickle, freck frecklèd," where the initial consonant alliterates. Sometimes, the alliterated sound falls inside a word, but it must begin a stressed syllable, such as "adazzle, dim," where the *d* is the repeated sound. Alliteration is one of Hopkins's most characteristic poetic techniques and his heavy reliance upon it is another borrowing from the Anglo-Saxon and Welsh verse traditions. In the Anglo-Saxon poem *Beowulf*, for example, each line is divided into two half-lines, and the first stressed word of the second half-line must alliterate with at least one of the stressed syllables in the first half-line. Other words may alliterate as well.

Curtal Sonnet

"Pied Beauty" is one of Hopkins's three curtal or shortened sonnets, the others being "Peace" and "Ash Boughs." It differs from the standard Petrarchan sonnet (named after Petrarch, the fourteenth-century Italian poet) in that while the Petrarchan form is divided into an octave

COMPARE & CONTRAST

- **1870s:** Hopkins's innovative use of sprung rhythm, alliteration, compound words, and condensed syntax, in part borrowed from Anglo-Saxon and Welsh poetic techniques, is considered radical, strange, and shocking.

  Today: Poetic techniques pioneered by Hopkins have entered the mainstream of literature, having influenced such poets as T. S. Eliot, W. H. Auden, Dylan Thomas, Stephen Spender, C. Day Lewis, and Ted Hughes. Modern poets use a variety of regular and irregular metrical styles, alliteration, and compound words to express their meaning.

- **1870s:** The Industrial Revolution reaches its height in Britain, prompting writers to comment on the profound social, environmental, and economic changes it brings in its wake. It also brings a renewed interest in the beauty and sacredness of nature, expressed in keenly observed detail in Hopkins's poetry.

  Today: Environmentalists and social commentators continue to draw attention to the effects of industrialization on man and nature, and the topic continues to inspire writers. Governments have taken some

  measures, such as creating national parks, to protect certain areas from industrial development.

- **1870s:** Following the expulsion of the Society of Jesus from the Catholic European nations and their colonies in the latter half of the eighteenth century (this was a secular act prompted by resentment of the Jesuits' intervention in governmental policies such as slavery), in the early 1800s, the Jesuits are restored in most countries. Throughout the nineteenth century, the society expands and sets up many colleges and universities in Britain, the United States, and other countries.

  Today: Jesuits are free to practice their faith and, in most places in the world, to work in their ministries. In the second half of the twentieth century, following a trend in the Catholic priesthood in general, the numbers of members of the Society of Jesus decline. However, according to the official website of the British Province of the Society of Jesus (www.jesuit.org.uk), as of 2006, the society has around 20,000 members worldwide, engaged in a variety of ministries.

(eight lines) and a sestet (six lines), in the curtal sonnet, the octave becomes a sestet and the sestet becomes a quatrain (four lines), followed by a half-line tail-piece. In the traditional Petrarchan sonnet, the octave sets up a proposition or problem, while the sestet provides the resolution. "Pied Beauty" does not follow this pattern, but the sonnet form is still used to create a turnabout in focus. The first stanza or sestet ranges from God, then the heavens (in the Biblical account of creation in Genesis, God's first act was to create the heavens), and then the individual beings of creation. The progression is from the vast and infinite to the small and particular. The second

stanza or quatrain reverses this process, ranging from the particular and varied "All things," to the more abstract qualities such as swiftness and slowness, thence to God's act of creation ("He fathers-forth,") and ultimately, to the unchanging nature of God himself.

Rhyme Scheme

The standard rhyme scheme of the octave of a Petrarchan sonnet is a-b-b-a, a-b-b-a. For the sestet the commonest rhyme schemes are c-d-e-c-d-e or c-d-c-c-d-c, though other variants are to be found. The rhyme scheme of "Pied Beauty" is a-b-c-a-b-c for the sestet, and d-b-c-d-c for the quatrain and tail-piece. It can be seen that Hopkins brings over two of his rhymes from the sestet into the quatrain and tail-piece. This creates a continuity that unifies the two stanzas and reinforces the sense of resolution and completeness at the poem's end. The poem's regular rhyme scheme adds to the chiming effect created by the sprung rhythm and alliteration. The rhymes in the poem are masculine, meaning that the rhyme falls on a stressed syllable. This has a stronger, more emphatic effect than feminine rhymes, where the rhyme falls on an unstressed syllable.

HISTORICAL CONTEXT

The Society of Jesus (Jesuits)

St. Ignatius of Loyola (born Iñigo López de Loyola, 1491–1556) founded the Society of Jesus, or the Jesuits, as they are commonly known, in 1534. The Jesuits are a religious order of Catholics who profess direct loyalty and service to the pope. They are often called "Soldiers of Christ" and "Footsoldiers of the pope," partly because St. Ignatius was a soldier before he became a priest. St. Ignatius emphasized the importance of love for God and believed that man was created to praise and serve him (as, for instance, the poet of "Pied Beauty" does, while exhorting his readers to do likewise). In the process, he will save his own soul. Unusual among Christian teachers, St. Ignatius believed that emotions were important and taught that a person should be sensitive to the emotions that shaped him (a factor that may well have appealed to the emotionally sensitive Hopkins). At the same time, he taught that a person should be indifferent to the comfort or discomfort of his circumstances, to whether he was enjoying his activity or not, and to cultivate a state of serene acceptance. In addition, St. Ignatius taught that God is present in all things, so there is no division between the sacred and profane. This idea would accord well with Hopkins's ecstatic love and appreciation for the natural world and mankind, which are expressed in "Pied Beauty." Possibly as a result of this aspect of St. Ignatius's philosophy, Jesuits have been prominent in the arts and sciences.

As of 2006, Jesuit ministries were established worldwide and focused on education, missionary work, and ministry in human rights and social justice. Hopkins began training to be a Jesuit priest in 1868 and was ordained as a priest in 1877, the year in which he wrote "Pied Beauty." The poem begins and ends with variations of the Jesuit mottoes and thereby takes on the flavor of a Jesuit devotional exercise.

Duns Scotus, Nature, Inscape, and Instress

Blessed John Duns Scotus (1266–1308) was an English theologian and philosopher. Gardner, in *Gerard Manley Hopkins (1844–1889): A Study of Poetic Idiosyncrasy in Relation to Poetic Tradition*, believes that it is most likely that it was the work of Scotus, which Hopkins began to read in 1872, that influenced Hopkins to arrive at a metaphysical fusion of God and nature. Scotus was of the Franciscan tradition, which emphasized the importance of love of nature, God's creation, as a means of loving and praising God. Gardner comments: "Scotus taught that God the Son 'personifies' nature; yet a pantheistic heresy [a belief that identifies God with the universe] is carefully avoided, since although He is *in* the world, He is not *of* it." Gardner cites a journal entry by Hopkins as expressing this notion: "I do not think that I have ever seen anything more beautiful than the bluebell I have been looking at. *I know the beauty of our Lord by it.*"

Hopkins's poetry, including "Pied Beauty," shows an exquisite sensitivity to, and sharp observation of, nature. His is not a generalized vision but a particular one that identifies, for example, the exact pattern and color of a trout's skin, and this habit of particularity, too, may have been influenced by Scotus. Scotus used the term *haecceitas* (this-ness) to express the individuation of natural being and object as it comes into manifestation. This has some similarity with Hopkins's concepts of *inscape* and *instress*, terms that he coined to express his perception of nature. While the exact definitions of these terms were probably only known to Hopkins, inscape may be defined as the unified group of characteristics that give each thing its uniqueness. Instress is defined variously (depending on context) as the force of being that holds the inscape together or the impulse from the inscape which carries it whole into the mind of the beholder. Hopkins acknowledged his debt to Scotus in forming these concepts in a journal entry, cited by Gardner: "when I took in any inscape of the sky or sea I thought of Scotus."

The Industrial Revolution and Nature

The Industrial Revolution began in England in the late eighteenth century and from there, spread around the world. By the time Hopkins wrote "Pied Beauty" in 1877, it was in full flow and had radically and permanently changed the landscape and social organization of Britain. Hopkins's own family relocated in order to escape the rapidly industrializing environment of their hometown, Stratford in Essex. Hundreds of thousands of rural people migrated to the industrialized towns in search of work, including those in which Hopkins worked as a priest: Manchester, Liverpool, and Glasgow. Many found jobs in factories, but the work followed the fluctuations of markets, and poverty, disease, and hardship were widespread. For the first time, a large sector of the population lost access to land to grow food, leading to problems of hunger. Meanwhile, rural areas fell into decline as the center of the economy shifted to the towns.

Writers such as the poet William Blake (1757–1827), the novelist Elizabeth Gaskell (1810–1865), and the social and art critic John Ruskin (1819–1900) wrote at length about the social problems caused by the Industrial Revolution. In parallel, there grew among romantic and other writers an appreciation of the beauty of nature (which was under threat due to the sprawl and pollution of industrialization) and of fast-disappearing rural skills and trades (which were viewed as tying man to nature, unlike dehumanizing factory work). Hopkins showed a keen awareness of the problems, as is clear from his poem "God's Grandeur" (published in *Gerard Manley Hopkins: The Major Works*), which contains the line, "all is seared with trade; bleared, smeared with toil." The trades mentioned in "Pied Beauty," with their "gear and tackle and trim," do not appear to be tainted with industrial associations; they are the rural trades that tie man to the "plotted and pieced" landscape and enable him to bring order to it.

CRITICAL OVERVIEW

With a few exceptions of uncharacteristic poems appearing in minor periodicals, Hopkins's poems were not published during his lifetime and were read only by friends and fellow poets. Hopkins resisted the entreaties of his friends to publish. His reluctance was probably due to his anticipation of responses such as that of the poet and critic Coventry Patmore after wrestling with a number of Hopkins's poems. Patmore, cited in Paul L. Mariani's *A Commentary on the Complete Poems of Gerard Manley Hopkins*, complained that the poems required "the whole attention to apprehend and digest them." He added that Hopkins's poetry was "arduous" enough without the added difficulty of "*several entirely novel and simultaneous experiments in versification and construction*," together with an "altogether unprecedented system of alliteration and compound words."

Patmore was perhaps vindicated in his view by the slow sales of the 1918 publication of the first collected edition of Hopkins's poems, *Poems of Gerard Manley Hopkins*, edited by Robert Bridges, in which "Pied Beauty" was included. The English poet A. E. Housman gave his opinion of the collection in a letter of 1918 to Robert Bridges, cited in the University of Glasgow website article "Paper 17. Literature 1830–1914 (Victorian)." Housman dismisses Hopkins's attempts at sprung rhythm as being less competent than "many a humble scribbler of words for music-hall songs" has written. He accuses Hopkins of doing more "violence" to the English language than even the poet John Keats, and of trying to "compensate by strangeness for the lack of pure merit."

"Pied Beauty" subsequently appeared in the second complete edition of Hopkins's poetry, published in 1930. This time, popular taste had begun to catch up with Hopkins's innovative style. The edition met with considerable critical and public acclaim and established Hopkins's influence on twentieth-century poets. Not everyone was wholly impressed, however. T. S. Eliot (in his 1934 essay "After Strange Gods," as cited in the University of Glasgow website article "Paper 17. Literature 1830–1914 (Victorian)") noted that while Hopkins's innovations were good, "like the mind of their author, they operate only within a narrow range." Eliot wrote that they sometimes come close to being "purely *verbal*, in that a whole poem will give us more of the same thing, an accumulation, rather than a real development of thought or feeling."

Donald Davie, in his 1952 book *Purity of Diction in English Verse* (cited in the University of Glasgow website article, "Paper 17. Literature

WHAT DO I READ NEXT?

- All of Hopkins's poems, along with extracts from his journals and letters, and some of his sermons and devotional writings, are collected in *Gerard Manley Hopkins: The Major Works* (1986), edited by Catherine Phillips. Readers new to his poetry may enjoy "The Windhover," "God's Grandeur, and "As Kingfishers Catch Fire." For an example of his so-called terrible sonnets, "No Worst" may be of interest.

- *Gerard Manley Hopkins: A Very Private Life* (1991), by Robert Bernard Martin, is an interesting biography that argues that Hopkins projected his suppressed homoerotic impulses onto God and nature, producing some of the most sensually ecstatic religious poetry in English literature. Martin gained unprecedented and unrestricted access to Hopkins's notebooks to write this biography.

- *Christ Plays in Ten Thousand Places: A Conversation in Spiritual Theology* (2005), by Eugene H. Peterson, is a popular book written for the general reader in which the author explores the meaning of Biblical texts through the beauty of creation and the tragedies of history. Peterson, a pastor and professor, argues that spirituality is a sensual process.

- Readers who enjoy Hopkins's poetry may also appreciate that of the seventeenth-century English metaphysical poet John Donne. Most of his poems, including his love poetry and religious poems and writings, are collected in *John Donne: The Major Works, including Songs and Sonnets and Sermons* (2000).

1830–1914 (Victorian)"), lambasts Hopkins for his "self-regarding ingenuity," which "may be called decadent." Hopkins, Davie writes, is the greatest poet of a decadent age, "because he cultivates his hysteria and pushes his sickness to the limit." Part of Hopkins's decadence, Davie added, lies in "the refinement and manipulation of sensuous appetite": his work tries to restore "to a jaded palate the capacity for enjoyment." Davie, like Housman, objects to what he sees as Hopkins's lack of respect for the English language and his forcing it into "a muscle-bound monstrosity."

Over the decades, readers and critics have become used to many of the poetic innovations that were once considered so strange and difficult in Hopkins's poetry, allowing his strengths to come to the fore. His work gained particular admiration from many adherents of the New Criticism that dominated the study of English literature in Britain and the United States from the 1920s until the 1960s. The New Critics' emphasis on close reading of the text led them to appreciate Hopkins's short and condensed poetry, to such an extent that in 1952, the critic F. R. Leavis was able to begin his essay on Hopkins, "Metaphysical Isolation" (published in *Gerard Manley Hopkins: A Critical Symposium*) with the bold statement, "That Hopkins has a permanent place among the English poets may now be taken as established beyond challenge: academic scholarship has canonized him." "Pied Beauty" is among the most frequently anthologized of Hopkins's poems, and it is widely taught in schools and colleges. Kevin Heller, in his article for *Explicator* (2001) entitled "Hopkins's 'Pied Beauty,'" surely expresses the views of many modern critics and readers when he praises the poem for its "creativity and brilliance."

CRITICISM

Claire Robinson

Claire Robinson has an M.A. in English. She is a writer and editor and a former teacher of English literature and creative writing. In the following essay, she examines how Hopkins uses the poetic techniques of the oral traditions of Anglo-Saxon and traditional Welsh poetry to express his meaning in "Pied Beauty."

Gerard Manley Hopkins's experimentation with the poetic techniques of Anglo-Saxon and Welsh poetry was entirely geared to his intention that his poems be read aloud with the ear, not on the page with the eye. In a letter of August 21, 1877 to Robert Bridges (cited in *Gerard Manley*

REGULAR RHYTHM TENDS TO SOOTHE AND LULL READERS WITH ITS INCANTATORY EFFECT, WHEREAS IRREGULAR RHYTHM SUCH AS HOPKINS USES WAKES THEM UP AND SHOCKS THEM INTO SOMETHING APPROACHING A STATE OF ASTONISHMENT, AWE, OR WONDER."

Hopkins: The Major Works), he writes, "My verse is less to be read than heard . . . it is oratorical, that is the rhythm is so." In another letter to Bridges in 1886 (cited by Paul L. Mariani in *A Commentary on the Complete Poems of Gerard Manley Hopkins*), enclosing his sonnet, "Spelt from Sibyl's Leaves," he writes:

> Of this long sonnet above all remember what applies to all my verse, that it is, as living art should be, made for performance and that its performance is not reading with the eye but loud, leisurely, poetical (not rhetorical) recitation, with long rests, long dwells on the rhyme and other marked syllables, and so on.

One of the tools that Hopkins took from the Anglo-Saxon and Welsh oral traditions was alliteration, the repetition of initial consonant sounds in neighboring words, sometimes called consonant-chiming. For example, every line of the Anglo-Saxon poem *Beowulf* contains three alliterations. The Welsh-language poetic genre called *cynghanedd* (meaning harmony), a traditional form dating from ancient times and continuing into the present day, relies heavily on alliteration and internal rhyme (in which two or more words in the same line rhyme). Hopkins was studying the Welsh language and literature in the years prior to writing "Pied Beauty."

In "Pied Beauty," Hopkins includes such alliterative phrases as "skies of couple-colour as a brinded cow," where the initial letter "c" is repeated three times, and "Fresh-firecoal chestnut-falls," where the alliteration lies in the letter "f." The effect of alliteration is similar to rhyme in that it sets up an expectation of repetition that is later satisfied, thereby carrying the listener through the poem. (For one who

recites, the alliteration is an aid to memory.) It also has a musical, incantatory effect similar to that of metrical rhythm, due to the repetition of sounds. Often, Hopkins reinforces the chiming effect of the alliteration by making the alliterations fall on strongly stressed syllables, in the Anglo-Saxon style. This point is illustrated in all the above examples.

Hopkins's use of compound words is another conscious borrowing from the Anglo-Saxon tradition. *Beowulf* is laden with such constructions, called *kennings* (literally, knowings). A king is called a ring-giver (a king rewards his warriors with gifts of rings), a burial mound is an earth-hall, and a ship is a sea-rider. Such descriptions lend a concrete and picturesque quality to the object described; they pull it from the realm of the abstract into the more directly felt world of the senses, turning an idea into an object. For example, Hopkins's "couple-colour" conjures up a concrete image of a pair, perhaps a pair of people, while the word *two* and the prefix *bi-*, which have the same meaning, completely fail to stir the senses. The expression "Fresh-firecoal" invokes the familiar image of a burning coal breaking open and glowing red, but it is lent a new twist by the addition of "Fresh-," an adjective that connotes both newness and vitality.

The Anglo-Saxon language abounds in words describing the concrete and tangible world, as opposed to the often more abstract and cerebral Latin- and Greek-derived words that entered the English language with the Norman conquest of 1066. Anglo-Saxon-derived words are also usually shorter than Latin- or Greek-derived words, creating a more forceful sound effect. Hopkins's poetry is laden with words with Anglo-Saxon roots, which he prefers to those with Latin or Greek roots. Everyday speech has far more Anglo-Saxon-derived words than does formal speech or writing, and Hopkins wanted to approximate normal speech in his poetry. He also used many dialect and archaic words that hark back to the Anglo-Saxon past. An example from "Pied Beauty" is "brinded," an archaic and dialect word meaning striped or streaked, which is derived from the Anglo-Saxon *bernen* or *brinnen*, to burn.

The most important influence of Anglo-Saxon verse on Hopkins's poetry lay in its metrical system. Hopkins's sprung rhythm is based on a metrical style that was common in Anglo-Saxon poetry such as *Beowulf* and William

Langland's *Piers Plowman*. This metrical style has a set number of strong stresses per line. Each line is divided into two half-lines; there are two strong stresses per half-line and alliteration only occurs on stressed syllables. Each line can contain any number of syllables. "Pied Beauty" has four or five strong stresses per line, and many of the strong stresses alliterate also. For example, in the line, "Fresh-firecoal chestnut-falls; finches wings," three of the four strong stresses fall on the syllables beginning with the letter "f" the other strong stress falls on "chest-."

The Anglo-Saxon and sprung meters are different from the traditional meter of English verse written after the Norman invasion of 1066. The Norman style, which became the traditional English style, counts both stresses and syllables, rather than just stresses. It contains a regular number of syllables per foot, with the stress generally falling in the same place within each foot except when the rhythm is deliberately changed for emphasis. In his "Author's Preface" to the 1918 edition of his poetry, reproduced in *Gerard Manley Hopkins: The Major Works*, Hopkins called such traditional meter "Running Rhythm." He noted that while he himself made use of it, if strictly adhered to, it made verse become "same and tame."

Hopkins favored sprung rhythm because he believed it was the rhythm of common speech. It may be added that this rhythm is uniquely well-suited to Hopkins's declamatory, ecstatic, and enthusiastic style in general, and to the hymn of praise "Pied Beauty" in particular. Hopkins noted in a letter of April 2, 1877, to Robert Bridges (cited in *Gerard Manley Hopkins: The Major Works*) that sprung rhythm was "the most rhetorical and emphatic of all possible rhythms." Robert Lowell, in his essay "Hopkins' Sanctity," in *Gerard Manley Hopkins: A Critical Symposium by the Kenyon Critics*, notes the perfect correspondence between Hopkins's rhythmical style and his personality: "Hopkins' rhythms even when he is not writing sprung-rhythm have the effect of a hyperthyroid injection. As we know from the letters and personal anecdotes, he lived in a state of exhilaration."

Hopkins's sprung rhythm draws its power from the tension between the regular rhythms of poetry, which were usual in the poetry of his time, and his deliberately disturbed rhythms, which he called counterpointed rhythm. Regular rhythm tends to soothe and lull readers with its incantatory effect, whereas irregular rhythm such as Hopkins uses wakes them up and shocks them into something approaching a state of astonishment, awe, or wonder. An example is the first stanza of "Pied Beauty," in which Hopkins employs emphatic and sometimes staccato rhythms that load each line with a sense of exhilaration. In the second stanza, the shift in focus from outward creation to inward reflection is reflected in a slowing down of the rhythm and tempo. This is reinforced by the longer vowel sounds of line 7; it is impossible to read it as quickly as the first stanza. Line 9, with its list of opposite qualities, speeds up, as is usual with a list, but then the tempo slows markedly in the momentous lines 10 and 11: "He fathers-forth whose beauty is past change: / Praise him." The combination of a number of strongly stressed long vowel sounds and the four consecutive strong stresses falling on the final four words forces the reader to slow down.

The changes in rhythm and tempo between the lively first stanza and the more ponderous second perfectly reflect the meaning. The first stanza is quick and lively and expresses the variety of God's creation; the second is slower and more reflective and expresses both the poet's wondering introspection. The final one-and-a-half lines are slowest and grandest of all, and express the unchanging nature of God.

Hopkins never used innovative poetic techniques for their own sake. Rather, he used them to express and deepen the meaning of his poems. His theories of sprung rhythm and his study of the Anglo-Saxon and Welsh traditions have proved taxing for students of literature to research and understand. What matters is the end result: verse that shimmers with a sensual passion for life and its creator. This can only be fully realized by reading his poetry aloud, which is where the study of Hopkins's verse should begin and end.

Source: Claire Robinson, Critical Essay on "Pied Beauty," in *Poetry for Students*, Thomson Gale, 2007.

Kevin Heller

In the following essay excerpt, Heller gives an interpretation of Hopkins's "Pied Beauty," in which attention is given to the prayer form of the poem and how the "pied" poetic elements reflect the topic.

Through the use of various poetic devices in "Pied Beauty," Gerard Manley Hopkins causes the words of his poem to take on meaning beyond their dictionary definitions. By alluding to common prayers and manipulating both sound effect and stanza form. Hopkins makes his poem itself an example of pied beauty: it is pied, ordered and beautiful, and is an imitation of the creative act of God written to praise him in the form of a poem-prayer.

With the opening line, "Glory be to God [...]" (1), Hopkins alludes to the "Glory Be"—"Glory be to the Father, and to the son, and to the Holy Spirit, as it was in the beginning, is now, and ever shall be, world without end. Amen." By beginning "Pied Beauty" with those words, Hopkins forces the reader to recall the entire prayer and asks the reader to consider his poem a prayer. The "Glory Be" itself is unclear just what, exactly, about the Father, Son, and Holy Spirit is deserving of glory, but Hopkins provides an answer: the pied beauty of so many of God's creations is what causes God to be deserving of glory. In "Pied Beauty," God deserves glory for having created such beautiful things out of nothing, and humans have no idea what magnificent creation God will place on the earth in the future, just as the "Glory Be" discusses the past, present, and future.

The last line of Hopkins's poem, "Praise him" (11), is significant, just as the last line of the "Glory Be" is "Amen." Granted, "amen" does not mean "praise him," but rather "certainly" or "truly." Hopkins implies, however, that "Praise him" and "Amen" should be equated, and the context makes sense: Hopkins believes "Certainly" or "Truly" one should "Praise him." Readers can imagine listening to "Pied Beauty" being read (as it was intended to be read) aloud and nodding in assent to the last line. They might even be tempted to call out "Amen" or "Praise him."

The sounds that Hopkins's audience hears are brilliantly construed sentences and words that illustrate just why God deserves glory for his myriad creations: By combining words in such a new, unique, and beautiful manner, just as God created so many things in the world, Hopkins creates pied sounds—and both God's and Hopkins's creations are beautiful in their pied nature: God creates "brinded cows" the "couple-colour" (2) of the sky, and Hopkins creates beautiful sounds, such as, "Fresh-firecoal chestnut-falls; finches' wings" (4). This phrase

alliterates with *f* four times and contains six sprung rhythm feet—three single stresses, and three trochees—just as three separate God-created natural things are discussed. Further. Hopkins highlights the pied nature of the three things, because the reader cannot easily distinguish between the subject noun and the modifier in the sets "fresh-firecoal," "chestnut-falls," and "finches' wings." One word does not modify the other, but both work in conjunction to heighten the pied nature of their pairings. God creates "rose-moles all in stipple upon trout that swim" (3)—a line rich in imagery and sound. Hopkins creates a fraction of a line. "who knows how?" (8) in which the letter *o* is pronounced differently—in a pied fashion—in three separate words: these words utilize *w*'s and *h*'s to make the pattern "whwhw." Hopkins combines things in ways that do not at first seem to go together. But both God and Hopkins give their creations order, and within that order is beauty. Or within that beauty is order. In the line "With swift, slow; sweet sour; adazzle, dim" (9), Hopkins uses four *w*'s and four *s*'s, two *a*'s, two *d*'s, and two *z*'s, creating the pattern "aba-bababcdceed" (fourteen letters, just as a sonnet is fourteen lines) and Hopkins uses a modified form of the sonnet in "Pied Beauty."

A ten-and-a-half-line poem is not standard; it is "counter, original, spare, strange" (7). But the beauty of the form comes from its complexity and ingenuity within the boundaries of order: A typical sonnet could be eight and six lines, but Hopkins writes "Pied Beauty" in six and four and half lines—exactly proportionate to a regular fourteen-line sonnet (8/6 and 6/4.5; $8 \times 4.5 = 36$ and $6 \times 6 = 36$). The form of "Pied Beauty" is Hopkins's way of praising God through imitation: Hopkins created something pied and beautiful—the ten-and-a-half line sonnet—while maintaining order.

Whereas a prose version of the points Hopkins makes may be lucid, the effect that allusion, sound effect, and stanza have in "Pied Beauty" cannot possibly be captured in anything but poetry. Hopkins's poem and God's creations are both deserving of glory for their creativity and brilliance, but God created Hopkins: possibly an example of pied beauty himself.

Source: Kevin Heller, "Hopkins's 'Pied Beauty,'" in *Explicator*, Vol. 59, No. 4, Summer 2001, pp. 191–92.

John Ferns

In the following essay, Ferns gives a critical analysis of Hopkins's work.

While Gerard Manley Hopkins's importance as a Victorian poet is well established, his significance as a Victorian prose writer is not as fully recognized. This is, perhaps, because his prose did not appear in single works, like John Ruskin's *Modern Painters*, Matthew Arnold's *Culture and Anarchy*, or Walter Pater's *Studies in the History of the Renaissance*, published in his lifetime but is found in such varied forms as essays, notes, sermons, and letters which were not collected and published until well after his death. Nevertheless, Hopkins is demonstrably one of the great writers of Victorian prose just as he is one of the era's great poets. He deserves consideration alongside such acknowledged masters of Victorian prose as Arnold, Ruskin, Thomas Carlyle, and John Stuart Mill. As a literary critic, for example, Hopkins is surely the most important and perceptive critic of English poetry between Arnold and T. S. Eliot and an important link in the critical tradition they represent. His achievement in prose is intimately related to his achievement in poetry. In fact, the two achievements are really one; in his prose as well as in his poetry there is the same "strain of address" (as Hopkins called it), the same enthusiasm, feeling, love, inspiration, and sincerity—a unity of purpose confirmed in his Catholic faith and reaching back from Aquinas to Aristotle through Christ, whom Hopkins regarded as the best judge of literary ventures as well as of human lives.

Hopkins was born at Stratford, Essex, on 28 July 1844 to Manley and Kate Smith Hopkins. He was the eldest of their eight children who survived childhood. Manley Hopkins was a prosperous marine insurance adjuster and a minor poet. Gerard attended Highgate Grammar School (1854-1862) where he became an excellent student of Greek and Latin. He won an Exhibition scholarship to Balliol College, Oxford, in 1863.

In July 1866 Hopkins decided to become a Roman Catholic. He was received into the Catholic Church by John Henry Newman in October 1866. In 1867 he graduated with a double-first class degree in classics. The following year he decided to enter the Society of Jesus, and as a consequence of this decision he burned his early poetry, inadvertently overlooking some working drafts. His nine years of Jesuit training

> THE CHIEF INFLUENCE ON THE TECHNIQUE OF HOPKINS'S DETAILED NATURE OBSERVATIONS WAS LIKELY THE ART CRITIC JOHN RUSKIN, WHO IN VOLUME ONE OF HIS *MODERN PAINTERS* (1843) ADVISED THAT 'EVERY LANDSCAPE PAINTER SHOULD KNOW THE SPECIFIC CHARACTERS OF EVERY OBJECT HE HAS TO REPRESENT, ROCK, FLOWER, OR CLOUD.'"

took place at various Jesuit houses throughout Britain, in particular Roehampton, Stonyhurst, and St. Beuno's. In 1877 Hopkins was ordained a priest and during the next seven years carried out pastoral duties that included preaching and teaching in London, Oxford, Bedford Leigh, Liverpool, Glasgow, and Stonyhurst. The poverty and distressing social conditions that he witnessed in these industrial towns caused him to express deep concern in his letters to Robert Bridges and others.

He was appointed professor of Greek at Royal University College, Dublin, in 1884, a position he held until his early death from typhoid fever on 8 June 1889. The poetry which he began to write again late in 1875 and which he shared only with his family and a few friends, such as Robert Bridges, Richard Watson Dixon, and Coventry Patmore, was eventually published in an edition prepared by Bridges in 1918, nearly thirty years after Hopkins's death. The earliest extant letters, diary entries, and notebooks date from his later school days and earliest undergraduate years at Oxford University. The volume *The Notebooks and Papers of Gerard Manley Hopkins* (1937), edited by Humphry House in the 1930s and enlarged with the help of Graham Storey as *The Journals and Papers of Gerard Manley Hopkins* (1959) in the 1950s, contains, as well as early diaries and journals, undergraduate essays on a range of subjects. Besides book lists, the volume includes etymological notes and Lenten self-admonitions. Its focal point is an extended journal mainly of nature observations but also of spiritual experiences that Hopkins kept from 1866 to 1875.

The chief influence on the technique of Hopkins's detailed nature observations was likely the art critic John Ruskin, who in volume one of his *Modern Painters* (1843) advised that "Every landscape painter should know the specific characters of every object he has to represent, rock, flower, or cloud." Together with this was the classical-Arnoldian wish which Hopkins shared to represent the object "as in itself it really is." These notes, then, written during an extended period of self-elected poetic silence become, at times, almost prose poems in their impassioned contemplation of nature—for example, bluebells, described by Hopkins in May 1871: "This day and May 11 the bluebells in the little wood between the College and the highroad and in one of the Hurst Green cloughs. In the little wood/ opposite the light/they stood in blackish spreads or sheddings like the spots on a snake. The heads are then like thongs and solemn in grain and grape-colour. But in the clough/through the light/they come in falls of sky-colour washing the brows and slacks of the ground with vein-blue, thickening at the double, vertical themselves and the young grass and brake fern combed vertical, but the brake stuck the upright of all this with light winged transoms. It was a lovely sight.—"

This dense and detailed prose—which it took the greater selectivity of the beautiful sonnets of six years later, such as "Pied Beauty" and "Hurrahing in Harvest," to turn into poetry—is a prose that hardly knows what prose is. It is prose that lacks the discipline of writing for an audience, other than oneself. Much later, Hopkins was to complain to his friend and fellow poet Coventry Patmore about Patmore's and John Henry Newman's prose. The comments that follow he would no doubt have been willing to apply to his own early prose. To Patmore in October 1887 he wrote a passage that gives a good sense of what Hopkins thought successful prose should be: "It is that when I read yr. prose and when I read Newman's and some other modern writers' the same impression is borne in on me: no matter how beautiful the thought, nor, taken singly, with what happiness expressed, you do not know what *writing prose* is. At bottom what you do and what Cardinal Newman does is to think aloud, to think with pen to paper. In this process there are certain advantages; they may outweigh those of a perfect technic; but at any rate they exclude that; they exclude the belonging technic, the

belonging rhetoric the own proper eloquence of written prose. Each thought is told off singly and there follows a pause and this breaks the continuity, the *contentio*, the strain of address, which writing should usually have."

Hopkins goes on to argue that the beauty and eloquence of good prose cannot come wholly from the thought expressed. He offers Edmund Burke as an example of a prose writer who colorlessly transmitted his thought in prose. However, because Burke was an orator his writing emerged from an oratorical tradition and thus possessed the "strain of address" that Hopkins believed necessary to successful prose. John Henry Newman, Hopkins believes, does not follow the common tradition of English prose. He seems, Hopkins suggests, to write from the assumption that Edward Gibbon was the last master of traditional English prose as well as from the point of view that, since Gibbon cannot be emulated, it is best to "begin all over again from the language of conversation, of common life." Hopkins, then, tells Patmore that he (Patmore) writes prose from a conviction that the style of prose must be different from the style of poetry. But, Hopkins argues, prose style must be a "positive thing and not the absence of verse forms; . . . pointedly expressed thoughts are single hits and give no continuity of style." In Hopkins's view, good prose must always possess "continuity of style" and "strain of address." What Hopkins had discovered between 1871, when he wrote the bluebell passage, and 1887 was that to make his prose successful he needed to write with an audience in mind. Perhaps the bluebell passage shows "strain of address" and "continuity of style" but it does not possess them to the degree that the letter to Patmore does. Nevertheless, the journal of 1866-1875 does contain examples of moving prose when, for instance, Hopkins expresses the simple certainty of his religious belief. If Augustan prose lost the ability to express religion, Hopkins marvelously recovers that capacity for Victorian prose in the following passage from his journal for 8 October 1874, which possesses both "strain of address" and "continuity of style" even though Hopkins continues, here, to serve as his own audience. He had visited St. Winefred's well at Holywell with his Jesuit colleague Barraud, and there is a significant movement in the passage from natural observation to something approaching religious rapture: "Bright and beautiful day. Crests of snow could be seen on the mountains. Barraud and I walked over to Holywell and bathed at the well and returned very joyously. The sight of the water in the well as clear as glass, greenish like beryl or aquamarine, trembling at the surface with the force of the springs, and shaping out the five foils of the well quite drew and held my eyes to it. Within a month or six weeks from this (I think Fr di Pietro said) a young man from Liverpool, Arthur Kent (?), was cured of rupture in the water. The strong unfailing flow of the water and the chain of cures from year to year all these centuries took hold of my mind with wonder at the bounty of God in one of His saints, the sensible thing so naturally and gracefully uttering the spiritual reason of its being (which is all in true keeping with the story of St. Winefred's death and recovery) and the spring in place leading back the thoughts by its spring in time to its spring in eternity: even now the stress and buoyance and abundance of water is before my eyes."

The passage begins, like many of his earlier nature observations, in notes rather than with continuous prose: "Bright and beautiful day. Crests of snow could be seen on the mountains." The images are more sharply differentiated than are those in the bluebell passage, but essentially Hopkins uses the same method of recording observation. What distinguishes this passage from the earlier one and leads to increasing "strain of address" and "continuity of style" is the consideration of the miraculous cure. Hopkins's reflection, then, deepens and, as he would in the poetry he was shortly to recommence writing, he moves from a sense of the natural to a perception of the divine. "The Windhover" and "Hurrahing in Harvest" provide analogies from the poetry to what is happening here. The prose style in the journal passage is affected and changes from the fragmentariness of the nature observation of "Bright and beautiful day" to the continuity of the long, concluding, perfectly clear and moving sentence. What impresses is the wonder of Hopkins's simple faith, the realization that despite the fact that he lived in an age of doubt he believed in miracles. As F. R. Leavis observed in the second annual Hopkins Lecture, published by the Hopkins Society in 1971, "Hopkins, in a wholly unpejorative sense, was simple. There is nothing equivocal in his verse, and in the letters we see the simplicity as that of a man of high intelligence, fine human perception, irresistible charm and complete integrity."

Once Hopkins was ordained a priest at St. Beuno's Seminary, North Wales, in the fall of 1877, he had to assume priestly duties, one of which was preaching. His preaching, in London, Oxford, and eventually in Bedford Leigh and Liverpool, as well as the poetry he had recommenced writing in 1875, helped to extend the flexibility and range of his developing prose style. We should note, in this connection, that the sprung rhythm which he introduced into his poetry was, in his own words, "the nearest to the rhythm of prose, that is the native and natural rhythm of speech, the least forced, the most rhetorical and emphatic of all possible rhythms, combining, as it seems to me, opposite and, one wd. have thought, incompatible excellences, markedness of rhythm—that is rhythm's self— and naturalness of expression." For surely in recovering the alliterative rhythms of medieval verse in such poems as *The Wreck of the Deutschland* (1876), Hopkins was also recovering the rhythms of early English prose, with its two-beat phrases held together by stress patterns within and between phrases, its dependence on rhythm more than syntax to determine meaning, and its stringing together of main clauses connected by *and* and *but*. Just as Hopkins's poetry was influenced by Old and Middle English alliterative verse, his prose was influenced by early English prose. Understanding Hopkins's relationship to medieval prose and verse traditions helps to lead us to the heart of Hopkins's literary achievement. He brought poetry closer to the rhythm of prose. What he failed to achieve in prose as a preacher, he succeeded in presenting as a poet in such works as *The Wreck of the Deutschland*. But as his poetry and prose matured they came together in such a manner that in his later years Hopkins expressed similar thoughts in similar ways in both his meditation notes and in his sonnets of desolation.

The Sermons and Devotional Writings of Gerard Manley Hopkins, unpublished until 1959, contains both his less successful sermons and his deeply moving meditations. Though Hopkins was not thought by his Jesuit superiors or, apparently, by his audience to be a successful preacher, his sermons were clearly very carefully prepared. They demonstrate all the expected oratorical features such as repetition and accumulation, and Hopkins obviously took great care in his sermons to suit his matter to the capacity of his hearers. His painstaking preparation is perhaps clearest in his sermons delivered to his largely working-class parishioners at Bedford Leigh in Lancashire. The following passage from a sermon delivered on 23 November 1879 shows that by that date Hopkins was completely aware of the importance of "strain of address" and "continuity of style." His sermon oratory is also carefully shaped, though it is not Hopkins's best prose. He is speaking of Christ: "I leave it to you, brethren, then to picture him, in whom the fulness of the godhead dwelt bodily, in his bearing how majestic, how strong and yet how lovely and lissome in his limbs, in his look how earnest, grave but kind. In his Passion all this strength was spent, this lissomness crippled, this beauty wrecked, this majesty beaten down. But now it is more than all restored, and for myself I make no secret I look forward with eager desire to seeing the matchless beauty of Christ's body in the heavenly light. . . ."

Despite his sensitive handling of repetition and accumulation here, Hopkins would not be remembered as a prose writer for prose like this. Its alliteration is a little too self-conscious and the passage exudes, in places, an air of almost Pre-Raphaelite or decadent loveliness.

It is in the three published volumes of his letters—to Robert Bridges, to his former schoolmaster Richard Watson Dixon, and to others, including his parents and his Oxford friend Alexander Baillie—that Hopkins's claim to importance as a writer of Victorian prose lies. And the claim must be made in this way: Hopkins's prose is of interest because it is important literary criticism which also illuminates the creative practice of a major English poet. The letters, moreover, reveal a sense of the discovery and lively development of fresh thought.

One important aspect of Hopkins's contribution to literary criticism in the letters is his striking out against Tennyson's Parnassian style in the hope of restoring a language of inspiration to English poetry. Hopkins's essential critique of Tennyson occurs in an early letter to his friend Baillie, written in September 1864 when Hopkins was twenty years old. He announces somewhat melodramatically to his friend, "Do you know, a horrible thing has happened to me. I have begun to *doubt* Tennyson." The reason for doubt is that Tennyson writes too much "Parnassian," which Hopkins differentiates from the language of inspiration in the following way: "I think then the language of verse may be divided into three kinds. The first and highest is poetry proper, the language of inspiration. The word inspiration need cause no difficulty. I mean by it a mood of great, abnormal in fact, mental acuteness, either energetic or receptive, according as the thoughts which arise in it seem generated by a stress and action of the brain, or to strike into it unasked. . . . the poetry of inspiration can only be written in this mood of mind, even if it only last a minute, by poets themselves."

Hopkins's best prose is inspired writing as is his best poetry. The sense of intense concentration on the object that Hopkins himself speaks of as *contentio* or "strain of address" is perceptible in Hopkins's prose especially when he feels the force of divine inspiration, as he does in the 1874 journal account of the visit to Holywell and as he does in a later letter to Dixon discussing Wordsworth's Immortality Ode. Parnassian, in contrast to the language of inspiration, is the "second kind" of poetic language that Hopkins argues can "only be spoken by poets but it is not in the highest sense poetry. . . . It is spoken *on and from the level* of a poet's mind, not, as in the other case, when inspiration which is the gift of genius, raises him above himself." He goes on to offer an analysis of a passage from *Enoch Arden* to establish his point that Tennyson palls because he writes too much Parnassian. Hopkins's own return in his poetry from the mellifluous, Latinate diction of Tennyson to a more Germanic, Anglo-Saxon diction in the writing of *The Wreck of the Deutschland* involves an important shift in the language of English poetry which is also reflected in Hopkins's prose. When Hopkins counters Bridges's dislike of Dryden in a letter of November 1887, he describes Dryden's language in a way that characterizes his own poetry and prose, "he is the most masculine of our poets; his style and his rhythms lay the strongest stress of all our literature on the naked the and sinew of the English language, the praise that with certain qualification one would give in Greek to Demosthenes, to be the greatest master of bare Greek. . . ."

Hopkins was remarkably faithful, throughout his life as a critic, to his early judgment of Tennyson. He simply came to believe more and more fully that inspiration, whether in poetry or prose, came from God. A later judgment of Tennyson, in a letter to Dixon written in February or March 1879, shows the continuity in Hopkins's critical thought and is, as well, a representative example of his mature critical prose. The following passage shows a comprehensive grasp of Tennyson's canon to 1879 and a maturity of critical judgment: "You call Tennyson 'a great outsider'; you mean, I think, to the soul of poetry. I feel what you mean, though it grieves me to hear him depreciated, as of late year has often been done. Come what may he will be one of our greatest poets. To me his poetry appears 'chryselephantine'; always of precious mental material and each verse a work of art, no botchy places, not only so but no half wrought or low-toned ones, no drab, no brown-holland; but the form, though fine, not the perfect artist's form, not equal to the material."

Hopkins goes on to argue that Tennyson is at his best when inspired by personal feeling as in *In Memoriam* which Hopkins considers a divine work. Also, he admires Tennyson the pure rhymer and simple imaginer of "The Lady of Shalott," "Sir Galahad," "The Dream of Fair Women," and "The Palace of Art." However, Hopkins thinks that the want of perfect form in Tennyson's imagination comes out in his longer works—*Idylls of the King*, for example, which Hopkins considers "unreal in motive and incorrect. He shd. have called them *Charades from the Middle Ages*. . . ." Galahad, in one of the later *Idylls*, Hopkins considers "a fantastic charade-playing trumpery Galahad, merely playing the fool over Christian heroism." Although Hopkins finds the individual scenes from the *Idylls* triumphs of language and "of bright picturesque," the overall effect is that of a charade and not as dramatically convincing as the plays on Drury Lane. Tennyson's opinions are neither original nor independent in Hopkins's view and often sink into vulgarity. "Locksley Hall," *Maud, Aylmer's Field*, and *The Princess* are "ungentlemanly rows," though Tennyson, Hopkins notes, lacks the real rakishness and rascality of Goethe or Burns. For Hopkins, Tennyson is at his worst in such rhetorical pieces as "The Lord of Burleigh" and "Lady Clare Vere de Vere." He concludes, however, by reaffirming his admiration for Tennyson—"a glorious poet and all he does is chryselephantine."

Hopkins's assessment of Tennyson is typical of his critical prose in that it is both generous and critical, his language is colloquial ("no botchy places . . . no drab, no brown-holland"), and he provides a criticism of Tennyson that the common reader can grasp. Even the dubious criticism of *Maud* and *The Princess* as "ungentlemanly rows" gains point when we understand

that Hopkins was making a moral rather than a merely social judgment. Hopkins thought that the perfect gentleman was Christ. In an 1879 letter to Bridges he makes a further comment on Tennyson and an account of truly gentlemanly qualities he believes that the best poetry should possess: "Tennyson: his gift of utterance is truly golden, but go further home and you come to thoughts commonplace and wanting in nobility (it seems hard to say it but I think you know what I mean)." Then, speaking of Bridges's poetry he observes, "Since I must not flatter or exaggerate I do not claim that you have such a volume of imagery as Tennyson, Swinburne, or Morris, though the feeling for beauty you have seems to me pure and exquisite; but in point of character, of sincerity or earnestness, of manliness, of tenderness, of humour, melancholy, human feeling" are those of true gentlemanliness that, for Hopkins, characterize the best literature.

Another excellent example of Hopkins's critical prose is found in his letter of 23 October 1886 to Dixon when he defends Wordsworth's 1807 Immortality Ode against Dixon's indifference to the poem. In the latter part of the letter, Hopkins speaks of Wordsworth and Plato: "human nature in these men saw something, got a shock; wavers in opinion, looking back, whether there was anything in it or no; but is in a tremble ever since. Now what Wordsworthians mean is, what would seem to be the growing mind of the English speaking world and may perhaps come to be that of the world at large/is that in Wordsworth when he wrote that ode human nature got another of those shocks, and the tremble from it is spreading. This opinion I do strongly share; I am, ever since I knew the ode, in that tremble. You know what happened to crazy Blake, himself a most poetically electrical subject both active and passive, at his first hearing: when the reader came to 'The pansy at my feet' he fell into a hysterical excitement. Now commonsense forbid we should take on like these unstrung hysterical creatures: still it was proof of the power of the shock."

Hopkins continues by arguing that the ode is better than anything else by Wordsworth. Wordsworth was an imperfect artist capable of deep insight in some instances and little in others, but the subject matter of the ode is "of the highest, his insight was at its very deepest, and hence to my mind the extreme value of the poem." Wordsworth's poetic execution, in

Hopkins's view, rises to the occasion of his subject. His rhymes are "musically interlaced," his rhythms successful. Wordsworth's diction throughout the ode Hopkins considers "charged and steeped in beauty and yearning." Hopkins's oratorical and rhetorical style in the letter and the strain of his address reach their height in his final comment: "For my part I shd. think St. George and St. Thomas Canterbury wore roses in heaven for England's sake on the day that ode, not without their intercession, was penned. . . ." Again we have the sense of an enthusiastic critical intelligence, alive in its admiration of Wordsworth's ode. As in his criticism of Tennyson, Hopkins shows the acute critic's capacity to go directly to the heart of his subject. Whereas Tennyson is suspect in his inability to sustain inspiration, Wordsworth provides an inspired insight into the nature of immortality. Such significant perceptions, written from moral conviction and expressed with point, place Hopkins in the English critical tradition that includes Johnson, Coleridge, Wordsworth, Arnold, and culminates in the literary criticism of T. S. Eliot and F. R. Leavis. In both the passages on Tennyson and Wordsworth, Hopkins's moral and religious convictions, his "strain of address," and his capacity to sustain an argument or perception, his "continuity of style," are evident as they are, too, throughout his nature, sermon, and meditation writing. In addition to the commentaries on Tennyson and Wordsworth, Hopkins, in his letters, offers equally perceptive critical discussions of Milton, Browning, Barnes, and others. We see throughout the letters the delicacy, the fineness of Hopkins's sensibility, the warmth of his friendship, and the strength of his moral intelligence.

Two further aspects of Hopkins's prose deserve to be considered. His seriousness is frequently leavened by a sense of humor which helps to give freshness and vitality to his writing. His April 1871 letter describing to his sister Kate his response to a smallpox vaccination is spontaneous and amusing: "We were all vaccinated the other day. The next day a young Portuguese came up to me and said 'Oh misther 'Opkins, do *you* feel the cows in *yewer* arm?' I told him I felt the horns coming through. I do I am sure. I cannot remember now whether one ought to say the calf of the arm or the calf of the leg. My shoulder is like a shoulder of beef. I dare not speak above a whisper for fear of bellowing—there now, I am going to say I am obliged to speak low for fear of lowing. I dream at night

that I have only two of my legs in bed. I think there is a split coming in both my slippers. Yesterday I could not think why it was that I would wander about a wet grass-plot: I see now. I chew my pen a great deal. The long and short of it is that my left forequarter is swollen and painful (I meant to have written arm but I could not)." In a letter to Bridges of 2 August 1871 his awareness of prose style is revealed in amusing parodies of Carlyle, written in imitation of Carlyle's "most ineffacious-strenuous heaven-protestations, caterwaul, and Cassandra-wailings." Writing to Bridges from Ireland in August 1884, he records an amusing incident: "I must tell you a humourous touch of Irish Malvolio or Bully Bottom, so distinctively Irish that I cannot rank it: it amuses me in bed. A Tipperary lad, one of our people, lately from his noviceship, was at the wicket and another bowling to him. He thought there was no one within hearing, but from behind the wicket he was overheard after a good stroke to cry out 'Arrah, sweet myself!'" And in the same year, in a letter to his sister, he produces a marvelous parodic transcription of Irish speech: "And now, Miss Hopkins darlin yell chartably exkees me writin more in the rale Irish be raison I was never rared to ut and thats why I do be slow with my pinmanship, bad luck to ut (saving your respects), and for ivery word I delineate I disremember two, and thats how ut is with me."

For Hopkins, however, the other side of this humor is the sense of melancholy present in the early letters and ever increasing through the last five years of his life, which he spent as professor of Greek at what is now University College, Dublin. The following paragraph from his retreat notes written at St. Stanilaus' College, Beaumont, on 1 January 1889 is surely the seed for one of his last sonnets of desolation, "Thou Art Indeed Just Lord": "I was continuing this train of thought this evening when I began to enter on that course of loathing and hopelessness which I have so often felt before, which made me fear madness and led me to give up the practice of meditation except, as now, in retreat and here it is again. I could therefore do no more than repeat *Justus es, Domine, et rectum judicium tuum* and the like, and then being tired I nodded and woke with a start. What is my wretched life? Five wasted years almost have passed in Ireland. I am ashamed of the little I have done, of my waste of time, although my helplessness and weakness is such that I could scarcely do otherwise. And yet the Wise Man warns us against excusing ourselves in that fashion. I cannot then be excused; but what is life without aim, without spur, without help? All my undertakings miscarry: I am like a straining eunuch. I wish then for death: yet if I died now I should die imperfect, no master of myself, and that is the worst failure of all. O my God, look down on me." In this disturbing passage one perceives the anguish that animates Hopkins's need to write. His final auditor is God.

Hopkins's prose underwent considerable and rapid development during his short career. From brief nature observations he moved to religious meditations on the divine origins of nature. After his ordination, he turned his developing awareness of the possibilities of prose to the writing of sermons. Throughout his life he was a lively and, when his religious duties allowed, prolific letter writer. His letters, with their moral intelligence, critical estimates of English poetry, and sensitivity to the dynamism and to the spiritual and physical poverty of his times, establish him as an important writer of Victorian prose. As a literary critic he has been unduly neglected, though it is perhaps not surprising that Hopkins's prose has been slower to gain acceptance than his poetry. It did not begin to be published until nearly twenty years after the first collection of his poetry appeared. However, the prose has been used by most critics of Hopkins's poetry because in expressing the drama of his inner life it provides the best introduction we have to that poetry. W. H. Gardner, in his two-volume *Gerard Manley Hopkins (1844-1889)* (1944, 1949), and F. R. Leavis, in *The Common Pursuit* (1952), are two critics who have realized the importance of Hopkins's prose particularly in relation to his poetry. Nevertheless, full-length studies of Hopkins as a Victorian prose writer and literary critic remain to be written.

Source: John Ferns, "Gerard Manley Hopkins," in *Dictionary of Literary Biography*, Vol. 57, *Victorian Prose Writers After 1867*, edited by William B. Thesing, Gale Research, 1987, pp. 130–38.

SOURCES

Gardner, W. H., *Gerard Manley Hopkins (1844–1889): A Study of Poetic Idiosyncrasy in Relation to Poetic Tradition*, Vol. 2, Oxford University Press, 1949, pp. 21, 22, 367.

Heller, Kevin, "Hopkins's 'Pied Beauty,'" in *Explicator*, Vol. 59, No. 4, Summer 2001, p. 192.

Hopkins, Gerard Manley, "Author's Preface," in *Gerard Manley Hopkins: The Major Works*, edited by Catherine Phillips, Oxford University Press, 1986, p. 106.

———, "God's Grandeur," in *Gerard Manley Hopkins: The Major Works*, edited by Catherine Phillips, Oxford University Press, 1986, p. 128.

———, Letter to Robert Bridges, August 21, 1877, in *Gerard Manley Hopkins: The Major Works*, edited by Catherine Phillips, Oxford University Press, 1986, p. 229.

———, Letter to Robert Bridges, April 2, 1878, in *Gerard Manley Hopkins: The Major Works*, edited by Catherine Phillips, Oxford University Press, 1986, pp. 228, 229.

———, Letter to Robert Bridges, February 15, 1879, in *Gerard Manley Hopkins: The Major Works*, edited by Catherine Phillips, Oxford University Press, 1986, p. 235.

———, "Pied Beauty," in *Gerard Manley Hopkins: The Major Works*, edited by Catherine Phillips, Oxford University Press, 1986, pp. 132–33.

"Jesuits Worldwide," in *Jesuits in Britain*, the official website of the British Province of the Society of Jesus, http://www.jesuit.org.uk/overseas/worldwide.htm (accessed December 5, 2006).

Leavis, F. R., "Metaphysical Isolation," in *Gerard Manley Hopkins: A Critical Symposium by the Kenyon Critics*, Burns & Oates, 1975, p. 115.

Lowell, Robert, "Hopkins's Sanctity," in *Gerard Manley Hopkins: A Critical Symposium by the Kenyon Critics*, Burns & Oates, 1975, p. 92.

Mariani, Paul L., *A Commentary on the Complete Poems of Gerard Manley Hopkins*, Cornell University Press, 1970, pp. xviii, 198.

Milward, Peter, S.J., *A Commentary on the Sonnets of G. M. Hopkins*, Hokuseido Press, 1969, p. 30.

"Paper 17. Literature 1830–1914 (Victorian)," website of the Faculty of Arts at the University of Glasgow, http://www.arts.gla.ac.uk/SESLL/EngLit/ugrad/hons/materials/hopkins2.htm (accessed December 5, 2006).

FURTHER READING

Brown, Daniel, *Gerard Manley Hopkins*, Northcote House Publishers, 2002.
This book provides an accessible introduction to Hopkins's poetry in the light of his prose writings, which are used to illuminate Hopkins's thinking on nature, prosody, language, philosophy, science, and theology, as well as his ideas on *inscape* and sprung rhythm.

Heaney, Seamus, ed., *Beowulf: A New Verse Translation*, W. W. Norton, 2001.

In his translation of the epic Anglo-Saxon poem, the Irish poet Seamus Heaney has preserved the alliterative and rhythmical patterns and the profusion of kennings that characterized the original. The poem tells the story of the warrior Beowulf and his battles with three monsters.

Muller, Jill, *Gerard Manley Hopkins and Victorian Catholicism: A Heart in Hiding*, Routledge, 2003.
Muller examines Hopkins's life, writings, and spirituality in the context of a newly industrialized, anti-Catholic, and increasingly secular England. She shows how the preoccupations and disappointments of Hopkins's career reflect the deflation of Catholic hopes during the second half of the nineteenth century.

Sheehan, Sean, *Student Guide to Gerard Manley Hopkins*, Greenwich Exchange, 2005.
This critical study explores the relationship between Hopkins's poetry and his philosophy. Sheehan shows the intimate relationship between Hopkins's perceptions, his poetic expression, and his idea of *inscape*.

Russian Letter

JOHN YAU

2002

"Russian Letter," published in 2002, in the collection *Borrowed Love Poems*, is a quirky little poem that at first seems to promise to offer a deep meaning of life and the passage of time and what all that means to the individual. Then in the middle of this poem, the narrator appears to change his mind. First, the narrator offers a standard philosophical theory about the makeup of the past and the present and how one reflects upon the other. This philosophical theory is offered through some source, referred to in the phrase, "it is said." Then the poet casts doubt on the theory; the narrator suggests that maybe this philosophical message goes too far. Just as the reader anticipates an alternative statement by the narrator, the poem offers a surprise ending, which neither provides an argument against the theory nor offers a more stimulating one. Instead, the narrator inserts an artistic memory, an image as beautiful as a Rembrandt painting, leaving the reader with a picture to ponder rather than an answer. If there is an answer to the questions in life, this poem hints that those answers cannot be easily handed over like a gift.

Yau's "Russian Letter" is the first in a series of six poems, all with the same title. Reading all six of these poems does not necessarily offer an easier task of understanding Yau's poetry, but it might help the reader to relax in the reading of Yau's poetry. Rather than attempting to make literal sense of Yau's poems, the reader needs to merely enjoy the images, the individual couplets,

John Yau *(© Christopher Felver/Corbis)*

their works have been published in various books dedicated to art criticism. In addition, Yau is the author of two collections of short stories, *My Symptoms* (1998) and *Hawaiian Cowboys* (1995), which, despite its title, contain stories mostly about people living in New York City. Yau has taught both art criticism and poetry at several schools, including Pratt Institute in Brooklyn; Brown University in Providence, Rhode Island; and the University of California at Berkeley.

Over the years, Yau received many awards for his poetry, including the Lavan Award from the Academy of American Poets and the Jerome Shestack Prize from the *American Poetry Review*.

POEM TEXT

It is said, the past
sticks to the present

like glue,
that we are flies

struggling to pull free   5
It is said, someone

cannot change
the clothes

in which
their soul   10

was born.
I, However,

would not
go so far

Nor am I Rembrandt,   15
master of the black

and green darkness,
the hawk's plumes

as it shrieks
down from the sky   20

and the sounds of the language. Or as Paisley Rekdal, writing for the *International Examiner*, described Yau's poetry, his "writing attempts to mimic the effects of abstract painting in that words or sentences become isolated images that are irreducible as narratives: they exist simply as line and color and tone." Yau's poem, "Russian Letter" is like a painting, in other words, one that uses language as its medium.

AUTHOR BIOGRAPHY

John Yau was born in Lynn, Massachusetts, in 1950, shortly after his parents left Shanghai, China. In 1972, at the age of twenty-two, Yau graduated from Bard College with a bachelor's degree. Six years later, he received his M.F.A. degree from Brooklyn College.

After that, Yau wrote seventeen books of poetry. Three of these, published in the early 2000s, are *Borrowed Love Poems* (2002), in which the poem "Russian Letter" appears; *Ing Grish* (2005); and *Paradiso Diaspora* (2006). He also wrote several books about artists, including one on the famous modern American artist Andy Warhol. Yau's essays about artists and

POEM SUMMARY

Lines 1 through 5

John Yau's "Russian Letter" is a short poem of ten couplets (pairs of lines), with each couplet offering the reader a brief but fascinating image. Yau has stated that the couplet is one of his favorite poetic forms, offering short but concise reflections on specific themes.

The first couplet in Yau's "Russian Letter" opens with an image of time and the memories and experiences associated with the passage of time. However, this opening image is not offered as coming from the narrator. Rather, the narrator suggests that the first thoughts of this poem belong to someone else. The narrator begins with the phrase, "It is said." In other words, there is a widely recognized and affirmed theory that the narrator wants to discuss. This theory is stated as "the past / sticks to the present." The narrator offers this philosophical statement in such a way that the reader senses (because of the "It is said" phrase) that the narrator will either reinforce or refute this belief later in the poem. By using this opening phrase, "It is said," the narrator implies both an inherent weakness in the philosophical statement and an awareness that it has perpetuated and is well known. The pronoun "it" locates the power of the statement in tradition, away from the narrator. This signals that the narrator may not agree with the statement at all or, at least, may be skeptical that this statement reflects truth as far as the narrator understands it.

In the second couplet, the narrator expounds on the stickiness of the past to the present. The past is stuck "like glue" to the present. This simile provides an image for the statement. What does it mean for the past to be stuck to the present? And how powerful is the adhesion? After all, some glues can be easily washed away. In the next lines, the narrator makes clear there is a lot of stickiness, using a metaphor, creating the image of flies stuck on tacky paper. Flies are small and frail. If flies are caught on a sticky tape, there is little or no chance for them to escape. This image of flies stuck on a gummy surface conveys the serious, even dire nature of the adhesive that connects the past to the present. So by the end of the second couplet, it appears that according to the philosophy of the statement, one has no chance of escaping one's past. The past holds each person in it or in place. No matter what is done, there is no escape. Then by the fifth line of this poem, the action intensifies. Not only is the past stuck to the present, like flies in a sticky trap, but everyone is "struggling to pull free" of it. This adds an element of desperation and futile effort. The past has now turned into something negative, something that one wrestles with in order to escape from it. This is, according to the philosophy introduced at the beginning of the poem, a fruitless effort.

Lines 6 through 11

Line 6 at the end of the third couplet repeats the opening phrase: "It is said," thus signaling a continuation of this authoritative philosophy or offering another philosophical statement that is equally uncomfortable for the narrator. "It is said, someone / cannot change," the narrator states in lines 6 and 7. The reader might wonder, at this point, if the narrator believes this statement or if the narrator is going to argue against it. The idea of someone not being able to change seems to run contrary to the evidence because people change all the time. Children grow up; people change professions; single people become married people, and so on. What kind of change is the narrator talking about? The narrator provides a hint in the next few lines.

The idea that people cannot change is not true on some level, perhaps, but the narrator is referring to transitions on a deeper level than mere appearance. As the poem continues, readers learn that the narrator means that people "cannot change / the clothes / in which / their soul / was born." The word "clothes" does not refer to wardrobe but rather to the physical self, perhaps suggesting the composition of DNA, the make-up of one's personality, and other essential traits that each baby has in place at birth. What is interesting in this part of the poem is how the poet has chopped up the components of this statement, keeping the reader in suspense as each new line adds more pertinent information. As readers continue into the next lines of the poem, they discover what the narrator is really talking about. The "clothes" are the full-blooded body in which a person is born, that which the soul inhabits and animates. The body of each person houses the intellect, talents, and the personality that determine how each person chooses to use these faculties. These factors or traits cannot change, this philosophy contends. The parallel is drawn here: the past is stuck to the present just as the prenatal characteristics are stuck to the newborn baby.

Lines 12 through 20

In the twelfth line the narrator sets himself apart from the statement of the first section of the poem. The narrator states, "I, however," suggesting an alternative statement to come. The narrator's full declaration is given in degrees; he "would not / go so far" as to claim that no one can change or that the past is stuck like glue to the present or that "we are flies / struggling to

TOPICS FOR FURTHER STUDY

- Since John Yau, the author of "Russian Letter," is also very much involved with art, imagine this poem in a visual art form. Sketch or paint an image that you think the poem inspires. Present your image to the class and explain how it arose from the poem.

- Yau can be compared to other poets, for example, Bob Dylan. Take one of the themes of this poem (freedom, change, nonconformity, time) and compare it to one of Dylan's lyrics. (The book called *Lyrics*, published in 2005, contains Dylan's poetry.) How similar are the images that these two poets use? Do they agree with one another? Is one clearer in his meaning than the other? Present your findings to your class.

- Present a PowerPoint display of Rembrandt's paintings, suggesting how the painter might be referred to as a master of "the black and green darkness." Research critical commentary on how Rembrandt used the darkness in his paintings and present both the images and the information to your class to more fully illuminate Yau's reference to the artist.

- Write a melody for Yau's poem and either sing or play the tune for your class. Then ask them to join with you, as you teach them the song.

pull free." The narrator backs off from these beliefs, but what is not clear is what the narrator would replace these beliefs with. Maybe that is the narrator's point: Maybe the narrator cannot agree fully with the first assertions but, while he places himself in a more moderate position, he has no counterstatement to offer.

At the fifteenth line, Yau, the poet, brings art into his poem. Yau's poetry is known for jumping from one image to another without necessarily providing a bridge between the two images, defying convention, just as the narrator refuses to subscribe to a well-known philosophical or psychological concept that the past and present are inevitably stuck to one another. At the fifteenth line, the narrator suddenly claims that he is not the famous Dutch painter Rembrandt, "master of the black / and green darkness." Rembrandt's paintings were often highly contrasted, with large portions of the canvas in dark colors, which directed the viewer's focus to the subject, which might be painted in comparatively bright colors. So the "black / and green darkness" that is mentioned in the poem could be a reference to the dark tones of the oil paints that Rembrandt used. The narrator then describes a hawk that "shrieks / down from the sky." One can imagine Rembrandt painting such a piece with dark skies above and dark earth below and all the light centered on the hawk.

In ending his poem with the seemingly disconnected reference to Rembrandt, the poet might be making the statement that he paints his poem with words but does not claim to define life or philosophy through his poetry. With the phrase, "Nor am I Rembrandt," the narrator might be also saying that he claims no mastery, no super statement that answers life's most important questions, for example, those pertaining to what remains the same through time. The poem offers images only, like a painting.

THEMES

Time

The shortness of Yau's poem "Russian Letter" dictates that the themes are only briefly mentioned or suggested. The subject given the most words is the idea that the past is stuck to the present. Clearly time passes, and yet the poem asserts that it is commonly believed that the past is always determining the present. Too, the poem points out that as much as people may struggle to escape the past, they have as much chance of doing so as flies stuck on gummy paper. The statement is fatalistic or pessimistic. The plot is already fixed in and by the past, and no matter what effort is exerted, the past dictates present circumstances, no matter how much one may struggle against that. This is a common way of seeing the time-bound human condition. It is a belief that strikes the narrator as extreme, one that he chooses to step back from, trying to find a less extreme view. But then the narrator does not offer an alternative; all readers get is the narrator's inability to agree. The narrator does

In this poem, Yau suggests that humans try to pull themselves away from their personal histories the way flies try to pull free from the flypaper that traps them (© Jack Sullivan/Alamy)

not offer an alternative view from the one stated as commonly held.

Change

Yau's poem also points out that it is widely believed that people "cannot change." While the narrator separates from this position, too, he explains that commonly it is asserted that what happens to people is determined by the nature they have at birth, by those factors of the physical self that the soul inhabits. The narrator is able to imagine something more to causation than this idea that "someone / cannot change / the clothes / in which / their soul / was born." There must be more factors that conspire to shape people's lives, but the narrator questions his own ability to say what they are. The narrator would not "go so far," and yet, he admits, he is no "Rembrandt / master of the black / and green darkness." The narrator is not a master of subtlety, not a master of things that are dark enough to blend black and green. The image of the hawk is ominous; this bird of prey "shrieks / down from the sky" when it is

intent on making a kill. There must be factors, the image suggests, that create change that are not determined by one's innate features, factors of risk and chance, perhaps another being's innate nature. The narrator suggests these potential determinants in the final image.

Authority

The phrase, "It is said," appears twice in the poem. The phrase repeats in the poem, which makes sense since the common or widely believed verities that might be introduced with this phrase are themselves repeated frequently. The phrase suggests tradition and a history of repetition. The truths that are repeated come with a certain authority. They come with the authority of tradition or of scripture or of widely circulated philosophical or psychological premises. These are not the facts of nature but rather the theories about nature. With repetition through time, like the momentum of often repeated clichés, they gather weight and apparent validity, though they may nonetheless be incorrect or disproved by empirical evidence. Given the familiarity of the observation or interpretation, such statements may be accepted blindly as indisputable fact. The narrator does not subscribe to the often repeated belief, but he admits to not being clever enough to come up with a substitute, something that might persuade others to see the accepted verity as no longer valid.

Nonconformance

The narrator's resistance to the often repeated observation suggests that the poem recommends resistance to conformity, resistance to blind acceptance of what others have repeatedly said is true. Nonconformity requires not going along with common beliefs just because they have been accepted by the majority. The narrator suggests that there are more ways of seeing the nature of human circumstances, more ways of understanding what causes human events to turn out as they do. The narrator's refusal to align with the dominant belief seems to serve as the poet's recommendation to readers to think independently and to search beyond the pat explanations. Those who believe in the fatalistic idea are as doomed as the flies stuck to a sticky surface; those who seek a larger, more inclusive perspective on the nature of things have the hope of escaping the past through their larger understanding of it.

STYLE

Couplets

Yau's poem "Russian Letter" is composed of couplets, a unit of verse made up of two successive lines. The poem consists of ten couplets. No couplet is complete unto itself, however, as both the subject and the grammar continue from one couplet to the next. The poem has only one full stop: a period appears at the end of the first line of the sixth couplet.

Yau has stated that couplets allow him to present brief images. In this way, the poet contends, he can concentrate on the two lines, each in their own time, without thinking ahead and trying to determine what the whole poem will be about. Although in this poem most of Yau's couplets do not contain complete thoughts, many do create interesting images, which might be explained by another statement that the poet has made. Yau has also compared couplets to a painter's individual brush strokes that eventually make up a whole painting. In the first couplet of "Russian Letter," Yau states the central idea of the poem and in the phrase, "it is said," suggests that the idea is widely recognized. In just the first two lines (the first couplet), the reader gains a sense of what the first half of the poem is about. The second couplet offers a simile that draws a picture of the philosophical idea. Yau uses the couplets in a free verse format, in which there are no end rhymes and no fixed beats per line.

Enjambment

Enjambment occurs when a full stop does not occur at the end of a line and the grammatical arrangement continues into or beyond the next line. This happens throughout Yau's poem, beginning with the first two lines, which read: "It is said, the past / sticks to the present." The second line here does not end with the word "present" but continues with a simile in the third line: "the past / sticks to the present / like glue." That completed statement does not end either. Rather a concrete illustration for the abstract statement is given in the fourth and fifth lines which compares the past stuck to the present to flies stuck on adhesive paper. However, the added point here is the use of "we." The fourth and fifth lines read: "that we are flies / struggling to pull free." So the comparison conveys the idea that just as flies stuck on adhesive paper struggle to get free, so do people stuck in their pasts struggle to free themselves from their histories. Sometimes enjambment is used for emphasis: the line break forces readers' eyes to skip down and left to the beginning of the next line and doing so puts emphasis on the word the begins the next line. Enjambment might also create a sense of ambiguity, with one line appearing to mean one thing until the next line is read and the meaning changes. This last point occurs in Yau's poem between the third and fourth couplets. At line six, "It is said, someone," continues unto the fourth couplet with "cannot change." People cannot change is the meaning that the reader brings out of this. However, continuing with line eight, the reader discovers that the narrator is really saying that people "cannot change the clothes," not literally change dress but rather, as the next line clarifies, "the clothes / in which / their soul / was born." Reaching the end of the sentence readers see that the word "clothes" is a metaphor for the innate self, the body with all of its features, which is animated by the soul. By line eleven the statement is completed. But during the passage from line six until line eleven, several misinter-pretations, or guesses, about what the narrator is trying to say are made, thus keeping the reader off balance and misunderstanding through the use of enjambment.

Imagery

Imagery provides a picture through words. In "Russian Letter" several images occur. The first image is of "glue," a way of conveying how the past clings to the present. To clarify further and to add a sense of impending doom, the poem presents a more vivid picture in a metaphor, "we are flies," and like flies, we struggle "to pull free." Thus the philosophical statement about the ever-presence of the past is conveyed through the image of flies struggling to free themselves from sticky paper. Just as the flies are doomed, so are people in their struggle to escape the past.

The next image uses the common experience of getting dressed and compares that to the soul inhabiting the body at birth. While people change their clothes literally quite frequently, the soul cannot escape the body it animates and get into a different one. Two assertions are being made here: first, the narrator states that it is commonly held, often "said," that people cannot change; second, this idea is equivalent to saying that the soul is contained in one body, all of the features of which are determined at birth. The image of clothes and the fact that people do change their clothes may anticipate the narra-tor's refusal to agree that people cannot escape the determinants fixed at birth.

The last image of the hawk suggests a vari-able that may conflict with the commonly repeated fatalistic statement. The hawk's nature is to shriek "down from the sky" in its dive to kill its prey The timing or chance that brings its prey into view and makes it vulnerable to the hawk are factors not so much associated with either creature's past as with current circumstances. In other words, the predestination suggested in the commonly held belief does not take into consid-eration factors of chance and timing. The hawk image intrudes as a fact of nature that disrupts the philosophical statement the poem has pre-sented as common knowledge and with which the narrator cannot fully agree.

Connotation

Connotation is meaning that is recognized through common usage in a particular community. Words have literal meaning, but they can also connote other meanings by the way they are used. The phrase, "It is said," connotes repetition through the years, a widely repeated and recognized truth that comes into the present as though it were can-onical because it has been repeated so often that it is now virtually taken for granted. The statement that is so introduced has more power because it has a history or tradition behind it, because it is famil-iar and frequently repeated. It may be an old say-ing, not substantiated by empirical evidence, but through its longstanding recognition it has accu-mulated validity with many people. The poet con-veys this validity through the connotation that can be inferred in the phrase, rather than in the phrase's literal meaning.

HISTORICAL CONTEXT

Rembrandt

Rembrandt Harmenszoon van Rijn (July 15, 1607–October 4, 1669), one of Europe's greatest painters, was born in Leiden in the Netherlands. He was a prolific artist, creating more than 600 paintings, 400 etchings, and 1400 sketches. His portrait paintings show his expertise in handling light and texture and his ability to convey per-sonality in the look in a subject's eyes. Some of his more famous paintings are "St. Paul in Prison" (1627); "Supper at Emmaus" (1630); "The Anatomy Lesson of Dr. Nicolaes Tulp" (1632); "Young Girl at an Open Half-Door" (1645); "The Mill" (1650); "Aristotle Contem-plating the Bust of Homer" (1653); and "The Return of the Prodigal Son" (sometime after 1660). Rembrandt's subjects included his own face, which he depicted in more than sixty self-portraits. Other models that he used for his paintings included members of his family, such as his mother, his wife, and his children. One third of his paintings contain Biblical themes. His treatment of religious subjects illustrates how he found ways to make the spiritual event a human one.

Bob Dylan

Yau's poetry has sometimes been compared to the lyrics of Bob Dylan. Dylan, who was born in 1941, is best known for his music. However, his lyrics have been studied as poetry. Dylan became famous in the 1960s during the upheaval over civil rights and the U.S. involvement in Vietnam.

He was one of the leaders of the counterculture movement during that turbulent decade. His lyrics were often used to inspire protests or to explain them. Some of his more famous lyrics, including "Blowin' in the Wind" and "Times They Are a-Changin,'" became anthems against the war and in support of the civil rights movement. His poetry includes political, religious, social commentary, literary, and philosophical themes. Dylan was named *Time* magazine's most influential folk singer of the twentieth century. He has also been referred to as a master poet. In 2006, Dylan was inducted into the Rock and Roll Hall of Fame. Although Dylan has been honored and praised as a poet, he resists the literary label. Dylan recorded over forty albums of his original lyrics, and in 2006, he was still touring around the world performing his music.

John Ashbery

Yau's poetry is often compared to John Ashbery, a Pulitzer Prize-winning poet and recipient of the so-called genius prize, the MacArthur Award. As of 2007, Ashbery had written over twenty books of poetry, including *Chinese Whispers* (2002); *Your Name Here* (2000); *Girls on the Run: A Poem* (1999); *Wakefulness* (1998); and *Can You Hear, Bird* (1995). His 1975 publication, *Self-Portrait in a Convex Mirror* won him the Pulitzer Prize for Poetry, the National Book Critics Circle Award, and the National Book Award. His work often focuses on the meaning of reality or the ultimate truth about life and whether a person can actually fully grasp it. Much of his poetry attempts to expose how people's minds are so locked into the conventional language of science, technology, and journalism that they are unable to grasp what reality is all about. People blindly accept what others tell them is true. Ashbery tries to point out that clichés hide the truth rather than preserving it. Like Yau, Ashbery was, at one time in his life, dedicated to the visual arts. Early on, he took drawing and painting classes at the Art Institute of Rochester, and as an adult, he served as an art critic. Ashbery taught literature classes at Brooklyn College, where Yau was one of his students. Ashbery also taught language and literature at Bard College. Between 2001 and 2003, Ashbery served at the poet laureate of New York state.

L = A = N = G = U = A = G = E Poets

Yau has been linked by some literary critics to the L = A = N = G = U = A = G = E poets, a loosely connected group of avant-garde poets who, for one thing, tend to recognize the role of the reader in interpreting a poem. L = A = N = G = U = A = G = E poetry is said to have begun in the 1970s. However, poets from earlier eras, such as Gertrude Stein (1874–1946), William Carlos Williams (1883–1963), and Frank O'Hara (1926–1966) influenced those who call themselves L = A = N = G = U = A = G = E poets. This group of poets focuses on the political implications inherent in language. In attempts to break down language, some L = A = N = G = U = A = G = E poets create poems that make no sense, such as making up a poem from the index of a book or using only prepositions in the entire poem. Some L = A = N = G = U = A = G = E poems supposedly contain no meaning and are, therefore, considered nonsense poems. In many L = A = N = G = U = A = G = E poems, seemingly random thoughts or arbitrary observations are considered the norm. There is also a lack of personal expression generally, as if the poet does not exist. This feature distinguishes these works from, for example, confessional poetry, in which the poet reveals personal aspects of his or her life through poetry. L = A = N = G = U = A = G = E poems put little stock in the stanza but rather concentrate on each line individually, shaping it to illustrate fragmentation and obscurity. Poets associated with the L = A = N = G = U = A = G = E poetry movement include Yau, John Ashbery, Kit Robinson, Douglas Barber, Charles Bernstein, and Lyn Hejinian, among others.

CRITICAL OVERVIEW

"Russian Letter" was published in Yau's collection *Borrowed Love Poems*, which was reviewed by Joshua Clover in *Artforum*. Clover calls the collection "vivid, mysterious, unsettling, and laconically charming in shifting degrees." Clover then adds that "it's a terrific and variegated book of poems." Throughout the collection, Clover writes, Yau's poetry exemplifies many of the underlying principles of the L = A = N = G = U = A = G = E poets, who question language, meaning, and identity. Clover finds Yau's poetry very satisfying, "fun," and full of "tonal richness."

WHAT DO I READ NEXT?

- In his *Paradiso Diaspora* (2006), Yau continues his exploration of language and its shortcomings. However, a more personal side of the poet shows in this collection as Yau explores his relationship with his daughter, Cerise Tzara, to whom he dedicated his collection *Borrowed Love Poems*.

- In Yau's 2005 collaboration with artist Thomas Nozkowski called *Ing Grish*, the poet creates often humorous lyrics to go along with Nozkowski's abstract paintings.

- For a taste of Yau's prose, readers may enjoy his short story collection *Hawaiian Cowboys* (1995). Here are thirteen stories about strange characters that live outside the mainstream. They include exhibitionists, prostitutes, and heroin addicts. Sometimes sad and sometimes humorous, Yau's characters struggle with loneliness and frustration.

- John Ashbery won the Pulitzer Prize for his *Self-Portrait in a Convex Mirror* (1975), a collection of poems that has been both praised and criticized. Ashbery's poems can be difficult to understand, but they are filled with beautiful and thought-provoking images.

- Frank O'Hara's influence on the L=A=N=G=U=A=G=E poets is important; O'Hara's 1964 collection *Lunch Hour* is one of the best places to start for readers who want an introduction to his poetry. Using music, art, and movies, O'Hara explores his relationship with New York City and the people he encounters there.

- Founder of the magazine L=A=N=G=U=A=G=E (from which the L=A=N=G=U=A=G=E poets derived their name), Charles Bernstein is also a well recognized poet. His 2006 collection, *Girlie Man*, explores what one critic refers to as Bernstein's dedication to what poetry is not in order to find what poetry can ultimately become.

- David Citino edited *The Eye of the Poet: Six Views of the Art and Craft of Poetry* (2001), which contains the writings of six published poets who also teach poetry. One of their topics is the concept behind the works of L=A=N=G=U=A=G=E poets.

Although Yau, in general, received critical consideration for his poetry, that attention has not been extensive, especially in terms of the featured collection, *Borrowed Love Poems*. One other reviewer, however, Paisley Rekdal, writing for a Seattle-based journal, the *International Examiner*, refers to Yau's "writing aesthetic" as well as his "prolific writing career." Yau's writing, Rekdal states, "is almost completely devoid of the autobiographical, the confessional, the personal of any kind." This, Rekdal finds, makes Yau's poetry "both refreshing and irritating to read." Yau's writing is hard to extract meaning from, Rekdal writes. His poetry is not based on "linear or concrete narratives of physical or emotional experience," like so much other popular poetry that is easier to understand. Unlike the poetry that readers become accustomed to in college or in popular magazines, Rekdal continues, Yau's poetry is an expression of "the inauthentic." Rekdal understands the fact that one of the purposes of Yau's poetry, true to the beliefs shared by other L=A=N=G=U=A=G=E poets, is to present the idea that language is a poor transmitter of meaning. However Rekdal questions why anyone would want to read poetry that lacks meaning. Language has it shortcomings, Rekdal admits, but, after all, language is what gives "our life shape and, what's more, meaning."

Although critic Lisa Chen, writing for *Asian Week*, finds Yau's "nonlinear flights of unadulterated invention" sometimes "wearying," she compliments the poet for his "ingenuity," which she states "never lets up." Chen continues: Yau's "poems tell us that if we don't create our own terms, our own vision of the world that doesn't put the mainstream view or dominant culture perspective at its center, we risk reinforcing that center." Another critic, Christopher A. Shinn, writing for the *International Examiner*, describes Yau as having a "rich and complex poetic imagination." Evaluating another collection of poetry in this review, (Yau's *Forbidden Entries*, 1997), Shinn states that Yau's work "combines wit, good humor and literary and artistic complexity." He concludes that Yau is "one of the best Asian American writers."

CRITICISM

Joyce Hart

Hart has degrees in literature and creative writing. In the following essay, she examines the spiritual images in Yau's poem.

If literary critics are accurate in describing Yau as a L=A=N=G=U=A=G=E poet, one who believes that meaning is not inherent in a poem and that the only meaning that can be found is that which is discovered by the reader, then that opens the door for reading spirituality in Yau's poem "Russian Letter" whether or not the poet intended it to be there. Given the mention of "soul," a spiritual interpretation seems logical. Only the poet knows for sure what his mood was or where his thoughts came from when he wrote this poem. But there are images in this poem, besides that of the soul, that conjure up a sense of the spiritual. Whether this spirituality is inspired by the poet, his language, his images, or the reader who ponders them is not the point. What matters is that if readers look close enough and allow themselves the freedom to explore their own interpretations, a sense of the spiritual can be discovered in this poem.

The first phrase in this short poem is the statement, "It is said," which could be heard as of the voice of a preacher standing in the pulpit in front of a congregation and reading from some holy, or highly respected, book. The preacher's finger might be pointing to a particular sacred passage in the book, suggesting that

THERE IS NO DIRECT MENTION OF ANY SPIRITUAL TRUTH THAT THE NARRATOR TRUSTS OR WILL USE TO COUNTER THE IDEAS PUT FORTH SO FAR IN THIS POEM. THE NARRATOR ONLY STATES A LACK OF BELIEF OR AT LEAST A LIMIT TO THE BELIEF THAT PEOPLE ARE STUCK IN GLUE LIKE FLIES...."

what he or she is about to say are the inspired words of scripture. One can almost hear the preacher's voice ringing out over the pews, resounding off the tall ceilings of the house of worship. The preacher might pause to make sure he or she has the attention of the people and then repeat the phrase, adding the full course of the message. "It is said," the preacher repeats, that "the past / sticks to the present / like glue." This is how Yau opens his poem, somewhat like that preacher, as he has his narrator proclaim these words, which, for some people, might be a sacred precept, one that is completely honored and believed.

Looked at in another way, this statement could be simply delivered in a classroom, one focused on comparative religions or spiritual beliefs. The narrator could be explaining, as if he were a professor standing in front of a group of students, that the statement that "the past / sticks to the present" is similar to the Buddhist concept of karma, through which one's past lives determine the present one, contaminating the present with past mistakes or blessing it with favors for good deeds performed in previous lives. Or the narrator could be pointing out that the belief of original sin. For example, according to some Christian faiths, babies are born with original sin, inherited from the disobedient first parents, the Biblical Adam and Eve. The original sin is stuck like glue to the babies' souls and must be cleansed through the sacrament of baptism.

Yau's poem continues with the statement that not only is the past stuck to the present but "that we are flies / struggling to pull free." The past, in other words, is this huge strip of sticky paper to which all humans, in the present situation of their lives, are stuck. Not only are all humans stuck to the past, they are also struggling to flee from the negative effects of the past on their present lives. This sense of struggle is an underlying theme in many religions. Some religions teach that people need to free themselves from past weaknesses so they can avoid possible future temptations. Another spiritual belief is that this struggle to free oneself is a lifelong work, because even if people tend to get free from that sticky paper, they foolishly forget to look where they are going and fly right back into it. The practice of some spiritual beliefs is to train people to avoid the traps and therefore to avoid the struggle. Even if temptations are not sinful, a struggle is implied in the work of remaining focused on the more spiritual aspects of life rather on the temporary worldly pleasures it offers. Yau's poem brings all of these spiritual ideas into readers' thoughts.

In line six, the narrator of Yau's poem repeats the phrase: "It is said." Again, one thinks of that voice bellowing out to the congregation as the preacher emphasizes the next message, which is: "Someone / cannot change / the clothes / in which / their soul / was born." The spiritual or religious concept of the "soul" connects the poem to a religious interpretation. One of the basic elements that many religions teach is that people can change. Religious teachers try to lead people from their sinful ways and into lives filled with grace. If successful, this transition would mark a very big change. Conversion from one religion to another is also change. Baptism implies change, as does the Buddhist concept that all life is change. Who would preach the idea that people cannot change? Maybe the narrator has given the reader an incomplete thought. Perhaps the complete thought is that people cannot change without Buddha, Jesus, or Mohammed. That, at least, would make more sense. Despite the confusion over this statement of the inability to change, the spiritual connotation remains apparent. Only a person who has some sense of the spiritual would make mention of a soul, no matter what religious practice is followed or even if that person has no affiliation with a religion. If Yau's narrator mentions a soul, then Yau's narrator seems to be talking about the world of the spirit, which reinforces (or at least encourages) a spiritual interpretation of the poem to this point.

But the narrator in line twelve denies absolute authority to the statement "It is said." The narrator "would not / go so far" as agreeing completely. It is not clear if this means that the narrator would not go so far as to declare that people have souls or if he would not go so far as to state that people cannot change. Also, it is not known if the narrator himself has a spiritual belief that counters the statement that people are stuck and cannot change. There is no direct mention of any spiritual truth that the narrator trusts or will use to counter the ideas put forth so far in this poem. The narrator only states a lack of belief or at least a limit to the belief that people are stuck in glue like flies, unable to correct their mistakes or the mistakes of their parents; unable to free themselves from sins they might have committed in past lives and therefore continue to find themselves stuck and unable to move forward.

The narrator does not mention his own spiritual beliefs outright and may dispute the spiritual concepts that are mentioned in this poem. However, he uses the word, "soul." Where is the narrator of Yau's poem taking this concept of soul if not into a spiritual context? And how does his reference to Rembrandt fit into all of this?

Well, for one thing, Rembrandt is a creator. Not only does Rembrandt create but, as the narrator refers to the artist, Rembrandt was also a "master." Rembrandt took the basic elements of color and turned paint and canvas into a reflection, or a picture, of life as he saw it. He created something out of nothing. The narrator of this poem could be using Rembrandt as a metaphor of a supreme being. The narrator might be offering this image to the readers to give them a more concrete belief, one that will counter the more abstract statement that begins with "It is said." Rembrandt created images, just as various religions teach that there is a spiritual first force that created the world, the animals and fish, and all humans. The narrator could be referring to this master creator as one who paints life similar to the way that Rembrandt created his images.

Yau does not end his poem at this point though. He takes the discussion one step further. Not only does he mention that Rembrandt has created a picture but that, in the narrator's presentation of this painting, the hawk appears to come alive. Out of the "black / and green darkness," the hawk dives through the air as if he has been animated, as if it has freed itself from the "glue" of the canvas and paint (or the hawk's past) and is gliding through the air. The darkness that the narrator mentions could symbolically be the void, and it is out of the void that Rembrandt draws his creation. To prove that Rembrandt has truly brought this hawk to life, the poet imbues the bird with a sound, a voice. The hawk "shrieks" as he plunged out of the sky. Rembrandt, the narrator might be saying, is like a god, one capable of creating life through his mastery of oil paints, brushes, and strokes, one that instills his creations with a soul that is free from the past.

Finally, as the hawk "shrieks / down from the sky," readers can imagine the bird traveling from the heavens to the earth, an image that could be related to the journey of the soul as it travels from heaven to a new physical body. After all, Yau could have said that the hawk flies across the sky, but instead the poet has the bird soaring downward, coming "from" the sky. This could be seen as the soul in hawk's clothing.

Source: Joyce Hart, Critical Essay on "Russian Letter," in *Poetry for Students*, Thomson Gale, 2007.

David Kelly

Kelly is an instructor of creative writing and literature. In this essay, he looks at how Yau uses dichotomies, or directly contrasting ideas, to help a short poem cover two philosophical positions.

John Yau's "Russian Letter" is a short, focused poem that packs a lot of ideas into few words. Yau is able to create a thought-provoking piece with such spareness by opposing complex ideas. Rather than leaving out important information, though, Yau accomplishes this by trimming things down to basic opposites. By presenting ideas in dichotomies, he is able to invoke thoughts that represent whole systems of human thought. A nuanced portrait of the world might be required to examine objects on a one-by-one basis, but creating dichotomies allows the poet to categorize ideas into either of the two groupings mentioned. The opposing concepts are coupled: each one incorporates half the world, while its corresponding member incorporates the other half. This arrangement allows the poet to be economical with words as he alludes to complex matters that concern the whole of the human condition. Yau's poem is structured around this principle, a plan perfectly suited to the poem's statement.

"Russian Letter" consists of ten stanzas, each stanza a couplet, and no line is longer

> LIKE ALL OF THE BEST POEMS, 'RUSSIAN LETTER' GIVES ITS READERS A FAMILIAR FEELING— GIVEN THAT ONE OF ITS THEMES IS THE FEAR OF BEING TRAPPED BY THE PAST, THIS SENSE OF RECOGNITION COULD BACKFIRE. BUT IT DOES NOT."

than five syllables. Eight of the twenty lines contain only two words. It does not seem short, though. It feels longer than these figures suggest.

Most of the lines are enjambed, making Yau's ideas seem qualified or tentative, more hesitant or uncertain, than they would be if presented in end-line completed units. The resulting flow from one line to the next reminds readers of the complexity of the world, even while Yau's word choices work to simplify the world's nature. The enjambment gives the sense that the ideas Yau touches on in the poem's basic dichotomies hide within them more than his words have room to explain. Plus the narrator seems conflicted about his own possible over-simplification, even as that simplification allows the poem to progress directly through the issues that it raises.

There are quite a few places where "Russian Letter" pairs up opposites. The most significant dichotomy, the one at the poem's center, is the distinction between inertia and motion. The first half of the poem introduces the human struggle against the past, which is presented here as an inhibiting force. The poem ends, though, with the hint that some action might be even more fearful than being stuck in one place. Yau uses the images of the fly stuck in flypaper and the hawk swooping down from the sky to convey these opposites. Most readers would not like to consider themselves as either the helpless insect or the predator's victim, yet these opposite images represent two ways of looking at the human condition: one sees it as predestined by the past, including physical traits; the other sees it as determined by arbitrary or at least unanticipated events, including the actions of others.

This distinction between being stuck and being seized reflects the distinction between nouns and verbs, the most basic tools of language. Nouns, in and of themselves, are names for inert and active subjects—they represent objects, like glue or adhesive, that cannot move on their own. They are important to speech because they mark or label the physical world. In "Russian Letter," concrete nouns dominate: "glue," "flies," "clothes," "plumes," and "hawk." They are augmented by occasional abstractions such as "soul" and "darkness."

Verbs show up less frequently in the poem, but they have considerable impact. This is particularly true of what is arguably the most important word in the poem, "shrieks": a horrifying action, adapted from a noun, the word evokes both the hawk's sharp call and the precision with which it swoops in with its talons stretched out for attack. In a poem that, until this point, has been focused on philosophical statement and theoretical musing, that shriek cuts through with a sudden and frightening clarity. The other notable verb, which characterizes the first half of the poem, is a form of the verb, to struggle. Yau uses the word "struggling" to describe the ongoing human inability to act freely without encumbrance, which connects effort with futility and hopelessness. In effect, the abrupt swoop of the hawk as it "shrieks / down from the sky" is the opposite of the weighty pondering of the first half of the poem and the substantial nouns that are, in this poem, associated with the past.

Moreover, the contrast between arduous inaction and sudden, deadly action is linked to the division between the past and future. The first five stanzas analyze backward, focusing on the past's ability to adhere to and determine the present. In effect, despite human efforts to the contrary, the past is as capable of cementing present circumstances as flypaper is to hold flies. Indeed the past is both fixed (in the sense that it cannot be changed) and fixing (in the sense that it holds in place). Though the logic might seem strained, this does make sense. For one thing, the past *is* frozen, in the sense that it cannot be changed. Moreover, a commonly held theory is that this relationship between the past and the present is inevitable and inescapable. If one believes that anything that is happening now is a result of factors established in the past, then one can conceptualize the past as gripping the present. Many people who believe in determinism, in original sin, or in fate might easily accept this image of the past as adhering to and controlling the present.

One concept of the present, though, is that as it unfolds (as the future is realized in it) the unanticipated and unknowable occur. Through current factors such as timing, coincidence, intersection, through the crosscurrent of opposing entities, events that are unpredictable occur. The shrieking hawk can swoop down into the field and snatch the unsuspecting mouse; risk and danger can unexpectedly and violently determine events. The pull of the past might tend to make life too predictable for the speaker's tastes, but the speaker also recognizes that there is no real way of knowing what is to come either, and therefore the future always represents a certain potential for danger.

If the present were to have as much control of the future as the past has of the present, there would be nothing to fear: all possibilities could be determined. It could then be said that Yau is presenting a balanced equation, with the same effect distributed equally across the past, present, and future. But his whole point is that while some see the past as always a drag on what is happening now, the empirical fact is the future is unpredictable. These differing ideas do make sense, but they are not as tidy as a simple dichotomy would be. In a poem of so few words, Yau is taking a chance when he introduces a complicated idea such as this one.

There is one other dichotomy raised in the poem that serves to explain Yau's main point: it is the distinction between what could be referred to as "common knowledge" and the rare genius of certain individuals. Yau uses the phrase "it is said" twice. The phrase introduces an idea that comes with a certain authority or tradition of repetition behind it, an idea that has weight and is widely recognized and accepted by many. What "is said" is that life is trapped by the past. This is the concept that has wide acceptance. But the narrator in the poem cannot passively accept the statement, cannot go so far as to subscribe to it without pulling back and seeking some more moderate position.

The speaker in the poem does not support what "is said," at least not without qualification. He expresses his own disbelief, a matter of restraint: "I, however, / would not go so far" is the way he expresses his hesitancy to fully accept the idea. He does not entirely agree with this idea of being unable to resist fate, but he does not wholeheartedly disagree with it either. He has no clear, strong argument to offer in opposition to what is "said," but the idea of human beings being bound by the past just seems too extreme to be completely true for the narrator.

In opposition to what is said by authoritative and often quoted sources is the narrator who is unable to accept blindly or fully. Also in opposition to the narrator is someone as creative as, say, the artist Rembrandt who is a "master" of the "black / and green darkness" of the "hawk's plumes." The poem suggests that Rembrandt, since he could depict darkness and sudden unexpected events such as a hawk's swooping descent, must have been able to conceptualize the potential threat in the future. The shrieking hawk, harbinger of the unknowable that is just out of sight, is the kind of image Rembrandt was able to depict in his paintings. The suggestion may be that someone like Rembrandt would be able to control in art what is unexpected in life. Rembrandt sees the complexity of life so clearly that he is able to distinguish the blacks from the greens, and he is able to make beauty out of the mystery that others fear.

But the speaker of the poem says that, much as he might admire such mastery, Rembrandt's world is not quite the world he sees, either. The narrator resists believing in the idea of being trapped by the past, and he shrinks from claiming he is capable of capturing the future in an artistic medium. He appreciates the accomplished skill of Rembrandt, even though he is unable to match it.

The poem's finest achievement is its refusal to take an emphatic position in the philosophical debate. It is a work in tune with the contemporary audience. In another culture, at another time, the balance of anxieties would be tipped in a different direction. For instance, the baby boom generation spent the late 1950s and 60s trying to shake off the numbed complacency that their parents acquired from decades of economic depression and war, so the threat of being held back by the past might have resonated more with them. "Russian Letter" was written in a time when the destruction of the World Trade Center in New York had given people across the United States the awareness that, though they had defined their destiny in one way, sudden attack could occur and disrupt the illusion of preordained safety.

Yau's accomplishment here is in recognizing that conflicting ideas coexist. The balance might shift slightly, according to events, but it is a function of modern sensibilities that the past can be considered as much a threat as the future. Fear of being stuck in the past has become so prevalent that people not only worry about what is to come, they also worry about what has happened. Like all of the best poems, "Russian Letter" gives its readers a familiar feeling—given that one of its themes is the fear of being trapped by the past, this sense of recognition could backfire. But it does not.

The key is Rembrandt. If this poem were only a polemic on modern sensibilities, a lecture about opposing philosophical positions and the fears they evoke, readers would be left with nothing but gloom. The past, according to this poem, is something from which to escape, while the future is something to shrink back from with fear. When Yau introduces a greater artistic skill, he is offering a solution. The poem confirms that the present, despite being positioned between two unpleasant alternatives, does not have to be thought of as a waste or as a pending disaster. Rembrandt, a figure from the past, embraced the darkness, and in using him as a model the poem tells its readers that they can, too.

Overall, "Russian Letter" has a broader range of concerns than just identifying bad situations: for the most part, it says that life itself is a bad situation. By the end, though, it does offer a vision of hope, letting readers know that there is a sane path to follow, a way of looking at the world that will not fill people with despair or dread. If Rembrandt can make art of darkness, then darkness can at least be put to some constructive use. It is a powerful and convincing way to end such a terse poem. Some poems offer a vision of life: "Russian Letter" points readers in two directions that Yau wants them to consider anew. He trusts his readers to either understand his point or at least believe in the wisdom of a master like Rembrandt, as the poet himself clearly does, in order to realize that the current situation, however, dire can be transformed into art.

Source: David Kelly, Critical Essay on "Russian Letter," in *Poetry for Students*, Thomson Gale, 2007.

Sheri Metzger Karmiol
Karmiol holds a Ph.D. in English literature and is a university professor. In this essay, she considers the importance of titles and what understanding the title of John Yau's poem, "Russian Letter,"

contributes to the readers' understanding of the poem.

In his essay, "Try Titles," Arthur Minton points out that "in a curious way titles partake of the nature of two kinds of expression that are otherwise incongruous—poetry and advertising." The title sells the poem to the reader, who after all has many poems from which to choose. Minton explains that "in poetry and advertising every word is heavy-laden; the whole effect depends on the balance of connotations, overtones, and colors." Writers choose their words carefully. Every word in a poem is carefully considered, laden with meaning and measured for effect. A title receives the same attention from the poet. The most interesting titles are ones that beguile and beckon, not promising too much but hinting at an enigma to be solved. John Yau's poem, "Russian Letter," presents his readers with a brief title that suggests simplicity but in reality delivers complexity. In his poem, "Russian Letter," Yau employs a title with a subtext that captures the author's love of abstract expressionism.

The title of Matthew Rohrer's 2002 profile of Yau's thirty-year writing career, "Where Art and Poetry Collide," identifies an important feature of Yau's poetry—the poet's efforts to integrate concepts from abstract visual art into his poetry. Rohrer describes how as a youth, Yau was friends with the son of Chinese abstract painter, John Way. This friendship stimulated Yau's interest in art, and as a youth Yau spent much of his free time at art museums. After college, he moved to New York City, where he began writing reviews of art gallery shows and began studying art criticism in a M.F.A. program at Brooklyn College. In his formal study of art, Yau no doubt learned that abstract expressionism began at least a generation earlier than the American art movement of the 1940s that first interested him. In fact, two of the originating artists were Russian painters, Wassily Kandinsky and Kasimir Malevich. Kandinsky and Malevich initiated the style that came to be called abstract expressionism. They appear to be the Russian connection in "Russian Letter."

The word, "letter," in the title invites the reader to think about the nature of written communication. Letters convey messages. People write to others about their experiences and their views. In their content, letters relate memories, current circumstances and thoughts, and plans for the future.

> UNDERSTANDING THE TITLE, AND INDEED THE POEM, REQUIRES THE READER TO ACCEPT YAU'S CHALLENGE TO FOREGO RULES AND TO THINK BEYOND CONVENTION. IT ALSO REQUIRES DOING SOME RESEARCH TO UNCOVER RELEVANT INFORMATION."

As a medium of exchange, a letter is written in one moment and then later, when it is received, it is read. One could say that the letter is time-bound in several ways: it contains the past, is written in the present, and is read in the future. Both in terms of the news they contain and the sequence in which they are composed and later read, letters move from the past to the present. This means that letters make narrative. They communicate stories and their writing and reading are actions that might serve as events in a plot. In other words, letters participate in a time-bound frame, are part of narrative. This shift between moments in time connects to the content of Yau's poem, especially in the opening lines: "the past / sticks to the present." Yau's poem is a letter to his readers—but with a difference. Yau, as the writer of this letter, resists communicating what he thinks: he cannot agree to what is commonly said; nor is he the kind of artist that depicts objects from life as Rembrandt did. This resistance to communicate subject matter makes the poem abstract and thus there is a link here to abstract expressionism.

The avant-garde style, called abstract expressionism, became popular in the United States in the period just after World War II. Abstract expressionists focused on design, form, color, arrangement of shapes, but not on figures or objects. The emphasis in this style is emotion without narrative, in which the content is reduced to elements of shape and line. So for many new viewers, the work of abstract expressionists seemed to lack subject matter. Yau's debt to these painters is hinted in the title of another poem from *Borrowed Love Poems*. The poem that follows the six "Russian Letter" poems, is titled, "830 Fireplace Road." The poem title is, in fact, the Hampton, New York, address of American abstract expressionist Jackson Pollack. The poem is a fourteen-line sonnet, but in reality Yau composed only thirteen lines, since the first line is a quotation from Pollock. Just as Pollock broke the conventional rules about subject matter and technique (his paintings are filled with dripped lines), in this poem, Yau breaks the accepted rules for composing sonnets. Similarly, in "Russian Letter," Yau presents readers with what appears to be a letter that refuses to communicate, one written from someone who is not identified. Understanding the title, and indeed the poem, requires the reader to accept Yau's challenge to forego rules and to think beyond convention. It also requires doing some research to uncover relevant information.

It is the rejection of rules, both in painting and in poetry that appeals to Yau. Although poetry, especially free verse, may seem to be free of rules, in reality, poetry is governed by many rules about structure, meter, rhyme, language, and even—apparently—ethnicity. Yau rejects the label of Asian-American poet. Yau tells Rohrer that "If you are an Asian-American, as I am, many people expect you to write transparent or autobiographical poems, poems about garlic, soy sauce, ginger, etcetera." But Yau rejects what is expected in favor of the unexpected, which explains why he would appreciate art that disrupts viewers' expectations and refuses to give what is expected but gives something surprising instead.

Yau's attraction to abstract expressionism sheds light on the final six lines of the poem. The poet's sudden shift in line 15 to "Nor am I Rembrandt," initially seems incongruous with the lines that precede it. What has Rembrandt to do with the earlier idea that people struggle "to pull free" from the past? Yau's interest in abstract expressionism and the role of the Russian painters in this movement suggest reasons why the speaker in the poem does not identify with a seventeenth-century Dutch poet. Rembrandt's work is all about narrative. His portraits, interiors, and depictions of biblical scenes all evoke story. The speaker's assertion that he is not Rembrandt combined with Yau's interest in abstract expressionism suggests that Yau would not be able to envision himself creating poetry reminiscent of the formality of Rembrandt's portraiture or his religious art. Yau's title adds just another layer to understanding the poem's content.

It is unlikely that Yau would want his poem defined by its title. The title serves as the introduction to the poem and to the poet, but that introduction should only hint at the composition that follows. In choosing the title for his poem, "Russian Letter," Yau acknowledges his debt to the abstract expressionist painters and embraces the notion that poetry can be as abstract as abstract expressionist paintings are. Both the painter and poet traverse the connections between image, word, and expression, and both kinds of artists find new ways to express their ideas. The emotional intensity of abstract impressionist art can be expressed in poetry, just as it can be expressed in painting. It makes sense then that the speaker reports what is commonly said, widely accepted, but he is unable himself to subscribe to the cliché. In his review of *Borrowed Love Poems*, Thomas Fink claims that Yau chooses "to dignify linguistic experiments that keep reminding us how slippery language is, how resistant it is to stable contextual framing." Yau's title is like this—slippery and resistant to conventional meanings.

Source: Sheri Metzger Karmiol, Critical Essay on "Russian Letter," in *Poetry for Students*, Thomson Gale, 2007.

Nicholas Birns

In the following essay, Birns gives a critical analysis of Yau's work.

Some readers know John Yau only as an art critic and prolific writer of essays for art catalogues. Others know him as a veteran avant-garde poet who has kept both the excitement and the standards of the experimental poetic tradition alive and who wittily and unpredictably deploys images of Chinese American identity throughout his work.

Yau was born in Lynn, Massachusetts, on 5 June 1950; he was the first child of Arthur Yau, a bookkeeper, and Jane Chang Yau. Both parents had left Shanghai in the wake of the Communist takeover of China the previous year. Yau is partly of English descent: his paternal grandfather had lived in England and married an English farmer's daughter before moving the family to the United States, where Arthur Yau was born in 1921, and then to China. John Yau's brother, Arthur, was born in 1960. The family moved to Boston and then to Brookline, where Yau attended junior high and high school. He studied at Boston University from 1967 to 1969, then transferred to Bard College in Annandale-on-Hudson, New York, where he studied with the poet Robert Kelly. He received his B.A. in 1972. He continues to be involved with Bard, lecturing and giving workshops and contributing to the journal *Conjunctions*, which is headquartered there.

While studying under the poet John Ashbery at Brooklyn College, Yau had his first book published by Bellevue Press in Binghamton, New York. *Crossing Canal Street* (1976) appeared in an edition of 750 copies, 50 of which were signed by the author. This procedure set a precedent for the majority of his hardcover poetry books, which tend to have small press-runs, and reflects his interest in the book as a physical and potentially collectible object. *Crossing Canal Street*, for which Kelly wrote the preface, explores some of the subtleties of Yau's relationship with the New York avant-garde. Canal Street in lower Manhattan forms the border between Chinatown to the south and SoHo to the north; at the time the book was published, SoHo was becoming the heart of the New York downtown art gallery scene. The title of the volume thus implies the question of the direction in which Yau is crossing Canal Street. His Chinese American identity is visible in "Cameo of a Chinese Woman on Mulberry Street": Mulberry Street is one block west of Mott Street, the main north-south artery of Chinatown; when it crosses Canal Street northward, Mulberry becomes the main street of Little Italy. Yau's Chinese woman is thus at once in and out of her assigned "place." The eight-line poem is written almost entirely in monosyllabic words, with no line exceeding nine syllables. The first line of each of the four nonrhyming couplets has three stresses, as in "Her face this moon a house." The conjunction of the woman's face with the moon gives rise to the surreal imagery of "place fur" and "silver talons," but the initial

grounding of the poem in an observed place has the effect of making the surreal tangible. Other poems in the volume, such as "Suggested by a Chinese Woman Alone on Mott Street," capture the dual aura of Chinatown as both home and a place of exile; but it is Chinatown seen through an anamorphic lens, perhaps from the vantage point of SoHo. "Their Shadows" explores how the marriage of Yau's paternal grandparents was affected by war and racial stereotypes. "Ten Songs" is primarily concerned with language: using verbs as the overwhelming element of his diction, Yau shows how the process of trying to make sense leads, against his intention, to a linguistic proliferation that, paradoxically, ends up making sense after all. Thus, Yau's first volume has a metaphorical presence on both "sides" of Canal Street. It launches the riddling, playful rumination that has characterized the way he relates to his implied reader throughout his career.

Yau received his M.F.A. from Brooklyn College in 1977. That same year his collection *The Reading of an Ever-Changing Tale* was published by another upstate New York avant-garde press: Nobodaddy Press in Clinton, the home of Hamilton College. Harold Bloom commented on it briefly in an omnibus review in the *New Republic* (26 November 1977) in which he saw Yau as being of the Ashbery school; Ashbery himself reviewed the book in *The Nation* (11 November 1978).

The Reading of an Ever-Changing Tale did not make as much of an impact as *Sometimes* (1979), which includes two of Yau's best-known poems. "Robert Herrick," which alludes to the song-like lyrics of the seventeenth-century English poet, is an offbeat postmodern love poem that honors the ideals of beauty by refusing them. The poet assumes the persona of a man working in a filling station "that stands neatly clustered on a wedge / formed by a fork in the road"; though the speaker is exposed to nature by going to a nearby lake, the things he sees in the filling station are enough to spur him to dream and to inquire. At the end of the poem the speaker likens the smoothness of the lake to that of a Cadillac he has just polished, and the significance of the Herrick title becomes clear: the poem is addressed to the speaker's beloved, as the lake "has that bottomless dark feeling about it / that only cars and lakes and you can have." In "January 18, 1979" the speaker, watching a woman brush her hair, likens her to a traditional artist's model: like a face in a picture, the woman appears to both know and not know that she is being observed. The speaker sees "Someone half in love with yourself / and half in love with the world." The woman's narcissism, perhaps half-imputed to her by the male observer, does not preclude a reciprocal interaction with what is outside her. Other poems in the volume, such as "Serenade" and the title piece, balance mystery and banality or imply that the most satisfying mystery is to be found within banality. The publication of this volume, along with his receipt of a fellowship from the National Endowment for the Humanities for 1977-1978 and the Ingram-Merrill Foundation Grant in 1979, helped put Yau on the map of contemporary poetry.

In 1980 Yau began a seven-year relationship with Rachel Stella, the daughter of the painter Frank Stella and the art historian Barbara Rose. Published that year, *The Sleepless Night of Eugene Delacroix* marks a new stage in Yau's career: it is dominated by longer sequences of prose poems, rather than the short, enigmatic pieces of the previous volumes. The series "Postcards from Nebraska" limns an arid, prosaic landscape in which exciting things nonetheless happen. "Predella" and "A Different Prince" are pastiches that refer to artists, musicians, and writers. Many of the other pieces, including the title poem, tell stories. "Toy Trucks and Fried Rice" describes the annual Christmas party of the Chinese Benevolent Association; the speaker feels almost arbitrarily assigned a category of Chinese "identity" that overrides differences of dialect (his mother is from Shanghai) and class (his grandfather had been ambassador to Belgium under Sun Yat-Sen), as well as his own highly inexact sense of his heritage. Chinese identity is also defined by opposition to certain icons of the "Americans": every year Santa Claus is played by a white man who has studied Chinese. Nonetheless, the speaker remembers the satin embroidery on the chairs at the Christmas banquet hall as an emblem, however tawdry and inauthentic, of being Chinese American.

Broken off by the Music (1981) returns to the lyric form of Yau's first three books. "Scenes from the Life of Boullee" includes references to various aspects of art and experience and turns upon the apothegm "the perfection of greed is the sign of the times." "The Dream Life of a

Coffin Factory in Lynn, Massachusetts" is set during Yau's boyhood and is an elegy for the old industrial order in which prefabrication and conformity coexisted with a kind of egalitarian security: "It was a time when the century had gone to sleep / and everyone glistened with pride." The title piece is a classic American road poem, presenting everyday scenes of collective life and finding, amid the sights and sounds of much-traveled highways, "the remnants of sufficient enchantment." Yau's fascination with unlikely sorts of beauty and with the manifestation of beauty in unlikely places is a constant in his poetry of the late 1970s and early 1980s.

Yau returned to the prose poem in *Corpse and Mirror* (1983). The book represented an increase in visibility for Yau as he moved from small, if prestigious, avant-garde publishers to the mainstream trade house Holt, Rinehart, and Winston. The title of the volume is derived from a series of poems, all of which have the title "Corpse and Mirror," as in series of paintings by Abstract Expressionist painters; the poems have a provisional, experimental quality, a sense of being tentative exercises that may accumulate to a definitive meaning but do not in themselves constitute one. "Carp and Goldfish" contrasts a carp in a prince's pond in China that is overwhelmed by turmoil with a goldfish in a boy's tank in America that needs to be excited by the boy simulating the turbulence of waves.

In the early 1980s Yau began to devote a considerable amount of his time to writing criticism for major art magazines, such as *ARTnews*, as well as for more-specialized periodicals and for little magazines. In 1985 he received another Ingram-Merrill Grant Fellowship; that same year he was named distinguished visiting critic at the Pratt Institute Graduate School of Art in Brooklyn, a position he held until 1990. He also taught at the Milton Avery Graduate School of the Arts at Bard College. In 1988 he received the New York Foundation for the Arts Award, the Lavan Younger Poets Award from the Academy of American Poets, a New York Foundation for the Arts Award, and a General Electric Foundation Award, and his poetry was included in David Lehman's anthology *Best American Poets 1988*, guest edited by Ashbery. Also that year he married the painter Jane Hammond.

Radiant Silhouette: New and Selected Work, 1974-1988 was published in 1989 by Black

Sparrow Press; it includes selections from Yau's previous books, as well as a substantial body of previously uncollected poems titled "Dragon's Blood," which was published as a separate volume by a small press in France later in 1989. The poems in *Radiant Silhouette* deal, in a more sustained manner than Yau had previously attempted, with the poet's Chinese American background. "Halfway to China" plays on Christopher Columbus's supposition that in exploring the Americas he was near China. China, deployed as a symbol for both a yearned-for paradise and a lost past, provides a locale both for fantasy and for death. In the grim "We Are All Vultures" Yau continues the meditation on lapsed time begun in "Halfway to China," musing that "What is terrible (and beautiful) about the past is its remoteness." Language provides no solution, no compensating permanence, to this loss of the past: "Whatever is left behind will soon be gone, devoured by words." "No One Tried to Kiss Anna May Wong" uses the actress Wong, the first Asian American woman to become a truly iconic figure in American popular culture, as an example of the victim role often required of Asian women in European-derived culture, while it also recognizes that a real person existed behind the roles Wong played. The poem also describes Wong's alluring, if remote, sexuality. "Genghis Chan Private Eye" is a sequence of seven poems that combines Genghis Khan, the thirteenth-century Mongol conqueror, and Charlie Chan, the Chinese American Honolulu detective created by the white American novelist Earl Derr Biggers and played in movies by the white actors Warner Oland and Sidney Toler and on television by the white actor J. Carrol Naish.

The "Dragon's Blood" sequence is written in unrhymed quatrains of four stressed syllables. It is a pantoum, a form invented in Malaya in the fifteenth century, introduced into France in the nineteenth century by Ernest Fouinet, made fashionable there by Victor Hugo and Charles Baudelaire, and popularized in the United States by Ashbery. In the pantoum, lines are repeated in a rigorously set, though not immediately apparent, sequence. This veneer of regularity, rare in the distinctly unformalistic poetry of Yau, fortifies the theme of the poems, which is that poetic forms reflect formal qualities found in nature. "Eskimo Villanelle" uses another repetitive, highly engineered form imported from France and championed by Ashbery: the

villanelle consists of five stanzas of three lines and one stanza of four lines, with only two rhymes; the first and third lines alternate as the last lines of the second, third, and fourth stanzas and form the last two lines of the fifth stanza. "Choral Amphisboena" is a monologue about personal identity. In "Spin, Spell, Spill" a January day in Bozeman, Montana, serves as a premise for a dizzy cavalcade of bumptious phenomena. "Picture Book" describes a toy car made of tin that was produced in China and ends: "Both car and box were produced in a country where the bicycle is the most widely used form of transportation." The closing line is characteristic of Yau in its humorous yet tangible signal of Chinese American identity. Juliana Chang points out in a 1998 article in *MELUS* that "Because Yau's writings in general do not address racialized identity in a straightforward, explicit manner, it is difficult for critics of multicultural literature to read his work as 'representative' of ethnic/racial experience."

Although it was printed in an edition of only 401 copies, *Radiant Silhouette* was widely reviewed. An issue of *Talisman: A Journal of Contemporary Poetry and Poetics* was devoted to Yau in 1990, and his poems began to find their way into syllabi in courses in contemporary poetry and Asian American literature. Yau's poetry continued to appear in avant-garde and experimental magazines and was also published in more mainstream outlets, such as the *American Poetry Review*, which included fifteen of his pieces in the November 1992 issue. Yau's marriage to Hammond had ended in divorce in 1990; in 1992 he began a four-year relationship with another painter, Jenny Scobel.

Of all of Yau's books, *Edificio Sayonara* (1992) is the most heavily dominated by poems in series: in addition to more Genghis Chan poems, the volume includes the series "Odes to My Desk," "Big Island Notebook," "Tropical Bulbs," "Postcard," "Avila," "Each Other," and "Angel Atrapado." By placing individual poems in unsystematic, if not totally random, progressions, Yau strategically resituates the lyrical "I." *Edificio Sayonara* received the Jerome Shestack Prize from the *American Poetry Review* in 1993.

In the 1990s Yau became so well known as a critic that he conferred prestige and recognition on many of the artists about whom he chose to write. He also arranged and curated exhibitions, including one as Ahmanson Fellow at the Museum of Contemporary Art in Los Angeles in 1996. While he admires major artists such as Andy Warhol, Jasper Johns, and A. R. Penck, on each of whom he has written monographs, he has also paid attention to figures he considers underrated. He is especially sympathetic to eccentrics such as Forrest Bess, saying in his introduction to a 1988 exhibition catalogue that the Texas artist "belongs to the tradition which fights to invest symbols with meaning," as well as to unrecognized artists whose work is animated by formal and political motives, such as the Chinese American Martin Wong and the Argentine Miguel Angel Rios. Yau also writes sympathetically and insightfully of younger artists such as Brenda Zlamany, Henry Brown, and Kathleen Kucka. The essay Yau wrote for *Young + Brash + Abstract*, the catalogue of an exhibition at the Anderson Gallery of Virginia Commonwealth University in early 2002, shows his confidence in the continuing provocations of twenty-first-century American art:

> This exhibition focuses on younger abstract artists who have transformed what may seem like the end of painting into the beginning. They recognize that history isn't over, that it is always beginning, that it is always being told and simultaneously revised. It seems to me that in drawing, and being committed to drawing, these artists depart from the art historical narrative that claims that Pollock dissolved drawing, made gesture become a part of the field. Drawing, their work tells us, still has many places to go.

What Yau says of Zlamany's portrait painting in his essay "The Skin and Body of Looking" in a 1998 catalogue of an exhibition of her work might well be said of his own poetry: it "shifts effortlessly and provocatively between paint and illusion, insistent thing and detailed image."

During this period Yau's prose poetry developed to the point that his pieces became recognized as short stories. In *Hawaiian Cowboys* (1995) and *My Symptoms* (1998) he uses narrative to entertain and to undermine, to explain and to puzzle. In *Hawaiian Cowboys*, the more immediately accessible of the two volumes, "Family Album" explores the situation of the narrator's transvestite brother with key words such as *television, photograph*, and *makeup* repeated like the teleutons (end-words) in a sestina. "A Little Memento from the Boys" uses the escapades of a trio of workmen renovating a woman's apartment to muse on the strange ways in which individual lives come together. "How to Become Chinese" is Yau's most direct treatment of racial stereotyping of Asian Americans:

> Finally, when we stopped at a red light, he looked over his shoulder and asked me if I was Chinese. After I had answered him, he asked me where I was born. I told him. He turned his head, snorted as if he were a horse, and said: You are not Chinese, you are an American. There's no Chinese left in you. He repeated this when he learned that I didn't speak Chinese either. I must have stayed too long in the bar, because I feel as if I had pissed away some part of my identity without even knowing it. . . . it was clear that the cabby thought it was disgraceful that I hadn't learned to speak Chinese. For if I had, then it wouldn't have been so bad that I was an American.

A theme of several pieces in the collection is how male aspirations for sex, for social acceptance, and for career success both motivate the protagonists to ambitious deeds and cheapen their moral vision. Reviewing *Hawaiian Cowboys* in the avant-garde journal *The Review of Contemporary Fiction* (March 1996), Brian Evenson said: "Often focusing on what it means to be partly Chinese, to be between cultures, Yau refuses to accept easy answers."

My Symptoms includes "Treasure Hunt," in which a man realizes that his girlfriend is plotting to murder him and concludes, "Maybe I shouldn't have been so sure she was the kind of perfection I needed and wanted, that I had to have." This collection, like *Hawaiian Cowboys*, was well received by a *Review of Contemporary Fiction* critic: Dennis Barone (September 1998) commented that "Yau's characters, his poetic paragraphs, talk of guilty pleasures and masks of innocence, of various freedoms and a multitude of constraints." More-mainstream readers, however, felt puzzled. Sybil S. Steinberg complained in *Publishers Weekly* (20 July 1998) that the stories "read more like a sketch or the openings of a story than the finished products of an author's craft."

Yau has also maintained his interest in the prose poem proper, publishing in 2001 a book of nonnarrative prose poems titled *My Heart Is That Eternal Rose Tattoo*. No more than three or four pages long, the poems have the succinctness and the linguistic implication of the lyric. Many seem to describe scenes that exist only in the poet's imagination. Often, as in "Heraclitus's Parking Lot," a poem begins with a collection of evidence ("A loaf of honeysuckle bread sits on the kitchen counter . . . "), moves to a consideration of abstract questions ("Or is the aging process obvious to the clocks mounted inside stones?"), and concludes with an enigmatic anecdote ("still I managed to join in, and stomp on the beetles with my stolen parasol and borrowed sandals"). The one-line "Caption to a Postcard from the 20th Century" is a Zen-like statement: "The municipal parking lot finally reaches the horizon." *My Heart Is That Eternal Rose Tattoo* was hailed for its ingenuity and verbal power. Evenson described it in *The Review of Contemporary Fiction* (Spring 2003) as "an effective *esquisse* on the history of prose, with Yau gleefully straddling genres in all possible ways."

Yau returned to the lyric form with *Borrowed Love Poems* (2002); the title sequence had appeared in *Best American Poetry 2000*, edited by Rita Dove. The collection represents Yau's most prominent book publication in nearly two decades; it is part of the Penguin Poets series, which includes writers identified with the mainstream lyric such as Carl Dennis and Stephen Dobyns. It displays a formal and thematic unity that is unusual for Yau; gnomic yet lucid, it is Yau's most direct and emotional volume. The lyrics do not pretend that the ego can prevail over everything: "we are flies / struggling to be free." Longtime preoccupations of Yau's, such as movie stars, impersonations, and anecdotes about paraphernalia, are restated here in a clearer and tighter vein. The term "borrowed" implies a kind of ventriloquism, a displacement of the voice into a flimsy, yet strangely substantive, exile, as can be seen in "Autobiography of Pink and Blue": the speaker asserts that "I am not an Egyptian napkin. I am not even a retired cosmonaut or guileless barber," implying that the absurdity of being those things is no more extreme than the absurdity of being anything with only one ascribed identity. Yau's lyricism is, thus, always tempered by wry, observed detail and by an overlay of often corrosive irony.

In the fall 2002 on-line edition of the journal *Rain Taxi* Tom Devaney called *Borrowed Love Poems* "a dazzling exploration of deft and unforgiving openness. The poems engage the reader with a wide and wild array of characters, disembodied and otherwise, with an imaginative and capacious use of the lyric 'I.'" Matthew Rohrer wrote in *Poets & Writers* (May-June 2002), "Yau is eclectic, independent, and fiercely committed to the freedom of artistic expression—to finding his own way." F. D. Reeve described *Borrowed Love Poems* in *Poetry* (August 2002) as characterized by "dash and luster, a verbal shine, a tricky idiosyncrasy that make him seem eternally avant-garde." In *Bookforum* (Summer 2002) Joshua Clover praised *Borrowed Love Poems* as "vivid, mysterious, unsettling, and laconically charming in shifting degrees." That poet-critics ranging from Reeve, a senior figure in American literature, to young writers such as Rohrer and Clover all recognized Yau's achievement speaks to the wide and positive critical reception of *Borrowed Love Poems*. Although it was one of the New York Public Library's recommended poetry titles for 2003, however, the volume, and Yau's reputation, continued to hover just below the horizon of an educated general readership.

In a 2003 exhibition catalogue of works by Kucka, Yau asks: "What if identity isn't fixed? What if identity is fluid? What parameters would we either set for others or ourselves?" In a career that has spanned decades, Yau has asked these questions with eloquent and wry persistence. John Yau lives in New York City with the artist Eve Aschheim, whom he married in 1997, and their daughter, Cerise Tzara, and teaches at the Mount Royal Graduate School of Art of the Maryland Institute in Baltimore.

Source: Nicholas Birns, "John Yau," in *Dictionary of Literary Biography*, Vol. 312, *Asian American Writers*, edited by Deborah L. Madsen, Thomson Gale, 2005, pp. 348–58.

Zhou Xiaojing

In the following essay excerpt, Xiaojing defines postmodernism and uses Yau's own theoretical comments to explore the "Genghis Chan: Private Eye" poems. Xiaojing comments on the nature of the speaker in the poem, the "I" of the poem, and the experience of Otherness for an Asian American poet writing in the United States.

Alluding to critical reception of his poetry, John Yau refers to himself as "the poet who is too postmodern for the modernists and too modern for the postmodernists" (1994, 40). Yau's poems evoke different schools of poetry and mix multiple genres. "I am an indigestible vapor rising from the dictionary / you sweep under your embroidered pillow." says the speaker in his poem "Peter Lorre Records His Favorite Walt Whitman Poem For Posterity" (1999c 159). Elements of Surrealism, popular culture, history, and deconstruction coexist in Yau's poetry. In one of his recent prose poems, "Boris Karloff in *The Mummy* Meets *Dr. Fu Manchu*," "a heavily jacketed though unpimpled boy points out the newly severed head of the evening moon, which, elsewhere, is floating directly above the Bank of Shanghai's misaligned ideograms and misplaced radicals" (2002a, 43). These poems not only shed light on the apparently conflicting labels for Yau as a poet, but also suggest the multiple, heterogeneous characteristics of postmodernism. The term postmodernism has meant many things to many readers. Its multiplicity and contingency have generated provocative debates over subjective agency and the politics of representation. While engaging with some major critical views on Yau's work, my reading of Yau's "Genghis Chan: Private Eye" series breaks away from approaches which assume a false dichotomy that renders agency of the Othered subject and postmodern poetics mutually exclusive. I would argue that Yau's work connects postmodernism in poetry to debates about postmodernism and Asian American identity in ways that engage larger issues concerning the relationship between postmodern discourses and minority American literatures...

Yau employs the subversive possibilities of postmodern aesthetics of fragmentation, indeterminacy, and multiplicity to problematize representation, and to denaturalize language and images as transparent means for constructing identities. Combining investigation of language with interrogation of identity construction, Yau undermines the representation of Asian Americans in American popular culture, exposing not only the effects, but also the naturalizing techniques of racial stereotyping. At the same time, he explores the relation between language and the self, between the lyric "I" and the raced subject, mostly through parody, which at once alludes to and demolishes racial stereotypes. It is precisely through parody as such that postmodern aesthetics of multiplicity, fragmentation, and indeterminacy in Yau's serial poems become situated in the social and historical conditions of the raced subject. In fact, ... his subversive parody of Chinese American stereotypes produces an irreducible, uncontainable Otherness that disturbs dominant notions about the racial, cultural Other...

> ... HIS SUBVERSIVE PARODY OF CHINESE AMERICAN STEREOTYPES PRODUCES AN IRREDUCIBLE, UNCONTAINABLE OTHERNESS THAT DISTURBS DOMINANT NOTIONS ABOUT THE RACIAL, CULTURAL OTHER."

Even though Yau does not believe in the notion of the death of the author or of the self, he suggests that the self is necessarily multiple, indeterminate, and fragmented. "I do not subscribe to the death of the author, the postmodern belief that there is no self writing," Yau states in his essay, "Between the Forest and the Its Trees" (1994, 40) However, Yau asks "Might it not be possible that the self is made up of many selves, incomplete and fragmented? Might it not be possible that none of them know the whole story, not even the one who is speaking, the one who is in this sentence, the I which is writing these words?" (41). For Yau, the possibilities and limits of representing or knowing the "I" are conditioned by the structure of language and by the speaker's identities and subject position (ing). "Where the I begins is in a sentence," Yau contends. He continues: "I am obeying the rules of language, the illusions of order it casts upon the swiftly metamorphosizing-metamorphosing [sic] world. If the I continues the structures of language—the accepted narratives, their little boxes—as they are used (and abused), then might not this I continue to oppress and be oppressed? (38)

In addition to linguistic and generic constructions and constraints, Yau suggests that the identity of "I" is not isolated in—nor does it originate from—the textual space when the I begins to write. Rather, the speaking subject has a history in terms of the social and discursive constructs of identities, as the name "Genghis Chan" grounded in social histories and popular cultures suggest, and as the debates over the "lyric I" indicate. Yau opens the same essay with the statement: "I (or another faceless one with my name) was sentenced to sentences before I spoke, before walking toward the ones who named me" (1994, 37). He asks, "How does the I shift through the accumulations of sentences he or she must serve, move beyond the pages the I must copy, and move over the pages written on by others? How does the I emerge from the sentences imposed on it by others?" (38).While locating the identities of the Chinese American "I" in their social, historical formations, Yau seeks to allow this racially marked yet private "I" to move through and beyond those identities imposed by the dominant culture.

In his "Genghis Chan: Private Eye" poems, Yau explores the possibilities of articulating the ambivalence and complexity of the self that is at once a social construct and a self invention through language. The title "Ghengis Chan: Private Eye" draws the reader's attention to both the historical and the fictional, while creating a tension between the public and the private "I." Indeed, it sets up the reader's expectation for the familiar, which the "I" in the poems frustrates and contravenes. In the first poem of the series, for instance, the speaker shows no immediate resemblance to the stereotypes the title alludes to. Rather, the "I" reveals a self whose identity evokes that of Charlie Chan, and yet refuses to be identical with him, thus remaining elusive and open to alternative identities:

> I was floating through a cross section
> with my dusty wine glass, when she entered,
> a shivering bundle of shredded starlight.
> You don't need words to tell a story,
> a gesture will do. These days,
> we're all parasites looking for a body
> to cling to. I'm nothing more
> than riffraff splendor drifting past the
>   runway.
> I always keep a supply of lamprey lipstick
>   around,
> just in case. (Yau 1989, 189)

The "I" in this poem is unsettling because the speaker resists being identified according to any definitive race or gender codes which we expect to find—codes that are implicated in the name in the title. In other words, the "I" in this poem breaks down the correspondence between the name and its identity, or, between the signifier and its referent. In discussing the relationship between names and identities, Slavoj Zizek writes that "the only possible definition of an object in its identity is that this is the object which is always designated by the same signifier—tied to the same signifier. It is the signifier which constitutes the kernel of the object's

'identity'" (1989, 98). Therefore, Zizek emphasizes that it is "the name itself, the signifier, which supports the identity of the object." Thus "naming itself retroactively constitutes its reference" (95). . . .

The reader, then, is forced to rely on narrative and the speaker's statements in order to figure out who the speaker is, and what is happening in the poem, but all these remain elusive because the narrative and language Yau employs are deliberately ambiguous. . . .

Breaking away from conventional ways of using words is for Yau a mode of resisting the "little boxes" of identity categories in order to articulate elusive, multiple selves and the "Others." As he writes in his essay: "You have your labels, their falsifying categories, but I have words. I—the I [who] writes—will not be spoken for" (1994, 40).

In both his Language and lyric poems, Yau has found a way of using language and voice to break away from the solipsism of the poet-I without ignoring his own subject position or ethnic background. He has developed strategies for using language in such a way so as to hear the Other and to let the Other speak. Yau's insistence on using language as such in his poetry enables him to develop a poetics of resistance that enacts a politicized aesthetics as an ethical relationship with the Other.

Through a critical engagement with postmodern aesthetics from the positions of the Other, John Yau develops an anti-assimilation poetics. His deployment of postmodernist poetics demonstrates possibilities of a politically enabling postmodernism for minority American literatures. In seeking to address identities of race and to articulate a self that is historically and socially situated, yet refuses to be merely a social construct, Yau extends the possibilities of postmodern discourses for investigating raced subject, for articulating Otherness, and for enacting resistance and intervention. By employing postmodern aesthetics to articulate an irreducible, uncontainable, and challenging Otherness, Yau's "Genghis Chan: Private Eye" series participates in shaping the meanings of the postmodern, particularly in developing a politically charged postmodern poetics for minority American literature.

Source: Zhou Xiaojing, "Postmodernism and Subversive Parody: John Yau's 'Genghis Chan: Private Eye' Series," in *College Literature*, Vol. 31, No. 1, Winter 2004, pp. 73–74, 77, 80–82, 89, 98–99.

SOURCES

Chen, Lisa, "Of Genghis Chan and Geishas: John Yau's Work Defies Categorizations, Helps Define APA Aesthetic," in *Asian Week*, Vol. 18, No. 34, April 17, 1997, p. 17.

Clover, Joshua, Review of *Borrowed Love Poems*, in *Artforum*, Vol. 9, No. 2, Summer 2002, p. 19.

Fink, Thomas, "Poetic I.D.'s," February–March 2003, http://www.bostonreview.net/BR28.1/fink.html (accessed February 4, 2007).

Minton, Arthur, "Try Titles," in *English Journal*, Vol. 27, No. 10, December 1938, pp. 809–10.

Rekdal, Paisley, "John Sees, John Writes, John Laughs: The Multi-Faceted Satiric Vision of John Yau," in *International Examiner*, Vol. 30, No. 16, September 2, 2003, p. 16.

Rohrer, Matthew, "Where Art & Poetry Collide: A Profile of John Yau," in *Poets & Writers Magazine*, Vol. 30, No. 3, May–June 2002, pp. 26, 28–29.

Shinn, Christopher A., "A Fresh Description of Old Expressions: *Forbidden Entries*," in *International Examiner*, Vol. 24, No. 8, May 6, 1997, p. S29.

Yau, John, "Russian Letter," in *Borrowed Love Poems*, Penguin Group, 2002, p. 3.

FURTHER READING

Addonizio, Kim, and Dorianne Laux, *The Poet's Companion: A Guide to the Pleasures of Writing Poetry*, W. W. Norton, 1997.
> Praised as one of the best books about creating poetry, teacher Addonizio and poet Laux help students understand and prepare for the process of writing poetry.

Henry, Brian, and Andrew Zawacki, eds., *The Verse Book of Interviews: 27 Poets on Language, Craft, and Culture*, Wave Books, 2005.
> The editors present interviews with some of the world's emerging contemporary poets. The book covers poets from all of the world, including those from Australia, Slovenia, the Czech Republic, and Kashmir, as well as a strong representation of U.S. poets who are known for their experimental writings.

Schwartz, Gary, *The Rembrandt Book*, Harry N. Abrams, 2006.
> Schwartz, one of the leading authorities on Rembrandt, provides a look into the life and work of the Dutch master. Over the centuries many controversies have arisen about Rembrandt, and Schwartz's research answers some of the more imposing questions.

Yau, John, *The United States of Jasper Johns*, Zoland Books, 1997.
> An example of Yau's critical writing on art, this book examines the works of Jasper Johns, considered the father of minimalism in art.

Sentimental Education

MARY RUEFLE

2000

Mary Ruefle has become an important voice in contemporary American poetry, praised often for her fresh, inventive style. She has published several collections of her works, including *Tristimania* (2004), *Among the Musk-Ox People* (2002), *The Adamant* (1989, winner of the 1988 Iowa Poetry Prize), and *Post Meridian* (2000), which became one of her most successful. The poems in this collection reflect her whimsical treatment of language, her startling and often obscure images, and her exploration of the interaction between imagination and human experience.

In one of the best poems in that collection, "Sentimental Education," Ruefle focuses on a classroom of children who must face a series of injustices as they interact with each other and with their teacher. The title of the poem, an allusion to Gustave Flaubert's novel of the same name, is an ironic statement about the nature of education. In her construction of lists of each child's loves and of the prayers that they recite in the classroom, Ruefle reveals how the students are confronted with the harsh realities of human experience and of traditional, parochial education, and how they learn to face these realities through active, imaginative engagement with their world.

AUTHOR BIOGRAPHY

Mary Ruefle was born in Pittsburg, Pennsylvania, in 1952. She spent her first twenty years traveling around the United States and Europe with her mother and her father, a military officer. Ruefle earned a degree in literature from Bennington College in 1974. Upon graduation, she attended the writing program at Hollins College. She has been quoted as claiming that she began writing poems as soon as she could read.

Ruefle's work has appeared in numerous magazines and journals, and as of 2007, she was the author of seven books of poetry, including *Post Meridian* (2000), which includes "'Sentimental Education," all of which have been well-received. Her poems have been anthologized in *Best American Poetry*, *The Extraordinary Tide*, and *Great American Prose Poems* and her collection *The Adamant* won the 1988 Iowa Poetry Prize. She also won fellowships from the National Endowment for the Arts and the Guggenheim Foundation. She won the American Academy of Arts and Letters Award in Literature and the Whiting Foundation Writer's Award in 1995. Ruefle has taught at Bennington College, Colby College, the University of Michigan, and in China. As of 2007, she lived in New England, where she was teaching in the M.F.A. in Writing program at Vermont College. She has also been a visiting faculty member with the University of Iowa Writers' Workshop.

POEM SUMMARY

Ruefle's "Sentimental Education" creates a classroom scene in which the students are reciting prayers, revised in terms of their own awareness of one another and the relationships that exist between certain students. In the first stanza, the speaker notes that Ann, a girl in class, loves a boy named Barry. In the second stanza, the class is asked to pray for someone named Lucius Fenn, who "suffers" while shaking hands, suggesting that he is painfully shy. It is not clear whether Lucius is a student in the class.

The third and forth stanza continue this pattern. In the third, the speaker claims that a girl named Bonny Polton loves a pug, which is a type of dog. In the fourth, the children are asked to pray for Olina Korsk, who is missing several fingers.

In the fifth stanza, the speaker notes that Leon Bendrix loves Odelia Jonson, but it seems as if his love is not returned since Odelia loves Kurt. Similarly not reciprocating in feeling, Kurt

"loves Carlos who loves Paul." The love one boy feels for another could be an expression of friendship or a suggestion of homosexual feelings. In the sixth stanza, the students are asked to pray for Cortland Filby, probably a boy in class since his action of handling a dead wasp is described in the present tense. The wasp is "a conceit for his mother." Conceit is a literary device which draws a striking comparison between two extremely different things, in this case between the dead wasp and Cortland's mother. Since Cortland is not identified as having a specific problem, as Lucius and Olina have been, this prayer gives a vague sense that he may be troubled by something or that a boy with a waspish mother needs the prayers of his peers.

In the seventh stanza, the speaker notes Harold's pleasure in examining Londa's hair under the microscope. Similarly intrigued, Londa enjoys braiding her pony's mane. Fancy Dancer, the focus of the prayer in stanza eight, is likely the name of Londa's pony who "is troubled by the vibrissa [the stiff hairs growing] in his nostrils."

Stanza nine returns to the love Nadine St. Clair feels for Ogden Smythe who loves "blowing his nose on postage stamps." The directive for the prayer for William Shakespeare in the next stanza may come from a student who wants the children to think of him often or it may come out of the children's sense that the teacher wants them to appreciate Shakespeare's poetry.

In stanza eleven, Yukiko Pearl is said to love "the bits of toffee / that fall to the floor" as Jeffrey eats his snack.

The call for the prayer in the next stanza seems to come from one of the children who knows Marieko, a florist who rings up the wrong code for the flowers that he sells.

The focus shifts in stanza thirteen when the speaker notes that Muriel Frame is fixated on an event that occurred on "the afternoon of November third" and likes to talk about it. The year of the incident is not given. Ruefle chooses not to reveal the date's significance to Muriel. According to the Roman Catholic Church, this is the feast day of several saints. The date also marks the day of independence for Panama in 1903, for Dominica in 1978, and the Federated States of Micronesia in 1986. But it is likely the event that fascinates Muriel is a more personally relevant one.

TOPICS FOR FURTHER STUDY

- Read Ruefle's "When Adults Talk," which appears on the facing page in *Post Meridian*, and compare its treatment of the tensions between adults and children to those depicted in "Sentimental Education." Does Ruefle raise any different points in "When Adults Talk" about the problems of communication between the two groups? Write a paper in which you compare and contrast the two poems.

- Write an additional four stanzas in the same format (one stanza focusing on what one of the children loves; the other directing a prayer) that would fit the thematic focus of "When Adults Talk."

- Research the Tartar invasion of Asia and Europe during the Middle Ages. What details about the invasion could be related to the situation(s) in the poem? Make a presentation on your findings.

- Prepare to lead a class discussion on the obscurity of contemporary poetry. Present examples of work from other poets such as Leslie Scalapino (*Zither & Autobiography*), Dean Young (*Skid*), and Joan Aleshire (*Litany of Thanks*). You could also include a poem by a modernist such as Wallace Stevens (for example, "Thirteen Ways of Looking at a Blackbird"). Organize a classroom debate about the value of poetry that is clearly not written for the common reader.

The call for prayer in the fourteenth stanza comes from one of the children who asks that classmates pray for their teacher who does not know even half of what the students know. She also appears not to recognize the suffering she has caused one of her students as described in the next stanza, or perhaps she does not care.

Ruefle breaks the couplet and contrapuntal pattern in the last two stanzas. In the fifteenth, the speaker describes a little girl who has been forced to sit in the corner with a dunce cap on her head. Her utter humiliation is apparent in her downcast face, her trembling chin, and her "fervent wish to die."

One reading of the final stanza is that "it" refers to the "fervent wish to die," and speaker wants that wish to be given "to the Tartars / who roll gloriously into battle." In other words, let the wish to die be on the battlefield and not in the classroom. The word Tartars refers to a group of Turkic people from Eastern Europe and Central Asia who banded together in their invasion during the Middle Ages of central and western Asia and Eastern Europe. The term can also refer to a person with an irritable or violent nature, usually a female. The definitions could merge in a call for the girl's sorrow and humiliation to be given to the marauding Tartars who might also be imagined as battling the forces that oppress her.

THEMES

Lack of Awareness

Ursula Twombly, the children's teacher, who "does not know the half of it," may well not know the content of the children's prayers. Moreover, she appears not to notice the hypocrisy of the system that she supports. Part of the ritual in her classroom is the recitation of prayers to help alleviate the suffering of others. But the teacher seems not to recognize how her own actions have caused the suffering of the child singled out as a dunce. Ruefle may be suggesting that in order to devote oneself to the system by following convention, one must ignore the hypocrisies of that system. She may also be suggesting that the children's creative engagement with their world helps them to be more aware of it, unlike adults who require them to follow certain rules. The teacher's last name may be a child's mispronunciation of the name, Trombly, which suggests how young the children are. Ironically, they may be much more aware than their teacher is.

Compassion

The children show remarkable compassion for others considering that their teacher does not seem to model that virtue. In the prayers that they make up, they show concern for one child who is painfully shy, another who is missing several fingers, and for a pony that is "troubled

This poem describes students in a classroom praying for people while citing their quirks or shortcomings
(AP Images)

by the vibrissa in his nostrils." Even the local florist who makes mistakes while ringing up his flowers gets their consideration, which reveals the children's sense that even adults make mistake and ought to be treated compassionately. The final prayer reveals the children's compassion for their clueless teacher even after she has caused one of them so much pain, revealing in addition the ability of children to forgive. Moreover, the children's prayers reveal their awareness of connections and relationships among themselves of which the teacher is unaware. It seems to be, also, that the children in their prayers are more inclusive than the teacher's formulaic prayer allows.

STYLE

Allusion
The title, "Sentimental Education," is most likely an allusion or reference to *Sentimental Education*, a novel by Gustave Flaubert (1821–1880) which chronicles the life of Frederic

Moreau during the time of the French Revolution of 1848. Through his depiction of Frederic's experiences in Paris where the young man gains his "sentimental education" concerning the workings of society, Flaubert satirizes France's social classes, customs, and political institutions by focusing on the moral corruption and hypocrisy that he finds there. Frederic, whom Flaubert presents as a representative of his generation, enters the privileged bourgeois society with a passive acceptance of its social order. Unable to think independently, he becomes a voice for social conformity and prejudices in his refusal to recognize the injustices committed by those of his milieu. The allusion to Flaubert's novel could suggest a thematic link to the poem's focus on injustice. Clearly, there is nothing sentimental (sweet and attractive) in the education these children are really receiving in the parochial school.

Repetition of Sound
The repetition of vowel sounds in the poem (a technique called assonance), especially in the lines that note one child's love for another, are

euphonious, or pleasant sounding. For example, Ruefle repeats the "a" in Ann Galbraith's name as well as the "o" sounds in "love" and the boy Ann loves, Barry Soyers. The repeated "r" and "y" sound (a technique called consonance) in Barry's name adds to the euphony. The "o" sound appears five times in the third stanza in its declaration that "Bonny Polton loves a pug named Cowl." (italics added). This pleasing repetition of sound intensifies the connection between the child and the beloved pet.

Repetition of Words

Words are repeated for emphasis in the poem. The two words most often repeated are "love" and "pray," which reinforce the sense of the children's devotion and compassion for each other. Another image is repeated for a different effect. In stanza twelve, the speaker describes Marieko the florist wrapping roses in a paper cone, an object that also appears in the penultimate stanza. When Ruefle describes the child's dunce cap as a paper cone rolled to a point, she suggests what is wrong in the situation. Paper cones should be used for wrapping flowers, not for humiliating a child.

Liturgical Form

The word "litany" has two meanings: a series of prayers spoken or sung at a religious service, asking for God's blessing; and a long list of complaints or problems. Ruefle constructs the poem in the form of a litany, employing both definitions of the term. The poem moves back and forth from a list of children and the things that they love to a prayer. This serves two purposes: it reinforces the connection between the children and the disconnection between the children and the teacher who is directing them to pray. The pattern is broken at the end of the poem when the child is described sitting in the corner wearing a dunce cap, which reinforces the sense of isolation the child feels in being punished by being separated from the class.

HISTORICAL CONTEXT

Contemporary Poetry

In "Difficult and Otherwise: New Work by Ruefle, Young, and Aleshire," Peter Harris determines that a good number of contemporary poets write obscure poetry that refuses to cater "to the illusive ideal of a 'common reader' who

has a need to 'get it.'" The goal of poets such as Leslie Scalapino (*Zither & Autobiography*, 2003), Mary Ruefle, Dean Young (*Skid*, 2002), and Joan Aleshire (*Litany of Thanks*, 2003) is, Harris maintains, to "elude closure, embrace discontinuity, celebrate polyvalence" (the use of language that can have more than one meaning). The poets in this group came to be known as "local" poets, writing poetry, Harris explains, for readers "who know how to break a particular code" in a poem and thus find meaning. Reading their poetry can be a frustrating experience, however, for those who expect the images of a poem to come together to provide them with a clear understanding of its themes.

In this sense, these contemporary poets echo the work of the modernist poets, including T. S. Eliot (1888–1965), Ezra Pound (1885–1972), and Wallace Stevens (1879–1955). These poets wrote for an elite readership that could understand the allusive nature of their work and appreciate the poets' experiments with the dislocation of language. Modernists determined that continuity, a clear relationship between parts of the poem, did not accurately reflect the fragmented nature of experience and so refused to use transitions to facilitate the reader's comprehension in moving from one image to another, creating a sense of disjunction in their work.

In his review of four collections of poetry, Stephen C. Behrendt argues that poems that were published in 1999 and 2000 exhibit a "remarkable sadness" which echoes that of the romantic poets, especially the poetry of William Wordsworth (1770–1850), who "paints Nature in darker tones than we usually think." The romantic poets, including Wordsworth, Shelley (1792–1822), Byron (1788–1824), and Keats (1795–1821), were characterized by their devotion to the free expression of human emotions. They rejected the preference in the previous period for reason and instead promoted a return to nature and a contemplation of the beauty found there.

Behrendt likens the contemporary revolutionary age to that of the romantics two hundred years ago. While the poets he places in this contemporary group—Robert Wrigley (*Reign of Snakes*, 1999), Robin Chapman (*The Way In*, 1999), Dan Bellm (*Buried Treasure*, 1999), and Mary Ruefle—sound their sadness "in a new and particularly contemporary key," they, like their predecessors, live "in no less troubled times, in a culture in which the future was no more clear than our own is." The tensions of the Romantic Age that were expressed in its poetry were caused by such events as the French Revolution, which began in 1789; the rise of dissenting religious views; and the exploitation of workers during the industrialization of Britain. This period dates from the beginning of the revolution in 1789 to the death of Wordsworth in 1850.

CRITICAL OVERVIEW

Hadara Bar-Nadav, in *American Review*, insists that Mary Ruefle is "at her best ... wry, edgy, and infinitely surprising," an assessment echoed by reviewers of the poems collected in *Post Meridian*. A review of the collection in *Publishers Weekly* states that the collection contains "elegantly worked poems" that slip "behind screens of language, dazzling the reader." Noting the sometimes obscure nature of her work, the reviewer explains, "within the poems, Ruefle concocts circular patterns of sound that seduce the reader away from the hunt for logical development." Yet, the review concludes, "Readers will find ample verbal threads here for their own happy picking."

Mark Halliday, in his review of the collection, also comments on Ruefle's obscurity, insisting that the first poem, "Perfect Reader," stands as "a warning" to readers as they prepare to read the rest of the book. Halliday explains that this poem states: "*it is beautiful to try to be a perfect reader of poems. And you are fated to try. But your imaginative efforts will be tiring and endless.*" He finds though that the poems move "along in what seems a whimsical, impulsive way, but when we read [them] thoughtfully . . . we find ourselves inhabiting an emotional coherence."

Stephen C. Behrendt writes in the *Prairie Schooner* that the poems in *Post Meridian* are "wildly exuberant exercises in fanciful juxtaposition, in the imagination let loose on a world of possibilities." Behrendt determines that what sets the poems in this collection apart from Ruefle's previous ones is "the very different route by which they arrive at their cumulative intensity." He notes that "In these poems the oddly juxtaposed images resolve themselves again and again into an almost comforting texture rather than a discordant one." They are, he

WHAT DO I READ NEXT?

- Dana Gioia's "The Litany," which can be found in his collection *Interrogations at Noon* (2001), contains a series of prayers that make powerful statements of love and loss and reveal the search for a way to comprehend the nature of suffering.

- James Merrill's "Lost in Translation" (1974), collected in his *The Book of Ephraim*—one of a group of three books in Merrill's *Divine Comedies* (1976), is a complex study of loss and the artistic rendering of experience in its focus on the speaker's often painful memories of his childhood.

- Ruefle's "When Adults Talk" appears on the page facing "Sentimental Education" in *Post Meridian* (2000). The two poems share a similar focus: the separation between adults and children caused by problems with communication.

- Ruefle's "Cold Pluto" (1996), from her collection by the same name, focuses on the active role of the imagination in the contemplation of experience, which is a recurring theme in her work.

- Ruefle has admitted that she was most influenced by poet Wallace Stevens, whose work shares the same focus on the power of the imagination. His "Thirteen Ways of Looking at a Blackbird," which can be found in *The Collected Poems of Wallace Stevens* (1990), is one such poem.

claims, "lively in their language and voice, deft in their verbal variety" and "wonderfully detailed, their images sharp and crisp as woodsmoke in mountain air." He concludes, "It takes an adept juggler as well as a crafty illusionist—and a skillful poet—to keep everything in motion and to maintain at least the illusion of a still-possible reassuring and restorative order."

CRITICISM

Wendy Perkins

Perkins is a professor of twentieth-century American and English literature and film. In this essay, she examines the theme of injustice and the interplay of the imagination.

Several critics have noted that readers often find Mary Ruefle's poetry inaccessible due to the seemingly irreconcilable images it contains. Much of the language of her poems is ambiguous, frustrating the search for meaning. Mark Halliday, in his review of *Post Meridian*, insists that when "confronting a poem, we often have to work hard to decide whether its oddity or difficulty comes from a wonderfully forgivable, or from a repulsive arrogance." Ruefle's "Sentimental Education" falls decidedly in the former category. Each of the stanzas contains separate statements that the reader must interpret. The reflective reader can find that under careful consideration, Ruefle's strikingly fresh and sometimes unnerving images come together to form a coherent, imaginative vision of the injustices of human experience.

In "Sentimental Education," Ruefle juxtaposes two types of litany in her inquiry into the nature and consequences of injustice as she centers on the parochial classroom experiences of a group of young boys and girls. She constructs prayers and lists based on anaphora, the use of the same word or phrase at the beginning of several sentences or lines, to emphasize her themes. Each item in the list opens with the name of a student and the repeated word, "loves," while each line of prayer begins with "Please pray for."

The title of the poem appears obscure unless we understand it as an allusion to Flaubert's novel of the same name, which focuses on a young man in Paris in the nineteenth century who is unable to gain a clear understanding of the injustices of his world; thus his education becomes "sentimental," as it reinforces convention, rather than challenging it. Flaubert, however, exposes to the reader the moral corruption and hypocrisy he finds in the social classes of the age by satirizing the young man's experiences. In the same sense, Ruefle exposes to her readers the injustices the children suffer while she suggests that the teacher, who is conducting a conventional "sentimental" education for them, is unaware of their condition.

ONE OF THE MAIN KINDS OF INJUSTICE THE CHILDREN EXPERIENCE IS THE CONDITION OF LOVING SOMEONE OR SOMETHING THAT DOES NOT LOVE THEM BACK."

One of the main kinds of injustice the children experience is the condition of loving someone or something that does not love them back. In a seemingly mundane sequence, Ruefle constructs lists that fix a distinct powerful emotion felt by the children. Their love is not actively rejected but it is not acknowledged by the objects of their affection. Leon, for example, loves Odelia, but she "loves Kurt who loves Carlos who loves Paul." This produces an ironic relationship between the children as each child who loves reveals a strong connection to another while the unrequited nature of that love suggests rejection or at least indifference. The love that Kurt feels for Carlos and Carlos for Paul may suggest the young age of the children, their being in a stage in which boys and girls are as likely to form homo- as heterosexual pairs of friends. Or it could suggest a further problematic note if readers interpret it to suggest homosexual urgings, which could cause the children not only to feel cut off from the person loved but also from the society that dictates what kind of love is acceptable and what kind of love is not.

The children's feelings of affection for others are made more poignant by their incongruity. For some unknown reason, "Harold loves looking at Londa's hair under the microscope," while Nadine loves Ogden, whose only identifiable characteristic is "blowing his nose on postage stamps." Ruefle suggests that these children, along with Yukiko who loves to look at "the little bits of toffee that fall to the floor" from Jeffrey's snack, are able to engage on an imaginative level with the world, discovering significance that is not as apparent to adults, especially teachers who follow convention without examining the hypocrisies contained within it.

The children are required, as part of their conventional education to participate in the ritual of prayer in their school, asking for God's

2 1 0

Poetry for Students, Volume 26

blessing for their loved ones and those less fortunate than they. Their ability to creatively envision their world prompts them, however, to individualize the prayers and so they become more meaningful. The prayers also reflect the injustices endured by others, including Okina, "who holds the record for missing fingers" and Lucius, whose shyness causes him to "suffer greatly."

Their final prayer is for their teacher, "who does not know the half of it," especially concerning the hypocrisy of the educational system in her classroom as well as the injustice it inspires. Ruefle breaks the contrapuntal pattern of her poem in the last lines to illustrate this point.

She uses straightforward free verse to describe a heartbreaking scene in the classroom. A little girl is forced to sit in the corner with a dunce cap on her head as a form of punishment. The child's utter humiliation over "having been singled out like this" is evident in her bowed head, her trembling chin, and her sincere and "fervent wish to die." Here Ruefle satirizes the conventions of an educational system that requires students to pray for the misfortunes of others while, at the same time, being actively responsible for the abject humiliation experienced by the little girl in the corner. The irony is compounded by the fact that the children are reciting their prayers while their classmate suffers.

The acute sadness that results from Ruefle's list of the injustices endured by the children is periodically relieved by her comic descriptions of their sometimes incongruous emotions and by the children's genuine concern for their classmates. This sadness is also relieved by the power of the imagination, especially regarding the little girl in the dunce cap. At the end of the poem, the speaker, perhaps voicing the children's directive, extols her to "take it away and give it to the Tartars." The "it" the speaker refers to could be the humiliation the child feels or her wish to die to escape her shame. Giving it to the Tartars, perhaps a subject they have studied in school, may imaginatively eradicate the feelings. These marauders, known for their violent invasions of foreign lands, would take those feelings into battle with them.

In "Sentimental Education," Mary Ruefle asks her readers to actively engage in the process of interpretation by opening themselves up to the unexpected in order to see things in a fresh

> SHE IS THE UNLOVED AND THE UNWANTED, A SYMBOL OF THOSE PEOPLE IN THE WORLD FOR WHOM THE PASSIONS *AND* THE SUFFERINGS OF LOVE REMAIN FOREVER A PROMISE IN POETRY AND NOVELS."

way. She illustrates the power of imaginative engagement in her focus on the children in the poem, who are able to deal with the injustices that they experience through their playful, poignant, and ultimately exhilarating interaction with their world.

Source: Wendy Perkins, Critical Essay on "Sentimental Education," in *Poetry for Students*, Thomson Gale, 2007.

Klay Dyer

Dyer holds a Ph.D. in English literature and has published extensively on fiction, poetry, film, and television. He is also a freelance university teacher, writer, and educational consultant. In this essay, he discusses "Sentimental Education" in terms of the philosophy of love introduced in the eighteenth century in the writings of Rousseau and Goethe.

The mid-eighteenth century saw the publication of two novels that changed dramatically the ways that writers and poets thought and wrote about love and romance. In Jean-Jacques Rousseau's *Julie, ou La Nouvelle Héloïse* (1761) and Johann Wolfgang von Goethe's *The Sorrows of Young Werther* (1774), the longstanding cultural idea of love as either a contract that authorizes sexual relations or a financial arrangement was changed forever. These two novels imagined a new concept of love, one shaped more by emotion and spirituality than sex and money. Following the wide success of these novels, love was reimagined as an affair of almost religious intensity, marked by total devotion on the part of at least one partner, which inevitably seemed to necessitate remarkable sacrifices.

Love in this new sense became a secular version of the intense passion that a religious person feels toward God. Glorifying the pain as well as the joys of a love relationship, this concept of sentimental love also celebrated relationships as commitments of a lifetime. Sentimental love suggested the idea that men and women in love should be considered equals: equally noble their spiritual connection, equally passionate in their sexual experiences, and equally free as intellectual beings.

Attached to this new view of love and relationships came a new understanding of human nature that prizes emotion and passion over reason as well as individual instincts over the social constructs of duty or civility. Rousseau had long insisted that people were naturally good, so removing the constraints of social rules and ethical frameworks was a freedom that he endorsed. Accordingly, he argued, love as an intensification of a natural feeling of goodness would simplify human relationships, serving as a kind of spiritual counterbalance to the corrupting taint of modern society, with its dogmatic attention to greed, power, and materialism.

Mary Ruefle gives many of these eighteenth-century ideas a contemporary spin in the aptly titled "Sentimental Education." In her opening couplet, for instance, Ruefle uses familiar expression that renders love as both an active, present tense verb ("loves") and an articulation of the emotion itself. In this sense, the statement "Ann Galbraith / loves Barry Soyers" is an *unpoetic* statement of the complex emotion of love. Such an expression of apparent devotion, seen everywhere in contemporary culture from tattoos to bathroom graffiti, has become so familiar as to be cliché, that is, an expression that has been used so often that it has become stale and lacking in imagination.

But even with its staleness, this couplet expresses an idea or fact that is to be understood in definite terms. There can be no doubt in the mind of the reader about what it means. Moreover, the statement "Ann Galbraith / loves Barry Soyers" is a public announcement of a private feeling, much like children would use who spread gossip about one another. But unrevealed is whether Barry Soyers loves Ann Galbraith in return.

Goethe, in particular, was fascinated with the idea of love that is not reciprocated. His protagonist, Young Werther, presents an intimate account of his own unrequited love for a beautiful young girl, Lotte, who is already engaged to Albert. Werther spends months becoming a trusted friend of the couple, despite the suffering that he feels as his love for Lotte is reinforced and remains unreturned. After several failed attempts to disconnect from this self-destructive relationship, Werther writes a farewell letter, borrows two pistols from Albert, and kills himself.

From this opening couplet, Ruefle builds a series of couplets that move in two directions. Following the first path, the poem begins to take shape as a catalogue of the various tribulations that might befall the sentimental lover whose affection is not returned. For example, Leon Bendrix "loves Odelia Johnson / who loves Kurt who loves Carlos who loves Paul." Then there is Harold who "loves looking at Londa's hair under the microscope" but not necessarily at Londa herself, and Muriel Frame, who loves the story of "the incident / that happened on the afternoon of November third" so much that she recounts it incessantly, probably to the disinterest of her listeners. This poem is, as its title promises, an education in what people talk about when they talk about love in contemporary culture.

Following Ruefle's second path through this poem, readers find alternating couplets that underscore the intersection in the sentimental model between love as an emotional, physical act and love as a devotional, spiritual act. The repetition of the opening words "Please pray" in the even number couplet stanzas (2, 4, 6, 8, 10, 12, 14) suggests the poem's balanced emphasis on the notion of love and the religious devotions it might elicit.

Significantly, these devotional couplets, each of which invoke a plea to "Pray for" someone, use words associated with the sentimental lover's heightened emotions. Such words as "suffers greatly," "missing," "dead," and "troubled" balance with the possible joy of the interlocking stanzas, making suffering a component of love and love a component of suffering. As the fourteenth and final couplet of this opening series suggests, to understand only the joy side of love *or* the suffering side of love is to "not know the half of it."

But Ruefle's education does not end with this synthesis of love and suffering. Rather it moves in the fifteenth stanza of the poem, a septet (group of seven lines), to describe "a little girl" who is isolated and unloved. She has been "singled out," for punishment and left to sit "by the radiator in a wooden chair" and wears "a dunce's cap." The girl sits with head bowed,

THE YOUNG GIRL IS COMPLETELY

OVERWHELMED BY HER TEACHER'S INABILITY TO SEE

HER WORTH AND WANTS NOTHING MORE THAN TO DIE."

"sincere in her fervent wish to die." She is the unloved and the unwanted, a symbol of those people in the world for whom the passions *and* the sufferings of love remain forever a promise in poetry and novels. While Werther and those who take him as a symbol of a sentimental education might long to die for love, Ruefle's little girl longs to die because she feels unloved.

The "it" of the final couplet, perhaps a reference to all of this girl's feelings, conveys the other children's hope that whatever hurts her will be taken far away by warring soldiers. The final couple seems to say, in effect, let the Tartars take that wish for death into the battle and leave this little girl free of it.

Source: Klay Dyer, Critical Essay on "Sentimental Education," in *Poetry for Students*, Thomson Gale, 2007.

Joyce Hart

Hart has degrees in literature and creative writing. In this essay, she examines Ruefle's poem to discover the underlying tone, dissecting the phrases to find the hidden emotions that are reflected in the images.

Ruefle's poem "Sentimental Education" is filled with a variety of emotions, from empathy to despair. Unlike the suggestion in the title, these emotions are not overly romanticized as the word "sentimental" suggests but rather are often understated. The success of this poem, which at first appears to be a random collection of childlike observations, is that the feelings are expressed almost as if the narrator is not even aware that she is exposing them. By using concrete nouns, such as the first and last names for the subjects of the narrator's observations, readers are led to believe that the poem makes literal sense and is only what it appears to be on the surface. However, by looking closer and examining what might be behind the narrator's choice of words and selection of images, the reader gains insight into the emotional content of this poem.

The first thing that one might notice in reading this poem is that the narrator speaks in the present tense. This places the narrator in the midst of the observations being made and thus suggests that the narrator is a child describing her classmates. Although some of the vocabulary (such as "conceit" and "vibrissa") are unusual for a child, there is an innocence present in the observations that suits the young student. Apparently, the emotions expressed or described are those of children. It is possible to imagine that the young narrator is capable of recording the events around her as she sees them without being able to completely comprehend their hidden emotions. Thus, the deep feelings expressed by the narrator come through as authentic.

The next thing the reader might notice is the distance that the narrator places between herself and the people who are the subjects of her observations. This distance is greatest at the beginning of the poem, where the subjects of the narrator's focus seemed removed from the narrator. As the poem progresses, this distance slowly disintegrates, and the emotions are fully expressed. For example, in the first two lines (or couplet), the poem reads: "Ann Galbraith / loves Barry Soyers." This is a simple statement. The narrator does not describe this love or offer any further insight into the two characters. In using both the first and the last names, the narrator suggests a schoolroom decorum where students are referred to by the full names. The children named are fellow classmates, and the narrator may be passing on rumors. But then in contrast to this observation is the one about Lucius Fenn, who "suffers." Suffering and loving both involve feelings, but the narrator offers more information about Lucius Fenn's suffering than she does about Ann and Barry's love. Lucius Fenn suffers "whilst shaking hands." Although this too is a statement of fact, the narrator has intrigued the reader's imagination, leaving tantalizing gaps that the reader must fill in. First, there is the use of the word "whilst," which is an unusual word for a child. The reader might wonder if this is the result of the narrator's love of William Shakespeare (whom the narrator mentions later in the poem), an author in whose Elizabethan English this word is quite common. Another possibility is that the narrator is merely repeating the vocabulary of Lucius Fenn himself, who might have described his suffering this way. Is Lucius Fenn afraid to touch others? Is he shy? Withdrawn? Or is it the case that his own hands shake? Whatever the answer is, the narrator rouses empathy in the reader for Lucius, a response slightly stronger than that for the first two classmates mentioned in the poem. This rising emotional reaction continues to grow as the poem progresses.

The gap between the narrator and her classmates continues to narrow as the reader continues with the poem. "Bonny Polton" is also in love. But the object of her love is a dog, a "pug named Cowl." The word "cowl" gives the impression that Bonny Polton is to be felt sorry for in some way. The word "pug" is not quite as endearing as the word "dog," and the word "cowl" brings up images of a hood that covers one's head. Perhaps the narrator is suggesting that Bonny Polton might not be popular enough to have a boyfriend. That is one possibility.

The fourth couplet also presents a more serious departure from the first four lines of the poem, when the narrator brings up the image of Olina Korsk, "who holds the record for missing fingers." Whereas Lucius Fenn "suffers greatly" when he must shake hands, poor Olina may not be able to shake hands at all. Not only does Olina have digits missing from her hands, she holds the record for such a fact, which suggests the youthfulness and inexperience of the narrator who sees Olina's deformity as an extreme case or just uses that expression to convey the shocking nature of her deformity.

The reader's emotional response may intensify with the next few lines, with their depiction of unrequited love, with Leon loving Odelia, and Odelia loving Kurt, and Kurt loving Carlos "who loves Paul." There appears to be no reciprocation of love in either the seemingly heterosexual or homosexual attractions. Individuals are chasing others, who in turn are seeking love from someone else. It sounds a bit like a game of tag on a playground.

In the next line, there is a suggestion of another type of lack of affection. In the sixth couplet Cortland Filby is portrayed. Cortland's mother is compared to a "dead wasp." The word "conceit" here makes clear the extreme comparison between the mother and the insect. Whether he compares the stinger of the wasp, or the fact that the wasp is dead, to his mother, one could conclude that his relationship with his mother is definitely uneasy and uncomfortable. The fact that the narrator asks for prayers for Cortland implies that she knows that Cortland, like

Lucius and Olina, is suffering. The fact that the narrator understands, or at least is aware of, this suffering suggests that the narrator is more familiar with Courtland's family life than she is in the lives of the characters when they are at home. As the narrator's emotional involvement increases, so too does that of the reader.

Through the next several couplets, the narrator's observations record less serious emotions. Harold loves to study Londa's hair under a microscope, and Londo loves to braid her horse's mane. The narrator then feels sorry for Fancy Dancer, presumably the horse, who is bothered by whiskers in its nose. The idea of the horse's nose leads the narrator to think of "Ogden Smythe / who loves blowing his nose on postage stamps." By this point in the poem, the word love has been used in many ways, even ridiculous ways like this one.

The narrator brings up the subject of the students' teacher, Ursula Twombly, in the fourteenth couplet. All of the observations that the narrator has made so far have been missed by Ursula Twombly, the teacher, "who does not know the half of it." One should note too that at this point of the poem the structure completely changes. The narrator has presented a picture of her classmates in circumstances and relationships that are not created by the teacher. The teacher is unaware of these circumstances, to the gossip the narrator is passing on about the class members. By contrast, one student's circumstances are the product of the teacher's actions: the child who sits in the corner wearing the dunce cap.

The girl has on "woolen stockings" but is sitting next to the radiator. Like the florist Marieko, mentioned earlier, this little girl is also involved with a "paper cone." Also like Marieko, this little girl has done something wrong. Unlike Marieko, though, who places flowers in a paper cone, this little girl is humiliated because she must wear the paper cone on her head. Marieko's mistake (punching in the wrong code) can be easily rectified, one can assume. The error might cause momentary hardship (frustration, possible confusion in inventory, and maybe even a loss of money), but the emotional consequences are nothing in comparison with this little girl's humiliation. This child, who sits with "her hands / in her lap and her head bowed down," has lost all sense of self-worth.

She is fighting back tears, unable to look at all the other students; while her classmates are in a group, she is isolated. All this little girl wants is to die.

Readers might question why the narrator does not ask for prayers for this girl. Instead, the narrator asks the reader to pray for the teacher who must be indifferent to the pain of her students and especially unaware of the despair she has caused by singling out this child for punishment. A dunce cap implies a slow learner, someone who is too stupid to do adequate work. The young girl is completely overwhelmed by her teacher's inability to see her worth and wants nothing more than to die. If there is a slow learner in this poem, the narrator implies that it is not the little girl but the teacher, which makes the image of the little girl even more disheartening.

In the last couplet, however, there is a glimmer of hope. Like Genghis Khan who gathers the Tartars into his ranks as they spread out of Mongolia into Eastern Europe to conquer the lands, maybe this little girl is also ready to "roll gloriously into battle." Maybe her wish to die is not a gesture of surrender or a sign of defeat. Maybe her "sincere" and "fervent wish to die" can be turned into a willingness to fight on a battlefield to free herself from the unreasonable will of the adults who try to control her. Maybe while she sits on that stool, someone prays for her, and that prayer is to give her the courage to defy those who try to oppress her. In this case, the teacher's efforts, both in teaching the children to pray and in enforcing some kind of discipline through punishment and example, fail. What is learned by these children has more to do with the circumstances of their separate lives and the compassion they feel for each other.

Source: Joyce Hart, Critical Essay on "Sentimental Education," in *Poetry for Students*, Thomson Gale, 2007.

Thomson Gale

In the following essay, the critic gives a critical analysis of Ruefle's work.

Prolific poet and educator Mary Ruefle is a professor of English in the M.F.A. program at Vermont College. In addition to appearing in several anthologies, Ruefle's works have won her numerous prizes and prestigious fellowships, including a National Endowment for the Arts fellowship, a Guggenheim fellowship, and an American Academy of Arts and Letters award in literature.

In *Cold Pluto*, the "audacious" Ruefle "writes lyrical poetry that stays afloat above the riptides of intense emotion by virtue of fierce concentration on strong images," observed Peter Harris in the *Virginia Quarterly Review*. In the poem "Peeling the Orange," for example, she turns the act into a symbolic experience in which the peel resembles "Pile of hides. Strips & scraps of flannel," and in which the small spray of juice becomes a "burst of mist, an aerosol attempt/at speaking." In "Merinque," the poet asks a series of questions, those early in the sequence seemingly mundane, but each fixing a distinct, emotionally charged and physically focused moment or activity: "Did you rip up the photo?/Did you pick up the baby/And kiss its forehead?/Did you drive into a deer?" Each question is "poignant in its evanescence, but overwhelming unless we understand what principle links them," Harris commented. "Have you been born?," the poet asks, bringing into focus a theme of living a rich and fulfilled life, and experiencing all the small and simple acts and sensations it provides. In the final lines, the poem embraces the mundane aspects of mortality: "What book will you be reading when you die?/If it's a good one, you won't finish it./If it's a bad one, what a shame." This poem, like others of Ruefle's works, "are about living one's life with great intensity, with interrogative adamancy; they challenge us more or less literate readers, drowsed by the fume of poppies, to wake up before we're beheaded," Harris concluded.

The collection titled *Post Meridian* contains "short, elegantly worked poems" paired on facing pages by subject, frame of reference, or poetic style, observed a reviewer in *Publishers Weekly*. Carefully constructed "patterns of sound" serve to "seduce the reader away from the hunt for logical development" within the works, the reviewer added. In one poem the lines "The circle of flame over the stove/is blue and I walk towards it./Picking a thread from my mouth," inspiring the *Publishers Weekly* reviewer to conclude that readers "will find ample verbal threads here for their own happy picking."

Ruefle's collection *Tristimania* "keeps the whimsy" of many of her earlier works while adding "a strong undertone of bleak regret," noted another *Publishers Weekly* critic. The poems contemplate the poet's failures at other undertakings; the sadness of those close to her; and her "wonderment, that the world was full/of so many absent things." Ruefle's longtime readers "might sense more depth here, if a more constrained range," the critic reviewer remarked.

A *Publishers Weekly* reviewer called the poems collected in *Among the Musk Ox People* to be "fast-moving" and "jittery," observing that, "in fluently unpredictable free verse (mostly) and discursive poetic prose (on occasion), Ruefle's work can take in almost anything, the more unexpected the better." The collection "teems with questions, from arch to heartfelt to zealous," remarked *Poetry* reviewer Steven Cramer. Ruefle's intense interrogatories are part of her process of throwing off "stale literary conventions" within her work with a set of techniques that also include "cultivat[ing] a sense of the absurd" where needed, Cramer added. The poet "initiates her best poems with a charged event; a fresh, apt image; a statement with something at stake, then accelerates into the turns," the critic continued, citing the opening lines of the poem "Blood Soup": "The last time I saw father alive he was using/a black umbrella, closed, to beat off some pigeons." Ruefle's "more serious side continues to give her work depth and necessity," the *Publishers Weekly* reviewer concluded of Ruefle's expanding oeuvre.

Source: Thomson Gale, "Mary Ruefle," in *Contemporary Authors Online*, Thomson Gale, 2005.

Stephen C. Behrendt

In the following excerpt, Behrendt's review of the collection praises the language and voice, noting a pervasive sadness that is transformed and unified by the poems themselves.

. . . Although I am undoubtedly writing against the grain to say it, I also find in Mary Ruefle's new collection, *Post Meridian*, a striking element of sadness, even though—or perhaps *because*—the poems are such wildly exuberant exercises in fanciful juxtaposition, in the imagination let loose on a world of possibilities. The word "madcap" comes to mind, with all its paradoxes bright and apparent. For despite all their energy and their startling images, the chaotic world they trace in Ruefle's poems becomes too familiar and too omnipresent for one not to grow uneasy, even to wonder whether the author herself does not see it all as rather too much to bear, too overwhelming, the imaginative overload of our crushing, devouring, daily existence.

A man jumps from a bridge
falling vertically.
I cannot think of a word for this,
for I am thinking of something else,
a plate of lentils in a Dutch painting,
the unknown shoemaker in The Hague
who bought them for a sack of the same,
      dried.
("White Fleck")

Now that the brown mule is dead,
who will transport the roses as they come off
      the mountain?

But a thousand acres of celery
will not row me to the floodgates
so I can put castanets on his tomb.

Now that the brown mule is dead
I want a cargo of tin horns
to keep the flies away
and an agate-handled spoon.
("The Brown Mule")

Ruefle's poems are lively in their language and voice, deft in their verbal variety. They are also wonderfully detailed, their images sharp and crisp as woodsmoke in mountain air. And yet the wood that's being burned is curious, exotic, and one can never quite identify the fragrance, although one seems to trace familiar elements, unfamiliarly combined.

What is the different about *Post Meridian*, in contrast to the other collections, is the very different route by which they arrive at their cumulative intensity. In these poems the oddly juxtaposed images resolve themselves again and again into an almost comforting texture rather than a discordant one, a coming-into-coherence that for the readerly moment draws design from chaos, calm from turbulence. The images and incidents themselves are grounded in familiar life: sorting socks, walking through corn, soccer, the rain, literature itself. Their familiarity, which the poems first render unfamiliar, then familiar again, yields a curious tranquility in the reading of this constantly darting collection. But an unwritten tension seems always to hover just beneath the surface—a need to intervene, somehow, to draw that external (and internal) order and tranquility from elements that seem irreconcilable in their natural state. That intense drive to organize and to civilize imperfectly camouflages a residual sadness, it seems to me, perhaps in the melancholy realization that it is forever necessary to do just this, that left to their wholly natural devices, things will—and do—fall apart.

It takes an adept juggler as well as a crafty illusionist—and a skillful poet—to keep everything in motion and to maintain at least the illusion of a still-possible reassuring and restorative order. This is what Ruefle does in *Post Meridian*.

Source: Stephen C. Behrendt, Review of *Post Meridian*, in *Prairie Schooner*, Vol. 76, No. 3, Fall 2002, pp. 176–77.

SOURCES

Bar-Nadav, Hadara, "Lost Knowledge," in *American Book Review*, January–February 2005, p. 17.

Behrendt, Stephen C., Review of *Post Meridian*, in *Prairie Schooner*, Vol. 76, No. 13, Fall 2002, pp. 171, 176, 177.

Halliday, Mark, "The Arrogance of Poetry," in *Georgia Review*, Vol. 57, No. 2, Summer 2003, pp. 220, 221.

Harris, Peter, "Difficult and Otherwise: New Work by Ruefle, Young, and Aleshire," in *Virginia Quarterly Review*, Vol. 73, No. 4, Autumn 1997, pp. 680, 681.

Review of *Post Meridian*, in *Publishers Weekly* Vol. 247, No. 2, January 10, 2000, p. 58.

Ruefle, Mary, "Sentimental Education," in *Post Meridian*, Carnegie Mellon University Press, 2000, pp. 39–40.

FURTHER READING

Flaubert, Gustave, *Sentimental Education*, Penguin Classics, 2004.

Ruefle borrows the title for her collection of poetry from Flaubert, who in this 1869 novel satirizes the conventions of bourgeois society.

Perkins, David, *A History of Modern Poetry*, Vol. 2: *Modernism and After*, Belknap Press, 2004.

Perkins examines the works of individual poets published up to the twenty-first century as well as important movements such as modernism, beat poetry, and confessional poetry. He notes the distinctiveness and the interconnectedness among the poets in these movements and addresses the critical response to them over the years.

Spiegelman, William, *The Didactic Muse: Scenes of Instruction in Contemporary American Poetry*, Princeton University Press, 2006.

Spiegelman finds parallels between contemporary American poetry and modernist poetry. His focus is on poets as teachers and how contemporary poets have embraced that role.

———, *How Poets See the World: The Art of Description in Contemporary Poetry*, Oxford University Press, 2005.

Spiegelman investigates how poetry makes connections between the word and the image and offers insight into the processes of reading and interpretation. He also explores how word and image are influenced by biographical and cultural factors.

Walch, Timothy, *Parish School: A History of American Catholic Parochial Education from Colonial Times to the Present*, Herder and Herder, 1996.

The text presents a comprehensive overview of Catholic parochial education and its impact beyond the boundaries of the Church, including its influence on immigration and public education.

Walk Your Body Down

J. T. BARBARESE

2005

J. T. Barbarese's poem, "Walk Your Body Down,," published in 2005 in the award-winning collection *The Black Beach*, presents a few intense moments from the narrator's point of view as he observes an urban scene in some undisclosed city and contemplates the meaning of life. Through this poem, the reader witnesses a variety of emotions, including loneliness, frustration, and anger, as the narrator projects his feelings on and draws conclusions about his fellow city dwellers.

Barbarese's narrator observes life around him and tries to make sense of it all. He observes the sounds and sights around him—the arguing couple, the crying baby, the man walking down the middle of the street—and weaves them together with the feelings and collected experiences of his own life, hoping that this will explain the fragmentation he sees. He sees stressful and maniacal behavior and wants to smooth the ragged edges. He senses death and wants to put a comfortable face on it. He tries to remind his readers to claim the lives that have been offered to them as gifts and to enjoy the present moment, before it is too late.

AUTHOR BIOGRAPHY

J. (Joseph) T. Barbarese was born in Philadelphia on May 18, 1948. He attended Franklin and

J. T. Barbarese *(Photograph by Rob McCarron)*

Marshall College, Duke University, and Temple University, where he earned his doctorate. He taught writing at Friends Select School in Philadelphia, as well as at Rutgers University in New Jersey. As of 2007, he had written four books of poetry: *Under the Blue Moon* (1985), *New Science* (1989), *A Very Small World* (2005), and *The Black Beach* (2005), the collection in which "Walk Your Body Down" is found. *Black Beach* won Barbarese the Vassar Miller Prize.

In addition to his poetry, Barbarese also wrote short stories, essays, and literary reviews, which appeared in various magazines, including the *Atlantic, Story Quarterly, Journal of Modern Literature, New York Times*, and *Georgia Review*. Barbarese also translated Euripides's plays, which appeared in *Euripides 4, Ion, Children of Heracles, The Madness of Heracles, Iphigenia in Tauris, Orestes* (1999). He also wrote an afterword for the revised edition of Louisa May Alcott's *Little Men* (2004).

As of 2007, Barbarese was married and had three children.

POEM TEXT

The couple on the left of me
is breaking up, the baby
on the ramp beside us
sings maniacally,
and a middle-aged black guy comes walking   5
down the center of the street,
and he looks rather like me—average build,
gathered into himself like an Arctic bird,
his aloneness at home here,
aloof as an element   10
yet who but he would care,
alone as earth or air
he knows nobody else is like him anywhere,

nothing is more memorable than ourselves.
Look at the way he stutter-steps down the
       center line,   15
look at the way he strides, as if to say,
walk your body proudly into the twilight
past that budded arrangement of sun and
       cloud,
past caskets of neighborhoods,
and all you remember, care for, is yourself   20
up to the moment when the mind leaves the
       curb in its black cab

and the conversations break up, and the people too,
and manic children sing on, in their minds still
       immortal,
and so is their pain
hurled up and down the ramp where the babies
       go up and down   25
like physics experiments
o, walk your body down, don't let it go it alone.

POEM SUMMARY

First Stanza, Lines 1–13

Barbarese's poem "Walk You Body Down" begins with a very ordinary phrase. The narrator sits somewhere, possibly waiting for a bus or train, with strangers all around him. The narrator mentions a couple on his left. He is aware of them, eavesdrops on their conversation, but appears not to know them.

The narrator relates that the couple "is breaking up, the baby." If the reader overlooks the punctuation in this line, the image that is created is violent, and the brutality of this image forces the reader to pay attention, which is probably exactly what the poet intended. Looking more closely, the reader sees the comma in the second line and realizes that the couple is breaking up, arguing, but they are not hurting the baby. The tension between them might be flaring, which may make the narrator uncomfortable.

The baby is sitting on a ramp "beside us," the narrator states. The baby is separated from the couple and the narrator, on a ramp, which implies a taking off point of some kind. The baby, "sings maniacally," setting a tone for the scene. The baby is singing as if it has gone mad. The baby might be feeling the emotions conveyed by the couple. The couple's discomfort is affecting the people around them. But while the narrator just sits there and tries to control his own negative reactions to whatever the couple is doing, the baby sings, letting the whole world around it know exactly how it feels to be in the company of the couple whose relationship is ending. If the baby belongs to the couple, then the emotional discomfort becomes more understandable. Although too young to understand the situation, the baby feels the emotional strain of the couple.

By the fifth line of the poem, the narrator observes a man walking down the street, a man who reminds the narrator of himself. This man seems ordinary enough: he is middle-aged and of average build. However, he is doing something extraordinary: he is walking down the center of the street. The narrator immediately jumps to conclusions about the man, and these reactions are more about how the narrator feels about himself than about what he knows of this man. The narrator projects how he feels onto this stranger. The narrator notices little quirks about him. He then projects how he himself would feel if he were doing what this man is doing. For example, the narrator believes the man is "gathered into himself like an Arctic bird." The fact that the narrator conjures up an image of an Artic bird, as opposed to a tropical bird, makes the reader think about the cold. An Artic bird must find some way to keep warm. When a man is cold, he might wrap his arms around himself in an attempt to contain his body heat. This is what the narrator suggests when he states that the man has "gathered into himself," as if to protect himself from the cold. But the cold is not necessarily physical. It could be an emotional cold, the chill of "aloneness." The narrator sees is his own loneliness. Sitting in the middle of a city of many people, the narrator feels alone in the crowd. Perhaps the couple feel it, too, as they face separating. Separation is also

conveyed by the image of the baby, who is sitting on the ramp without anyone taking care of it. So far in the poem, most images have a touch of this loneliness.

In a strange way, the narrator, in line nine, attempts to create something positive from this sense of aloneness, which he states in the phrase "at home here." This phrase usually conjures a warm feeling. There is a sense of belonging in being at home. However, the home that the narrator is talking about is not warm or friendly but rather one of shared grief or lack of caring. Everyone that the narrator has mentioned is in one way or another ill at ease. Sure, the Artic bird man who is walking down the middle of the street has learned to adapt to the cold, but that does not mean that he is comfortable. He is "aloof as an element," the narrator states. The man has adjusted to his loneliness by detaching himself from his surroundings. He walks down the middle of the street as if he owns it, unaware of eyes scrutinizing him. After all, the narrator states, "who but he would care." In other words, although the streets are crowded, everyone is a stranger to everyone else. No one knows anything about the other people who fill the sidewalks, cars, and buses. No one really cares.

But then the narrator contradicts himself. When this man in the street first appears, one of the first things the narrator comments on is that the man looked like him (the narrator). However, by line thirteen, the narrator switches from this position, stating that this man "knows nobody else is like him anywhere." Not only does this contradict with the narrator's earlier statement in which he is relating to this stranger, but this concept of being unlike everyone else can be taken in two ways. First, it could be a pessimistic sentiment. People look for similarities in other people, so they can relate to one another. If a person cannot find something comparable in another person, it may be hard to share an experience. If everyone felt this way, then that feeling of breaking up would be everywhere. The world would be made up of separated individuals with nothing in common. In a second, more positive reading, the narrator could be referring to a person who enjoys celebrating his uniqueness, his own special gifts or talents that are different from everyone else's. It is hard to know which way the narrator intends this comment until the reader continues on to the next few lines of the poem.

TOPICS FOR FURTHER STUDY

- J. T. Barbarese mentions in his poem "Walk Your Body Down" "manic children" who, like the babies on the ramp, "go up and down." This is possibly an allusion to bipolar disorder or manic depressive illness. Find out what this illness is. What are the symptoms? How does it affect children? What are doctors doing to help children with this illness? Present your research findings to your class.

- Form a panel to discuss Barbarese's use of race, as in the passage, "middle-aged black guy." Pose the question: Why does the poet mention that this man is black? If race is important, why is the couple sitting next to the narrator not described in terms of race? Why are the children not identified by race? What do you think is the purpose of mentioning race at all? To prepare for the panel, make a survey of news articles (print, television, Internet) to see how many times race is an issue. If the focus person is white, is his or her race mentioned? What happens when the focus person is black? Use your findings to open the panel discussion.

- Write a description (about 300 words) of something you have observed that affected you in some way. The subject could be something simple but beautiful, like a walk along a beach, or it could be dramatic, such as witnessing a car accident or the death of a pet. Write this in the form of prose narrative, a story. When you are finished, arrange the lines of your story so that it looks like free verse. Use enjambment to emphasize certain points. Isolate certain phrases that you think represent key descriptions. Rearrange or change words and delete whatever is not necessary so that your poem fits on one page. Read both versions, the prose narrative and the free verse poem to your class. Which one do class members like better? Which one do you prefer? Why?

- Barbarese's poem depicts a city scene. Draw or paint a picture that represents this scene as you imagine it.

Second Stanza, Lines 14–21

In the second stanza, the narrator concentrates on the man in the street. All memories are centered in the body, the narrator points out, and then the body takes on the task of representing oneself to the world. The narrator turns to the man who "stutter-steps down the center line," so out of synch with what everyone else is doing. The man is practically dancing down the street. Not on the sidewalk, he walks in traffic. All the narrator sees is the man's pride. The man is acting as if he owns the world, just as he owns his body, which he is walking "proudly into the twilight." This image suggests impending death. However, this death does not bring with it a connotation of suicide or carelessness. Instead there is a feeling here of performance. The man, at least in the mind of the narrator, is making a statement with his walk. The message to all onlookers, as the narrator interprets it, is to be proud of all those memories that are stored in the body and to walk that body toward the light, past both the beauty of nature (the "budded arrangement of sun and cloud") and the ugliness of manmade structures (the "caskets of neighborhoods"). The last two lines of this stanza deliver the man's message, which is to care for the self, because that is all one has. Until the last breath ("when the mind leaves the curb in its black cab"), one should stay mindful.

Third Stanza, Lines 22–27

At the beginning of the third stanza, the narrator returns to the earlier image of the arguing couple. The narrator repeats the phrase "break up." This time the breaking up is extended, though, to include conversations. Words, the narrator might be inferring, do not always convey the full meaning behind them. The "conversations break up" because of poor reception, a weak connection, or some other distraction, such as a lack of understanding. This results in people not understanding one another, not empathizing with one another. This situation may be the narrator's reason for emphasizing, in the previous stanza, that "all you remember, care for, is yourself." Conversations are difficult, relationships are challenging, and both are susceptible to falling apart. Babies, who believe they are immortal, go on singing. But even they suffer. They are manic. Babies are on the ramp, where they "go up and down / like physics experiments." They are much more susceptible to the up-and-down emotions of the people around them.

Before the poem ends, the narrator reflects, once again, on the man's message, asking the reader to stay aware of his own body and to engage fully in living in the body. Some people, the narrator might be saying, are empty shells. They have abandoned their bodies, walking around on the earth like lost souls, detached from their own experiences. To emphasize this in the final lines, the narrator reminds the reader: "o, walk your body down, don't let it go it alone."

THEMES

Urban Living
The narrator in Barbarese's poem "Walk Your Body Down" sets the scene in the first few lines, making it clear that this is an urban setting. The narrator does so not by talking about groups of people but by insinuating that he is sitting in the midst of strangers, who do not appear happy. The narrator is aware of an argument going on by two people near him; he suspects they are breaking up. The narrator's mention of a ramp, a man walking in the street, and "caskets of neighborhoods," all convey the city setting. The poet seems to be saying that people are in proximity in the city, but that does not mean they relate to one another or feel connected as a group.

Isolation and Loneliness
A sense of isolation and loneliness pervades this poem. First, there is the breaking up of the two

people who sit next to the narrator. The baby sitting on a ramp without being attended to also suggests isolation of individuals. A ramp is an in-between place. It is neither where the narrator is sitting nor some place else, but a bridge connecting two different levels. The ramp signifies the place "where the babies go up and down / like physics experiments." In this sense, the narrator may be suggesting the emotional rise and fall that people experience. In the scene, the baby is not moving but is stuck on the ramp, isolated from the adults.

Another image of isolation is that of the man in the street. Everyone else, it can be assumed, is walking on the sidewalks or driving in cars. This man is in the street, making it a stage in a sense, seemingly very much into himself. Although his separation from others does not seem negative, he still is alone.

The phrase "caskets of neighborhoods" also adds to the separation. Caskets are boxes big enough for only one body. They are the ultimate enclosures of separation since they contain the corpse to be buried. Although the word "neighborhoods" implies congregations of many people, when used with the word "caskets," the image of neighborhoods implies not so much a co-mingling of people as a kind of stacking up of individuals, a collection of individuals each packaged in his own cell or box.

Specific phrases in this poem refer to isolation and aloneness, such as "his aloneness at home here" and "alone as earth or air." But the last line in the poem attempts to counteract the theme of loneliness: the narrator suggests, "don't let it [the body] go it alone."

Mortality
The first reference to death in this poem occurs in the second stanza, when the narrator is watching the man walk in the street and describes him as walking "proudly into the twilight." Twilight may suggest death, as in the twilight of one's life, marking the end of it. Even the "budded arrangement of sun and cloud" seems to suggest the floral displays that often surround a person's casket. Reinforcing this allusion is the narrator's mention, in the next line, of "caskets." As the second stanza ends, the narrator refers to the "moment when the mind leaves the curb in its black cab." Here, the word "leaves" also implies death, with the "black cab" reminiscent of a hearse. Then as the third stanza continues with

Cities are often seen as lonely places in spite of the large crowds that may live there. People may stand or live close to others without ever speaking a word (© *Michael Klinec/Alamy*)

this image, the narrator brings forth the image of not only conversations breaking up but also people. This could be a reference to what it may feel like at the moment of death, when ties to life are slowly broken, as the mind slowly releases all its memories. Then the narrator states that only babies go on singing at this moment; that is because they still believe they are immortal. Adults know better. Adults are well aware of their mortality. They know that one day, they will die.

End of Relationships

There are several different endings of relationships in this poem. The most obvious is the couple who are "breaking up." This relationship, the narrator suggests, somehow affects the baby who is singing "maniacally," perhaps sensing that its relationship with the couple, as the baby has known it up to this point, is also breaking up.

There are also references to the end of life. That the "mind leaves the curb" implies an end of relationship between the mind and body. The leave-taking occurs, as the mind faces death. In the last stanza, there are more endings, as "conversations break up, and the people too." Conversations are no longer being maintained because communications does not occur. People are falling apart too, no longer relating to others or to themselves.

STYLE

Imagery

Imagery is used in poetry to convey meaning through pictures. Where concrete words alone fall short of providing the meaning the poet wants to convey, images are used so the reader can better envision the subject. For example, the "baby on the ramp" is an image that the poet uses to imply the baby's isolation. Another image comes in the simile of the man, whom the narrator describes as "gathered into himself like an Artic bird." This same man is also "aloof as an element," the narrator states. Here, the poet defines an emotional state with a scientific term. In creating this image, the poet emphasizes the man's singleness. What could be more separate than an element, a fundamental form of matter? The poet creates a similar image in the phrase "alone as earth or air."

In the phrase "budded arrangement of sun and cloud," the poet accomplishes two things. First, there is the image of floral arrangement, such as those given at a funeral. In this interpretation, the poet imbues the image with a sense of death. However, the poet creates another interesting effect. By referring to the sun and cloud as a "budded arrangement," the poet encourages the reader to look at nature in a new way. Clouds and the sun are so much a part of everyday experience that people might forget to notice them. However, the poet is telling the reader to look again, to see the sky as extraordinary and renew his relationship with nature.

In the third stanza, the poet refers to children, who although they are singing are in pain, "hurled up and down the ramp where the babies go up and down like physics experiments." The children are, in some ways, like pawns, the poet suggests, at the mercy of the emotions and actions of the adults around them. The poet suggests that the emotional up-and-down ride that children are subjected to is like some kind of physics experiment that measures relationships between objects. This image suggests that children are seen as having no emotions. They are likened to the elements by the adults who handle them. They are hurled from one place to another (that is why they are on the ramps) as the adults fail in their communications. All of this is implied through imagery.

Tone

The tone of the poem reflects the poet's attitude toward the subject. Tone can also imply mood. Barbarese's "Walk Your Body Down" expresses many emotions, the frustration of the baby, the depression of the couple, the self-absorbed contentment of the man in the street. However, the narrator's tone seems didactic, as if the poet has a message that needs to be conveyed to the reader. First, the poet exposes various negative emotions, pointing out the break down in relationships and communications and the pain that it causes the children. Next, the poet offers a reminder: life is too short to waste in on these feelings. One needs to walk through the congested highways of life, enjoying the moment. One should live fully in

one's own body, where all the memories and experiences are stored. Emphasizing this message is the tone of the last sentence in the poem; in the last line, the narrator directly tells the reader to walk in the body. Thus the poem ends by repeating the title's statement.

Enjambment

Enjambment occurs when the subject of one line continues grammatically into the subsequent lines. Enjambment occurs in the second, third, and fourth lines of the first stanza: "the baby / on the ramp beside us / sings maniacally." The line breaks emphasize the isolation of the baby. Too, the enjambment requires the reader to move toward the period without pausing, causing the poem to read more quickly through the syntax of the sentence.

Free Verse

Some formal poetry has a strict rhyme and metrical structure. Lines are measured by the number of beats or syllables, each line containing the same number. However, in free verse, there is no specific structure that dictates line length, rhythm, or rhyme scheme. Therefore the length of the line, that is, the number of beats in each line, can vary.

In free verse, the poet decides to end a line for the poem's sake or for the effect that the poet wants to create for the poem. For example, in the fourth line, the poet has the phrase "sings maniacally" alone on the line. Isolating the phrase like this emphasizes it. A baby singing maniacally is an unusual image. This image emphasizes the weirdness of the scene. The baby sounds strange, unnatural. In the sixth line, the poet isolates the phrase "down the center of the street." The poet emphasizes the man's location by isolating this image on a line. The poet repeats this type of isolation for the phrase, in line twelve, "alone as earth or air," once again emphasizing the man's separate location. Then in the third stanza, in line 24, the poet wants to emphasize the pain of the children. The poet first mentions that the children are singing, which one would assume is a sign of happiness. This is not what the poet intends, though. It is their pain that the poet wants to point out: the phrase "and so is their pain" is given its own line.

HISTORICAL CONTEXT

Married Couples Breaking Up

In 2005, over 2 million people were married, according to the National Center for Health Statistics. A large number of these marriages, according to statistics, were anticipated to end in divorce. Divorce statistics for 2005 include figures such as those found in the state of Florida, where over 81,000 divorces occurred in comparison to a little over 158,000 marriages. In the state of New York, a little more than 53,000 divorce papers were filed, compared to little more than 135,000 marriage in that same year. The center concluded that for 2005, for every 1000 marriages, about 20 would end in divorce. Although the number of divorces dropped sharply after the 1980s, so did the number of people getting married. Living together without getting married seemed increasingly popular, in which cases people can separate without getting a divorce.

Children are affected by divorce, and their problems can be overlooked by divorcing parents who are coping with by their own challenges. According to the American Academy of Child and Adolescent Psychology (http://www.aacap.org), children whose parents go through a divorce can have problems sleeping, can become depressed, and can go through withdrawal due to stress and their sense of loss, which can then lead to poor grades in school, lowered self-esteem, and troubles in their own relationships with friends.

Increasing Urban Populations

According to an article by the British Broadcasting Corporation (BBC), the United Nations stated that in the early 2000s more than half the world's population lived in urban settings. The trend toward living in the city began in the early twentieth century, with an increase from 14 percent of all people living in cities around the world in 1900 to 47 percent doing so by the end of the century.

Worldwide, cities with one million or more people went from 83 in 1950 to 411 at the beginning of the twenty-first century. With the world's population anticipated in 2007 to double in about thirty-eight years, an increasing number of very large cities, with populations of over 10 million, was expected. In 2000, there were only eighteen mega-cities, for example, New York, Tokyo, Mexico City, and Bombay. In 2005, that number had increased to twenty. By 2010, the United Nations predicted that the number would rise to twenty-two mega-cities worldwide.

As of 2007, about 80 percent of the U.S. population lived in an urban setting, and the tendency to live in cities was predicted to continue. However, movement to the city was anticipated to slow for very large cities. In the case of cities with over ten million, the area becomes saturated, with little additional room for growth. Then midsize cities become the destination for people seeking urban locations. In the early 2000s, Phoenix, San Antonio, San Diego, Jacksonville, Columbus, and Seattle were some of the midsize cities that were experiencing rapid growth.

Children's Literature

Children are often represented in Barbarese's poetry. In his poem "Walk Your Body Down,," Barbarese uses children to show the effects of adult actions, reactions, and breakdowns. Moreover, Barbarese taught children's literature on the college level, having made a study of this genre. Given this focus on children in Barbarese's work and his life, it is relevant to take a look at children's literature and its historical development.

Although fables, fairytales, and other stories have been used for many centuries to teach and to delight children, the credit for initiating the publication of children's literature is given to John Newbery (1713–1767), a British bookseller. Newbery, for whom the Newbery Award in children's literature is named, is supposedly the first person to offer books specifically geared to children. These books varied from alphabet books to novels for children, a new idea in the realm of bookselling at that time. One of the first novels to be published was reportedly Newbery's own (although some historians believe that Oliver Goldsmith might have been the real author of this story), *The History of Little Goody Two Shoes* in 1764, a variation on the fairytale *Cinderella* and the source of the saying that someone is a "goody-two-shoes," a reference to someone who always does what is right or good.

During the nineteenth century, children's literature continued to develop. Lewis Carroll (1832–1898) wrote his *Alice's Adventures in Wonderland*, published in 1865; Rudyard Kipling

(1865–1936) published his *Jungle Book* in 1894; and Robert L. Stevenson (1850–1894) penned his most famous work *Treasure Island* in 1883. The popularity of these books indicates the large audience of children they had.

During the twentieth century children's literature continued to grow. Moreover, children's literature became a subject taught in college, and several critical studies appeared on the subject, including those done through research centers such as the one at Rutgers where as of 2007 Barbarese worked at the Center for Children and Childhood Studies.

CRITICAL OVERVIEW

Although the poetry of J. T. Barbarese can be found in many literary magazines and journals, his poetry collections have not been widely reviewed. This is true for Barbarese's collection *The Black Beach*, in which the poem "Walk Your Body Down" appears. Some poets, such as Eleanor Wilner (*Reversing the Spell*, 1998) have commented positively on Barbarese's work, and Maxine Kumin (*Jack and Other New Poems*, 2005) has stated how she enjoyed Barbarese's depictions of urban life.

The Black Beach won the 2004 Vassar Miller Prize, an award sponsored by the University of North Texas Press. Yet one of the few reviews available for Barbarese's collection is not very complimentary. Dan Chiasson, writing for *Poetry*, states: "If you choose the everyday as your subject matter, you risk inconsequence," which is how Chiasson sums up some of Barbarese's poems. Chiasson claims that Barbarese has a tendency to write poetry in a style that Chiasson calls "gritty-pretty." Barbarese, Chiasson writes, often begins with something pretty, such as a field of flowers then ends with a gritty image such as a truck driver. At another time, Barbarese opens a poem with an image of the narrator's daughter and closes with reference to the Holocaust. This pattern does not sit well with Chiasson, who concludes his review with the statement: "gritty-pretty has got to go."

In contrast, a reviewer for the *Wisconsin Bookwatch* praises Barbarese's collection. This reviewer points out that the collection "contrasts between everyday acts, such as putting children to bed or coaching Little League, and the mysteries that linger beyond the commonplace." The

WHAT DO I READ NEXT?

- Barbarese in his 1986 collection *Under the Blue Moon* focuses on everyday events and uses them to help depict and explain the world.

- Recipient of the MacArthur Prize (often referred to as the Genius Prize), Eleanor Wilner's 1997 collection, *Reversing the Spell*, contains previously published work along with new poems. Wilner has been called a lifelong civil rights advocate, and her poems reflect her vision of art and life.

- Maxine Kumin's *Jack and Other Poems* (2005) centers on nature, such as found around her New Hampshire farm, and on political history. The poet looks for answers to the bloodshed and political upheaval that bombards her in the news.

- Pulitzer Prize–winning poet Mary Oliver has written a guide for budding poets, *The Poetry Handbook* (1994). Oliver explains various aspects of the craft of writing a poem and provides examples from such great poets as James Wright and Elizabeth Bishop. Oliver even offers her views on the merits of writers' workshops for poetry.

reviewer maintains: "*The Black Beach* is a profoundly inspired view of God and the cosmos as surely as it is a celebration of unsung heroes of parenting."

CRITICISM

Joyce Hart

Hart has degrees in literature and creative writing. In this essay, she explores the title's meaning in Barbarese's poem.

J. T. Barbarese's poem "Walk Your Body Down" offers clear images of city life that

> THE MAN IS TALKING TO THE PEOPLE AROUND HIM THROUGH HIS ACTIONS. HE IS THE BEARER OF THE MESSAGE, AND THE MESSAGE, ACCORDING TO THIS POEM, IS THAT PEOPLE NEED TO STAY AT HOME IN THEIR BODIES AND LIVE THEIR EXPERIENCES THROUGH THEIR BODIES."

include a couple arguing, a baby singing, crowded living conditions typical of urban living, and a sense of isolation felt by individuals in the midst of city crowds. There is little abstraction in the images, and the meanings or connotations are rather easily grasped. However, the title of the poem, as well as its message, is a little more difficult to understand. Just what exactly does the narrator mean by the recommendation to "walk your body down?" How does one do it? And is there anything in the poem itself that helps the reader answer these questions and understand the meaning of the title?

There is no way for a reader to know what the title means as the poem begins. After all, "walking one's body down" could refer to something negative, such as wearing one's body out until it falls down. In the second line of the poem, there is mention of breaking up, which could also be a reference to running something down until it no longer works. So at the beginning of the poem, there is no clue offered as to whether the title refers to something good or something bad.

In the first stanza, the narrator also offers a distressed baby that is sitting on a ramp, neither here nor there, alone and seemingly unprotected. Included with the arguing couple, the opening images, so far, suggest a breakdown of some kind, either in relationships, communications, or emotions. But when the narrator focuses attention on the middle-aged man something positive occurs. Here, the reader can grasp that this man and his way of walking, as well as the title, are meant to contradict the negative energy of the scene. The way the man walks down the center of the street ties him to the title, and readers can assume that the man is also connected to

the meaning or message of the poem. The man in the street probably conveys what the title means.

This middle-aged man is described as self-contained and aloof, and no one cares about him. The narrator describes this man as he sees him, of course, through the lens of his own projections. Immediately the narrator relates to him, recognizing something familiar in the way the man moves and acts. It is interesting to note that the motion of the poem changes at the end of the first stanza. Here, the narrator distinguishes this man from the crowd, separating him from the city scene and from the narrator himself. Despite the fact that he identifies with the man, the narrator states that this man is unlike anyone else. Up until this point, everyone mentioned in the poem seems to be a bit off kilter. The couple is arguing or discussing breaking up. The baby is maniacal or a bit crazed. But the man in the street seems completely disconnected from reality. Who else would put his life in danger for no apparent reason? But at this point in the poem, the narrator says this man is unique, and from this statement on, something positive begins to happen. The narrator starts to admire the man for his walking down the center of the street, despite the irrationality of that act. At first it seems that the narrator praises the man merely because the man is different from all the people around them. However, in the next stanza, the narrator's thoughts become a bit clearer, as does the meaning of the title.

The second stanza gives a sense that the opening images, which feel tense and agitated, run contrary to the title. The images that are provided are negative, whereas the title offers hope or, at least, some sense of direction. In the beginning of the poem, everything appears to be breaking up or breaking down. There are repeated images of suffering. But in the second stanza, in the middle of all this negativity, the narrator becomes focused on something else, something that is not breaking up at all: the man, who is now dancing, or making "stutter-steps," down the center line. The narrator is amazed. "Look at the way he strides," the narrator tells the reader, demanding that the reader pay attention. As the narrator watches, he is filled with pride because the middle-aged man is so confident and perfectly aware of what he is doing. The man is enjoying himself, more so than anyone else in the poem.

Why has the narrator chosen this man to deliver the message of the poem? What does this man represent? First, given his age, the man may be more aware of his mortality than a young couple or children are. He may realize time is precious. He is less likely to waste time in arguments, marrying for the wrong reasons, ignoring children who are in need. Time, like life, is to be appreciated, the narrator seems to be saying. Then, too, the man walks toward the twilight. In other words, this man approaches the end of his life. He is not afraid of death. He is not hiding from death. He is fully aware of it, and that is what motivates him. If one ignores one's own mortality, there is the chance that one may not live each moment fully. To be aware of death is to be mindful that time runs out, which in turn makes one appreciate every moment, every experience, and every emotion. This man walks not just for himself, according to the narrator, but for everyone who is watching him. "He strides," the narrator states, "as if to say, walk your body proudly into the twilight." The man is talking to the people around him through his actions. He is the bearer of the message, and the message, according to this poem, is that people need to stay at home in their bodies and live their experiences through their bodies.

Then the narrator states: "nothing is more memorable than ourselves." In other words, people are memorable, worth remembering. "O, walk your body down," the narrator states at the end of the poem. "Don't let it go it alone." In other words, people should dance through their lives as the man stutter-steps down the street. The man sees the "caskets of neighborhoods," the negative aspects of life, but this does not stop him from dancing. Although the man has withdrawn into himself in order to protect his warmth, he still takes chances. Regardless of the fact that he knows he is "alone as earth or air," he strides proudly. Because he recognizes his own uniqueness, he not only enjoys his life but also becomes the messenger to others, reminding other people how to benefit from theirs.

Source: Joyce Hart, Critical Essay on "Walk Your Body Down," in *Poetry for Students*, Thomson Gale, 2007.

Klay Dyer

Dyer holds a Ph.D. in English literature and has published extensively on fiction, poetry, film, and television. He is also a freelance university

> *IMAGINING AHEAD IN TIME TO THE MOMENT OF HIS OWN DEATH, WHEN THE MIND/SPIRIT AND BODY SEPARATE PERMANENTLY, THE SPEAKER REACHES HIS LYRIC EPIPHANY, A MOMENT OF PROFOUND ILLUMINATION WHEN THE IMPLICATIONS OF HIS EARLIER STANCE (WALKING ALONE DOWN THE CENTER LINE) IS REVEALED."*

teacher, writer, and educational consultant. In this essay, he discusses "Walk Your Body Down" as a poem that explores the speaker's realization that leading a controlled life, a wholly structured life, is what denies him access to the experiences of walking his body through a richly textured, albeit often painful, world.

Lyric poetry stresses emotional responses to personal struggles and to the fears associated with living in the contemporary world. For the speaker in J. T. Barbarese's "Walk Your Body Down" these fears come from a fragmenting sense of self and from a world that is no longer a familiar place. Trapped in a world that appears to be defined by the dynamics of "breaking up" and maniacal singing, the speaker finds himself in a world he struggles to understand. He finds himself withdrawing into an isolating "aloneness," an "aloof[ness]" from the society of which he is a part. He feels, like the "middle-aged black guy" he sees "walking / down the center of the street" as though he has been displaced from a harsh and uncaring world. It is a world, he acknowledges in the opening stanza, that leaves him feeling disconnected, "gathered into himself like an Arctic bird." In this poem, the speaker is doomed to feel "alone as earth or air," locked forever in his belief that "nobody else is like him anywhere."

Trapped by angst about a world that is shifting its values and definitions, Barbarese's speaker explores his own unconscious, only to find, or so he believes, that he is essentially alone in the world, walking down the center line of his life in order not to touch the feelings or ideas that invite him to either side. The life he lives is an inward looking one that refuses, by the power of his will, to avoid interaction with the world around him. He chooses, as the poem opens, to remain a man of disconnection rather than a man of engagement, a man who confuses his dedication to the center line with superiority and with safety.

Barbarese imagines his speaker as someone struggling with his sense of displacement in the world. From the opening moments of the poem, Barbarese leaves readers with the picture of a man trapped in his own private space, unable to escape and unwilling to believe that others can help. The speaker establishes clearly the psychological tone of his introspections: these are the ideas of a man who has given himself over to a sense of loss and to a physical, spiritual, and psychological isolation.

Despite an overwhelming sense of isolation and disconnection, the speaker describes community when he comes across a "middle-aged black guy" walking a center line. Whether this man is, in fact, another person or the speaker of the poem seeing himself from a different perspective is irrelevant. What is important is that in this other walker the speaker comes to recognize the inclusivity of "ourselves" as distinct from the more exclusive and limiting "myself." The shift in language to include recognition of someone else on the line is a signal that the speaker of the poem is not as isolated as he first appears. As the poem unfolds, the speaker evolves toward companionship and through that companionship toward a sense of wholeness and the motivation to mobility. The speaker's language, for instance, suggests that he and the other man will join together on the center line in the spirit of the journey being undertaken.

Balancing between the exclusiveness of the first person pronoun (the I/me voice of the poem) and the more inclusive you, us, and our connections of the poem, the speaker begins to combine his sensitive inner character and his more cynical, outward self. In these moments of imaginative negotiation with another man walking down the same center line, the speaker addresses his own personality, as if looking into a mirror and speaking to and about his own reflection. It is as though in these opening images of break ups and infant wailings that the speaker sets himself on a threshold, dancing carefully along a ledge of connecting and disconnecting with the world around him.

Shifting to mobility from immobility, the poem uses action verbs "look," "walk," and "remember," to convey a possibility of movement and connection that expands the perspective of the speaker. In the actions of the second stanza, the poem begins to move "past" (another often repeated word) the stagnancy and dullness of the world that the speaker had seemed determined to inhabit as the poem opened.

Tellingly, the second stanza concludes with the speaker imagining a moment when, as he puts it, "the minds leaves the curb in its black cab." Imagining ahead in time to the moment of his own death, when the mind/spirit and body separate permanently, the speaker reaches his lyric epiphany, a moment of profound illumination when the implications of his earlier stance (walking alone down the center line) is revealed. As the second stanza closes, in other words, the speaker realizes that he can move from a position of displacement toward placement within the community of wailing babies, arguing couples, and people holding conversations. Having moved "past" his limiting dedication to "the center line," the speaker sees life through a different lens and as having a whole new range of possibilities.

The discoveries of this new and inclusive opportunity brings the speaker into two related and potentially problematic states. He is exposed to a new world that slips beyond his ability to articulate its complexities. The discoveries that he encounters are not themselves poetic musings on a life lived joyfully but are more like "stutter-steps" or mutterings that slide inevitably into incompleteness. "Conversations break up" and are deferred into promises of maturity. He looks to celebrate the cries of the "manic children" for what they are, raucous declarations of youthful vigor, while at the same time hoping for something more substantive and harmonious in the future.

At the same time, and even in the celebratory squeals of the children, the speaker comes to recognize that a life lived off the center line will involve an acknowledgement of "pain." With openness comes *both* comfort (of connection and belonging) and pain, that takes hold inevitably, like the laws of physics.

Life is not about walking down the center line, the speaker comes to recognize, but is more akin to being "hurled up and down [a] ramp" on the edge of having control and losing it. But as the speaker learns during the course of the poem, to engage life fully is not to avoid the ramp (the ups and downs) but to engage the contours and dynamics of its angles with knowledge and with openness. The ramp is to be engaged with pride and companionship. As the speaker observes of the other line walker in the poem, the message is to "walk your body proudly into the twilight" and to ensure that it does not "go it alone."

At first trapped in a veritable *cul de sac* of psychological inertia that collapses the energy of the poem into a straight line, the speaker transcends his sense of living trapped in a world that is fractured in terms of his psychology and his language. The angst he feels, however deep and existential, is finally dismantled by his willingness to focus on the world's complexities. A perception that once denied circularity and elevation in favor of a flat line of control is expanded in the poem in such a way that the speaker identifies himself, finally, as a "memorable" part of a complex world. Exhausted from struggling to remain centered, the speaker steps away from the line and into a reality within which fullness of experience, both sensory and revelatory, will be realized.

Source: Klay Dyer, Critical Essay on "Walk Your Body Down," in *Poetry for Students*, Thomson Gale, 2007.

David Kelly

Kelly is an instructor of creative writing and literature. In this essay, he examines the ways that this poem implicitly talks about the problem of alienation, and the answers that it offers to the problem

Poetry can be powerfully, breathtakingly effective when it gives a clear and concrete vision of life. It can also, however, be simply too concrete sometimes, when the vision of the world that it offers is so tightly focused that readers can only recognize objects and events in the poem but cannot make meaning of them. And then there is the other extreme, the poem that is all about what goes on in the writer's mind, filled with ideas that never quite relate to the physical world. When poetry goes wrong, it often means that the poet was unable to strike a workable balance between observation and meditation, between objectivity and subjectivity. Readers can feel left out of the poetic process if either the world of the mind or the world of the body is too dominant.

J. T. Barbarese is one poet who strikes a clear balance between observation and emotion without tilting too strongly toward either side.

> READERS MAY THINK THAT THEY KNOW THE SPEAKER'S ISOLATION BECAUSE IT IS REFLECTED BY THE MAN IN THE STREET, BUT THEN THEY NEED TO ASK THEMSELVES: CAN THE SPEAKER REALLY BE ISOLATED IF HE SEES HIMSELF REFLECTED IN ANOTHER PERSON?"

He often takes this balance as the subject of his work, as in his poem "Walk Your Body Down." In this poem, Barbarese describes what seems to be an everyday street scene. With strategic placement of his observations, though, and careful arrangement of the details, the poet is able to reveal more about the poem's speaker than letting the speaker explain himself ever could.

From the very start, "Walk Your Body Down" approaches the question of subjectivity by addressing what an individual is. The first few lines of the poem give quick sketches of characters that may be in physical proximity to each other but are trapped in their isolation. There is a couple in the process of breaking up. There is a baby whose uncomfortable crying is described as maniacal singing. And then there is the poem's speaker, observing the others—the distinction between him and them is a clear-cut one. They are the described subjects, and his is the subjective point of view, commenting on them. The poem gives the speaker's perspective, but without really revealing his views.

The only physical detail given about the setting is that these characters are on a ramp. The poet does not give readers much about the objective world, but they can piece it together if they are willing to speculate and take suggestions to their logical conclusions. This is obviously a public place, one that is modern enough in design to accommodate wheeled conveyances and casual enough that a baby would be brought there. It is outside. The signs point to a park: a pleasant setting for walking a baby, even if it is possibly too bucolic for a break-up. Since no one else is mentioned, and since babies do not go to public places by themselves, it is quite likely that the baby referred to as being "on the ramp beside us" is, in fact, with the speaker and may be his own. Using such a strained, abstract expression to refer to one's own child indicates the speaker's sense of alienation, the poem's main concern.

As the first stanza progresses, the speaker takes notice of what turns out to be the poem's most interesting, most clearly described character. He is introduced as a "middle-aged black guy" with an "average build," which tells readers practically nothing about him. There are two things, though, that make him important. First, the speaker thinks that this stranger resembles him. He sees himself reflected in the man walking up the middle of the street. Also, the man distinguishes himself with his unusual behavior, which just looks odd at first but ends up being a key to the question of subjectivity and objectivity that troubles the speaker.

There is no clear reason for why the speaker should identify with this man. That his build is average means that he is similar to many other people. His racial identity makes him similar to others. The thing the speaker seems to relate to most is that he is "gathered to himself like an Arctic bird." Given what has already been established about the speaker's sense of isolation—that he observes his child with curiosity and sees hostility around him—this observation says much more about the speaker than it does about the man he is describing. This speaker does not have to mention his feelings in order to convey the fact that he feels distanced from people. Barbarese then complicates his readers' chances of understanding the speaker's emotions by adding a self-contradicting element. Readers may think that they know the speaker's isolation because it is reflected by the man in the street, but then they need to ask themselves: can the speaker really be isolated if he sees himself reflected in another person?

The solitary figure in the street introduces the following discussion of loneliness. Though the speaker knows nothing about the man, having never met him, he purports to be able to instantly read his body language well enough to claim that aloneness is, for him, natural, like one of the atomic elements, like "earth or air." This connection between alienation and the mechanical nature of the material universe is echoed later in the poem, when the speaker refers to babies (not just his own, but others too) as being pushed up and down the ramp "like physics experiments." Both descriptions share a stubborn refusal to acknowledge an internal, subjective life in the speaker or the babies.

It is this sort of casual associations that makes "Walk Your Body Down" able to imply much more beyond the events described in it. Barbarese draws a connection, via physics, between infancy and the man in the street, and then he goes on to draw a connection, via recognition, between the man and the speaker of the poem. Once this circuit is complete and accepted by the reader, the poem's speaker has a right to claim he understands the thoughts going on within all parties mentioned.

What is not made clear, however, is whether the jump made by his identification is real or imaginary. The structure of "Walk Your Body Down" does not allow Barbarese any room to comment on whether it is interpretation or psychological projection that makes the poem's narrator think he knows how the man in the street feels. If it is interpretation, then readers can accept his claims about the man as the truth, but there are good odds that the speaker is just projecting his own sense of loneliness onto the other man. When the speaker says of the other man that "his aloneness [is] at home here," he is clearly speaking of his own feelings, but do these feelings really apply to both of them? The actual nature of the relationship between these two men is the poem's greatest mystery.

Whether the narrator shares the other man's feelings or is just making up a fantasy about him in order to understand himself, the important thing is that, in the end, the poem offers a cure for loneliness, a way to resolve the pain caused by the estrangement of mind from body. This is what the speaker learns from the man walking in the street. Regardless of whether the other man finds this a good resolution—and, from his cool demeanor, it is likely that he does—the important thing is that the speaker of the poem feels it is true.

The process of overcoming isolation starts early, even before the problem is identified. Soon after the other man's arrival on the scene, the narrator begins, interestingly, to address another person. The second and third lines of the second stanza direct some unnamed and unexplained person to "look at" the other man's movements. This is more than a case of the poetic convention that lets a speaker address the audience in the second person. For one thing, it comes in late, more than half way through the poem, and even then it is not carried consistently throughout the remaining lines, and so cannot really be considered a shift in the poem's style.

Another thing that makes this form of address stand out is that it bears such a slight relationship to the lives of those addressed or the person doing the addressing. Instead of discussing the events that have already been described, it directs readers' attention to physical details that they cannot see: things that are happening in the world of the poem, but that have not yet been explained. Giving commands in this way is a more emphatic, more excited way of calling attention to the details that the speaker is pointing out, as if the speaker of the poem cannot contain himself, but it also makes a sublime statement about loneliness. The alienated speaker of the first few lines of the poem suddenly feels that there is someone to talk to, someone with whom he can share the marvel of the extraordinary individual that he is observing.

Having covered loneliness and bonding, there is one other major element to the mind/body duality that the poem faces: death. This is eased into the poem with the mention of walking "into the twilight," but in subsequent lines it becomes a major part of the poem's focus. Neighborhoods are describes as caskets, and, eventually, the body is reduced to being nothing more than a black cab—a hearse—in which the mind rides away.

Here, the speaker reveals his anxieties most clearly. This concern about death, of existing in the lifeless physical world and then, eventually, the mind being separated from the lifeless body, turns out to be what is concerning him and him alone. There is no indication that the man in the street or the poem's other characters share this concern. It might be thought that the awareness of death is supposed to be assumed as an underlying factor behind all of the crying, conversing, and breaking up, but the poem does not really make this an issue. When death is brought into the poem, the issue being examined becomes much clearer, as does the poem's basic relationship: the speaker of the poem understands the problem and the man in the street knows the solution, and peace will come when each is able to learn from the other.

The world that the poem's speaker sees is a harsh one. Babies know pain and they expect it to go on for eternity; couples get together, but the illusion of human connection can only last a short while before they break up; and then there is death. For the man walking up the street, however, the world is a placid place, even though he is physically separated from everyone else, at risk of being run over, and unable to walk straight. There is no question that he is isolated: what the speaker needs to find out is how he can cope so well with the isolation. The man walking up the middle of the street is immune to the pain, alienation, and knowledge of death that complicate life, and the poet's task is to find out how others can reach the same attitude.

Clearly, the solution is not to simply be or play ignorant. This is probably what others see when they view the walking man: he seems unaware of how strange his behavior is, of the danger of walking in the middle of the street. It is common in most urban areas to find such people, people who stand out because of their odd behavior, and usually they are ignored or pitied. The fact that the poem's speaker identifies with this man, finds kinship with him, may be left unexplained because it violates a basic social principle, which is that those who take no stock of life's miseries are assumed to have some sort of mental problem, an inability to see that such misery exists. Simply acknowledging the man, taking him as someone who might be important, takes this poem at least halfway toward the solution that it seeks.

In the end, the solution to alienation turns out to be nothing about social relationships at all, but all about the relationship that the mind has with the body. The key phrase in the last line, "walk your body down," is a mirror of the line from stanza 2, "Walk your body proudly into the twilight." At the end of the poem, though, it takes on a religious tone, starting with "O" and including an echo of the language of old spirituals such as "Go Down, Moses." This is clearly meant to be the bottom line, the heart of the poem. And Barbarese finishes off the thought with "don't let it"—that is, your body—"go it alone."

What is so compelling about the man walking in the street is that, estranged from other people, he is still a complete person, because he is comfortable within his own body. Though the poem does still, in the end, admit that the body is a separate thing from the mind/spirit/personality, it puts the relationship between the two into perspective. The body must be taken care of, because it is just a physical thing, but, even more importantly, one must be a companion to it. There may be duality, but there is also equality.

"Walk Your Body Down" is written with the kind of passivity that a casual observer might have about common events that are going on around him on a typical day. As every good poem should, though, it uses its observations to reveal complex truths. In this case, the alienation of the individual, viewing the objective world from a subjective perspective, that becomes more and more torturous as one reads deeper. The speaker of the poem fixates on one lone individual, and it takes a while to understand why: that individual, with his erratic behavior, is the only person in the poem who knows what the body and soul have to do with one another.

Source: David Kelly, Critical Essay on "Walk Your Body Down," in *Poetry for Students*, Thomson Gale, 2007.

SOURCES

Barbarese, J. T., "Walk Your Body Down," in *The Black Beach*, University of North Texas Press, 2005, p. 3.

Chiasson, Dan, "Eight Takes," in *Poetry*, Vol. 187, No. 2, November 2005, pp. 143–55.

Review of *The Black Beach*, in *Wisconsin Bookwatch*, September 2005.

FURTHER READING

Collins, Billy, ed., *Best American Poetry 2006*, Scribner, 2006.

> Poetry in this annual collection is gathered from current literary magazines and other publications in the given year.

Ferguson, Margaret, ed., *Norton Anthology of Poetry*, 5th edition, W. W. Norton, 2004.

> This poetry volume includes 340 poets, ranging from Shakespeare to contemporary poets. Also included are guides to reading and understanding poetry.

Fry, Stephen, *The Ode Less Traveled: Unlocking the Poet Within*, Gotham, 2006.

> Fry is all in favor of having fun with writing poetry. His book covers various aspects of writing poetry, including rhythm, rhyme, and several poetic forms.

Sitomer, Alan Lawrence, *Hip-Hop Poetry and the Classics*, Milk Mug, 2004.

> A high school teacher, Sitomer has put together a comparison of hip-hop poetry and classic poems. Comparisons include Robert Frost's poetry and Public Enemy and Shakespeare's poetry with lyrics by Eminem. This book offers a different way of reading the classics and appreciating the lyrics of contemporary poetry.

The War Correspondent

CIARAN CARSON

2003

"The War Correspondent," by Irish poet Ciaran Carson, appears in Carson's collection, *Breaking News* (2003). It consists of seven poems, all but one of which are set in the Crimea at the time of the Crimean War. This war took place between 1854 and 1856 and pitted a British and French alliance against Russia for influence in the Near East. The Crimea is a region off the Black Sea in present-day Ukraine.

"The War Correspondent" is based on dispatches from the Crimea written by Anglo-Irish war correspondent William Howard Russell for readers of the *Times*, a London newspaper. In his notes to *Breaking News*, Carson writes that "The War Correspondent" is "especially indebted to his [Russell's] writing; in many instances I have taken his words *verbatim*, or have changed them only slightly to accommodate rhyme and rhythm." Taken together, the seven poems in "The War Correspondent" convey a sense of the wastefulness and destruction of war, set against the ever-recurring rhythms of nature.

AUTHOR BIOGRAPHY

Ciaran Carson was born on October 9, 1948, in Belfast, Northern Ireland, the son of Liam Carson, a postman. He acquired his taste for language and storytelling very early. He recalls that when he was two or three, his father would tell his children stories in Gaelic every evening, and each story would continue (at least it seemed that way to the child) for weeks.

Carson was educated at Queen's University in Belfast, from which he received a Bachelor of Arts degree in English. From 1974 to 1975, he worked as a schoolteacher in Belfast, after which he became the Traditional Arts officer for the Arts Council of Northern Ireland, in Belfast, a position he held until 1998.

Carson's first volume of poetry was *The New Estate* (1976), followed by *The Irish For No* (1987). In the latter collection, Carson, who was raised as a Catholic, reflects with humor and satire on the violent situation in Belfast. This book appeared during the civil conflict in Northern Ireland known as "the Troubles," in which the majority Protestants, who wanted Northern Ireland to remain part of the United Kingdom, clashed with the minority Catholics, many of whom wanted a united Ireland free of British rule. The conflict, which also involved the terrorist organization, the Irish Republican Army (IRA) and the British Army, began in 1969 and lasted nearly three decades and resulted in thousands of deaths. Carson's *Belfast Confetti* (1993), which was highly acclaimed by critics, also examines Belfast and its violent history.

Carson's fourth volume of poetry, *First Language* (1994), focuses on language, examining how in Belfast, English, Gaelic, and slang intersect, often resulting in a failure of communication. It was awarded the first ever T. S. Eliot Prize for the outstanding book of poetry published in Great Britain in 1994.

Opera Et Cetera (1996) is notable for its puns and other wordplay, as well as its form. Each ten-line poem is written in rhyming couplets. Other poetry collections by Carson are *The Alexandrine Plan: Versions of Sonnets by Baudelaire, Mallarmé, and Rimbaud* (1998), *The Twelfth of Never* (1998), and *Selected Poems* (2001). *Breaking News* (2003) won the prestigious Forward Prize for best collection of poetry. This volume includes the seven poems that make up "The War Correspondent." In 2006, Carson published *The Midnight Court*, a translation of Brian Merriman's eighteenth-century poem in Irish.

Carson has also published fiction in other genres, including *Shamrock Tea* (2000), a novel set in 1950s Belfast, and *Fishing for Amber: A Long Story* (2000). He has also written nonfiction, including *The Star Factory* (1997), a memoir of his life growing up in Belfast, and *Last Night's Fun: A Book about Irish Traditional Music* (1996). Carson is an accomplished musician who plays the flute. He also published a translation, *The Inferno of Dante Alighieri: A New Translation* (2002), which was awarded the Oxford Weidenfeld Translation Prize.

In 1998, Carson was appointed a professor of English at Queen's University of Belfast. As of 2006, he was director of the Seamus Heaney Centre for Poetry.

Carson married in 1982, and the couple had two sons and a daughter.

POEM TEXT

1 Gallipoli
Take sheds and stalls from Billingsgate,
glittering with scaling-knives and fish,
the tumbledown outhouses of English farmers'
   yards
that reek of dung and straw, and horses
cantering the mewsy lanes of Dublin;   5

take an Irish landlord's ruinous estate,
elaborate pagodas from a Chinese Delftware
   dish
where fishes fly through shrouds and sails and
   yards
of leaking ballast-laden junks bound for
   Benares
in search of bucket-loads of tea as black as tin;   10

take a dirty gutter from a back street in
   Boulogne,
where shops and houses teeter so their pitched
   roofs meet,
some chimney stacks as tall as those in
   Sheffield
or Irish round towers,
smoking like a fleet of British ironclad
   destroyers;   15

take the garlic-oregano-tainted arcades of
   Bologna,
linguini-twists of souks and smells of rotten
   meat,
as labyrinthine as the rifle-factories of
   Springfield,
or the tenements deployed by bad employers
who sit in parlours doing business drinking
   Power's;   20

then populate this slum with Cypriot and Turk,
Armenians and Arabs, British riflemen
and French Zouaves, camel-drivers, officers,
   and sailors,
sappers, miners, Nubian slaves, Greek money-
   changers,
plus interpreters who do not know the lingo;   25

dress them in turbans, shawls of fancy
    needlework,
fedoras, fezzes, sashes, shirts of fine
    Valenciennes,
boleros, pantaloons designed by jobbing tailors,
knickerbockers of the ostrich and the pink
    flamingo,
sans-culottes, and outfits even stranger;   30

requisition slaughter-houses for the troops,
and stalls with sherbet, lemonade, and rancid
    lard for sale,
a temporary hospital or two, a jail,
a stagnant harbour redolent with cholera,
and open sewers running down the streets;   35

let the staple diet be green cantaloupes
swarming with flies washed down with sour wine,
accompanied by the Byzantine
jangly music of the cithara
and the multi-lingual squawks of parakeets—   40

O landscape riddled with the diamond mines of
    Kimberley,
and all the oubliettes of Trebizond,
where opium-smokers doze among the Persian
    rugs,
and spies and whores in dim-lit snugs
discuss the failing prowess of the superpowers,   45

where prowling dogs sniff for offal beyond
the stench of pulped plums and apricots,
from which is distilled the brandy they call
    'grape-shot',
and soldiers lie dead or drunk among the
    crushed flowers—
I have not even begun to describe Gallipoli.   50

2 Varna

On the night of August 10th, a great fire broke
    out,
destroying utterly a quarter of the town.
A stiff breeze fanned the flames along the
    tumbledown
wooden streets. Things were not helped by the
    current drought.

It began in the spirit store of the French
    commissariat.   55
The officers in charge immediately broached
    the main vat,
but, as the liquid spouted down the streets, a
    Greek
was seen to set fire to it in a fit of drunken
    pique.

He was cut down to the chin by a French
    lieutenant,
and fell into the blazing torrent. The howls of
    the inhabitants,   60
the clamour of women, horses, children, dogs,
    the yells
of prisoners trapped in their cells,

were appalling. Marshal St Arnaud displayed
    great coolness
in supervising the operations of the troops;
but both the French and we were dispossessed   65
of immense quantities of goods—

barrels of biscuit, nails, butter, and bullets,
carpenters' tool-boxes, hat-boxes, cages of live
    pullets,
polo-sticks, Lord Raglan's portable library of
    books,
and 19,000 pairs of soldiers' boots.   70

A consignment of cavalry sabres was found
amid the ruins, fused into the most fantastic
    shapes,
looking like an opium-smoker's cityscape
or a crazy oriental fairground—

minarets, cathedral spires of twisted blades,
    blades   75
wrought into galleries and elevated
    switchbacks,
railroad sidings, cul-de-sacs, trolleyways, and
    racing tracks,
gazebos, pergolas, trellises, and colonnades.

Such were the effects of the great fire of Varna.
Next day the cholera broke out in the British
    fleets   80
anchored in the bay, then spread into the
    streets,
and for weeks thousands of souls sailed into
    Nirvana.

3 Dvno

Once I gazed on these meadows
incandescent with poppies,
buttercups and cornflowers   85
surrounded by verdant hills

in which lay deep shady dells,
dripping ferns shower-dappled
under the green canopy
of live oaks and wild apples,   90

aspens, weeping-willow, ash,
maple, plane, rhododendron,
sweet chestnut, spruce, Douglas fir,
and Cedar of Lebanon,

round which vines and acacias   95
vied with wild clematises
to climb ever on and up
to twine the trunks of the trees,

and I thought I was in Eden,
happily stumbling about   100
in a green Irish garden
knee-deep in potato flowers.

But at night a fog descends,
as these woods breed miasmas,
and slithering through the brush   105
are snakes thick as a man's arm;

the vapours rise and fatten
on the damp air, becoming
palpable as mummy shrouds,
creeping up from the valleys   110

fold after fold in the dark,
to steal into a man's tent,
and wrap him, as he's sleeping,
in their deadly cerements.

One day, down by the sea-shore,   115
I scraped my name with a stick
on the sand, and discovered
the rotting face of a corpse;

and by night in the harbour
phosphorescent bodies float   120
up from the murky bottom
to drift moonward past the fleet

like old wooden figureheads,
bobbing torsos bolt upright.
Tiger, Wasp, Bellerophon,   125
Niger, Arrow, Terrible,

Vulture, Viper, Albion,
Britannia, Trafalgar,
Spitfire, Triton, Oberon:
these are vessels I remember.   130

As for the choleraic dead,
their names have been unravelled
like their bones, whose whereabouts
remain unknown.

4 Balaklava

The Turks marched in dense columns, bristling
    with steel.   135
Sunlight flashed on the polished barrels of their
    firelocks
and on their bayonets, relieving their sombre
    hue,
for their dark blue uniforms looked quite black
when viewed *en masse*. The Chasseurs
    d'Afrique,
in light powder-blue jackets, with white car-
    touche belts, scarlet   140
pantaloons, mounted on white Arabs, caught
    the eye
like a bed of flowers scattered over the valley
    floor.

Some, indeed, wore poppies red as cochineal,
plucked from the rich soil, which bore an
    abundance of hollyhocks,
dahlias, anemones, wild parsley, mint, white-
    thorn, rue,   145
sage, thyme, and countless other plants whose
    names I lack.
As the Turkish infantry advanced, their boots
    creaked
and crushed the springy flowers, and delicate
perfumes wafted into the air beneath the April
    sky:

the smell of sweating men and horses smoth-
    ered by flora.   150

Waving high above the more natural green
of the meadow were phalanxes of rank grass,
    marking the mounds
where the slain of October 25th had found their
    last repose,
and the snorting horses refused to eat those
    deadly shoots.
As the force moved on, more evidences of that
    fatal day   155
came to light. The skeleton of an English
    horseman
had tatters of scarlet cloth hanging to the bones
    of his arms;
all the buttons had been cut off the jacket.

Round as shot, the bullet-skull had been picked
    clean
save for two swatches of red hair. The remains
    of a wolfhound   160
sprawled at his feet. From many graves, the
    uncovered bones
of the tenants had started up, all of them lack-
    ing boots.
Tangled with rotted trappings, half-decayed
    horses lay
where they'd fallen. Fifes and drums struck up
    a rataplan;
so we swept on over our fellow men-at-arms   165
under the noon sun in our buttoned-up jackets.

5 Kertch

A row of half a mile
across the tideless sea
brought us to a beautiful beach

edged by a green sward   170
dotted with whitewashed houses
through which the French

were running riot, swords
in hand, breaking in windows
and doors, pursuing hens: 175

every house we entered
ransacked, every cupboard
with a pair of red breeches

sticking out of it, and a blue
coat inside of it; barrels of lard,   180
bags of sour bread, mattress feathers,

old boots, statues, ikons, strewn
on the floors, the furniture
broken into kindling—

such an awful stench   185
from the broken jars of fish oil
and the rancid butter,

the hens and ducks cackling,
bundled up by the feet
by Zouaves and Chasseurs,   190

who, fancied up in old calico
dresses, pranced about
the gardens like princesses.

I was reminded of Palmyra
after we had sacked it: 195
along the quay a long line

of walls, which once
were the fronts of storehouses,
magazines, mansions, and palaces—

now empty shells,   200
hollow and roofless, lit from within
by lurid fires,

as clouds of incense
rose from the battered domes
and ruined spires,   205

all deadly silent
save for the infernal noise
of soldiers playing on pianos

with their boot-heels,
and the flames crackling   210
within the walls

and glassless windows,
the great iconostasis
of the Orthodox cathedral

shot to bits, the golden   215
images and holy books ablaze
amid the crashed candelabras

and broken votive lamps,
while the Byzantine mosaics
were daubed with excrement.   220

Thus did we force the straits
of Kertch, and break the Russian forts.
Corn, oil, naval stores,

prodigious quantities of guns,
bullets, grapeshot, brandy of a high degree— 225
all fell into our hands.

And we spread terror and havoc
along the peaceful seaboard
of that tideless sea.

6 Tchernaya

After only two or three days, the soil   230
erupted with multitudes of snowdrops,
crocuses, hyacinths, gladioli,
marigolds, daffodils, and buttercups.

Finches and larks congregated in little flocks.
Buntings, gold-crested wrens, yellowhammers, 235
linnets, wrens, and tomtits formed little claques,
piping, and twittering and shimmering.

Strange to hear them sing about the bushes
in the lulls between the thud of the bombs,

or to see between the cannon-flashes   240
the whole peninsula ignite with blooms,

spring flowers bursting through the crevices
of piles of rusted shot, and peering out
from under the shells and heavy ordnance.
A geranium waved from an old boot.   245

The insides of our huts became gardens.
Grapes sprouted from the earth in the sills,
the floors, and the fireplace. As in a trance,
we watched the vines crawl slowly up the walls.

Albatrosses, cranes, pelicans, and gulls   250
haunted the harbour. Eagles, vultures, kites
and hawks wheeled over the plateau in squalls,
vanishing for two or three days at a time.

Then they'd return, regular as clockwork,
after feeding behind the Russian lines.   255
I know, for I remember my watch stopped,
and we made a sundial with white stones.

The Tchernaya abounded with wildfowl.
Some of the officers had little hides
of their own where they went at night to kill 260
time. This was deemed highly exciting sport,

for the Russian batteries at Inkerman,
if their sentries were properly alert,
would send two or three shells at the
        sportsmen,
who took short odds on escaping unhurt.   265

In the daytime, they'd take two or three French
soldiers down with them to act as decoys,
who were only too glad of the break. Hence
we coined the old saying, 'dead as a duck.'

Then there was betting on how many flies   270
would fill a jar in which lay a dead dove,
and the two-or-three-legged dog races—
little to do? There was never enough.

Thus we spent the time by the Tchernaya,
making it up as we went along, till   275
long before the battle of Tchernaya,
we each had two or three life-stories to tell.

7 Sedan

Cavalry men asleep
on their horses' necks.
In the fields, heaps   280

of sodden troops,
the countryside charming,
covered with rich crops,

but trampled
underfoot, vines and hops   285
swept aside by the flood

of battle, the apples blasted
from the trees, scattered
like grape-shot.

Gutted knapsacks, boots,
cavalry caps, jackets, swords,
mess-tins, bayonets,   290

canteens, firelocks, tunics,
sabres, epaulettes,
overturned baggage cars,   295

dead horses
with their legs in the air,
scattered everywhere,

dead bodies,
mostly of Turcos and Zouaves,   300
picked over by pickpockets,

one of them staggering
under a huge load of gold
watches and teeth.

Hands hanging in the trees   305
in lieu of fruit,
trunkless legs at their feet.

I will never forget one man
whose head rested
on a heap of apples,   310

his knees drawn up
to his chin, his eyes wide
open, seeming to inspect

the head of a Turco or Zouave
which, blown clean off,   315
lay like a cannonball in his lap.

What debris a ruined empire
leaves behind it!
By the time I reached Sedan

with my crippled horse,   320
it was almost impossible
to ride through the streets

without treading on
bayonets and sabres, heaps
of shakos, thousands   325

of imperial eagles
torn off infantry caps,
or knocking into stooks

of musketry and pikes.
I thought of Sevastopol,   330
mirrors in fragments

on the floors, beds
ripped open, feathers
in the rooms a foot deep,

chairs, sofas, bedsteads,   335
bookcases, picture-frames,
images of saints, shoes, boots,

bottles, physic jars,
the walls and doors
hacked with swords,   340

even the bomb-shelters
ransacked, though in one dug-out
I found a music-book

with a woman's name
in it, and a canary bird,   345
and a vase of wild flowers.

POEM SUMMARY

Gallipoli

"Gallipoli" is the first of the seven poems that make up "The War Correspondent." It gives a vivid description of the slum regions of Gallipoli, Turkey, at the time when British and French forces were billeted there on their way to the Crimea. The ten-stanza poem presents Gallipoli as a teeming, cosmopolitan, polyglot city. The first four stanzas all begin with the word "take," as the poet, drawing on the work of the war correspondent William Howard Russell, evokes the sights and smells of various places around the world to give the reader a picture of the impoverished areas of Gallipoli.

The first reference is to Billingsgate, a well-known fish market in London, with its "scaling-knives and fish." This is followed by a reference to outhouses in "English farmers' yards" that "reek of dung and straw," then horses in Dublin, Ireland. The next three stanzas extend the range of associations almost worldwide, beginning with references to pagodas from a "Chinese Delftware dish." (Delftware is a Dutch imitation of Chinese porcelain from the Ming Dynasty that was first imported into the Netherlands in the early seventeenth century.) The scope of the comparisons then expands to ships bound for Benares, India, to collect massive amounts of tea.

Stanza 3 describes the houses in Gallipoli, introducing them with a reference to a "back street in Boulogne," a city in France, then to chimney stacks in Sheffield, a town in northern England, that belch out smoke like a fleet of British ships. There is another comparison to "Irish round towers." These are early medieval stone towers, still found in Ireland, which may originally have been bell towers or places of refuge. (They are generally found in the vicinity of a church.)

Stanza 4 begins with an evocation of the rich scents in the arcades of Bologna, a city in Italy, including garlic, oregano and "rotten meat." These arcades are "as labyrinthine as the rifle-factories of Springfield." This is a reference to the Springfield Armory in Springfield, Massachusetts, which has manufactured weapons for the U.S. armed forces since 1835, including the Springfield rifle.

Stanza 5 moves from descriptions of what Gallipoli is like to descriptions of its inhabitants. The heterogeneous nature of the city is emphasized, populated by Cypriots, Turks, Armenians, Arabs, Greeks, and "Nubian slaves" (Nubia is a region in the south of Egypt and in northern Sudan), as well as British and French soldiers. Zouaves was the name given to a French infantry corps that was first created in 1831. By 1854, there were four regiments of Zouaves, and the Crimean War was the first time they served outside Algeria.

In stanza 6, the variety of dress worn by all these nationalities that live in Gallipoli is described, from "turbans" to "fedoras," from "pantaloons" to "knickerbockers" and "sans culottes."

Stanza 7 describes the creation of quarters for the troops in a slaughter-house, as well as the presence of a temporary hospital and a jail. The unsanitary nature of the city is clear from the last two lines, which mention that cholera flourishes there and open sewers run down the streets.

Stanza 8 describes what people in Gallipoli eat, the standard diet being green cantaloupe "swarming with flies" and sour wine, which people consume as they listen to music played on the cithara (a stringed instrument) and the squawking of parakeets.

Stanza 9 extends the frame of reference still further, with mention of the diamond mines of Kimberley. Kimberley is a town in South Africa, famous for its diamond mines. It would appear that there are also diamond mines in the regions near Gallipoli, since the poet states that the landscape is "riddled" with them, as well as with "oubliettes of Trebizond." Trebizond was a small Greek state that acquired an empire out of the remains of the Byzantine empire in the thirteenth century. The Trebizond empire fell in the fifteenth century, but it appears that it was known for its oubliettes. An oubliette is a concealed dungeon with a trap door at the top. It was used for people condemned to life imprisonment or those whom the authorities wished to leave to die secretly. The word comes from the French verb, oublier, which means to forget. The second part of this stanza returns to descriptions of the people who can be found in Gallipoli,

including opium smokers who "doze among the Persian rugs" and spies and whores who discuss the political situation in "dim-lit snugs."

The last stanza returns to the smells of the city, as dogs sniff for offal, and pulped plums and apricots, ready to be distilled into brandy, give off a stench. The final image, of soldiers lying dead or drunk among crushed flowers, reminds the reader of the reality of war.

But even with all these dense, rich descriptions of the city of Gallipoli, the poet/journalist concludes, in the last line, "I have not even begun to describe Gallipoli," which suggests that no description could ever capture the full flavor of what the war correspondent Russell, in his *The British Expedition to the Crimea,* called "a wretched place . . . horribly uncomfortable."

Varna

In eight four-line stanzas, "Varna" describes a fire that took place at the port city of Varna, Bulgaria, on the western shores of the Black Sea, on the night of August 10, 1854. The fire destroyed a quarter of the town. It broke out after French officers opened up a vat in the "spirit store" of the French commissariat. The liquid poured into the streets and a drunken Greek deliberately set fire to it. He was immediately killed by a French lieutenant. As the fire raged, there was a great commotion among the inhabitants as they tried to escape. Some prisoners were trapped in their cells. The commander of the French forces, Marshal St. Arnaud, supervised his troops well, although both British and French armies lost considerable amounts of equipment and supplies, including butter, bullets, "Lord Raglan's portable library of books" (Lord Raglan was the commander of the British forces), and nineteen thousand pairs of soldiers' boots.

Stanza 6 reveals that after the fire, a consignment of cavalry sabres was found in the ruins, "fused into the most fantastic shapes." The following six lines elaborate on what those shapes looked like, everything from a "crazy oriental fairground" to "gazebos, pergolas, trellises, and colonnades."

The final stanza records that the day following the fire there was an outbreak of cholera in the British fleet anchored in the bay. It spread to the town, killing thousands of people within weeks.

Dvno

During the Crimean War, British forces set up a camp in a valley near the village of Dvno, often spelled Devno. In this poem, the first four stanzas form a series of subordinate clauses, before the subject and verb of the sentence ("I thought") appears in stanza 5. In these first four stanzas, the poet (following the journalist Russell) recalls an occasion when he looked out on the beauty of the meadows with their many flowers and trees, and thought he was in the Garden of Eden, which he then illustrates in terms of "a green Irish garden / knee-deep in potato flowers."

The poem takes a turn beginning at stanza 6. After the description of the beautiful, idyllic valley, the poet reveals a darker side to the scene. At night a fog would descend, thick snakes would slither through the brush, and poisonous vapors would arise and creep up from the valleys into the tents of the men, infecting them as they slept.

In stanza 9, the speaker recalls how one day, at the sea shore, he scraped his name on the sand with a stick and laid bare the rotting face of a corpse. The following stanza tells that at night, dead bodies float in the harbor, past the ships of the British fleet. The names of some of the ships are listed. The final stanza reveals an irony. The names of the ships may be known, but the names of those killed by cholera are not, just as their bones have been scattered to whereabouts unknown.

Balaklava

Balaklava is a port city near Sevastopol in the Crimea, in the present-day nation of Ukraine. "Balaklava" begins with a description of Turkish infantry soldiers marching in columns in their dark uniforms. The Chasseurs d'Afrique, in their light blue jackets and mounted on horses also catch the eye. The Chasseurs d'Afrique were a light cavalry corps in the French Armée d'Afrique (Army of Africa), the mounted equivalent of the French Zouave infantry. The Chasseurs d'Afrique wore exactly the colorful uniforms described in the poem, which catch the eye "like a bed of flowers scattered across the valley floor."

Stanza 2 lists some of those flowers and plants, from dahlias to sage and thyme. It is April 1855, and everything is in bloom; the

perfume of the flowers fills the air. But as the Turkish infantry marches, the soldiers crush some of the flowers beneath their feet.

Stanza 3 changes the emphasis from the present to the recent past. Above the green of the meadow, tall grass waves in the breeze. This grass marks the burial mounds of the soldiers who died in a battle that took place the previous fall, on October 25, 1854 (in which British forces repelled a Russian attack). The horses of the soldiers refuse to eat this grass.

As the soldiers move on, there are more signs of the battle, including the skeleton of an English horseman. The skull is clean except for two tufts of red hair. The remains of a wolfhound are at the horseman's feet. From the graves, uncovered bones can be seen, all of them without boots. There are also remains of horses. Fife and drums play as the living army sweeps over the remains of the dead soldiers.

Kertch

The narrator describes an expedition in which he and some unspecified others (probably British troops) row half a mile across the sea to a beach around which are some houses. They find French soldiers, both Zouaves and Chasseurs, with swords drawn, ransacking the houses. Windows and doors are broken, and various items, from barrels of lard to old boots, are strewn all over the place; closets are open and furniture broken. There is a stench from broken jars of fish oil and rancid butter. Hens and ducks cackle. The soldiers even put on dresses and prance around the gardens "like princesses."

In stanza 10, the scene reminds the speaker of what the ancient city of Palmyra, in Syria, must have looked like after it had been sacked by the Romans in A.D. 272. Storehouses, mansions, and palaces have been ruined and left as empty shells, and clouds of incense rise from ruined places of worship. Everything is silent except for the noise of pianos being played on by soldiers with the heels of their boots and the sound of crackling flames. The Orthodox cathedral has been destroyed, and holy artifacts set ablaze. The mosaics are smeared with excrement.

In stanza 11, the poet explains that this was the way the Russian forts were broken during the war. All kinds of supplies, from corn to guns and bullets, fell into the hands of the British and

French, who spread "terror and havoc" along the otherwise peaceful seaboard. (This poem refers to a British and French expedition to Kertch in May 1855, in which Russian communications and supply lines were successfully disrupted.)

Tchernaya

Tchernaya is a river in the Crimean peninsula, and this poem, set in the spring of 1855, tells of incidents that took place in the vicinity of the Tchernaya. These were preludes to the struggle that took place for possession of Sevastopol later that year.

The poem begins by evoking the sudden coming of spring. After just a few warm days, all kinds of flowers and plants, from snowdrops to buttercups, start to spring up from the soil, and many different kinds of birds burst into song. The birds can be heard in the intervals between the sounds of the cannons firing. The flowers bloom among "piles of rusted shot" and from under "shells and heavy ordnance." Even the huts in which the soldiers are billeted show signs of the coming of spring. Grapes sprout through the floors and the fireplace, and vines climb the walls. "Albatrosses, cranes, pelicans, and gulls" can be seen in the harbor, and "eagles, vultures, kites and hawks" can also be spotted in the region. These birds disappear for a few days at a time and then return after feeding behind the Russian lines.

The river Tchernaya is full of wildfowl, as stanza 8 explains. Some of the British officers go out at night and hunt them. This is an exciting and dangerous sport, since the Russian batteries at nearby Inkerman (the site of another great battle in the Crimean War), if their sentries were awake, would fire shells at them. During the daytime, the officers would take some French soldiers with them on these expeditions; the French, who were glad to take a break, would act as decoys.

The men also passed the time with various trivial activities. They would bet "on how many flies would fill a jar in which a dead dove lay," and they would organize races between two- or three-legged dogs. In this way, the men amused themselves long before the actual battle took place, and each man accumulated several stories to tell.

Sedan

"Sedan" is the only poem in "The War Correspondent" that does not refer entirely to events and places in the Crimean War. Instead, Sedan was the site of a battle that took place in France, on September 2, 1870, during the Franco-Prussian War. The battle resulted in a catastrophic defeat for the French. The French emperor, Napoleon III, was taken prisoner along with a hundred thousand of his soldiers.

The poem is based on the report made by William Howard Russell of his visit to the scene immediately after the battle. He finds dead cavalry men slumped on their horses' necks and piles of corpses of the troops. The countryside is covered with rich crops that have been trampled underfoot by the tide of battle. Apples have been "blasted from the trees" and lie around "like grape-shot." (Grape-shot consisted of small iron balls connected together and fired from a gun.) Military equipment is lying around everywhere, including knapsacks, boots, swords, bayonets, and sabres. Dead horses are scattered around, "their legs in the air." The dead bodies of the soldiers have been "picked over by pickpockets." One of those pickpockets is seen carrying a load of gold watches and teeth.

There are also dismembered bodies at the scene. Hands hang from trees, and legs lie at the foot of the trees. The speaker says he will never forget the sight of one man in particular, whose head rested on a pile of apples. His eyes were open, and he seemed to be inspecting the severed head of another soldier, which lay in his lap.

The speaker then recalls the sights that greeted him as he first entered Sedan, which cause him to exclaim, "What debris a ruined empire / leaves behind it!" He explains that it was almost impossible to ride through the streets without treading on all kinds of discarded military equipment, from bayonets and sabers to shakos (a shako is a tall, cylindrical cap and was standard military dress during the nineteenth century), musketry and pikes. The sight makes the speaker think back to how Sevastopol in the Crimea was ransacked after the battle. He recalls houses and bomb shelters in chaos, with debris scattered everywhere: shattered mirrors on the floors; beds torn open; furniture, walls, and doors hacked at with swords. He recalls finding in one dug-out "a music book / with a woman's name in it," a canary, and a vase holding wild flowers.

TOPICS FOR FURTHER STUDY

- Research the Charge of the Light Brigade and make a class presentation explaining what happened and why. Why was the order to charge given? What did the Light Brigade do? Was the charge a classic military blunder or did it accomplish something?

- Read "The Indian Mutiny," by Carson, in *Breaking News*. Like "The War Correspondent," it is based on a report by William Howard Russell. Research and describe the historical event that gave rise to the poem. Does "The Indian Mutiny" resemble any of the poems that make up "The War Correspondent?" How are the themes similar? Write an essay in which you explain your findings.

- Take any newspaper or magazine article that describes conditions in Baghdad, Iraq, or Kabul, Afghanistan, or any other place in the world where there is a current or recent conflict. Following Carson's example in "The War Correspondent," write a poem based on the article.

- Write an essay in which you discuss how war reporting has changed from the Crimean War to World War II, the Vietnam War, and the war in Iraq that began in 2003. Examine relations between governments and the press during these wars. Has the press been subject to censorship? Is censorship in war necessary or should the press have complete freedom? How does war reporting by press and television affect government decisions made in times of war?

THEMES

War's Destruction and the Beauty of Nature

A theme that runs through the seven-poem sequence is the juxtaposition of opposites: destruction caused by war and disease and the ever-renewing beauty of nature. This is first

hinted at in the last stanza of "Gallipoli"; the final image to describe the reality of that city is "soldiers lie dead or drunk among the crushed flowers." In that image, the beauty of flowering nature is overwhelmed by the folly of men, either through war or the escape from it in drunkenness. The image is echoed in "Balaklava," one of three poems in the series that is set in spring, the time of nature's renewal of life. The speaker first presents the soldiers marching, followed by a description of the manifold flowers that are blooming on that April day, including dahlias, anemones, wild parsley, rue, sage and thyme. The two sets of images come together in the lines, "their boots creaked / and crushed the springy flowers." A similar image occurs in "Sedan," in which the countryside is:

> covered with rich crops
>
> but trampled
> underfoot, vines and hops
> swept aside by the flood
>
> of battle

Similar images occur also in "Tchernaya," but in that poem, flowering nature, instead of being crushed by the onslaught of human conflict, is present within it. When spring suddenly comes, all kinds of flowers appear and the birds break out in song. But their presence cannot be separated from the reality of the war that afflicts the region:

> Strange to hear them sing about the bushes
> in the lulls between the thud of the bombs,
> or to see between the cannon-flashes
> the whole peninsula ignite with blooms.

That last image, of the area igniting with blooms, fuses the two realties (the renewal of natural life and the destruction caused by war), since flowers are not usually described as "igniting" with blooms; the word suggests rather the firing of the cannons.

The juxtaposition of opposites continues throughout the following stanza:

> spring flowers bursting through the crevices
> of piles of rusted shot, and peering out
> from under the shells and heavy ordnance.
> A geranium waved from an old boot

The image of the geranium waving from an old boot is perhaps an answer to the earlier images in which flowers were crushed by soldiers' boots. The theme here is that nature will always spring up in new life, no matter how much destruction and death occurs in the human world. While the

The Crimean War dispatches of William Howard Russell served as the inspiration of this poem
(*Library of Congress*)

conflict lasts, however, it may produce some strange, even macabre reversals of the natural order of things. This can be seen in "Sedan," in which apples have been blasted prematurely from the trees by the force of the gunfire (stanza 4), and instead of apples, the speaker sees "Hands hanging in the trees / in lieu of fruit / trunkless legs at their feet." The final image of that poem, the vase of wild flowers that remains even though the bomb shelter in which it has been found has been ransacked, returns to the juxtaposition of natural beauty and war.

In "Dvno," there is a similar juxtaposition, the Eden-like environment that the speaker describes in the first five stanzas yields to a darker reality, the presence of the deadly disease cholera, a disease that is aggravated by the unsanitary conditions of war.

Throughout the sequence of poems, images of death (skulls, bones, rotting or floating corpses, both human and animal), are juxtaposed with the upsurging of new life. The eternal rhythms of nature are set against the transience of individual lives.

STYLE

Rhyme

The seven poems that make up "The War Correspondent" contain a wide variety of form and structure. In "Gallipoli," the entire ten stanzas, each consisting of five lines, consist of a single sentence. Most of the stanzas end in semi-colons; one ends in a dash, and one with a comma; the only period comes after the last word. The most noticeable poetic device in this poem is the rhyme scheme, which operates in units of two stanzas. The stanzas do not for the most part contain end rhymes within themselves. (An end rhyme occurs at the end of a line of verse.) Instead, for example, line 1 of stanza 1 ("Billingsgate") rhymes with line 1 of stanza 2 ("estate"), line 2 in stanza 1 ("fish") rhymes with line 2 in stanza 2 ("dish"), and so on. Stanzas 3 and 4 follow this same structure, although there is one change: the rhyme in the last two lines is reversed, so stanza 3, line 4 ("towers") rhymes with stanza 4, line 5 ("*Power's*"), and vice versa. Stanzas 5 and 6 follow this modified rhyme scheme also. Stanzas 7 and 8, and 9 and 10, follow broadly the same scheme, although they all include one end-rhyme within the stanza: in stanza 7, lines 2 and 3 rhyme ("sale" and "jail"), as do lines 3 and 4 in stanza 9 ("rugs" and "snugs").

Some of the rhymes are masculine; that is, they involve a single, stressed syllable, as in the previous two examples. "Billingsgate" and "estate" (in stanzas 1 and 2) are also considered masculine rhymes, since the rhyme occurs only on the last stressed syllable. This applies also to "streets" and "parakeets," and "troops" and "cantaloupes" in stanzas 7 and 8.

Rhymes that consist of a stressed syllable followed by an unstressed syllable are known as feminine rhymes. An example occurs in "sailors" and "tailors" in stanzas 5 and 6. "Lingo" and "flamingo" in those stanzas also use feminine rhyme. This type of feminine rhyme is also referred to as double rhyme, since the rhyme occurs in two syllables.

In one instance, the poet rhymes words identical in spelling and sound but different in meaning. In stanza 2, "yards," used as an unit of measurement, rhymes with "yards" (stanza 1), used in the sense of a piece of land around a house. In stanza 4, "meat" is used to rhyme with "meet." The words are identical in sound but not in meaning or spelling. In both cases, the rhyme is classified as a "rich rhyme."

"Varna" has shorter, four-line stanzas, with three different rhyme schemes: abba (which means that line 1 rhymes with line 4, and line 2 rhymes with line 3) in stanzas 1, 6, 7, and 8; aabb (stanzas 2 and 3); abab (stanza 4); and aabb (stanza 5).

The poet makes use of imperfect rhyme, in "troops" and "goods," since the vowel sounds only approximate each other. The same applies to "books" and "boots" in stanza 5. The latter might qualify as an "eye-rhyme," in which the printed words look as if they should rhyme but in fact do not. Such rhymes can vary according to different regional accents; some English speakers might pronounce the vowels in these two words in a more similar way than others.

"Dvno," like "Kertch" and "Sedan," makes little use of end rhyme, but "Balaklava" has a rhyme scheme similar to "Gallipoli," operating in units of two stanzas.

In "Tchernaya," end rhyme is used only occasionally; the poetic effect is achieved by use of alliteration at the end of the lines. That is, the consonants are repeated but the vowels do not rhyme. In stanza 3, for example, the "b" in the final word of line 1, "bushes," is echoed by "bombs" (end of line 2), and "blooms" (end of line 4). Other examples of this technique, which can also be found frequently in "Dvno," are "sills" and "walls" in stanza 5; "gulls" and "squalls" (stanza 6); "stopped" and "stones" (stanza 7); "decoys" and "duck" (stanza 10), and "till" and "tell" in the final stanza. The poet took some of these words directly from the prose descriptions of William Howard Russell. The following is an example from Russell's dispatches: "The Tchernaya abounded with duck, and some of the officers had little decoys of their own." It is the poet's artful placement of the words at the end of the line that produces the poetic effect.

HISTORICAL CONTEXT

The Crimean War

In 1853, war broke out between an expansionist Russia and a declining Turkish empire (known as the Ottoman Empire). Russia's initial actions, including the invasion of the Baltic provinces of Moldavia and Wallachia (in present-day Romania)

and the destruction of the Turkish fleet at Sinope, aroused opposition in Britain and France. Britain viewed Russian control of the eastern Mediterranean and possible expansion into Afghanistan as a threat to its interests in India. France was an ally of Turkey, and under Emperor Napoleon III (reigned as emperor, 1852–1870) was keen to show its imperial ambitions. Britain and France therefore declared war on Russia in March 1854.

British and French forces camped at Varna in Bulgaria during the spring and summer of 1854 while Turkish forces engaged the Russians a hundred miles to the north. The Russians withdrew from the Balkan provinces, and the British and French forces were ordered to invade the Crimea and take control of the Russian fortress of Sevastopol. (The region known as the Crimea is the peninsula on the Black Sea, situated in present-day Ukraine.)

The British and French allies landed in the Crimea in September 1854, about thirty miles north of Sevastopol. On September 20, they were victorious over the Russians in the battle of the Alma, about fifteen miles from Sevastopol, although they suffered heavy losses. The following month the allies began their siege of Sevastopol. The Russians tried but failed to relieve the siege at the battle of Balaklava, a small port about eight miles from Sevastopol. This was the occasion of the most famous incident of the Crimean War, the heroic but ill-advised charge of the Light Brigade, in which British cavalry charged entrenched positions of Russian artillery. Of the 673 soldiers who took part in the charge, 113 died and 134 were wounded.

On November 5, the Russians were defeated at the Battle of Inkerman. The siege of Sevastopol continued, but military action was suspended during the winter of 1854–1855. The dire conditions the troops endured during the harsh winter, with bad housing, inadequate food, and almost no proper medical care, caused an outcry in England, causing the government to fall and the new government to establish several commissions to report on and alleviate the problems.

In May 1855, as the siege of Sevastopol continued, the allies captured Kertch and Yenikale in a sea expedition. In June, the Malakoff Tower and the Redan, two forts built to defend Sevastopol, were attacked, but the Russians beat back the assault. On August 16,

"The Valley of Death" as seen after the British army lost more than half of their horses and almost a third of the 650 soldiers who took part in the Charge of the Light Brigade (Library of Congress)

Russian forces attempting to come to the aid of Sevastopol were defeated by the French and Sardinians (the latter had joined the war in January 1855) in the battle of the Tchernaya. By mid-September the Russians were forced to evacuate Sevastopol. In March 1856, the Treaty of Paris was signed, officially ending the Crimean War.

Sir William Howard Russell

Pioneering war correspondent William Howard Russell was born in Lilyvale, County Dublin, Ireland, in 1820. His introduction to journalism came when he reported on Irish elections in 1841, and in 1845, when he was living in England, he was sent by the *Times* of London to report on events in Ireland. The *Times* then sent him as a special correspondent to Denmark to cover the Danes' war with Schleswig-Holstein from 1849 to 1850. On the outbreak of the Crimean War, Russell again went out as

special correspondent for the *Times*. He accompanied the light division to Gallipoli in March 1854, and then he proceeded with the first detachment to Varna, where in August he witnessed the great fire that destroyed one-quarter of the city.

On the embarkation for the Crimea, Russell was attached to the British second division, which landed on September 14, 1854. "Few of those who were with the expedition will forget the night of the 14th of September," he wrote. "Seldom or never were 27,000 Englishmen more miserable." The problem was that no tents had been sent ashore, and torrential rain fell throughout the night on the troops, who had only their coats and blankets to protect them from the storm.

On September 20, Russell was present on horseback at the battle of the Alma, although riding around behind the action he was not able to see much for himself. For his reports to the *Times* he depended on the accounts given him by the soldiers and officers he questioned. He had a much better view of the battle of Balaklava on October 25 in which he witnessed the calamitous charge of the Light Brigade. His account of the charge was published in the *Times* on November 14, 1854:

> They swept proudly past, glittering in the morning sun in all the pride and splendour of war. We could scarcely believe the evidence of our senses. Surely that handful of men were not going to charge an army in position? Alas! It was but too true—their desperate valour knew no bounds, and far indeed was it removed from its so-called better part—discretion.

Russell also witnessed the battle of Inkerman on November 5, 1854, which he described as "the bloodiest struggle ever witnessed since war cursed the earth. The bayonet was often the only weapon employed in conflicts of the most obstinate and deadly character."

During the winter of 1854–1855, British troops in the Crimea suffered severe privations due to bad weather, poor management, and inadequate supplies. There were no facilities to care for the wounded and not even enough linen for bandages. In his dispatches to the *Times*, Russell brought attention to the serious situation, claiming that the army had been ruined by mismanagement. Demands from the public for improvements led to the sending of Florence Nightingale (1820–1910), a nurse who was to become famous for her care of the troops, to the Crimea. Russell's critical reports were also a factor in the downfall of the British government led by prime minister Lord Aberdeen. According to Philip Knightley, in *The First Casualty*, Russell's war reporting was "considerably closer the truth than anything the public had previously been permitted to learn, and his influence on the conduct of the Crimean campaign was immense."

In May 1855, Russell accompanied the expedition to Kertch but did not return to the Crimea until August. In September and October he described the attacks on the forts of Malakoff and Redan, and the occupation of Sevastopol.

After the Crimean War, Russell went on to cover the Indian Mutiny in 1857 (his report on it was adapted by Carson for his poem, "The Indian Mutiny" in *Breaking News*), the American Civil War, the Austro-Prussian War, the Franco-Prussian War (including the battle of Sedan),

the Paris Commune, and the British expedition to quell a Zulu uprising in 1879.

Russell, who received many honors and awards, was knighted in 1895. He died in 1907.

CRITICAL OVERVIEW

Breaking News, the collection in which "The War Correspondent" appears, received high praise from critics. Sean O'Brien in the *Times Literary Supplement*, comments that the collection, which ends with the seven poems that make up "The War Correspondent," "concludes with the teeming plenitude of atmospheric and material detail which has marked Ciaran Carson's work since his poetry came fully to life in the 1980s." O'Brien goes on to describe "The War Correspondent" as "a rich and remarkable piece of work.... the poems never read as antiquarian works of reconstruction." He singles out "Gallipoli" for particular comment, describing it as a characteristic Carson poem, "its thousand details all somehow got on board the poem's sixty-line sentence, only for the poet-correspondent to declare: 'I have not even begun to describe Gallipoli.'" O'Brien describes this last statement as a "boast, an admission of failure and a profession of faith... [it] means that the world, however terrible, is inexhaustible."

In another favorable review, David Gardiner, in *Irish Literary Supplement*, comments that "Every poem within *Breaking News* addresses or alludes to political conflict and its results." He comments in particular on the final images in "Sedan,"—the music-book, the canary, and the vase of wild flowers—seeing them as characterizing the poet's "entire effort." He explains as follows: "Carson presents the poet as effete looter, taking part in none of the barbarity but trying to preserve it for later generations while looking for beauty for himself."

John Taylor, in the *Antioch Review*, describes "The War Correspondent" as a "richly detailed long poem." He contrasts this with the shorter poems elsewhere in *Breaking News* which are so "stripped of rhetoric... they resemble mere on-the-scene jottings."

When *Breaking News* was awarded the Forward Prize, the largest poetry award in the United Kingdom, the chairman of the judges, Sir Peter Stothard, said Carson had written "powerfully about war and politics—taut, truthful poems" (quoted in the *Guardian*).

WHAT DO I READ NEXT?

- Carson's *Selected Poems* (2001) is a representative selection of Carson's poetry taken from each of his seven books up to *The Twelfth of Never* (1998). The selection shows how Carson's poetry has progressed and changed over the years.

- *The Oxford Book of War Poetry*, edited by Jon Stallworthy (new edition, 2003), contains 250 poems from all ages, including Homer's *Iliad*, poems of World War I and World War II, the Vietnam War, and the later conflicts in Northern Ireland and El Salvador. Poets represented include Lord Byron, Thomas Hardy, Wilfred Owen, Siegfried Sassoon, and Seamus Heaney.

- Leo Tolstoy's *Sebastopol Sketches* contains three sketches by the great Russian writer who served in the Russian army during the Crimean War. The sketches give vivid insight into the lives of the ordinary Russian soldiers, and Tolstoy tells his story with a concern for truth and for his own feelings rather than what the authorities expect him to say. Some parts of the sketches were at the time subjected to censorship by the Russian authorities. The sketches are available in a Penguin Classics edition published in 1986.

- "The Charge of the Light Brigade," a poem by Alfred, Lord Tennyson, famously records the disastrous charge of the British Light Brigade during the Crimean War. Tennyson was inspired to write the poem after reading the description by William Howard Russell of the courageous but ill-fated charge. The poem is available in Tennyson's *Selected Poems*, published in 2003 by Phoenix Press.

CRITICISM

Bryan Aubrey

Aubrey holds a Ph.D. in English and has published many articles on poetry. In this essay, he discusses the

> THE POET CARSON, HOWEVER, HAD LITTLE INTEREST IN RUSSELL'S PATRIOTISM OR HIS ACCOUNTS OF THE SUFFERING OF THE WOUNDED. WHAT MOST CAUGHT HIS EYE WAS THE JOURNALIST'S KEEN OBSERVATION, HIS EYE FOR DETAIL, HIS GIFT FOR THE TELLING IMAGE."

war reporting of Sir William Howard Russell and the use Carson made of it in "The War Correspondent."

Ciaran Carson's "The War Correspondent" is a tribute to the war reporting of Sir William Howard Russell, whose words written in the mid-nineteenth century come to new life in the work of the Irish poet. Reading Russell's vivid, richly descriptive dispatches from the Crimean War, it is not difficult to see why they have exerted such an influence on the poet, who dedicates the entire volume, *Breaking News*, in which "The War Correspondent" appears, to Russell. Russell was an Irishman in the days before Irish independence; Carson is an Irish poet from a region of Ireland that remains part of the United Kingdom, who lived through thirty years of sectarian violence that turned his home city of Belfast into a virtual war zone. In *Breaking News*, Carson becomes a kind of war reporter himself, recording the sights and sounds of Belfast in the years following the uneasy peace settlement of 1998, during which tension and fear still pervade the air, British Army helicopters still fly overhead, and the memory of sudden, deadly violence remains clear. Carson also links the present-day reality of Belfast with the wars that have gone before it, including the Crimean War, an imperial war the traces of which can still be seen in the early 2000s in Belfast in the commemorative names of the streets: Sevastopol, Crimea, Inkerman. As Carson writes in "Exile":

> Belfast
> is many
>
> places then
> as now

The work of Russell marked the beginning of a new era in war reporting, through which the educated public became more fully informed about current wars than ever before. Although some of Russell's dispatches took nearly three weeks to reach London and get printed in the *Times*—by contrast to instant satellite communications that enable war correspondents in the early 2000s to be heard and seen live by millions of television viewers—in their accuracy and detail they represented considerable progress over former times. Only sixty years earlier, news of a great English naval victory over the French was conveyed by courier to the British Admiralty, and no less a personage than the Duke of Clarence went personally to the theater at Covent Garden and told the manager to announce the news to the audience. It was common during the French Revolutionary wars and the Napoleonic wars to make such announcements in streets and theaters. Newspapers were not the sources of such information; without reporters on the spot, they were dependent on the government, which controlled the channels of communication, to tell them what had happened.

In the Crimean War, the first major war in Europe since the end of the Napoleonic wars in 1815, the dry official dispatches that purported to describe events at the battlefront were eclipsed by the rise of a new type of newspaper reporter, the special correspondent, the greatest of whom was Russell. Russell's reports not only informed the public about the nature and outcome of key battles but also exposed the mismanagement that led to the extreme hardships suffered by British troops in the severe winter of 1854–1855. Working for the *Times* enhanced Russell's influence, since in the early 1850s it had a circulation of forty thousand, greater than that of all its rivals put together.

Russell's reports give the reader plenty of insight into the brutality of war and the suffering it inflicts. His descriptions of the aftermath of battles are particularly memorable, although they do not make for comfortable reading. After the fall of Sevastopol, Russell entered a hospital to which Russian casualties had been taken. He described what he saw as "the most heartrending and revolting" example of the horrors of war that had ever been presented. Here is part of his description of the wounded Russians:

> Many lay, yet alive, with maggots crawling about in their wounds. Many, nearly mad by the scene around them, or seeking escape from it in their extremest agony, had rolled away under the beds and glared out on the heart-stricken spectator. Many, with legs and arms broken and twisted, the jagged splinters sticking through the raw flesh, implored aid, water, food or pity, or, deprived of speech by the approach of death or by dreadful injuries in the head or trunk, pointed to the lethal spot.

Although Russell's horror at sights such as these is entirely genuine, he also had a belief, in keeping with the age in which he lived, in the glory of war. He had his fair share of patriotic fervor regarding the "sublime efforts" of his countrymen in the "great struggle" that was the Crimean War (these words are from a preface he wrote when his account of the war was published as *The British Expedition to the Crimea*). In this respect, his writing is clearly from another era, as in this stirring account of a moment in the battle of the Alma, which reads almost as if it is from a comic strip designed to inculcate patriotic pride in British schoolboys:

> Sir George Brown . . . rode in front of his Light Division, urging them with voice and gesture. Gallant fellows! they were worthy of such a gallant chief. . . . Down went Sir George in a cloud of dust in front of the battery. He was soon up and shouted, "23rd, I'm all right. Be sure I'll remember this day," and led them on again.

The poet Carson, however, had little interest in Russell's patriotism or his accounts of the suffering of the wounded. What most caught his eye was the journalist's keen observation, his eye for detail, his gift for the telling image. In "Gallipoli," for example, the first four stanzas, which consist in effect of a series of similes that create a picture of what the city looks like, spring directly from Russell's description of Gallipoli, written when he arrived there with British forces in early April 1854. Russell's first sentence begins "Take the most dilapidated outhouses of farmers' yards in England," which Carson adopts almost word for word in line 3 of stanza 1: "the tumbledown outhouses of English farmers' yards." The very first line of the poem is also taken directly from Russell's "carry off sheds and stalls from Billingsgate," which becomes "Take sheds and stalls from Billingsgate" in "Gallipoli." Russell's "borrow a dirty gutter from a back street in Boulogne—let the houses in parts lean across to each other so that the tiles meet" becomes "take a dirty gutter from a back street in Boulogne, / where shops and houses teeter so their pitched roofs meet" in stanza 3 of the poem.

Sometimes, the poet makes changes in Russell's account simply to create a rhyme. In stanza 3 of "Varna," for example, the French soldier who kills the man who started the fire is a "lieutenant," whereas in Russell's account he is identified only as an "officer." Carson makes the change so he can create at least a partial rhyme between "lieutenant" and "inhabitants" in the next line. In stanza 1, he takes Russell's phrase "fanned the flames as they leapt along the wooden streets" and writes, "fanned the flames along the tumbledown / wooden streets." The poet needed to add "tumbledown" in order to create a rhyme with "town" in the previous line. Similarly, Russell's "casks of spirits" becomes "the main vat" in order to create a rhyme with "commissariat" in the previous line. The "yells of the Turks" become "the yells / of prisoners trapped in their cells," which has the advantage not only of creating a more vivid image but also of providing the necessary rhyme. In stanza 6, Russell's description of the cavalry sabres "fused into the most fantastic shapes" as a result of the fire stimulates the poet to his inventive similes, in which the sabres are "looking like an opium-smoker's cityscape / or a crazy oriental fairground."

The final images in "Sedan," the last poem of "The War Correspondent" are among the most striking of all the images in these poems. Carson has plucked them almost verbatim from Russell's description of the scene he encountered at the site of the Redan fort after it had fallen to the British. Referring to bomb shelters, Russell wrote, "in one of them a music-book was found with a woman's name in it, and a canary bird and vase of flowers were outside the entrance." The only changes Carson makes, other than placing the line breaks appropriately to fit the form of the poem, is to put the journalist's discovery in the active voice ("I found") rather than the passive "was found," to add the adjective "wild" to describe the flowers, and to omit "outside the entrance," so as to create a more compact image of these items all being found in the bomb shelter. Thus does Carson fuse the prose of war reportage with the stuff of poetry to convey the irony of natural beauty and human culture found in the midst of wholesale, man-made destruction.

Source: Bryan Aubrey, Critical Essay on "The War Correspondent," in *Poetry for Students*, Thomson Gale, 2007.

> " AS CARSON HAS MOVED FORWARD FROM MUSIC TO LANGUAGE ITSELF, HE HAS NOW FOCUSED ON THE LANGUAGE THROUGH WHICH THE VAST MAJORITY OF THE ENGLISH-SPEAKING WORLD NOW GETS ITS 'NEWS,' THOSE TAGS, REFERENTS, AND SNIPPETS OF SPEECH WHICH PORTRAY WAR AND IMPACT POETRY."

David Gardiner

In the following review, Gardiner points out that many of the poems map the city of Belfast, Ireland, while the prose of William Howard Russell gives a distant echo of the British imperial battles which can still be seen in the names of Belfast streets. In "The War Correspondent," "Carson presents the poet as effete looter, taking part in none of the barbarity but trying to preserve it for later generations while looking for beauty for himself."

As the third generation of poets after Yeats has entered mid-career, their mature works turn towards questions and topics which may quickly make generational classifications more obsolete than useful. This is, we are told, the first truly European generation of Irish poets, as comfortable in Moscow, Barcelona, or Omaha, as they are in Montenotte, Balldoyle, or Oughteraard. (Well, perhaps not Omaha.) As a poet whose work has remained imaginatively rooted in Belfast, Ciaran Carson easily commutes between the richness of his native city and wider reading publics. Evidence of this is presented by the awarding of the Forward Prize, poetry's version of the Booker Prize, in October to Carson's *Breaking News.*

The award is well deserved but comes as no surprise. Since the Alice Hunt Bartlett Award (1987) for *The Irish For No*, Carson's work has been recognized with the Irish Times Literature Prize for Poetry (1990), the T. S. Eliot Prize (1993), and the Yorkshire Post Book Award (1997), among others. Throughout his career, Carson has been one of the Irish poets most willing to challenge himself publicly and aesthetically. The decade-long break from poetry between his firm collection and *The Irish For*

No saw Carson's devotion to, and mastery of, traditional music and scholarship yield results within his newly-fashioned long line. Then again, his continued work in experimental prose forms as varied as, and in some sense similar to, the music which his prose first addressed, moved over the course of the next decade from occasional pieces into novels. Accompanying this work; there was also a logical expansion of his translation work from Irish to include Latin, French, and even Dante's *Inferno* itself, which is likely material for a writer who has plumbed the history and topography of his own city as intimately and imaginatively as did that of the exiled Florentine.

Most recently, certainly since *First Language*, it has become commonplace to propose that Carson's subject is language itself. *Breaking News* does subject language to this continuing interrogation, but it might also be seen as another of Carson's very public departures from his previous techniques. In many ways, the collection indicates not only Carson's place among the continuing generations of Irish writers, but also his place apart. It presents Carson as a poet fully capable of simultaneously challenging and building upon his body of work while engaging in some of the most difficult questions poetry itself has to face.

The tired conversation about the relationship between poetry and politics, or more specifically, poetry and war, might continue academic pronouncements but it is a damning cliché for poets to face head on. The more tendentious the critical or creative approach the less likely it is to succeed, or simply to last. In *Breaking News*, Carson leaps directly into this lion's den and potential dead-end and comes out (relatively) unscathed. Comprised of 34 poems and dedicated to William Howard Russell, the nineteenth-century Anglo-Irish war correspondent, in both form and content the work marks a break, if not changing direction, from Carson's previous work. In *Breaking News*, conflict is no longer addressed obliquely, through the nod and wink poetics of *The Irish For No* (1987) or *Belfast Confetti* (1990). Perhaps building upon the hallucinogenic revisions of Irish political ballad in *The Twelfth of Never* (1999) and *The Ballad of HMS Belfast* (1999), Carson directly depicts and details the events and occasions of war.

Every poem within *Breaking News* addresses or alludes to political conflict and its results. The state of war which permeates the volume even creates a background pulse for poems such as the seven line, "Shop Fronts":

Cheek by jowl

Chemist
Tobacconist

Wilkinson Sword

Razor-blades

Warhorse

Plug

This is an example where context is all. Without the backdrop of the other poems in the collection and Carson's other collections, this seems to be a spare poem indeed. One of the strengths of *Breaking News* though is the attention with which this has been shaped as a collection, a poetic sequence, addressing the relation between past and present conflict and language's role within them. Other reviewers have pointed to the eerie silences of the collection which resemble the same state of post-cease fire Belfast. Within the collection itself, Carson economically uses line length and allusion to create a dialogue with the reader that is at once familiar and alienating, thus encouraging such echos.

Readers of Carson have become used to the long lines since *The Irish For No*. That collection marked Carson's recognition and use of his backgrounds in traditional Irish music that has since—with a healthy dose of MacNeice, Whitman, C. K. Williams, Rimbaud, inter alia—marked his work. Not entirely unexpected, the short poems of *Breaking News* resemble the Basho haiku which demarcated *Belfast Confetti*. Except for the poems, "The War Correspondent," "The Indian Mutiny," and "The Forgotten City," there are few lines longer than a mere four syllables. In the three longer-lined poems, all depend upon others' lines for their length: "The Forgotten City" is *after* William Carlos Williams, and the other two poems borrow heavily from the prose of William Howard Russell.

Considered one of the founding fathers of war journalism, W. H. Russell's accounts of the disastrously led Crimean War (1845–46) almost single-handedly swayed public opinion against that war. In his notes to *Breaking News*, Carson writes that his poems are "especially indebted to his [W. H. Russell's] writing; in many instances I have taken his words *verbatim*, or have changed them only slightly to accommodate rhyme and rhythm" (59). Always surprising in his juxtapositions and location of sources, Carson looks back to not only the founder of war journalism—the way in which the reading public learns to speak about war—but to one of the first people to share with the English reading public the locations that would later become the street names and neighborhoods of many late Victorian cities, including Belfast. In this way, *Breaking News* continues to map the city of Belfast while Russell's prose provides the distant echo of the imperial battles which named Inkerman, Crimea, Odessa, and Balaklava as streets in Belfast.

In "The Indian Mutiny," Carson moves to the later, desperate battles in India. The translation, or adaptation, of the Anglo-Irishman's prose to poetry is truly remarkable. The full effect of both Carson's work on the original and its potential can be seen in a juxtaposition of just one of Russell's complete excerpts against this poem from *Breaking News*. In his original account of the siege, Russell writes:

> I was looking through my glass at the time, and I distantly saw the gunners laying the piece for our humble selves just as he finished speaking. It is an unpleasant thing to look down the muzzle of a hostile gun with a glass. "I think," said I, modestly, 'they are going to fire at us.' As I spoke, pluff came a spurt of smoke with a red tongue in it—a second of suspense, and whi-s-s-s-h, right for us came the round shot within a foot of our heads, plumped into the ground, with a storm of dust and small stones, beyond us, then rising rushed over the wall into the chief's camp....Just some twelve inches lower, and where had been the brains of some of us, or the subtler part? Of all horrid sights, I know none so bad as seeing a man's brains dashed out like froth from a canon-ball! One would never feel it one's self—for the time is come, when brains are out, that men will die. 'My telegraph wires will be exposed to fire,' said Stewart; and so we sauntered over to the Dilkusha, which was filled with Highlanders [93rd Highlanders who Russell earlier famously termed "a thin red line tipped with steel"]. No one asked us for our passes—we crossed the courtyard, ascended the flight of steps of the hall, and thence, through heaps of ruin, broken mirror-frames, crystals of chandeliers, tapestries, pictures, beds of furniture, mounted to the flat roof. A vision, indeed!
>
> A vision of palaces, minars, domes azure and golden, cupolas, colonnades, long facades of fair perspective in pillar and column, terraced roofs—all rising up amid of calm still ocean of

the brightest verdure. Look for miles and miles away, and still the ocean spreads, and the towers of the fairy-city gleam in its midst. Spires of gold glitter in the sun. Turrets and gilded spheres shine like constellations. There is nothing mean or squalid to be seen. There is a city more vast than Paris, as it seems, and more brilliant, lying before us. Is this a city in Oudh? Is this the capital of a semi-barbarous race, erected by a corrupt, effete, and degraded dynasty? I confess I felt inclined to rub my eyes again and again.

A reader of Russell may be struck with the exoticism, but the poetry may not normally be apparent. In his poem, "The Indian Mutiny," Carson simply adapts the lines from Russell:

> There I was
> looking down the muzzle
> of a hostile gun
>
> with a spyglass—
> I think, said I, they're
> going to fire at us,
>
> and as I spoke, pluff
> came a spurt of smoke
> with a red tongue in it—
>
> a second of
> suspense, when whi-s-s-h, right
> for us came the round-shot
>
> within a foot
> of our heads, and plumped
> into the ground a storm
>
> of dust and grit
> with which we upped and away
> and into the courtyard.
>
> No one asked us
> for our passes
> as we climbed the staircase
>
> to the upper room through
> heaps of glass and broken mirrors,
> tapestries and beds of silk,
>
> to stare into the blue beyond
> of palaces and azure minarets,
> domes, temples, colonnades
>
> and long facades
> of fair perspective. Look for miles
> away, and still
>
> the ocean spreads,
> the towers of the city
> gleam amidst it,
>
> spires of gold
> and constellated spheres
> so bright

I had to rub my eyes
before this vision
vaster and more beautiful

than Paris . . . (ln. 1–40)

What is included in the poem is clear, but it's what is left out that provides the real echo. Within Russell's accounts, we learn that this Siege of Lucknow was relieved largely through the efforts of Henry Kavanagh, an Irish civilian employed in India who volunteered to slip out from the besieged 33 acre colonial compound. Dressed as a sepoy, Kavanagh eventually made his way to the British forces. In a sort of perverse echo of the Siege of Derry, this troop of 1700 trapped Europeans and loyal sepoys fought their way out and abandoned the city with the help of the 93rd Highlanders. Carson's very careful identification of source materials leads the readers towards such background information while distinctly letting the materials literally speak for themselves.

It is a dangerous project to let what we would call if not yellow journalism outright propaganda speak for itself. This assumes a wry knowledge on the readers' part, but it also challenges the reader to draw their own distinctions between the changed significations of the writing which lie beneath what they represent of war. In Carson's 1996 reflection *Last Night's Fun*, Carson wrote in "Ask My Father":

'Last Night's Fun', to take an example, is a name or a label for a tune: it does not describe its musical activity nor impute experience to it. It is not about frolics reveled in on some particular night, although the name might put you in mind of them. In other words, the tune, by any other name, would sound as sweet; or as rough, for that matter, depending on who plays it, or what shape they're in. So, the names of tunes are not the tunes: they are tags, referents, snippets of speech which find themselves attached to musical encounters."

As Carson has moved forward from music to language itself, he has now focused on the language through which the vast majority of the english-speaking world now gets its "news," those tags, referents, and snippets of speech which portray war and impact poetry.

In *Breaking News*, Carson sketches out new demarcations that have yet another, unrecognized model—John Montague. In *A New Siege*, which would later become the tenth canto of *The Rough Field* (1972), Montague wrote in the same two-beat lines as he incorporated verbatim the

words of Rev. Seth Whittle from during the Siege of Derry. There too, Montague carefully reworked the referents of this staunch defender of the loyal city so as to refer to the Northern Irish Civil Rights Association during the late 1960s. Montague sought to trace the "seismic lines" of Paris, Berkeley, Belfast, and Derry during the summer of 1968.

Breaking News ends with the seven poem sequence, "The War Correspondent," which could just have easily been titled, "Meditations in Times of Equally Trumped Up Imperial War." In the first poem, "Gallipoli," the previously careful abbca rhyme scheme breaks down as the narrative voice describes a place

where opium-smokers doze among the
    Persian rugs,
and spies and whores in dim-lit snugs discuss
    the failing prowess of sugarpowers."

These contemporary resonances coexist with echoes of Yeats's "Stare's Nest" from "Meditations in Times of Civil War," as Carson continues:

The insides of our huts became gardens. Grapes sprouted from the earth in sills, the floors, and the fireplace. As in a trance, We watched the vines crawl slowly up the wall.

Finally, Carson provides the image which may characterize his entire effort as it concludes the work:

. . . even the bomb-shelters
ransacked, though in one dug-out
I found a music-book

with a woman's name
in it, and a canary bird,
and a vase of wild flowers.

Carson presents the poet as effete looter, taking part in none of the barbarity but trying to preserve it for later generations while looking for beauty for himself.

In a sense, Carson may be affirming that as an artist, or reader, you can't "make" anything out of the subject of war which destroys. John Montague's experiment with his public meter resulted in a search for the rhythm which united the entire world. Retrospectively, there might be an air of late-1960s, or simply republican, triumphalism in Montague's work. In *Breaking News*, Carson's "I" is gone. In "Home," he writes:

Hurtling from
The airport down
The mountain road

Past barbed wire
Snagged with
Plastic bags

Fields of scrap
And thistle
Farmyards

From the edge
Of the plateau
My eye zooms

Into the clarity
Of Belfast
Streets

Shipyards
Domes
Theatres

British army
Helicopter
Poised

Motionless
At last

I see everything

Like so many poems of *Breaking News*, this poem moves on without an end stop. Juxtaposing these spare lines and images with some of the most loaded words in the English language, this poem joins the others of the collection in questioning not just the conditional nature of "home," but the need to fill in those equations. *Breaking News* does indeed continue Carson's explorations of language and war but in a uniquely challenging way by addressing not the literary utterance—the typical traffic of the poets—but what Eliot called "the language of the tribe." Other than Russell, there is little of the sophisticated wordplay of recent collections or the contemporaries with whom Carson is often compared. This collection starts humbly enough—a poem entitled "Belfast" is followed by "Home." With his translation of Dante's *Inferno* behind him, no structural aspect of Carson's work can be taken as accidental. *Breaking News* is an important installment in the divine comedy that Carson is writing of Belfast. In engaging the beginnings of empire through Russell, it is also an important contribution to the linguistic forces that have not only shaped Belfast, but much of the globe that continues to wrestle with the inheritance of empire.

Source: David Gardiner, "The Effete Looter," in *Irish Literary Supplement*, Vol. 25, No. 1, Fall 2005, pp. 27–28.

Thomson Gale

In the following essay, the critic gives a critical analysis of Carson's work.

> CARSON'S POEMS, ESSAYS, AND FICTION ARE ALL INFUSED WITH A DISTINCTIVE, IRISH STYLE OF TALE TELLING."

A poet and storyteller from Belfast, Northern Ireland, Ciaran Carson is a gifted teller of tales who won a T. S. Elliot for his poetry and has been nominated for the Booker Prize. He inherited his love of storytelling from his father, Liam, who would tell his children stories in Gaelic. "As far back as I remember, the age of two or three I think, " Carson said on the Radio Netherlands Web site, "every evening, my father would sit us down and say, 'Now, here's a story for you.' And the story would appear to go on night after night for weeks. Whether in fact he did tell us stories each night, for weeks and months and years on end, I'm not sure, but in my imagination it was that way."

Carson's poems, essays, and fiction are all infused with a distinctive, Irish style of tale telling. A common motif is his native Belfast, which is a living landscape to the author, scarred and worn by its violent recent history, yet alive with its people, culture, and history.

Carson's poetry reflects the pain that natives of Belfast stubbornly endure. "Reading Carson's poetry is a vicarious experience, " commented William Pratt in a *World Literature Today* review of *Selected Poems*, "a bloodbath that is bloodless but thoroughly convincing, and for such a testimony to human endurance one has to be grateful despite the misery." John Kerrigan observed in an *Essays in Criticism* article comparing and contrasting Carson with fellow poet Seamus Heaney, "Carson writes with Proustian intensity about the elusiveness of memory in poems which thickly describe the fashions, songs, and smells of vanished Belfast." Kerrigan also noted the poet's fascination with cartography in his imagery about Belfast. Drawing a parallel between Carson and other Irish poets, the critic explained that "Carson is interested in the dubiety of maps which seem authoritative: no more permanent than place, they keep changing along with the city, and shape perceptions of the territory through censorship and velleity."

The sense of the transitoriness and mutability of Belfast, as in his poetry, is seen in Carson's autobiographical novel *The Star Factory,* in which he recaptures images of his youth before the time of terrorism between the Protestants and Catholics in Northern Ireland began. Compared by some critics to James Joyce's writing about Dublin and Seamus Heaney's memories of Ulster, *The Star Factory* reconstructs the poet's childhood memories in what *New Statesman* contributor Terry Eagleton called a "wonderfully evocative book" in which Carson "ransack[s] his Belfast boyhood for gleaming, sensuous treasures." In the book, the poet reflects on subjects ranging from school and his father to his boyhood friends and remembered objects. There is no real plot, and the book is not faithful autobiography, as it is tinged with Carson's artful eye. However, "Carson does not seek to fictionalise his history," wrote *Sunday Times* critic Walter Ellis. "Instead, he allows his finely honed mind to wander, unfettered, through the labyrinths of memory." Ellis concluded, "The funny thing is that *The Star Factory* is a splendid, easy read, packed, however obliquely, with wonderful reminiscences of old Belfast, a city much maligned."

In addition to capturing the past in *The Star Factory,* Carson also captures the musical essence of Ireland in *Last Night's Fun: A Book about Irish Traditional Music,* which was published in the United States as *Last Night's Fun: In and out of Time with Irish Music.* Less direct than his earlier *Pocket Guide to Irish Traditional Music,* which is more of an encyclopedia on the subject, *Last Night's Fun* seeks to convey the feeling of Irish music through thoughtful essays and poetry. Carson, a musician himself who plays the flute, touches not only on music, however, but also on such subjects as Irish cooking, homemade whiskey, the Gaelic language, history, and other subjects that one might hear spoken about while in an Irish pub. As one *Publishers Weekly* reviewer described the book, "It is an endless pub crawl in the labyrinthine soul of a remarkable writer who dares to play unfamiliar tunes." Alix Madrigal, writing in the *San Francisco Chronicle,* called it an "impressionistic meditation on Irish traditional music." Madrigal continued, "Carson is full of asides and digressions, funny and learned both, " concluding that the book "is a joy to read."

Carson's works of fiction are similarly quirky pieces. *Fishing for Amber: A Long Story,*

for example, is unconventional and difficult to categorize. "I hesitate to call it a novel, " said Erica Wagner in the London *Times,* ". . . it is a leitmotif." Divided into twenty-six chapters that are connected by several literary devices: the narratives are told by Jack the Lad, who is, in turn, telling stories from Irish mythology to a fairy audience; they are, furthermore, tales that were originally told to him by his father. "Another loose connection comes from the narrator's father's fascination with Holland, and his correspondence—in Esperanto—with a Dutchman," said Wagner. This part of the book comes right out of Carson's own life; his father had a similar correspondence with a Dutchman whom the family called Uncle Are. Carson then uses this device to write about such subjects as Dutch art and science, but he also touches on such diverse topics as stamp collecting and microscopes, among other seemingly unrelated things. "This is a strange work," Wagner concluded, "multifaceted, not entirely satisfying. But it is consistently intriguing, consistently original."

The troubles in Northern Ireland come to the center of Carson's fiction in his *Shamrock Tea,* another odd tale involving a magical tea that allows its main character, Carson, and his cousin Berenice to enter the painting "The Arnolfini Wedding" by Jan van Eyck, where they meet interesting people from history and have various adventures. But there is a serious side to the tale, for the fictional Carson has been sent into the painting by his Uncle Celestine, who wants his nephew to locate more shamrock tea, which is concealed in the painting. The tea has the additional quality of allowing those who use it to see the world more clearly and understand the oneness of all people. Carson's uncle plans to pour the tea into Belfast's drinking water, thus putting an end to the Protestant-Catholic fighting. This strange tale is a challenging but potentially rewarding read, according to critics. Nancy Pearl called it "maddening, entrancing, and mysterious" in a *Booklist* review, while a *Publishers Weekly* contributor warned that "because the disparate tales do not coalesce until late in this work, readers may lose patience, especially as the characters are 'allowed no inner thoughts.'" However, Ian Sansom, writing in the *Guardian,* felt that *Shamrock Tea* is "perhaps [Carson's] most potent blend to date."

Source: Thomson Gale, "Ciaran Carson," in *Contemporary Authors Online,* Gale, 2003.

IN TRUTH, GALLIPOLI IS A WRETCHED PLACE—
PICTURESQUE TO A DEGREE, BUT, LIKE ALL
PICTURESQUE THINGS OR PLACES, HORRIBLY
UNCOMFORTABLE."

William Howard Russell

In the following excerpt, Russell describes the three places Carson presents in "The War Correspondent": Gallipoli, Varna, and Kertch.

...When morning came we only felt sorry that nature had made Gallipoli, a desirable place for us to land at. The tricolor was floating right and left, and the blue coats of the French were well marked on shore, the long lines of bullock-carts stealing along the strand towards their camp making it evident that they were taking care of themselves.

Take some hundreds of dilapidated farms, outhouses, a lot of rickety tenements of Holywell-street, Wych-street, and the Borough—catch up, wherever you can, any of the seedy, cracked, shutterless structures of planks and tiles to be seen in our cathedral towns—carry off odd sheds and stalls from Billingsgate, add to them a selection of the huts along the Thames between London-bridge and Greenwich—bring them, then, all together to the European side of the Straits of the Dardanelles, and having pitched on a bare round hill sloping away to the water's edge, on the most exposed portion of the coast, with scarcely tree or shrub, tumble them "higgledy piggledy" on its declivity, in such wise that the lines of the streets may follow on a large scale the lines of book-worm through some old tome—let the roadways be very narrow, of irregular breadth, varying according to the bulgings and projections of the houses, and paved with large round slippery stones, painful and hazardous to walk upon—here and there borrow a dirty gutter from a back street in Boulogne—let the houses lean across to each other so that the tiles meet, or a plank thrown across forms a sort of "passage" or arcade—steal some of the popular monuments of London, the shafts of national testimonials, a half dozen of Irish Round Towers—surround these with a light gallery about twelve feet from

the top, put on a large extinguisher-shaped roof, paint them white, and having thus made them into minarets, clap them down into the maze of buildings—then let fall big stones all over the place—plant little windmills with odd-looking sails on the crests of the hill over the town—transport the ruins of a feudal fortress from Northern Italy, and put it into the centre of the town, with a flanking tower at the water's edge—erect a few wooden cribs by the waterside to serve as *café*, custom-house, and government stores—and, when you have done this, you have to all appearance imitated the process by which Gallipoli was created. The receipt, if tried, will be found to answer beyond belief.

To fill up the scene, however, you must catch a number of the biggest breeched, longest bearded, dirtiest, and stateliest old Turks to be had at any price in the Ottoman empire; provide them with pipes, keep them smoking all day on wooden stages or platforms about two feet from the ground, everywhere by the water's edge or up the main streets, in the shops of the bazaar which is one of the "passages" or arcades already described; see that they have no slippers on, nothing but stout woollen hose, their foot gear being left on the ground, shawl turbans (one or two being green, for the real descendant of the Prophet), flowing fur-lined coats, and bright-hued sashes, in which are to be stuck silver-sheathed yataghans and ornamented Damascus pistols; don't let them move more than their eyes, or express any emotion at the sight of anything except an English lady; then gather a noisy crowd of fez-capped Greeks in baggy blue breeches, smart jackets, sashes, and rich vests—of soberly-dressed Armenians—of keen-looking Jews, with flashing eyes—of Chasseurs de Vincennes, Zouaves, British riflemen, *vivandières*, Sappers and Miners, Nubian slaves, Camel-drivers, Commissaries and Sailors, and direct them in streams round the little islets on which the smoking Turks are harboured, and you will populate the place.

It will be observed that women are not mentioned in this description, but children were not by any means wanting—on the contrary, there was a glut of them, in the Greek quarter particularly, and now and then a bundle of clothes, in yellow leather boots, covered at the top with a piece of white linen, might be seen moving about, which you will do well to believe contained a woman neither young nor pretty. Dogs, so large, savage, tailless, hairy, and curiously-shaped, that

Wombwell could make a fortune out of them if aided by any clever zoological nomenclator, prowled along the shore and walked through the shallow water, in which stood bullocks and buffaloes, French steamers and transports, with the tricolor flying, and the paddlebox boats full of troops on their way to land—a solitary English steamer, with the red ensign, at anchor in the bay—and Greek polaceas, with their beautiful white sails and trim rig, flying down the straits, which are here about three and a half miles broad, so that the villages on the rich swelling hills of the Asia Minor side are plainly visible,—must be added, and then the picture will be tolerably complete.

In truth, Gallipoli is a wretched place—picturesque to a degree, but, like all picturesque things or places, horribly uncomfortable. The breadth of the Dardanelles is about five miles opposite the town, but the Asiatic and the European coasts run towards each other just ere the Straits expand into the Sea of Marmora. The country behind the town is hilly, and at the time of our arrival had not recovered from the effects of the late very severe weather, being covered with patches of snow. Gallipoli is situated on the narrowest portion of the tongue of land or peninsula which, running between the Gulf of Saros on the west and the Dardanelles on the east, forms the western side of the strait. An army eucamped here commands the Ægean and the Sea of Marmora, and can be marched northwards to the Balkan, or sent across to Asia or up to Constantinople with equal facility. . . .

On the night of Tuesday (Aug. 10th) a great fire broke out at Varna, which utterly destroyed more than a quarter of the town. The sailors of the ships, and the French and English soldiery stationed near the town, worked for the ten hours during which the fire lasted with the greatest energy; but as a brisk wind prevailed, which fanned the flames as they leapt along the wooden streets, their efforts were not as successful as they deserved. The fire broke out near the French commissariat stores, in a spirit shop. The officers in charge broached many casks of spirits, and as the liquid ran down the streets, a Greek was seen to set fire to it. He was cut down to the chin by a French officer, and fell into the fiery torrent. The howling of the inhabitants, the yells of the Turks, the clamour of the women, children, dogs, and horses, were appalling. Marshal St. Arnaud displayed great vigour and coolness in superintending the operations of the troops, and by his exertions aggravated the symptoms of the malady from which he had long been suffering. The French lost great quantities of provisions, and we had many thousand rations of biscuit utterly consumed. In addition to the bread (biscuit) which was lost, immense quantities of stores were destroyed. 19,000 pairs of soldiers' shoes and an immense quantity of cavalry sabres, which were found amid the ruins, fused into the most fantastic shapes, were burnt. The soldiers plundered a good deal, and outrages of a grave character were attributed to the Zouaves during the fire. Tongues and potted meats, most probably abstracted from sutlers' stores, were to be had in the outskirts of the camp for very little money soon after the occurrence, and some of the camp canteen keepers were completely ruined by their losses. To add to our misfortunes, the cholera broke out in the fleets in Varna Bay and at Baltschik with extraordinary virulence. The *Friedland and Montebello* suffered in particular—in the latter upwards of 100 died in twenty-four hours. The depression of the army was increased by this event. They "supped full of horrors," and listened greedily to tales of death, which served to weaken and terrify. . . .

Highlanders, in little parties, sought about for water, or took a stray peep after a "bit keepsake" in the houses on their way to the wells, but the French were always before them, and great was the grumbling at the comparative license allowed to our allies. The houses were clean outside and in—whitewashed neatly, and provided with small well-glazed windows, which were barely adequate, however, to light up the two rooms of which each dwelling consisted, but the heavy sour smell inside was most oppressive and disagreeable; it seemed to proceed from the bags of black bread and vessels of fish oil which were found in every cabin. Each dwelling had outhouses, stables for cattle, pens, bakeries, and rude agricultural implements outside. The ploughs were admirably described by Virgil, and a reference to *Adams's Antiquities* will save me a world of trouble in satisfying the curiosity of the farming interest at home. Notwithstanding the great richness of the land, little had been done by man to avail himself of its productiveness. I never in my life saw such quantities of weeds or productions of such inexorable ferocity towards pantaloons, or such eccentric flowers of huge dimensions, as the ground outside these cottages bore. The inhabitants were evidently graziers rather than agriculturists. Around every house were piles of a substance like peat, which is made, we were informed, from the dung of cattle, and is used as fuel. The cattle, however, had been all driven away. None were taken that I saw, though the quantity which fed in the fields around must have been very great. Poultry and ducks were, however, captured in abundance, and a party of Chasseurs, who had taken a huge wild-looking boar, were in high delight at their fortune, and soon despatched and cut him up into junks with their swords. The furniture was all smashed to pieces; the hens and ducks, captives to the bow and spear of the Gaul, were cackling and quacking piteously as they were carried off in bundles from their homes by Zouaves and Chasseurs. Every house we entered was ransacked, and every cupboard had a pair of red breeches sticking out of it, and a blue coat inside of it. Vessels of stinking oil, bags of sour bread, casks of flour or ham, wretched clothing, old boots, beds ripped up for treasure, the hideous pictures of saints on panelling or paper which adorned every cottage, with lamps suspended before them, were lying on the floors. Droles dressed themselves in faded pieces of calico dresses or aged finery lying hid in old drawers, and danced about the gardens. One house, which had been occupied as a guard-house, and was marked on a board over the door "No. 7 Kardone," was a scene of especial confusion. Its inmates had evidently fled in great disorder, for their greatcoats and uniform jackets strewed the floors, and bags of the black bread filled every corner, as well as an incredible quantity of old boots. A French soldier, who, in his indignation at not finding anything of value, had with great wrath devastated the scanty and nasty-looking furniture, was informing his comrades outside of the atrocities which had been committed, and added, with the most amusing air of virtue in the world, *"Ah, Messieurs, Messieurs! ces brigands! ils ont volés tout!"* No doubt he had settled honourably with the proprietor of a large bundle of living poultry which hung panting over his shoulders, and which were offered to us upon very reasonable terms. We were glad to return from a place which a soldier of the 71st said "A Glasgae beggar wad na tak a gift o'." . . .

Source: William Howard Russell, "Excerpts," in *The British Expedition to the Crimea*, George Routledge and Sons, 1877, pp. 13–14, 61–62, 269–70.

SOURCES

Carson, Ciaran, "The War Correspondent," in *Breaking News*, Wake Forest University Press, 2003, pp. 42, 45–57, 59.

Gardiner, David, "The Effete Looter," in *Irish Literary Supplement*, Vol. 25, No. 1, Fall 2005, pp. 27–28.

Gibbons, Fiachra, "Triumph for 'Breakfast' Poet and a Comic Rival for Blake's Jerusalem," in *Guardian*, October 9, 2003, http://books.guardian.co.uk/news/articles/0, ,1059043, 00.html (accessed December 2, 2006).

Knightley, Phillip, *The First Casualty: From the Crimea to Vietnam: The War Correspondent as Hero, Propagandist, and Myth Maker*, Harcourt Brace Jovanovich, 1975, p. 5.

Mathews, Joseph J., *Reporting the Wars*, University of Minnesota Press, 1957, p. 71.

O'Brien, Sean, "Belfast and Beyond," in *Times Literary Supplement*, No. 5228, June 13, 2003, p. 10.

Russell, William Howard, *The British Expedition to the Crimea*, New and Revised Edition, George Routledge and Sons, 1877, p. v.

———, *Russell's Despatches from the Crimea, 1854–1856*, edited by Nicolas Bentley, Hill and Wang, 1966, pp. 28, 29, 30, 54, 67, 88, 127, 132, 176, 263, 264, 265.

Taylor, John, Review of *Breaking News*, in *Antioch Review*, Vol. 62, No. 2, Spring 2004, p. 372.

FURTHER READING

Crotty, Patrick, *Modern Irish Poetry: An Anthology*, Blackstaff Press, 1995.
> This anthology of Irish poetry includes selections from the work of established poets such as Seamus Heaney, Eavan Boland, Derek Mahon, Michael Longley, and Paul Muldoon, as well as some new and less well-known voices.

Lewis, Jon E., ed. *Mammoth Book of War Correspondents*, Carroll & Graf Publishers, 2001.
> This book highlights 150 years of war reportage in the reporters' own words, beginning with Russell's coverage of the Crimean War and concluding with the 1990s conflicts in Bosnia and Chechnya. The one hundred pieces of war correspondence, which are arranged chronologically, include work by Stephen Crane, Rudyard Kipling, Ernest Hemingway, George Orwell, Edward R. Murrow, Seymour Hersh, Peter Arnett, and Ernie Pyle.

Royle, Trevor, *Crimea: The Great Crimean War, 1854–1856*, Palgrave Macmillan, reprint edition, 2004.
> Royle is an expert on military history, and this book is widely considered the definitive work on the Crimean War. It describes in detail the

causes of the war, the military action and diplomatic maneuvering, and the long-term consequences.

Warner, Philip, *The Crimean War: A Reappraisal*, Taplinger Publishing, 1973.

Warner provides a fresh examination of the Crimean War, suggesting that the traditional view, that the war was a classic model of military and medical incompetence, may not be the complete truth.

What the Poets Could Have Been

JULIANNA BAGGOTT

2001

"What the Poets Could Have Been" is from Julianna Baggott's first collection of poetry, *This Country of Mothers*, published in 2001. The poetry in this collection can best be defined as stories of family and of change and growth. These are poems of childhood, of parents and grandparents, of miscarriage and childbirth, and of the metamorphosis from daughter to mother. This collection is dedicated to Baggott's mother, Glenda, and to her daughter, Phoebe, which is appropriate, since the poems are drawn from Baggott's own memories of being a daughter and mother. "What the Poets Could Have Been" fits neatly into this collection of memories and transformation.

Like her novels, Baggott's poetry is autobiographical. "What the Poets Could Have Been" is from chapter four of the collection, which includes poems that do not seem to fit neatly into the other four chapters of this book. The poems in this chapter are about spirituality and religion, about death and torture during war, and about being a poet. What they all have in common, though, is the poet's response to events or people. "What the Poets Could Have Been" recognizes the journey that Baggott undertook in becoming a poet. In this poem, Baggott explores several aspects of the poet's creative process, including the importance of imagination and creativity in producing poetry. One important aspect of "What the Poets Could Have Been" is Baggott's conjecture regarding what poets might

have done with their lives had they chosen different career paths. Baggott speculates on the role
that poetry plays in the poet's life. She also wonders what poets would have done instead had
they chosen not to write. She finally wonders if
paying more attention to lectures in school might
have made them more content.

AUTHOR BIOGRAPHY

Julianna Baggott was born on September 10,
1969, in Wilmington, Delaware, and was raised
in the nearby town of Newark. Baggott attended
Loyola College in Baltimore, Maryland, where
she studied creative writing and French. While
she was at Loyola, she also studied abroad at the
Sorbonne in Paris, where she received a certifi-
cate in language proficiency in 1990. After she
completed a bachelor's degree in 1991, Baggott
went on to earn an M.F.A. in creative writing
from the University of North Carolina in 1994.
Baggott soon married David Scott, who was also
a creative writing student at North Carolina.

In 1998, Baggott received a call from an agent
asking if she was interested in writing a novel, and
so she turned a short story, "Girl Talk," into a
novel by the same name, which was published in
2001. At the same time, Baggott had a collection
of poetry ready for publication. "What the Poets
Could Have Been" is one of the poems in *This
Country of Mothers*, Baggott's first collection
which appeared in 2001. These first two books
were quickly followed by two more novels, *The
Miss America Family* (2002) and *The Madam*
(2003). In 2004, Baggott published her first children's novel under her pen name, N. E. Bode. Her
children's novels, *The Anybodies* (2004), *The
Nobodies* (2005), and *The Somebodies* (2006),
were a huge success with young readers. However,
Baggott returned to adult readers with another
book of poetry in 2006, *Lizzie Borden in Love:
Poems in Women's Voices*, and a novel, *Which
Brings Me to You: A Novel in Confession*, written
in collaboration with Steve Almond. Baggott's
third book of poetry, *Compulsions of Silkworms
and Bees*, was published in 2007.

Baggott has received a number of awards for
her writing. Her first book of poetry, *This
Country of Mothers*, received the Crab Orchard
Award for Poetry in 2000. Her third novel, *The
Madam*, was nominated for the National Book
Award in 2003. In 2004, Baggott's children's

book, *The Anybodies*, was nominated for the
Mark Twain Award in Missouri, the Diamond
State Award in Delaware, the Maine Student
Book Award, the Master List for the Pennsylva-
nia Young Readers Choice Award, the Massa-
chusetts' Children's Book Award, and the Nene
Award in Hawaii. *The Anybodies* was as of early
2007 under development with Nickelodeon
Movies at Paramount Studios.

*Lizzie Borden in Love: Poems in Women's
Voices* was a 2006 nominee for the Pulitzer
Prize. Baggott won the Lena-Miles Wever
Todd Poetry Series Award for *Compulsions of
Silkworms and Bees*. As of 2007, Baggott was
teaching creative writing at Florida State
University. She was living in Florida with her
husband and their three children.

POEM TEXT

If every time their minds drifted,
they'd thought instead of a grocery list—
milk, eggs, shoe polish, liniment—
if they could have smelled lemon
and thought of lemons, not their mother's
    hands,   5
if they'd been more attentive
to Mr. Twardus's lectures on manliness
while sanding garden boxes in shop class
and more exacting of the apron hem
in Mrs. Niff's home economics,   10
if they'd been, in some cases, just a little taller
and hadn't fallen so deeply in love each time,
hopping the fence to swim naked with a lover
in the county park pool, their buoyant bodies
    drifting up
the way words bubble to the mind's surface,   15
if there were, in general,
less shine, blueness, ticking,
less body and earth, they could have been
repressible, contented. Imagine Hudgins
your minister bent over chapel weeds;
    Lauterbach   20
your librarian reading travel books,
pictures of le Tour Eiffel spread open
on her desk; Shapiro your basketball coach,
his thick glasses sliding down his nose
as he calls you off the bench; Levine,   25
having stuck it out at Detroit Transmission,
now your father's boss, his face
lined hard, eyes squinting.
Imagine if they were your aunts and uncles,
    tired, smiling
as they drink beer on the back porch—   30
the simplest things make them happy—
you, for example, twirling your baton up
into the moonlit, mosquito-singing sky,

and all you must do—not this, not words—
is spin and try to catch it   35
in your unsteady, opening hand.

POEM SUMMARY

Lines 1–5

In "What the Poets Could Have Been," Baggott begins with the word, "if." She repeats this word several times in the first lines of the poem and uses this repetitive format to imagine what poets might have done, had they not been poets, had they been able to hold their minds in check and not let their thoughts drift beyond what was expected of them. The "if" is what might have been. The title of the poem makes clear that the subject is an exploration of what poets could have been, had they been different; it points to this poem's inquiry.

Baggott makes the differences between poets and other people clear in her opening lines. When the minds of people not destined to be poets are distracted, their thoughts turn to grocery lists. The minds of such people wander to commonplace errands of the day, trying to remember if they need milk and eggs or shoe polish. When most people smell the scent of lemons, they wonder if they need to buy more. But that is not true of the poet. According to Baggott, when poets smell lemons, they associate the scent with memories, in this case with a mother's hands that smelled of lemon. In the first line, Baggott refers to poets as a group of people who get distracted in similar ways. She repeats the use of plural pronouns throughout these first few lines, using "they'd" and repeating the use of "their" several times. Baggott suggests that poets share certain traits. The use of "if they'd" or "if they" establishes both the imaginative possibilities and the connectedness of all poets, who can be identified through their inability to be commonplace or like the majority.

Lines 6–10

In line 6, Baggott uses the conditional "if" to refer to those times when the poets' minds drifted in school, such as when the shop teacher, Mr. Twardus, lectures during shop class or when the home economics teacher, Mrs. Neff, expects careful attention to the hem of the apron being sewn. It is easy for a student's mind to wander

from a teacher's lecture, and it frequently happens, but in these two examples, Baggott leads the reader to consider that for poets, this inability to pay attention to teachers is a sign of their creativity or of the talent that will be developed after high school. If the future poets had listened more in school, they might not have developed into poets later on.

Lines 11–19

Line 11 repeats the use of "if" to remind readers of yet another distraction, but "only in some cases." These words present yet another qualifier. If these future poets had been taller or less likely to fall deeply in love each time, if the world have been less tactile, with "less shine, blueness, ticking," then these people would have been "repressible, contented." In other words, they would not have developed into poets.

Future poets are impulsive in love; they jump the fence to "swim naked with a lover." When in the water, these kinds of lovers, their "buoyant bodies drifting up" to the surface, are inspired by words, which also "bubble to the mind's surface." Soon-to-be poets are the type of people who are spontaneous, intense, and impetuous; They abandon the ordinary and spring toward the unusual.

In these last three lines before the poem's first period, the poet provides of list of words, which are preceded once again by the word, "if." The list consists of sensory perceptions: the "shine" of the sun, the "blueness" of the sky, the "ticking" of the clock, as time passes. The poet sees and feels these things more vividly than those non-poets. "If there were . . . less" of these beautiful sensations, Baggott concludes that the potential poets might have been "repressible, contented."

Lines 19–28

Mid way through line 19, Baggott switches from the possibilities the lie before high school students to the realities of ordinary adult lives and work. The poet asks her readers to "imagine" adults engaged in ordinary work-related activity. In lines 19 and 20, the minister is weeding the church property; the librarian, who cannot take a trip to Paris, placates herself with a photograph of the Eiffel Tower; the coach with sweat on his face deals with the students; Levine has a lined face from having "stuck it out at Detroit Transmission." These adults have settled for less than perhaps what they hoped for.

TOPICS FOR FURTHER STUDY

- Baggott's poetry is autobiographical. Make a list of at least seven to nine memories that are important to you. These should be the things that first come to mind when you think of your life. You might try to pick one or two items from each of the past several years. After you have a list, arrange them in order of importance. This order does not have to be chronological, but it can be. When you have brought some sort of order to your list, rewrite the list as a poem. Baggott's poem proposes that memories are interpreted differently by poets. After you complete your poem, write a brief critique in which you consider if your memories change when transformed into poetry.

- Select a poem by any nineteenth-century female poet and compare it to Baggott's poem "What the Poets Could Have Been." Compare such elements as content, theme, tone, and word choice. In your evaluation of these two works, consider the modernity of Baggott's poem. Do you think it is different in tone and content from the poem by the nineteenth century poet that you chose? How are the two poems similar or different?

- Take the first line of Baggott's poem "What the Poets Could Have Been," and use it as the first line of your own poem. Write a poem of at least twenty-five lines, using the same strategy of asking "what if" that Baggott uses. Choose a different career, perhaps that of movie star, politician, or singer, and create a poem exploring the kinds of traits that go into the career that you have chosen and how life would be different. Your poem should also incorporate a similar style. For instance, you should try to create a lengthy dependent clause that then

leads into the main point of the poem, whatever that might be.

- Artists are often inspired by poets to create some of the most beautiful art imaginable. For instance, William Blake was inspired by John Milton's poetry to create illustrations of the poet's finest work, *Paradise Lost*. Spend some time looking through art books in the library and select a picture or illustration that you feel best illustrates Baggott's poem. Then, in an essay, compare the art that you have selected to the images that Baggott creates in her poem, noting both the similarities and the differences between the art and the poem.

- One of the best ways to learn about poetic form is to write poetry. Place yourself in Baggott's life or the life of any modern female poet whom you admire, and using her work as a guide, write at least one or two poems that imitate both her style, meter, and content. When you have completed your poems, write a brief evaluation of your work, comparing it to the poet's work. What have you learned about the difficulty of writing modern poetry?

- Baggott's novels are autobiographical and, in some cases, like poetry transformed into prose. Stories can also be transformed into poetry, which is what you will do. Instead of writing a research paper, this assignment asks you to write a research poem. Choose a famous woman from history and use at least one or two important events from her life to create a narrative poem about her. Remember that sometimes the most interesting poetry does not rhyme. Instead, try to use free verse to capture the emotion and intensity of this woman's life.

Baggott introduces the word "you" into the poem, and for the first time, she pulls the reader into the poem, making the poem about the

reader as well as the poet. By using "you," Baggott offers readers a chance to see themselves as a youngster again, a high school athlete, a baton twirler, a future poet. Readers are given the chance to imagine themselves as a part of this new world, in which the possibilities lie in the future.

Lines 29–36

The first word of the third sentence of the poem, at line 29, is once again "Imagine." Finally, the poet moves away from the people who inhabit schools, church, library, and business, and asks the reader to imagine the poet's family. The family sits all together on the back porch. They are made happy by "the simplest things," sitting there together, smiling, drinking beer. They do not need much to make them smile—the company of family, a warm evening, a cold beer, and a twirling baton in the hands of a beloved child. They smile as they watch the child perform. They are made happier by watching the child's attempts to catch the baton, in her "unsteady, opening hand." The simple act of tossing the baton and catching is all that is required, but that is not enough for the child. Baggott inserts only a short phrase to suggest that for the child, the performance is not rewarding. The words, "not this, not words" reminds readers that the poet's words are not what is making the aunts and uncles smile, even as the tossing of the baton does not fulfill the child's dreams. These "words" demand more from the child than the act of twirling the baton.

THEMES

Conformity

The whole premise of Baggott's poem is that future poets are not like other people when they are young. Those people who are not poets do not let their minds drift; instead they do what is expected. They conform. But they are not poets, whose minds drift from lemons to their mother's lemon-scented hands. Poets let their minds drift at school, as well. They do not conform, as other so-called good students do. Poets are not "attentive / to Mr. Twardus's lectures on manliness," nor are they "exacting of the apron hem" in home economics class. Poets do not conform in matters of love either. Poets fall more "deeply in love each time," and they are impetuous as well, "hopping the fence to swim naked with a lover."

Poets fail to conform in other ways as well. For instance, in lines 17 through 19, Baggott suggests that if poets were less connected to the world around them, they would more easily be contented and repressed. But they are stimulated a lot by the sensations nature works, by the "shine, blueness, ticking." They feel their bodies too much to be repressed. For poets, the sun is more intense and the sky more blue. They see the world intimately and respond to it, and this responsiveness causes their edgy discontent and their inability to be repressed or held back. Poets cannot conform, and they cannot settle for less.

Imagination

At line 19, Baggott asks her readers to "imagine" some very ordinary adults—the minister, the librarian, and the basketball coach, all working in their everyday, attending to their obligations. There is nothing ideal or special about what these adults are doing. The minister is weeding the chapel garden. The librarian, Lauterbach, may dream about Paris and seeing the Eiffel Tower, but the closest she gets is the open book on her desk with a photo. Clearly, the minister and the librarian have aspirations and dreams, but these scenes suggest those dreams were unfulfilled.

The next two people are the basketball coach and a boss. The reader identifies more intimately with the poet and poem if he or she also recognizes people and events from his or her past. Baggott uses the second person, "your," in the final segment of the poem, transporting the reader back into childhood and into a family gathering. Using the pronoun, "your," the poet invites the reader to recall moments in childhood when the act of pleasing the family was not what the reader really wished for herself.

Self-Discovery

In "What the Poets Could Have Been," the poet-speaker takes readers on a journey of self-discovery, in which they imagine for a few moments the possibilities that exist for young people. She creates images of a world that is much more interesting for poets than for non-poets, and she leads readers to imagine different choices. Rather than the boredom of high school class, the poet escapes, letting his or her mind drift away from the drone of a teacher's lecture. This is an enviable escape that many readers will recognize. Instead of growing up to become one of those teachers, the young people whose minds

Baggott suggests that poets find themselves distracted from the mundane details in life, much as this woman's thoughts appear to have drifted from the ironing set before her (© *George Robinson/Alamy*)

drift grow up to be poets. These are the kind of people who fall more "deeply in love each time," and they "swim naked with a lover / in the county park pool." Readers may not identify with these images, but they are invited to see the beauty in the ability to feel more deeply or behave more impetuously. The intensity of experience that Baggott describes, even if not what the reader desires, leads readers toward understanding how individuals develop as they do and how adult work gets chosen. Modern poets in particular want readers to see a new world that is different from the old. Readers who are able to visualize the poet's world can learn more about their own world and more about themselves.

STYLE

End-Stopped Lines

End-stopped lines occur when a phrase or sentence ends at the end of a line with a mark of punctuation. In a few cases, such as at the end of lines two and three, Baggott uses a dash to signal a pause for the reader, but except for the dash, she rarely employs an end-stop, preferring instead to continue the thought into the next line.

Enjambment

Enjambment occurs when the grammatical sense of a line continues beyond the line's end into the next line. In this poem, Baggott uses enjambment to continue the thought through several lines, from the first line to line 19, where a period finally closes the opening thought.

Free Verse

Free verse is poetry with no predictable structure, rhyme scheme, or meter. Free verse allows the poet to fit the poetic line to the content of the poem. The poet is not restricted by the need to shape the poem to a particular meter but can instead create complex rhythm and syntax. Free verse is not the same as blank verse, which is unrhymed iambic pentameter. Free verse relies on line breaks and word choice to create rhythm. Baggott's poem is an example of free verse. There is no pattern of rhyme or meter to "What the Poets Could Have Been," and instead, the irregular line breaks give the poem its rhythm, which is best appreciated by reading it aloud.

Line Breaks

Line breaks are a defining element of poetry. They are one characteristic that is used to impart meaning or to place emphasis on an idea, to create a rhyme or rhythm, or to lend a specific appearance to the poem on the page. Baggott uses line breaks to create a brief pause and to emphasize ideas. The use of a line break at line 16 emphasizes the importance of the list of words that follows at line 17: "if there were, in general, / less shine, blueness, ticking." Line breaks are not the same as the use of the dash at line 34, where Baggott wants to create more tension and put more emphasis on the words "not this, not words." The line breaks force the reader's attention on those words, whose meaning is just the opposite of the words that come before and follow.

Repetition

Repetition of a word, sound, or phrase is useful in emphasizing ideas in a poem. This stylistic device is one way to cue readers about what matters most. Baggott uses repetition to emphasize the idea that when other people are paying attention to some things, poets are distracted by other things, and in some cases, poets may look like they are not paying attention, but the fact is they are paying attention to what matters to them. For example, in the first line, the poet uses "drifted" to describe the poet's mind moving away from the immediate subject—not to what follows in the poem (a grocery list, for example) but something else not all that explicitly identified in the poem. The next time the poet uses this word, she describes the lovers' bodies in the pool, poetry (in the form of a metaphoric comparison) taking over in the phrasing: "their buoyant bodies drifting up / the way words bubble to the mind's surface." Here, the poet illustrates what in the first line a would-be poet's mind drifts to: it drifts to words "that bubble to the mind's surface," irrepressibly and naturally coming into consciousness to describe the sensations of the fully lived experience. This immediacy of words and experience explains why the high-school-age future poets' minds drift. The repetition cues readers to see the point not directly stated elsewhere in the poem.

HISTORICAL CONTEXT

Education and Hard Work

"What the Poets Could Have Been" was not published prior to its inclusion in *This Country of Mothers*, which was published in April 2001. Although the exact date of composition is unknown, it seems reasonable that the poem was probably composed late in the twentieth century, at some point close to its publication date. Baggott was readying her first collection of poems for publication against a backdrop of social, economic, and technological change.

The late twentieth century was a period of economic boom in the United States, and it was also a period that saw a greater emphasis on hard work, with U.S. citizens choosing to work longer hours and take fewer vacation days than workers in many other countries. This period also witnessed the birth of mass technology, with online use changing the way that people communicated with one another, shopped for clothing and other goods, or chose entertainment. While all this technology fed an economic boom, with low unemployment and huge growth in the stock market, for families the change was also felt in education. While the percentage of teens that completed high school rose significantly during the last years of the twentieth century, to a graduation rate of about 80 percent, the actual mechanics of education changed dramatically. It became clear that for many attending so-called brick and mortar schools was not the answer. Many parents decided that their children could be home schooled, and many others used online distance learning programs to augment traditional community schooling. There were special schools for teenagers who had become parents and special schools for troubled students who could not adapt to a traditional school setting. Some students wore uniforms and some students went to school year round. Unfortunately there were also school shootings, which reminded parents everywhere that not all schools were safe.

Baggott takes her readers back to high school and reminds them of shop class and home economics, and through a careful choice of words, she reminds readers of how bored students could be in class. It was not only poets whose minds drifted during these classes. But perhaps those who were attentive were, as Baggott proposes, more "repressible, [and] contented." Maybe those students did grow up to be more restrained and subdued, and maybe they were so controlled that they never thought about writing poetry. The use of the drug Ritalin increased dramatically in the 1990s as more students were diagnosed with attention deficit disorders, and teachers made more attempts to create "repressible, contented" students. Schools clearly had changed, but bored students had not, which accounts for the variety of options designed to keep students engaged in their education.

Dreams of Escape

In her poem, Baggott suggests different ways to escape mundane everyday life. The minister may escape in thought while he weeds the church garden. The librarian can imagine a dream escape to Paris while browsing through a picture book, and the basketball player gets called off the bench and is finally given the opportunity to play. Although life expectancy climbed to nearly seventy-seven years, in the United States many people spend more of that time at work. The International Labor Organization reported that by 1997, U.S workers were working the longest hours of any workforce in a major nation of the world. U.S. workers put in 77 more hours per year than Japanese workers and 234 more hours than Canadian workers. U.S. workers also worked 234 more hours than workers in Germany and 567 more hours than workers in Norway. All of this extra work added to the stress of everyday living. Americans chose many different ways to escape the stress of late-twentieth-century life, and there were plenty of things to make life stressful.

Iraq invaded Kuwait in 1990, leading to Operation Desert Storm and the Gulf War. The Bosnian civil war in 1992 and the killing fields of Rwanda in 1995 proved that genocide did not end with the World War II Holocaust. Both the World Trade Center bombing of 1993 and the Oklahoma City bombing of 1995 caused U.S. citizens to increasingly worry about terrorism, and in 1998, there was additional cause for concern when both Pakistan and India tested nuclear weapons. The world was undergoing many changes. The Taliban took over Afghanistan in 1996, and Hong Kong became part of China in 1997. NASA scientists announced in 1996 that a rock from Mars might once have known living creatures, and in 1997 Dolly became the first successfully cloned animal. In the United States, people found different ways to

escape their concern about a world that seemed to defy control. Huge crowds flocked to theaters to see the ship, *Titanic*, sink and to see the long-awaited prequel to *Star Wars*. Other people dove into the latest John Grisham escapist story or tuned into *Seinfeld*. No matter the choice, there were many ways to escape the stresses of late-twentieth-century life. Baggott offers one other form of escape—the method employed by poets, who use words to imagine different lives.

CRITICAL OVERVIEW

This Country of Mothers, Baggott's first published collection of poetry, won the Southern University Press Crab Orchard Award, which included a cash prize as well as an agreement to publish the book. As quoted in a release from the Southern Illinois University Press, in awarding the Crab Orchard prize, one of the judges, Rodney Jones, is reported to have stated that Baggott "is an accomplished poet of the eye and ear, of the definitive feminine experience, and her poems of private life are expansive enough to suggest a vision of a political and historical era." Although Jones does not specifically mention "What the Poets Could Have Been", he does point out that Baggott "draws themes as sharp as razors" and that her poems are "marvelously accessible." Jones's comments include the observation that "*This Country of Mothers* announces a poet of substantial powers."

The book also earned praise from several other reviewers. In a review for *Book Page*, Joanna Smith Rakoff links Baggott's poetry to her very successful novels, noting that the poems "wrestle with the same themes and ideas" as her first novel, *Girl Talk*. Rakoff points out that the poems are "narrated by a young American Everywoman, navigating her way through a generic and often cruel landscape." These are narrative poems, in which the speaker "strives to reconcile her growing spirituality with her intense skepticism." Rakoff claims that the narrative quality of the poems creates "compelling, breathless" works that should be read almost like a novel, "as the narrator engages with the literal and metaphysical worlds."

In the online forum, *Emerging Authors*, Dan Wickett's review of *This Country of Mothers* points out that "Baggott is not afraid to discuss

WHAT DO I READ NEXT?

- *Lizzie Borden in Love: Poems in Women's Voices*, Baggott's second collection of poetry and nominated for a Pulitzer Prize in Poetry in 2006, uses the voices of many women to offer commentaries about their lives. These poems include portrayals of Mary Todd Lincoln, Katherine Hepburn, and Monica Lewinsky, among others.

- *The Madam* is Baggott's third novel. Published in 2003, this novel is a fictionalized account of Baggott's great-grandmother's bordello, which operated in 1920s West Virginia.

- Baggott and Steve Almond collaborated on *Which Brings Me to You: A Novel in Confessions* (2006). This epistolary novel tells the story of two people who have an immediate attraction to one another and who use letters as a way to learn each other's romantic history.

- *The Anybodies* is Baggott's first children's novel under her pen name, N. E. Bode. This novel, published in 2004, is about the adventures of an eleven-year-old girl, who discovers she was switched at birth.

- Marian Coe's 2007 collection, *Between Us: Women's Voices Sharing Confidences, Earned Wisdom and Moments from Life: A Gift Package of Stories*, is a collection of poems, short stories, and essays that present brief vignettes drawn from women's lives.

- *Innovative Women Poets: An Anthology of Contemporary Poetry and Interviews* (2007), edited by Elisabeth A. Frost and Cynthia Hogue, is a collection of fourteen interviews with female poets from the last half of the twentieth century. These interviews provide an opportunity to understand the historical and cultural context of contemporary women's poetry.

her fears through her poems, to question both the positives and negatives of daily life and offer opinions." Wickett claims that in this collection of poetry Baggott "has nicely followed up on some of the themes of her debut novel," looking at the process of motherhood and moving through the "very personal journey of chronicling her own life." Wickett also compliments Baggott on the ease of understanding of her poems, which are "written so cleanly" that they are "entirely accessible." Wickett concludes that while Baggott's "poems are emotionally wrenching at times, and while certainly written from a feminine perspective, they should not be looked at as exclusive to women." Sales for this first collection of poetry were successful enough that the book went to a second printing, which is unusual for a book of poetry.

CRITICISM

Sheri Metzger Karmiol

Karmiol holds a Ph.D. in English literature and is a university professor. In this essay, she discusses the self-conscious awareness of the poet, who uses her talent as a way to justify the poet's existence and give meaning to her work.

The desire to use poetry as a way to either justify its creation or explain its purpose is not new. Julianna Baggott's "What the Poets Could Have Been" is only one of many attempts to explore the power of poetry and its importance, which some poets think extends far beyond words on paper. In ancient Greece, poets wrote about the purpose of poetry, the need for poets to fulfill certain functions, and the importance of poetry in the world of human affairs. After the Roman conquest of the Greek city-states, Roman poets adopted the Greek value of poetry. Horace's *Ars Poetica* (Art of Poetry or Nature of Poetry) became the standard attempt by poets to define what poetry means. When, in the first century B.C.E., Horace warned writers to "Examine well, ye writers, weigh with care, / What suits your genius; what your strengths can bear," he was only repeating Aristotle's earlier warnings. The power of poetry to influence people and actions, even political events, was well known. Horace claimed that poets should "Be delicate and cautious in the use / And choice of words," because he understood that words have power that extends beyond their value as

> THE POET IS THE ONE WHO RESPONDS TO THE 'SHINE, BLUENESS, TICKING' OF LIFE. TO NOT RESPOND MEANS SETTLING FOR LIFE LESS FULLY LIVED. POETS DELIVER THE FULLY LIVED LIFE TO THEIR READERS."

literature. The lessons of two thousand years ago have not been lost on Baggott. In "What the Poets Could Have Been," Baggott focuses on the role that poetry plays in the poet's life and what it means to the reader, as well.

As early as 1956, an English professor named Robert Preyer lamented the fact that his academic colleagues did not read poetry. After acknowledging the complaints that readers express about the difficulty they have in appreciating poetry, Preyer tried to explain the importance of poetry and how poetry can enhance understanding. In his essay, "The Prejudice against Poetry: A Diagnosis and an Appeal," Preyer defends the importance of reading poetry, claiming that poetry is "an organization of experience capable of altering the present and creating new significances." For Preyer, poetry is a way to alter reality into something vastly different and perhaps more appealing. This is also true of Baggott's poem, which plays with reality and experience. In "What the Poets Could Have Been," Baggott captures the importance of poetry as a means to being alive fully in the world and through words bringing others to greater appreciation of sensory experience. For example, Baggott writes that people who have the potential to be poets are likely to hop a "fence to swim naked with a lover." The words conjure an image of impetuous desire, of living in the moment. Indeed, Baggott refers to the poet's many loves as having been felt more "deeply," somehow suggesting that the poet feels love with an unusual intensity. Moreover, the intensity stimulates words that, like lovers' "buoyant bodies," drift to the surface of the poet's mind. The link between passion and poetry illustrates the value of the words and connects Baggott's point to an ancient tradition of using poetry to convey romantic love and the risks it may induce lovers to take. Only poetry engages others in the lived experience in such an intimate

way. Photography or paintings cannot capture the same intensity. The photographic image is flat and two-dimensional, but the poem brings the reader inside the world the words create, animating a sensed experience that exists off the page, as well as on it.

Like Preyer, Baggott understands the nature of the prejudice against poetry. Her poem, "What the Poets Could Have Been," is both a justification for being a poet and a defense against those who do not pay attention to poetry. The lengthy dependent clause that begins the poem, with "If every time their minds drifted" and that ends only at lines 18 and 19 with "they could have been / repressible, contented," makes clear that for Baggott, non-poets are those who are content with less emotion in their lives, who are more easily repressed. These non-poets are not the naked lovers. The non-poets are those who are likely to pay attention in class, to follow directions in sewing a hem; they are the ones who grow up to stick it out in jobs that line their faces. The poet is the one who responds to the "shine, blueness, ticking" of life. To not respond means settling for life less fully lived. Poets deliver the fully lived life to their readers.

Robert W. Blake, an English professor at SUNY College in New York, agrees that poetry alters the perceptions people have of the world. In his 1990 essay, "Poets on Poetry: Writing and the Reconstruction of Reality," Blake asserts, "When one writes poetry, one reconstructs reality." For example, Baggott asks readers to imaginatively jump from high school experience to the mundane work lives most adults make for themselves. She uses the minister and the librarian as examples of people, who may well have unlived dreams. The minister weeds the church property, while he may well wish he could as easily separate the bad from the good for his congregation. The librarian sits at her desk with an open travel book, displaying a photo of the Eiffel Tower. She may well have wanted to visit France, but she settles for a picture instead of reaching for the firsthand experience. "Poets," Blake writes, "see the value of poetry in various ways. Poetry is like a lens or prism through which one views the world in a heightened way. Poetry is for telling people what they hadn't noticed or thought about before." Baggott makes her readers see inside the minister and librarian to intuit their hidden desires. In his essay, Blake argues that "poetry is using chosen words to reveal what people and living creatures are really like." This revelation is the work of poetry.

Baggott is not the first woman to use poetry as a way to delve into the self-conscious, even as she creates a more intense reality for the reader. In the 1860s, Emily Dickinson visualized the poet as someone who "Distills amazing sense / From ordinary Meanings." Ordinary flowers find their scent intensified to become a perfume, an "attar so immense" that it exceeds the flower's common origins. The poet is someone who reveals meaning hiding in things and becomes, "Of Pictures, the Discloser." Dickinson understood that the poet's role in helping readers to imagine greater meanings from their experience. Dickinson also injects a certain amount of irony. Given the poet's invaluable role in society, Dickinson acknowledges that those who are not poets lead poor lives by contrast: "The Poet—it is He—/ Entitles Us—by Contrast—/ To ceaseless Poverty." Baggott no doubt appreciates Dickinson's reference to poverty, but sees in it a different meaning. In several interviews, Baggott mentions how poor she and her poet husband were when they first began writing. For instance, in a fall 2001 interview with Cheryl Dellasega, Baggott states that when she completed her bachelor's degree in creative writing and French, "her father called it 'a degree in starvation and poverty.'" Baggott and her husband were poor enough that they took in boarders to help cover the cost of housing for their growing family. Still, there are rich compensations for a person who lives life as a poet, one who engages in the magical transformation of the ordinary.

In her poem, "What the Poets Could Have Been," Baggott justifies choosing to live as a poet. To have not become a poet would mean for her becoming something less, something more "repressible, contented," but she does not use the word, "happy." Baggott refers to "the simplest things" making her aunts and uncles "happy" as they sit on the back porch, but the child with the hidden words is not described as happy twirling her baton. Baggott shows her readers what these people kept hidden within and so transforms their reality into something magical. In his essay on the need for poetic recreations of reality, Blake captures the essence of the poet when he writes:

Poetry is for representing the sacredness of human existence. Poetry creates something that didn't exist before without destroying something else in the process. And poetry is for naming all the concrete things in our universe and, by naming, acknowledging their existence and ultimately placing them in an intuitively perceived order, which I call reconstructing reality.

Source: Sheri Metzger Karmiol, Critical Essay on "What the Poets Could Have Been," in *Poetry for Students*, Thomson Gale, 2007.

Nikki Tranter

In the following interview, Baggott discusses books, writing, girls, and her indifference about the successful Harry Potter *books.*

Writing as N. E. Bode, Julianna Baggott's *Anybodies* series is a coupling (soon to be tripling) of books featuring Fern Drudger, a young girl on her pre-pubescent path to enlightenment courtesy of a wild imagination and a whole lot of girl-power gumption. Though odd-looking, a little nutty, and open to moments of deep desperation concerning her place in the world, Fern is also bright, funny, and unafraid of asking important questions of her elders. Baggott has something to say, and with her resilient and intellectually advanced teen protagonist, she says it loud: Girls rock.

That's, of course, how her YA audience might describe it, but Baggott's explanation of her objectives with Fern are lot more complex. According to Baggott, not only are books with strong girl characters in need of a Renaissance, so are serious female writers interested in genre-crossing. Baggott has spent much of her career attempting to make literary inroad by adopting what she considers a male approach to writing. As far as she was concerned, this was her ticket to a sustainable career. As it turns out, it wasn't until she wrote *Girl Talk*, about a young New Jersey girl searching for her biological father, that success came her way.

The irony of a writer so set on giving voice to bold young women not outwardly trusting her own is hardly lost on Baggott. Yet she still finds herself frustrated at clichéd and even patronizing responses to women writers by readers and critics. *Girl Talk* wasn't so much a response to this as a catalyst for opening Baggott's eyes to the amount of work needed (or, at least, the amount of explaining) in order to remain strong-willed and confident as a commercial literary writer.

She's one of the lucky ones, in fact, writing to critical approval and decent sales. It's no surprise, then, that lately, Baggott's confidence is looming large.

This is especially noticeable throughout *The Nobodies* (released through HarperCollins in June) and its precursor, *The Anybodies*, (out in paperback in September). Baggott steams into the story with humor and intelligence as she explains just how far from heavenly it is for the crazily inventive Fern to comprehend her parents, Mr. And Mrs. Drudger—the most boring people alive. They didn't like to take vacations from [work]," Bode writes. "But . . . didn't want to cause a stir by not taking them either."

The dull Drudgers are opposed to anything resembling super, awesome, or cool, and so Fern's creative mind is ordered to a standstill. The problem is, Fern's about three-parts normal and all the rest creativity. Her dreamer qualities (can she or can't she make stuff drop from books by shaping them really hard?) and devotion to literature (she's read every books for kids there is) fill her up. Her very personality is has been fuelled throughout her short life by the books she's read, the adventure stories and fairytales she's immersed herself in as escapism and for sheer entertainment's sake.

Fern desires her own adventure, though. She gets it at the beginning of *The Anybodies* when she receives a visit from a man proclaiming to be her real father. A hospital mix-up meant that math-loving Howard ended up going home with him, and Fern with the Drudgers. Her father, known as The Bone, makes a deal with the Drudgers to swap kids for the summer and gag just how well, or not so well, they fit.

So begins Fern's own girl's adventure. She soon learns that her overactive imagination might just be a product of her DNA. She, like her father and late mother, is an Anybody. She learns, too, that a book containing the secrets of the Anybodies entitled, *The Art of Being Anybody* is her birthright and so sets herself on a quest to find the book and thus learn everything possible about being an Anybody. She is going to have to be quick smart about it, though, as someone else—an evil and miserly someone—is also on the hunt for the book and its treasures. Fern is suddenly on a race through literature and fantasy to get her book and discover her true purpose.

Fern's race, continued in *The Nobodies* in which she and Howard attend a camp for Anybodies and discover something's not quite right about the camp counselors who seem to all be suffering fun-transplants, is about a whole lot more than a simple quest for a book. Along the way, she comes to learn that being an Anybody is about understanding the true effect of literary life, and that the world is ever changing and that she can change along with it, so long as she doesn't alter her personal beliefs and ideals unless she does so on her terms. As a mystical fellow Anybody tells her in *The Nobodies*:

> Thing are always changing. You have to be in tune with that, the world's flux. You know that Heraclitus was a great Anybody. He was the one who said that you can't step in the same river twice. And Kafka was dating an Anybody when he wrote Metamorphosis, of course.

Heady stuff for kids, but effective. The point here, that Fern comes to know, is how important it is for young people to understand the level of control they have over their own life paths. Fern soon realizes that her parents' dispositions need not be her own, and that if she desires avenues considered unworthy by anyone at all that she thoroughly believes in, she should have the will to go forward. She is, essentially, the god of her own world, the writer of her own story.

Baggott, as N.E. Bode, brings this intricate message to young readers in style reminiscent of Roald Dahl, by way of P. L. Travers. There's a snappy buoyancy to her prose, which is offset (but never overrun) by an eerie, dramatic undertone. It's not a kiddie spookiness that hides beneath the giggles of *The Anybodies'* opening chapter, but a feeling that, as the books jacket reveals, things are not as they seem. This feeling culminated at the end of chapter one in the revelation that Fern's mother died in childbirth:

> . . . the mother, with large brown eyes, wet as pools, lashes soft as moth wings, began to lose blood. She would lose so much, in fact, that she would die.

While the book's comedy is its high point, it's Baggott's (or Bode's) ability to convey such solemnity with sensitivity and skill that gives these stories weight. Her reluctance to alter her writing style in terms of language and vocabulary to suit a child's ear and remain entirely accessible to those children is her true gift. She's direct, she's concise, and above all, her drive to make a role model out of Fern comes across as natural and unforced.

On the eve of *The Anybodies* paperback debut, Julianna Baggott spoke to *PopMatters* about girls, books, the joys of writing, and why she's not too concerned that *Harry Potter* continues to dominate the book charts.

[*PopMatters*:] *When you first had kids, what books could you not wait to introduce them to?*

[Julianna Baggott:] I was raised during the crazy days of the *Little House* comeback where girls were force-fed bonnets and prairie dresses. I confess I was completely into the bonnets, but when it came to books, I was going for something a little less devoted to realism and more interested in the unusual. I was dying to read *The Lion, The Witch and The Wardrobe* to my kids, but I started in when they were way too young—the oldest antsy for more pictures, the youngest still relatively blobby. I had to put it down and be patient. Luckily picture books these days are astounding—*A Day At Wilbur Robinson's House, Weslandia, A Bad Case of Stripes, Alpha Beta Chowder*—so the kids and I were kept well-fed while awaiting C. S. Lewis and Dahl. I also loved Judy Blume and Beverly Cleary—and by thirteen had turned quickly into a David Mamet diehard

What makes a book or a story memorable? Why are we still reading for example, Charlotte's Web *and* Anne of Green Gables—*or are we? Have the new age Harry Potters and Lemony Snickets erased those classics?*

Charlotte's Web is a phenomenal book. It's easy to see how and why it lives on. But take White's *Stuart Little*. It's a messy narrative with no real resolution. But, still, it lives on for its situation—a baby mouse?—and Stuart's character and, I think, because the novel's inventive premise allows children's minds to riff off of it. *Charlie and the Chocolate Factory* is one of the tightest novels I've read—a tidy, bizarre, sadistic morality tale—but *Charlie and the Great Glass Elevator* is a disaster. I think it only lives on because it's the sequel to something quite brilliant. *Potter* and *Snicket* haven't erased anything. In fact their popularity has brought adults back to the more wildly imagined terrain of books for kids—classics and new works alike.

Have you always wanted to join the ranks of adult writers creating for kids?

No, not at all. I wanted to be taken seriously as a writer and to do so I was pretty sure that I should write like a man. I wrote like a man for years and published many manly stories. But it was my first story about woman that got the attention of an agent. When my agent sold *Girl Talk*, I was married with two kids, a third on the way, and, without hearing anything about the book, people assumed that I'd written a children's book—an assumption I don't think they'd have made if I'd been a man. When I told them that it was for adults, the second question was often asking if it was a romance novel . . . You see what I mean. It was frustrating. Books for children, like novels more geared toward women—literary or not—are dismissed in a way that novels written by men aren't. But, frankly, it's my books about women and now girls that have worked for me. The biases still exist however.

What broke me of my own bias against writing for kids—I was as much to blame as anyone—was reading the children's books to my kids, remembering that I'd signed onto the writing business because I loved magical realism; Marquez and Calvino, the poems of Adelia Prada. There a great quote from Michael Chabon—who made the post-Pulitzer leap into kid-lit with *Summerland* (2002)—talking about the age when he finally wanted to be a writer, 10 or 11: "Back then I didn't want to write a novel about an overweight, pot-smoking, philandering teacher whose mistress is pregnant; I wanted to write the books I loved to read, fantasy and novels about contemporary children."

I'd gotten tired of realism, tired of my own desire to be taken seriously, and wanted to go back to my roots.

How does having children influence writing for children? Could have written these books ten years ago?

If I'd wanted to really dive back into my own childhood, sure, I could have come up with novels for the younger set without children of my own. But there's something to be gained by being steeped in my kids' lives—seeing their drawings, listening to them recount bad dreams—that gives me a deeper insight and helps me remember my own childhood needs.

Can you pinpoint some specific differences between writing for adult and writing for kids? In both The Anybodies *and* The Nobodies, *your language has hardly been watered down for a young audience—did you deliberately decide to blend a very literary style with that fantastic, simple language?*

It's ironic but adults are a babyish audience who need a lot of narrative handholding. I have to warn them before anything unusual happens. I have to couch my most imaginative moves in metaphor. But the kid audience is always ready to leap. It's been really liberating.

I wrote *The Anybodies* using whatever language came naturally to me, knowing my editor would dumb it down when necessary. She never once changed a word based on the notion it might be too challenging. I found that remarkable and admired her for her respect for the kid audience.

Why do think it's important that Fern be a girl? Is there a lack of female protagonists in modern kid-lit?

I met with my editor before I wrote the book, and we both agreed that we wanted a book about an empowered girl in a wild adventure. *The Anybodies* is hugely feminist.

The first round in Hollywood, pitching the first book to execs, I was told point blank that girl movies were a hard sell because boys and girls go to movies about boys, but only girls go to movies about girls. As a result—a calculated move that actually gave me structure and turned out to work out very well for the series—Howard became more important in *The Nobodies*—a real buddy book.

What was your aim with Fern? Did you deliberately decide on her specific strengths and weakness?

I have oversized eyes and hair that sticks up wildly, rooster-like, on top of my head. Fern and I have much in common. I didn't think about her in terms of strengths and weaknesses. In many ways, I just thought of myself at that age—though with a deeper sadness.

Together, the books present a clear message that imagination and the ability see the world almost in an absurd, existentialist way, are the keys to discovering the magic of the individual's world. Was this the message you set out to impart from the beginning?

I don't set out with a message, but it's no surprise that this is the message that's come to light. I certainly believe that the world is a bizarre place and that each person's reality has many levels, and that if you pay attention to the world around you, you'll see truly magical thing.

The philosophy behind Fern's quest was heavy enough for me to follow—I'm thrilled at the possibility that kids could begin to investigate and interpret existence and life as Fern eventually does. Are younger readers understanding this idea?

This again was a criticism from Hollywood execs in the first round. What's the philosophy that governs *The Anybodies*? I had no answer. It was plaguing me when I sat down to write *The Nobodies* and I was determined to understand the book on a simpler but deeper level.

Now, my therapist at the time was a Buddhist, and although he turned out to be a crummy therapist, he was a good Buddhist, and the philosophies of Buddhism work very well with Anybodies—the idea that the world is always in flux and that Anybodies, who are truly in tune with this constant state, can enter it and transform themselves or the things around them—like books, making the figurative real, etc.

This vision was a huge relief on an artistic level, but it also worked for Hollywood. Now I had a more present boy character to attract the boy audience and I had a philosophy that made sense. It was in this second round that the series was optioned by Nickelodeon Movies at Paramount Pictures.

Do you buy into the idea that kids would rather go to the movies than read a book?

I'm inundated with stories of kids who love to read—fan mail, letter from parents. I think kids want to read and do, and there's no question that Rowling's books single-handedly taught an entire generation not only to love to read but to wait white-knuckled for, of all things, a book. Rowling's success also flew in the face of the publishing industry's claim that adult American readers want realism, and if not realism than at least something that acts like it. Rowling's success has forced publishers to reconsider the adult audience's appetite for more magical fiction, and it's certainly made more room in the children's section for magical fiction. Chabon has said that [he believes] his publisher would not have been so interested in *Summerland* if it weren't for *Harry Potter*. This is an interesting notion. True or not, I certainly feel it and believe I owe Rowling a debt.

Do you see any disadvantages with the popularity of the Harry Potter series? To you, other authors, other readers?

The publication of *The Nobodies* overlapped with the *Half-Blood Prince* hype and so it was harder to fight for review space. A columnist, and there aren't tons in kids lit, might do four columns a month but this July, three of the four went to Potter-mania. That said, I'll take the traffic I don't know the *Potter* stats, but when Oprah's book club was in full swing, readers who walked into a store to buy an Oprah pick also bought two to three other books on average. I imagine that the Potter stats aren't too far off. It's healthy for booksellers and that helps the industry, which helps my books as well.

Why do you think Harry Potter has been as successful with adult readers as with kids?

Stephen King wrote an essay that I've heard about though haven't ever seen with my own eyes, in which he speculates at what point Rowling stopped writing for kids and turned to the adults as her main audience. I think that the books have gotten hugely complicated which can be a natural consequence of writing in series. *The Somebodies* becomes much more complicated than the first two [in *The Anybodies* series]. I think that Rowling's books exploded in a way that no one could have ever predicted or masterminded. But I do think that she didn't stagnate with the age group—whereas *Lemony Snicket*'s books remain true to their audience, which is good and bad. I see *Snicket*'s books literally as a series of events—brilliant and hilarious—but not accumulating much in terms of real character growth from book to book.

How do you think your books differ from these others? Do you get tired of the comparisons?

The Anybodies series is truly American and full-color. *Potter* and *Snicket* are both gothic and British in tone—thick with the feel of capes and quills and antiquated dramatics—even with the contemporary references. I think of *The Anybodies* as fully contemporary—magical like Rowling with a smirky tone like *Snicket*—but now, really and truly. I don't mind the comparisons—at all.

What age did you aim The Anybodies *at? Do you keep up with modern kids and YA books? Has your response to these genres been generally positive?*

The Anybodies was written to suit a seven-year-old in a read-aloud setting up to 13 or so when *The Sisterhood of the Traveling Pants* should take over. I still write adult fiction, and poetry, and for kids, and I'd love to do something non-fiction, so the answer is no to keeping up. I don't feel like I can keep up with any of those genres as I should—especially since most of my reading [as a teacher] consists of manuscripts that have yet to be published. But I try to. Again, I'm picky and slow—I do so admire [Neil Gaiman's] *Coraline* and many [Terry] Pratchett books.

How did you find Peter Ferguson? Did you work together throughout the illustrating process? What do you think of his interpretations of your characters?

His portfolio was the first take on the characters. It's spooky how much Fern looks like me and my daughter, frankly. He'd never seen pictures of us but through my descriptions of the giant eyes and the wild hair and scrawniness, well, there we were. I love his drawings—even more so in *The Nobodies*, which I didn't thing was possible. My editor edits his drawings so they work with the text, but I don't interact with him at all really. I just sit back and see his translations. It's an amazing process to be translated visually like that.

What did books mean to you growing up? What's it like, if such is the case, to see your own children discovering the magic of reading?

The truth is I was a reluctant reader—slow and picky. I would start ten books to find one I might want to finish. Discerning would be a euphemism. Dunderheaded might be more on target. I still am slow and picky. And frankly, my daughter just stopped hating reading this year. She's ten, and she's had a really hard time with the words on the page. So I've worked hard on all of this and have a defense of the reluctant reader on my website—a letter to parents. I started out giving my daughter all of these magical books and funny books—things that I loved as a kid to get her going. But found that she really wanted serious biographies (Harriet Tubman and Joan of Arc), and books on the development of animal species. She loves research. Recently, my son was reading to himself and stopped, looked up, and said: "Listen to this.", And then he repeated the line—a description of snow. He just liked the way sounded and the image, and wanted me to hear it. That was a fantastic moment.

Source: Nikki Tranter, "Magical Things: An Interview with Julianna Baggott," in *PopMatters*, August 29, 2005, pp. 1–8.

Thomson Gale

In the following essay, the critic gives a critical analysis of Baggott's work.

As a young writer, Julianna Baggott watched as many of her contemporaries headed for the publishing capital of the world, New York City, to make their mark on the literary scene. After receiving her master's degree, however, Baggott and her poet husband headed for a small Delaware city, where she went to work writing short stories and then poetry as she began to raise a family. Baggott wisely wasn't all that interested in the literary scene. "I just wanted to write," she told Dirk Westphal for an article in *Poets & Writers Magazine*. "I didn't want to 'be a writer.'"

The distinction paid off for Baggott. In 2001 at the age of thirty-one, her first two books, a novel and volume of poetry, were published within months of each other. Baggott had arrived on the literary scene whether she liked it or not.

Baggott's novel *Girl Talk*, which appeared in bookstores a month before her collection of poetry titled *This Country of Mothers*, is a mother-daughter, coming-of-age tale in which thirty-year-old Lissy Jablonski, pregnant and unmarried, reflects back to the summer when she was fifteen. That summer, Lissy and her mother took a road trip after Lissy's father had run off with another woman. During the trip, Lissy and her mother engage in nights of "girl talk," and Lissy soon discovers secrets about her mother's past, including the fact that her mother once tried to commit suicide and that her biological father is actually the dwarfish Anthony Pantuliano, who is her mother's only true love.

Writing in the *Washington Post Book World*, Abby Frucht found the novel charming but lacking in substance. Although she described Baggott's novel as "clever," Frucht noted that the novel does not lead "to anything truly persuasive." Most critics, however, praised the book for its serious subject matter , which the author handles with humor and flair. "Baggott's biting, darkly comedic, and brutally honest narrative takes a sardonic look at suburbia and family dysfunction," wrote Carolyn Kubisz in *Booklist*. A *Publishers Weekly* reviewer called the novel a "touching . . . story that delivers more depth than its title might imply." The reviewer went on to note, "Baggott's multilayered, psychological tale is told with a deceptively light tone." Jan Blodgett, writing in the *Library Journal*, commented that the "juxtaposition of stories" between Lissy's present life and her mother's past "turns this first novel . . . from just a thirty-something coming-of-age tale into a wise look at mother-daughter legacies."

This Country of Mothers is a collection of poems in which Baggott reflects on her experiences as a mother and as a daughter. In her poems, Baggott talks both about love and destruction in a manner that seems entirely personal while, at the same time, embracing universal themes. For example, in her poem "What We Didn't Talk about at Fifteen," Baggott writes about the discovery of a drowned girl who was "found naked and raped." The poem's narrator comments, "Didn't each of our mothers warn it could have been us?"

In her interview with Westphal for *Poets & Writers Magazine*, Baggott related that she turned from focusing solely on fiction to writing poetry, in part, to explore her feelings after giving birth. "I felt kind of betrayed by the animalness of it, and the physicality of [having kids], and the huge emotion of it," she told Westphal. "I wondered why no one had mentioned this to me."

In her second novel, *The Miss America Family*, Baggott once again focuses on a dysfunctional family. She tells her story from the views of two characters: Pixie Kitch, who was crowned Miss New Jersey and longed to become Miss America, and Pixie's sixteen-year-old son Ezra, an awkward teenager who is trying to make sense of a world turned topsy-turvy after his mother shoots her dentist husband and Ezra is sent to stay with his biological father, only to learn that his father is gay. "Baggott takes family dysfunction to a new level," wrote a reviewer in *Publishers Weekly*, noting that Baggott uses "wit and humor" to explore the failings of a seemingly perfect family. Carolyn Kubisz, writing in *Booklist*, called the novel "darkly comedic, and brutally honest." In her *Library Journal* review, Karen Traynos noted that *The Miss America Family* "establishes Baggott's remarkable talent for creating characters who resonate with readers."

As for her own reading preferences, Baggott told Westphal that, although she "fell in love with the novel as a form," she loves reading poetry. "If I'm going to get a book out of the library, I get poems," she said. "Poems have the ability to make me read them for pleasure. They

THE EMOTIONAL MONSOON OF GIVING BIRTH ALTERED NOT ONLY WHAT SHE WANTED TO WRITE ABOUT BUT HOW SHE WANTED TO WRITE IT."

demand it. They say, 'You have to love me.' Whereas other things don't; I read them because I'm taking a clock apart."

Source: Thomson Gale, "Julianna Baggott," in *Contemporary Authors Online*, Gale, 2003.

Joanna Smith Rakoff

In the following essay interview, Baggott discusses the process and business of getting published, motherhood, and writing.

Julianna Baggott doesn't miss a beat. When Theo, her chubby-checked nine-month-old, begins to fuss a little. Baggott picks him up and begins to nurse him without losing her train of thought or even pausing for a breath. But then again, we're talking about her favorite subject: poetry. Not about the ephemeral stuff, the hard stuff, not about the making of poetry, but about the making of poets, the behind-the-page dirt that no one wants to discuss. We're talking about money.

When Baggott recently discovered that one of her favorite writers—an established and highly respected American poet who publishes with a major publishing company—receives a mere thousand dollars for her lauded volumes, the news sent her reeling. Baggott is outraged and, in a certain way, energized by such injustices. For though she would never describe herself as an activist, Julianna Baggott—novelist, poet, screenwriter—has something of a mission. Poets, she believes, don't market themselves, don't fight for their work, don't make themselves nearly visible enough. And in behaving so meekly, she feels, they harm not only themselves but potential readers of poetry. Baggott, by virtue of example, is out to change all that. "I want to apply marketing to poetry—and that's really looked down on," she says. "The poems are the poems, but once you've written them you go and you sell them. You have a book, you promote the book. You act intelligently and

business-like and professional. I feel like there's a certain lack of professionalism among poets."

Indeed, what's most intriguing about Julianna Baggott, aside from the sheer talent evident in her work and her warm, generous personality, is this hyperprofessional attitude toward both the act of writing and the work of being a writer, an attitude noted by both her editor and her agent, who sing her praises with undiluted awe. "Professionalism" to Baggott doesn't mean that she places her writing—or her self-promotion—above all else in the world, but rather that she treats writing as though it's a job, as opposed to a lifestyle.

This spring Baggott has the rare pleasure of seeing her first two books—*Girl Talk*, a novel, and *This Country of Mothers*, a collection of poetry—published within a month of each other (the first in mid-February, the second in March). This is no small feat considering, first of all, her rather tender age (she's 31); secondly, that she wrote her first poem three years ago; and finally, that she has three small children: baby Theo, four-year-old Finneas, and six-year-old Phoebe.

The story of Baggott's success incites from most writers the same rash of questions: Is she in possession of an independent income? Good connections—perhaps she's the daughter of an editor or a famous writer? Did she have full-time child care? And how did she end up with three kids, anyway—by accident? The answer to all of the above is no.

Baggott's story—the way she's decided to live her life—defies all conventional wisdom about young writers. Which is just as she intended it.

In 1994 Julianna Baggott completed her MFA in fiction at the University of North Carolina at Greensboro (UNC-G). The majority of her friends from graduate school moved, as is the wont of young writers and artists, to New York City to complete their novels or collections of poetry or memoirs. Or, some might say, to live the writerly life: drinking Jameson at book parties, hobnobbing with editors, embarking on careers in journalism or book publishing. But the literary life of myth and legend—as immortalized in too many memoirs and novels to name—held little appeal for Baggott. "I just wanted to write," she explains. "I didn't want to 'be a writer.'" Baggott chose UNC-G's solid but not terribly well known MFA program precisely because she wasn't interested in the more unpleasant side effects of high-profile programs: competition among students, gossip about agents and advances.

Upon arriving at UNC-G, Baggott—then 22—met and fell in love with David Scott, a poet in the class ahead of her. The courtship was quick—after four months of dating they were engaged; they married the following spring. Not long afterward Baggott became pregnant with Phoebe. By choice.

"We wanted to have a family, and we wanted to write," she recounts over sandwiches at a café populated largely by University of Delaware faculty. Scott is at home watching the kids. "If we didn't have a family, we would resent our work. If the kids stopped us from writing, we would resent our kids. The only way for us to not be bitter was to do both, to be bullheaded about it."

And so, while their friends headed to Manhattan, Scott and Baggott settled in Newark, Delaware, a small city known less for its arts community and more for being home to corporate chemical giant DuPont. It was a move based completely on practicality: Baggott's parents live in Newark, where she grew up. "We came back to Newark because we had no money and if I wanted help, which I knew I would need in order to write, I would have to be near family. My parents have been extremely helpful. There's no way I could do it without them."

During the first years of their marriage, Baggott and Scott tried desperately to find ways to earn money that would not impinge on their nearly nonexistent writing time. "Dave and I were living under the poverty level when the first two kids came along," she says. "To make ends meet we ran a boardinghouse of sorts, renting two bedrooms in our house to foreign students and cooking meals for them. It paid for the house." For a while, the two worked as tag-team freelance writers, mainly writing for local magazines and newspapers. "Dave would go out and get the story," Baggott says, "then he would come home and write the story up. He's the *fast* writer. I would come in and rewrite it. I would be the hay-to-gold person."

Previously, the two had rarely shared or critiqued each other's creative work, a dynamic established soon after they became involved. "The very first thing I ever showed him, he read

the first sentence and said, 'You know, this sentence doesn't work.' And I said, 'Oh no. Put it down. You'll never read anything of mine again. Never.'" But collaborating on articles led to an epiphany. "That system taught us a lot about how much we need each other. We realized that we are assets to each other and we need to exploit that."

And exploit it they did. They joined workshops together in Newark and, perhaps more important, found a balance—due, in part, to Scott's taking a full-time job in print production—that freed up Baggott's time, allowing her to write despite the constant din and interruption of the kids. But when she turned back to her writing, she found that she "couldn't write short stories anymore." It was simply too difficult to "enter" a short story in the little snippets of time she had while the kids were napping.

But there was more to it: The emotional monsoon of giving birth altered not only what she wanted to write about but how she wanted to write it. "I felt kind of betrayed by the animalness of it, and the physicality of [having kids], and the huge emotion of it. I wondered why no one had mentioned this to me." Poetry seemed the right vehicle to explore these feelings, in part because Baggott had found "role models in poetry: female poets writing about birth and menstruation and female things."

Just as she began publishing her poetry in magazines like *Poetry* and the *Southern Review*, Baggott found herself pulled out of poems and, as she says, "screwed into writing a novel." One afternoon in the fall of 1998, she received a call from literary agent Nat Sobel. He had read her story "Girl Talk" in *New Delta Review* and was impressed. "Lots of times I can tell from a short story whether or not a writer has the storytelling ability to sustain a novel," Sobel says, "and Julianna's story led me to believe that she was a *real* storyteller. It was filled with funny, interesting characters. Little did I know that Julianna is a fireplug. She can do *anything.*"

Sobel's call took Baggott completely by surprise. "I gave the kids a jar of jelly beans so that I could talk to him," Baggott remembers. "He asked if I was working on a novel and I said, 'As a matter of fact, I *am.*'" Baggott, however, wasn't working on a novel. "I had no intention of *ever* writing a novel. I was strictly a short story writer." But Sobel's call came at a time when she was beginning to feel frustrated with the market for short story collections. "I was having trouble getting my collection published," she says, "so I thought as an act of love for my short story collection I would maybe write a novel. I was at that point where I felt I really had to do something—as a first-time author I just couldn't get the collection published."

And so Baggott told Sobel that she needed about a month to polish the first 50 pages of the novel that didn't yet exist. Baggott and Scott agreed that this was a huge opportunity for her and that she should simply throw herself into it. "I have a great husband," Baggott says. "He said, 'Okay, we're just going to buckle down.' The first fifty pages I wrote with no baby-sitters. Dave would get home from work, and I would begin to write immediately. My office was in my living room, so I would write whenever I could during the day, when the kids were napping. I would work late at night, and as I was falling asleep I would take notes about what I was going to work on the following day. I always knew exactly what I needed to write the next time I sat down." Sobel liked the first 50 pages and asked Baggott to send on the rest. Which meant, of course, that she had to actually write the rest. And she had just found out that she was pregnant again.

Battling morning sickness, Baggott set out to write the bulk of *Girl Talk*, letting almost everything else in her life fall by the wayside. "The house was a wreck. The bills were not paid. *Green Mountains Review* had sent me galleys—I found them after I had finished the novel. Everything just went completely undone. I just did what I had to do with the kids and didn't lift a finger in any other way. I basically went underground. My friends never saw me. I disappeared." As she had been almost exclusively writing poems—short pieces—for two years, she eased herself into the novel by writing it in short segments. "There was no other way to get through a novel. My attention span was tight and small, a coiled spring. Once I went back to revise I joined things together and made things bigger."

Filled with characters both comic and threatening—characters who inevitably reveal strange and startling secrets—*Girl Talk* consists of three interwoven episodes in the lives of the narrator, 30-year-old Manhattan advertising executive Lissy Jablonski, and her mother, Dotty. The novel's plot begins in the present, when an unmarried and pregnant Lissy finds Church Fiske, the family friend with whom she lost her virginity as a teen, at the door of her dilapidated Chelsea apartment. Church's appearance sends Lissy back to her 15th summer—"the summer that never happened"—when her dad ran off with another woman and her mom took Lissy on a trip to Bayonne, New Jersey, during which Dotty both revealed "the bare, naked truth" about her past and taught Lissy "the art of omission, how to tell the perfect lie, or . . . how you can choose the truth . . . from the assortment of truths life has to offer."

Though it's anything but autobiographical, the novel was inspired by Baggott's relationships with her mother and grandmother. Sobel was correct in her suspicions that Baggott possesses a strong feel for storytelling. "Both my parents are storytellers, and *Girl Talk* is definitely about how you teach people through stories," she says. "My mother and my grandmother, especially, tell stories to teach lessons, to pass on history. But the novel is just as much about what is not told and how such secrets affect those who are kept in the dark.

Soon after starting in on the body of the novel, Baggott miscarried. "I was three months along. At that point, I was so ready to fall in love with that child. And the child wasn't coming. So I fell in love with my characters. I wrote the rest of that book *very* quickly." She finished in April—about six months after Sobel's initial call. Baggott was determined to finish the novel before Sobel's interest in her faded. "I thought, 'I have an audience, even if it's just one person, and I'm going to keep it.' But I also didn't want to get lost in a novel for five years. I just know too many people who go into novels and never come out. I refuse to do that, because how many poems am I not going to write; how many short stories am I not going to write?" She signed a contract for *Girl Talk* a few months later with Greer Kessel Hendricks at Pocket Books, an editor only slightly older than Baggott who has a proven track record with young and first-time novelists. The entire process took less than a year.

Hendricks, who fell in love with *Girl Talk* after reading the first 50 pages ("I sat and read it at my desk. I *never* have time to read at my desk"), described Baggott as being "cool as a cucumber, self-assured and confident" during the interviews that led up to her novel's auction. "She just was very smart and savvy about [talking to editors]."

After *Girl Talk*'s sale, Baggott immediately went back to work. She continued to send out her poetry manuscript—which had been a finalist in the Bread Loaf and Kent State first-book contests—and after a few months was notified that she had won second prize in the *Crab Orchard Review* Award and that her book would be published by Southern Illinois University Press. Soon after, she completed and sold her second novel, *The Miss America Family*, to Hendricks (it's scheduled for a February 2002 release, to coincide with the paperback release of *Girl Talk*). "I thought, 'I have an audience. These people are interested.'" Last fall, she finished a screenplay, *The Madame*, a fictionalized biography of her great-grandmother, a bordello-keeper. Sobel helped her find the Los Angeles agent who is currently shopping the screenplay around.

Although busy with her numerous projects, Baggott always had *Girl Talk* on her radar screen. And when Pocket began having problems with the cover—Baggott liked the first design, Hendricks hated it; Hendricks liked the second, Baggott hated it—she geared herself for action. Fearing that the third design would be no better than the second, she and Hendricks collaborated on a letter to the art department explaining their thoughts on what the cover should look like. Then Baggott took matters into her own hands. "I turned to Dave and said, 'Look, we're screwed. We have to come up with something that's excellent right now. Today.'" After their evening workshop in Newark, Scott returned to his office—a 45-minute drive—and picked up his iMac and digital camera. "He took a picture of me, designed the cover, laid out where the text would be, and the next morning we e-mailed it in." Both Hendricks and Pocket's marketing department loved the design—which is simple but striking—and decided to use it. And so Baggott—or part of Baggott (her face is turned away from the camera)—adorns the cover of her book.

The early reviews of *Girl Talk*—in *Kirkus* and *Publishers Weekly*—were favorable, and initial sales were strong: Two weeks after its release, both Barnes & Noble and Borders had restocked. One can only imagine that the success is due, at least in part, to Baggott's vast network of friends and acquaintances in the writing and publishing world, to the sleekly designed Web site she launched to help promote the book

(www.juliannabaggott.com), to the national tour Pocket Books has sent her on, and to a blurb in the February issue of *Glamour* magazine. And it is *Girl Talk*—a breathless novel that manages to be both funny and bleak, both poignant and bitchy—that will make Baggott famous.

Still, though she says she unexpectedly "fell in love with the novel as a form" while writing *Girl Talk*, her heart lies more with poetry. "I love to read poems. That's what I read. If I'm going to get a book out of the library, I get poems," she says, explaining that she first started reading poetry because of the availability of her husband's extensive collection. "Poems have the ability to make me read them for pleasure. They demand it. They say, 'You have to love me.' Whereas other things don't; I read them because I'm taking a clock apart."

Back at Baggott and Scott's charmingly disarrayed home—"total Americana," she calls it, sounding like the smart-alecky narrator of *Girl Talk*—Baggott is the epitome of patience. She and Scott feed me birthday cake left over from Finneas's party that morning. The kids cavort around us while Baggott feeds the baby and, miraculously, manages to continue our conversation, telling me stories about UNC-G. "When I was working as an editor at the *Greensboro Review* I would think, 'Nobody's called me to see where their manuscript is? I've been sitting on this thing for three months. Why hasn't this writer called me?' I would write rejection letters saying, 'I had to struggle with this piece. I really liked it. Send me something else.' And then I would never hear from them. I mean, when you get a letter like that you send something. The next day! Somebody wants it. You have an audience. There are so few times when people are listening. You have to take advantage of it."

Source: Joanna Smith Rakoff, "Julianna Baggott: How to Be the Next Big Thing," in *Poets & Writers*, Vol. 29, No. 3, May–June 2001, pp. 32–37.

Cheryl Dellasega
In the following interview, Baggott talks about being a writer and mother and how being a mother has improved her writing.

... Julianna Baggott does double duty as a poet and novelist, as well as triple duty with her children: oldest daughter Phoebe is six, son Phineas is four, and baby Theo is nearly one and a half. A resident of Newark, Delaware,

Baggott appreciates the proximity of her parents, and it isn't hard to understand why.

When Julianna got a bachelor's degree in creative writing and French from Loyola University in Baltimore, her father called it "a degree in starvation and poverty." She is more philosophical, reflecting that at least she finally got to put her foreign language skills to use when she went to France to promote her book. An MFA from the University of North Carolina at Greensboro in 1991 further honed her writing skills.

Julianna began publishing stories while in graduate school for her MFA at the University of North Carolina at Greensboro where she was a Greensboro Scholar, studying fiction. Her work has appeared most recently in magazines such as *Poetry*, *The Southern Review*, *Indiana Review*, *Quarterly West*, *Crab Orchard Review*, and *Cream City Review*. Andrew Hudgins nominated her book for a prize sponsored by the Sewanee Writers' Conference.

Her collection of poems was a 1999 finalist in Kent State's first book contest and Middlebury College's Bakeless Prize through Bread Loaf, where she was awarded a scholarship to attend the Bread Loaf Writers' Conference for summer 2000. In the last two years, she has placed nearly thirty poems, in addition to publishing fiction. She's been awarded two fellowships from the Delaware Division of Arts, one in poetry and the other in fiction. Few of us will ever top her accomplishments in the year 2001: two of her books, one collection of poems and the other a novel, were published.

Her poetry, in *This Country of Mothers: Crab Orchard Award Series in Poetry* (Southern Illinois University Press, 2001), won the university's prestigious prize, which provided her with cash as well as publication. That book has currently gone into a second printing, which confirms the publisher's belief that poetry can be profitable. In addition to selling well, *In This Country* has garnered glowing reviews from an array of established poets. Linda Pastan, author of *Carnival Evening: New and Selected Poems, 1968–1998*, (W.W. Norton & Company, 1999), comments that: "Julianna Baggott has a fierce imagination which probes the ordinary details of a woman's life and lights up both the sacred and profane." Poet Andrew Hudgings describes her work as possessing "a full vision," and says that: "In these large, passionate, compelling

poems, the speaker's family and the holy family merge in love and suffering—wholly family, wholly loved, wholly suffered for." Another well-known poet, Rodney Jones (*Elegy for a Southern Drawl*, Houghton-Mifflin, 1999), comments that: "Against a backdrop of family stories, Julianna Baggott draws themes as sharp as razors. She is an accomplished poet of the eye and ear, of the definitive feminine experience, and her poems of private life are expansive enough to suggest a vision of a political and historical era."

Her novel, *Girl Talk: A Novel*, was also published by Simon & Schuster in 2001, and is currently being released overseas. Reviews for it were equally positive, *Booklist* says: "As much as this story is touching, Baggott's supporting characters succeed in making it funny and entertaining, as well. *Publishers Weekly* describes the book as: "a touching coming of age story," while *Poets and Writers* notes that: "And it's *Girl Talk*—that manages to be both funny and bleak, poignant and bitchy—that will make Baggott famous." *The New York Times* review of her debut novel claims: "The title misleadingly suggests that this novel will have a good-natured, gossipy tone, but Baggott's brand of witty, psychological observation is dark and corrosive."

[*Cheryl Dellasega:*] *What inspired you to write?*

[Julianna Baggott:] I was raised to be a writer in some ways. My mother's family is Southern, so I came from a strong storytelling history. Stories were used for everything: cautionary advice, passing history, entertainment. Also, when I was younger, I got to go to New York City to see all the plays my sister was in. She's an actress who is nine years older than me, so that taught me about drama. My parents took me everywhere, and that developed my ear. I was in church every Sunday, which was a great lesson in literature and symbols, and what they mean. I knew very young that I wanted to be a writer.

My first job was teaching grades six through eight after I graduated from college. The next year, I did odd jobs to support my writing, including ballroom dancing and raking leaves. It was another year and a half before I could start graduate school, which is where my first short story was published in *Farmer's Market*, a western literary journal.

After graduate school, I met my husband, who is a poet, and got married. We knew we wanted to have children and write, but we needed to be close to my family to do so. An artist's grant from Delaware enabled us to move back to my hometown, where I was soon pregnant and living below poverty level. My husband and I ended up taking in boarders and he worked as an editor, which gave him a lot of different skills (including the ability to design the cover of *Girl Talk*).

Still aspiring to reach poverty level, we did freelance work together for six months, and made good money. Our process was smooth: he would go out and get the story, come back, write it, and give it to me. I would add the finesse. That experience gave me a huge amount of confidence. By the time I decided to write a novel, I felt I could write anything. Around this same time, my husband got a job developing publications for a private school, which meant we finally had enough money to move into a bigger house and make an office in the living room, but we still couldn't afford babysitters.

After my second child was born, I began writing poetry, partly because my time shrank, and partly because I found my writing becoming more autobiographical. Being a mother and a daughter was a big theme for me. Then I became pregnant with my third child, was very sick, and had a miscarriage. During this time, I realized that when I'm upset, I write. I worked through a lot of grief in poetry. All the love I was preparing to lavish on a child, I lavished on my poems and novel.

How did you get an agent?

I had a short story collection but couldn't get a publisher interested, which was really frustrating. At my moment of despair, an agent called who had read my short story "Girl Talk" and discussed developing it into a novel. I wrote the first 50 pages, and he liked them.

How old were you children when you started to write?

I was writing long before they arrived! In fact, I had my own journal before I could write. I would dictate to my sisters what I wanted to write.

From a practical standpoint, how has being a mother affected your writing?

At times it has been frustrating, especially with *Girl Talk*, since I didn't have sitters. My husband was extremely supportive, so I knew I could count on having time to write. He was

crucial, as was living in my hometown. My parents are near the library, so lots of times I would drop the kids off on my way to write.

My kids are used to going to Kinko's and stuffing envelopes. Anything I can include them in, I do. When I was writing *Girl Talk*, I had a one and a half hour block of time I could count on when one was in preschool and the other napping. Of course, there needs to be family time too, so I used weekends to write. Not that children imprison me, but sometimes, I felt like a prisoner with a spoon. I could dig away, doing little bits at a time, hoping I would see the light. A small amount every day added up—two pages a day, and in 30 days I had 60 pages.

I constantly think of what I can do here and there? I read while the kids play on the playground, and am very good at musing. Before I fall asleep I sort of untether myself mentally and think about what I want to work on the next day. I keep paper next to the bed.

We all went to the Breadloaf Writers Conference while I was still nursing. I had been nominated for a scholarship and applied. When I got accepted, we decided to go as a family. We rented a house nearby; everyday my husband would drop me off, and then he took the kids. When it was time, he would bring the baby in to nurse. We managed to muddle through. It was crazy but worthwhile. I also went to a writers colony at the Virginia Center for the Creative Arts which was very bucolic. I went in two week stints, just to write. When I was six months pregnant, I went to Ragdale writers colony in Lake Forrest outside of Chicago, but I wasn't as productive. I couldn't fall in love with writing because of being so concentrated on my pregnancy.

Does it make your children uncomfortable to have a mother who is a writer?

My oldest gets a little more frustrated. When all the hoopla for *Girl Talk* was going on she would get upset at times, and ask if we had to talk about the book so much. At my premier in Newark, she was there handing out cookies, though. My older son thinks everyone is a writer, since his parents are both writers, as are most of our friends.

In spite of the writing, our priority has always been to have one person at home. There was a time from February to May where I was on a big tour for *Girl Talk* and we had to get a sitter.

We weren't living our priorities, which is why my husband decided to work from home. Still, it's very hard to do a tour with a family.

Has there ever been something from your child's life you wanted to write about but didn't for privacy reasons?

My poetry really reflects the kids. *Girl Talk* isn't about my kids. My second novel, *The Miss America Family* isn't about them either. But they're in the poetry.

Actually, my kids make their own books all the time. Phoebe loves stories, and draws pictures to go with them. My son is a narrator. There's the world and then there's what's going on in Phineas's head. He always has a story in his head.

How did your own mother influence you as a writer—if at all?

My mother was a concert pianist and a stay at home mom. My dad was an engineer and corporate lawyer. They were both very encouraging of my writing and having a creative life, but that runs in our family. My older sister is an actress, my brother is a musician who works with computers, and my other sister paints.

My third novel is called *The Madame*. It's based on my grandmother who was raised in a whorehouse. She had three kids she put in an orphanage. To understand how she could do this, I had to put myself in that position and my kids in that position. It's so very different from the way I am, the only way I could write about it was to project myself into her situation. So she influenced me in an indirect way.

Any other thoughts on how being a mother has influenced you as a writer?

Motherhood has helped me become a better writer for several reasons. I thought I had a depth before, but children mine that so much deeper. I have so much more love than I ever thought myself capable of. The success and failure of my writing often hinges on my ability to fall in love with it. That takes so much generosity, which children give you. They develop your capability to love. Being a mother brought me to a deeper level in my willingness to give to my characters and be aware of how much attention they needed.

Being a mom has also improved my concentration. The amount of time I wasted before I had kids astounds me now! That old saying, "If you want something done, ask someone who's busy" is really true for me. I've gotten so much better at a zen mindset, turning it on and off. Where I used to need a lot of time to get into a short story, I now juggle a huge to-do list and stay within a story as well.

Other kinds of jobs take up your musing time while filing, typing, etc., but with children, you can muse while nursing, chopping apples, or making peanut butter sandwiches. Rocking my youngest to sleep is good musing time for me. When Phoebe, my oldest, was born, I had to go away to a writers' colony after she was a year old because I couldn't write. With my second it was six months and poetry until I could write, then with my third it was five days.

What are you working on now?

My second novel *The Miss America Family* is the story of a former Miss New Jersey, the point of view of a 16 year old who is coming of age, like *Girl Talk* with bipolar disorder. I've also been doing some screenplays. Because my family stories are so complex, I actually wrote *The Madame,* my third book, as a screenplay first to get a handle on it.

What are your writing habits?

I have done a lot with writing groups off and on, which is especially helpful for poetry. I led a women's writing group for about five years until I wrote *Girl Talk*. My husband is always in groups too, but now, with him home at home, he reads my work. Sometimes what he says is brilliant but I don't realize it immediately.

Do you have any advice for other mothers/ writers?

I try to be encouraging. Once I was in a chat room where I said writing was "doable," and a woman got upset with me, because she felt I was saying if you don't get it done you've failed. That made me feel really bad, because that's not what I meant.

Be kind to yourself. If it's not getting done, be gentle. Recognize your priorities. If it's not getting done, understand that it's okay. Wanting to be a writer is compatible with motherhood. Being an astronaut or lawyer with long hours wouldn't work, but writing can. Don't impose your schedule on them. The closer you can get to their natural rhythms the better your writing will be.

Source: Cheryl Dellasega, "Mothers Who Write: Julianna Baggott," in *Writers Write: The Internet Writing Journal*, October–November 2001, pp. 1–6.

SOURCES

Baggott, Julianna, "What the Poets Could Have Been," in *This Country of Mothers*, Southern Illinois University Press, 2001 pp. 57–58.

Blake, Robert W., "Poets on Poetry: Writing and the Reconstruction of Reality," in *English Journal*, Vol. 79, No. 7, November 1990, pp. 16, 20, 21.

Dellasega, Cheryl, "Mothers Who Write: Julianna Baggott," November 2001, http://www.writerswrite. com/journal/nov01/baggott.htm (accessed December 11, 2006).

Dickinson, Emily, "This Was a Poet," in *The Complete Poems of Emily Dickinson*, edited by Thomas H. Johnson, Little, Brown, 1955, p. 215.

Horace, "The Art of Poetry," in *Horace: The Odes, Epodes, Satires, and Epistles*, Frederick Warne 1892, lines 55–56, 64–65, http://www.classicpersuasion.org/ pw/horace/horacepo.htm (accessed December 13, 2006).

Jones, Rodney, Review of *This Country of Mothers*, in Southern University Press, 2001, http://www.siu.edu/ %7Esiupress/titles/s01_titles/baggott_mothers.htm (accessed September 27, 2006).

Preyer, Robert, "The Prejudice against Poetry: A Diagnosis and an Appeal," in *College English*, Vol. 18, No. 2, November 1956, p. 84.

Rakoff, Joanna Smith, "Celebrating the Joys of Poetry," in *Book Page*, April 2001, http://www.bookpage.com/0104bp/ nonfiction/poetry_roundup.html (accessed December 11, 2006).

Wickett, Dan, "Review of *This Country of Mothers*," in *Emerging Writers Forum*, August 27, 2002, http:// www.breaktech.net/emergingwritersforum/View_Review. aspx?id = 197 (accessed December 11, 2006).

"Working Families," in *Bernie Sanders: Vermont's Independent Congressman*, http://bernie.house.gov/economy/ today.asp (December 11, 2006).

FURTHER READING

Behn, Robin, *The Practice of Poetry: Writing Exercises from Poets Who Teach*, Collins, 1992.

This book is ideal for anyone who wants to learn to write poetry. The book consists of a series of exercises designed to help would-be poets begin writing and finding their own poetic voices.

Germin, Pamela, *Sweeping Beauty: Contemporary Women Poets Do Housework*, University of Iowa Press, 2005.

This appropriately titled collection of poems focuses on what women most often do in the home—housework. Many of the poems in this collection, which includes a poem by Baggott, make readers laugh, but many more will cause readers to notice the exceptional female poets included in this book, who can turn even housework into art.

Mullaney, Janet Palmer, ed., *Truthtellers of the Times: Interviews with Contemporary Women Poets*, University of Michigan Press, 1999.

This collection of fifteen interviews includes a broad spectrum of women's voices, representing diversity in race, ethnicity, and age. Although Baggott is not included in this collection, these poets speak of the same topics that interest all women poets—women's stories and women's survival as poets.

Prins, Yopie, and Maeera Shreiber, eds., *Dwelling in Possibility: Women Poets and Critics on Poetry*, Cornell University Press, 1998.

This book is a collection of feminist critical essays that have been interwoven with poetry. The book includes the work of female poets and feminist literary critics, who explore new ways to write and think about poetry.

Rankine, Claudia, ed., *American Women Poets in the 21st Century: Where Lyric Meets Language*, Wesleyan University Press, 2002.

This book presents a collection of ten contemporary American women poets and focuses on the issue of whether gender influences the work of female poets.

Rees-Jones, Deryn, *Consorting with Angels*, Bloodaxe Books, 2001.

In this collection of critical essays, Rees-Jones examines that different ways that twentieth-century female poets have tried to create feminist poems within a cultural and societal framework that confines what female poets can write.

Witness

LIZ WALDNER

2000

Liz Waldner's "Witness" is the final poem in the fifth section ("Triangle") of Waldner's Euclidian-inspired *A Point Is That Which Has No Part* (2000), following sections named "Point," "Line," "Circle," and "Square." Developing an extended metaphor that likens the coming of dawn (and the new day) to a wild horse, "Witness" exemplifies what is strongest in Waldner's poetry: diction, intellectualism, and an appreciation of science and nature. The combination of poetry and science characterizes much of Waldner's poetry. In her later work *Saving the Appearances* (2004), for instance, she uses Plato's idea, which was later applied by Copernicus, that there is a fundamental spirit that links the empirical world (its appearances) and the revelations it causes.

AUTHOR BIOGRAPHY

As of 2007, very little biographical information was available concerning Liz Waldner. She was born in Cleveland, Ohio, but was raised primarily in rural Mississippi before moving on to St. John's College, where she earned a B.A. in philosophy and mathematics. She later earned an M.F.A. from the University of Iowa and thereafter worked with various musicians and visual artists.

Waldner's poetry has appeared in the *Colorado Review*, *Denver Quarterly*, *New American Writing*, and *Ploughshares* as well as in such

collections as *Etym(bi)ology* (2002) and *Saving the Appearances* (2004). A number of her books have been recognized with prestigious awards. *A Point Is That Which Has No Part*, in which "Witness" appears, received the 2000 James Laughlin Award. *Self and Simulacra* won the Alice James Books Beatrice Hawley Prize in 2001, and *Dark Would (the missing person)* won the University of Georgia Contemporary Poetry Series in 2002. Waldner was awarded grants from the Massachusetts Cultural Council, the Boomerang Foundation, and the Barbara Deming Memorial Money for Women Fund as well as fellowships from the Vermont Studio Center, the Djerassi Foundation, and the MacDowell Colony.

The poems in her most celebrated collection, *A Point Is That Which Has No Part* blend mathematical questions with an experimental lyricism reminiscent of Gertrude Stein (1874–1946) and with a stream of consciousness that echoes such modern writers as James Joyce (1882–1941) and Virginia Woolf (1882–1941). The collection takes both its title and inspiration from Euclid's *Elements of Geometry*.

POEM TEXT

I saw that a star had broken its rope
in the stables of heaven—

This homeless one will find her home
in the foothills of a green century.

Who sleeps beside still waters, wakes.   5
The terrestrial hands of the heaven clock

comb out the comet's tangled mane
and twelve strands float free.

In the absence of light and gravity,
slowly as dust, or the continents' drift,   10

sinuous, they twine a text,
one letter to an eon:

I am the dawn horse.
Ride me.

POEM SUMMARY

Lines 1–2

The title of "Witness" identifies the subject at hand as bearing witness to an event (in this case, the appearance of a comet). The opening words of the poem, "I saw," stated in the past tense, indicate that the witnessed moment happened in the past and now remains clear in memory.

In the first couplet, readers are also asked to bear witness to the initiation of a metaphor that has both empirical and philosophical connotations. A "star" is compared to a horse breaking the rope that has kept it confined to "the stables." The rope of dust streams from the comet in the direction away from the Sun which it orbits. Without gravity the Earth (the speaker's vantage point) would not be held together as one sphere, and its orbit would not be fixed by its attraction to the Sun. Gravity affects locations of heavenly bodies and how and why they can be viewed by the speaker from the Earth. The speaker's imagination is shaped, then, by both the physical laws of the universe and by the poet's inclination to use metaphoric language.

Lines 3–4

Moving beyond its former location in the orbit/stable, the star/horse is imagined as "homeless." It appears dislocated and moving. The speaker asserts that the star/horse will find another "home." This new home is identified both in terms of time ("a green century") and space ("the foothills"). She gives a poetic version of the more complicated concept which physicists call spacetime. The anxiety associated with "homelessness" is counterbalanced by the comfort of knowing that the coordinates involved can determine future location. The idea that the star will settle in a new century suggests that it is actually a comet traveling its elliptical orbit around the Sun, which accounts for why the comet is visible from Earth for a certain period and then appears again at a distant time in the future.

In this couplet, too, the freed star/horse is described as female, which gives Waldner's metaphor another dimension. "Witness" becomes a poem that is about viewing a heavenly body that is described as a star, a horse, and a woman.

Lines 5–8

The third and fourth couplets form two sentences and can be treated together. Line 5 and 6 refer to space and time in new ways. The one "who sleeps besides still waters, wakes"; and "terrestrial hands" (human hands and the hands of a clock) mark the "heaven clock." The fourth couplet continues the second sentence: the "terrestrial hands" comb out

TOPICS FOR FURTHER STUDY

- Research the history and mythology surrounding a single star (Eta Carinae or Krzeminski's Star, for instance) or a constellation (Orion, for example) from its classical origins through to modern times. Write a poem or interconnected series of poems that recounts this history and mythology.

- Do some research on quantum mechanics or string theory. Write a story or poem in which you imagine your life as it might be lived in a reality that is shaped by some of these concepts associated with either subject. How would one's sense of self be shifted by living in a world defined more by absence than by presence? How would such familiar themes as love, truth, and family life be different in this new world?

- Compose (using words—and pictures if necessary) the story of the life of a star or constellation from its birth to its death or transformation into a black space in the cosmos. Feel free to arrange and rearrange the fragments of this life as you deem necessary to represent the totality of this existence.

- Compile a collection of children's poems or nursery rhymes that focus on the night sky and on stars. Write a brief introduction to your collection, and provide illustrations for selected poems.

"the comet's tangled mane / and twelve strands float free." The suggestion seems to be that the waking observer organizes the night sky in terms of time or degrees and analyzes (combs out) the comet's tail. In the line, "comb out the comet's tangled mane" the metaphor of the horse appears in the use of "mane" and the "star" of the first line is now identified as a comet.

Lines 9–12

The fifth and six couplets describe a huge expanse of time, "an eon," which is a unit of time determined by estimates of geologic periods. The "strands" of comet dust mentioned in line 8 "twine a text" as slowly as "one letter" to "an eon." In such a period, the continents drifted to their present location, which might mean the period here spanned contained somewhere between 100 million and 275 million years. The poet imagines the swirling dust of twelve freed strands and how they weave themselves into "a text," so slowly only a letter appears for each eon. The colon that ends line 12 indicates that the twined text that ultimately appears is printed below, in italics.

Lines 13–14

The poet imagines that over this vast expanse of time, the comet's tail forms a statement in the sky: "I am the dawn horse. / Ride me." The witness on Earth imagines that over the eons in which the comet appears in the sky, the dust tail shapes this directive to any who can observe it. The message identifies the comet in the metaphor of "a dawn horse" and directs the viewer, the witness, to "ride" it.

THEMES

Connections between Science and Art

"Witness" argues against understanding reality only in terms of mathematics and physics; it suggests through metaphor that heavenly bodies can be understood by acts of the imagination and the poetry these acts produce. This poem challenges the notion that science and art are mutually exclusive. The close observation of the night sky, the study of astronomy, can be transformed into poetry. A comet can be understood in terms of a metaphor. The physics involved in understanding how a comet orbits the Sun can morph into images of "the foothills of a green century." The concept of time provides the poet with an idea of how "terrestrial hands" (literal and metaphoric) allow one to *read* "the heaven clock." Humans tell time by the location of stars; geologists estimate the Earth's age by the location of tectonic plates, by theorizing about the movement of continents. All of this science is material for a poet to use in shaping a poem.

Identity and Language

In another sense, "Witness" attempts to unrope words from their traditional meanings. Cole

Swenson in *Boston Review* explains that "every word points in several directions," and every reader comes to sense that "there is more than one way to move through language, and therefore language can never be entirely in control." Highlighting this absence of control, Waldner underscores one theme in her poetry, what Swenson describes as "the disintegration, or at least the radical transformation of identity... [that] is disintegrated into language." People know the world through the words and ideas that they attach to it, Swenson suggests. When a poem or a story challenges the relevance of words, this understanding of the world and of a person's place in the world is questioned.

The speaker of the poem, the "I," is the key witness. At the same time, though, the poem displaces this position, like the word assigned to "her," which dissolves into the *me* in the closing line. Who is speaking in these final lines? The comet's tail becomes the writer of text here, personified, speaking directly to the witness. The idea seems to be that the unroped star is invested over the eons with sentience and sentence; the metaphoric horse bids to be ridden.

The Significance of the Number Twelve

The number of strands in the comet tail, significantly, is twelve, a number that resonates through the poem. The number twelve coincides with the twelve months of the year, and there are two periods of twelve hours each in the day (midnight to noon, and noon to midnight). Twelve is a divisor of the basic units of the worldly clock. There are sixty seconds to the minute, sixty minutes to the hour, and twenty-four (twelve times two) hours to the single day. Moreover, both the western and Chinese zodiac systems have twelve signs, each of which is related in various ways to constellations and planetary movements of a universe roped by gravitational fields.

The number twelve is significant in several other disciplines. It is an important number, for instance, in what is known as the mathematical Kepler conjecture, which deals with the implications of Euclidean space. Geometry reveals that it is possible to construct a perfect circle from straight lines shaped into twelve sections of thirty degrees each. Twelve, in this latter sense, is understood as the most natural division of the perfect circle. The human brain (arguably the seat of both the reason and imagination) has twelve cranial nerves, while

the Bible tells of the twelve sons of Jacob, the twelve tribes of Israel, and twelve apostles of Jesus. In ancient Greek religion, the twelve Olympians were the principal members of the pantheon, while the powerful Norse god Odin boasted twelve sons. The number brings numerous layers of possible meanings to a poem that is increasingly determined to avoid being confined by a single meaning or interpretation.

STYLE

Metaphor

Metaphor is figurative language that compares one thing, idea, or image (a star, for instance) to something else (a horse). Metaphors are traditionally divided into the tenor (the subject) and the vehicle (the object to which the subject is compared). In this poem, the comet is the subject and the horse that has broken its rope and moves free from its stable is the vehicle to which the subject is compared. The metaphor creates a correspondence, a poetic pairing, and that allows the poet to draw upon related associations. If the metaphor continues over a number of lines, as it does in this poem, it is called an extended metaphor. Parallels continue, new pairs of traits appear, extending across several lines of text. In this case, the metaphor culminates in the final lines when the comet's text in the sky beckons the viewer to ride the horse.

Metaphor expands readers' understanding of both the tenor and the vehicle. Metaphor allows both parts to be understood in new ways. Metaphor is an appropriate device for Waldner to use in "Witness," a poem that asks readers to view heavenly bodies from both a scientific and a poetic perspective.

Alliteration

Alliteration is the repetition of initial consonant sounds in close proximity within lines and stanzas. Examples of alliteration include such groupings as "float free" (repeating the f- sound), "dust... drift," and "twine a text." The repetition of sounds underscores Waldner's engagement with the physical elements of the world and the sound of the language attached to it. The alliterative passages turn language into music.

HISTORICAL CONTEXT

Poetry and Science

Plato thought science and poetry were antithetical. Aristotle, in his *Poetics*, challenged Plato's opinion. Aristotle explained that science and art more generally are complementary (rather than opposing) ways of understanding the world. Science studies the tangible, empirical world, and poetry expresses human perception and feeling about the world. Both seek truth. Dante in the thirteenth century argued that science is truth achieved through reason and poetry is truth achieved through imagination.

During the Renaissance, thinkers outlined a broader context for the arts, sciences, and philosophy. These disciplines were understood as interrelated and virtually inseparable. Artists used what they learned from scientific experimentation to design paintings that correctly conveyed a sense of depth and proportion. The human body was depicted in drawings, paintings, and frescos that proved the artist's efforts to convey correct anatomy. Indeed, one of Da Vinci's paintings is of an autopsy being performed. Also, paintings of outdoor scenes and landscapes incorporated realistic depictions of plants and flowers, thus revealing the artist's careful study of botany.

The rise of modern sciences through the seventeenth and eighteenth centuries established an intellectual climate that was in many ways inimical to poetry. One seventeenth century rationalist, for instance, René Descartes saw the world as controlled by mind and asserted that matter has little significance by comparison to the workings of the mind. Descartes' theories, referred to as Cartesian philosophy, influenced others throughout this period, along with the works of other prominent rationalists, such as Thomas Hobbes and John Locke.

William Shakespeare and John Donne produced poetry that incorporated science and traditionally literary subjects. This enterprise of drawing from various disciplines and weaving the ideas from them into a given work continued through the eighteenth and nineteenth centuries, as seen in the writings of William Blake, Matthew Arnold, and Thomas Hardy in England and, on the other side of the Atlantic, by Ralph Waldo Emerson and Edgar Allan Poe, among others.

Waldner's poetry explores the interrelationships between poetry and science (especially physics, geology, astronomy, and mathematics). This blending of systems contributes to a postmodern skepticism about the nature of reality. Waldner's poems invite readers to consider new ways of seeing and conceptualizing the physical world. "Witness" creates a world of shared knowledge and shared perspective. This synthesis brings together the cognitive (analytical) and the psychological (emotional) in such a way as to illuminate the correlations between the two ways of seeing and understanding.

CRITICAL OVERVIEW

In a long review of *A Point Is That Which Has No Part* for the *Boston Review*, Cole Swensen notes Waldner's skill at using "language at the very end of its tether." Swenson observes "a thrilling tension and an almost visceral suspense" in the poetry. Admiring her craft, Swenson points out that Waldner "capitalizes on rhyme, off-rhyme, rhythm, and alliteration, and turns language into a muscled force that controls the choices she makes."

A reviewer for *Publishers Weekly* applauds Waldner's ability to mix "sassiness, smarts and lyricism, intellectual querulousness with personal bitterness, vigor and exasperation." Despite what this reviewer calls a propensity for "metalinguistic obsessions," the poems in this collection never "prevent [Waldner] from seeing a real world with people in it." The reviewer recommends this "debut" as "worth seeking out."

Although reviewer Wayne Miller focuses actually on Liz Waldner's collection *Saving the Appearances* in his 2005 article for the *American Book Review*, his comments are relevant to readers of "Witness. Waldner is "at her best" as a poet, Miller observes, when "building off" the big ideas of such thinkers as Plato and Euclid, and when "playfully addressing how thought shifts" over time while moving always "toward a clarity of statement." He notes, she "is wonderful at quietly and subtly articulating the complexity of how one apprehends the physical world" and how that process at times collides with people's more emotional responses to the world.

Miller also maintains that Waldner seems to reach "for [a] spiritual principle" that will harmonize the complexities of the world. At other times, the poet is "equally good at [creating] mysterious, duplicitous endings" to her poems.

WHAT DO I READ NEXT?

- Liz Waldner's 2002 collection, *Dark Would (the missing person)*, is a tough and often funny group of poems that uses Dante's idea of the dark wood and incorporates references to pop songs, other poems, and gender politics.

- Brian Greene's *The Fabric of the Cosmos: Space, Time, and the Texture of Reality* (2004) discusses concepts of spacetime and relativity and the fundamental nature of matter.

- For readers interested in the complex relationships between art and perception, John Berger's *Ways of Seeing* (1972) remains a useful book. These essays discuss art, feminism, politics, and the business of publicity and self-promotion.

- Henry David Thoreau's *Walden* (1854) is a classic exploration of the intimate relationships between man and nature.

Her most profound assertions occur, Miller concludes, in those poems in which the voice of "the heart selflessly and unselfconsciously reveals itself" to the pressures and idiosyncrasies of the world in which it exists. Deterred, on occasions, by a feeling of "scatteredness" in the poems, Miller is unwavering in his assessment of Waldner's poetry. Her "intellectual search for humanistic meaning and stability is an important one . . . that should continue to be engaged," he concludes. "At its best," Waldner's poetry "captures this noble and perpetual search both movingly and beautifully."

CRITICISM

Klay Dyer

Dyer holds a Ph.D. in English literature and has published extensively on fiction, poetry, film, and

> BOTH STAR *AND* HORSE EXIST SIMULTANEOUSLY IN THE IMAGINED SPACE OF THE POEM. METAPHOR IS SUDDENLY RENDERED UNNECESSARY AS THE DISTINCTIONS INHERENT IN COMPARISON DISSOLVE INTO A POETIC SPACE THAT IS DEFINED BY AN 'ABSENCE' AND BY 'DRIFT.'"

television. He is also a freelance university teacher, writer, and educational consultant. In this essay, he discusses Waldner's "Witness" as a poem that rewards a reading that transcends traditional interpretations of metaphor.

Science tells readers that even the hardest, densest rock is made up mostly of empty space or, in a more abstract sense, of absence rather than presence. Such a radical subatomic reality cannot be perceived by humans, of course, despite the fact that there is an overabundance of data to serve as proof. Liz Waldner's "Witness" asks these same readers a number of deeply philosophical questions: Why is it that humans cannot see what science tells them is the reality of the world that exists beyond the world perceived by the senses? Why are most humans seemingly limited to a reality in which the idea of matter is more a useful fiction than a scientific reality? And, finally, is it possible for individual readers to develop so they can perceive things that are currently beyond the grasp of their imaginations?

Waldner's poems question the way the world is understood in the present. Her poems spring from an interest in paradoxes uncovered regularly in science. Interested in what she perceives as a skewed perspective of the world, Waldner plays on the still unimaginable aspects of science (a rock that is more empty space than hardness, for instance) in order to lend the mysterious to the everyday. To Waldner, poetry provides a way to explore the paradoxes of scientific discovery. It is a path into a world that is surprising, elegant, and imaginative. Like Lewis Carroll, who invited readers down a rabbit hole into an eccentric world of looking-glass oddities, Waldner invites readers to enter the mysterious.

Waldner asks readers to move beyond an era when the concepts of space and time provided a constant language that made the world knowable and comfortable. These two terms (space and time) informed an age of belief during which the act of being in a specific place (a train station, for instance) at a specific time (noon) might actually mean something. Traditionally, such coordinates provided basic measures of a knowable reality. There was a physical certainty that allowed a traveler to visit the same station day after day. There was no need to debate the substance of the building and its environs. The traveler also knew that the restaurant next to the train station would be in its same space when the train returned in the evening. The world of the station remained stable and knowable.

Within this world of space and time, what came to be known as the poetic imagination embraced metaphor a tool of investigation. With metaphor the train station could become whatever the poet might wish it to become. Metaphor as a device allows for a comet to become an exuberant horse that breaks the rope that tethers it in a stable. Metaphor allows the imagination of the poet to break free of the logic of time and space and to venture beyond what the eye can see. Metaphor allows poets a safe way to imagine outward beyond culture's sometimes dogmatic belief in literal meaning.

Quantum mechanics gave people a more relativistic view of the world than previous science considered possible. Albert Einstein realized that the traditional understanding of space and time was flawed, that neither exists as an absolute. According to Einstein, the once thought-to-be permanent train station, like the once solid rock, became a matter of question. Whereas classical understanding of reality framed the existence of the train station in terms of a relationship of spaces (the station is either in one place or in another), quantum mechanics allowed for a reality in which both spatial arrangements occur at the same time. According to quantum mechanics, the train station exists in numerous places at the same time. The station, in other words, exists as a kind of possibility that exists here and there simultaneously. The reality of the train station, in other words, becomes defined by the presence of an observer who, through the act of seeing, makes the station real in the moment. Should this observer move or turn away, the station returns to the haze of possibility, awaiting another observer to recreate it in another moment of reality.

Waldner's "Witness" explores the limits of imagination and metaphor and the nature of reality itself. By witnessing the star, Waldner's speaker creates the reality of a star that moves untethered across the galaxy. The speaker's imagination creates the horse of the poem, an animal that breaks its rope and runs from "the stables of heaven." While a traditional view of the poem might explain this arrangement as a metaphor (the star is compared to a horse), a quantum reading would see the relationship as less comparative and more an instance of double identity. Both star *and* horse exist simultaneously in the imagined space of the poem. Metaphor is suddenly rendered unnecessary as the distinctions inherent in comparison dissolve into a poetic space that is defined by an "absence" and by "drift." Freed from rigid spaces of comparison, both star and horse run free in the parallel worlds made possible by the presence of the witness.

"Witness" allows the now parallel worlds of star and horse to call out to their observer. In the line "*Ride me*" horse and star speak together, fusing in the word "*me*." Thus, the language of the poem acts out the science of the poem, allowing imagination and reason to merge and to "twine a text, / one letter to an eon."

To mount the horse or ride the star is, as Waldner's poem suggests, a dramatic revision of the reality in which both poem and reader exist. To step across the breach of language and to become one with the poem dissolves the observer's position, turning the speaker of the poem from watcher (of the night sky, of the horse) to a rider being watched by another, unspecified witness to the events of the poem. If the witness acts, does she cease to be a witness and become a participant? And if she acts, who steps into the role of witness, a position necessary to observe? Or is that stabilizing position necessary at all in a poem that celebrates multiplicity rather than singularity and that carries metaphor to new meaning? And what of the reader's role in this exercise? Does the new reader become the new witness, making the poem real in the moment of its reading? And should the reader, like Alice, be prepared for an invitation to ride the quantum poem into a new reality unlike any yet imagined?

Source: Klay Dyer, Critical Essay on "Witness," in *Poetry for Students*, Thomson Gale, 2007.

Thomson Gale

In the following essay, the critic gives a critical analysis of Waldner's work.

Liz Waldner's poetry has often been compared to that of experimental writer Gertrude Stein (1874-1946) for its innovative voice and style, which has been described as audacious, witty, intelligent, and sarcastic. Waldner is said to push the edge in terms of meaning and language.

Waldner's most celebrated publication is *A Point Is That Which Has No Part* (2000), a collection of poems that mix math and science with modern poetics. Whether she is discussing sex, time, or death, the subjects of her poems are colored with emotions that express longing and loss. This is a book that a reviewer for *American Poet* described as "deliberately unpredictable in its forms and subjects," referring to Waldner's ability to write as if her words were coming straight from her unconscious onto the page. This excerpt from "Wednesday Morning Pray Time" provides an example:

"Thumb, plum sex in a nutshell, plumb line, heart line, throw out the live line (phone sex) I mean lifeline, Jesus is coming for me. When he washed oh when he washed when my Jesus washed he washed my sins away. O happy day with thunder clouds, O dunder-head, O Donner, O Blitzen, all alone (a sorry pass) in the wrack of the roof of history."

In this passage, Waldner wanders through nursery rhymes, Biblical stories, lines from hymns, and finally historical events and pop culture. A reviewer for the *American Poet* quoted Waldner's description of her method of writing, in which, she says, there is "no transition from 'out of it' to 'right back in.'"

Although Waldner does not define her writing as such, her poetic style calls to mind the stream-of-consciousness writing that James Joyce (1882-1941) first popularized, a process through which the author tries to capture meaning by exploring his own random thought processes. That is why Waldner's poems read as if she is flowing through snatches of her memories, stopping only briefly at one image, which quickly reminds her of a somewhat related but different one. In the words of the *American Poet* reviewer, Waldner's writing is similar to observing "an animator drawing the hand of an animator drawing a bridge as the mouse crosses over it. Waldner seems to compose a line from moment to moment as we watch."

The poetry in Waldner's writing resides mostly in the sounds of, her choices of, and her combinations of words. The sounds rush out as the words cross the page, "not in nonsense," though, as Cole Swensen, for the *Boston Review*, pointed out, "for in part what Waldner demonstrates is that nonsense doesn't exist—where sense is not, something else is." And that something else, Swensen believes, is "a deep engagement with sound."

For a reviewer in *Publishers Weekly*, that something else in Waldner's work is deeply felt emotion. This reviewer appreciated Waldner's poetry for the fact that she "mixes sassiness, smarts and lyricism, intellectual querulousness with personal bitterness, vigor and exasperation."

Waldner's work elicits a variety of effects on her readers. Some critics attempt to understand her work on an intellectual level, trying to comprehend all her allusions, puns, and hidden meanings. Others enjoy the linguistic challenge that she offers in presenting words in unusual patterns and forms; while still others relinquish the need to understand her words and instead simply enjoy the musicality of her poetry.

Waldner has released additional collections, including *Self and Simulacra*, in 2001. In this volume, she more precisely addressed the issues of women as she explored the influences that help create female identity. Her most recent work includes *Dark Would: (The Missing Person)* and *Etym(Bi)Ology*, both published in 2002.

Source: Thomson Gale, "Liz Waldner," in *Contemporary Authors Online*, Gale, 2003.

SOURCES

Miller, Wayne, Review of *Saving the Appearances*, in *American Book Review*, May–June 2005, pp. 19, 24.

Review of *A Point Is That Which Has No Part*, in *Publishers Weekly*, February 7, 2000, p. 69.

Swenson, Cole, Review of *A Point Is That Which Has No Part*, in *Boston Review*, December 2000, http://bostonreview.net/BR25.6/swensen.html (accessed January 7, 2007).

Waldner, Liz, "Witness," in *A Point Is That Which Has No Part*, University of Iowa Press, 2000, p. 66.

FURTHER READING

Albright, Daniel, *Quantum Poetics: Yeats, Pound, Eliot, and the Science of Modernism*, Cambridge University Press, 2006.

A scholarly yet accessible study of the complex intersection between science and poetry in the work of three of the most influential poets of the modern era, this book examines the appropriation of scientific metaphors in the writing of the early twentieth century.

Levy, David H., *Starry Sky: Astronomers and Poets Read the Sky*, Prometheus Books, 2001.

The acclaimed science writer David Levy shows in this diverse and rich collection how the starry night sky has long captured the imagination of poets and scientists alike. This collection includes works by Galileo, Shakespeare, Milton, and Keats, among others.

Lockwood, Michael, *The Labyrinth of Time: Introducing the Universe*, Oxford University Press, 2007.

Starting from the physicist's assumption that the universe is a much stranger place than either science or poetry imagined, Lockwood enquires into the nature of things. This book is an engaging introduction to the physics of time and the structure of the universe that takes readers through the basics of relativity theory and quantum physics, including the ideas of Newton, Einstein, and Hawking.

Wudka, Jose, *Space-time, Relativity, and Cosmology*, Cambridge University Press, 2006.

This book is an undergraduate-level historical discussion of modern cosmology. The book traces the roots and evolution of the ideas from antiquity to Einstein. The topics are presented in a non-mathematical manner, with the emphasis on the ideas that underlie each theory. The book also includes discussion of data gathered by the Hubble telescope.

Glossary of Literary Terms

A

Abstract: Used as a noun, the term refers to a short summary or outline of a longer work. As an adjective applied to writing or literary works, abstract refers to words or phrases that name things not knowable through the five senses.

Accent: The emphasis or stress placed on a syllable in poetry. Traditional poetry commonly uses patterns of accented and unaccented syllables (known as feet) that create distinct rhythms. Much modern poetry uses less formal arrangements that create a sense of freedom and spontaneity.

Aestheticism: A literary and artistic movement of the nineteenth century. Followers of the movement believed that art should not be mixed with social, political, or moral teaching. The statement "art for art's sake" is a good summary of aestheticism. The movement had its roots in France, but it gained widespread importance in England in the last half of the nineteenth century, where it helped change the Victorian practice of including moral lessons in literature.

Affective Fallacy: An error in judging the merits or faults of a work of literature. The "error" results from stressing the importance of the work's effect upon the reader—that is, how it makes a reader "feel" emotionally, what it does as a literary work—instead of stressing its inner qualities as a created object, or what it "is."

Age of Johnson: The period in English literature between 1750 and 1798, named after the most prominent literary figure of the age, Samuel Johnson. Works written during this time are noted for their emphasis on "sensibility," or emotional quality. These works formed a transition between the rational works of the Age of Reason, or Neoclassical period, and the emphasis on individual feelings and responses of the Romantic period.

Age of Reason: See *Neoclassicism*

Age of Sensibility: See *Age of Johnson*

Agrarians: A group of Southern American writers of the 1930s and 1940s who fostered an economic and cultural program for the South based on agriculture, in opposition to the industrial society of the North. The term can refer to any group that promotes the value of farm life and agricultural society.

Alexandrine Meter: See *Meter*

Allegory: A narrative technique in which characters representing things or abstract ideas are used to convey a message or teach a lesson. Allegory is typically used to teach moral, ethical, or religious lessons but is sometimes used for satiric or political purposes.

Alliteration: A poetic device where the first consonant sounds or any vowel sounds in words or syllables are repeated.

Allusion: A reference to a familiar literary or historical person or event, used to make an idea more easily understood.

Amerind Literature: The writing and oral traditions of Native Americans. Native American literature was originally passed on by word of mouth, so it consisted largely of stories and events that were easily memorized. Amerind prose is often rhythmic like poetry because it was recited to the beat of a ceremonial drum.

Analogy: A comparison of two things made to explain something unfamiliar through its similarities to something familiar, or to prove one point based on the acceptedness of another. Similes and metaphors are types of analogies.

Anapest: See *Foot*

Angry Young Men: A group of British writers of the 1950s whose work expressed bitterness and disillusionment with society. Common to their work is an anti-hero who rebels against a corrupt social order and strives for personal integrity.

Anthropomorphism: The presentation of animals or objects in human shape or with human characteristics. The term is derived from the Greek word for "human form."

Antimasque: See *Masque*

Antithesis: The antithesis of something is its direct opposite. In literature, the use of antithesis as a figure of speech results in two statements that show a contrast through the balancing of two opposite ideas. Technically, it is the second portion of the statement that is defined as the "antithesis"; the first portion is the "thesis."

Apocrypha: Writings tentatively attributed to an author but not proven or universally accepted to be their works. The term was originally applied to certain books of the Bible that were not considered inspired and so were not included in the "sacred canon."

Apollonian and Dionysian: The two impulses believed to guide authors of dramatic tragedy. The Apollonian impulse is named after Apollo, the Greek god of light and beauty and the symbol of intellectual order. The Dionysian impulse is named after Dionysus, the Greek god of wine and the symbol of the unrestrained forces of nature. The Apollonian impulse is to create a rational, harmonious world, while the Dionysian is to express the irrational forces of personality.

Apostrophe: A statement, question, or request addressed to an inanimate object or concept or to a nonexistent or absent person.

Archetype: The word archetype is commonly used to describe an original pattern or model from which all other things of the same kind are made. This term was introduced to literary criticism from the psychology of Carl Jung. It expresses Jung's theory that behind every person's "unconscious," or repressed memories of the past, lies the "collective unconscious" of the human race: memories of the countless typical experiences of our ancestors. These memories are said to prompt illogical associations that trigger powerful emotions in the reader. Often, the emotional process is primitive, even primordial. Archetypes are the literary images that grow out of the "collective unconscious." They appear in literature as incidents and plots that repeat basic patterns of life. They may also appear as stereotyped characters.

Argument: The argument of a work is the author's subject matter or principal idea.

Art for Art's Sake: See *Aestheticism*

Assonance: The repetition of similar vowel sounds in poetry.

Audience: The people for whom a piece of literature is written. Authors usually write with a certain audience in mind, for example, children, members of a religious or ethnic group, or colleagues in a professional field. The term "audience" also applies to the people who gather to see or hear any performance, including plays, poetry readings, speeches, and concerts.

Automatic Writing: Writing carried out without a preconceived plan in an effort to capture every random thought. Authors who engage in automatic writing typically do not revise their work, preferring instead to preserve the revealed truth and beauty of spontaneous expression.

Avant-garde: A French term meaning "vanguard." It is used in literary criticism to describe new writing that rejects traditional approaches to literature in favor of innovations in style or content.

B

Ballad: A short poem that tells a simple story and has a repeated refrain. Ballads were originally intended to be sung. Early ballads, known as folk ballads, were passed down through generations, so their authors are often unknown. Later ballads composed by known authors are called literary ballads.

Baroque: A term used in literary criticism to describe literature that is complex or ornate in style or diction. Baroque works typically express tension, anxiety, and violent emotion. The term "Baroque Age" designates a period in Western European literature beginning in the late sixteenth century and ending about one hundred years later. Works of this period often mirror the qualities of works more generally associated with the label "baroque" and sometimes feature elaborate conceits.

Baroque Age: See *Baroque*

Baroque Period: See *Baroque*

Beat Generation: See *Beat Movement*

Beat Movement: A period featuring a group of American poets and novelists of the 1950s and 1960s—including Jack Kerouac, Allen Ginsberg, Gregory Corso, William S. Burroughs, and Lawrence Ferlinghetti—who rejected established social and literary values. Using such techniques as stream of consciousness writing and jazz-influenced free verse and focusing on unusual or abnormal states of mind—generated by religious ecstasy or the use of drugs—the Beat writers aimed to create works that were unconventional in both form and subject matter.

Beat Poets: See *Beat Movement*

Beats, The: See *Beat Movement*

Belles- lettres: A French term meaning "fine letters" or "beautiful writing." It is often used as a synonym for literature, typically referring to imaginative and artistic rather than scientific or expository writing. Current usage sometimes restricts the meaning to light or humorous writing and appreciative essays about literature.

Black Aesthetic Movement: A period of artistic and literary development among African Americans in the 1960s and early 1970s. This was the first major African-American artistic movement since the Harlem Renaissance and was closely paralleled by the civil rights and black power movements. The black aesthetic writers attempted to produce works of art that would be meaningful to the black masses. Key figures in black aesthetics included one of its founders, poet and playwright Amiri Baraka, formerly known as LeRoi Jones; poet and essayist Haki R. Madhubuti, formerly Don L. Lee; poet and playwright Sonia Sanchez; and dramatist Ed Bullins.

Black Arts Movement: See *Black Aesthetic Movement*

Black Comedy: See *Black Humor*

Black Humor: Writing that places grotesque elements side by side with humorous ones in an attempt to shock the reader, forcing him or her to laugh at the horrifying reality of a disordered world.

Black Mountain School: Black Mountain College and three of its instructors—Robert Creeley, Robert Duncan, and Charles Olson—were all influential in projective verse, so poets working in projective verse are now referred as members of the Black Mountain school.

Blank Verse: Loosely, any unrhymed poetry, but more generally, unrhymed iambic pentameter verse (composed of lines of five two-syllable feet with the first syllable accented, the second unaccented). Blank verse has been used by poets since the Renaissance for its flexibility and its graceful, dignified tone.

Bloomsbury Group: A group of English writers, artists, and intellectuals who held informal artistic and philosophical discussions in Bloomsbury, a district of London, from around 1907 to the early 1930s. The Bloomsbury Group held no uniform philosophical beliefs but did commonly express an aversion to moral prudery and a desire for greater social tolerance.

Bon Mot: A French term meaning "good word." A *bon mot* is a witty remark or clever observation.

Breath Verse: See *Projective Verse*

Burlesque: Any literary work that uses exaggeration to make its subject appear ridiculous, either by treating a trivial subject with profound seriousness or by treating a dignified subject frivolously. The word "burlesque" may also be used as an adjective, as in "burlesque show," to mean "striptease act."

C

Cadence: The natural rhythm of language caused by the alternation of accented and unaccented syllables. Much modern poetry—notably free verse—deliberately manipulates cadence to create complex rhythmic effects.

Caesura: A pause in a line of poetry, usually occurring near the middle. It typically corresponds to a break in the natural rhythm or sense of the line but is sometimes shifted to create special meanings or rhythmic effects.

Canzone: A short Italian or Provencal lyric poem, commonly about love and often set to music. The *canzone* has no set form but typically contains five or six stanzas made up of seven to twenty lines of eleven syllables each. A shorter, five- to ten-line "envoy," or concluding stanza, completes the poem.

Carpe Diem: A Latin term meaning "seize the day." This is a traditional theme of poetry, especially lyrics. A *carpe diem* poem advises the reader or the person it addresses to live for today and enjoy the pleasures of the moment.

Catharsis: The release or purging of unwanted emotions—specifically fear and pity—brought about by exposure to art. The term was first used by the Greek philosopher Aristotle in his *Poetics* to refer to the desired effect of tragedy on spectators.

Celtic Renaissance: A period of Irish literary and cultural history at the end of the nineteenth century. Followers of the movement aimed to create a romantic vision of Celtic myth and legend. The most significant works of the Celtic Renaissance typically present a dreamy, unreal world, usually in reaction against the reality of contemporary problems.

Celtic Twilight: See *Celtic Renaissance*

Character: Broadly speaking, a person in a literary work. The actions of characters are what constitute the plot of a story, novel, or poem. There are numerous types of characters, ranging from simple, stereotypical figures to intricate, multifaceted ones. In the techniques of anthropomorphism and personification, animals—and even places or things—can assume aspects of character. "Characterization" is the process by which an author creates vivid, believable characters in a work of art. This may be done in a variety of ways, including (1) direct description of the character by the narrator; (2) the direct presentation of the speech, thoughts, or actions of the character; and (3) the responses of other characters to the character. The term "character" also refers to a form originated by the ancient Greek writer Theophrastus that later became popular in the seventeenth and eighteenth centuries. It is a short essay or sketch of a person who prominently displays a specific attribute or quality, such as miserliness or ambition.

Characterization: See *Character*

Classical: In its strictest definition in literary criticism, classicism refers to works of ancient Greek or Roman literature. The term may also be used to describe a literary work of recognized importance (a "classic") from any time period or literature that exhibits the traits of classicism.

Classicism: A term used in literary criticism to describe critical doctrines that have their roots in ancient Greek and Roman literature, philosophy, and art. Works associated with classicism typically exhibit restraint on the part of the author, unity of design and purpose, clarity, simplicity, logical organization, and respect for tradition.

Colloquialism: A word, phrase, or form of pronunciation that is acceptable in casual conversation but not in formal, written communication. It is considered more acceptable than slang.

Complaint: A lyric poem, popular in the Renaissance, in which the speaker expresses sorrow about his or her condition. Typically, the speaker's sadness is caused by an unresponsive lover, but some complaints cite other sources of unhappiness, such as poverty or fate.

Conceit: A clever and fanciful metaphor, usually expressed through elaborate and extended comparison, that presents a striking parallel between two seemingly dissimilar things—for example, elaborately comparing a beautiful woman to an object like a garden or the sun. The conceit was a popular device throughout the Elizabethan Age and Baroque Age and was the principal technique of the seventeenth-century English metaphysical poets. This usage of the word conceit is unrelated to the best-known definition of conceit as an arrogant attitude or behavior.

Concrete: Concrete is the opposite of abstract, and refers to a thing that actually exists or a description that allows the reader to experience an object or concept with the senses.

Concrete Poetry: Poetry in which visual elements play a large part in the poetic effect. Punctuation marks, letters, or words are arranged on a page to form a visual design: a cross, for example, or a bumblebee.

Confessional Poetry: A form of poetry in which the poet reveals very personal, intimate, sometimes shocking information about himself or herself.

Connotation: The impression that a word gives beyond its defined meaning. Connotations may be universally understood or may be significant only to a certain group.

Consonance: Consonance occurs in poetry when words appearing at the ends of two or more verses have similar final consonant sounds but have final vowel sounds that differ, as with "stuff" and "off."

Convention: Any widely accepted literary device, style, or form.

Corrido: A Mexican ballad.

Couplet: Two lines of poetry with the same rhyme and meter, often expressing a complete and self-contained thought.

Criticism: The systematic study and evaluation of literary works, usually based on a specific method or set of principles. An important part of literary studies since ancient times, the practice of criticism has given rise to numerous theories, methods, and "schools," sometimes producing conflicting, even contradictory, interpretations of literature in general as well as of individual works. Even such basic issues as what constitutes a poem or a novel have been the subject of much criticism over the centuries.

D

Dactyl: See *Foot*

Dadaism: A protest movement in art and literature founded by Tristan Tzara in 1916. Followers of the movement expressed their outrage at the destruction brought about by World War I by revolting against numerous forms of social convention. The Dadaists presented works marked by calculated madness and flamboyant nonsense. They stressed total freedom of expression, commonly through primitive displays of emotion and illogical, often senseless, poetry. The movement ended shortly after the war, when it was replaced by surrealism.

Decadent: See *Decadents*

Decadents: The followers of a nineteenth-century literary movement that had its beginnings in French aestheticism. Decadent literature displays a fascination with perverse and morbid states; a search for novelty and sensation—the "new thrill"; a preoccupation with mysticism; and a belief in the senselessness of human existence. The movement is closely associated with the doctrine Art for Art's Sake. The term "decadence" is sometimes used to denote a decline in the quality of art or literature following a period of greatness.

Deconstruction: A method of literary criticism developed by Jacques Derrida and characterized by multiple conflicting interpretations of a given work. Deconstructionists consider the impact of the language of a work and suggest that the true meaning of the work is not necessarily the meaning that the author intended.

Deduction: The process of reaching a conclusion through reasoning from general premises to a specific premise.

Denotation: The definition of a word, apart from the impressions or feelings it creates in the reader.

Diction: The selection and arrangement of words in a literary work. Either or both may vary depending on the desired effect. There are four general types of diction: "formal," used in scholarly or lofty writing; "informal," used in relaxed but educated conversation; "colloquial," used in everyday speech; and "slang," containing newly coined words and other terms not accepted in formal usage.

Didactic: A term used to describe works of literature that aim to teach some moral, religious, political, or practical lesson. Although didactic elements are often found in artistically pleasing works, the term "didactic" usually refers to literature in which the message is more important than the form. The term may also be used to criticize a work that the critic finds "overly didactic," that is, heavy-handed in its delivery of a lesson.

Dimeter: See *Meter*

Dionysian: See *Apollonian and Dionysian*

Discordia concours: A Latin phrase meaning "discord in harmony." The term was coined by the eighteenth-century English writer Samuel Johnson to describe "a combination of dissimilar images or discovery of occult resemblances in things apparently unlike." Johnson created the expression by reversing a phrase by the Latin poet Horace.

Dissonance: A combination of harsh or jarring sounds, especially in poetry. Although such combinations may be accidental, poets sometimes intentionally make them to achieve particular effects. Dissonance is also sometimes used to refer to close but not identical rhymes. When this is the case, the word functions as a synonym for consonance.

Double Entendre: A corruption of a French phrase meaning "double meaning." The term is used to indicate a word or phrase that is deliberately ambiguous, especially when one of the meanings is risque or improper.

Draft: Any preliminary version of a written work. An author may write dozens of drafts which are revised to form the final work, or he or she may write only one, with few or no revisions.

Dramatic Monologue: See *Monologue*

Dramatic Poetry: Any lyric work that employs elements of drama such as dialogue, conflict, or characterization, but excluding works that are intended for stage presentation.

Dream Allegory: See *Dream Vision*

Dream Vision: A literary convention, chiefly of the Middle Ages. In a dream vision a story is presented as a literal dream of the narrator. This device was commonly used to teach moral and religious lessons.

E

Eclogue: In classical literature, a poem featuring rural themes and structured as a dialogue among shepherds. Eclogues often took specific poetic forms, such as elegies or love poems. Some were written as the soliloquy of a shepherd. In later centuries, "eclogue" came to refer to any poem that was in the pastoral tradition or that had a dialogue or monologue structure.

Edwardian: Describes cultural conventions identified with the period of the reign of Edward VII of England (1901-1910). Writers of the Edwardian Age typically displayed a strong reaction against the propriety and conservatism of the Victorian Age. Their work often exhibits distrust of authority in religion, politics, and art and expresses strong doubts about the soundness of conventional values.

Edwardian Age: See *Edwardian*

Electra Complex: A daughter's amorous obsession with her father.

Elegy: A lyric poem that laments the death of a person or the eventual death of all people. In a conventional elegy, set in a classical world, the poet and subject are spoken of as shepherds. In modern criticism, the word elegy is often used to refer to a poem that is melancholy or mournfully contemplative.

Elizabethan Age: A period of great economic growth, religious controversy, and nationalism closely associated with the reign of Elizabeth I of England (1558-1603). The Elizabethan Age is considered a part of the general renaissance—that is, the flowering of arts and literature—that took place in Europe during the fourteenth through sixteenth centuries. The era is considered the golden age of English literature. The most important dramas in English and a great deal of lyric poetry were produced during this period, and modern English criticism began around this time.

Empathy: A sense of shared experience, including emotional and physical feelings, with someone or something other than oneself. Empathy is often used to describe the response of a reader to a literary character.

English Sonnet: See *Sonnet*

Enjambment: The running over of the sense and structure of a line of verse or a couplet into the following verse or couplet.

Enlightenment, The: An eighteenth-century philosophical movement. It began in France but had a wide impact throughout Europe and America. Thinkers of the Enlightenment valued reason and believed that both the individual and society could achieve a state of perfection. Corresponding to this essentially humanist vision was a resistance to religious authority.

Epic: A long narrative poem about the adventures of a hero of great historic or legendary importance. The setting is vast and the action is often given cosmic significance through the intervention of supernatural forces such as gods, angels, or demons. Epics are typically written in a classical style of grand simplicity with elaborate metaphors and allusions that enhance the symbolic importance of a hero's adventures.

Epic Simile: See *Homeric Simile*

Epigram: A saying that makes the speaker's point quickly and concisely.

Epilogue: A concluding statement or section of a literary work. In dramas, particularly those of the seventeenth and eighteenth centuries, the epilogue is a closing speech, often in verse, delivered by an actor at the end of a play and spoken directly to the audience.

Epiphany: A sudden revelation of truth inspired by a seemingly trivial incident.

Epitaph: An inscription on a tomb or tombstone, or a verse written on the occasion of a person's death. Epitaphs may be serious or humorous.

Epithalamion: A song or poem written to honor and commemorate a marriage ceremony.

Epithalamium: See *Epithalamion*

Epithet: A word or phrase, often disparaging or abusive, that expresses a character trait of someone or something.

Erziehungsroman: See *Bildungsroman*

Essay: A prose composition with a focused subject of discussion. The term was coined by Michel de Montaigne to describe his 1580 collection of brief, informal reflections on himself and on various topics relating to human nature. An essay can also be a long, systematic discourse.

Existentialism: A predominantly twentieth-century philosophy concerned with the nature and perception of human existence. There are two major strains of existentialist thought: atheistic and Christian. Followers of atheistic existentialism believe that the individual is alone in a godless universe and that the basic human condition is one of suffering and loneliness. Nevertheless, because there are no fixed values, individuals can create their own characters—indeed, they can shape themselves—through the exercise of free will. The atheistic strain culminates in and is popularly associated with the works of Jean-Paul Sartre. The Christian existentialists, on the other hand, believe that only in God may people find freedom from life's anguish. The two strains hold certain beliefs in common: that existence cannot be fully understood or described through empirical effort; that anguish is a universal element of life; that individuals must bear responsibility for their actions; and that there is no common standard of behavior or perception for religious and ethical matters.

Expatriates: See *Expatriatism*

Expatriatism: The practice of leaving one's country to live for an extended period in another country.

Exposition: Writing intended to explain the nature of an idea, thing, or theme. Expository writing is often combined with description, narration, or argument. In dramatic writing, the exposition is the introductory material which presents the characters, setting, and tone of the play.

Expressionism: An indistinct literary term, originally used to describe an early twentieth-century school of German painting. The term applies to almost any mode of unconventional, highly subjective writing that distorts reality in some way.

Extended Monologue: See *Monologue*

F

Feet: See *Foot*

Feminine Rhyme: See *Rhyme*

Fiction: Any story that is the product of imagination rather than a documentation of fact. Characters and events in such narratives may be based in real life but their ultimate form and configuration is a creation of the author.

Figurative Language: A technique in writing in which the author temporarily interrupts the order, construction, or meaning of the writing for a particular effect. This interruption takes the form of one or more figures of speech such as hyperbole, irony, or simile. Figurative language is the opposite of literal language, in which every word is truthful, accurate, and free of exaggeration or embellishment.

Figures of Speech: Writing that differs from customary conventions for construction, meaning, order, or significance for the purpose of a special meaning or effect. There are two major types of figures of speech: rhetorical figures, which do not make changes in the meaning of the words, and tropes, which do.

Fin de siecle: A French term meaning "end of the century." The term is used to denote the last decade of the nineteenth century, a transition period when writers and other artists abandoned old conventions and looked for new techniques and objectives.

First Person: See *Point of View*

Folk Ballad: See *Ballad*

Folklore: Traditions and myths preserved in a culture or group of people. Typically, these are passed on by word of mouth in various forms—such as legends, songs, and proverbs—or preserved in customs and ceremonies. This term was first used by W. J. Thoms in 1846.

Folktale: A story originating in oral tradition. Folktales fall into a variety of categories, including legends, ghost stories, fairy tales, fables, and anecdotes based on historical figures and events.

Foot: The smallest unit of rhythm in a line of poetry. In English-language poetry, a foot is typically one accented syllable combined with one or two unaccented syllables.

Form: The pattern or construction of a work which identifies its genre and distinguishes it from other genres.

Formalism: In literary criticism, the belief that literature should follow prescribed rules of construction, such as those that govern the sonnet form.

Fourteener Meter: See *Meter*

Free Verse: Poetry that lacks regular metrical and rhyme patterns but that tries to capture the cadences of everyday speech. The form allows a poet to exploit a variety of rhythmical effects within a single poem.

Futurism: A flamboyant literary and artistic movement that developed in France, Italy, and Russia from 1908 through the 1920s. Futurist theater and poetry abandoned traditional literary forms. In their place, followers of the movement attempted to achieve total freedom of expression through bizarre imagery and deformed or newly invented words. The Futurists were self-consciously modern artists who attempted to incorporate the appearances and sounds of modern life into their work.

G

Genre: A category of literary work. In critical theory, genre may refer to both the content of a given work—tragedy, comedy, pastoral—and to its form, such as poetry, novel, or drama.

Genteel Tradition: A term coined by critic George Santayana to describe the literary practice of certain late nineteenth- century American writers, especially New Englanders. Followers of the Genteel Tradition emphasized conventionality in social, religious, moral, and literary standards.

Georgian Age: See *Georgian Poets*

Georgian Period: See *Georgian Poets*

Georgian Poets: A loose grouping of English poets during the years 1912-1922. The Georgians reacted against certain literary schools and practices, especially Victorian wordiness, turn-of-the-century aestheticism, and contemporary urban realism. In their place, the Georgians embraced the nineteenth-century poetic practices of William Wordsworth and the other Lake Poets.

Georgic: A poem about farming and the farmer's way of life, named from Virgil's *Georgics.*

Gilded Age: A period in American history during the 1870s characterized by political corruption and materialism. A number of important novels of social and political criticism were written during this time.

Gothic: See *Gothicism*

Gothicism: In literary criticism, works characterized by a taste for the medieval or morbidly attractive. A gothic novel prominently features elements of horror, the supernatural, gloom, and violence: clanking chains, terror, charnel houses, ghosts, medieval castles, and mysteriously slamming doors. The term "gothic novel" is also applied to novels that lack elements of the traditional Gothic setting but that create a similar atmosphere of terror or dread.

Graveyard School: A group of eighteenth-century English poets who wrote long, picturesque meditations on death. Their works were designed to cause the reader to ponder immortality.

Great Chain of Being: The belief that all things and creatures in nature are organized in a hierarchy from inanimate objects at the bottom to God at the top. This system of belief was popular in the seventeenth and eighteenth centuries.

Grotesque: In literary criticism, the subject matter of a work or a style of expression characterized by exaggeration, deformity, freakishness, and disorder. The grotesque often includes an element of comic absurdity.

H

Haiku: The shortest form of Japanese poetry, constructed in three lines of five, seven, and five syllables respectively. The message of a *haiku* poem usually centers on some aspect of spirituality and provokes an emotional response in the reader.

Half Rhyme: See *Consonance*

Harlem Renaissance: The Harlem Renaissance of the 1920s is generally considered the first significant movement of black writers and artists in the United States. During this period, new and established black writers published more fiction and poetry than ever before, the first influential black literary journals were established, and black authors and artists received their first widespread recognition and serious critical appraisal. Among the major writers associated with this period are Claude McKay, Jean Toomer, Countee Cullen, Langston Hughes, Arna Bontemps, Nella Larsen, and Zora Neale Hurston.

Hellenism: Imitation of ancient Greek thought or styles. Also, an approach to life that focuses on the growth and development of the intellect. "Hellenism" is sometimes used to refer to the belief that reason can be applied to examine all human experience.

Heptameter: See *Meter*

Hero/Heroine: The principal sympathetic character (male or female) in a literary work. Heroes and heroines typically exhibit admirable traits: idealism, courage, and integrity, for example.

Heroic Couplet: A rhyming couplet written in iambic pentameter (a verse with five iambic feet).

Heroic Line: The meter and length of a line of verse in epic or heroic poetry. This varies by language and time period.

Heroine: See *Hero/Heroine*

Hexameter: See *Meter*

Historical Criticism: The study of a work based on its impact on the world of the time period in which it was written.

Hokku: See *Haiku*

Holocaust: See *Holocaust Literature*

Holocaust Literature: Literature influenced by or written about the Holocaust of World War II. Such literature includes true stories of survival in concentration camps, escape, and life after the war, as well as fictional works and poetry.

Homeric Simile: An elaborate, detailed comparison written as a simile many lines in length.

Horatian Satire: See *Satire*

Humanism: A philosophy that places faith in the dignity of humankind and rejects the medieval perception of the individual as a weak, fallen creature. "Humanists" typically believe in the perfectibility of human nature and view reason and education as the means to that end.

Humors: Mentions of the humors refer to the ancient Greek theory that a person's health and personality were determined by the balance of four basic fluids in the body: blood, phlegm, yellow bile, and black bile. A dominance of any fluid would cause extremes in behavior. An excess of blood created a sanguine person who was joyful, aggressive, and passionate; a phlegmatic person was shy, fearful, and sluggish; too much yellow bile led to a choleric temperament characterized by impatience, anger, bitterness, and stubbornness; and excessive black bile created melancholy, a state of laziness, gluttony, and lack of motivation.

Humours: See *Humors*

Hyperbole: In literary criticism, deliberate exaggeration used to achieve an effect.

I

Iamb: See *Foot*

Idiom: A word construction or verbal expression closely associated with a given language.

Image: A concrete representation of an object or sensory experience. Typically, such a representation helps evoke the feelings associated with the object or experience itself. Images are either "literal" or "figurative." Literal images are especially concrete and involve little or no extension of the obvious meaning of the words used to express them. Figurative images do not follow the literal meaning of the words exactly. Images in literature are usually visual, but the term "image" can also refer to the representation of any sensory experience.

Imagery: The array of images in a literary work. Also, figurative language.

Imagism: An English and American poetry movement that flourished between 1908 and 1917. The Imagists used precise, clearly presented images in their works. They also used common, everyday speech and aimed for conciseness, concrete imagery, and the creation of new rhythms.

In medias res: A Latin term meaning "in the middle of things." It refers to the technique of beginning a story at its midpoint and then using various flashback devices to reveal previous action.

Induction: The process of reaching a conclusion by reasoning from specific premises to form a general premise. Also, an introductory portion of a work of literature, especially a play.

Intentional Fallacy: The belief that judgments of a literary work based solely on an author's stated or implied intentions are false and misleading. Critics who believe in the concept of the intentional fallacy typically argue that the work itself is sufficient matter for interpretation, even though they may concede that an author's statement of purpose can be useful.

Interior Monologue: A narrative technique in which characters' thoughts are revealed in a way that appears to be uncontrolled by the author. The interior monologue typically aims to reveal the inner self of a character. It portrays emotional experiences as they occur at both a conscious and unconscious level. Images are often used to represent sensations or emotions.

Internal Rhyme: Rhyme that occurs within a single line of verse.

Irish Literary Renaissance: A late nineteenth- and early twentieth-century movement in Irish literature. Members of the movement aimed to reduce the influence of British culture in Ireland and create an Irish national literature.

Irony: In literary criticism, the effect of language in which the intended meaning is the opposite of what is stated.

Italian Sonnet: See *Sonnet*

J

Jacobean Age: The period of the reign of James I of England (1603-1625). The early literature of this period reflected the worldview of the Elizabethan Age, but a darker, more cynical attitude steadily grew in the art and literature of the Jacobean Age. This was an important time for English drama and poetry.

Jargon: Language that is used or understood only by a select group of people. Jargon may refer to terminology used in a certain profession, such as computer jargon, or it may refer to any nonsensical language that is not understood by most people.

Journalism: Writing intended for publication in a newspaper or magazine, or for broadcast on a radio or television program featuring news, sports, entertainment, or other timely material.

K

Knickerbocker Group: A somewhat indistinct group of New York writers of the first half of the nineteenth century. Members of the group were linked only by location and a common theme: New York life.

Kunstlerroman: See *Bildungsroman*

L

Lais: See *Lay*

Lake Poets: See *Lake School*

Lake School: These poets all lived in the Lake District of England at the turn of the nineteenth century. As a group, they followed no single "school" of thought or literary practice, although their works were uniformly disparaged by the *Edinburgh Review*.

Lay: A song or simple narrative poem. The form originated in medieval France. Early French *lais* were often based on the Celtic legends and other tales sung by Breton minstrels— thus the name of the "Breton lay." In fourteenth-century England, the term "lay" was used to describe short narratives written in imitation of the Breton lays.

Leitmotiv: See *Motif*

Literal Language: An author uses literal language when he or she writes without exaggerating or embellishing the subject matter and without any tools of figurative language.

Literary Ballad: See *Ballad*

Literature: Literature is broadly defined as any written or spoken material, but the term most often refers to creative works.

Lost Generation: A term first used by Gertrude Stein to describe the post-World War I generation of American writers: men and women haunted by a sense of betrayal and emptiness brought about by the destructiveness of the war.

Lyric Poetry: A poem expressing the subjective feelings and personal emotions of the poet. Such poetry is melodic, since it was originally accompanied by a lyre in recitals. Most Western poetry in the twentieth century may be classified as lyrical.

M

Mannerism: Exaggerated, artificial adherence to a literary manner or style. Also, a popular style of the visual arts of late sixteenth-century Europe that was marked by elongation of the human form and by intentional spatial distortion. Literary works that are

self-consciously high-toned and artistic are often said to be "mannered."

Masculine Rhyme: See *Rhyme*

Measure: The foot, verse, or time sequence used in a literary work, especially a poem. Measure is often used somewhat incorrectly as a synonym for meter.

Metaphor: A figure of speech that expresses an idea through the image of another object. Metaphors suggest the essence of the first object by identifying it with certain qualities of the second object.

Metaphysical Conceit: See *Conceit*

Metaphysical Poetry: The body of poetry produced by a group of seventeenth-century English writers called the "Metaphysical Poets." The group includes John Donne and Andrew Marvell. The Metaphysical Poets made use of everyday speech, intellectual analysis, and unique imagery. They aimed to portray the ordinary conflicts and contradictions of life. Their poems often took the form of an argument, and many of them emphasize physical and religious love as well as the fleeting nature of life. Elaborate conceits are typical in metaphysical poetry.

Metaphysical Poets: See *Metaphysical Poetry*

Meter: In literary criticism, the repetition of sound patterns that creates a rhythm in poetry. The patterns are based on the number of syllables and the presence and absence of accents. The unit of rhythm in a line is called a foot. Types of meter are classified according to the number of feet in a line. These are the standard English lines: Monometer, one foot; Dimeter, two feet; Trimeter, three feet; Tetrameter, four feet; Pentameter, five feet; Hexameter, six feet (also called the Alexandrine); Heptameter, seven feet (also called the "Fourteener" when the feet are iambic).

Modernism: Modern literary practices. Also, the principles of a literary school that lasted from roughly the beginning of the twentieth century until the end of World War II. Modernism is defined by its rejection of the literary conventions of the nineteenth century and by its opposition to conventional morality, taste, traditions, and economic values.

Monologue: A composition, written or oral, by a single individual. More specifically, a speech given by a single individual in a drama or other public entertainment. It has no set length, although it is usually several or more lines long.

Monometer: See *Meter*

Mood: The prevailing emotions of a work or of the author in his or her creation of the work. The mood of a work is not always what might be expected based on its subject matter.

Motif: A theme, character type, image, metaphor, or other verbal element that recurs throughout a single work of literature or occurs in a number of different works over a period of time.

Motiv: See *Motif*

Muckrakers: An early twentieth-century group of American writers. Typically, their works exposed the wrongdoings of big business and government in the United States.

Muses: Nine Greek mythological goddesses, the daughters of Zeus and Mnemosyne (Memory). Each muse patronized a specific area of the liberal arts and sciences. Calliope presided over epic poetry, Clio over history, Erato over love poetry, Euterpe over music or lyric poetry, Melpomene over tragedy, Polyhymnia over hymns to the gods, Terpsichore over dance, Thalia over comedy, and Urania over astronomy. Poets and writers traditionally made appeals to the Muses for inspiration in their work.

Myth: An anonymous tale emerging from the traditional beliefs of a culture or social unit. Myths use supernatural explanations for natural phenomena. They may also explain cosmic issues like creation and death. Collections of myths, known as mythologies, are common to all cultures and nations, but the best-known myths belong to the Norse, Roman, and Greek mythologies.

N

Narration: The telling of a series of events, real or invented. A narration may be either a simple narrative, in which the events are recounted chronologically, or a narrative with a plot, in which the account is given in a style reflecting the author's artistic concept of the story. Narration is sometimes used as a synonym for "storyline."

Narrative: A verse or prose accounting of an event or sequence of events, real or invented. The term is also used as an adjective in the sense "method of narration." For example, in literary criticism, the expression "narrative technique" usually refers to the way the author structures and presents his or her story.

Narrative Poetry: A nondramatic poem in which the author tells a story. Such poems may be of any length or level of complexity.

Narrator: The teller of a story. The narrator may be the author or a character in the story through whom the author speaks.

Naturalism: A literary movement of the late nineteenth and early twentieth centuries. The movement's major theorist, French novelist Emile Zola, envisioned a type of fiction that would examine human life with the objectivity of scientific inquiry. The Naturalists typically viewed human beings as either the products of "biological determinism," ruled by hereditary instincts and engaged in an endless struggle for survival, or as the products of "socioeconomic determinism," ruled by social and economic forces beyond their control. In their works, the Naturalists generally ignored the highest levels of society and focused on degradation: poverty, alcoholism, prostitution, insanity, and disease.

Negritude: A literary movement based on the concept of a shared cultural bond on the part of black Africans, wherever they may be in the world. It traces its origins to the former French colonies of Africa and the Caribbean. Negritude poets, novelists, and essayists generally stress four points in their writings: One, black alienation from traditional African culture can lead to feelings of inferiority. Two, European colonialism and Western education should be resisted. Three, black Africans should seek to affirm and define their own identity. Four, African culture can and should be reclaimed. Many Negritude writers also claim that blacks can make unique contributions to the world, based on a heightened appreciation of nature, rhythm, and human emotions—aspects of life they say are not so highly valued in the materialistic and rationalistic West.

Negro Renaissance: See *Harlem Renaissance*

Neoclassical Period: See *Neoclassicism*

Neoclassicism: In literary criticism, this term refers to the revival of the attitudes and styles of expression of classical literature. It is generally used to describe a period in European history beginning in the late seventeenth century and lasting until about 1800. In its purest form, Neoclassicism marked a return to order, proportion, restraint, logic, accuracy, and decorum. In England, where Neoclassicism perhaps was most popular, it reflected the influence of seventeenth-century French writers, especially dramatists. Neoclassical writers typically reacted against the intensity and enthusiasm of the Renaissance period. They wrote works that appealed to the intellect, using elevated language and classical literary forms such as satire and the ode. Neoclassical works were often governed by the classical goal of instruction.

Neoclassicists: See *Neoclassicism*

New Criticism: A movement in literary criticism, dating from the late 1920s, that stressed close textual analysis in the interpretation of works of literature. The New Critics saw little merit in historical and biographical analysis. Rather, they aimed to examine the text alone, free from the question of how external events—biographical or otherwise—may have helped shape it.

New Journalism: A type of writing in which the journalist presents factual information in a form usually used in fiction. New journalism emphasizes description, narration, and character development to bring readers closer to the human element of the story, and is often used in personality profiles and in-depth feature articles. It is not compatible with "straight" or "hard" newswriting, which is generally composed in a brief, fact-based style.

New Journalists: See *New Journalism*

New Negro Movement: See *Harlem Renaissance*

Noble Savage: The idea that primitive man is noble and good but becomes evil and corrupted as he becomes civilized. The concept of the noble savage originated in the Renaissance period but is more closely identified with such later writers as Jean-Jacques Rousseau and Aphra Behn.

O

Objective Correlative: An outward set of objects, a situation, or a chain of events corresponding to an inward experience and evoking this experience in the reader. The term frequently appears in modern criticism in discussions of authors' intended effects on the emotional responses of readers.

Objectivity: A quality in writing characterized by the absence of the author's opinion or feeling about the subject matter. Objectivity is an important factor in criticism.

Occasional Verse: poetry written on the occasion of a significant historical or personal event. *Vers de societe* is sometimes called occasional verse although it is of a less serious nature.

Octave: A poem or stanza composed of eight lines. The term octave most often represents the first eight lines of a Petrarchan sonnet.

Ode: Name given to an extended lyric poem characterized by exalted emotion and dignified style. An ode usually concerns a single, serious theme. Most odes, but not all, are addressed to an object or individual. Odes are distinguished from other lyric poetic forms by their complex rhythmic and stanzaic patterns.

Oedipus Complex: A son's amorous obsession with his mother. The phrase is derived from the story of the ancient Theban hero Oedipus, who unknowingly killed his father and married his mother.

Omniscience: See *Point of View*

Onomatopoeia: The use of words whose sounds express or suggest their meaning. In its simplest sense, onomatopoeia may be represented by words that mimic the sounds they denote such as "hiss" or "meow." At a more subtle level, the pattern and rhythm of sounds and rhymes of a line or poem may be onomatopoeic.

Oral Tradition: See *Oral Transmission*

Oral Transmission: A process by which songs, ballads, folklore, and other material are transmitted by word of mouth. The tradition of oral transmission predates the written record systems of literate society. Oral transmission preserves material sometimes over generations, although often with variations. Memory plays a large part in the recitation and preservation of orally transmitted material.

Ottava Rima: An eight-line stanza of poetry composed in iambic pentameter (a five-foot line in which each foot consists of an unaccented syllable followed by an accented syllable), following the ababcbcc rhyme scheme.

Oxymoron: A phrase combining two contradictory terms. Oxymorons may be intentional or unintentional.

P

Pantheism: The idea that all things are both a manifestation or revelation of God and a part of God at the same time. Pantheism was a common attitude in the early societies of Egypt, India, and Greece—the term derives from the Greek *pan* meaning "all" and *theos* meaning "deity." It later became a significant part of the Christian faith.

Parable: A story intended to teach a moral lesson or answer an ethical question.

Paradox: A statement that appears illogical or contradictory at first, but may actually point to an underlying truth.

Parallelism: A method of comparison of two ideas in which each is developed in the same grammatical structure.

Parnassianism: A mid nineteenth-century movement in French literature. Followers of the movement stressed adherence to well-defined artistic forms as a reaction against the often chaotic expression of the artist's ego that dominated the work of the Romantics. The Parnassians also rejected the moral, ethical, and social themes exhibited in the works of French Romantics such as Victor Hugo. The aesthetic doctrines of the Parnassians strongly influenced the later symbolist and decadent movements.

Parody: In literary criticism, this term refers to an imitation of a serious literary work or the signature style of a particular author in a ridiculous manner. A typical parody adopts the style of the original and applies it to an inappropriate subject for humorous effect. Parody is a form of satire and could be considered the literary equivalent of a caricature or cartoon.

Pastoral: A term derived from the Latin word "pastor," meaning shepherd. A pastoral is a literary composition on a rural theme. The conventions of the pastoral were originated by the third-century Greek poet Theocritus, who wrote about the experiences, love affairs, and pastimes of Sicilian shepherds. In a pastoral, characters and language of a courtly nature are often placed in a simple setting. The term pastoral is also used to classify dramas, elegies, and lyrics that exhibit the use of country settings and shepherd characters.

Pathetic Fallacy: A term coined by English critic John Ruskin to identify writing that falsely endows nonhuman things with human intentions and feelings, such as "angry clouds" and "sad trees."

Pen Name: See *Pseudonym*

Pentameter: See *Meter*

Persona: A Latin term meaning "mask." *Personae* are the characters in a fictional work of literature. The *persona* generally functions as a mask through which the author tells a story in a voice other than his or her own. A *persona* is usually either a character in a story who acts as a narrator or an "implied author," a voice created by the author to act as the narrator for himself or herself.

Personae: See *Persona*

Personal Point of View: See *Point of View*

Personification: A figure of speech that gives human qualities to abstract ideas, animals, and inanimate objects.

Petrarchan Sonnet: See *Sonnet*

Phenomenology: A method of literary criticism based on the belief that things have no existence outside of human consciousness or awareness. Proponents of this theory believe that art is a process that takes place in the mind of the observer as he or she contemplates an object rather than a quality of the object itself.

Plagiarism: Claiming another person's written material as one's own. Plagiarism can take the form of direct, word-for-word copying or the theft of the substance or idea of the work.

Platonic Criticism: A form of criticism that stresses an artistic work's usefulness as an agent of social engineering rather than any quality or value of the work itself.

Platonism: The embracing of the doctrines of the philosopher Plato, popular among the poets of the Renaissance and the Romantic period. Platonism is more flexible than Aristotelian Criticism and places more emphasis on the supernatural and unknown aspects of life.

Plot: In literary criticism, this term refers to the pattern of events in a narrative or drama. In its simplest sense, the plot guides the author in composing the work and helps the reader follow the work. Typically, plots exhibit causality and unity and have a beginning, a middle, and an end. Sometimes, however, a plot may consist of a series of disconnected events, in which case it is known as an "episodic plot."

Poem: In its broadest sense, a composition utilizing rhyme, meter, concrete detail, and expressive language to create a literary experience with emotional and aesthetic appeal.

Poet: An author who writes poetry or verse. The term is also used to refer to an artist or writer who has an exceptional gift for expression, imagination, and energy in the making of art in any form.

Poete maudit: A term derived from Paul Verlaine's *Les poetes maudits* (*The Accursed Poets*), a collection of essays on the French symbolist writers Stephane Mallarme, Arthur Rimbaud, and Tristan Corbiere. In the sense intended by Verlaine, the poet is "accursed" for choosing to explore extremes of human experience outside of middle-class society.

Poetic Fallacy: See *Pathetic Fallacy*

Poetic Justice: An outcome in a literary work, not necessarily a poem, in which the good are rewarded and the evil are punished, especially in ways that particularly fit their virtues or crimes.

Poetic License: Distortions of fact and literary convention made by a writer—not always a poet—for the sake of the effect gained. Poetic license is closely related to the concept of "artistic freedom."

Poetics: This term has two closely related meanings. It denotes (1) an aesthetic theory in literary criticism about the essence of poetry or (2) rules prescribing the proper methods, content, style, or diction of poetry. The term poetics may also refer to theories about literature in general, not just poetry.

Poetry: In its broadest sense, writing that aims to present ideas and evoke an emotional experience in the reader through the use of meter, imagery, connotative and concrete words, and a carefully constructed structure based on rhythmic patterns. Poetry typically relies on words and expressions that have several layers of meaning. It also makes use of the effects of regular rhythm on the ear and may make a strong appeal to the senses through the use of imagery.

Point of View: The narrative perspective from which a literary work is presented to the reader. There are four traditional points of view. The "third person omniscient" gives the reader a "godlike" perspective, unrestricted by time or place, from which to see actions and look into the minds of characters. This allows the author to comment openly on characters and events in the work. The "third person" point of view presents the events of the story from outside of any single character's perception, much like the omniscient point of view, but the reader must understand the action as it takes place and without any special insight into characters' minds or motivations. The "first person" or "personal" point of view relates events as they are perceived by a single character. The main character "tells" the story and may offer opinions about the action and characters which differ from those of the author. Much less common than omniscient, third person, and first person is the "second person" point of view, wherein the author tells the story as if it is happening to the reader.

Polemic: A work in which the author takes a stand on a controversial subject, such as abortion or religion. Such works are often extremely argumentative or provocative.

Pornography: Writing intended to provoke feelings of lust in the reader. Such works are often condemned by critics and teachers, but those which can be shown to have literary value are viewed less harshly.

Post-Aesthetic Movement: An artistic response made by African Americans to the black aesthetic movement of the 1960s and early '70s. Writers since that time have adopted a somewhat different tone in their work, with less emphasis placed on the disparity between black and white in the United States. In the words of post-aesthetic authors such as Toni Morrison, John Edgar Wideman, and Kristin Hunter, African Americans are portrayed as looking inward for answers to their own questions, rather than always looking to the outside world.

Postmodernism: Writing from the 1960s forward characterized by experimentation and continuing to apply some of the fundamentals of modernism, which included existentialism and alienation. Postmodernists have gone a step further in the rejection of tradition begun with the modernists by also rejecting traditional forms, preferring the anti-novel over the novel and the anti-hero over the hero.

Pre-Raphaelites: A circle of writers and artists in mid nineteenth-century England. Valuing the pre-Renaissance artistic qualities of religious symbolism, lavish pictorialism, and natural sensuousness, the Pre-Raphaelites cultivated a sense of mystery and melancholy that influenced later writers associated with the Symbolist and Decadent movements.

Primitivism: The belief that primitive peoples were nobler and less flawed than civilized peoples because they had not been subjected to the tainting influence of society.

Projective Verse: A form of free verse in which the poet's breathing pattern determines the lines of the poem. Poets who advocate projective verse are against all formal structures in writing, including meter and form.

Prologue: An introductory section of a literary work. It often contains information establishing the situation of the characters or presents information about the setting, time period, or action. In drama, the prologue is spoken by a chorus or by one of the principal characters.

Prose: A literary medium that attempts to mirror the language of everyday speech. It is distinguished from poetry by its use of unmetered, unrhymed language consisting of logically related sentences. Prose is usually grouped into paragraphs that form a cohesive whole such as an essay or a novel.

Prosopopoeia: See *Personification*

Protagonist: The central character of a story who serves as a focus for its themes and incidents and as the principal rationale for its development. The protagonist is sometimes referred to in discussions of modern literature as the hero or anti-hero.

Proverb: A brief, sage saying that expresses a truth about life in a striking manner.

Pseudonym: A name assumed by a writer, most often intended to prevent his or her identification as the author of a work. Two or more authors may work together under one pseudonym, or an author may use a different name for each genre he or she publishes in. Some publishing companies maintain "house pseudonyms," under which any number of authors may write installations in a series. Some authors also choose a pseudonym over their real names the way an actor may use a stage name.

Pun: A play on words that have similar sounds but different meanings.

Pure Poetry: poetry written without instructional intent or moral purpose that aims only to please a reader by its imagery or musical flow. The term pure poetry is used as the antonym of the term "didacticism."

Q

Quatrain: A four-line stanza of a poem or an entire poem consisting of four lines.

R

Realism: A nineteenth-century European literary movement that sought to portray familiar characters, situations, and settings in a realistic manner. This was done primarily by using an objective narrative point of view and through the buildup of accurate detail. The standard for success of any realistic work depends on how faithfully it transfers common experience into fictional forms. The realistic method may be altered or extended, as in stream of consciousness writing, to record highly subjective experience.

Refrain: A phrase repeated at intervals throughout a poem. A refrain may appear at the end of each stanza or at less regular intervals. It may be altered slightly at each appearance.

Renaissance: The period in European history that marked the end of the Middle Ages. It began in Italy in the late fourteenth century. In broad terms, it is usually seen as spanning the fourteenth, fifteenth, and sixteenth centuries, although it did not reach Great Britain, for example, until the 1480s or so. The Renaissance saw an awakening in almost every sphere of human activity, especially science, philosophy, and the arts. The period is best defined by the emergence of a general philosophy that emphasized the importance of the intellect, the individual, and world affairs. It contrasts strongly with the medieval worldview, characterized by the dominant concerns of faith, the social collective, and spiritual salvation.

Repartee: Conversation featuring snappy retorts and witticisms.

Restoration: See *Restoration Age*

Restoration Age: A period in English literature beginning with the crowning of Charles II in 1660 and running to about 1700. The era, which was characterized by a reaction against Puritanism, was the first great age of the comedy of manners. The finest literature of the era is typically witty and urbane, and often lewd.

Rhetoric: In literary criticism, this term denotes the art of ethical persuasion. In its strictest sense, rhetoric adheres to various principles developed since classical times for arranging facts and ideas in a clear, persuasive, appealing manner. The term is also used to refer to effective prose in general and theories of or methods for composing effective prose.

Rhetorical Question: A question intended to provoke thought, but not an expressed answer, in the reader. It is most commonly used in oratory and other persuasive genres.

Rhyme: When used as a noun in literary criticism, this term generally refers to a poem in which words sound identical or very similar and appear in parallel positions in two or more lines. Rhymes are classified into different types according to where they fall in a line or stanza or according to the degree of similarity they exhibit in their spellings and sounds. Some major types of rhyme are "masculine" rhyme, "feminine" rhyme, and "triple" rhyme. In a masculine rhyme, the rhyming sound falls in a single accented syllable, as with "heat" and "eat." Feminine rhyme is a rhyme of two syllables, one stressed and one unstressed, as with "merry" and "tarry." Triple rhyme matches the sound of the accented syllable and the two unaccented syllables that follow: "narrative" and "declarative."

Rhyme Royal: A stanza of seven lines composed in iambic pentameter and rhymed *ababbcc*. The name is said to be a tribute to King James I of Scotland, who made much use of the form in his poetry.

Rhyme Scheme: See *Rhyme*

Rhythm: A regular pattern of sound, time intervals, or events occurring in writing, most often and most discernably in poetry. Regular, reliable rhythm is known to be soothing to humans, while interrupted, unpredictable, or rapidly changing rhythm is disturbing. These effects are known to authors, who use them to produce a desired reaction in the reader.

Rococo: A style of European architecture that flourished in the eighteenth century, especially in France. The most notable features of *rococo* are its extensive use of ornamentation and its themes of lightness, gaiety, and intimacy. In literary criticism, the term is often used disparagingly to refer to a decadent or over-ornamental style.

Romance: A broad term, usually denoting a narrative with exotic, exaggerated, often idealized characters, scenes, and themes.

Romantic Age: See *Romanticism*

Romanticism: This term has two widely accepted meanings. In historical criticism, it refers to a European intellectual and artistic movement of the late eighteenth and early nineteenth centuries that sought greater freedom of personal expression than that allowed by the strict rules of literary form and logic of the eighteenth-century neoclassicists. The Romantics preferred emotional and imaginative expression to rational analysis. They considered the individual to be at the center of all experience and so placed him or her at the center of their art. The Romantics believed that the creative imagination reveals nobler truths—unique feelings and attitudes—than those that could be discovered by logic or by scientific examination. Both the natural world and the state of childhood were important sources for revelations of "eternal truths." "Romanticism" is also used as a general term to refer to a type of sensibility found in all periods of literary history and usually considered to be in opposition to the principles of classicism. In this sense, Romanticism signifies any work or philosophy in which the exotic or dreamlike figure strongly, or that is devoted to individualistic expression, self-analysis, or a pursuit of a higher realm of knowledge than can be discovered by human reason.

Romantics: See *Romanticism*

Russian Symbolism: A Russian poetic movement, derived from French symbolism, that flourished between 1894 and 1910. While some Russian Symbolists continued in the French tradition, stressing aestheticism and the importance of suggestion above didactic intent, others saw their craft as a form of mystical worship, and themselves as mediators between the supernatural and the mundane.

S

Satire: A work that uses ridicule, humor, and wit to criticize and provoke change in human nature and institutions. There are two major types of satire: "formal" or "direct" satire speaks directly to the reader or to a character in the work; "indirect" satire relies upon the ridiculous behavior of its characters to make its point. Formal satire is further divided into two manners: the "Horatian," which ridicules gently, and the "Juvenalian," which derides its subjects harshly and bitterly.

Scansion: The analysis or "scanning" of a poem to determine its meter and often its rhyme scheme. The most common system of scansion uses accents (slanted lines drawn above syllables) to show stressed syllables, breves (curved lines drawn above syllables) to show unstressed syllables, and vertical lines to separate each foot.

Second Person: See *Point of View*

Semiotics: The study of how literary forms and conventions affect the meaning of language.

Sestet: Any six-line poem or stanza.

Setting: The time, place, and culture in which the action of a narrative takes place. The elements of setting may include geographic location, characters' physical and mental environments, prevailing cultural attitudes, or the historical time in which the action takes place.

Shakespearean Sonnet: See *Sonnet*

Signifying Monkey: A popular trickster figure in black folklore, with hundreds of tales about this character documented since the 19th century.

Simile: A comparison, usually using "like" or "as", of two essentially dissimilar things, as in "coffee as cold as ice" or "He sounded like a broken record."

Slang: A type of informal verbal communication that is generally unacceptable for formal writing. Slang words and phrases are often colorful exaggerations used to emphasize the speaker's point; they may also be shortened versions of an often-used word or phrase.

Slant Rhyme: See *Consonance*

Slave Narrative: Autobiographical accounts of American slave life as told by escaped slaves. These works first appeared during the abolition movement of the 1830s through the 1850s.

Social Realism: See *Socialist Realism*

Socialist Realism: The Socialist Realism school of literary theory was proposed by Maxim Gorky and established as a dogma by the first Soviet Congress of Writers. It demanded adherence to a communist worldview in works of literature. Its doctrines required an objective viewpoint comprehensible to the working classes and themes of social struggle featuring strong proletarian heroes.

Soliloquy: A monologue in a drama used to give the audience information and to develop the speaker's character. It is typically a projection of the speaker's innermost thoughts. Usually delivered while the speaker is alone on stage, a soliloquy is intended to present an illusion of unspoken reflection.

Sonnet: A fourteen-line poem, usually composed in iambic pentameter, employing one of several rhyme schemes. There are three major types of sonnets, upon which all other variations of the form are based: the "Petrarchan" or "Italian" sonnet, the "Shakespearean" or

"English" sonnet, and the "Spenserian" sonnet. A Petrarchan sonnet consists of an octave rhymed *abbaabba* and a "sestet" rhymed either *cdecde, cdccdc,* or *cdedce.* The octave poses a question or problem, relates a narrative, or puts forth a proposition; the sestet presents a solution to the problem, comments upon the narrative, or applies the proposition put forth in the octave. The Shakespearean sonnet is divided into three quatrains and a couplet rhymed *abab cdcd efef gg.* The couplet provides an epigrammatic comment on the narrative or problem put forth in the quatrains. The Spenserian sonnet uses three quatrains and a couplet like the Shakespearean, but links their three rhyme schemes in this way: *abab bcbc cdcd ee.* The Spenserian sonnet develops its theme in two parts like the Petrarchan, its final six lines resolving a problem, analyzing a narrative, or applying a proposition put forth in its first eight lines.

Spenserian Sonnet: See *Sonnet*

Spenserian Stanza: A nine-line stanza having eight verses in iambic pentameter, its ninth verse in iambic hexameter, and the rhyme scheme ababbcbcc.

Spondee: In poetry meter, a foot consisting of two long or stressed syllables occurring together. This form is quite rare in English verse, and is usually composed of two monosyllabic words.

Sprung Rhythm: Versification using a specific number of accented syllables per line but disregarding the number of unaccented syllables that fall in each line, producing an irregular rhythm in the poem.

Stanza: A subdivision of a poem consisting of lines grouped together, often in recurring patterns of rhyme, line length, and meter. Stanzas may also serve as units of thought in a poem much like paragraphs in prose.

Stereotype: A stereotype was originally the name for a duplication made during the printing process; this led to its modern definition as a person or thing that is (or is assumed to be) the same as all others of its type.

Stream of Consciousness: A narrative technique for rendering the inward experience of a character. This technique is designed to give the impression of an ever-changing series of thoughts, emotions, images, and

memories in the spontaneous and seemingly illogical order that they occur in life.

Structuralism: A twentieth-century movement in literary criticism that examines how literary texts arrive at their meanings, rather than the meanings themselves. There are two major types of structuralist analysis: one examines the way patterns of linguistic structures unify a specific text and emphasize certain elements of that text, and the other interprets the way literary forms and conventions affect the meaning of language itself.

Structure: The form taken by a piece of literature. The structure may be made obvious for ease of understanding, as in nonfiction works, or may obscured for artistic purposes, as in some poetry or seemingly "unstructured" prose.

Sturm und Drang: A German term meaning "storm and stress." It refers to a German literary movement of the 1770s and 1780s that reacted against the order and rationalism of the enlightenment, focusing instead on the intense experience of extraordinary individuals.

Style: A writer's distinctive manner of arranging words to suit his or her ideas and purpose in writing. The unique imprint of the author's personality upon his or her writing, style is the product of an author's way of arranging ideas and his or her use of diction, different sentence structures, rhythm, figures of speech, rhetorical principles, and other elements of composition.

Subject: The person, event, or theme at the center of a work of literature. A work may have one or more subjects of each type, with shorter works tending to have fewer and longer works tending to have more.

Subjectivity: Writing that expresses the author's personal feelings about his subject, and which may or may not include factual information about the subject.

Surrealism: A term introduced to criticism by Guillaume Apollinaire and later adopted by Andre Breton. It refers to a French literary and artistic movement founded in the 1920s. The Surrealists sought to express unconscious thoughts and feelings in their works. The best-known technique used for achieving this aim was automatic writing—

transcriptions of spontaneous outpourings from the unconscious. The Surrealists proposed to unify the contrary levels of conscious and unconscious, dream and reality, objectivity and subjectivity into a new level of "super-realism."

Suspense: A literary device in which the author maintains the audience's attention through the buildup of events, the outcome of which will soon be revealed.

Syllogism: A method of presenting a logical argument. In its most basic form, the syllogism consists of a major premise, a minor premise, and a conclusion.

Symbol: Something that suggests or stands for something else without losing its original identity. In literature, symbols combine their literal meaning with the suggestion of an abstract concept. Literary symbols are of two types: those that carry complex associations of meaning no matter what their contexts, and those that derive their suggestive meaning from their functions in specific literary works.

Symbolism: This term has two widely accepted meanings. In historical criticism, it denotes an early modernist literary movement initiated in France during the nineteenth century that reacted against the prevailing standards of realism. Writers in this movement aimed to evoke, indirectly and symbolically, an order of being beyond the material world of the five senses. Poetic expression of personal emotion figured strongly in the movement, typically by means of a private set of symbols uniquely identifiable with the individual poet. The principal aim of the Symbolists was to express in words the highly complex feelings that grew out of everyday contact with the world. In a broader sense, the term "symbolism" refers to the use of one object to represent another.

Symbolist: See *Symbolism*

Symbolist Movement: See *Symbolism*

Sympathetic Fallacy: See *Affective Fallacy*

T

Tanka: A form of Japanese poetry similar to *haiku*. A *tanka* is five lines long, with the lines containing five, seven, five, seven, and seven syllables respectively.

Terza Rima: A three-line stanza form in poetry in which the rhymes are made on the last word of each line in the following manner: the first and third lines of the first stanza, then the second line of the first stanza and the first and third lines of the second stanza, and so on with the middle line of any stanza rhyming with the first and third lines of the following stanza.

Tetrameter: See *Meter*

Textual Criticism: A branch of literary criticism that seeks to establish the authoritative text of a literary work. Textual critics typically compare all known manuscripts or printings of a single work in order to assess the meanings of differences and revisions. This procedure allows them to arrive at a definitive version that (supposedly) corresponds to the author's original intention.

Theme: The main point of a work of literature. The term is used interchangeably with thesis.

Thesis: A thesis is both an essay and the point argued in the essay. Thesis novels and thesis plays share the quality of containing a thesis which is supported through the action of the story.

Third Person: See *Point of View*

Tone: The author's attitude toward his or her audience may be deduced from the tone of the work. A formal tone may create distance or convey politeness, while an informal tone may encourage a friendly, intimate, or intrusive feeling in the reader. The author's attitude toward his or her subject matter may also be deduced from the tone of the words he or she uses in discussing it.

Tragedy: A drama in prose or poetry about a noble, courageous hero of excellent character who, because of some tragic character flaw or *hamartia*, brings ruin upon him- or herself. Tragedy treats its subjects in a dignified and serious manner, using poetic language to help evoke pity and fear and bring about catharsis, a purging of these emotions. The tragic form was practiced extensively by the ancient Greeks. In the Middle Ages, when classical works were virtually unknown, tragedy came to denote any works about the fall of persons from exalted to low conditions due to any reason: fate, vice, weakness, etc. According to the classical definition of tragedy, such works present the "pathetic"—that which evokes pity—rather than the tragic. The classical form of tragedy was revived in the sixteenth century; it flourished especially on the Elizabethan stage. In modern times, dramatists have attempted to adapt the form to the needs of modern society by drawing their heroes from the ranks of ordinary men and women and defining the nobility of these heroes in terms of spirit rather than exalted social standing.

Tragic Flaw: In a tragedy, the quality within the hero or heroine which leads to his or her downfall.

Transcendentalism: An American philosophical and religious movement, based in New England from around 1835 until the Civil War. Transcendentalism was a form of American romanticism that had its roots abroad in the works of Thomas Carlyle, Samuel Coleridge, and Johann Wolfgang von Goethe. The Transcendentalists stressed the importance of intuition and subjective experience in communication with God. They rejected religious dogma and texts in favor of mysticism and scientific naturalism. They pursued truths that lie beyond the "colorless" realms perceived by reason and the senses and were active social reformers in public education, women's rights, and the abolition of slavery.

Trickster: A character or figure common in Native American and African literature who uses his ingenuity to defeat enemies and escape difficult situations. Tricksters are most often animals, such as the spider, hare, or coyote, although they may take the form of humans as well.

Trimeter: See *Meter*

Triple Rhyme: See *Rhyme*

Trochee: See *Foot*

U

Understatement: See *Irony*

Unities: Strict rules of dramatic structure, formulated by Italian and French critics of the Renaissance and based loosely on the principles of drama discussed by Aristotle in his *Poetics*. Foremost among these rules were the three unities of action, time, and place that compelled a dramatist to: (1) construct a single plot with a beginning, middle, and end that details the causal relationships of action and character; (2) restrict the action to the events of a single day; and (3) limit the scene to a single place or city. The unities were observed faithfully by continental European writers until the Romantic Age, but they were never regularly observed in English drama. Modern dramatists are typically more concerned with a unity of impression or emotional effect than with any of the classical unities.

Urban Realism: A branch of realist writing that attempts to accurately reflect the often harsh facts of modern urban existence.

Utopia: A fictional perfect place, such as "paradise" or "heaven."

Utopian: See *Utopia*

Utopianism: See *Utopia*

V

Verisimilitude: Literally, the appearance of truth. In literary criticism, the term refers to aspects of a work of literature that seem true to the reader.

Vers de societe: See *Occasional Verse*

Vers libre: See *Free Verse*

Verse: A line of metered language, a line of a poem, or any work written in verse.

Versification: The writing of verse. Versification may also refer to the meter, rhyme, and other mechanical components of a poem.

Victorian: Refers broadly to the reign of Queen Victoria of England (1837-1901) and to anything with qualities typical of that era. For example, the qualities of smug narrow-mindedness, bourgeois materialism, faith in social progress, and priggish morality are often considered Victorian. This stereotype is contradicted by such dramatic intellectual developments as the theories of Charles Darwin, Karl Marx, and Sigmund Freud (which stirred strong debates in England) and the critical attitudes of serious Victorian writers like Charles Dickens and George Eliot. In literature, the Victorian Period was the great age of the English novel, and the latter part of the era saw the rise of movements such as decadence and symbolism.

Victorian Age: See *Victorian*

Victorian Period: See *Victorian*

W

Weltanschauung: A German term referring to a person's worldview or philosophy.

Weltschmerz: A German term meaning "world pain." It describes a sense of anguish about the nature of existence, usually associated with a melancholy, pessimistic attitude.

Z

Zarzuela: A type of Spanish operetta.

Zeitgeist: A German term meaning "spirit of the time." It refers to the moral and intellectual trends of a given era.

Cumulative Author/Title Index

Cumulative Nationality/Ethnicity Index

Subject/Theme Index

Cumulative Index of First Lines

Cumulative
Index of Last Lines

Die soon (We Real Cool) V6:242

Do what you are going to do, I will tell about it. (I go Back to May 1937) V17:113

down from the sky (Russian Letter) V26:181

Down in the flood of remembrance, I weep like a child for the past (Piano) V6:145

Downward to darkness, on extended wings. (Sunday Morning) V16:190

Driving around, I will waste more time. (Driving to Town Late to Mail a Letter) V17:63

dry wells that fill so easily now (The Exhibit) V9:107

dust rises in many myriads of grains. (Not like a Cypress) V24:135

dusty as miners, into the restored volumes. (Bonnard's Garden) V25:33

E

endless worlds is the great meeting of children. (60) V18:3

Eternal, unchanging creator of earth. Amen (The Seafarer) V8:178

Eternity of your arms around my neck. (Death Sentences) V22:23

even as it vanishes—were not our life. (The Litany) V24:101–102

every branch traced with the ghost writing of snow. (The Afterlife) V18:39

F

fall upon us, the dwellers in shadow (In the Land of Shinar) V7:84

Fallen cold and dead (O Captain! My Captain!) V2:147

filled, never. (The Greatest Grandeur) V18:119

Firewood, iron-ware, and cheap tin trays (Cargoes) V5:44

Fled is that music:—Do I wake or sleep? (Ode to a Nightingale) V3:229

For I'm sick at the heart, and I fain wad lie down." (Lord Randal) V6:105

For nothing now can ever come to any good. (Funeral Blues) V10:139

forget me as fast as you can. (Last Request) V14:231

from one kiss (A Rebirth) V21:193–194

G

garish for a while and burned. (One of the Smallest) V26:142

going where? Where? (Childhood) V19:29

H

Had anything been wrong, we should certainly have heard (The Unknown Citizen) V3:303

Had somewhere to get to and sailed calmly on (Musée des Beaux Arts) V1:148

half eaten by the moon. (Dear Reader) V10:85

hand over hungry hand. (Climbing) V14:113

Happen on a red tongue (Small Town with One Road) V7:207

Has no more need of, and I have (The Courage that My Mother Had) V3:80

Has set me softly down beside you. The Poem is you (Paradoxes and Oxymorons) V11:162

Hath melted like snow in the glance of the Lord! (The Destruction of Sennacherib) V1:39

He rose the morrow morn (The Rime of the Ancient Mariner) V4:132

He says again, "Good fences make good neighbors." (Mending Wall) V5:232

He writes down something that he crosses out. (The Boy) V19:14

here; passion will save you. (Air for Mercury) V20:2–3

History theirs whose languages is the sun. (An Elementary School Classroom in a Slum) V23:88–89

How at my sheet goes the same crooked worm (The Force That Through the Green Fuse Drives the Flower) V8:101

How can I turn from Africa and live? (A Far Cry from Africa) V6:61

How sad then is even the marvelous! (An Africian Elegy) V13:4

I

I am black. (The Song of the Smoke) V13:197

I am going to keep things like this (Hawk Roosting) V4:55

I am not brave at all (Strong Men, Riding Horses) V4:209

I could not see to see— (I Heard a Fly Buzz—When I Died—) V5:140

I cremated Sam McGee (The Cremation of Sam McGee) V10:76

I didn't want to put them down. (And What If I Spoke of Despair) V19:2

I have just come down from my father (The Hospital Window) V11:58

I hear it in the deep heart's core. (The Lake Isle of Innisfree) V15:121

I never writ, nor no man ever loved (Sonnet 116) V3:288

I romp with joy in the bookish dark (Eating Poetry) V9:61

I see Mike's painting, called SARDINES (Why I Am Not a Painter) V8:259

I shall but love thee better after death (Sonnet 43) V2:236

I should be glad of another death (Journey of the Magi) V7:110

I stand up (Miss Rosie) V1:133

I stood there, fifteen (Fifteen) V2:78

I take it you are he? (Incident in a Rose Garden) V14:191

I turned aside and bowed my head and wept (The Tropics in New York) V4:255

If Winter comes, can Spring be far behind? (Ode to the West Wind) V2:163

I'll be gone from here. (The Cobweb) V17:51

I'll dig with it (Digging) V5:71

In a convulsive misery (The Milkfish Gatherers) V11:112

In balance with this life, this death (An Irish Airman Foresees His Death) V1:76

in earth's gasp, ocean's yawn. (Lake) V23:158

In Flanders fields (In Flanders Fields) V5:155

In ghostlier demarcations, keener sounds. (The Idea of Order at Key West) V13:164

In hearts at peace, under an English heaven (The Soldier) V7:218

In her tomb by the side of the sea (Annabel Lee) V9:14

in the family of things. (Wild Geese) V15:208

in the grit gray light of day. (Daylights) V13:102

In the rear-view mirrors of the passing cars (The War Against the Trees) V11:216

In these Chicago avenues. (A Thirst Against) V20:205

in this bastion of culture. (To an Unknown Poet) V18:221